PREVIOUS

CONVICTIONS

by N O R A

S A Y R E

RUTGERS UNIVERSITY PRESS

New Brunswick, New Jersey

P REVIOUS

CONVICTIONS

A
JOURNEY
THROUGH
THE
· 1950S

GRATEFUL ACKNOWLEDGMENT IS MADE TO THE ESTATES OF JAMES M. CAIN AND
S. J. PERELMAN, BOTH REPRESENTED BY HAROLD OBER ASSOCIATES, INCORPORATED,
FOR PERMISSION TO QUOTE FROM AN UNPUBLISHED LETTER BY EACH WRITER.

WALKER EVANS, *MAIN STREET, SARATOGA SPRINGS, NEW YORK, 1931* REPRODUCED BY
PERMISSION OF THE WALKER EVANS ARCHIVE, THE METROPOLITAN MUSEUM OF ART.

PORTIONS OF THIS BOOK HAVE BEEN PREVIOUSLY PUBLISHED IN *THE NEW YORK TIMES BOOK
REVIEW, GRAND STREET*, AND *THE PROGRESSIVE*.

LIBRARY OF CONGRESS CATALOGING-IN-PUBLICATION DATA

SAYRE, NORA.
    PREVIOUS CONVICTIONS : A JOURNEY THROUGH THE 1950S / NORA SAYRE.
    P.   CM.
    INCLUDES BIBLIOGRAPHICAL REFERENCES (P.   ) AND INDEX.
    ISBN 0-8135-2231-5 (ALK. PAPER)
    1. UNITED STATES—CIVILIZATION—1945– 2. ANTI-COMMUNIST
MOVEMENTS—UNITED STATES—HISTORY. 3. AUTHORS, AMERICAN—20TH
CENTURY—POLITICAL AND SOCIAL VIEWS. 4. RADICALISM—UNITED STATES—
HISTORY—20TH CENTURY. 5. SAYRE, NORA—CHILDHOOD AND YOUTH.
I. TITLE.
E169.12.S295   1995
973.9—DC20   95-15826
                                                                      CIP
BRITISH CATALOGING-IN-PUBLICATION INFORMATION AVAILABLE

For

Lily Emmet   *Nora Johnson*   *Emily Taylor*   *Eleanor Townsend*

Friends of then and now

Contents

SEQUELS TO THE THIRTIES

HINDSIGHT FROM THE NINETIES

Acknowledgments

I am extremely grateful to the friends, acquaintances, and strangers who shared their recollections and their insights. I began to gather material for this book long before I was free to write it. Hence some of the interviews date back to a time when memories were very fresh among people who have since died. But I don't wish to separate the living and the dead: they inhabit an equal space in history. Some of my sources chose to be anonymous because they felt their political history might still be harmful to their children's careers. Others won't agree with my views—and I want them to know that I appreciate their generosity.

Parts of the book also emerged from old notebooks, where I'd recorded what I heard and saw without foreseeing that I would one day write about it. Letters I wrote during the Fifties—coaxed back from the recipients—were full of quotes and some of the scenes that appear here.

A fellowship from the John Simon Guggenheim Foundation and grants from the National Endowment for the Arts and the Ludwig Vogelstein Foundation were vital to my research. Here are my special thanks to the providers.

The section on the Twenties was enriched by conversations with Douglas Auchincloss, Malcolm Cowley, Frances Goodrich and Albert Hackett, Edith Haggard, Emily Hahn and Helen Hahn Smith, Ann Honeycutt, Nora Johnson, Nunnally Johnson, Percy Knauth, Jeannette Lowe, Joseph Mitchell, Joel Sayre, Helen Thurber, and Florence Willison.

My thanks to Joseph Blotner and Robert W. Hamblin for background material on Faulkner and my father.

For memories of Walker Evans I am indebted to Calvert Coggeshall, Lily Emmet, Paul and Dorothy Grotz, John T. Hill, Leslie Katz, Jane Mayhall, John McDonald, William McDonough, Hank O'Neal, Elizabeth Shaw, James and Tania Stern, John Szarkowski, Jerry L. Thompson, and Erik Wensberg.

Dr. Christian Beels, Dr. Katherine Rees, and Dr. Eleanor Townsend gave me illuminating information about the psychiatric treatments of the Fifties (also described in chapter 16: "Excavations").

For overviews of the Fifties I had rewarding conversations with Harriet Barlow, Ann Birstein, David Caute, Lillian and Phillip Gerard, Lis Harris, Parker Hodges, and Seymour Krim.

Revisiting the New Criticism, I was guided by William Alfred, Jane Cooper, Malcolm Cowley, Edwin Honig, Alfred Kazin, Milton Kessler, and Erik Wensberg.

For reflections on the loyalty oath crisis at Berkeley, my great thanks to Hans Lewy, Leon F. Litwack, Charles Muscatine, Nevitt Sanford, and Kenneth M. Stampp. F. Coffey, Douglas Dowd, Joseph W. Garbarino, Peter Goldschmidt, Norman Jacobson, and Joseph Tussman were also most helpful.

I am especially grateful to Autherine Lucy Foster for her willingness to recall her experiences at the University of Alabama in 1956. My particular thanks to J. Jefferson Bennett, E. Culpepper Clark, Rose Gladney, Donna Gloeckner, Judge Hobart H. Grooms, Judge Constance Baker Motley, and Arthur Shores.

The Poets' Theatre came vividly alive in talks with William Alfred, Edward Gorey, Molly Howe and her daughters Susan Howe and Fanny Howe, F. M. Kimball, Felicia Lamport, Peter Sourian, Bronia S. Wheeler, Nicholas Wahl, Arnold Weinstein, Bronia S. Wheeler, and David Wheeler.

For the investigation of *The New York Times* I had the good fortune to talk with Herbert Mitgang, John Oakes, Seymour Peck, A. H. Raskin, Nan Robertson, Richard Shepard, Alden Whitman, and Joan Whitman.

For material on the radicalism of the Thirties, blacklisting, investigating committees, American exiles, and Cold War history, interviews with the following were invaluable: Larry Adler, James and Grambs Aronson, Cedric Belfrage, Sally Belfrage, Walter Bernstein, Alvah Bessie, Arthur Birnkrant, Betsy Blair, Dorothy Bloch, Leonard and Jean Boudin, Victor Chapin, Harold Clurman, Lester Cole, Malcolm Cowley, Henry Steele Commager, Sarah Cunningham, Philip Dunne, Elizabeth Faragoh, James T. Farrell, Carl Foreman, Marvin Gettleman, Joanne Grant, Morris Greenbaum, Mildred Grossman, Dorothy Healey, Alger Hiss, Alice and Ian Hunter, Elia Kazan, Alfred Kazin, Reata Kraft, Sam Kushner, Ring Lardner, Jr., Herman and Betty Liveright, Ephraim London, Dwight Macdonald, Albert Maltz, Josephine Martin, Carey McWilliams, Arthur Miller, Florence Mischel, Jessica Mitford, Sam Moore, Karen Morley, Victor Navasky, Eileen O'Casey, Abraham and Sylvia Polonsky, Victor Rabinowitz, Maurice Rapf, William Reuben, Al Richmond, Sidney Roger, Harold Rosenberg, Arthur Schlesinger, Jr., Budd Schulberg, Ellen Schrecker, Wilma Shore Soloman, Donald Ogden Stewart, Gloria Stuart, Paul Sweezy,

Norma Sullivan, Edith Tiger, Robert Treuhaft, Joseph Wershba, H. H. Wilson, Ella Winter, Florence Willison, and Mary Yohalem. Many details in "Blacklist in Exile" came from my notebooks of 1955–1959, as well as interviews that occurred years later.

In Columbus, Ohio, I learned a great deal from Robert Bremner, Walter Bunge, Lewis and Marjorie Branscomb, Jack G. Day, Judge Robert Duncan, Edith Smilack, Carolyn Moore, Megan Mountain, Elisabeth Sterner, Dennis Toth, Robert Thurber, Benson Wolman, and Allen and Leslie Zak. Robert A. Tibbetts, Curator of Rare Books and Mss. at the Ohio State University Libraries, went out of his way to unearth some of the Thurber papers. Olaf Prufer and James Murphy provided extensive material about Richard Morgan.

I am thankful for the help I received from the American Anthropological Association (Washington, D.C.); the Bancroft Library at the University of California (Berkeley); the Brodsky Collection, Center for Faulkner Studies, Southeast Missouri State University; the Carnegie Library (Columbus, Ohio); archivist David J. Haight at the Dwight D. Eisenhower Library (Abilene, Kansas); the Film Study Center at the Museum of Modern Art; the Harvard Theatre Collection at the Nathan M. Pusey Library; the Louis B. Mayer Library at the American Film Institute (Los Angeles); the NAACP Legal Defense and Educational Fund Inc.; the New York Public Library; the New York Society Library; the Schomburg Center for Research in Black Culture; and the James Thurber Collection at Ohio State University.

Between bouts of research I left Manhattan and immersed myself in the manuscript at the MacDowell Colony, Yaddo, the Virginia Center for the Creative Arts, the Millay Colony for the Arts, Blue Mountain Center, and the Alfred University Summer Place. These splendid working retreats enabled me to double my time: to do two weeks' writing in one, two months' writing in a month. I thank all of them for privacy and silence.

The idea for this book grew out of a conversation with James Chace, who also read several sections and gave particular attention to the passages on foreign affairs. Erik Wensberg read every chapter while the book was in progress: to him I owe immense thanks for detailed editorial guidance. Ellen Schrecker and Marvin Gettleman contributed many helpful suggestions and valuable facts.

Sally Belfrage, Edith Tiger, and Florence Willison gave me inestimable support along the way. I am grateful to Ileene Smith of Summit Books, Leslie Mitchner of Rutgers University Press, and my agents, Georges and Anne Borchardt. I thank Stuart Mitchner for meticulous copy editing.

Fletcher DuBois, Josephine Martin, and Joseph Mitchell contributed photographs that I could never have obtained without their help.

PREVIOUS

CONVICTIONS

"America is not finished, perhaps never will be"
—*Walt Whitman*

Prelude

After Hiroshima, Stalin—spurred by our nuclear monopoly—pressured Soviet physicists to produce an atomic bomb so swiftly that small attention was given to the safety of scientists or technicians exposed to dangerous levels of radiation, and communal graves received the corpses of prisoners who died mining uranium. In the Fifties the CIA suspected that the Russians might "overrun" Western Europe; retired agents have recalled how they organized armed "resistance groups" in Scandinavia, France, Italy, West Germany, the Netherlands, Belgium, and Luxembourg. In a world prepared for war I sang madrigals and medieval music, read Henry James and Yeats but not the newspapers, fell in and out of love, bicycled through the cobbled streets of Aix-en-Provence, and sensed the acute anxieties in the air but didn't try to trace them to their sources. Like many young Americans I was uninterested in public affairs, and I felt that Eisenhower and McCarthy could never be as important as John Donne or Bach. While I was in college the Korean War ended, a CIA coup overthrew Iran's Prime Minister Mohammed Mossadegh, Dien Bien Phu fell to Ho Chi Minh, and the Supreme Court ruled that segregation in the public schools was unconstitutional; I did not hear those events discussed. Hence parts of this book explore what I didn't follow while many of us were seeing *Beat the Devil* and *Kiss Me Deadly*, puzzling over abstract expressionism—called subversive by conservatives and decadent by some left-wing critics—and making fun of the Reverend Billy Graham's airborne evangelism.

I hope readers who remember the national convulsions of the Fifties will hold still when I refer to some history which isn't familiar to those who were born after Carl Perkins recorded "Blue Suede Shoes" in 1956. This isn't a survey of the decade; instead I've drawn on much that I witnessed—and written about a good deal that was unknowable at the time, when there was no Freedom of Information Act, when "Communists" were almost mythical beings (it seemed as if few Americans had ever met one), when many facts as well as feelings were suppressed. Since the death of J. Edgar Hoover, we've heard secrets that neither he nor his quarry ever intended to reveal. And the emotional inhibitions of the era now seem as archaic as the 1953 Studebaker coupes.

Historians may never agree about the origins of the Cold War. But given all the evils of Stalin's dictatorship, his hostility toward the West, and Khrushchev's homicidal response to the Hungarian uprising, the idea that both the United States and the Soviet Union were responsible for perpetuating the animosities is no longer unacceptable. Our belligerence toward the Russians was fueled not only by their conquests in Eastern Europe but by our opposition to change in almost any nation—on the chance that Communism might lurk behind any kind of change. Supporting despotic governments—in South Korea, South Vietnam, Iran under the Shah—mainly because they were anti-Communist, our country was said to be "the leader of the free world," proclaiming its strength abroad while riddled with fears of vulnerability at home. The waning American Left was made to seem so powerful that the prospect of internal betrayal appeared even more ominous than an external threat.

Yet the decade was also a time of immense optimism, which meant that the consequences of racism and indigence were hardly acknowledged while many black Southerners were moving to Northern cities, exchanging rural poverty for urban destitution. (When John Kenneth Galbraith began to write *The Affluent Society*, he planned to call the book *Why People Are Poor*.) Few pundits had foreseen the postwar prosperity which enabled middle-income Americans who had grown up during the Depression and lived through World War II to dwell in comfort for the first time. In the early and mid-Fifties—years of minimal inflation—millions were able to earn and save and spend all at once. No longer worried about money, they could concentrate on building homes and raising families and fulfilling aspects of themselves which had been undernourished—they were taking piano or saxophone lessons and painting pictures, vacationing in Europe—and many would later think of that period as the happiest they'd known.

Today only the wealthy could live as the middle class did then. And when public figures assured Americans that they were well-off, some spent much more than they could afford. Installment plans made them rich in objects instead of cash, but the gleaming upholstered cars could make them feel successful despite the debts. Instructed that they had more free time than ever before, they bought boats and skis and Aqualungs, reclining lounge chairs, inflatable rubber dragons for the new pools, trampolines, elaborate tool kits and gardening equipment, tons of grass seed and fertilizer. They did parachute jumping or needlepoint, shot pheasants or gave bridge parties, and the sale of lawn furniture tripled. Universities created departments of leisure studies. Working people started to play golf. Complicated camping equipment was purchased to take multitudes back to nature; the garages were full of tents and knapsacks. It became desirable to cook outdoors as well as indoors: smoke from the charcoal grills rose over the leafy suburbs, fathers in striped navy blue denim aprons poked the glowing coals. Some underground fall-out shelters designed for the same backyards had windows or landscapes painted on the walls; a thirty-five-hundred-dollar model contained a Geiger counter and a telephone. Yet much of the public did not wish to seem extravagant: the caption for one of Plymouth's 1959 advertisements was "Good Taste Is Never Extreme," though the car had soaring white tailfins outlined in chrome. Consumers seemed to want the reassurance that what they owned was "tasteful," and if a car was colossal, it should not differ greatly from the others on the block.

A *Life* magazine editorial of 1959 announced that our civilization "ought to be freer and bolder than the Greek, more just and powerful than the Roman, wiser than the Confucian, richer in invention and talent than the Florentine or Elizabethan, more resplendent than the Mogul, prouder than the Spanish, saner than the French, more responsible than the Victorian, and happier than all of them put together." This state of affairs could be realized because leisure would liberate Americans to improve themselves. The editorial criticized the culture's wasted opportunities and "our mass consumption," yet it implied that ancient or foreign societies could never match the marvels that the United States offered to its citizens. Indeed *Life* sounded rather like *Partisan Review*'s 1952 symposium, "Our Country and Our Culture," in which most contributors celebrated the nation almost without reservation. In *The Genius of American Politics*, the historian Daniel Boorstin asked, "Why should *we* make a five-year plan for ourselves when God seems to have a thousand-year plan ready-made for us?"

• • •

This book is a memoir of mentalities—plus certain elations and disasters—which were shared by some Americans in the middle of this century. It's also a journey through three generations and the variety of their own voyages. By examining the cultural educations along with the political and sexual sensibilities of my predecessors and contemporaries, I'm indicating what can be learned from each group: from their achievements and illusions and mistakes. There are many flashbacks because others' memories of the past are featured. But there is no suggestion that any one generation was more enlightened than another. The stress is on the great differences between them—and on the baggage they carried with them: the ideas that some retained from their formative decades, although almost everything around them had changed. In fact this is a book of changes, and readers will be aware of historical cycles. They may also see parallels to the present, but I leave comparisons to them.

The notion that we are to some extent creatures of specific periods was unpopular in the Fifties, when individuality was thought to be stronger than zeitgeist. (Meanwhile the New Critics were telling us that a poem should be read as though it had no historical context, that it existed "apart from its time.") I've long been intrigued by the relation between our private lives and public events, whether the personal experiences reflect what occurs beyond one's doorstep—as when Scott Fitzgerald felt his own life mirrored the sprees of the Twenties and the bankruptcies that followed—or whether one is in conflict with an era—as Jack Kerouac and Allen Ginsberg were during the Fifties. By thirty we may have shed a few of the convictions acquired earlier on, but others can last for a lifetime, whether they are rust-proof or not. And I'm interested in how people subsist in a time they find unsympathetic, even repellent.

The first section of the book is devoted to individuals who came of age in the Twenties: as I remember them in the Fifties, when they were middle-aged. I'm recalling my parents' friends: most were New York writers, the still adventurous and quite cynical heirs of H. L. Mencken. The atmosphere of the jazz age permeated the rooms where these men and women gathered: their lifelong gaiety was palpable and so were the casualties. Among them were some of the best storytellers I've known, and the tales often echoed the carefree nature of the years after World War I, when many Americans were confident that there would never be another war of that magnitude. Frequently the stories were hilarious, yet many of them dwelt on the precariousness of ordinary life, the perilous balance between sanity and madness. I loved the jokes and dreaded the explosions: mood swings were almost as punctual as sunset. The writers in our living room believed in hard work and in enjoying themselves as much as possible; they seemed as productive as they were reckless, and their scorn for the commercialism of the Twenties was revived in a lively contempt for Wall Street and Madison Avenue in the Fifties. As the parents and teachers of what was called the silent generation, they were influential not only because of their views, but because their daring helped to make us circumspect. The wit and the charm masked some of the pessimism which is common to writers: on dark days the stories and the laughter built a barricade against dejection, against the cheapening of the culture around them, against the fact that no one lives forever.

The second section concentrates on those of us who came of age in the Fifties. We mystified our elders because we lived cautiously, anxious not to repeat their turbulent history. Probably some of us were overburdened with a sense of consequences. Hiding our passions and apprehensions from everyone but our intimates, we were almost invisible—by choice. As undergraduates, many of my friends were out of step with the era: timid rebels with no channel for dissent. Here I'm looking at Harvard: not for its own sake but because it represents other Ivy League institutions where young aesthetes could reside at a cosmic distance from the pressures and compulsions of the period. Comparative literature and seeing foreign movies and obtaining contraceptives were far more important to us than the Army-McCarthy hearings or rhythm-and-blues. Neither apathetic nor cynical, but mistrustful of authority, addicted to the arts and unconcerned with politics, my friends and I were romantics wary of risk, would-be explorers who were also self-protective. And we had a horror of sentimentality (even though some of us wrote sentimental letters).

Much of this section shows what it was like to retreat from public controversy and into personal life. But I've included three documentaries that distill some of the key issues of the time: the loyalty oath crisis at Berkeley, the Autherine Lucy case in Tuscaloosa, Alabama, and the Senate Internal Security Subcommittee's assault on *The New York Times*. Each of these chapters reveals how liberals and conservatives behaved, how they sometimes resembled one another, and how principles were often sacrificed in the onrush of battle. The Berkeley chapter shows a renowned university racked by wayward charges of Communism, all unproven. Autherine Lucy—the first black student to enter the University of Alabama—and her experiences highlight the violent resistance to desegregation in the South. The search for Communists at *The Times* demonstrates how the country's most powerful newspaper responded to its adversaries. These documentaries are deliberately plain, even stark, providing a sharp contrast to the self-absorption of the young.

The apolitical aspects of the Fifties concern me just as much as the political fervors, and I think they are equally significant. But it should be remembered how the Montgomery bus boycott at the end of 1955 gave momentum to the modern civil rights movement, that *Dissent* began publication in 1954 and *The Village Voice* in 1955, that SANE (The National Committee for a Sane Nuclear Policy) was founded in 1957 and so was SLATE, a radical political party at Berkeley; the seeds of the Sixties were being planted, though the majority of Americans knew little about them.

The third section focuses on radicals who came of age in the Thirties. When I first encountered American leftists in the mid-Fifties, most were blacklisted. Some were exiles in London; deprived of their passports and writing movie scripts under pseudonyms, they formed a close community: angry at their government, homesick for their country. (This section comes last because that was my own route: I became acquainted with the radicals after I knew the writers of the Twenties.) Except in the headlines, the Left was inconspicuous during the domestic Cold War. Perhaps no group of Americans has been so exhaustively defined by others—who never consulted or even met them. Most outsiders weren't interested in what they thought; instead the suspects were called on to prove what they were not—that is, agents of Stalin plotting insurrection in the midst of enormous prosperity. What they said about themselves hardly mattered, since almost no one was going to believe them anyway.

When I started this book I felt my territory was anti-Communism; I didn't plan to write about the Communist Party. But in the course of many interviews a number of people chose to tell me about their years as Communists. Like the independent radicals, they would not talk about the blacklist without describing what came before it: their activities in the Thirties and Forties. Quite a few non-Communist leftists remarked that just as one cannot understand the Fifties without a grounding in the Thirties, one can't discuss the unaffiliated Left without considering the role of the Party before and during World War II. Of course the independent Left was a great deal larger than the Party, and within it there were socialists and Trotskyists who detested Communists as much as the latter despised them. But the Communists' efforts on behalf of the unemployed during the Depression, their commitment to the rights of black Americans, and their endeavors in developing the CIO, had a substantial influence on some left-wingers who disagreed with them in other realms, especially about the virtues of the Soviet Union or the value of "class struggle."

The names of former Communists I spoke with are used with their permission, and most had already made the record public. But some of my sources must remain nameless, mainly because they worried that their history could be harmful to their adult offspring, particularly if they were scientists or lawyers or employed by the government. At first I wondered if such caution might be excessive. But when I interviewed certain traditional liberals of the same generation, "Commies" and "Stalinist stooges" were vilified as often as McCarthy; some of those liberals had opposed the Vietnam War in the Sixties, but the vehemence of their domestic anti-Communism showed me why ex-Communists did not think the Cold War was over inside the United States.

Recently opened Comintern archives indicate that American Communist leaders had contacts with the Soviet intelligence agencies, that they received funds from Moscow (not quite news), that some confidential State Department correspondence was stolen in Washington and passed via New York Party headquarters to the Comintern. In the Thirties there was an underground Communist group in Washington, but the extent of its activities is not yet known. Other Soviet documents (as well as FBI files) had already shown that the Manhattan Project was penetrated by spies; the German Communist Klaus Fuchs, nuclear physicist and a member of the British team at Los Alamos, provided vital information. Decoded cables exchanged between Moscow and New York confirm that Julius Rosenberg was the head of a network that passed on national defense research—about radar or types of aircraft—obtained from war plants in 1944 and 1945. He was also involved with intelligence gathering about the Manhattan Project, though perhaps not extensively. It appears that Ethel Rosenberg was not a spy—and that the FBI knew that well before she was executed.

The question of comprehensive spying by Americans remained speculative in 1995, when much of the archival material was fragmentary. But even if some Communist leaders were spies (Rosenberg was a follower), it's plain that most of the ordinary Party members were kept clueless—after all, espionage relies on secrecy. Until certain documents were made public, the ex-Communists I talked with had not believed that the Party contained spies—because it seemed so improbable that the Soviets would employ individuals who were already closely watched by the FBI. Yet that is what the Soviets did.

My own interest is in the American Left per se, rather than in its violators. In a later section I've examined the strengths and failings of the American Communist Party of long ago from the perspective of some of its former members. Most I've known were neither bitter nor nostalgic, and I saw that the Party had attracted rebellious temperaments as well as doctrinal dissidents. But most hadn't abandoned the Left after they decided that the postwar Party was not a useful institution. In my quest for the hidden history of the period, I've aimed for a balance between non-Communist radicals and ex-Communists; the experiences of the two overlapped while their views diverged. These people are seen during the best and worst chapters of their lives: recalling the exhilarations of political involvement in the Thirties, the ruined careers of the

Fifties, and reflecting on the tremendous diversity of the American Left. This section of the book also conveys the trepidation that was prevalent at a time when many apolitical citizens feared the investigating committees: it was not irrational to be frightened—even if one had no reason to be afraid.

• • •

A word that will not appear in this book is "McCarthyism," nor will there be any references to "the McCarthy era": terms which reduce the whole history of anti-Communism to the behavior of one person. The senator was a by-product of the period, not its creator. Although he'd assailed *The Capitol Times* of Madison, Wisconsin, as a "Red mouthpiece," he was not pledged to the crusade in the late Forties. Then he capitalized on an already fertile movement when he needed a campaign issue. In January 1950, when he was still an obscure figure outside of Wisconsin, he dined with three fellow Catholics to seek advice on a theme for his bid for re-election in 1952; an attorney proposed promoting the St. Lawrence Seaway, and McCarthy considered developing a new pension plan. Then a priest suggested Communism, and McCarthy seized on the subject that would make him famous one month later.

Many misunderstand the Fifties because they assume that "McCarthyism" died when the man did—or when he lost his power in 1954. And some who called him "dreadful" really meant that someone else could do a better job, that McCarthy was besmirching the cause of anti-Communism: with the sleaziness of his style, his panoramic lies, and his zeal in abusing the establishment—as when he said that General George Marshall was "always and invariably serving the world power of the Kremlin" and that Truman and Dean Acheson were "the Pied Pipers of the Politburo," or when he called Henry Luce "a debased, degraded, degenerate liar." Many of McCarthy's critics were incensed because he molested numerous non-Communists, but the civil liberties of Communists was hardly a popular issue.

McCarthy thrived for a little over four years because of his talent for manipulating the media and because he gave the impression that Communists had already perverted parts of our government, and especially because politicians feared that he could wreck their careers by turning the voters against them. He was skilled at galvanizing hatred and outrage, particularly among those who felt they'd been disdained or ignored by Northeastern liberals. For a time he succeeded in paralyzing Truman, and then Eisenhower, by keeping them on the defensive while he sabotaged many in their administrations. Richard Rovere of *The New Yorker*, who often interviewed McCarthy, felt he was a nihilist without any interest in the social order. Rovere also viewed him as "a political speculator, a prospector who drilled Communism and saw it come up a gusher. He liked his gusher, but he would have liked any other just as well." After 1945 many politicians had found that reviling Communists (real or imaginary) was beneficial to their careers. No doubt some believed what they were saying—or came to; repetition usually strengthens conviction.

McCarthy was riding a tide that had swelled years before he learned how to swim in it. In the Thirties numerous states had passed anti-Communist legislation; the House Committee on Un-American Activities was established in 1938; the Smith Act (under which Communists could be prosecuted for allegedly conspiring "to teach and advocate the overthrow of the government by force and violence") was passed in 1940; the 1940–1941 investigations by the Rapp-Coudert Committee led to the firing of professors and staff at the City College of New York. Antipathy toward radicals, unionists, and other forerunners of the American Communist Party dated back to the 1870s and 1880s; even then socialism had been regarded as a foreign and therefore sinister import, and immigrants were held responsible for "labor unrest." The government's drive against radicals quickened early in this century.

There was another wave of passionate aversion to foreigners when the United States entered World War I in 1917. Many Americans could see no compelling reason why their country should be involved, but they were rapidly persuaded by politicians, the press, clergymen, and infinite orators that the Huns were monstrous, vile beyond imagination. On home soil it was dangerous to have a German accent: Americans of German descent were characterized as traitors. President Woodrow Wilson had already lambasted Americans "born under other flags . . . who have poured the poison of disloyalty into the very arteries of American life." Ex-President Theodore Roosevelt demanded that German publications be suppressed, that teachers be fired if they wouldn't sign a loyalty oath. In the introduction to a book of his speeches and articles, *The Foes of Our Own Household*, Roosevelt wrote, "In the long run we have less to fear from foes without than from foes within," a sentiment which roused emotions that would outlive him for most of the century.

Fear (of an enemy next door) and pride (in the superiority of the United States) spiraled into a whirlwind of nationalism; recalling those days, George Kennan wrote, "all was righteousness and hatred." German-Americans were persecuted throughout the nation, hounded from their homes and neighborhoods, beaten and threatened with lynching. Certain orchestras stopped playing Bach and Beethoven, and Wagner's operas were banned in many cities. Some patriots even blamed the Germans for outbreaks of diarrhea and a devastating epidemic of Spanish influenza, deducing that German spies had infected the water supply. Immigrants of many nationalities were expected to be pro-German, as were pacifists. In the meantime Roosevelt was calling for "100 per cent Americanism"—a phrase adopted by the American Legion when it was founded in 1919.

At its first national convention the Legion promised to fight against "all anti-American tendencies, activities, and propaganda." The Legion also supported the censorship of liberal and left-wing periodicals. (Referring to unnamed writers with "wildly socialistic ideas," *Photoplay Journal* probably spoke for many others when it commented, "There is much freedom of thought that should be imprisoned.") One of the Legion's missions was to assist the government in combating Communism; by then Bolsheviks had supplanted the Huns as the arch-enemy (as the Soviets would replace the Nazis as villains soon after World War II). Ever since the Russian Revolution of 1917, Bolshevism was seen as a menace, as were its sympathizers in the United States, particularly because many unions aimed to reduce—if not destroy—the power of management. The militant Industrial Workers of the World (the Wobblies), founded in 1905, represented unskilled laborers, hoped to create "one big union," and eventually to eradicate capitalism; many of the IWW leaders were imprisoned when they opposed participation in World War I. The Wilson government was intent on crushing dissent: the Socialist leader Eugene Debs was arrested for making a pacifist speech and jailed for speaking in violation of the Espionage Act. Both the Wobblies and the Socialist Party were fatally wounded when the federal government defined their ideas as criminal.

The demonizing of radicals and foreigners reached new heights with the Palmer raids of December 1919 and January 1920. Attorney General A. Mitchell Palmer claimed that aliens were planning a revolution modeled on Russia's, and the young J. Edgar Hoover arranged the sweeping arrests of some ten thousand foreign-born people; over five hundred of them were deported. "The chief evil of the Red movement," Palmer said, was that "it accomplishes a constant spread of a disease of evil thinking." Amid the violence of the raids, Walter Lippmann wrote to a friend that the nation was passing through "a reign of terror in which honest thought is impossible, in which moderation is discountenanced, in which panic [supersedes] reason." Justice William O. Douglas later observed that we had "dishonored our Constitution" by violating the rights of "innocent men and women, whose only crime was being foreigners." The Red Scare ebbed in 1920 because Hoover and Palmer could produce no evidence that immigrants were trying to demolish the government, and because politicians and prominent lawyers condemned the far-flung illegalities of the raids. But Hoover, then the head of the Radical Division of the Justice

Department, would spend fifty-two years expanding the campaign against the American Left, and his influence on his country would far outdistance McCarthy's.

• • •

The people in this book are presented as figures in a landscape. The landscape is the era. But no era can be explored in isolation. Hence I'm also looking at the aftermath of earlier decades, at what was left behind when the tide pulled out. I myself will wander in and out of the narrative; at times I was a participant, at others simply a listener. Because the book is a memoir of a period, not an autobiography, there are passages where I disappear altogether: when I'm writing about events I didn't witness or experiences I never shared. Recurrently I found I was depicting communities that no longer exist—not only because the members have died but because the energies that united them have dwindled. Many of those I consulted did not write their memoirs. So I'm intent on preserving the kind of history that could be lost.

Often we treat the past as if it were inscribed on a child's magic slate: when you lift up the top page, what was written vanishes, and the sheet beneath it holds no trace of the words that were there. Once the past is relinquished we can easily be deceived: about laws which once protected our rights but have since been rewritten, about official corruption, about the necessity of waging particular wars or spying on our own citizens. And when we forfeit our history we also lose the chance to understand ourselves; just as we need to know a certain amount about our grandparents if we're to make sense of our families, we need to learn what our American precursors thought and did if we are to comprehend the conflicts that besiege us in the present.

The socialist Michael Harrington wrote that the Fifties were "a moral disaster, an amusing waste of life." Yet although that was a reactionary era, a time of manipulation and hypocrisy, it was also the decade when the ground was prepared for some of the major civil rights legislation of the Sixties. After Sputnik encircled the earth in 1957, the money poured into universities gave millions the educations they might never have had. There was an international exchange of a sort which had been rare since the Twenties: fellowships took American students abroad while thousands of young foreigners came to study in the United States, and American writers who weren't academics were invited to universities in countries they'd always longed to visit. At home great European emigrés who'd settled here in the Thirties—such as the architect Mies van der Rohe and the choreographer George Balanchine—were infusing the culture with excitement, the audiences for classical music were growing larger and greedier, while New York became the capital of the art world and the Actors Studio was testing the talents of some of our finest performers: Marlon Brando, Eli Wallach, Kim Stanley, Montgomery Clift, and Julie Harris among them. From the beat writers to Elvis Presley, mutineers were challenging the patterns of propriety. And from the Lower East Side of Manhattan to North Beach in San Francisco, no artist needed to spend much on daily life; experiment was not expensive.

Yet Americans of different backgrounds dwelled far apart in the Fifties. The economic classes and the races knew next to nothing about one another, and people with or without college degrees were usually ignorant about those beyond their own turf, whether the setting was the university or the factory, a weekly magazine or a city hospital. Here I'm writing mainly within the framework I knew then: the educated urban middle class, a world of cultural privileges and slender salaries, where nonconformists were quite plentiful and it was usually a compliment to be called an outsider.

It may seem that I've confined myself to an elite. But most of the writers of the Twenties and the radicals of the Thirties had made their own way—through their work. Their children of my generation were at an advantage because the achievers wanted us to go to better schools or colleges than some of them had. Their expectations had differed hugely from ours; the writers thought their freewheeling way of life would alter the behavior and morals of other Americans—and it did; the radicals believed that they could change a whole society, including what Americans would ask and receive from their government—as they partly did, due to the New Deal. (Though socialism never came to America, many conservatives felt it was looming; the Left's frustrations coincided with the Right's alarm.) My quiet generation didn't expect to change anything; we hoped the conventions surrounding us wouldn't stifle us, that we would be able to pursue our personal destinies without interference—and many did.

I like complicated subjects and am a student of change and contradictions. So this is a book of ruminations; I never intended to write a comprehensive account of the Fifties. I haven't portrayed the religious revival of the period because it did not involve the two older generations in the book, and the young Catholic converts of my age were extremely private, even reclusive, about their faith: they didn't seem to feel they were part of a movement. (Nor have I discussed Gestalt therapy, which was popular but didn't attract those I knew.) Naturally I've been stimulated by hindsight. But I have tried to show the difference between what I knew then and what we know now, and sometimes to express opinions and feelings that I no longer have. I've had to say how certain things seemed at the time—instead of how they appeared years afterward. (I was surprised to find how easy it was to re-enter states of mind which are alien to me today.) Many readers' perspectives will differ from mine, but perhaps the book may tempt some to review their own experiences, even to interview themselves.

In my early twenties I noticed that Americans love to talk about generations, to compare them or denounce them. While my schoolmates and I were trying to define ourselves, to find a foothold, I took a close look at our seniors and saw that they'd known more about many kinds of freedom when they were young. Raymond Carver once said that "good fiction is partly a bringing of the news from one world to another," and that's my nonfictional purpose here. In any period the generations in this country can seem as remote from one another as the largest planets. Since I've had the good fortune to travel between several spheres which did not exchange many bulletins, I'm acting as a messenger who carries tidings from one realm to the next. Much of the news casts light on the most demanding issues of the century, and how some Americans did (or didn't) confront them—when confidence was high and fears were abundant, when life had rarely seemed so comfortable or so uncertain.

LEGACIES

FROM THE

TWENTIES

It was an age of miracles, it was an age of art,
it was an age of excess, it was an age of
satire. . . . We were the most powerful nation.
Who could tell us any longer what was
fashionable and what was fun?
—*F. Scott Fitzgerald,*
"Echoes of the Jazz Age"

All the wars are over and there will never be
another one. . . . At last, at last,
everything's ahead.
—*Toni Morrison,* Jazz

1

Blame It on the Moon

Smoke rose and thickened until it swayed across the room in a wavering canopy: the harsh tang of Chesterfields and Camels and Lucky Strikes mingled with the fumes of Scotch sloshing against the ice cubes—which rattled with the impatience of enthusiastic listeners who nonetheless wanted to talk themselves, or simply wanted another drink.

When I remember my parents' friends I think of them indoors, in living rooms, laughing, eating salted nuts and drinking whiskey, talking expansively—with a group rather than to one person. The setting would shift from New York to Beverly Hills and Cape Cod, occasionally to Connecticut. And one or two guests might spend the night, perhaps on sofas: next morning there would be the long silent trip to the bathroom, the speechless breakfast, and then a few jokes about hangovers. But no perceptible remorse.

To their timid juniors of the Fifties, their gatherings seemed astoundingly gay: how could such a variety of individuals relish one another's company with such ease? Shyness might never have been invented; even though one heard it attributed to E. B. White and Edmund Wilson, diffidence was rarely apparent in those rooms where conversation was a form of play as well as exercise. Still, Wilson sometimes looked most comfortable if he sat next to Peggy Bacon—who loved to remind him that his dog had given her fleas—or the novelist Dawn Powell; he'd known both of them well for many years. Bacon, whose satirical drawings had been compared to Daumier's, could rarely resist an opportunity to tease: that was her style of affection.

The companions of the Twenties were then approaching fifty or recently past it. Quite a few of them had worked together on newspapers when they were very young—Nunnally Johnson, James Thurber, John O'Hara, James M. Cain, St. Clair McKelway, and my parents, Joel Sayre and Gertrude Lynahan—and the camaraderies of the city room at *The Herald Tribune* and *The New York World* had persisted. Later many had *The New Yorker* in common; a number had served time in Hollywood. Not all of them were intimates, but the mobile affinity groups included S. J. and Laura Perelman, the screenwriters Frances Goodrich and Albert Hackett, Edmund and Anne Duffy (cartoonist and decorator), the novelist and art critic Robert Coates, Random House editor Robert Linscott, William Faulkner when he was in Manhattan or Los Angeles, and the clothes designer Muriel King.

Ceremony didn't suit them and daily life did not entail much planning: they liked to drop in for drinks after dinner. Yet even when the speakeasies belonged to the past, the excitement that swirled through the living rooms resembled what John Dos Passos described in his autobiography: "There is a time in a man's life when every evening is a prelude. Toward five o'clock the air begins to tingle. It's tonight if you drink enough, talk enough, walk far enough, that the train of magical events will begin."

Few of the writers were born New Yorkers; most had come to Manhattan from provincial cities or towns: from Shelby, Ohio, or Corning, New York, or Marion, Indiana, and had made their way as absolute beginners, testing their talents against their obscurity. In a world of strangers they had won the battle against anonymity at an early age, and had also found each other in the shabby Greenwich Village boardinghouses or around the water coolers in the hallways of the magazines which began to publish them: *The American Mercury, The New Republic, Vanity Fair, The Nation,* and *Scribner's Magazine.* Some had visited Europe in the Twenties but hadn't wished to live there; for them New York had been the place of all potentialities: a liberated zone.

Even in the Fifties, some who were older or much younger than they called them bohemian—which was not how they saw themselves. Naturally they had enjoyed shattering the codes of Victorianism in their youth. Freewheeling sex and floating parties were still taken for granted as a part of normal life, but ongoing escapades did not often deflect them from working, from trying to write a better sentence than the last one, to build a better paragraph or essay or book. Committed to extreme professionalism, they had no respect for anyone who was careless about his or her work. While they might not have been as stern as Scott Fitzgerald sounded when he wrote to his daughter that work was "the only dignity," they made it plain that a productive life was the only one worth leading.

And despite the (sometimes manic) gaiety of those rooms where they regrouped, most over fifty probably considered themselves to be respectable citizens—who were also free to behave as outlaws whenever they pleased. Of course they had long ago rejected the ethos of their own middle-class parents, along with the precepts of the Midwest. Some looked back on their hometowns as oppressively stagnant and shamefully ignorant, grateful to have escaped the main streets satirized by Sinclair Lewis. And yet I think they felt that they were guardians of certain decencies: honesty, loyalty to friends, and the concept of equality—at least among men. Their educations and their gifts—and by the Fifties, their professional standing—had advanced them beyond the social class of their forebears. But few were social snobs: O'Hara was mercilessly razzed for his weakness in that realm, and it was thought that Fitzgerald's fascination with the rich had sometimes been debilitating for him as a writer. So their children could have the illusion of growing up in a classless society, where talent and achievement were the ruling standards.

Their community was loosely meshed and it seemed open to newcomers. Yet most tended to abide with their own generation, born early in the century, though there were a few younger exceptions, like the *New Yorker* writer Philip Hamburger. Fairly remote from *Partisan Review* and the Jewish intellectual circles of New York, they were irreverent toward academics. For them academia was associated with the genteel tradition which had helped to stifle experimental work. "Professors" were expected to be pedants who misunderstood literature and committed crimes against language. Cherishing education for its own sake, the writers I knew had great respect for the erudition of individuals such as Edmund Wilson, who was even harder on academics than they were. But their disdain for universities was probably an extension of their profound mistrust of all institutions. And they scoffed at the establishment although they were a part of it.

Indeed most were still the offspring of their decade, even though some thirty years had passed. The values and tropisms of the Twenties were very much alive in our living room of the Fifties. Not that the visitors seemed dated. But they had shared a species of exuberance in their unshadowed early years that none of their successors had known—certainly not those who came of age only to enter the Depression or World War II, nor those of us who were girdled by the constraints of the Eisenhower era. And most behaved as though they were thoroughly unfettered in middle age: for them authority didn't even seem to exist. I think they felt quite young at fifty, and they laughed at an unpublished Thurber drawing when it was handed around our living room: a small shocked man drops his drink as a woman cheerfully tells him, "I believe I have accomplished a great deal in my thirties, but I just peed my twenties away."

Except for Dorothy Parker, few of my parents' friends had spent much time at the Algonquin Round Table, which was said to have been draining and self-conscious. In the Fifties, although they didn't seem nostalgic for the jazz age, they did perpetuate its music: sometimes the melodies of the period drifted through the smoke: "Button Up Your Overcoat," "Don't Bring Lulu," and "Blame It on the Moon." My father was an expert on the Tin Pan Alley songs of World War I: "Don't Bite the Hand That's Feeding You," "Wind Up the Watch on the Rhine" ("We don't want the bacon / All we want is a piece of the Rhine"), and "Would You Rather Be a Colonel with an Eagle on Your Shoulder Than a Private with a Chicken on Your Knee?" The occasional singers had not kept the banjoes or ukeleles which they'd played decades before. But they remembered ballads like "My Freckle-faced Consumptive Sarah Jane": "Some say that you are crazy, but I know that you're insane."

As for their children, who passed the crackers and cheese and refilled the ice trays, a number of us felt colorless in comparison to our seniors, who still lived (as someone said) as though something wonderful would happen in the next twenty minutes. To us it seemed as if they had done everything first— as though there were no fresh fields for us to discover. There was surely no way to shock them. They could be exasperated by bad grades or mulishness and they insisted on "manners": we were raised to practice a politeness they didn't expect from their peers. On the whole they were quite strict with us. But it seemed impossible to surprise them.

I've long thought that the largest sexual revolution of the century occurred in the Twenties. The gulf that gaped between my grandparents' generation and their children's was clarified for me in the Sixties, when a woman born in 1880 told me she wished that prostitution might be legalized—so that "those poor college girls" wouldn't feel they had to "sleep with men." Sex, she said, was excusable only when the motivation was "a nice baby."

Yet it was very hard for me to imagine the puritanism which pervaded my seniors' upbringing. Those who grew up in the Midwest had been instructed that the lights must not be dimmed when a group of young people were merely talking together, and holding hands was taboo. It was indefensible for a woman to adjust her hat in public and cosmetics were reviled. In some communities dancing was subversive: the social historian Herbert Asbury wrote that "every-where in my section of Missouri the waltz and the two-step were considered Steps toward Hell. . . . One man in our town was even criticized for [dancing] with his wife."

Despite the feverish Sunday sermons about omnipresent dens of prostitution, many townships were bereft of brothels because, as Asbury explained, "There were not enough cash customers to make the scarlet career profitable." His adolescent fantasies conjured up houses "full of handsome young women, all as loose as ashes," but he knew there were none in his neighborhood. In Farmington, Missouri, there was just one part-time prostitute, known as Hatrack "in deference to her figure": a domestic servant who had time for her trade only on Sundays, when she took her Protestant clients to the Catholic cemetery, and her Catholic clients to the Masonic cemetery. But the young men and women who left the Midwest for Manhattan soon felt as free to enjoy one another as they did to enjoy their new city—and some were vastly amused when the issue of *The American Mercury* that carried Asbury's account of Hatrack was briefly banned in Boston.

During my teens it was clear to many of us that our parents loved sex. But we also realized that it complicated their lives. The sexual cavortings didn't diminish with their youth. Most had married rather late, after abundant exploration. In their forties and fifties some acted so swiftly on spontaneous attractions that few could be astounded if a wife or a husband or lover suddenly took off with a new acquaintance or an old friend. Long before, many had assured each other that they were all free and rational spirits, that no one had the right to be possessive. However, affairs among the married were supposed to be inconsequential. But some became deeply involved with one another's partners—and then most were wounded or outraged. Feelings didn't always jibe with the principles: messy middle-class jealousies had not been erased after all, and there were many enduring ruptures. Those who kept getting divorced and remarried were called "big marriers." Of a husband who didn't stray, it was said that he was "a very married man." As Lincoln Steffens had written to his niece in 1925, "Nowadays we do not regard love and marriage as necessarily permanent."

Some of the former Midwesterners agreed with Harold Ross of *The New Yorker* that "clinical" or "functional" details did not belong in the magazine, and I heard no four-letter words from them until I was almost twenty; cries of "Shoot!" or "Fudge!" rose when someone stubbed a toe or broke a glass. But decorum vanished in private and in their letters. In the late Thirties my father wrote to my mother from Hollywood about a San Diego fishing trip with Nathanael West, Edward Paramore—a writer with many girlfriends— and S. J. Perelman: "The only catch of the day was an eerie Will-Beebeish object Paramore fished up which Sid identified as a marine vulva. We threw it in a bucket. When anybody but [Paramore] looked at it, it lay inert on its side. But when he gave it a peek it would shoot out its fronds and eject a cloud of purple effusion." When Edmund Wilson's *Memoirs of Hecate County* was published, Joseph Mitchell overheard my mother and Katharine White talking outside his *New Yorker* office after they'd been to lunch. The narrator of Wilson's novel had referred to his penis as his "club." The two women were laughing; one exclaimed, "His *club!*" and the other said, "Bunny's club." Mitchell told me that their mirth wasn't unkind, that it seemed like a response to the machismo inherent in all cultures, and he also thought they were amused "because they knew how unreliable a club could be."

Many have called the Twenties generation romantic, and the word certainly applied to their individualism and their hedonism. But I sensed that few had been romantic about love. (Scott and Zelda Fitzgerald and Edna St. Vincent Millay and Dorothy Parker seemed like exceptions; Fitzgerald had told Wilson that he wouldn't care if Zelda died, but he couldn't bear it if she married anyone but him.) Perhaps romance depended on variety, on having a number of lovers; my mother's friends urged me and my contemporaries to "Play the field!" and were baffled when their juniors spoke wistfully about "relationships." Emily Hahn recalled a man who wrote many poems about love—to different women; she added that "a fixation" on one person could become "pretty dull." Some admitted that they had been looking for love but were wary of intimacy, and that they had often pretended to themselves that they were in love, mainly when sex was exhilarating. Even so, I was told, love was rarely as romantic as the first ocean voyage to a foreign country. It seemed as though quite a few were emotional claustrophobes: if "love" threatened to tie them down, it ceased to be alluring, and there was an impulse to look for the exit sign before the question of commitment could arise.

But most eventually got married because that was part of experience—you couldn't postpone it forever. (Even in New York, unmarried lovers didn't live openly together for long.) The decision to marry had little connection with domesticity: acquiring a home and putting down roots were not attractive. A first marriage had sometimes been undertaken as a fling: an extension of good times, a venture. Some also hoped it might be glamorous. Later on, most male writers wanted to be looked after—they seemed to be a batch of helpless men who couldn't change a light bulb because they didn't know where bulbs were kept, who were unable to boil water—and some second wives (like Helen Thurber and Belle O'Hara) or third wives (Katharine O'Hara) or fourth wives (Elena Wilson) were exceptionally supportive of their husbands' talents. But there wasn't much desire to "build families"; most of the couples had one child, partly because they couldn't afford more during the Depression, but also because both sexes wanted to travel lightly. The fact that some became enthusiastic parents was startling to them: they hadn't guessed that children would be interesting.

Whether the women had full-time careers or not—and many did—most writers' wives were expected to be able to earn at short notice or for years at a stretch. Domestic help had been cheap in the Twenties and was still inexpensive in the Fifties, so a middle-aged woman didn't have to be tethered to her household. Few of the wives were keen on cooking: like my mother, they'd learned to make fudge in college, but while they were apt to overcook the meatloaf or the canned succotash on the maid's night off, they made sure that the maids ironed the husbands' shirts, dusted their desks without disturbing the papers, and reordered their favorite foods from the grocery.

If there were feminists within this group, I did not know it; perhaps women who'd held jobs since the Twenties had persuaded themselves that the issue was outmoded. Yet I didn't see them deferring to men, and I'm sure that most regarded themselves as men's equals. So the history and the perpetuation of inequality were unacknowledged. And although I later learned that Thurber was a misogynist, I hadn't guessed that he regarded the American woman as his "mortal enemy," because he was in favor of daughters—his own and his friends'. But in his letters and theirs, "a writer" was usually male; Thurber wrote to Malcolm Cowley, "Not long ago, [John] McNulty expressed surprise at having met a writer who had always wanted to be a writer, and I was surprised that he thought most men drifted into it." Thurber also liked to quote Robert Benchley's observation "that the free-lance writer is a man who is paid per piece or per word or perhaps." Still, Thurber was encouraging when I started to write, and he didn't suggest that I was intruding on masculine turf.

And if there was competition between spouses, I wasn't much aware of it: perhaps that was something that was hidden from the children. But there were some who rarely allowed each other to finish a sentence. I remember the cartoonist Edmund Duffy saying to his wife Anne, "You don't talk—you only interrupt!" When Nora Johnson, daughter of the screenwriter Nunnally Johnson, was taken by her father to see their friend Helen Hayes in *The Wisteria Trees*, Nora was impressed by the prolonged, explosive coughs that resounded throughout each of the play's climactic passages, and Nunnally explained that that was Charles MacArthur: he always hacked and choked during his wife's key scenes. Accustomed to his reflexes, the actress never faltered in delivering her lines.

Growing up in this world, I received almost no impression of the customary roles of husbands or wives, except that both should be pleasing to one another;

otherwise there was no point in being together. I also deduced that marriage required a lively amount of self-protection: each person must defend the psyche against invasion, and over-dependency was a transgression: being a burden was one step away from being a parasite. Therefore marriages which worked well indicated that both partners—especially the wives—were not overly demanding. Demands per se were offensive, and I concluded that it was wrong to ask for things: requests for time or money or love itself could violate the code of non-encroachment.

Needless to say, few marriages were exempt from mutual intrusions and the resentments that resulted were often dramatic: I remember the doors slamming and the bags rapidly packed and the tickets purchased by those who wanted an intermission in the middle of a marriage. Yet they took divorce hard: it might be inescapable but so was demoralization, and people who were heading for Reno received commiseration from many friends. Possibly some also felt a stirring of their traditional backgrounds: divorce implied failure, and it seemed like a short circuit in a promising life. But the conventions of marriage seemed unreasonable to most of them; on hearing that a friend was separating from her husband, Perelman wrote to her, "I suppose I incline to feel that monogamy is at best a very shaky and provisional arrangement invented by some rather smelly monks for the purpose of preventing the extinction of the race."

There was a story by O'Hara that I read in my early teens which described two married couples exchanging their underwear after three A.M., following a party given for one couple's wedding anniversary. Each man put on the other's wife's bra, and the women wore the husbands' undershirts and shorts. Although I hadn't seen anything like that, the story conveyed the possibilities that were in the air—I was struck by that at the time. I already knew that what people did or said when drunk ought not to matter the next day: you weren't supposed to judge anyone when he was loaded, and he had no reason to be embarrassed. But there was some disapproval of "thimble bellies" who couldn't hold two or three drinks without imperiling the furniture.

At times the group still seemed to be defying Prohibition, as though whiskey were hard to obtain. A. J. Liebling wrote, "People whose youth did not coincide with the Twenties never had our reverence for strong drink. Older men knew liquor before it became the symbol of a sacred cause. Kids who began drinking after 1933 take it as a matter of course. . . . Drinking, we proved to ourselves our freedom as individuals and flouted Congress. . . . It was the only period during which a fellow could be smug and slopped concurrently."

According to Police Commissioner Grover Whalen, there were at least thirty-two thousand speakeasies in New York City during Prohibition. The speakeasies had been the scene of social cementing: people were drawn together in response to the opposition, just as a population may be unified in time of war. Inevitably, what was forbidden was irresistible. And the boundaries of class evaporated when typesetters, judges, stagehands, college students, off-duty doormen in uniform, debutantes, prizefighters, and newspaper publishers drank with each other. But perhaps the greatest charm of the speakeasies was the opportunity to leave home, to *get out* of the house—to walk out the door and away from all restrictions. For many young New Yorkers, "home" had meant propriety, the correct behavior required in childhood. So saloon life was an enthralling emancipation.

Dos Passos recalled the bewitchment of "places [where] you whispered your name through a slot in the door. . . . From the moment the door clicked behind you, you had the feeling of being in the Fortunate Islands, where there were no rules and regulations, no yesterdays and no tomorrows." Meeting friends at Bleeck's or Costello's, mingling with songwriters and bootleggers and aviators or a man who booked horses out of the Frick Museum—when he saw all the empty telephone booths, he moved in and ran his business there—the young revelled in discovering the unknown and in dwelling in the present: nothing mattered but this evening, the hour or two that lay ahead.

Having escaped from their own homes, they didn't want to visit others': dinner parties made them feel trapped; when they needed to eat, they preferred the hardboiled eggs at Dan Moriarity's or the T-bone steaks and spaghetti at Tony Soma's. In the speakeasies they could sing and shout and throw things at each other, or initiate the mock-fights that alcohol can inspire: those who felt aggressive but not particularly angry could match insults and pretend to be offended, duel with words and jokes and call it a draw. The speakeasies also enabled them to get out of themselves—always a boon for writers. And they could depart whenever they wished to: the sidewalk was right out there. If they felt like dancing, they might dash up to Harlem, where they had learned to dance without holding on to their partners: men and women would dance away from one another for a few steps, and no one was guiding anyone. Home was where they went when the saloons were closed: it was a place for sleeping and working, not for self-expansion.

In middle age they still liked to go out, but the domicile was no longer so distasteful: the living room had become the speakeasy, and the presence of growing children was not the hindrance that their forebears' had been. And yet they were under observation—more so than they knew. As Manhattan teenagers we saw that our parents' drinking was a celebration: of the self and of friendship—they seemed to feel closer to each other once the whiskey had risen in them. Theirs was a rather athletic, activist style of drinking, so unlike the silent soakers we encountered. Yet we also noticed (and discussed) how isolated adults could appear when they were very high: there would be monologues by some who hardly seemed to know that there were others in the room.

But even those who had passed the flashpoint of drinking for pleasure were almost exultant about their appetites; Wolcott Gibbs had said there was no such thing as one martini. Ring Lardner was sometimes quoted: "How do you look when I'm sober?" Nunnally Johnson, who often came to New York from Hollywood, once complained that after four days in the city he'd had nothing to eat but hors d'oeuvres: all the drinks and hangovers had left no time for meals. Thurber, who briskly rejected Gertrude Stein's definition of the Lost Generation, wrote in a letter: "We weren't lost. We knew where we were, all right, but we wouldn't go home. Ours was the generation that stayed up all night. Indeed, we spent so little time in bed most of us had only one child." And a friend of my father's, a writer who was dying from the massive binge in Rome, brightly told the stretcher carriers in the ambulance that was speeding him to the hospital, "This is a self-inflicted wound."

• • •

My father drank lavishly when young, assertively in middle age, then tapered off after sixty. Yet he did not seem to be an alcoholic because he could stop easily and cheerfully for months or a year whenever he needed to shed weight. (Athletic in youth, he was fat as well as bald before thirty—which didn't diminish his attractions for women.) But one winter when he gave up cigarettes, coffee, and starches all at once, along with liquor, and began to lose his temper daily, he resumed smoking "because I don't want to be a slave to my will power." If excess was part of his nature, compulsion wasn't.

Raised in Columbus, Ohio, he took his degree in literature at Oxford, where his tutor was J.R.R. Tolkien, studied medicine for a year at Heidelberg, settled in Manhattan, and worked for *The New York Herald Tribune* and a couple of other newspapers. At first he hit the typewriter keys so hard that they cut through the paper. In the early Thirties he published two satirical novels: *Rackety Rax* (about gangsters who founded a university in order to muscle in on college football), which had splendid reviews and was later described as a "Voltairean masterpiece" by the British historian Dennis Brogan, and *Hizzoner the Mayor* (about two crooked New York mayors, a Democrat and a Republican), which critics praised for its sardonic depiction of corrupt city politics; one called him "an underground Swift." He wrote articles and fiction for

The New Yorker, but prose didn't earn enough to carry a family through the Depression, so he spent about five years in Hollywood, employed on over a dozen film projects. He longed to adapt Daudet's *Tartarin de Tarascon* for W. C. Fields, but no producer was tempted, even when Fields was available.

The only director he enjoyed working with was George Stevens; for him my father co-wrote *Annie Oakley*, which recharged Barbara Stanwyck's sputtering career, and he was the final screenwriter on Stevens's *Gunga Din*, much of which was filmed in the summer of 1938 at Lone Pine, California, in the High Sierra. Living in a tent village in the desert, the company sweltered through heat waves so ferocious that the ignition switch melted off the dashboard of my father's car. The troupe averted a couple of potential homicides on the set by disarming two heatstruck souls and sending them home. The blue-eyed Sam Jaffe, cast as Gunga Din, had been a Russian Grand Duke in Josef von Sternberg's delirious *Scarlet Empress*, starring Marlene Dietrich; at Lone Pine Jaffe and his wife, the actress Lillian Taiz, entertained the crew with wicked imitations of Sternberg directing Dietrich in a sado-masochistic fashion. For *Gunga Din*'s battle scenes, hundreds of cowboys were hired to play the cavalry and the kilted Scottish Highlanders. When Victor McLaglen—who'd fought with the British in the Boer War—was drunk, he would drill some extras and march them to a bar in a nearby town. In those days it was unusual for writers to work on location, but the script wasn't finished before the shooting began, and my father was racing to stay a few sequences ahead of the camera: expanding the role of the Hindu villain, Eduardo Ciannelli (a physician and opera singer before he became an actor), adding new lines for Robert Coote (the blustering sergeant), paring down Joan Fontaine's small but intrusive part, and helping to improvise the scene where medicine was fed to the elephant.

During World War II he was a foreign correspondent for *The New Yorker*. Heading for the Middle East via a series of short flights, he passed a night in a Brazilian jail (I never knew why). After traveling through North Africa and Egypt, he was in Iran for nearly a year, then wrote a book about the Persian Gulf Command, which delivered American arms, food, tanks, planes, and medicine across Iran to the Soviet Union. Perplexed by the enmities between Iranians and Arabs and between Shiite and Sunni Moslems, menaced by sunstroke and typhus and overdosed with Spam, the GIs said that P.G.C. stood for People Going Crazy and that F.B.I. meant Forgotten Bastards of Iran. Toiling through mountains, dust storms, and oceans of sand where itinerant tribes were expert with rifles and the kind of slingshot David used against Goliath, the American truck drivers, railroaders, engineers, and stevedores managed to provide the Red Army with supplies essential to defeating the Germans. By chance my father was one of four correspondents at the opening of the Teheran Conference of 1943, and he saw Churchill presenting the Sword of Stalingrad to Stalin: the weapon fell out of its scabbard and clanged on the floor before Stalin kissed it.

In the early spring of 1945, *The New Yorker* sent him to Germany for the last phases of the European war. He spent a week at Buchenwald right after the first American tanks arrived there in April, making daily excursions to talk with skeletal men who had not been hanged, shot, starved, or beaten to death. He also inspected the cross from which inmates were hung by the wrists until their arms were nearly wrenched out of their sockets, the gallows, the crematorium, and the lampshades and purses made from tattooed human skin for Ilse Koch, wife of the camp's commandant. Piles of naked corpses still awaited burial. After a week, a ceremony was held in front of a wooden monument built by survivors in memory of Buchenwald's sixty-five thousand dead: a gigantic crowd of former prisoners shouted in unison that fascism would be destroyed. The day after V-E Day on May 10th, he saw the surrender of the German army at Tyrol and visited Hitler's sumptuous chalet at Berchtesgaden, where Mussolini and the Nazi high command had strode across the marble floors and Eva Braun's bedroom closet was crammed to its ceiling with hoarded sanitary napkins, unobtainable in Germany for years. One of the first American correspondents to reach Russian-occupied Berlin, he explored Hitler's bunker when many Germans still doubted that the Führer had shot himself there.

My father remained in Berlin for more than a year after the war ended, a witness to the legacy of life under Hitler. He met citizens who had truly hated the Nazis—and was repelled by dozens who pretended they had. He was told that Berliners learned to recognize the smell of fresh human blood during bombing raids; it differed from the reek of corpses. He watched documentary footage that George Stevens had shot when Dachau was liberated; the unit had filmed the camp's Malaria Institute, where a thousand prisoners had been infected with germs to see how they would react; some of the skulls of non-survivors had been bleached and used as paperweights by the S.S. The unit also filmed the signs reading "It is your duty to be clean" outside the showerbaths where cyanide gas had streamed from the nozzles instead of water. He kept track of the postwar crime waves in Berlin as murders and muggings soared; most of the killings involved robbery—in a city where food was so scarce that when a draft horse fell dead in the street, bystanders rushed forward with knives and carved steaks before its harness was removed. Meanwhile suicides ran high.

In *The House Without a Roof*, his book about the experiences of a partly Jewish family during the Third Reich, he conveyed the sufferings of people who dwell with destruction and fear in any country ravaged by war, from the "twilight angst" before the nightly air raid to the death of those they love most. Occasionally objects were almost as eloquent as people: he found playing cards in the rubble where terminal fighting had occurred, realizing that German soldiers had whiled away their last hours with card games, and he saw how a bomb had shattered a glass case filled with Beethoven's ear trumpets and hurled them all over the floor. Heidelberg had delighted him in 1925; two decades later he sometimes wondered if he'd been beguiled by a mirage. His war reporting was some of his best writing: when he listened to a man who'd spent hideous months in a clinic for the insane, feigning hereditary madness so as not to be drafted into the S.S., or heard a fifteen-year-old tell how her closest friend had hanged herself when she expected to be sent to a concentration camp, also how she'd seen her neighbors being herded into a van—one had mislaid her baby's bottle, but an S.S. officer said that the baby wouldn't need it—he made tragedy concrete.

Following the war, his long article, "The Man on the Ledge"—about John Warde, who in 1938 leaped from the seventeenth floor of Manhattan's Gotham Hotel after vast crowds had watched him for eleven hours—drew wide attention before it was filmed. In the Fifties he went on writing for *The New Yorker*, *Holiday*, and other magazines, and for movies and television. But my mother had a severe breakdown from which she didn't recover; despite brief alleviations, there were enormous medical expenses as her illness and their financial crises fragmented their lives and his work. Writing editorials for *Life* and scripts for *Martin Kane, Private Eye* was like swimming in snowshoes, he said. But he still seized every opportunity to pursue his foremost interests, including the cultures of several Indian tribes in Arizona and New Mexico, and the inner workings of Scotland Yard. When he could leave his desk or home for the Grand Canyon or London or Provence, he was on the road or in the air and out of sight: no one, I was told, could pack so quickly.

It was a life lived in lunges: between two coasts, on trains and planes and in temporary sublets, among different women. (The three I came to know best were utterly unlike each other, and I was equally fond of them.) As he aged, his earliest friends still thought of him as the wild young man of the Twenties, whom Stanley Walker of *The Herald Tribune* had called "the wandering behemoth." Large-boned and barrel-chested, he was modest about his strength; when a Cape Cod neighbor decided to raze his old barn he gave a demolition party, inviting my father and his brother to swing from the rafters and ram themselves against the walls: dangling from the beams, the two redhaired young giants were nimble wreckers while the other guests danced until the building collapsed around them. A sensitive listener as well as a captivating storyteller, my father had no snobbery. The idea of social class meant nothing to him, and he was welcome wherever he went.

Recklessness was balanced by courtesy—he loathed rudeness—and although he could litter a room with papers and clothes until it looked as though a poltergeist had been there, he winced when anyone used a dinner plate as an ashtray; he was never unshaven and often immaculately dressed. Hopeless with money, he hardly knew where it went, but he was not extravagant—except about books: he had so many that when he couldn't find a particular volume, he bought a duplicate; Joyce's *Dubliners* was in every room in our apartment, Colette's novels and memoirs seemed to multiply on their own. My mother said we didn't need all those extra copies of Gide's *Les Faux Monnayeurs* and Adams's *Democracy* and Orwell's essays, nor the towers of foreign dictionaries. Languages thrilled him: he was fluent in French, Spanish, German, and Russian, and he loved grammatical texts. He read wherever he was: standing on a street corner while waiting for the traffic lights to change, throughout weddings or graduations (when some thought he was deep in prayer, because he hunched forward to conceal the book), in the bathtub and during family meals. Each new passion meant more books: learning to cook at fifty, he soon had a gourmet's library; the nomad could be hugely domestic. Bouillabaisse flowed through our home until he began to make cheesecake, then steak au poivre proliferated and he found a Scandinavian recipe for beer soup flavored with cinnamon.

He treated women as equals, but he rebelled when any woman called him unreliable: he resented that more from women than from men. He detested pressure of any sort. But when he dodged deadlines or didn't pay bills, he was forcing others to put pressure on him, and it was usually a woman who did so: his wife or an editor's assistant or an accountant's secretary. Yet he did struggle to be responsible, especially in the first years of my mother's sickness—when he took on many unappealing assignments and made daily casseroles which he brought to her in Bellevue and other hospitals—vowing to reform his habits and even his character. But as he wrote to a woman who was involved with him on and off for a lifetime, "Plans are always subject to change."

Frequently stricken with writer's blocks, he would embrace a new topic and foresake the last one. For him research was so enticing that it could carry him far off the track and he would miss another deadline. (In preparation for *Gunga Din* he ingested book after book about India, among them the *Kama Sutra*, which inspired a long erotic letter to my mother.) French and Russian history, the details of the Dred Scott case, Roger Casement's trial for treason in 1916, or the different pupae, nymphae, and larvae used as bait for California trout, or the life of Balzac, could rise like a mountain range between him and a movie treatment about Holland during World War II or a profile of a football coach. Compelled to continue learning all his life, he was relentless in his quest for information, whether he was investigating the aborted German revolution of 1848, the Mugwumps (dissident Republicans of the 1880s who backed the Democrat Grover Cleveland for president), or the identity of the Hairnet King of 1927.

Exuberant in discovery, he would talk about his material and pour it into his letters, diluting the urge to write it. He rarely relished the act of writing— "keeping the saw moving over the wood"—and he spoke of his detours as "going to Montreal via Miami"; my mother referred to them as "giant swings and snipe flights." Cooking could serve as an escape from the typewriter: creating a four-star feast was a substitute for "the bleak travail of putting it down." Yet he published a great deal for someone whose worst days meant sitting at his desk and "counting my feet." Discomfited by forethought or hindsight on his own behalf, he took parenthood seriously and entreated me to make decisions and choices for the future, as he hadn't. He kept warning me not to repeat his history: when I was sixteen he wrote, "You be an ant, kid; the hell with the grasshoppers; one in the family is more than plenty."

From twelve onward, my classmates were astonished that he was interested in our opinions; when my seventh- or eighth-grade friends dropped by after school, he asked what we'd discussed in classes that day and what we felt about a teacher's approach to Shakespeare's sonnets or *Julius Caesar*. And what did we think of the movie we'd just seen? Most of my friends told me their parents didn't encourage them to have views of their own or to express them; several exclaimed that it was exceptional for an adult to ask what they thought about anything. Now and then he and I clashed over my education; I balked when he tried to select my courses in high school, and he said I skipped medieval history mainly to defy him, which was true. But he didn't interfere with my college curriculum, although there was some protest when I took a semester of Milton: "When I consider how my dough is spent!" (I reminded him that I had a scholarship.) But his dislike of *Paradise Lost* and *Paradise Regained* dated back to his years at Oxford, where Milton was studied in terms of philology. Reproachfully he would declaim passages that pained him, and he showed me the essay in which T. S. Eliot had written that "Milton's poetry could *only* be an influence for the worse, upon any poet whatsoever," and that he had "done damage to the English language from which it has not wholly recovered."

Unlike many writers, he wasn't an egotist. Determined to make the most of life, he'd feared—even at twenty—that he wouldn't. Since his physical presence was so imposing and his public persona was gregarious, others didn't always perceive his vulnerability: the self-doubt that impeded writing, the guilt about unfinished work and his "centrifugal" behavior, about my mother's breakdowns and their corrosive marriage. When depressed he retreated into formidable silence. E. B. White accurately portrayed him in dejection; when my father's only stage play was pulled from production, White wrote to Thurber, "You don't need to be in a stalled car near Naples to be out of touch with Joe Sayre, you can be sitting right next to him at Bleeck's and get the same remote abandoned feelings. I have encountered him a couple of times at parties, but he just stares at you steadily for a minute and then goes phaaf, like your car, and sits down in a dark corner somewhere to continue brooding." (White added that "a blow like that" was harsher when you were over twenty-five and after "Hollywood has hung rhinestones all over your vest.") But when my father's friends were despondent, he gave them every kind of sympathy, and his jokes and stories were ready if they needed distraction. The attention he focused on those he cared about—and his concern for their welfare—forged loyalties that stayed firm for decades, and when Thurber, that angry and often bitter man, drew a map of his heart, a section of it was inscribed to Joel Sayre.

• • •

As college students, upright in our crinolines or tailored tweeds, we marveled at the random tales of our parents' youth: their past seemed utterly alien to our present. What they told us sounded daring yet somewhat alarming, since one story after another suggested that it was easy to lose control of your life or your sanity, or described situations where you couldn't trust your own judgment. For example:

As an Oxford student my father was often in Paris, where he saw a good deal of the cocaine trade in Montparnasse. But he didn't sample the drug himself, perhaps because of the experiences of a British classmate: "a snow-bird," as cocaine-users were called. The young man and his girlfriend had taken a hearty dose in their room at a small Parisian hotel, which had extremely thin walls. While they lay on the bed enjoying their responses, they heard a couple enter the room right next to theirs. Every word was audible and what began as a fierce quarrel soon became a horrendous fight, amplified by menacing shrieks and yells. In their highly sensitized state, the unwilling listeners were racked by the violence erupting a few feet away; the impact was especially agonizing because they seemed to be taking part in the battle themselves. Then they heard threats of murder and screams for help. But they found that they were incapable of moving at all. So they were grateful to hear the tough old concièrge and a flock of policeman battering down the door—although each blow on the splintering wood seemed to fall on their own skulls. Finally the howling pair was dragged away, and in the welcome silence that followed, the snowbirds slept for hours.

Next morning they asked the concièrge what had become of the couple: were they in jail? She was bewildered—what couple? She explained that no one had checked into the hotel since their arrival, and that the room next to theirs was empty—as it had been for weeks.

Left to ponder their joint hallucination they wondered if it expressed their feelings toward one another. My father added that at least they never got married. . . .

My mother, whose newspaper career was abetted by H. L. Mencken—whom she met in 1924 when she was reporting on the Democratic convention for *The Springfield Union*—later worked for *The New York World*, where she covered the Hall-Mills murder trial of 1926, the great coal strike of the mid-Twenties, and wrote the lead story on the first heavyweight championship fight between Jack Dempsey and Gene Tunney, subjects rarely assigned to a woman. When she was hired by *The World*, Mencken introduced her to editorial writer James M. Cain, advising, "If Cain makes any passes, call Arthur Krock. And if Krock does, call the police." (Krock was the assistant to the paper's publisher.) Joseph Mitchell, then a copy boy at *The World*, told me that in the days of her early achievements, "She walked like a queen with a swagger." That was long before my birth, and the assurance was gone well before I was old enough to pass the nuts and empty ashtrays. I never knew her well; then or now, I could not describe her "character," since her illness governed most of her conduct once she reached middle age. But I was eager to hear about her life before the depressions took over; she was said to have been delightful company. In old snapshots her smile is hopeful, though she looks anxious rather than confident.

Years after her death, Cain wrote to me that she had reproached him— over lunch at a "high-toned" speakeasy called Le Divan Parisien—for giving her the worst five minutes of her existence. That morning, when she was sitting at her desk in the city room of *The World*, meditating on the low quality of the gin of the night before, a shiny green shape as large as a chicken suddenly appeared on her typewriter: it glared at her. It looked like a frog, but she knew that no frog could be so huge. Dreading that it signaled an onslaught of delirium tremens, she forced herself to poke it with one finger and found it "cold and soft and horrible"—and real. She was saying that a copy boy had carried it away when Cain interrupted, recalling an editorial he'd written a couple of weeks before, complaining that the frog legs served in New York restaurants were far too small. In West Virginia they were much bigger. But a reader in Richmond wrote in to announce that he would prove that his county's frogs were even larger. So the man had mailed his evidence, addressed to the Frog Leg Editor, and the thing had escaped when the box was opened. It was promptly delivered to the New York Aquarium, where it was hailed as a rare species. Cain apologized to my mother for the shock to her equilibrium, and she replied that she was proud to have been part of a controversy, but that she would like another martini right away, if that wasn't asking too much . . .

The fragility of sanity—often jovially discussed by *New Yorker* writers who suffered from "bad nerves"—was a rondo theme throughout the tales recounted to entertain their friends. Small incidents could be reminders that mental balance was uncertain. I once heard Joseph Mitchell and S. J. Perelman chatting while they were waiting for a tardy elevator and standing on opposite sides of a noisy electric fan: one was talking about *Antic Hay* while the other was intent on Danny Kaye. Since they made no sense to one another, each stared at the other with acute concern. Finally I sprang forward to explain because both looked so worried—as though an old friend had just lost his mind. Their laughter echoed with relief as the elevator doors closed behind them, and I could still hear them whooping as they sank beneath the floor.

When incipient lunacy was the subject of humorous fiction, the joke was sometimes on the villains: in Thurber's *The Catbird Seat* and his fable, *The Unicorn in the Garden*, monstrous women were bested by their mild male victims, who convinced others that their persecutors were insane. Elsewhere an unstable universe threatened the blameless little man who reappeared in *New Yorker* casuals, especially Thurber's: a creature assailed by his environment, unable to cope with machinery or newborn kittens or train schedules, afflicted with buzzing ears and a turbulent stomach, dazed by the difficulty of distinguishing fact from illusion. He longed for peace and symmetry, but disorder was his element: for him, locks jammed and fuses blew, floods rose in the basement while mysterious strangers pounded on his door, demanding information he didn't have or delivering subpoenas that weren't meant for him. Mistaken for a burglar, he was likely to incriminate himself. Meanwhile others thought him crazed—not certifiable but imbecilic. So he felt guilty all the time: for his inadequacy, for attracting the abnormal, for not being able to repair the leak or to deflect the showers of meteors which were aimed at his house.

Dorothy Parker wrote of Thurber's characters, "They expect so little of life; they remember the old discouragements and await the new." And *The New Yorker* published so many pieces about the beleaguered male that Edmund Wilson suspected that Harold Ross may have found the character sympathetic due to his own "general feeling that everybody and everything was against him." If so, some of the writers Ross encouraged did appreciate the kinship between wit and sorrow. As Thurber wrote, "The little wheels of their invention are set in motion by the damp hand of melancholy."

In childhood I roared when Thurber reproduced the terrible sounds his brother Robert had made on first tasting buttermilk: the bellows were almost tragic. Encounters—with punitive food or malign plumbing, or objects that took on a life of their own—were essential to his vision of human existence as an obstacle race. The Thurber man's feelings of helplessness when faced with collapsing cots, stalled cars, falling ceilings, marriages, ghosts in the attic and global war, had to seem hilarious, because the author's own perceptions of chaos were sometimes intolerable. When I later read Graham Greene's reflections on comedy—"The man who falls downstairs must suffer if we are to laugh; the waiter who drops a plate must be in danger of dismissal. Human nature demands humiliation, the ignoble pain and the grotesque tear: the madhouse for Malvolio"—I felt that almost no one understood that better than James Thurber. And I was reminded of a story E. B. White used to tell— amid gusts of adult laughter—which seemed to me a literal nightmare.

In 1929, when his future wife, Katharine Angell, was traveling to Reno for a divorce from her first husband, White worried that she might change her mind about marrying him. After escorting her to the train station, he went home for a nap. White's sleep was dispersed by the telephone; he would subsequently learn that the caller was my mother, inviting him to a party. (They had been at Cornell together, where both were editors at the college newspaper, and they lived in the same Village rooming house.) Asleep once more he dreamed that Katharine had phoned to say that she'd decided against the divorce and that she would return to her husband. On awakening he still thought he'd received the message he dreaded: that day any woman's voice would probably have sounded like Katharine's to him.

Despite his misery he remembered that she would have to change trains at Chicago, so he was frantic to meet her there and to convince her to go through with the divorce. But how would he overtake the train? Friends helped him to charter a private plane; he hated the idea of flying, but the deadline of her arrival in Chicago was his sole obsession. A horrifying voyage ensued: lightning flashed and storms broke around the small craft, and it floundered so far off course that the frightened pilot asked White to read the map for him. It seemed that they would miss the train by many hours—if they survived at all. At last they landed on a golf course and then struggled through tempests to find transport to the city.

Distraught with grief and ill with terror, White was nonetheless on time: confronting Katharine in Chicago, he pleaded with her while she grappled with her amazement at seeing him. But she was finally able to persuade him that she had never made such a call, and that she had no intention of canceling their marriage.

She proceeded to Reno while White, almost prostrate with relief, returned to New York. Only a few days afterward, when my mother scolded him for not appearing at her party, was he able to piece together what had swept him off on his appalling journey.

2

Hanging Gardens

If the youthful behavior had lasted for a lifetime, it coexisted with an intense dedication to work: to writing as well as one possibly could. There was a conviction, which was passed on to the children, that work was enormously rewarding, that the primary task of any young person was to decide whatever he liked best, then to devote himself to it. And it was predicted that you were going to work like a dog all your life—whether you were a bus driver or the first violinist of the Philharmonic or a housewife or a designer of skyscrapers. Since your work would be so demanding it should be highly enjoyable as well. But the adults didn't seem to endorse the puritan work ethic, which asserted that work was good for the character. Instead most believed that work should be so pleasurable that it would expand your entire range of experience and be an adventure in itself.

When they were young, no one was supposed to sound too serious: that signified stuffiness and someone who approached pomposity could be told to "put some water in it." A person's most solemn thoughts were a private matter, or else they belonged on paper. But by the time I was around, the adults weren't afraid to be serious: about work, about war, about family problems. Still they shunned any nuance that suggested affectation. For example, few *New Yorker* writers might have called themselves artists; after all, essayists and reporters were not regarded as artists in the Fifties—academia saw to that. And since Mencken, their early mentor, had chosen "unwarranted pretension" as one of his chief targets, they might have thought it pretentious to speak of nonfiction as an art. But many had passed through a spell of youthful aestheticism. Some talked to me at length about Yeats and James and Joyce when I was immersed in them for the first time: the middle-aged pulled down the pencil-scarred copies from their shelves, reliving the delights of discovery. I remember that Thurber, who adored James, had a sardonic theory about *The Portrait of a Lady*: he claimed that all young American men had once been in love with Isabel Archer—therefore it was a good thing that her modern counterparts tended to settle down abroad, because she would have been a trial to live with.

When it came to earning, they had always expected to be paid to do exactly what they wished, and many were. Most held their employers—like any authority—in contempt. So the tales about the stupidities of Henry Luce or Bennett Cerf convulsed the rooms full of writers who mocked those who financed them. Most editors, apart from Mencken and Robert Linscott and Maxwell Perkins, were derided as frustrated writers who had no ear for language—only a longing to play with prose which didn't belong to them. In the Sixties Perelman wrote to me about magazine editors: "A pox on them. The chiefest function of the majority of editors is to act as a transmission belt for checks. . . . They fancy themselves mainly in the role of castrators, busily snooping through the prose they get to see how they can vitiate, weaken, or mildew it."

A. J. Liebling wrote that it was hard for writers to admire editors: "It is like asking a thief to approve a fence, or a fighter to speak highly of a manager." (Liebling then quoted an old boxer who stated, "Managers are pimps, they sell our blood.") Of Harold Ross, whom Liebling did respect, he observed, "We were eager to please him and cherished his praise, but we publicly and profanely discounted his criticism." Certain that *The New Yorker* editors had misread a couple of stories by Vladimir Nabokov, Edmund Wilson wrote to Katharine White that her colleagues were infected with "a truly alarming condition of editor's daze"; he added that they were "so afraid of anything that is unusual . . . that they put a premium on insipidity and banality." Few writers seemed to fear that their editors might be offended, or that they would use their power to bridle those who chastised them.

When Peggy Bacon, aged seventy-five, told me, "I'd rather have fun than security!" she could have been speaking for many of her friends, who assumed that pleasure and profit were polarities, that almost no one could have both. Bacon's devastating caricatures of the rich showed the disdain that her group felt for artists' patrons. In the Twenties, when Bacon's peers had minimal cash, they were sure it could be easily acquired, simply because dollars seemed to be floating around on every breeze and it appeared as if prosperity would never end. (Gene Fowler, a reporter and screenwriter, wrote, "Money is something to be thrown off the back end of the trains.") In the Fifties the same attitude was apparent. Scornful of those who took money too seriously, they were nonetheless very disciplined when a family illness or the needs of older relatives required them to work in Hollywood or for Time Inc.: the goal was to earn fast and get out quickly. (*The New Yorker* did not then pay well enough to carry a family through an unforeseen financial crisis.) But they were certain that hack work could be dangerous, that it could deaden the powers of invention.

Most of the New York writers were fairly cynical about movies, although they spoke more tolerantly about Hollywood years after they had left it and no longer feared that their energies would be sapped by the industry. While some had liked the prospect of working on screenplays, they loathed the studio system. And they'd resented the fiscal necessities which had taken them to the coast; Faulkner was there because (as he wrote in a letter) he had to provide "food, shelter, heat, clothes, medicine, Kotex, school fees, toilet paper, and picture shows" for a slew of relatives. James M. Cain wrote scripts when he was "sad in the pocketbook." Many disliked the collaborative nature of screenwriting, as well as the tradition of assigning a series of writers to the same script—that was "chain gang work." It was said that some eighty writers worked on the screenplay of Henry Hathaway's *Lives of a Bengal Lancer*; three received credit for it.

Faulkner and my father had the credits on Howard Hawks's *The Road to Glory*, but in truth almost all of the shooting script had been written by Nunnally Johnson. The screen team had been somewhat delinquent: my father was entranced by tales of the Snopes family, and he kept urging Faulkner to tell him more of them. Some that my father remembered never appeared in any of Faulkner's books. While the two were engrossed in legends of Mississippi rather than a movie about World War I in France, the novelist was writing *Absalom, Absalom!* But one afternoon, when he had a frightful hangover, he wrote a seventeen-page story about a cow as a comic Christmas present for my father. (It seems that Faulkner had had the idea for the tale some years before, but the Snopes sessions gave him the impetus to write it.) "Afternoon of a Cow" was self-parody, but some details from the story later resurfaced in *The Hamlet*, where the idiot Ike Snopes falls in love with a neighbor's cow.

Assignments were so arbitrary that one untalented writer was steadily rehired because he cooked spaghetti in a way that pleased Louis B. Mayer. And writers waxed more than weary of the formulae of the plots they were given, of remaking the same aviation or football picture, or vehicles in which the studio's child star played yet another version of Cupid. They also had to write parts for stars which dwelled on the performers' physical traits: Joe E. Brown's enormous mouth, Mae West's breasts, Jimmy Durante's nose. Cain wrote bleakly, "There is hardly an actor without an asset to be taken into account," and playwrights wistfully recalled that the theater does not rely on close-ups. And since typecasting was the norm, writers rarely had the fun of inventing an unfamiliar character. Although Hollywood was called the factory of fantasy, writers complained that they weren't allowed to use their imaginations. Dorothy Parker referred to her studio as Metro-Goldwyn-Merde. Perelman's letters from Hollywood seethed with disgust, as when he wrote that he and his wife Laura were "still flailing away" at "a treatment which is purest cat vomit. . . . From where we stand now, all we can see is a vast expansion of shit stretching away to the horizon."

The censorship of the late Thirties also maddened East Coast writers. A few years earlier some had gone to Hollywood to work on gangster films, but the censors soon decided that criminals set a dreadful example to American youth; because violent movies were so popular, more "morality" was necessary between the gun battles. Retribution was prescribed for all who erred, like divorced mothers—not just for those who broke the law. Scenes of sit-down strikes were forbidden. The censors were so obsessed with "brutality" that when a troop of Indians was scheduled to strangle its victims with handkerchiefs in *Gunga Din*, the Hays office sent a memo: "Please be careful in the strangling scene not to show any brutality." At the censors' suggestion the heroine of *Love Affair* was run over by a truck on her way to a tryst with her new lover; she had to atone for a premarital love affair before she could be happy with Charles Boyer. Albert Hackett said that almost the only kind of "infidelity" that could appear in movies "was one man taking another man's wife to lunch." (Mae West told *The New York Times*, "I like restraint if it doesn't go too far.") David O. Selznick was ordered to "Omit the action of Scarlett belching" in *Gone with the Wind*, and the Hays Office was vigilant when W. C. Fields starred in *The Bank Dick*: "Please eliminate the expression of 'nuts to you' from Egbert's speech."

Yet occasionally the censors and the Legion of Decency were foiled. When John Ford was directing *The Informer*, he worried that an essential scene in a brothel would be cut—how could he get away with filming "a cathouse"? J. M. Kerrigan, the Irish actor from the Abbey Theatre who played the little toady in the movie, solved the problem. "Put hats on the cats," he advised. Ford did so, and the censors never guessed that women who wore hats might be prostitutes. But such small triumphs were rare. Convinced that movies were growing more childish every year, writers were continually stunned by the ineptitudes of producers; it was said (perhaps unfairly) that Walter Wanger relinquished the chance to film *Wuthering Heights* because he didn't see any humor in it, and Frances Goodrich and Albert Hackett remembered that when a friend of theirs was commissioned to write a scene for a race horse picture in which a mare's foal dies, Hunt Stromberg commanded, "For God's sake, give me a whinny with a tear in it!" My father quoted George Stevens: "Nothing wrong with Hollywood except the toilet company that owns it." So I grew up knowing that moviemaking wasn't romantic.

A few who deservedly flourished as screenwriters—Nunnally Johnson, Goodrich and Hackett—were sometimes able to deal with the producers on their own terms. Johnson's talents were so widely appreciated that screenwriting became a satisfying vocation. But the Hacketts—who'd written *It's a Wonderful Life* (they loathed Frank Capra's rewrites) and whose credits included *The Thin Man, Easter Parade,* and the play and film of *The Diary of Anne Frank*— returned to New York and playwriting when unappetizing movie projects were offered. And many others, who wanted to resume writing books, were grateful to extricate themselves from Hollywood. For some, "selling out" had been less of an issue than "being bought": becoming dependent on stultifying institutions. Quite a few had written movies mainly to subsidize their fiction.

But despite the big hospital bills or debts that had led to stints in Hollywood or at *Time,* there seemed to be a challenge in "living by your wits"—another legacy from the Twenties. The first time I met Walker Evans, at a dinner given for my college roommate when we were sophomores, he told me how he had left Williams after a year and had gone to live in Paris. Excited by his recollections, I asked how he'd supported himself. "Oh," he said, aiming his large nose toward a snifter of magnificent brandy, "I lived by my wits." That sounded so dashing that I later ignored his stringent advice about the practicalities of earning a living.

Yet few of my elders seemed to feel that there was any point in planning for the future. Not only did they relish the unexpected, but many seemed optimistic about what lay ahead. They also appeared to have a sense of unending time: whatever one wanted, there would be plenty of time to achieve it. And their offspring were exhorted to live in the present. When difficulties arose, I was hazily assured that "Somehow, somewhere, some when" things would work out as they ought to; the assumption was that a decent or gifted person deserved a fine life: indeed the world owed it to him. For the older generation, worrying almost seemed to be a sin—not only because it wasted energy, but because apprehension was so unreasonable: for an imaginative being, nothing could ever be as bad as was anticipated. (The severe anxiety that surged through Thurber's writing and White's was supposed to be an artful exaggeration, not a natural human state.) Having regrets about the past was also wasteful: that was a drain on the present and even rather morbid. Problems would be coped with as they occurred, but surely one's overall existence would be freighted with rewards. These convictions undoubtedly came from the Twenties, when early publication had made many writers confident of their momentum.

In a world of cultural privileges and average salaries, most of my seniors lived very comfortably: modest wages went a long way in the Fifties. But since many had known austerity as apprentices in the Twenties, and far fiercer deprivations in the Thirties—except for those in Hollywood, who earned more during the Depression than they had ever had before—most didn't spend much on their surroundings. Possessions were impediments, a hindrance to wayfarers addicted to mobility. They didn't need elaborate belongings to announce their own worth to them, and home was a city (like New York) or a stretch of country landscape rather than any particular building, rented or owned. Their furnishings were quite traditional, even conventional: upright velvet upholstery, antique mahogany sideboards, discreet colors, and toile curtains had replaced the Salvation Army oddments they'd left behind in the cold-water flats of the Village.

The mistrust of lush living wasn't moralistic, and it was said to be healthy to enjoy money if it came one's way. But even in the affluent Fifties it was thought that writers should beware of costly lives; otherwise their freedom could be destroyed by the pressures to sustain them. And even those who had made a lot of money—like Thurber or the interior designer Anne Duffy—retained the outlook of wage-earners.

But money was not a thing one talked about, and writers who prospered shouldn't be boastful. Comparing royalty statements would have been boorish, almost as bad as referring to "status," a word that echoed through the Fifties. And like status, social class was not acknowledged—another characteristic of the period, as well as of this group of writers. So I was utterly unprepared for the reaction of my godfather, John O'Hara, when he asked where I would like to go to college. (Cozy and hectic and generous in my childhood, he had given me my first image of a dispenser—someone whose affections materialized as gifts: large stuffed lions from F.A.O. Schwarz, a diary that locked, charms for the charm bracelet, flowers, a gold pencil from Tiffany's.) When he laughed it sounded like a soda siphon: a hiss that began with a *k*. I'd been shielded from his priorities until the name of Radcliffe inspired a short sermon of disgust; it's nothing socially, he said, you should go to Vassar—no Harvard man will ever take a Radcliffe student to dinner, the girls are under a terrible stigma there.

Cheerfully I replied that people I knew didn't care about that social stuff, and that he must be out of date. His arm flew up and his wife Belle moved swiftly to restrain him, while my mother gestured in alarm. Belle led him quickly from their living room and my mother seized our coats, whispering that he was a writer who prided himself on getting everything absolutely right: you just don't tell that man he's out of date.

I had not yet read his novels—only some of the stories about Hollywood and Broadway and suburbia—in which I'd failed to detect his passion for privilege. Perhaps some buried envy had raised his arm to hit me: after all I was applying to the kind of college that his family's poverty had denied him. (His fixation on the Ivy League had prompted Hemingway to suggest that a fund should be started to send O'Hara—then thirty-seven—to Yale.) But as my mother hustled me out of his house, I was still unable to grasp that the issue at hand could be serious, or that he was as angry as he seemed.

My father wrote me, "Your godfather's predominating itch is that he wasn't born to the purple; nearly all his thinking, behavior, and writing have been efforts to combat this," and he quoted press agent Richard Maney's description of O'Hara as "the master of the fancied slight." But the breach was lasting; although he sent me a $100 check when I got married, I saw him only once again, eight years after I'd affronted him: on that occasion, he made a ritual of giving back some photographs of me that he'd had since I was a child.

In middle age he had traveled so far from the New York writers who lampooned his ideas of social prestige that he sometimes felt his later work was belittled because they envied his intercourse with the rich. Maybe he never quite knew that he had alienated his former companions by insisting that American society was still stratified: a notion that was considered so tasteless that it was hardly ever mentioned. At least I didn't hear it discussed. People were likable or not, gifted or not, successful or otherwise, solely on the basis of their individual traits. Earning a fortune did not signify success: anyone who thought so had succumbed to foolishness.

O'Hara, I was eventually told, was a victim of his own imagination: he'd believed that wealth and social standing were important, and that fantasy had damaged his talent. Once that was said, his early novels would be praised; his old friends were apt to speak of him in the past tense, even when he had almost twenty books ahead of him. But there were still affectionate memories of the buoyant young reporter who had been thrilled by his arrival in New York. It was also said that he had learned a lot from the city's press, even though he was discharged from *The New York Herald Tribune* after five months of hangovers and botched deadlines.

• • •

I heard many fond references to the newspaper life of the Twenties, when some young journalists had revelled in their jobs to a degree that was inconceivable in the Fifties, when our papers seemed flaccid and boring. New York had seventeen dailies when my father joined *The Herald Tribune* in 1926; he used to buy whole armloads of papers to read over lunch, tearing out stories and columns and editorials to compare them. *The New York World* was regarded as the most literate of all, and *The Tribune* was said to be more of "a writer's paper" than *The New York Times*, which was already "the newspaper of record." Respected for its thoroughness, *The Times* also had a reputation for flattening out a writer's style and for ponderous, conjunction-studded sentences. The paper was so overstaffed that star reporters battled with cubs for an opportunity to cover church bazaars or cornerstone layings, and the city desk was called Putterers' Field. *The Times* was known for two kinds of sobriety: the management was wary of jokes—"They carefully edited the smiles out of a story," my father said—and many of its writers didn't drink as much as those on *The Tribune*. Yet no one accused *The Times'* writers of prudery, and there was a rhyme that I heard repeated:

> Drink is the jinx of *The Tribune*
> And sex is the hex of *The Times*.

Ex-newsmen told me that until the New Deal switched the national focus to Washington, New York news was featured all over the country, and crime reporting was viewed as an art. Competing papers gleefully published one another's errors and fabrications. Quite a few reporters indulged their imaginations, but they and the editors who clamored for colorful stories—until their employees were willing to invent them—were frequently exposed. "Improving" a story might be a common practice, but absolute fiction aroused some awe. One famous lie of the Twenties concerned a giant floating speakeasy on a ship anchored well beyond New York's twelve-mile limit: the thing was splashed all over *The Tribune* and turned out not to exist at all. (The reporter, whose lead story described millionaires dancing with chorus girls to a jazz orchestra while champagne was guzzled amid the "revels de luxe," was fired after the hoax was discovered, but he was hired by numerous papers outside New York in the next three decades.) It was said that Reuters news service provided exotic or dubious stories: "A spider with a human face has been seen in Texas." But there was not much interest in foreign news, and that field did not develop until the ascendancy of Hitler and the outbreak of the Spanish Civil War.

It could take many months of filing unsigned copy to earn a byline; Joseph Mitchell compared the day when your name first appeared in a paper to the occasion when a bullfighter is given the bull's ear. Like many fledgling reporters, my father loved the unpredictability of daily assignments: shooting off on the subway to find himself in the midst of a congress of spiritualists in a remote part of the Queens waterfront, or covering the demonstrations against Mayor Frank Hague in Jersey City (eggs and stinkbombs were hurled at Hague's opponents) and a hobo convention in Newark and the demolition of a renowned Bowery beer palace and an evening gala in Harlem honoring the jazz composer W. C. Handy, who wrote "St. Louis Blues" and "A Good Man Is Hard to Find." Variety was a tonic: he interviewed a group of Mexican cowboys who were in town for the rodeo and then an Italian barber who was proud to resemble Mussolini, seven Ubangi women employed by the Ringling Brothers circus, the only Socialist in the *Social Register*, some entomologists who were at a loss to explain why hordes of praying mantises had suddenly appeared in several Manhattan skyscrapers, and Paul Poiret, the Parisian couturier, who predicted a revival of silk gloves, the demise of flesh-colored stockings, and the debut of the trouser-skirt.

For a while his regular beat was the Manhattan Criminal Courts. But he also wrote about conflicts between the Dean and the Bishop at the Cathedral of St. John the Divine, greyhound races in Staten Island, a crisis at Childs restaurants when the vegetarian stockholders tried to knock meat off the menu, women who startled the New York City Commission by demanding the right to be municipal streetcleaners, football games at Sing Sing prison, the contrasting character of crowds at Madison Square Garden during prizefights, political rallies, dance marathons, and horse or poultry shows, the 1929 opening of the Central Park Casino—where lobster dinners were served under the black and gold glass ceiling of the ballroom to the music of a string quintet—and a frigid day at Yankee Stadium when Babe Ruth's breath looked like smoke from a volcano. And he rejoiced in the fact that New York would never run out of stories and that readers in every state were greedy for more of them.

Because *The Tribune*'s salaries were meager he went to *The New York Telegram* for almost a year, found it provincial and returned to *The Tribune*. In those days a young reporter was often assigned a gangster of his own, whom he had to cover whenever the hood made news. My father's was Legs Diamond, unconvicted killer and owner of the Hotsy Totsy Club on Broadway. Diamond was distinguished for surviving four nearly fatal assaults on his life by rival mobs: on my mother's birthday or on the eve of a friend's wedding, Diamond would be shot in Manhattan or the Catskills, and my father would have to rush to his bedside in yet another hospital. The Sayres did not repine when he was finally dispatched in Albany in 1931. But those who followed criminals for *The Tribune* had to observe a certain delicacy, because Elizabeth Mills Reid, the publisher's mother, had banned some words from the paper: "coffin" (they had to refer to a gangster's "casket"), "honeymoon" (they felt silly alluding to a mobster's "wedding trip"), and—most difficult for crime reporters—"blood." Joseph Mitchell once wrote a brilliantly gory account of the aftermath of a shootout: he described crimson liquid and scarlet walls and floors without ever mentioning blood.

The political fraudulence and hypocrisy engendered by Prohibition meant that gangsters were in a semi-protected position, since bootleggers were popular figures—as well as adept at bribing policemen, judges, and politicians. As long as racketeers mainly murdered one another, the public didn't worry much about crime, and gangsters were thought to be entertaining. *The Tribune* sent Mitchell to many underworld funerals, which were often in Catholic churches in Little Italy or the Italian section of East Harlem. Mobs tried to outdo each other in providing their leaders with opulent rites. Mitchell gave special attention to hymns as well as the enormous wreaths and intricate flower pieces inscribed, "Goodbye, Old Pal" or "From the Boys." Vast floral clocks made of lilies and carnations—their gold hands pointing to the time of the dead man's murder—were customary; bronze or silver coffins were blanketed with roses. Yet Legs Diamond, abhorred for his foul temper, had only a small funeral.

Although some journalists of the era said the *Front Page* image of newspaper reporters was an exaggeration, my father wrote that the depiction of "iconoclastic young men wearing snap-brim hats with cigarettes dangling from their whiskey-wet lips and bent on insulting any and all individuals who stood in their paths, no matter how celebrated or sacrosanct," was accurate. But he did point out that *The Front Page* itself was set in Chicago, where newsmen seemed like "savages and barbarians" to New Yorkers, ready to do anything to get a story: betray a confidence, forge a signature, or sabotage a competitor's telephone. He laughed when he talked about the Chicagoans. But he revered facts and hated errors: writers who distorted their material were remembered with contempt. And since he disliked card games, he couldn't understand why some reporters loitered over poker in the newsroom when the city was overflowing with adventures.

Yet the alumni of the Twenties didn't seem sentimental about the papers of the past. Nunnally Johnson told me that the decade had nourished too many "whimsy boys" who wrote in "Biblical rhythms," and my father ridiculed the "word-painters" of the old *Telegram*: cub reporters from Minnesota or Oklahoma who were so dazzled by Manhattan that they wrote quaint articles about the Village and the Bowery in a style that A. J. Liebling called "Oklahoma Byzantine." Robert Benchley had claimed that *The World* folded because too many of its stories began, "Up the dark staircase crept a lonely figure." My father recalled a piece that was typical of the period—by a reporter who wrote up the drowning of two nuns and a child from the point of view of the wave. He and Johnson felt that the papers of the Twenties needed more specialists, particularly science reporters: Johnson complained of having to cover "the atrophy of the optic nerve" when his normal beat was Fifth Avenue parades. Both of them stressed that divorces received an extraordinary amount of space; even *The Times* gave extensive attention to the parting of Peaches and Daddy Browning six months after their marriage in 1926. The bridal night of the fifteen-year-old girl and the real estate tycoon, aged fifty-one, had also been immortalized by the press, which alleged that Daddy spent most of the night sandpapering a shoetree.

The former journalists I knew felt that the Newspaper Guild, organized by Heywood Broun in 1933, had been urgently needed. But a few still scoffed at the notion of "sending reporters home to their wives"; initially they had worked a six-day week without overtime pay. And they remembered that Mencken had argued that a forty-hour-a-week reporter was no more possible then a forty-hour archbishop. Most editors—other than Stanley Walker and Lessing Engelking of *The Tribune*—were known as "deskmen," and it was widely acknowledged that deskmen couldn't write, "they could just ruin." Teasing or outfoxing an editor was one of the fringe benefits of the trade.

Still, those who talked to me about their years in the city room were keen to convey how delightful it once was to be a New York reporter in what was called the nothing-sacred age of journalism. Almost by definition, the American newsman was a free spirit, heir to the country's best traditions of independence—at liberty to ignore the conventions imposed on other citizens. In the Twenties, my father said, "The town was crazy and wide open and full of scandal and uproar; there was no war, no bomb—just a perfectly wonderful murder now and then." He and his friends would have agreed with Stanley

Walker when he wrote in his memoirs that New York was "the paradise of the newspaperman." Surveying the city, Walker reflected, "Its hanging gardens are said to be superior to those of Babylon. . . . Its rackets are probably as brutal as those of Marseilles, and more devious and varied than those of Chicago. . . . It is deliriously beautiful and as ugly as a mildewed toad. Somehow, the city cannot be slandered, and anything that may be said of it in praise or abuse is more likely than not to be true." After meeting a deadline, a reporter leaving the *Tribune* building would hear the presses throb as they started to roll; at that moment, Joseph Mitchell told me, you could feel that you were truly at the heart of the center of the city.

3

Church and State

Politics was not often or ardently discussed in those living rooms of the Fifties. The idealism which had once made some men regret that they'd been too young to fight in World War I had disintegrated amid the mediocrities of Warren Harding's presidency: the postwar "normalcy" that he proclaimed inspired cynicism. And the execution of Sacco and Vanzetti in 1927 had suggested that justice was not obtainable in America; the system itself could not be trusted—not after two men whose guilt was widely doubted were put to death. Throughout the Twenties almost all politicians were regarded as fools by my parents' friends, and politics seemed irrelevant to those who were committed to literature. (Alvin Johnson of *The New Republic* said, "The only thing which has saved democracy is the indifference of the public to politics.") Even in the late Thirties, Thurber wrote to E. B. White, "All this concern about political forms is nonsense. . . . No government in the world is as big as a man's liver." In the Twenties and afterward, most of these writers were what Alfred Kazin has called "liberals by acquiescence"—mainly because "conservatism had become a joke," and also because it was allied with the small-town puritanism which their behavior had helped to discredit.

One catalyst of the national cynicism had been the Teapot Dome scandal and its consequences; in 1924 the extent of graft and bribery in President Harding's administration was revealed. But the widespread evidence of party corruption did not cripple the Republicans. Instead, the G.O.P. was returned to power in that year's election by a colossal majority, which was celebrating the greatest bull market Wall Street had ever known. Although the Democrats were supposed to be the liberal party, they were controlled by Irish ward heelers in the cities and by racists in the South. At the Democratic convention of 1924, throngs of hooded Ku Klux Klansmen (who backed William McAdoo, the Southern favorite) and phalanxes of Catholic priests (who supported Al Smith, the Tammany candidate) gathered at opposite ends of Madison Square Garden and howled at one another. The Klan, which had three hundred and forty delegates, was powerful enough to prevent Smith's nomination. The seventeen-day convention ended in a deadlock, and John W. Davis, the compromise candidate, was eviscerated by Calvin Coolidge in November. Understandably neither party appealed to educated young voters, who were also repelled when Coolidge said in 1925, "The business of America is business."

Much of the press, like most politicians, flattered the businessman. Shipping news was featured in the papers of the Twenties: reporters waited on the piers to question homecoming travelers emerging from the ocean liners. Docking in New York after excursions to Paris, embryo writers heard nut and bolt manufacturers from the Midwest being interviewed about international affairs after they'd spent two weeks abroad: the papers published their pronouncements at length, and their views carried far more weight than the opinions of most other Americans. Recalling "a world dominated by salesmen and brokers," Edmund Wilson wrote that he and his friends "had always resented its barbarism." Many years later Walker Evans said that, prior to the Wall Street crash, ours had been "a hateful society" for those who had no interest in business, and therefore "all authority was almost insulting to a sensitive citizen." The commercialism of the era seemed to perpetuate ignorance and bigotry as well as regimentation. So the sensitive were quite proud to know little about economics. And before they understood the enduring catastrophe of the Crash, some had felt as Wilson did early in 1932: "One couldn't help being exhilarated at the sudden unexpected collapse of that stupid gigantic fraud. It gives us a new sense of freedom." Evans remembered his "glee" on reading that brokers were "jumping out the window": "Capitalism is falling apart and none of those people has a cent of money. Good! Let them find out what it's like." In the Fifties the adults I knew still seemed to think that Wall Street was sleazy and so were bankers: there was something tainted about people who devoted a career to merely making money, and writers felt superior to anyone who wasted his life on the stock market.

Unquestionably the heritage of Mencken filtered through our home; his derision of "the boobus Americanus" lingered long after he had ceased to write (and I unwittingly inherited some Menckenism when I regarded the conformists of the Fifties as my enemies). The great arsonist who had put his torch to middle-class values, the editor whom Walter Lippmann had called "the most powerful personal influence on this whole generation of educated people," had inspired them to scorn businessmen, academics, reformers, and the genteel tradition in literature. Dedicated to the freedom of speech, Mencken had once seemed to embody civilization and wit in a nation of hacks and shoddy criminals.

Young aesthetes of the Twenties had relished paradox as a literary device, and Mencken's talent for hurling the reader off balance while shattering the accepted concepts of right and wrong had delighted his followers. He defined alimony as "ransom that the happy pay to the devil," and declared that "The plutocracy is comprehensible to the mob because its aspirations are essentially those of inferior men: it is not by accident that Christianity, a mob religion, paves heaven with gold and precious stones, i.e., with money." With impartial gusto he denounced Presidents Warren Harding (whose prose resembled "a string of wet sponges. . . . It is so bad that a sort of grandeur creeps into it"), Herbert Hoover ("a pathetic mud turtle"), and "the preposterous Truman, perhaps the cheapest and least honest man ever to sit in the White House." He called himself "a Tory in politics" and had a special animus for Franklin Roosevelt: "a demogogue pure and simple" and "a chartered libertine"; Mencken felt that FDR had "maneuvered the country into war and will bankrupt it in consequence," that American soldiers were dying overseas because of "Roosevelt's itch to glitter in history."

Contemptuous of democracy itself, he thought the idea of social progress was ridiculous: "Obviously, the human race, taking it by and large, is both ignorant and vicious . . . It is actually no more virtuous than a gang of rats." Government had "always been the great failure of mankind," and its problems were "inherently and incurably insoluble." Politicians were fundamentally useless: "the good ones, like the bad ones, seem to me to be unanimously thieves." For him Abraham Lincoln had been a slick opportunist and Marx was "the philosopher out of the gutter." Mencken was comfortable in his antipathies: "The simple truth is that I detest all movements and all uplifters." An energetic civil libertarian who had opposed the deportation of Emma Goldman to Russia in 1919 and campaigned for her readmission to the United States, he nonetheless castigated liberals who defended the rights of American Communists— although he thought Communists (like all Americans) were entitled to air their views. And he asserted that Communist professors should not be fired from Columbia in 1934.

In the mid-Twenties, when the Ku Klux Klan's membership was the largest in its history and the Klan helped to elect many congressmen and sixteen senators, Mencken assailed it regularly, supported desegregation, and battled all kinds of racists. He backed a bill that would have made lynching a federal offense and steadily published black writers in *The American Mercury*. Yet he frequently referred to black Americans as "darkies" and "blackamoors." In a favorable review of an anthology of essays by blacks, he also observed, "the vast majority of the people of their race are but two or three inches removed from gorillas." But his last piece—printed two weeks before his crippling stroke in 1948—urged that blacks be admitted to Baltimore's tennis courts and golf courses; of the city ordinance that excluded them, he wrote, "It is high time that all such relics of Ku Kluxery be wiped out of Maryland."

Many liberals appreciated Mencken, but the esteem wasn't mutual. In a self-portrait of 1923 he wrote that he was "unable to make the grade as a Liberal, for Liberalism always involves freeing human beings against their will—often, indeed, to their obvious damage, as in the cases of the majority of Negroes and women." Writing elsewhere that "the great curse of humanity . . . is idealism," he characterized "the so-called Reds" of 1920 as "humorless idealists . . . who took the platitudes of democracy quite seriously." That he totally misunderstood the Depression—in 1932, when he attended the political conventions, he implied that the overriding issue of the election was the legalization of beer—wasn't mentioned by those who spoke of him warmly in the Fifties. Disregarding his titanic inconsistencies and his dogmatism, they still quoted the ebullient iconoclast, the critic who had championed Joseph Conrad, Ibsen and Shaw, Sinclair Lewis and Scott Fitzgerald, and had published young radicals like Michael Gold and Josephine Herbst, whose views contradicted his own. (Malcolm Cowley, who disagreed with much of Mencken's literary taste, told me he never forgot what it had meant to read Joyce in *The Smart Set* when Mencken and George Jean Nathan were editing it.) Those whose first stories had appeared in *The American Mercury* were still proud to have appeared there, and our closets were full of old copies in their green covers. Mencken's memoirs—*Happy Days*, *Newspaper Days*, and *Heathen Days*—were prominent on our bookshelves along with the volumes of his *The American Language*. Some of his admirers managed to ignore the worst aspects of his political judgments because they continued to expect the worst from politicians—the very attitude that they had learned from him. Their Mencken was not the anti-Semite who had written to a friend in 1935, "My belief, often expressed, is that the Jews probably deserve their troubles," but the man who wrote, "My motto is that of Swift: 'the chief end I propose myself in all my labors is to vex the world rather than divert it.'"

Except for Edmund Wilson almost none of my parents' friends had been radicalized by the Depression, and he had retreated from politics well before I knew him. To the heirs of Mencken, the Spanish Civil War had been a "fashionable" cause, and parts of the New Deal were thought to be absurdly Utopian. Because I ate very slowly in childhood, I was called "a WPA spoon-leaner"; Mencken had made jokes about WPA workers as shiftless "shovel-leaners." In the Twenties he had said that genuine poverty did not exist in the United States, that only idiots could fail to prosper in such a rich country. For him, according to his friend Sara Mayfield, the Depression "was nothing more than a hangover after the financial binge of 1929." Despising Roosevelt's social programs and accusing the President of converting the government into a "milch cow with 125,000,000 teats," Mencken persisted in advocating laissez-faire capitalism. He sneered at Wall Street, but he owned stock in fifty-eight corporations, and all of it was paying dividends in the mid-Forties.

His disdain for religion suited a generation which had detached itself from Christianity and Judaism. Some had never felt any allegiance to the Presbyterianism or Methodism of their youth; the sermons and Sunday schools had bored them. Throughout their Midwestern childhoods, Sunday meant deprivation and dejection: baseball, fishing, buggy rides, playing the piano, and listening to the phonograph had been forbidden; some were not permitted to read anything but the Bible on the Sabbath, not even newspapers. Young Protestants were taught that levity belonged to Satan and that whatever was enjoyable was wicked. Righteousness also required a belief in questionable wonders like the Virgin Birth and Noah's ability to locate pairs of every animal in creation. Although they were told that their creed was rooted in love, the savage punishments of a vindictive God suggested that Christianity was based on revenge and hatred. So the piety of their elders became repugnant to them.

Ex-Catholics like O'Hara and my mother had decisively rejected the faith of their families. Jews like Perelman and Liebling were agnostics. These people did not attack the church, they just avoided it. I doubt if they would have gone as far as Mencken when he wrote, "One of the most irrational of all the conventions of modern society [is] . . . that religious opinions should be respected." But there was a suspicion that organized religion was a snare for the uneducated, who could be manipulated into fanaticism, especially through the fear of eternal suffering. To these New York writers, Christianity seemed downright unintelligent and the church represented hypocrisy and repression.

Perhaps my father's foremost religious experience occurred while watching a Hopi rain dance in Arizona—where he was terrifically impressed by the ensuing cloudbursts, followed by a tremendous electrical blackout; he talked about it for years. He and his friends were not hyper-rationalists and they didn't deny the spiritual dimensions of many works of art. But when they read Eliot and Faulkner and Waugh, they tended to bypass the Christian themes in their work. And when Allen Tate called Edmund Wilson a Christian, Wilson felt that was "a malicious, libelous, and baseless charge."

Like almost all their offspring, I was carefully protected from contacts with Christianity; the Greek legends were read aloud to me, but not the Bible. Hence my parents were dismayed to find me kneeling in prayer to Zeus when I was six; they hastily explained that the myths were "just stories." (From then on, I prayed to Apollo in secret.) At any rate, it was felt that children should grow up far from the contamination of all religions. So it was bewildering to be christened at the age of ten: which I was only because of the vagueness of my birth certificate. (I was born while my parents were visiting Bermuda, and they thought some American document was needed as proof of my existence.) There was an Episcopalian ceremony in a large church, and I was embarrassed because my godfather—horribly pale and sheeted with sweat—was wearing a tailcoat in mid-afternoon: I was later told that his costume was a self-imposed penance for being dreadfully hungover. O'Hara's trembling hands and his guilt and the crowd of adults waiting impatiently for the party to follow—a farewell bash for my father, who was leaving for Europe the next day—all intensified my impression of the discomforts of Christianity; I had never been in a church and it was years before I saw another altar.

Heywood Hale Broun, the son of feminist journalist Ruth Hale and the progressive columnist Heywood Broun, was even more sheltered than I was: "By making certain that I had no religious education of any kind, [my parents] were going to spare me from terror. They were convinced that their own lives were shadowed beyond saving by the vigorous 19th century Christianity that they had rejected but had not, in the darkness of their dreams and fears, escaped." As a child, Broun horrified his parents by announcing that he might like to go to a Universalist Sunday School along with some of his classmates. The distraught couple summoned a psychiatrist to their home "not so much to dissuade me as to comfort them that this terrifying symptom might be no more than a sign of some juvenile emotional rash. . . . Many years later he told me that their anxiety had been deep and genuine."

In the Fifties my seniors were distressed when some of my contemporaries embraced Catholicism: the parents had not guessed that theology and worship would seem like forbidden fruit—seductive because untasted. By then rereading Mencken could not have offered much consolation to the relatives of converts: "No sane man denies that the universe presents phenomena quite beyond human understanding, and so it is a fair assumption that they are directed by some understanding that is superhuman. But that is as far as sound thought can go. All religions pretend to go further. That is, they pretend to explain the unknowable. . . . Anyone who pretends to say what God wants or doesn't want, and what the whole show is about, is simply an ass. . . . The more ignorant the man, the more firm his faith." Mencken's followers also assumed that the church was just as venal as any corporate institution; after Nunnally Johnson made a movie for MGM in Italy, he told my father many stories about "how the Vatican really loves money and doesn't care a bit who does the palm-greasing, Leo the Lion or anybody."

Edmund Wilson had written that Mencken was "without question, since Poe, our greatest practicing literary journalist." But Wilson had also rebuked him for schooling a generation "to speak of politics as an obscene farce." Wilson felt that Mencken had actually increased the success of his adversaries, the bankers and the politicians, by encouraging young writers to believe that politics and commerce were inconsequential. Moreover, as late as 1942, although Mencken wrote unfavorably about Hitler, he added, "The German scheme is working better than Roosevelt's half orthodox and half Communist American scheme." (Mencken was reluctant to recognize the evils of the Nazis because he prized his Prussian ancestry and he was still reacting against the violent anti-German feelings that had endured in America after World War I.) Wilson concluded, "We never expected coherence from Mencken." He was rarely predictable: after Hiroshima he defined the atom bomb as "the greatest invention . . . since leprosy. . . . Try to imagine a decent cannibal throwing it on a town full of women and children."

But Mencken's pronouncements on war meant little to his former congregation. There had been passionate support for World War II within the Twenties generation, accompanied by a sharp flush of patriotism. Also some had become devoted to France and England when they visited those countries in their youth, and they felt we should fight on their behalf. And it was intolerable to many of them that a foreign dictator thought he could tackle the United States. For them there was no conflict between ridiculing their government and loving their country. Scott Fitzgerald wrote, "We were born to power and intense nationalism. . . . We were told, individually and as a unit, that we were a race that could potentially lick ten others of any genus." That certitude surrounded me early on—when the adults kept promising that we would win the war—and during the Korean War; no other nation could "push us around." These assurances came even when our troops suffered heavy casualties: our country could never lose a contest.

Yet most of my seniors were extremely well informed, especially on domestic matters: they gave an animated, almost scholarly attention to the news. It was crucial for them to know what was happening on a daily basis, and the events of the present were seen as ongoing history, although there wasn't much analysis of the issues. Social criticism—apart from Mencken's barbs—left them fairly cold. But the battles between boobs and charlatans made a marvelous spectacle, and observing the collisions was invigorating as well as amusing. Keeping up with the news was a recreation, almost a sport: good exercise that kept the mental muscles limber.

Although their liberalism wasn't directly political, I think it was sincere. Most responded swiftly to racism when it arose. (So I was later stunned to find casual references to "heebs" and "coons" in early letters between friends— words that were gone from their vocabulary after World War II began.) When I was eleven, a classmate who came to our apartment for dinner described the excitement of her first airplane trip: "Only I had to sit next to a big, sloppy, fat Jew!" As soon as she and a few visitors had left, my parents talked to me at length about the anti-Semitism which she must have absorbed from her family, and informed me that the three other guests at the table were Jews. I had never heard anyone identified that way before. I was invited to imagine how those three adults had felt: on hearing that remark from a child—who was unaware that she carried the disease that had infected all of Hitler's Germany. The lowered lids and the silence of those three people stayed with me as an image of the millions who died in the gas chambers.

I was raised to believe that black Americans suffered mainly in the South but not often in the North. So I was shaken when two elderly black men— bartenders at a university club who had offered my father and me a lift to a train—received no aid from motorists on a highway when they realized that the gas had been syphoned from their car. Impeccably dressed, they stood at the roadside signaling for help while cars rushed by. Then my father sprang out and seized their gas can: several vehicles stopped immediately at a gesture from a white man. Outraged by the treatment of our companions, he spoke afterward about the cruelties inflicted on black citizens by whites who behaved as though blacks didn't exist—as we had seen on the highway. In his Ohio and New York youth, he said, blacks had sometimes been depicted as comic figures, and it troubled him to remember the racial jokes of the Twenties, the blindness to civil rights.

Yet I didn't learn until much later that his grandfather had operated a station on the Underground Railway from his small country store in Wabash, Indiana. Periodically the storekeeper received a message that a load of wood was going to arrive that night; he would go to the crossroads, pull the wood off the wagon, and uncover an escaped slave bound for Canada at the bottom of the woodpile. His 1897 obituary noted that "many a hunted man has found refuge in his old cabin." But the fact that my great-grandfather had been an abolitionist was not the kind of family history that was often mentioned.

• • •

That New York and Hollywood had been the centers of American radicalism in the Thirties and Forties was something I would not know until well after I left my parents' home. The role of the Left in this country was hardly acknowledged in our living room, though a distinct but non-punitive anti-Communism was sometimes apparent among the writers I knew. During the Depression some of them had tangled with the Communists in the Screen Writers Guild, where their differences had been less ideological than stylistic: the not very political writers had resented the Communists' militancy and their attempts to gain control of the Guild (which they didn't). The Guild had been formed in 1933 after the employees of MGM had been pressured to take a 30 percent pay cut; when several other studios followed suit, the issue united the apolitical with the activists. While the liberal writers often agreed with the socialists and the Communists that the American system was corrupt, they didn't think it was their mission to alter it—indeed they doubted that it could be altered. They shared the hatred of Hitler, though few foresaw the expansion of fascism abroad. But most of them simply didn't understand the intensity of the commitment to change that infused all kinds of radicals. The cynicism of the Twenties had made them shun large causes; they disliked collective action, and they had no faith in the innate decency of human beings—or in the theory that human nature might improve if social conditions were amended—or in any vision of the future.

In the meantime they couldn't abide the Party's position in the arts or the idea that literature was valuable only as an instrument of social change, and they were indignant when the Communists dismissed Tolstoy and Faulkner as reactionaries. During the Depression Thurber had been infuriated by the attacks in *The New Masses* on *New Yorker* contributors who were reproached for writing about middle-class characters instead of working people; he retorted that, in America, "no sharp line [could be] drawn between the two." In two long letters to Malcolm Cowley, Thurber acknowledged that he and his friends did not know enough about the social upheavals of the era and that they were guilty of self-absorption while writing "little pieces about timid men afraid of the night that comes with sundown, oblivious of the night that comes with revolution." But he accused the Communists of trying "to put the artist in a uniform so like the uniform of the subway conductor that nobody would be able to tell the difference," and of a "desire to regiment and discipline art." He felt that "the literary Communists have almost got to the point where they believe that motherhood and passion and love and all that belong solely to the Communists. That you must be a Communist to make even your private life important."

Admitting that he was growing overheated, Thurber argued that the arrogance of the Communists was contributing to "the growing menace of fascism. . . . They won't debate, they won't listen. . . ." He was also incensed when the Left denigrated ethnic humor. Reviewing Granville Hicks's anthology, *Proletarian Literature in the United States*, for *The New Republic* in 1936 he wrote that proletarian fiction was "hysterical and overwrought," and many of his unpolitical friends felt the same. Later they thought it was hilarious when *Partisan Review* was excoriated by Communists as "a diversionist Trotskyite rag," and ludicrous when Party members were forbidden to read Arthur Koestler's *Darkness at Noon*.

Although these writers would have been incompatible with any political movement, a few teased the Communists they knew by pretending to espouse Trotskyism. Annoyed by the Communists' claim to possessing the right answers to all questions, they were also dubious that the radicals' commitments would last: "Next year, they'll have forgotten all about it—next year, it'll be perfumes," a writer named Sam Hoffenstein said to my father. Gradually much of the Hollywood Left ceased to mingle with those who mocked them, so there was little ongoing discussion between the activists and the writers who felt that art or entertainment should not be politicized.

But in the Fifties my family's friends were disgusted by the political inquisitions. Since they hadn't been attracted to radicalism in the Thirties, they had no reason to dissociate themselves from the Communists or to revile them— as many penitent ex-liberals did. They also thought the Cold War anti-Communists were extremely stupid: for implying that the American Communist Party had ever had substantial power. (They downgraded the influence of the Communists in the labor movement, perhaps because they had small affinity with unions, although few loathed unions in the way that Mencken did.) And since so many Communists of the Thirties had left the Party by 1950, some outsiders noted that the diminished membership was riddled with FBI agents—who were hardly about to overthrow the government. Also they were angered by the ferocious anti-Communism of religious dignitaries. In addition to feeling that American Communists were harmless and naive, there was a tendency to think of them as victims—not only of their leaders, but of generations of right-wing opportunists: some remembered the gross injustices of the Palmer raids, when about ten thousand radicals had been illegally arrested.

Perhaps my father's impression of the Communists as feckless derived partly from his memories of 1923, when he had lived in the attic of a former parish house on West 13th Street; on the ground floor there was a small French firm that manufactured pills to sweeten sour breath, and on the second floor were the Friends of Soviet Russia: a group of impoverished Russian refugees who stored some of the czar's crown jewels—smuggled out of Russia—in a straw suitcase. But until a policeman knocked on my father's door to question him about the theft of the gems, he'd had no notion that he'd been sleeping over part of the imperial treasure. To his knowledge the jewels were never recovered, and he wondered why the Communist Party had not protected them more carefully, or sold them before they were stolen from a cheap lodging house. Although the sanctimoniousness of some Hollywood Communists had irritated him, their forlorn forebears in Greenwich Village seemed characteristic of the Party too.

The Twenties' brand of liberalism insisted on the right of every person to think and do whatever he wished, short of homicide; therefore current and ex-Communists should not be persecuted. As impassioned nonconformists my parents' friends felt very strongly that everyone's freedom of behavior and expression must always be defended. In Hollywood the Committee for the First Amendment was organized by several liberals to oppose the procedures of the House Committee on Un-American Activities and to forestall censorship and blacklisting. In New York S. J. Perelman joined a number of writers and editors in filing an *amici curiae* brief on behalf of the Hollywood Ten. But few of the writers I knew involved themselves at any length in the defense of leftists, although most were extremely sorry for their former colleagues. Yet the FBI kept files on Perelman, Thurber, and White.

Despite White's feeling that a writer had "no obligation to deal with politics," he produced a series of "Comments" for *The New Yorker* which protested the investigation of American citizens, and he wrote two irate letters to *The Herald Tribune* after the paper ran an editorial that condoned the blacklisting of the Hollywood Ten: "Security, for me, took a tumble not when I read that there were Communists in Hollywood, but when I read your editorial in praise of loyalty testing and thought control. . . . Once men gain power over other men's minds, that power is never used sparingly and wisely, but lavishly and brutally and with unspeakable results. If I must declare today that I am not a Communist, tomorrow I shall have to testify that I am not a Unitarian. And the day after, that I never belonged to a dahlia club." *The Tribune* replied that dissenters like White were "nearly always as destructive as they have been valuable," and that they were "probably the most dangerous single elements in our confused and complicated society."

In a letter to his niece in 1952, White reflected, "We grow tyrannical fighting tyranny," and that "the most depressing thing that has happened in my lifetime" was "the official blacklist." In the same year, one of Perelman's letters described how "people are daily puking up their past to the Congressional sub-committees, and you can be fairly sure that anyone who ever contributed a dollar or signed a statement for any liberal cause whatsoever will be pilloried in due time . . . it's increasingly apparent that a process of brainwashing and thought control has stifled almost every bit of independent thinking." Thurber was enraged that writers in particular were singled out by the investigating committees: he was furious at the cooperative witnesses, and he refused to accept an honorary degree from Ohio State University when his alma mater began to scrutinize the politics of all visiting lecturers.

But for most of the writers in our living room, a belief in highly personal emancipation was the extent of their politics. And so the conversation would wheel away from Joseph McCarthy and Roy Cohn to the arts or education— or the murder trial of Dr. Samuel Shephard, or a recent Hemingway novel, or the ceremonies of the Hopi Indians.

4

"I Am Still Expecting Something Exciting"

I first met Edmund Wilson when he stashed his dog in my room. As a child I was sickly and I spent a lot of time reading in a bed surrounded by animals in cages and tanks. While I was immobile, my bedside seethed with activity. In addition to the horned toads, salamanders, several dozen white mice, canaries, tadpoles and frogs, snakes, the ant farm, and scores of newly hatched praying mantises which spilled out of egg cases called oothecae, the insectivorous plants, gallons of fish, generations of fruit flies bred to check out Mendel, a colony of meal worms to feed the reptiles, and a sequence of cats, I had some long-lived chameleons. In my somber little Yorkville bedroom, where creatures kept dying in the gritty, sunless air, I was proud of the chameleons' resilience. Their terrariums flourished with strong plants; they mated energetically and laid eggs and rarely stopped courting: red throats expanding, heads jerking up and down, bodies flushed green with sexual exuberance. The mice rattled in their cages, but backfires and loud street noises sometimes caused nervous mothers to decapitate their young; the mantises ate each other until only a few survived; birds collapsed mysteriously; some horned toads refused all food and withered from starvation; fish became sudden floating corpses; my liveliest cat was poisoned by roach crystals. But the chameleons thrived. Their health was important to me, since the recurrent deaths of the other animals almost seemed like a reproach of nature: for keeping captives in the city.

Few adults would enter my room: they said it stank of mice. So it did, but the odor of the fresh cedar chips on the bottoms of their cages, plus the aging bananas that sustained the fruit flies and the Liederkranz cheese I liked to eat, were the tang of my sanctuary and I didn't mind the aroma. I was quite flattered when grownups said that it "smelled like a zoo," since a zoo was what I wanted.

One night—I was eleven, and my parents were giving a dinner for someone I didn't know—my bedroom door sprang open and slammed violently. A dog had been tossed into the room: a butterscotch cocker spaniel which landed with out-flung paws beside my bed. The dog rose and shook itself. The door reopened at once, and a short, plump man walked in. He said nothing but went straight to the menagerie, inspecting each cage carefully. I watched him watching them: he took creatures seriously, he didn't sniff or sneeze or even seem to notice the reek. After working his way through the entire collection, he sat down next to the chameleons and peered into the terrarium from a number of angles. Finally he spoke—asking if I had invented the drainage system by myself.

I said I had.

He said it was good but it could be further improved, and called for a pair of wire-cutters. He suggested that there should be one more layer of wire mesh between the evaporating water at the tank's base and the gravel and soil above it. He introduced me to the dog (Bambi), asked what I was reading (*The Ingoldsby Legends*, as he reminded me long afterward), and was hacking away at a large sheet of metal mesh when my mother indignantly summoned him: the evening had been arranged at his request and included some people he'd wanted to meet. He seemed flustered on hearing this and went off with the wire-cutters.

Years later, when I often heard others accuse him of rudeness (and much worse), I remembered that total concentration, the absorption in one project that made him forget everything else. That singlemindedness was a component of his talent: for pursuing a topic until it was driven into a corner, where it was explored, completed, achieved. Once when he was talking about his method of learning languages, I asked how he could take on so much extra study without its interfering with his writing. He laughed briefly. "Well, how can I *drink* so much without its interfering with my writing?" he said gleefully. (He seemed to have scant understanding of writers' blocks, and was amused by Cyril Connolly's admission that writing was nearly impossible in wartime— and then that it was very hard to write in peacetime. Wilson responded, "Both peace and fighting keep Cyril from writing.") Whenever Wilson approached a new language, he hired a tutor—except when he studied German, and he volunteered that his German was still weak: he regretted that he'd tried to learn it on his own.

After our first meeting I saw him constantly until I went to boarding school; he lived across East 86th Street on Henderson Place, and he dropped in on my parents several times a week. (He and Mary McCarthy were in the final phases of their marriage; they separated and divorced while he was our neighbor.) I used to accompany him when he took Bambi to Carl Schurz Park, or earn a quarter by conducting Bambi's roadwork myself. When I returned the spaniel, Wilson usually gave me a ginger ale and then dove into discussions of natural history, for which he had a passion. He was fascinated by apes and he loaned me several books by people who had tried to raise chimpanzees and gorillas as though they were humans. He gave rapturous attention to the possibility that certain apes might be able to talk, and wondered if they might be able to *think* the words they couldn't pronounce but might, with training, be able to understand.

He was also intrigued by bees and their swarming patterns, and he described how they used dance as a form of communication: by performing specific dances one bee would tell the others where a source of honey was located. Wilson once gave me a demonstration of a bee dance, trotting in circles on his floor. Utterly unselfconscious at such moments, he appeared to enjoy slipping into improbable roles. One day when he came over to see if the chameleons' eggs had hatched, he gravely surveyed the sea of papers and books that rose high in my room, and then walked around intoning, "I am Langley Collyer. They are looking for me." (Collyer, a Manhattan recluse, had died with his brother Homer in an apartment so choked with refuse and newspapers that it took days to find his corpse.)

Now and then Wilson joined me in hypnotizing the horned toads: if you turned them on their backs and slowly stroked their stomachs, they would remain motionless for hours. But he cautioned against too much hypnosis for any reptile. (In his diaries of the Twenties, there was a reference to a woman whose alligator "was rather limp from being hypnotized so much.") Insectivorous plants also appealed to him. I had four varieties in one terrarium, and we would watch to see which one first entrapped the fly that I'd let loose. One morning a slew of boxes arrived at our door: he had sent me his complete works of Darwin. I was twelve at the time, and he was impatient when he learned that I was still working on them some years later.

In his fifties—perhaps for much of his life—he seemed far more relaxed with children than with adults, and probably I would not have come to know him as easily if I'd been twenty. He treated a child as an equal and seemed free to reveal the child in himself. As a boy he had revered Houdini, and he assumed that the very young would respond to his card and magic tricks—which they did, particularly because the sleight of hand often went awry, as cards fell out of his sleeves and onto his stomach and the floor—and he liked to give puppet shows. He had a series of catalogues from a magicians' supply house, and he longed to buy an item called the Floating Skull Illusion. The skull could glide all over a theater, stop and interview the spectators at the magician's will, and read minds. But it cost fifteen hundred dollars: an inconceivable sum for him.

Hatty, an elderly Southern black woman who had looked after him since the early Thirties, came to work for us too. She spoke rather sternly about Wilson's way of life, but she was so devoted to him that she transported our pot roasts and vacuum cleaners to his home across the street when she thought he needed them more than we did. During the Depression she'd tried to lend him money when he was hard up, and balked when he offered her a raise. (*To the Finland Station* entailed five years' work before it appeared in 1940; the publisher's advance was seventeen hundred dollars.) Extremely sensitive to his requirements, Hatty protected his writing schedule and provided hangover cures, and he was very fond of her. When we learned that he was going to marry his fourth wife, Elena Mumm Thornton, I was entranced by the thought of that portly, formal, but nervy figure in the throes of courtship. I was accustomed to the rituals of reptiles and birds—in my bedroom there was ceaseless foreplay—but hadn't yet seen humans going about it. I asked Hatty, What did he do when he proposed—did he go down on his knees? Hatty shook her head emphatically. "Uh-uh. He *doesn't* kneel." She added grimly, "They all think he's got money. And when they find out he doesn't—they leave." Untrue as that was, it showed the measure of Hatty's concern for him.

A few months after *Memoirs of Hecate County* was published, a couple of *New Yorker* writers used to read the erotic passages of the novel aloud at parties, imitating Wilson's voice: the treble that sounded as if he were suppressing a belch. One night I heard the mimics fluting away while the guests' laughter surged through the wall of my room, and I burst into the living room to berate them for disloyalty. I hadn't read the book, but I was sure that the author would be wounded. There was more laughter—Nunnally Johnson said, "Swell company your kid keeps!"—but I took some pleasure in slamming the door on the guffaws.

But Wilson didn't need vindicators. When I first knew him, he had already entered a particularly confident chapter of his life: *The New Yorker* furnished a stability that was quite new for him, while enabling him to cultivate his priorities. These were also the years of the integration of his aesthetic and political selves: the literary self of the Twenties and the radical sensibility of the Thirties. The two had not warred with one another—"Marxism never had the effect of destroying my belief in literature. All though the Thirties I was defending literature"—but his commitments became all the more cohesive after he turned fifty. His notes for an unfinished novel of "transformations" indicate that the metamorphoses in his protagonist's public and private lives "were really a consecutive development."

Soon after an interview with George Santayana in Rome, Wilson wrote, "He wants to conserve himself, to realize himself as he has never done before— I don't imagine that he is troubled by the thought of death—his present successful functioning absorbs, enchants, and satisfies him." Without comparing himself to Santayana, Wilson did seem to identify with him when he added that "the writer, when he ages . . . finds that he now knows his own business better and is in full command of his forces," and he noted that he was "feeling something of this." Eighteen months later, his fourth marriage supplied the reinforcement and the charms of a tranquility which had eluded him.

Wilson's diaries and letters show that he was highly conscious of being a survivor—in contrast to many of his friends. After the heavy drinking and jumbled love affairs of his twenties, a breakdown at thirty-five had made him dread that he might repeat his father's pattern of emotional "eclipses." (Yet the son's productivity never wavered: during his three weeks in the sanitorium, he had worked on *Axel's Castle*, gone through the page proofs of *I Thought of Daisy*, and finished a poem.) When he had lived long enough to relish his "continuity," the crack-ups and deaths and "peterings-out" of his contemporaries had made him especially grateful that he'd been able to renew himself in midlife.

When he and Elena Wilson called on Edna St. Vincent Millay—his early love, whom he hadn't seen for nearly two decades—a couple of years before Millay's death, "I reflected in dismay, but not without some satisfaction, at my own relative competence and health, on the tendency of the writers of my generation to burn themselves out or break down"—which made him think of Scott Fitzgerald and Elinor Wylie as well as Millay. "One didn't really believe until one saw it demonstrated that giving oneself up completely to art, to emotion, to enjoyment, without planning for the future or counting the cost, produced dreadful disabilities and bankruptcies later." Plainly he felt that he might have been a casualty like Millay had his new life with his new wife not rescued him from the "panics and depressions" of his earlier years. The marriage was often harrowing for Elena, though she brought ballast to his turbulence.

· · ·

When I went to Radcliffe, Wilson disapproved of my majoring in English— "Why are you doing *that?*" he asked, rather as though it were a program of miniature golf—and "What about your zoology?" That was a cry which I would hear for several years, mainly from writers. Many seemed convinced that any profession was more substantial than their own. (My father—not altogether joking—exclaimed, "Oh why didn't our parents teach us a *useful* trade? Like knife-grinding or putting sash weights in windows?") Wilson rather peevishly inquired about Walter Jackson Bate's lectures on Dr. Johnson, but grunted with approval when I described Bate's course. Still he would have preferred that I'd studied natural history.

Occasionally he seemed almost naive. For example, he was disturbed to learn that—at twenty-two—I'd met an old friend of his in London: a literary barrister who was one of the best hosts in town. I always felt fortunate to be one of his guests. But Wilson asked in real distress how I had come across him: "I didn't introduce you—I would never have done that—he's a *wolf*!" I couldn't persuade him that that kindly, punctilious man was not a slavering rapist. Wilson referred to the impropriety of my acquaintance with his friend for years, and it was rum to hear the word "wolf" repeated by the author of *Memoirs of Hecate County.*

After I'd spent five years living in England, we compared our loathing of Oxford and Cambridge: we spent a whole lunch trying to decide which we disliked most. Our experiences at those universities were similar, though they shouldn't have been, since the dons he met were going to drop his name all over their high tables. (I even encountered a don who had name-dropping dreams: in his sleep he was visited by T. S. Eliot and André Malraux and other distinguished nightly callers.) But we'd both recoiled from those communities where a gentleman—that is, a scholar—couldn't honorably discuss his own field. Many dons thought it was vulgar to disclose what one knew: talking shop was middle class. Hence the flight to small talk: stamp collections or comparative mustards or the cat that lived in the college kitchen—and above all electric blankets. Cambridge had many wiring systems: which brands of blankets worked best there? Mainly, it seemed, the kind that was turned on half an hour before bedtime and was turned off after one retired. The hallowed port hour in one college common room was drastically shortened because the oldest dons left early in order to switch on their blankets.

Some Londoners told me how lucky I was to live in Cambridge (as I did for five months)—because of the conversation. To me it seemed the worst in the world. But Americans were thought to lack refinement if they were bored by recitations of railway schedules or accounts of rain and snow. At any rate it was maddening to be in the presence of fine minds that would not expose their contents. Wilson told me that the last time he'd been in Cambridge, someone had given a lunch for him, and he'd hoped to meet some Dead Sea scroll dons, since he was updating and expanding his book on that subject. But the lunchers were academics of other sorts. For the first hour they spoke about tobacco—which he'd never smoked. Throughout the second hour they held forth on cars—which he didn't drive. Finally he fled to Heffer's bookstore, where the proprietor was "the only person in Cambridge who would talk to me about books." He swore that he would never go to Cambridge or Oxford again, and I don't think he did.

Previously, when he was in England for *The New Yorker* at the very end of the war, Wilson had found himself "estranged" from our British allies; galled by the persistence of imperialism, he remarked on "the passion for social privilege, the rapacious appetite for property" and "the dependence on inherited advantages," plus the "instinct . . . to make all these appear forms of virtue" in *Europe Without Baedeker*. Despising the British class system, he had been a fervent anglophobe throughout his life. Yet he seemed to be enjoying London when I saw him there in 1956, and he said that English writers had developed the insult until it was almost an art. But he was unhappy about the Americanization of postwar England: he wanted the two cultures to remain distinct. Since his youth he'd championed an evolving American literature that became less and less like that of Britain: he had long celebrated the independence of American culture.

But despite what he half-mockingly called "a lifetime of backbreaking patriotism," he was always a relentless critic of his own society and government. Appalled by the cascades of "nationalistic propaganda" which accompanied our quest for global power after World War II, he also exulted in the traditional role of the American rebel. His kind of rebellion meant assailing the institutions—from the Internal Revenue Service to the Modern Language Association—which he felt were betraying our civilization. "His" America was vanishing, but—although he didn't actively involve himself in politics after the Thirties—it was his instinct to correct the authorities that needed to be informed of their atrocious errors. When he was in Israel he read a speech of Eisenhower's about foreign policy "that sounded so incompetent and panic-stricken, I had the impulse to publish a commentary on it, taking it up paragraph by paragraph and showing the confusions and absurdities of the assumptions on which it was based."

In the Fifties, when he was absorbed in playwriting, the Bible, Gibbon, Chekhov and Pasternak, Swinburne, the literature of the American Civil War— he was building toward the book that took fifteen years to become *Patriotic Gore*—learning Hebrew, and spending time with the Indians of upstate New York, he sustained his lifelong habit of working on more than one project at the same time: "Am immersed in *Zhivago*, the Iroquois, and the Civil War all at once." He had several desks in his Wellfleet study: instead of moving his papers, he moved himself. Meanwhile his mounting abhorrence of the Cold War led him to denounce the "tyrannical power" exerted by the White House: the fear of the Soviet Union was no excuse for "spending billions for national defense," and in 1952 he had "an awful feeling" that "a war with Russia [is] all we seem to be planning for."

Outraged that some public figures behaved as if America could be "sub-verted" by the Soviets, he referred to "the periodical American panic, which dates from the Revolution, at the thought of being dominated by a foreign power." Deploring the "gigantic taxes here for atomic weapons and foreign occupations and a foreign policy consisting of the lies and ineptitudes of Dulles, who assures us from time to time that . . . the Soviet government is about to fall," he reprimanded those who extolled the serenity of Eisenhower's America.

Emphasizing the contradictions between "our pretensions to be the sanctu-ary of civil rights and our outbreaks of violent repression," he thought that we were sometimes "copying" the Russians: to him our loyalty investigations seemed like a crude parody of Stalinism; in 1956 he wrote, "Our recent security purges and political heresy-hunts must have been partially inspired by the Russian trials."

He had often disagreed with the American Communists during the Thirties; at first he'd supported them for the sake of the issues they raised, but by 1936 he felt that the cause of international socialism had been wrecked by Stalin. (His divergence was not forgiven: *The New Masses* titled its review of *Memoirs of Hecate County* "A Trotskyite in Love." It was forgotten that he had been very critical of the Trotskyists.) Yet he had some hopes for European socialism right after the war, and although he had once wanted "to take Communism away from the Communists," he could not tolerate their persecution. He was briefly heartened by Khrushchev's repudiation of Stalin, but since he expected nothing sensible or decent from "the government of oafs in Russia," it infuriated him to perceive parallels between the super-powers: "The Russians emulating America in their frantic industrialization and we imitating them in our prosecution of non-conformist political opinions."

• • •

It displeased him that he was primarily identified as a critic. His fiction and plays and poetry and reporting meant as much to him as his criticism—in some cases, more: *Memoirs of Hecate County* was his favorite among his books—and he tended to rebuke those who forgot that he had written in so many forms. His overwhelming interest in almost everything seemed like a living reproof to the Oxbridge dons: he'd composed a pantomime ballet for Charlie Chaplin while studying the Symbolists in preparation for *Axel's Castle*, and read *Electra* in Greek on the train to Hollywood, where he tried (but failed) to induce Chaplin to perform his ballet. (He read Alfred North Whitehead's *Concept of Nature* on the train that took him home.) The impassioned learner had no respect for boundaries: the American Civil War was as much his territory as the Russian Revolution, and he felt equally qualified to take on Hungarian along with Virgil and Swift and Flaubert and Thackeray and Dickens.

Always an internationalist, he was dedicated to illuminating "the general cross-fertilization" of literature, aiming "to make it possible for our literate public to appreciate and understand both our Anglo-American culture and those of the European countries." As he wrote in "A Modest Self-Tribute," "I have been working, as a practicing critic, to break down the conventional frames, to get away from the academic canons, that always tend to keep literature provincial." He thought most European critics had become insular due to their neglect of the Russian language and American literature, but that "for an American today it is natural to range" widely among "several cultures which have not always been in close communication." He felt a personal obligation to clarify the connections between civilizations which had "seemed inaccessible or incompatible with one another." At times he was also rather possessive about American culture. As an anonymous reviewer in *The Times Literary Supplement* wrote, "explaining the world to America and explaining America to itself" was his vocation.

The literary internationalism coexisted oddly with his isolationism in politics; he'd opposed America's entry into both world wars, a position that mystified and angered many of his friends. He wasn't a pacifist. But he argued that most wars were "not moral battles but battles for power": he did not believe the Civil War was fought to free the slaves, nor that World War II was waged because of the mass extermination of the European Jews. He objected strenuously to the "self-justificatory fantasy" that Washington concocted "about the nobility of our actions and aims." To Arthur Schlesinger, Jr., he wrote in 1958 that Americans "ought, I think, to recognize that we are really an expanding power unit, and that all our idealism is eyewash." Believing that our government served "the designs of big business" instead of the principles of democracy, he felt we should "train ourselves to disassociate our views of war from . . . moral attitudes." His peers continued to upbraid him for his stance long after the Axis was defeated, but he never altered his opinions.

Van Wyck Brooks had identified Wilson as "a vanishing type, the free man of letters," and his work was often belittled by academics. In the Fifties he was sometimes dismissed as "a journalist," mainly by the New Critics. But he had always defined himself as a literary journalist—in the tradition of De Quincey, Poe, and the young Bernard Shaw: he wanted to report on literature and to introduce the writers he admired to a broad audience, a goal that was foreign to many scholars. He also exhorted editors to venture beyond the predictable; chiding Allen Tate of *The Sewanee Review* for his "inhibitions" about publishing authors whose writing "differs strongly in tone and technique from the work of your own group," Wilson observed, "I am much more of a journalist than you and like to astonish people with startling discoveries and novel juxtapositions." (He also called himself a journalist in order to distinguish himself from prevailing critical conventions.) Hostile to literary fashions, he was scornful of professors who knew nothing *but* literature, and he was committed to exploring the relationship of literature to history at a time when the New Critics sought to disconnect the two. His "whole point of view about literature was affected by" Taine, who presented writers "as characters in a larger drama of cultural and social history, and writing about literature, for me, has always meant narrative and drama." The biographical approach was also unfashionable among the section men of the period. But he lambasted those who were "wandering" in "the vast academic desert of the structure of *The Sound and the Fury*, the variants in the texts of *The Scarlet Letter*, and the religious significance of *The Great Gatsby*."

At seventy he wrote, "The sole function I can have with young people seems to come down to instructing them." But that suggests one-way traffic, which was not my experience with him. His role was participatory: the listener was not a passive recipient. Although he imparted cataracts of information along with his judgments and enthusiasms, and had a headlong urge to share what he'd just unearthed—I remember calling on him when he was in bed with severe gout, and he was immediately impelled to read aloud from some A. E. Housman essays which delighted him—he was gifted at asking questions: whenever one saw him, he had a list of queries. Each conversation was charged with his titanic curiosity, the zeal of the investigator, which was powerfully reflected in his books. While being quizzed I was surprised by his memory for what I'd written: in the Sixties he wanted to know more about experimental movies or the "Objectivist" philosophy of Ayn Rand ("I am fascinated by that horrible woman") or the Free University in Greenwich Village—and why don't you like Anaïs Nin's writing? (He was annoyed when I wrote a negative review of the first volume of Nin's journals, and warned me that I had "a blind spot.") Had I read Angus Wilson's *Old Men at the Zoo*? And how has Balzac been taught at Harvard? Ineptly, he suspected—he was reading Balzac with gusto, savoring *La Comédie Humaine* more than he ever had before.

The mind which had voyaged through the literature and tongues of so many centuries, excavating the insights of Sophocles, the imagery of Pushkin, and the ambiguities of Henry James, would suddenly pounce and focus on an unfamiliar topic: the training of the New York City police. After all one's information had been exhausted, he would leap to another question: how could anyone read Tolkien? *The Lord of the Rings* seemed like trash to him, but he wanted to know what virtues others had seen which he couldn't detect. And have you read Hugh MacLennan and Marie-Claire Blais? If not, you should. The American ignorance about Canadian literature was a national disgrace. And where could he get some tree frogs? Were the mail order catalogues for schools still available?

Impressed by the opera *Bomarzo* by the Argentinian Alberto Ginastera, he was very eager to see the composer's other opera, *Don Rodrigo*, and I went with him; we left before the final act because he was feeling ill, but he was already disappointed. Having read the libretto beforehand, he went over it the next day, and he decided that the theme—defending the honor of a woman who'd been abandoned—was dramatically weak: "I couldn't see what all the fuss was about, could you?" Lost "honor" was appropriate to Racine and Corneille and *Don Giovanni*, but it wasn't a valid subject for a modern work. Testing a work of art against its time was compulsory for Wilson: he protested when some contemporary poets wrote verse drama—which belonged to the Elizabethans but was unsuitable for twentieth-century emotions. I had once been involved with a little theater which specialized in plays by poets, and he expressed a mischievous gratitude for having seen none of the performances.

• • •

I last saw one of his Punch and Judy shows in his Wellfleet house in 1966. The production was far more elaborate than it had been in my childhood: he had a tall stand-up theater and a huge collection of puppets, there was a written script, and he and his daughter Helen had practiced the songs. By then he had developed Punch and Judy into "a great ritual drama" in which "the ordinary man" vanquishes his enemies. Elena said he was much too wound-up that weekend and that the strain was bad for him. But the show went splendidly: Elena's small grandchildren roared in the front row, while a crowd of adults watched respectfully. As I listened to Wilson shouting his lines, while children chuckled and green branches tossed in the sun outside the windows, I realized the importance of a day like this one: time invested in an intricate diversion, a detour from the tensions that accompany writing for a living. The afternoon blended Wilson's sense of play with his intense professionalism: there had been rigorous rehearsals for the show and he was determined to make it as good as possible. None of the gentlemanly amateurism beloved by the British—for him play was also a form of work.

Wilson was in a fine mood afterward. I asked if he would contribute a piece to the American issue that the *New Statesman* was planning. (He'd written several essays for that magazine a few years before, and I was its New York correspondent.) He said no cheerfully, explaining that he had now mapped out everything he wanted to write before the end of his life. He had also devised a program of reading the classics he hadn't yet ingested, and it frustrated him that he was too old to learn Chinese. He didn't speak of dying. But he said that after you'd reached a certain age, you felt the pressure of time enormously: there was so much to do, and he'd had to make a detailed schedule. (He had six years—minus a few months—left.)

In his last years he hated to be called "mellow," and he wasn't. A year before he died, a friend of mine made the mistake of saying that he looked well. Wilson replied rather angrily. "No I don't. I know how I look. You must never tell anyone my age that he looks *well*—it simply isn't true." There was a little pocket of silence at the Princeton Club. Then he said more amiably that old people were easily offended when they felt others were patronizing them. I realized then that—despite his well-known assaults on his intellectual adversaries—I had not heard him patronize anyone. Of course I knew about the brusqueness and the quarrels, the insults and outbursts, the pugnacity for which he'd been notorious, especially when drunk. But I'd mainly seen him in contexts that brought out his generosity and warmth: my Yorkville home and his marriage to Elena, the extended family of the old *New Yorker*. So I hadn't witnessed him in an act of condescension toward those who knew less than he did.

In *Upstate* he had written, "As a character in one of Chekhov's plays . . . says that he is 'a man of the Eighties,' so I find that I am a man of the Twenties. I am still expecting something exciting: drinks, animated conversation, gaiety, brilliant writing, uninhibited exchanges of ideas." But unlike some of his intimates, he had never been a prisoner of the decade: the expectations had not immured him with attitudes that could destroy him. He'd assimilated the richest materials from the eras he had known, while discarding the debris of each period.

Although the years augmented his pessimism about this country and its culture, his disgust with the commercialism which pervaded small towns as well as cities, he tried hard to resist despair. Forty years before *Upstate*, he had written to the poet Louise Bogan, when she was in a sanitarium, about the "severe strain" that their generation had undergone while trying to adapt themselves to the tremendous ongoing changes in our society. "Still we have to carry on. . . . The only thing that we can really make is our work. And deliberate work of the mind, imagination, and hand . . . in the long run remakes the world."

5

"*A Flash of the Mind*"

"**W**atch me! I'm going to disappear": during the long intermission between the acts of *The Abduction from the Seraglio* at Glyndebourne, Walker Evans roved almost invisibly through the crowd, photographing the British opera-goers in evening clothes who squatted on the sopping lawns—rain had just receded—digging into vast picnic hampers crammed with pâté and cold meats: below a tiara, a jaw closed on a thick sandwich, while men in snowy dress shirts poured champagne into paper cups. Although Evans was everywhere with his camera, you wouldn't have noticed him unless you were paying very close attention to his movements. Several times I lost sight of him: he faded into the high laurel hedges, and his small, discreet presence never intruded on those whose gestures and expressions he was capturing in detail. Much as he relished photographing people in their surroundings—the Alabama share-croppers standing outside their cabins or the privileged audience at Glyndebourne—protecting the privacy of others seemed to be an obsession. His own privacy was sacred.

The facts of Walker Evans's life can be elusive. He kept revising his own history as the years went by, and although I never heard anyone call him a liar, his old friends have said his secrecy made him rather mystifying even to those who knew him for a lifetime. So I can only say how he seemed to me and repeat what he told me. When his interpreters differ and collide, I remember the faint smile that creased his narrow, triangular face before he vanished into the landscape at Glyndebourne and his chuckle at my surprise when he reappeared a few feet from me, or the brief crow of enthusiasm when he saw something he liked. If fantasy sometimes fed into his past, it was balanced by his insistence on honesty in a work of art, in a photograph or a novel. Though he chose to be enigmatic, his pictures were never abstruse. And he hated pretension or "artiness": he scoffed at the "tricks" that some visual artists employed to concoct a style that wasn't natural to them or to their subjects.

Evans told many people that he had waited almost fifteen years to publish the New York subway photographs he'd taken with a camera hidden inside his coat: the bleak faces on "the swaying sweatbox" of 1938 and 1941 weren't made public until their owners had lived much longer with their anxieties— or had ceased to live at all. Remarking that those subway riders had been caught without their masks, without defenses, Evans emphasized that he was guarding their privacy by delaying publication, although some of his colleagues thought a larger motive was the impulse to be secretive about his work. Yet the farming families of *Let Us Now Praise Famous Men* had been treated with sensitivity: James Agee and Evans—especially Agee—had wanted them to feel like participants, not objects.

The sanctity of privacy was a theme in my earliest conversations with Evans: he felt that the public owed it to every artist, just as artists owed it to strangers. He told me he'd deliberately turned his back on James Joyce when the writer had entered Sylvia Beach's Paris bookstore in the Twenties; as a young browser at Shakespeare & Company, Evans was careful not to look at the novelist he revered. In 1933, when he was in Cuba, he went to the coast with an American reporter who was planning to ambush Hemingway, whom Evans hadn't met. Hemingway was fishing from a boat: he resented the interruption and refused to be interviewed. Evans shrank from the altercation that followed, averting his eyes—and then Hemingway suddenly asked him to come aboard the boat. Retreating farther, Evans said, "No!" Hemingway laughed and slapped his shoulder, then hauled him off and talked to him about writing throughout a long afternoon. Evans said his inclination to shield others was rewarded again in the late Forties: when he was photographing "Faulkner's Mississippi" for *Vogue*—a dilapidated plantation house, railway tracks, tombstones, a mule-drawn wagon—the editor who accompanied him suggested that they should make a spontaneous call on Faulkner; Evans vetoed her idea. Faulkner heard about the incident and sent a message of thanks for Evans's tact—and an invitation to visit him in the future.

If these cautionary tales were at all fictional, I wouldn't have guessed it; they were so vividly recounted and the moral was exceedingly plain: one must never invade another's psyche. At twenty I was reproved for enjoying a glimpse of Gerard Philipe and Gina Lollobrigida as they walked out of a New York movie theater after a premiere. Though they smiled at the spectators and seemed to like being recognized, Evans frowned and led me quickly away from the throng. I protested that they were actors, that they'd chosen to live in the limelight. "No, no, come on," he muttered, "Awful for them!" He added that they should be "seen" only on the stage or screen.

Paradox seemed to run through his marrow: although photography is associated with exposure, he sometimes implied that there was something slightly indecent about looking at people. Agee had identified the camera as "a weapon, a stealer of images and souls, a gun, an evil eye," and his collaborator may have been disturbed by the metaphors of aggression. One of Evans's drafts for the text of a book of the subway pictures referred to American mothers telling their offspring, "Don't stare!" Americans didn't know how to "study" each other in public, he wrote, because staring was considered ill-bred. He claimed that sitting in Paris cafés in 1926 had liberated him from that training. But I doubt it. Some thought he was more comfortable photographing architecture and objects or urban landscapes than human beings. Yet he once took a picture of a vagrant lying in front of a tenement on Bleecker Street; nearby was the only Louis Sullivan building in New York, but Evans had photographed the shabby figure rather than the venerable building.

Given the brilliance of his portraits of anonymous faces, his photographs of his friends weren't always his best work. Here I'm no judge: I guiltily disliked some pictures he took of me at twenty-three because they quite harshly revealed the apprehensions I was trying to hide, even though they were taken during a pleasant meal. Perhaps the man who had called himself "a penitent spy and an apologetic voyeur" felt a bit unfair to his companions when he took their pictures. But he could burlesque his own aversion to invasion: when a woman who was organizing a reception for him asked if he would be willing to photograph the guests, he snorted and shuddered, envisioning an outlandish scene: "Delighted to meet you—Bang!" Momentarily he mimicked Chaplin, miming the snapping shutter and the eye-popping astonishment of the victims as flash bulbs burst in their faces.

He believed in a degree of solitude for the artist; he said he was fortunate to have begun his own work far from the mainstream and from any school of photography. He couldn't bear to be a member of a crowd: aware of his own value, arrogant but not vain, he had no confidence in collective intelligence. And when he was asked to analyze his art, he recoiled. "The thing itself is such a secret and so unapproachable," he told a group of Yale students. His evasive nature baffled some curators who dealt with him. For years he'd felt that his ideas had been stolen when he was employed by the New Deal's Farm

Security Administration in the Thirties, and he continued to fear that his style would be imitated or that he wouldn't receive full credit for his work—which may have been one source of his secretiveness.

Self-defense was mirrored in an affection for disguise. In the late Twenties not many men wore sunglasses, but Evans did; he also carried a cane, and it had once amused him to stand on a New York street, allowing passers-by to think he was blind; some dropped coins into his hat. A friend compared him to a performer with a whole trunkful of masks, which were necessary to his work; at times he needed protective coloration. A portrait (possibly a self-portrait) shows him behind a view camera, a dark cloth over his head: only the lower half of his body and the tripod can be seen. Yet that reclusive being could be expansive and convivial; his social life was ample, his acquaintance immense. And he excelled at friendship: two of his closest male friends told me that almost no one else had given such attention to their feelings, that few seemed to understand them as well. Despite his two marriages, one of his long-term friends used to call him an ideal bachelor; one evening he telephoned that friend from a small French restaurant to explain why he wasn't coming to a party: "I'm just having a little steak on my own"—the voice oozed with satisfaction. And he liked to travel or to appear in public by himself. When I first knew him, I thought he was divorced; several years later he announced that he and his first wife had separated.

The loner warned against early marriage—although he was too polite to comment when I married early myself—and he suggested that marriage was a ritual one might "go through" before entering the most important chapters of one's life. Yet I've never forgotten how he spoke with real horror about a woman who came to see him when he was hospitalized with ulcers: "She lives entirely alone." He had no intimate attachments at the time. But clearly, in spite of his allegiance to solitude, a certain kind of loneliness appalled him; he almost made it sound like death.

From him I learned that privacy and freedom often ride in tandem, and that neither is easily shared. Some lines of Yeats which I'd memorized in school reminded me of Evans:

> I turn away and shut the door, and on the stair
> Wonder how many times I could have proved my worth
> In something that all others understand or share;
> But O! ambitious heart, had such a proof drawn forth
> A company of friends, a conscience set at ease,
> It had but made us pine the more . . .

When I think of him now, two pictures appear side by side: in one he sits bunched up in a scuffed dark green velvet chair in the apartment of his friends Lily Emmet and Anthony West; there are cracks in the wall behind him and his expression is somewhat wistful, yet he looks content in isolation. I also see him in a dinner jacket, beaming and gesturing with a cigarette holder, surrounded by black ties and silk and tulle.

Disrespectful of "hostesses"—his voice would deepen when he ridiculed them—he accepted their invitations; afterward he might say how absurd the evening had been. (He disapproved of snobbery except for his own.) Although he took pains to know "the right people," he seemed just as interested in his barber or the waitress in a roadhouse near his home in East Lyme, Connecticut: what they said intrigued him as much as the conversation of worldlings. He didn't want to photograph celebrities and rarely did; the youthful portraits of Hart Crane and Lincoln Kirstein were made because those were his friends. He said he'd avoided taking pictures of Hemingway and e.e. cummings, and that photographing the famous was "an impure thing to do." I think he felt superior to those who were impressed by fame. He took pictures of his friends when they didn't ask him to, but not when they did. Requests of any kind inspired resistance.

• • •

Evans contradicted the art critics who classified him as a social critic: "I am not a social protest artist." (Perhaps some had credited him with a social conscience because Agee had one, and because the text of *Let Us Now Praise Famous Men* distilled the sensibilities of the Depression.) In the Twenties, when he'd worked briefly as a stock clerk on Wall Street, Evans had detested the industrialism of the era as well as the job: "When I was young . . . this was a very unpleasant society in the sense that if you weren't interested in commerce and business and commercialism in general, there was no place for you." But disgust with the business culture did not kindle any reverence for artists per se. When he turned to photography he spurned the romanticism that he felt was inherent in the work of Alfred Stieglitz, and he mocked the cloud pictures of which Stieglitz was so proud. Subsequently he said, "Nature rather bores me as an art form"—civilization was the subject that enthralled him.

Early on his work had rebelled against the optimism of the genteel tradition in the arts: like many in his generation, he was intent on challenging the William Dean Howells mentality, which held that "The smiling aspects of life are the more American." (Howell's own optimism deteriorated as he aged, but sunniness was his legacy.) Until 1929 the Pulitzer Prize for fiction was awarded to "the American novel published during the year which shall best present the wholesome atmosphere of American life and the highest standard of American manners and manhood." Since the establishment upheld "the affirmative" in the arts, Evans reacted by dwelling on subjects that the genteel thought depressing—as can be seen in the 1931 photograph of the rented room with a twisted iron bedstead backed by a badly plastered wall: the grimness of that interior unnerved me long before I learned that the room had been inhabited by the impoverished young John Cheever.

Evans said that at the beginning of his career, romanticism had given him something "to work against." Disliking "the painterly and over-artistic" photography of the late Twenties, which relied on soft focus and retouching, he was stimulated by newsreels and news photography. He informed the Yale students that "I got a lot of my early momentum from disdain of accepted ideas of beauty," and he declared, "I lean toward the enchantment, the visual power, of the aesthetically rejected subject"—the automobile graveyards, metal shavings scattered in a dark gutter, striped barber poles, ruined billboards, or the play of light on silvery corrugated tin nailed to the facade of a contractor's shack. He often spoke of having been influenced by Flaubert and Baudelaire, and said that he'd learned about objectivity from Flaubert. Sentimentality repelled him, and perhaps he found Baudelaire appealing because both of them were charmed by objects or faces that others thought ugly. Evans loved the black Model T Fords of the Thirties, and although his photograph of a long row of very similar cars on a rainy street in Saratoga might seem gloomy to some, he was celebrating a sight that delighted him. Today all those Fords could appear as an image of mass production, but he—who kept repainting his own Model T to maintain its original blackness—was probably exhilarated to see so many of them at once. (Cars were a ruling passion, and he was happy to own a Jaguar in his later years.)

Scornful of "introspection" in the arts—he used the word almost contemptuously—he wanted to be plain, direct, in no way unfaithful to fact. (He was impatient with the idea that photography itself was "an honest medium": it was easy for a camera to lie.) The photographer should operate outside the heat of battle and his personality ought to be absent from his pictures. Evans admitted to his friend the photographer and architect Paul Grotz that he was uncomfortable taking staged photographs, as when he asked a Southern family to stand on their porch and pose for a portrait—and Grotz enquired how he had managed to make them seem unaware of the camera. Evans replied that he'd pretended that he was there alone. Achieving an impersonal style required the discipline I'd witnessed at Glyndebourne: the ability to withdraw from participation, to be imperceptible and detached, while aiming for "the transcendent." Two days before his death in 1975, he told a class at Harvard that he was sometimes shocked by Agee's conviction that emotions and the ego were "*the* material" of the artist, that exploring them was one of the artist's primary tasks.

The almost triumphant understatement of Evans's photography does not suggest inhibition. Yet he had wrestled with that ogre at an early age—and in another medium. He often said that he had at first wished to be a writer. Later he confessed, "I wanted so much to write that I couldn't write a word," and that his standards had defeated him. Possibly he could not face the self-exposure that writing can entail. As he told his friend the writer Leslie Katz, director of the Eakins Press, "Writing's a very daring thing to do." He called himself a late starter, yet he didn't sound regretful; he had not begun to be a photographer until he reached the age of twenty-four in 1928. But although he abandoned the goal of writing, he did produce a few essays on photography, some film and art reviews for *Time*, brief texts to accompany his photographic series in *Fortune*, and a short memoir of Agee for the 1960 reissue of *Let Us Now Praise Famous Men*.

Self-taught, profoundly literary, he frequently cited his favorite authors, especially in conversations with the young. As he got older his newest friends grew younger: there was apt to be a distance of at least thirty years. He had stayed in touch with his own youth, and he often talked about his fledgling days in Paris, when that city was "the incandescent center, the place to be," when he'd "lived in a fiery cloud of excitement." And it was heartening—amid the formidable conventions of the Fifties—to listen to someone who was totally committed to the arts. For me he also amplified the mystique of Europe, where I assumed that the arts were more greatly respected than in the United States. But he would not say that foreign societies were more enlightened than ours—a notion that was common among my classmates; instead he said that Europe was a place for apprenticeship. He belonged to a generation of American artists who'd gone abroad and saturated themselves in the French avant-garde and then come home and experimented with native subjects and imagery: their materials were intrinsically American. Although Evans was a Francophile who also loved England, he had never wanted to be an expatriate.

He seemed to me to be the consummate aesthete—as well as a person animated by an historical imagination. The Model Ts and the Coca-Cola signs were brand-new when he first saw them, just as the melons held aloft by boys who sold them at the roadside were fresh that day, but they would become emblems of the American past as much as the Victorian architecture he photographed. Agee had written of "the keen historic spasm of the shutter" which Evans employed to show America to Americans. Yet although he recognized the scenes or artifacts that would speak for history—the ephemera that should be preserved—it's unlikely that he selected them on that basis, since he was responding "with a flash of the mind" to the moment. And he despised nostalgia: "To be nostalgic is to be sentimental." He wrote that nostalgia and sentimentality blurred one's vision and destroyed "the actuality of the past. Good old times is a cliché for the infirm mind."

Evans had a way of making you examine your priorities—especially in your approach to work—and he did dispense an urgency about "first things first." It was essential to trust your instincts, he kept saying, and he often stressed that his own art was "instinctive." And he was prescient about the dilemmas of those who were just starting out; there were many things one didn't need to tell him. His vulnerability made him sensitive to that quality in others and he volunteered much advice and many admonitions. There would be setbacks even when your work was progressing; as he told the Yale students, "Any venture is a rocky road." Moreover he was convinced that the embryo writer or artist must protect his gift, that it could quite easily be dispersed or damaged, and there were many sardonic references to Time Inc. (For nearly twenty years he had a flexible arrangement with *Fortune*, but although he chose most of his subjects and edited his own picture spreads, he resented his financial dependence on the Luce bureaucracy.) And he felt that the young should not be the protégés of older sophisticates, who could exploit their vitality, bewilder them with flattery, and be vengeful if rejected. He spoke very strongly about this, so I wondered if a senior succubus or two had depleted his stamina.

When I met Evans I wasn't skilled at using my eyes; almost all my training had been for the ear, for language and music. The reticent observer was generous with his insights when one took a walk with him. The walks were lengthy and no one could hurry him: as the writer James Stern said, he was "slow as a hearse." Wandering along Third Avenue or down the Chelsea Embankment, he would seize me by the shoulders—"Look!"—and wheel me around to focus on whatever he'd just seen: there was always a view or a detail I hadn't noticed. A Victorian lamppost or the texture of old stone, a batch of secondhand bathtubs for sale on a sidewalk, the juxtaposition of several buildings—each time Evans showed me where to stand, steering me into seeing from a fresh perspective. At such moments he seemed easily enraptured: how much pleasure he derived from a bit of iron grillwork or a reflection in a window. In 1931, writing in the magazine *Hound and Horn*, he had extolled "the lyrical understanding of the street" of Eugène Atget, the photographer of turn-of-the-century Paris, whose work had "electrified" him. In the development of his own lyricism, Evans had valued that stage in life when "the street becomes your museum," where he could discover the "American vernacular" which nourished him.

Years later he remarked that ours was not a visual culture, that our schools mainly taught us to read and think, while education of the eye was "slighted." A former student of his recalled how Evans would gaze at a single picture in silence for half an hour. Only then would he make comments, usually talking about light: how a photographer might record the quality of the light in the air between the camera and the object. The character of light in an attic—where there was dust in the air—or in the subway, where the air itself could seem noisy and chaotic, was central to the atmosphere of a photograph and to an artist who knew how to blend the prosaic with the profound.

He saw humor where many might miss it, as when he photographed the flowery backside of a young woman leaning over a railing at Coney Island. The 1936 Atlanta picture of two billboards in front of twin wooden houses with oval window frames was an intentional "witticism," because Carole Lombard's eyes (one of them blackened) in the poster of *Love Before Breakfast* repeated the eye-shaped design of the frames. Small objects he thought comic were sometimes given to friends: Leslie Katz received a champagne swizzler—an inch-long silver bottle with delicate wires springing from the top—and I have an old cloth button: Queen Victoria's face stares crossly from its surface. But he could be ruthless in acquiring what he craved: the poet and novelist Jane Mayhall reluctantly parted with a copper spoon-rest from the top of her stove after Evans said twice, "I *want* it."

His collections of picture postcards, antique tools, nineteenth-century labels, driftwood, folk art, matchbook covers, typographical wonders, feathers, poptops from soda and beer cans (especially those which had been run over by cars), even decrepit spectacle rims, swelled until storage was almost insoluble. He kept part of the engine of his mother's last car in his kitchen. Hardware stores and printers' outlets were irresistible. The art historian Beaumont Newhall told a class at the University of Michigan how Evans had fallen to his knees in an airport to pick up a piece of a discarded plane ticket: the magenta and black lettering that caught his eye seemed to belong in a collage. Near Saratoga he purchased a whole garage sale and had it brought in a truck to Leslie Katz's lawn. The battered signs he collected for years—STOP, PRIVATE, ONE WAY, DEAD END, DO NOT DISTURB, NO TRESPASSING—were often photographed, but there was also a glee in ownership; what others called trash was treasured.

In the Thirties he'd take pictures of a few skyscrapers under construction, including the Chrysler building, but his photographs of urban demolition displayed his esteem for what was vanishing: "the torn flower-designs, the wounded beams ... the entrails of iron." As he wrote in *Fortune*, once a building was leveled, there was still fascination in the "ground-leavings—two-thirds of a plaster acanthus, a serpent of electric wire from 1903, one ormolu table leg, a chipped porcelain plaque marked EXIT." He could have filled his own museum with items which had been thrown away or partially wrecked, each one endowed with a distinction that had been ignored. And the painter Calvert Coggeshall told me that Evans was the only person who fully understood his quest for "natural miracles": Coggeshall searched for objects in nature which inexplicably resembled one another, such as the stones he found in a Long Island potato field that looked exactly like potatoes, complete with eyes—which seemed far more magical than a caterpillar that looks just like a thorn or a leaf. But Evans's own way of seeing couldn't be predicted: the photographs show that he liked repetition—a block of identical houses—as much as contrast: a handsome classical building close to an ugly pseudo-castle. Discussing his 1935 picture of Easton, Pennsylvania, with Leslie Katz, he said of the "honest" edifice and the crenelated monster, "both are American," and he reveled in the "craziness" of the view.

A few critics have said that Evans seemed remote from—even unmoved by—the suffering apparent in his Depression photographs. But that is probably a misunderstanding of his commitment to objectivity. From listening to him, I felt that the experience of his own poverty had never left him: he knew about indigence well before Wall Street disintegrated. As a schoolboy he'd been summoned to the headmaster's office and told that he might have to leave school because his father hadn't paid the bills; having been "singled out" for that reason remained a pungent memory. In the Thirties, his father—once a prosperous Midwestern copywriter—died bankrupt, leaving the son a house and a car, neither of which had been paid for. Even when Evans was in his fifties he spoke of himself to me as "a stray waif"; clad in his Savile Row suit, he still seemed to fear penury.

But although he would later say that the Depression was "the worst thing that ever happened in this country, worse than the Civil War," he had not initially been perceptive about its consequences; in 1931, when Paul Grotz wrote from Germany to enquire about prospects for jobs and the state of the American economy, Evans had cheerfully replied that there was no need to worry. He had no interest in politics and he felt himself to be above "causes." Although he and Ben Shahn had been good friends and housemates, they had quarreled vehemently because Evans thought Shahn had sold out to the radical movement, that he'd ceased to be an artist and had become a tool of the Left. "Propaganda" seemed to be one of the most distasteful words in Evans's vocabulary, and he derided his contemporaries who thought they were going to refashion American society. While he was taking some of his greatest photographs for the Farm Security Administration between 1935 and 1937, he and his supervisor, the economist Roy Stryker, were in conflict about the purpose of the project: John Szarkowski, the director of the Department of Photography at the Museum of Modern Art from 1962 to 1991, wrote that Stryker "thought (most of the time) that the unit's function was to help reform the ills of the country, and Evans thought that an artist's function was to describe life." He was dismissed from the program after less than two years, when its budget was being trimmed.

Although some critics of the Thirties deduced that Evans was testifying about the injustices of the period, he was on a different wavelength. As well as photographing what he found beautiful or beguiling—the melted tin Ionic capitals and weathered clapboard and store windows filled with hats—he appeared to be attracted to tragedy. Like Berenice Abbott, he took pictures of the poor before the Depression. Feeling that society owed him a living, he didn't identify with the destitute. But perhaps what he saw in them were simply the tragic facts of life: the eyes that stare into emptiness, the faces that state a hopelessness which doesn't hide the desire for dignity. He also conveyed the small stabs at respectability that are crucial to the poor: in some of the subway photographs, the neatly folded scarf or the angle of a hat brim impart a remnant of self-respect—which may not last much longer.

Survival: he often returned to that topic—and he implied that any toehold would be temporary. Although he thought some early deprivations could be fruitful for young artists—he said that some developed their work during the Depression because few steady jobs were available—he told me "A man over fifty shouldn't have to earn his living," that he was weary of the necessity of assignments. By the time I knew him, fatigue appeared to be a part of him, and some of it seemed to stem from decades of exertion to support himself. Although he talked so much about his youth, I suspected that he might have been autumnal even in his twenties; some of the earliest snapshots hint that melancholy hovered over him. He laughed freely and often, but sadness shadowed his face between the smiles.

He spoke so frequently of Agee after the writer's fatal heart attack in a taxi in 1955 that I gradually came to think that Agee had been the most important person in his life: the irreplaceable being whose disappearance was mourned throughout Evans's last twenty years. In his sixties he said to John Hill, director of Graduate Studies in Photography at Yale, that he missed Agee every day. Agee's disregard for survival seemed to haunt Evans, and when he wrote that "Agee's rebellion was unquenchable, self-damaging, deeply principled, infinitely costly, and ultimately priceless," he was perhaps still trying to accept what was nearly unbearable.

• • •

Evans's first show at the Museum of Modern Art in 1938, and his first book, *American Photographs*, received many fine reviews. Although his audience was never large, he was always appreciated by a dedicated minority. None of his photographs were in the colossal "Family of Man" exhibition organized by Edward Steichen for the same museum in 1955, and Evans said he'd "kept out" of that show—which featured smiling or poignant children, radiant American households, nursing mothers, and clichés of "brotherhood." Funerals or calamities occurred mainly in Europe or Africa or Asia: the exhibition gave the impression that sorrow was rare in the United States. Carl Sandburg's introduction to the catalogue set the tone: "The wonder of human mind, heart, wit and instinct is here. . . . People! flung far and wide, born into toil, struggle, blood and dreams, among lovers, eaters, drinkers, workers, loafers, fighters, players, gamblers . . . one big family hugging close to the ball of Earth for its life and being."

Evans said the idea of the show "made no sense," that it was "rubbish" and full of "cheap feelings." The American optimism of the mid-Fifties was as alien to him as the affirmations of the conventional arts establishment of the Twenties. Maybe he had "The Family of Man" in mind while he was writing a wall label for his pictures in a group show at the Museum of Modern Art in 1956, when he was emphatic about what "valid photography" was not: "It is not the image of Secretary Dulles descending from a plane. It is not cute cats, nor touchdowns, nor nudes; motherhood. . . . Under no circumstances is it anything ever anywhere near a beach."

• • •

His playfulness could startle those who expected asceticism from a photographer of the Depression, or who knew of his despondencies. Elizabeth Shaw, then at the Museum of Modern Art, remembered an outdoor lunch in Connecticut when Evans suddenly snatched up a camera belonging to the art critic James Thrall Soby and danced around his friends seated under a tree: whirling and leaping, he photographed them for nearly an hour (and then found there was no film in the camera). When driving he liked to play a tape of "The Ride of the Valkyries": it was a celebration of his Jaguar. Often he used slang as though it were in quotes: "I'll be *darned*," "moom pitchers." (He loved movies, and had tried to make one with Ben Shahn.) Visual amusements persisted throughout a lifetime; he had a large collection of rubber stamps and a wealth of colored inks for decorating the envelopes of personal letters: Calvert Coggeshall said, "It was his way of saying ha-ha to the post office." Humor didn't desert him even when he became violently ill at a dinner and a couple of us called an ambulance, which we followed to New York Hospital; there he told us a few hours later that he'd unintentionally repeated Franklin Roosevelt's last words: "'I don't feel well,' he said—and died!" Laughing as he lay on the hospital bed, he distracted us from our fears about his health, though he had real cause to be worried.

Before John Szarkowski met Evans, he imagined that the person who had taken the photographs would resemble Lincoln—a rough-hewn man with big hands—and was astonished when he saw the self-contained little figure in polished summer cottons. And I was surprised that the perfectionist sometimes lived like a slob. The cautious bon viveur—"the diffident dandy," James Stern called him—who doted on luxuries like fine leather gloves and handmade English shoes and would go into debt to buy elegant clothes, had a Yorkville railroad flat of awesome grubbiness. (It had once been his work place, but he also lived there for a while.) Layers of soot and rotting food abuzz with flies didn't seem to bother him. He was prone to bacon fires: failing to pour away the liquid fat before it bubbled over the rim of his frying pan, he would grunt with irritation as flames streaked up his kitchen wall, while he casually swatted at them with a towel. Hearing him talk about "life as a work of art" while watching drops of fat falling near the contact sheets of the Glyndebourne gardens and the heaps of negatives, I wondered if some of his previous work had been damaged by its proximity to bacon or the cigarettes he left burning on the edges of tables and the arms of wooden chairs.

He seemed equally at home with order and disorder. As a young man he'd enjoyed observing a roommate's habit of preparing his breakfast table before he went to bed: the cup, the saucer, the spoon, and the doughnut were laid out in the same spot each night, and Evans had savored that ritual, the immaculate scheme for daily life. A decade later, looking up a word under M in his dictionary, he was amazed to find four one-hundred-dollar bills tucked into the page where "money" was defined: he'd squirreled them away for an emergency and forgotten all about them. Once he generously loaned me his apartment for two weeks while he was out of town and my parents' place was sublet; on departure I left a sack of sheets and towels at a Chinese laundry and promptly lost the ticket. For a month a mock-reproachful question— "Nora, *where* are my towels?"—was his greeting on the phone or when I saw him. He didn't really care, he said—they were not good towels (which was true)—but the loss became a running joke: he was tolerant of the disorganized.

Fastidious in his art, rather austere in his thinking, he succumbed to bouts of alcoholism in his last two decades, as well as recurrent ulcers and agonizing illnesses. When he was unexpectedly stricken, vomiting at a table in a restaurant didn't seem to embarrass him. (He told me he would rather throw up in the presence of friends than risk fainting on the way to the men's room.) And yet his aesthete's self was easily offended by lapses of conduct in others—when men weren't "gentlemanly" or women were "loud" or "aggressive." People who "lacked style" polluted the environment. Personal style engrossed him: he would analyze deportment or charm as if it were a talent. Severely critical of affectation, he placed a high value on graceful behavior: he spoke of his favorites as "civilized." However, he forgave some who weren't—no one has accused Hart Crane of being civilized, Agee's friends remembered his affinity for uproar—above all if they were artists.

There had been a good many women in his life, and his old friends said that he had given much pain to some of them. He described himself to me as someone who often fell in love. But I sensed his ambivalence about intimacy. It appeared that he was romantic about certain women because they were unavailable—hence their characters could be left to the imagination. I think he liked what wasn't going to happen: fantasies that needn't be fulfilled. Otherwise he seemed to mistrust most women, although young ones like myself were unthreatening since we weren't likely to challenge him on common ground. So it was possible to spend a lot of time with him without involvement—rewarded by his perceptions and reflections, his memories and his kindness—while he could relax in knowing that no demands would be made. That left him free to be courtly and flirtatious.

Long afterward the publication of John Cheever's letters and biography indicated that Evans had been bisexual; in the Fifties I had assumed he was, without giving the matter much thought. It could have been another reason for his secrecy: after all, a man born in 1903, reared in the middle class of the Middle West, would not have tended to be public about sex with other men when his own generation was overwhelmingly homophobic. And since he had been visited by FBI agents who came to his *Fortune* office to ask questions about Ben Shahn, Evans may have feared that the bureau was aware of his sexuality and that he might be threatened with exposure if he wasn't helpful to its agents. (Hoover kept files on the sexual adventures of celebrities but not unfamous citizens. In 1992 the FBI informed me that Evans had no file.)

Now and then he idealized his friends' relationships: "That's a beautiful marriage," he told me, when he should have known it wasn't, adding, "They do *everything* together"—when they didn't. And yet his antennae were usually extraordinary: for what was felt or half-said or unsaid. By the same token he could be suddenly affronted: by some shading or implication that he *thought* he'd heard. And because he seemed to listen to the unspoken, one sometimes didn't know why he was displeased, why he frowned or grew stern. Perhaps he preferred to guess what others meant, rather than hearing it directly; he didn't seem to welcome confidences. Meanwhile he had powerful intuitions concerning those who should know each other—and strong instincts about individuals who ought to avoid one another. He took great care to introduce some of his friends and just as carefully tried to prevent others from meeting. Keeping his life in compartments more than most do, he inhabited a number of different worlds: that suited his multi-faceted nature. But thanks to him, I met two people who would become my lasting friends—as he predicted. He arranged an evening that would give us plenty of time to talk. Then he made sure that I would soon see them again, even though he could not be present.

Fascinated by intimacies of all sorts, he loved to discuss them at length, to speculate about ties that were beneficial and not restricting. He'd been captivated by the sight of his friend Nigel Dennis and his two teenage daughters on the first night of Dennis's play, *Cards of Identity*, at the Royal Court Theatre in London. Backed by a streaming summer sunset, the playwright strolled toward us across Sloane Square in his tuxedo, a very young girl on each arm: both wore ballet-length chiffon dresses and gigantic sunglasses with blazing rhinestone rims. Dennis explained that when he'd asked what gifts they would like to commemorate his opening night—perhaps bracelets engraved with the date?—they'd eagerly requested the sunglasses.

As we sat in a restaurant before curtain time, the daughters—awkward, glowing, excited—plied Dennis with gin: "*Not* more coffee." Gin, they said, was better for his nerves. So he grinned at them and sipped at his drink slowly, while candlelight bounced off the rhinestone rims, which they wouldn't remove even in the dim restaurant. Years later Evans often mentioned that scene: he was touched by the bonds between the father and his daughters, the pace and congruence of their jokes. He seemed to marvel at that closeness—not that

I ever heard him say he wished he'd had children. In fact he told Paul Grotz when they were young that he would like children to be presented to him on a silver platter—when he called for them. Then, he said, they could disappear.

• • •

My most vivid memory of that private man in public comes from the end of the opening of the huge retrospective of his photographs at the Museum of Modern Art in 1971. He appeared shortly before the lights on one wall were turned off, laughing and nodding and looking truly delighted at the gathering of lifelong friends and admirers who were there to honor his work. His entrance—after an official dinner laden with tributes—was perfectly timed: he'd stayed out of sight until the museum was about to close—only then would he allow us to congratulate him, permit himself to be seen. The small figure rocked on its heels, chatting and smiling and emitting an exuberance that was scarce in a life ravaged by illnesses. Then the lights blinked a few times and scores of people surged toward the counter where their coats were checked, while several of us who searched for him in the crowd and among the shadows and in the dark street couldn't find him.

6

Derailments

Yolks streamed from his fingers, which he had accidentally plunged into the heart of his eggs benedict; his hands were too slippery to grasp a fork, and egg decked his lapels. Laughing and gasping, James Thurber repeated, "Oh, it is incredible—what is happening to me" in tones of mock-lamentation, while he pantomimed drowning in a tidal wave of egg. Everyone at the lunch table laughed with him.

As long as he could joke about his increasing blindness, he did so. He described trying to feed a nut to a faucet, thinking it was a squirrel, and frightening a woman on a bus by mistaking her white handbag for a lapful of chickens. When he was still able to drive, "flecks of dust and streaks of bug blood on the windshield look to me often like old admirals in uniform, or crippled apple women . . . and I whirl out of their way, thus going into ditches and fields and up on front lawns, endangering the life of authentic admirals and apple women." And he could be charmed by the unexpected: after a medical examination, when Thurber was informed that there was sugar in his urine and a murmur in his heart, he replied, "That's not a diagnosis, that's a song cue."

As his sight waned he pondered the dexterity of the handicapped in a letter to my father: "There is too much talk about the courage or the nobility of the afflicted, since I know damn well that the challenge is far greater than the handicap. Remember that one-legged newsboy in Columbus who went on the vaudeville stage . . . I saw an armless woman in a movie short wrapping bundles with her feet, and having more fun than you and I have with our hands.

Furthermore, I have been spared the sight of television." To his eye surgeon he wrote about the parallels between his optical illusions—"golden sparks, melting purple blobs"—and those reported by devout Christians whom he suspected of confusing their "retinal disturbances with holy visitation." He felt that hundreds of deluded persons had taken "their glory to the bishop rather than the eye doctor," adding, "I am a believer in miracles, since my own vision is a miracle, but I am opposed to people who can't tell one illusion from another." The gallantry endured for many years, although of course the ruined eyesight deepened the depressions which had long been natural to him.

He could be savage when drunk, and there were evenings when he turned on others who could see what he could not, who could take reading or drawing or typing for granted. I had watched him take swings at people he couldn't see well enough to slug, and once I heard his forlorn, tanked-up battle cry, which could rise when his self-assurance had sunk: "There are only three writers in America! Hemingway, Faulkner, and Thurber! There are only three writers. . . ." On those occasions his words could be as bruising as blows which landed on target. But he was also exceedingly loyal to his closest friends. Frequently he tried to raise the confidence of those who doubted their talents, sympathized about work that was poorly received, took the initiative to rekindle flagging careers, and offered money to some who shrank from borrowing. He was so faithful to friends in trouble that his intimates had a habit of relying on him even when he was desolate. He wrote about John O'Hara, "He would go through smoke and flame for a friend," but that was a more accurate depiction of Thurber than O'Hara. In my teens I thought of Thurber as someone who nurtured the sanity of others: when there was a crisis in my family, he and his second wife, Helen, arrived and dispensed unwavering support. Not that they were like paramedics. Yet as Peter De Vries remarked long after Thurber's death, "The bundle of nerves was a tower of strength." And until his very last years, when total blindness and pain and rage overwhelmed him, he shared his stamina with those who reached for the phone and summoned him in mid-disaster.

Despite the ebullience and productivity of the writers I knew, chronic depressions seemed to be a part of ordinary life. And some who'd had breakdowns would attempt to assist friends who were undergoing similar torments. Few of the emergencies had been foreseen. Perhaps the social drinking obscured the fact that someone was close to the edge; when most were full of whiskey, no one's behavior seemed odd. (Also some who were manic could drink a great deal without appearing to be higher than usual.) But then there would be an event: an armchair set on fire or a siege of screaming during dessert at a holiday dinner, or that moment when a person simply gets stuck in the middle of a staircase, unable to decide whether to go up or down, because all decisions have become impossible.

The event would be labeled as a breakdown, and then—for a while—no one would burden the sufferer with expectations of rationality. His friends would discuss the prelude to the collapse, the signals that he was becoming "unglued," as they called it. For the actor and playwright-director Elliott Nugent, one symptom was chartering airplanes: when he did that, it was time to call the Thurbers. For St. Clair McKelway, a *New Yorker* writer and editor who had introduced my parents to each other, manic depression could be a prologue to delusions. During World War II, when he was an Air Force information officer, he came to believe that Admiral Chester Nimitz was guilty of high treason, so he sent an official message of warning to the Pentagon. When McKelway was visiting Scotland in 1959, he thought the Russians were plotting to kidnap President Eisenhower, Queen Elizabeth, and Prince Philip— and that he himself was enmeshed in a counterplot devised by the CIA and the British Secret Service. Noticing that some license plates on cars he passed on Scottish roads displayed the initials of people he knew, including two CIA employees, he wondered if the apparent conspiracy might be a practical joke. But panic drove him to alert an American intelligence officer in Scotland to the international menace. McKelway later wrote jovial accounts of his temporary psychoses. But friends who went to see him in different hospitals over the years couldn't be confident that his latest derailment would be the last one.

If you had sick relatives, you kept trying to read their moods. Bouts of euphoria, or being unable to abide the company of others, or not being able to be alone, or thinking that no one else made any sense, could be overtures to prostration. Manic people often felt splendid: involving themselves in dozens of projects at once and making flurries of phone calls, they could not comprehend those who were trying to slow them down, obstructing the path to ecstasy.

Some of the sick felt that their own families were deranged. Others just became deeply withdrawn for weeks before the explosion, as did the depressive I saw oftenest but understood least of all: my mother. She had thrived in the Twenties and early Thirties, a successful journalist before my birth; in the Fifties she lost touch with her former self and living in the present was intolerable for her. There were no comforts in her life. The future—immediate or long-term—seemed horrific: she only wanted the agony of depression to end. To her old friends, she appeared to be a relic: a living reminder of another time, when everything had seemed possible. Her doctors weren't enlightening to my father when he sought clues to the causes or the nature of her illness;

he said they were vague or evasive. (Psychiatrists of that era rarely discussed a patient's condition with the family: that was thought to violate confidentiality and to hinder transference.) Sometimes I was asked if my mother was a schizophrenic, and I didn't know; the term was used very loosely in those days—by psychiatrists as well as by laymen—and it wasn't refined until much later. But eventually I was told she was considered to be a manic depressive.

Edward Paramore, a playwright, reporter, and screenwriter who had collaborated with Scott Fitzgerald on the movie of *Three Comrades*, used to stay with us between projects that didn't seem to hatch. The man who sat motionless for hours on our beige corduroy sofa was hard to associate with the clever, high-spirited adventurer who had been *The New Republic*'s correspondent in Russia during the Revolution, when he took more than a hundred American refugees through Siberia on a train whose engine was stolen three times, who'd played semi-professional baseball, had escaped from jail in Nicaragua two hours after he was imprisoned, and had made Edmund Wilson laugh throughout their youth; Wilson had loved to visit Paramore's family in Santa Barbara, and Wilson's diaries were full of Paramore's bawdy songs. But the pallid Paramore of the Fifties, whose stationary shoes I stumbled over as I dashed through our living room—he was as wooden as the furniture—seemed incapable of laughter. He took sleeping pills in the daytime and occasionally spoke in gibberish; at one point, he was afraid to go out on the street.

Once my mother, unused to our new record player, put on a Mozart quartet at the wrong speed: as the strings screeched at triple the velocity and pitch of normality, neither she nor Paramore noticed the hideous sounds; they sat quietly, so benumbed by dejection that they didn't know that Mozart was being murdered. As the noise became unbearable and I ran to rescue the record, Paramore spoke out of his long silence. "You know," he told my mother, "I've never cared much for this stuff." "No?" she said, straining to smile brightly, like a gracious hostess. They didn't seem to be aware of the difference when the music resumed at the right tempo. Disconnected from what they heard or saw or tasted, they dwelled at a distance from everyone around them, and probably we were as unreachable for them as they were for us.

When Dorothy Parker was mentioned, I remembered lots of dogs, a house in Bucks County, and a woman who shouted greetings and instructions to arriving guests, waving her arms toward the bedrooms, waving down the dogs. The adults all slept late the next day and didn't talk much on the way home. My parents saw less of her after politics became central to her life; my father had teased her about her commitment to radicalism. (He recalled a meeting of the Screen Writers Guild when a colleague had referred to her as a liberal—

whereupon she turned "white with passion" and cried "How *dare* you call me a liberal?") But he remained extremely fond of her and often quoted her. He described an evening when they went to a party for Janet Flanner, *The New Yorker*'s Paris correspondent, who was being very royal with those who were paying their respects to her. Parker stared at Flanner across the room, murmuring, "It's not enough to look like Voltaire, you gotta *be* Voltaire!"

I last saw Parker in 1959 at a small gathering at Donald Stewart, Jr.'s. By then she was something of a recluse. She arrived in a tottery state, eyes brimming; you couldn't guess if she was halfway drunk or if she'd had nothing. Tense and trembling with a watery smile, she seemed to be trying to act as "Dorothy Parker" was supposed to: the first thing she told Kenneth Tynan, who was eager to meet her, was that her poodle was named Cliché. She looked hopeful as she pronounced the word, waiting for laughter which never came.

Don led her carefully around the room, introducing her to each guest. When she heard my name, the wet eyes overflowed. "Oh," she said, gesturing at the level of a small child's head, "I knew you when you were . . ." then turned to Don—"And I knew him when he was . . ." (the other arm went out to pat an invisible skull), "And I remember when you were . . ." (patting the air again), "And he was . . ." Tears trickling slowly as we stood rigid, she continued to mumble, "I knew them when they were . . ." paddling the air with cupped palms, showing us how short we'd been some twenty years before. Words left her yet she persisted with the dumb show, sculpting our childhood heights in space. Her hands seemed unable to stop moving. But the loss of those two decades, and the grief that those years had given her, were almost paralyzing for all of us. She appeared to be physically lost, adrift in an unfamiliar room, dazed by the faces of polite young strangers fixed with expectant smiles. "My dog's name is Cliché": when she could speak again, she told each person that; it seemed to be the only sentence she was capable of uttering. Finally a close friend took her arm, walked her gently to the door, and took her home.

In the wake of the casualties, I sometimes thought about "stability"; did those who lived in Westchester or Nebraska and became lawyers have more resilience than the writers who were accustomed to each other's desperations? At heart I knew that no one was immune; early on I saw that no way of life protected the psyche: the lunacies of my schoolmates' relatives lunged out of every kind of background. I was sure that writing did not make people crazy and that some could renew themselves through work—indeed there were those who said that writing held them together. And one heard that physicians and psychiatrists had more crack-ups than members of other professions. But I used to look at the walls and furnishings of strangers, marveling at the facade of solidity: meals at regular hours, the bowl of nasturtiums in the center of the breakfast table, placemats that came from and were returned to the same drawer, orange juice squeezed the night before, even the neat lawns of New Canaan and Darien.

For us—and I began to identify with people more than twice my age—the news of emotional eclipses was almost routine. Then there were storms of asthma which made breathing like drowning, migraines or spastic colons, frozen hip joints, muscles that suddenly wouldn't move: legs that buckled, feet that didn't walk, hands that couldn't grip, bodies that gave in after despair had damaged the will. The physical impairments hadn't much to do with aging: some were so stricken in their forties that I used to wonder if or how they could resume their former lives.

• • •

Most of my parents' friends had known little about mental illness until it erupted in their homes. A previous generation had talked about "neurasthenia" and a few had taken "rest cures." But all that seemed rather remote from the mainstream of American experience, especially for those who had grown up in the Midwest. "Freud" was a literary influence, not a guide to private life; his stress on sexuality was seen as liberating, but his theories of neurosis were not taken personally or applied to one's companions. There was some skepticism about "noggin feelers" and "couch work." Nugent said of his contemporaries, "We had vastly greater respect for Henry James than for his brother William," and when E. B. White was recovering from a spell of "head trouble," he wrote to a friend: "Doctors weren't much help, but I found that old phonograph records are miraculous. If you ever bust up from nerves, take frequent shower baths, drink dry sherry in small amounts, spend most of your time with hand tools at a bench, and play old records till there is no wax left in the grooves."

Briefly a patient of Dr. Carl Binger's, White later wrote to him, "There isn't anything the matter with me that a guillotine wouldn't cure. My only trouble is in my head." For middle-aged writers, introspection could be the groundwork for fiction, but they were terribly uncomfortable with self-examination. (Perhaps the process was particularly unpleasant for the men, who may have felt that gazing inward was unmanly.) Still they were willing to try it; on all sides the depressed were in therapy, although most of the treatment did not seem to have much effect. At least I saw few lasting alleviations. In the Fifties antidepressants were not yet well developed, and people for whom daily life was anguish spent months recounting their childhoods to psychiatrists who seemed to deduce that what they needed was more love (when they were not lovable), or security (when that was unattainable), or to learn to express their anger (at which they had always excelled).

It was not then known that certain medications for anxiety—such as Miltown, which imitated the actions of barbiturates—were highly addictive. Patients who were acutely depressed were often kept in hospitals far longer than they are now, while the staff watched to make sure they didn't kill themselves. Electroshock was widely used for depression; although it was effective, it erased recent memories, which were supposed to return in a few months. After several treatments, some did not even remember why they were in a hospital. Many patients complained that they never regained their full memories. The techniques of shock were still crude: muscle relaxants were not yet employed, and an attendant had to hold the patient down during convulsions—otherwise the vertebrae could be fractured. Occasionally a leg was broken; heart attacks could occur during a seizure. The patient emerged in a wretched haze: his head and muscles ached, the joints were sore, the mind was thoroughly confused. He soon became submissive, which could be a relief to his relatives and doctors. Insulin shock, given to manic patients as well as schizophrenics, calmed people down but could make them feel frighteningly weak, almost as though they might be dying. At the time I heard that only a few I knew had had electroshock, and that two had received insulin. But later on I learned that other friends had been through electroshock in those years; since the treatment lasted just a few weeks, families could keep it secret if they wished.

• • •

Gradually I discovered that there were some differences between severe depressions and breakdowns. The depression could be grave but not incapacitating: the person could still write, teach, vote, balance the checkbook, roast a chicken, scramble the eggs. I used to think that simply being able to function was a proof of health. I did not know that there was such a thing as a functioning wreck. I could see that a few of the depressed were excellent managers: their lives were meticulously structured in an effort to keep blackness at bay. Some moved through their surroundings without disrupting them: there was no incident which caused friends to exclaim that someone "was perfectly all right last week." But one might some day learn that his pain had been as profound as that of people who had thrown ashtrays at the moon or sobbed all the way to the hospital. The melancholia could be so insupportable that the victim might try not to have emotions at all, to suppress every tremor of feeling. Then others would find him dim or cold or dull. Soon marriages and friendships could crumble, while the depressive courted the idea that "nothing mattered." He might even think of potential happiness as a threat: a new love could compel him to feel again, to be vulnerable.

You learned that strength and weakness were illusory: those who seemed robust might disintegrate sooner than some who appeared infirm. A writer whom I expected would be a triumphant survivor lost the compass of her memory and drifted into uncharted zones. In her last decade or so, drink became the current that bore her away from everything she had known: a lively career, lovers who remained her friends, passion and festivity. She had been a beauty and her work had had an ample audience. But aging—even handsomely—made her feel hopeless, worthless, unwanted. Then she couldn't remember the best years she'd had.

Mislaying whole chapters of her existence, she also spoke of things that hadn't occurred. One evening when she cooked a meal for the two of us, she asked me if the people we'd been talking with had left—adding that she hadn't liked them very much. I had to tell her that no one had been there. She didn't seem startled: clearly she assumed that I'd forgotten them. Anyway they weren't worth much attention, she said. The next night she rang to reproach me for being late for dinner: she did not know that I'd been at her table only twenty-four hours before. Once I heard her give a speech—on behalf of a school of the arts—in which she rambled piteously, kept alluding to Puff (her long-dead parents' Persian cat), and repeated that she wished she'd been a better writer. It was a public declaration of her atrophy. Afterward she stood smiling with a glass of wine in her hand, unaware that she had upset her listeners.

A few years later, when all alcohol was forbidden her, she was as bewildered in sobriety as she had been by drink. She often thought she was on a ship (she had adored ocean voyages when she was young). Confined to her apartment, controlled by nurses who prevented her from wandering out to buy bourbon, she kept preparing to travel, staying up all night to pack her bags. Over the phone she would tell me that she was about to go to Europe on a wonderful assignment— "I can't say much about it, but it's very big"—and her voice sounded as it always had: vigorous, calm, cheerful. When I said I wanted to come and see her, she explained that I couldn't, because she was in California— while I protested that I was just around the corner, in New York. Committed for a while to a psychiatric hospital, she somehow escaped and was found in her study, sitting at her desk and typing rapidly.

One of the last times I saw her, she told me she had been hallucinating and she was very straightforward about it. In great distress, she said there were days when images seemed to swim out from the television screen and entangle themselves with her perceptions. She was rational when she talked about the "illusions." But it was difficult for her to understand that she was at home, so a nurse had placed a note on her desk: "YOU ARE IN YOUR OWN APARTMENT." Yet she kept asking if she was at sea—she felt the motion of the waves, the pull of the tides. The nurse reminded her to look out the window and see the tree that was there: trees had roots, therefore she was on land.

She told me there was a new man in her life and that he was wildly attractive—and handed me a photograph of her ex-husband, taken some thirty years before. I said his name and she replied sharply, "No, that is *not* Jonathan." This was a man she'd met recently, though she couldn't quite remember what he was called. Always hale and active—she used to stride for hours along the beaches of Long Island, dive into surf that daunted others, cover miles of pavement while discovering the excitements of foreign cities—she seemed cursed with expanded energies once her sanity fled. Tall, she seemed to grow even taller: the large-boned body seemed to demand more space. Pacing to and fro in her living room, packing, typing, telephoning, getting ready for the next trip, she appeared to be trying to push back the walls which enclosed her. She wore out one nurse after another—at times, she hit them and wrestled with them when they wouldn't let her go out—and finally no one could restrain her. So she ended behind the barred windows of an institution, an explorer who became a prisoner.

Thinking of her, thinking of others in whom madness and alcohol seemed intertwined, I wondered if there might have been less turmoil without liquor. One couldn't be sure. Some seemed to drink because they were already very troubled or on poor terms with themselves. But no thoughtful person could have a good opinion of himself on a regular basis. Samuel Johnson had said he sometimes "required" wine "To get rid of myself, to send myself away." That could be understood by many writers. But at what stage did a respite from the self heighten a craving that became a disease? And when did craftiness start to conspire with the need? I knew a family that used to hunt for a hidden bottle: although they kept no alcohol at home, the daughters would return to find their mother sodden; having outsmarted them once more she would cock an eyebrow and grin while they looked through closets and under mattresses and lifted the lid of the toilet tank. When she was completely smashed she was quite peaceful. She could also become violent without liquor. Would she have been different without the daiquiris of her youth? No one was certain. But she—like the woman who sent herself away until she was put in custody forever—was one of those who seemed further crazed when alcohol swirled through their veins. After a few glasses these people did not seem merely drunk, they appeared to be out of their minds.

• • •

As for the successful suicides, they left a legacy that could not be disowned: a running battle with the dead. If suicide was someone's statement about his life, it was hard to acknowledge that he had had the final word: one went on arguing with his ashes, trying to persuade him not to kill himself. Fighting to foil an event which had already taken place, one wanted to believe that the act had not been planned far in advance—and that he could be called or reasoned back into existence, hauled back from the brink.

In the midst of fantasies about a resurrection, it was possible to unleash every sort of anger at the deserter: to chastise him for having tried to escape. But one also envisioned the long solo journey toward self-extinction—in retrospect it was like watching a figure receding across a desert, walking slowly away from his last human outposts, his back turned on the rest of us until he vanished into the distance. As he walked, choice abandoned him: there was only one thing left for him to do. Perhaps suicide had become a pledge that he had made to himself: if he'd felt like a failure, carrying through on one decision could seem like an achievement. Or perhaps—fearing that love and respect had ebbed away from him—he chose to disappear in hopes of regaining esteem: in memory.

One knew that people harbored many different motives for self-destruction. Some were enraged: their fury became the weapon they aimed at themselves. Some were avid for revenge—which would be fulfilled when the family saw the face shattered by the gunshot, the blood congealed on slashed wrists, the corpse choked on its vomit from the poison or the pills. (The newspapers would say that "the injuries are believed to have been self-inflicted," but the relatives were meant to feel that they had made the wounds.) Others hated their own sense of isolation: longing to eliminate that feeling, they eliminated themselves. And there were suicides who hadn't appeared to want comfort: if solace was offered, it wasn't accepted. And some would remain mysterious: no one would ever know why the departure had seemed imperative. But one inevitably imagined their last hours—speculating whether they had tried *not* to kill themselves, had resisted stepping off that window ledge or pressing the trigger or picking up the razor blade, while searching for a way to go on living. Or perhaps the final moments were spent in gearing up their courage: in forcing themselves—perhaps still reluctantly?—to die.

• • •

Usually it was adults who were derailed. But some of the writers were devastated by what happened to their offspring: the twenty-three-year-old suicide in the bathtub; the boy who menaced women with knives and was arrested for robbery and assault three times between the ages of fifteen and twenty-one; the schizo-phrenic who relapsed after each "recovery." Conferring with their children's psychiatrists, some found a son's or a daughter's condition so demoralizing that they too embarked on a course of treatment.

Family therapy was not widespread: it was new in the mid-Fifties, and many troubled families weren't aware that it was available. Among my parents' friends, the "bad seed" theory was in circulation: decent people could have a monstrous child and they should not be blamed for its deeds. "Wrong from the start" was a phrase that I remember after my companion of the sandbox cut his throat. It was true that he had once tried to strangle me when I stole a lot of his clay, but we had been close in our clumsiest years, and the relatives who urged me to avoid him couldn't convince me that he was "defective." The friends said that the knife-wielder was "born with a few buttons missing," and that the girl who kept being jailed for homicidal driving enjoyed disrupting the life of her lenient father—she was portrayed as almost demonic. When it came to "impossible" children there were some references to "bad blood" versus "good stock": the genes of one parent's mad forebear might have sullied the other's fine heredity. And when an adult learned that there had been a demented great-great uncle in the family, the news seemed all the more ominous because previous generations had concealed it for so long.

Living close to the breakdowns I couldn't help but feel that some of the sick were very powerful—almost as though their afflictions were fortifying: illness seemed to enlarge their ability to dominate the lives around them. The friends would debate whether the sickness was part of the invalid's character, or whether it should be regarded as a temporary aberration—a tornado which would pass. There was a desire to believe that the violence came from "outside" or elsewhere, or that it sprang from a situation, not that it was inherent in anyone's personality. Some of the more elderly psychiatrists seemed to encour-age this point of view: from an almost Victorian perspective, it would be implied that when the parish priest tried to burn down the chapel, that was only "an episode": he was "himself" again when he opened the church bazaar.

One was constantly advised not to judge an ailing person by his behavior: to forget what he did, since his actions did not represent his nature. What he said should not be taken too seriously. So the man who shouted to his children that he loathed them should not be believed: he did not mean it, he did not really wish they were dead. But the relatives of such a person could reach an impasse: when his statements were ignored, his frustration and wrath and fright could increase, and when he accused them of "misunderstanding" him, that was partially true. Moreover, if he felt they were being patient with him, he could come to detest their forbearance. But they might also fear for their own equilibrium: after dwelling with a certain amount of chaos, their own resources could start to erode, and mania might seem to be contagious.

There were so many avenues to misunderstanding. One was the invalid's misperception of himself. In Nugent's manic periods, he was positive that nothing was his fault: the policemen who kept arresting him for disorderly conduct were in error. When White was at his lowest, he thought he was not a writer. When Thurber had a breakdown—after five eye operations in one year, followed by the realization that he was unlikely to see again—he wept in the presence of a near stranger and asked if blindness was a punishment for having ridiculed others in his writings. How could anyone persuade the sufferers that their views of themselves were mistaken? Doctors tried, friends tried, but few seemed able to affect the cycle: the frenzy or the depression ran its course of weeks or months. Then there would be an improvement— which might last long enough to generate all sorts of hope. But usually it did not last. So the sick person and his intimates felt there had been a failure of understanding: they had thought he was well again, that life would be intelligible once more, that there was such a thing as progress. They had been wrong.

And then there was guilt. Guilt of wives and husbands and children toward the invalids: guilt for not loving them, when the doctors said that love was essential to the cure. And if there had been several attempts at suicide, one might miserably wish that the attempter had brought it off—or would just dry up and blow away, be gone without violence. But one might also be afraid that one had contributed to the breakdown, inspired the overdose. . . . Guilt of the casualty: for behaving in a way which meant that no one wanted to live with him any longer. He had plunged his family into a maelstrom, they were drowning in his disorders. Neither he nor they had many reasons to like themselves—or one another.

Trust had died over the years: a protracted silence or any sort of agitation, or an obscure joke, or a response to a book or a movie, could be a symptom— there might be a subtext to any remark. And it seemed that almost no kind of relationship could be counted on: if the other person sickened, everything could be altered—his character might appear to vary every day. Someone you still loved could become hateful. But you wouldn't know if he was helpless to curb his outbursts, or if he was sometimes indulging himself. He might also seem to have a rather magical capacity for turning into another being, and you had to be on the alert for the advent of his other self—or selves. Or else sedation had made him unrecognizable to himself: if his feelings had been leveled out by medication, he might miss the highs and lows—even if he knew how ravaging they were for everyone else.

Flight from the sick could be a temptation, but the families didn't flee: they were still in the apartment when the patient returned from the hospital; together they would work at some parody of family life. They had to accept the abnormal as the norm. Once that was understood, excursions to the outside world—time spent at college or on a bicycle trip—bestowed an appreciation of dualities: you could perceive what health was and try to measure up to it; meanwhile you knew what it wasn't—and knew how perilous the balance was.

At home the dialogues continued: friends of a lifetime asked one another if their generation was exceptionally unstable. Alcohol seemed to be an insufficient answer: many had used it without calamity, some abstained for months at a stretch. The gaiety of the Twenties did not have to end in madness. But had they been too careless about consequences? Were they too reckless? Or had they lived through too many upheavals? The bright certainties of their formative decade had been dispersed by a nation's poverty and global war. They'd had to keep adapting themselves to gigantic fluctuations. And yet—here a chorus of reassurance would commence—they had been skillful at living with changes and (unlike their predecessors) they had not asked history to hold still. Many were engaged in their best work, and the immediate future was teeming with opportunities. Why then were so many friends in hospitals? Why was it necessary to call the Thurbers (once again) to report that someone literally couldn't get out of bed—could not push the blankets aside or put one foot in front of another? Surely people of intelligence could remake their lives, and talent wasn't a transient: if a person had achieved a great deal in the past, the batteries could be recharged, the accomplishment could be repeated. Setbacks were perfectly natural. But life was a series of beginnings, of points of departure—if only everyone could realize that. It should be possible, they said, to take off once more, to start afresh, to astonish yourself and the world all over again. You could even go on the wagon.

7

Envoi

These memories should not end with illness. Few lives are free of turmoil, and the men and women in our living room had at least done what they'd chosen: they had followed their own imaginations wherever they led. Public opinion couldn't affect them, nor could it circumscribe their range. The readiness to challenge and then contradict official wisdom was supposed to be an American tradition, but that kind of autonomy was rare in the Fifties, and I was fortunate to come of age among people who took their independence for granted.

At the same time contempt for social snobbery enabled them to appreciate all sorts of Americans and their idiom, and that nourished their prose. A loathing of cliché—in thought as much as language—kept perceptions fresh and left them open to discovery. They believed in will and effort and they certainly liked achievers, but I never heard them deride the unsuccessful. They also seemed to respect the irrational—even if they didn't examine it closely, even though their sense of cause and effect was erratic. And the laughter that swept through the living room was restorative; moreover it was honest: when they joked about nightmares—real or imaginary—they were acknowledging that fear and pain could not be reasoned away.

Storytelling wasn't just a recreation: the narrators were dispensing tales and legends which reflected the wild diversities of American life, its character and textures. Thurber's Ohio, Nunnally Johnson's Georgia—where the sharecroppers of *Tobacco Road* would have "belonged to the country club set"—Albert Hackett's boyhood tours with a traveling theatrical troupe, and Faulkner's

Mississippi (my father's favorite regional lore of all), seemed to make Manhattan even more exciting than it was. Except for Thurber, few of the writers were performers: they told stories without fanfare, sharing what had amused or appalled them. *The New Yorker* had trained them to be scrupulous about facts in print, but in the living rooms some might soar into invention, and when a newcomer asked, "Is that true?" he could be answered with a faraway smile. But later on, when I checked out some of the stories, I found that many of them were. The narrators had revelled in the extraordinary—above all when it was true.

Some did forfeit their material by talking it away: I listened to marvelous tales that never reached the typewriter, and others which had lost their vitality when they finally were written. But few seemed aware of that peril; in many ways they were unacquainted with self-protection. And the survivors continued to behave as if they were indestructible. They thought that eating lots of steaks and eggs and lying in the sun were good for them, that liquor made men strong and women sweet, that many writers did their best work after midnight. (My father ate cream cheese, which he disliked, when he was dieting; he'd confused it with cottage cheese. When a couple of his friends had minor heart attacks, they drank extra whiskeys to benefit the cardiac muscles.) But although they didn't know how to take care of themselves or their talents, little energy was wasted on foreboding: the dread of consequence that would inhibit some of my contemporaries. Hesitation seemed as scarce as prudence: a writer should not risk missing anything that might stimulate him, whether it meant a sudden trip to Palermo or the library, a month among the Eskimos or in privacy on Cape Cod.

E. B. White was renewed by long sojourns at his farm in Maine until he settled there in the late Fifties. S. J. Perelman told me that excursions to unknown countries recharged him for writing, though he needed to hear the vocabulary and phrases of New York after being away from them. Edmund Wilson renovated his parents' old stone house in the Adirondacks, finding that the place attuned him to the past—not only his own, but the country's as he would analyze it in the throes of the Civil War. Rejoicing that the house now belonged "entirely" to him, no longer to his forebears, he saw that it also gave him a purchase on the future, that it primed him for the work he would do there after sixty and seventy. Reading and writing about the Dead Sea Scrolls, immersing himself in Turgenev and Genet, exploring the plight of the Iroquois, exhilarated by James Joyce's newly published letters, he admitted to "a certain satisfaction in outlasting and outworking" many of his colleagues.

When he was upstate he could follow a bit of the advice in one of the rhymes he sent to friends at Christmas:

> Beware of dogmas backed by faith,
> Steer clear of conflict unto death.
> Keep going; never stop; sit tight;
> Read something luminous at night.

Few of the writers I knew had avoided conflicts, but they were utterly undogmatic, and their responses to a book or a stranger or a situation couldn't be foreseen. When I first read Emerson's "Self-Reliance" and came across "a foolish consistency is the hobgoblin of little minds," I realized that such consistency was unfamiliar to me, that I was accustomed to the unpredictable.

Perhaps the individualists of the Twenties who became writers were more suited than some of their successors to leading double lives: the rewards of so much time spent alone, the ease with which they mingled after long days at the desk. If a friend was tired after his exertions, the others seemed tolerant: they didn't appear to ask one another to be lively on every occasion. Reclusive yet outgoing, most were probably solitaries at heart: the hours they enjoyed together may also have been a stimulant for withdrawal. Yet I didn't hear complaints of loneliness; although no one escapes it altogether, that state seemed alien to many of them. What they imagined or wrote could be as sustaining as the finest company—until they were ready to listen to voices that weren't their own. And I do remember a burst of laughter when someone mentioned the title of a new book called *The Lonely Crowd*.

ADMONITIONS

OF THE

FIFTIES

You had only to be careful and not immerse
yourself too deep in life, keeping one foot
always on dry land for a quick withdrawal
when the current got too strong.
—*Warren Miller,*
THE WAY WE LIVE NOW

Women had yet to see how the past made
the present, how the present rests in
untold ways on the subterranean world
of the past.
—*Lyndall Gordon,* SHARED LIVES

8

Maturity

During the Army-McCarthy hearings, a friend of mine at Radcliffe used to rise early (which she hated) and hasten downstairs to read our dormitory's only copy of *The New York Times* before some twenty-five other students crumpled it. Gradually she realized there was no competition: no one else wanted it. She could sleep until noon and still find the newspaper neatly folded, undisturbed on the coffee table where it was placed each day.

Harvard seemed to foster naiveté and irreverence at once; it enabled you to disdain the outside world and the inelegance of the era. You could be faithful to the arts and to your work while waxing skeptical about institutions (including Harvard) and growing rather hostile to authority. The New England traditions of independence that suffused our largest private universities helped to insulate students from the rest of America—as well as to screen them from some of the dismal uniformities of the Fifties. The education of the middle-class young could provide a shield but not much armor; no ammunition but some tactics of defense. For undergraduates the Northeastern universities were more like trenches than towers; perhaps there was a similarity to the dugouts of World War I, where troops not too near the battlefield were sheltered from the shells that soared overhead.

• • •

Writing long papers on the whiteness of the whale, analyzing Rilke's angels, acting in Yeats's plays, singing Bach cantatas and the music of the Renaissance, tracing Henry James's theories of art as expressed in *The Tragic Muse* ("The subject doesn't matter, it's the treatment, the treatment!"), following Persephone into the underworld and Theseus through the labyrinth, memorizing masses of Donne and Keats, pursuing the coin imagery in *Henry IV*, Part I and the eyesight metaphors in *King Lear* and the snakes in *Anthony and Cleopatra*, searching for Christian and pagan symbols in the Romanesque sculptures at Vézelay and Moissac, reveling in Palestrina and Proust, de Vigny and Rimbaud, replaying Dylan Thomas's recording of *Under Milk Wood* until students throughout the hallway protested vehemently, arguing that Dostoyevsky was better than Tolstoy (even though the professor said the opposite), silently reciting Eliot's lines while walking to class ("Eyes I dare not meet in dreams/In death's dream kingdom") trying to devise images as strong as Thoreau's, struggling to unravel *The Phoenix and the Turtle*: of course an eager saturation in the classics was as rewarding as it was exciting. Yet I feel somewhat rueful on recalling the aestheticism of the Fifties—certainly no regret for our education, but for what we were allowed to do with it. Unwittingly we used the past as an escape hatch, fleeing into literature and other centuries as though some safety or protection nestled there. For us the arts were severed from society, and I would have been astounded if I'd been asked to see a kinship between them.

To many of my friends there was no question that the past was superior to the present, just as Europe was superior to America, or art to politics. So it was easy to disregard what was happening: the election of Eisenhower simply couldn't be as significant as the rhythms of *Ulysses* or James's "designs" for *The Golden Bowl*. When a classmate of mine crooned, "I'd lay for Adlai," she was merely teasing her Republican uncles. Rehearsals of a baroque opera didn't prevent us from following the Rosenbergs' appeals for clemency; it was just that we didn't often think about them.

I remember only one evening in four years that touched on political matters: two young teaching fellows—William Alfred and Robert O'Clair—held a wake after Stevenson's defeat. My escort, a recent graduate, admitted that he'd voted for Eisenhower. They told him he would soon be drafted, because Eisenhower was going to expand the army (though he didn't), and they threatened to embroider ditty bags with quotations from English literature: to remind some of their former pupils that they'd voted themselves into military service. My friend—a romantic depressive—flinched when they chose the slogan for his bag: "I fall upon the thorns of life, I bleed!" But most of our other teachers didn't refer to politics in front of us: it was quite like the ancient taboo about mentioning sex or money in the presence of children or servants—a *pas devant* mentality.

The word "maturity" was prevalent in that period. Maturity could mean a genteel approach to the classics—namely, to the ideas and feelings they evoked; some tutors were anxious to raise their pupils above "the passions of faction," to nurture civility. In lectures we often heard the phrase "On the one hand . . . and on the other"; a "balanced" viewpoint was the goal. And eschewing strong social opinions meant being reasonable, sophisticated: that was a sign of political maturity. "Objectivity" should not be compromised by ingesting any ideology at all. (That "ideology" meant socialism wasn't made clear to students by the Cold War liberals.) The mature accepted society as it was and didn't seek to alter it. A certain stoicism was expected, which encouraged passivity in the young. And while our government suppressed the remnants of the American Left, and the Communist countries jailed or executed their own dissidents, politics per se fell into disrepute; to many young people all political philosophies seemed worthless.

At the heart of the end-of-ideology creed was the inference that all sorts of ideas might be masks for Communism; even "innocent assumptions" could be fronts for dangerous thinking. Words like "peace" and "freedom" were suspect because Communists had used them in petitions or as names for their organizations: a mistrust of language was a by-product of the Cold War. And perhaps some of my professors had come to feel that even the mildest form of socialism was a utopian fantasy, or that believing in any species of social system was a step toward extremism.

Yet it was absurd that the Communists were considered a menace to the young. Neither their deeds nor their aspirations had any reality for most of us: we weren't exposed to their views, we knew almost nothing about the issues that had engrossed them in the Thirties. In boarding school I'd had a history teacher who was later said to be a Communist. If he was, his perspective was not apparent: he trundled us through the Renaissance and the Reformation without a murmur of interpretation. Rarely addressing the class outright, he lectured from notes on little white cards held high before his face: the cards looked like blinders on a horse.

Consciously or not, many of our teachers censored themselves, while throughout the country their counterparts were being fired for their ideas or associations. After public figures like the Hollywood Ten and Alger Hiss went to jail, or were declared security risks like Robert Oppenheimer, the unfamous knew they should be careful. Our professors taught us, by their own example, that life was safer if you had no politics. Without knowing it we digested their fear—as though it were a tasteless, colorless potion that permeated whatever we ate or drank. They protected us from their own reactions to the headlines, we absorbed their inhibitions, and then they published articles that chided us for being apolitical. In distinguished monthly magazines they asked why we weren't out marching and picketing, as some of them had done in the Thirties.

But they didn't discuss the war in Korea, and it didn't occur to us to question it. Still a hush of foggy depression sometimes thickened the air in the Harvard dining halls: young men with indifferent grades did worry about the draft. Some could appreciate Holden Caulfield's response to war: "It wouldn't be too bad if they'd just take you out and shoot you or something, but you have to stay in the *Army* so goddam long." The Korean War was too intangible to be alarming, even though men of our age were dying there. Dying wasn't the issue. But many dreaded the army because it would be bruising to individuality—which we wistfully hoped to defend against the institutions which loomed larger within our landscape every year.

• • •

It was a bad time to be very young, a bad time to enter the early chapters of your life, bad for curiosity or the impulse to explore. You heard a lot about fitting in; molds were awaiting you: professional molds, marital molds, ways of comporting yourself so that others wouldn't think you were peculiar—and peculiar could mean sick, crazed, repellent. Small wonder that "molding" was a recurrent verb.

Moreover my generation had no advantage in being young. The youth worship which is intrinsic to our culture was in abeyance at that time. Then youth merely meant ignorance. The attitude of our seniors was that the young couldn't know anything, couldn't be interesting: go away and come back when you're older. We didn't feel disliked but we knew we were unwelcome. So we longed to be over thirty and tried to behave as if we had skipped a decade. Years afterward I realized why we seemed excessively raw to them: because we'd been born too late to have any direct perceptions of the Depression or World War II, we had none of their knowledge of poverty or devastation, of suffering or death. But that was exactly the kind of history they didn't and wouldn't share with us.

• • •

At the crest of the Harvard strike in 1969, a professor I'd known since the Fifties told me he missed the students of that period. We'd been such a small generation: "There were so few of you—it was easy to push you around." Indeed some of us who were born in the Thirties felt like the minority we were: overpowered by adults. In our quiet way we sought to please, and we didn't try to make changes.

No one I knew would have studied both Hegel and Mozart. And if you were wedded to literature, you weren't going to sully your mind with Richard Nixon, beyond remarking that he was "dreadful"; again the judgment was an aesthetic one. Politicians could not affect the standards and achievements of dead artists, who would outlive them. Besides, most of those who were ambitious for leadership were probably shallow, witless hacks. Surely no one of intelligence would want to run for office.

Yet there were occasional tremors of concern about world events: in November 1956 a group of Harvard undergraduates considered standing on the stairs outside Widener Library to protest the Soviet invasion of Hungary. But after some debate, they decided they would make an even stronger statement by *not* gathering in public. So the broad flight of stone steps remained empty in defiance of the Russians—and in tribute to the Hungarian resistance.

The connections between government and the citizen were dim to us, although we were groggily aware that the House Committee on Un-American Activities was dangerous. Harvard prided itself on its opposition to the Committee and to McCarthy's crusade against the "smelly mess" at Harvard, the Senator's favorite symbol of intellectual subversion. (McCarthy was particularly incensed when the Harvard Corporation did not fire physicist Wendall Furry on learning that he'd once been a Communist.) But students didn't then know that the university declined to hire or retain a small group of radical non-tenured teachers and graduate students because they had been Communists. Several of them, including the sociologist and historian Sigmund Diamond, were pressured by such Harvard administrators as Dean McGeorge Bundy to name Communists they'd known to the FBI. Diamond was willing to talk with the bureau's agents about his years in the Party but not to identify others, and he was fired for refusing to satisfy the FBI. But others were helpful: in 1953 the teaching fellow Henry Kissinger, who directed the Harvard International Seminar, opened some of his students' mail and gave flyers he found there to the FBI. (The flyers criticized the atomic bomb project.) Kissinger also gave the names of his students to the bureau, which investigated them. William Yandell Elliot, a professor of government and Kissinger's patron, was praised in FBI memoranda, which said he had "a most friendly and cooperative attitude and was an established contact of reliability of the [FBI's] Boston office."

A number of professors were upset by the contrast between Harvard's public policies and its private practices. Years later memos sent by federal agents to J. Edgar Hoover revealed that the university shared information with the FBI in hopes that cooperation would help to fend off ongoing assaults by congressional committees. (Furry was called to testify more than once; the Senate Internal Security Subcommittee held hearings in Boston and subpoenaed several Harvard employees; the House Committee probed the "infiltration" of Harvard.) The FBI, the CIA, and the State Department were deeply involved in the development and the character of Harvard's Russian Research Center. And the FBI leaked material to the university from its files on job candidates as well as members of the faculty and staff. As Diamond later wrote, Harvard's administrators "bartered what they knew to the FBI in exchange for what the FBI knew."

Although many Communists of the Thirties had resigned from the Party by 1950 and Communist professors were very scarce on postwar campuses, alleged subversives were discharged from Rutgers, the University of Washington, the City College of New York, MIT, Reed College, Boston University, New York University, Ohio State University, Temple University, the University of Michigan, and many others. But some Cold War liberals claimed, as did presidential counselor John P. Roche, that the universities "stood like fortresses" against the onslaughts of the investigators: academia was glazed with self-congratulation.

However Harvard's vaunted defense of academic freedom didn't instill the young with much regard for civil liberties. Soon after graduation a few of us were highly amused to learn that a schoolmate had been paid by the CIA to dispense information about political trends in Paris when he was there on a fellowship. Finding little to divulge about the French Left, he paraphrased what he read about French politics in *Partisan Review* (which he perused at the American library in Paris) and *Le Monde*. Then he left his typed report under a copy of *The Herald Tribune* in a café where his CIA contact sat at the next table. Delighted to hear that he'd been instructed to make a small hole in his *Tribune*—through which to peer at his contact—we thought his assignment was an enormous joke: informing or spying on behalf of the government couldn't be serious, couldn't cause harm.

9

Touchstones

Immersed in the New Criticism, we knew little about its origins: the purely aesthetic approach to literature had been advanced early in the century at Columbia University. But even before Eliot, Pound, and Yeats became the deities of the curricula of the Forties, the New Criticism had been developed by Southerners who eventually taught in the North: John Crowe Ransom, Robert Penn Warren, Cleanth Brooks, and Allen Tate. The Southern Agrarians' background was Christian and conservative, most were distinguished classicists, and they recoiled from egalitarianism and industrialism. Their theories overlapped with some of I. A. Richards's, R. P. Blackmur's, and Yvor Winters's, though the American critics had none of Richards's interest in psychology and he was an atheist. Warren later defected from the movement, but the textbook he wrote with Brooks in 1938, *Understanding Poetry*, was a New Critical testament for at least two decades.

The Southerners' aristocratic tradition was allied with a fixation on form and a conviction that the substance of great art could not be easily communicated, that art was inaccessible to the masses. Alfred Kazin wrote of Tate: "In a desperate effort to save literature from science and criticism from mere history or impressionism, he transformed the experience of literature into what I. A. Richards had called a set of 'isolated ecstasies.' The positivism was removed, the history forgotten, all extraneous vulgarities of circumstance disengaged. Only the poem remained, and its incommunicable significance."

While some New Critics disagreed with others, their disciples ruled many English departments in the Fifties. Revering T. S. Eliot, whose critical writings shaped the opinions of four or five generations of academics, they esteemed the metaphysical poets, rejected nineteenth-century Romanticism, and quickened the quest for symbols. Eliot had asserted that literature should be judged "from a definite ethical and theological standpoint." Certain New Critics maintained a moral stance toward poetry, though few (if any) would have gone as far as Eliot when he wrote, "The whole of modern literature is corrupted by what I call Secularism," or declared that D. H. Lawrence's characters lacked "any moral or social sense" because of "the deplorable religious upbringing which gave Lawrence his lust for intellectual independence."

Harvard's version of the New Criticism had emerged from Yale, where Warren and Brooks taught, and had traveled through Amherst. Our young tutors and instructors were in rebellion against the elderly historians and philologists who had discouraged an aesthetic response to the text, who had smothered poetry with pedantry. (Some may also have been reacting against the Marxist critics of the Thirties who had used literature as a springboard for social comment.) Identifying I. A. Richards as "the benign godfather" of the New Criticism, Walter Jackson Bate recalled that "the impelling motive" of Richards's followers was "to sweep the board clean of the huge accumulated learning of the past (biographical, historical, or otherwise) which was leading the subject to suffocate under its own rubbish." For the New Critics the text was sacred, and history and biography interfered with a proper understanding of the text.

So we examined literature as an object apart from its time; we used to hear that "a poem exists as it is printed on the page." It was "a fallacy of intention" to connect a writer's life with his work, and you weren't supposed to ask why Milton wrote *Paradise Lost* or what tuberculosis had meant to Keats. The fact that Yeats, Pound, and Eliot were political reactionaries wasn't mentioned in any lecture I heard. Nor did my professors refer to Pound's or Eliot's anti-Semitism. Evidence of racism need not have lessened their stature as poets; the splendors of *The Waste Land* and *Four Quartets* weren't diminished by Eliot's views. But the New Criticism stayed aloof from such matters. Yet while the New Critics strove to keep criticism pure of pertinence, they didn't quite succeed: if they recognized chronology—by acknowledging that one poem was written after another—history was introduced. Still they did their best to persuade us that context was trivia. And although they concentrated on poetry, their method was soon employed in the criticism of novels and plays, which had not been Richards's aim.

The poet Edwin Honig, then teaching at Harvard, later compared the removal of history from literature to deboning a chicken. Although a few courses gave us some historical guidelines for such writers as Benjamin Franklin and St. John de Crèvecoeur, we remained all too innocent of the events which had influenced many works of literature. In courses that weren't taught by New Critics, we retained habits that their attitudes instilled. Dodging history wasn't difficult: you could savor the eloquent defiance in Thoreau's *Civil Disobedience*—"I was not born to be forced"—while knowing little about his opposition to slavery or to the war against Mexico, or be racked by Malraux's *Man's Fate* without absorbing his analysis of revolution. You could worship the past in terms of its art—the masterworks of individuals—while ignoring what had happened during any artist's lifetime. So a literary generation grew up with the notion that history was unimportant—therefore contemporary history was of small consequence either. I believed that history obscured what really mattered.

• • •

In the Fifties it often sounded as though literary criticism was more important than what was criticized. Cultural historians have remarked that criticism almost replaced the novel in that period. Some joked that criticism had nearly supplanted religion. Small literary magazines were more apt to publish critical essays than avant-garde fiction. And since many poets were professors and vice versa, the new poetry was frequently shaped to satisfy the academy, where "the internal structure" of "the well-made poem" could be more significant than its language.

Eliot's essays were constantly cited by Harvard's New Critics, who dwelled on his commitments to classicism and objectivity. The famous sentences from *Tradition and the Individual Talent* were steadily quoted: "The progress of an artist is a continual self-sacrifice, a continual extinction of personality," and "The more perfect the artist, the more completely separate in him will be the man who suffers and the mind which creates." English majors were likely to know the summation by heart: "Poetry is not a turning loose of emotion, but an escape from emotion; it is not the expression of personality, but an escape from personality. . . . The emotion of art is impersonal." The issue seemed to be moral: no artist of quality would be forthright about his feelings on the page.

Because "the biographical fallacy" was despised by the New Critics, Eliot's compulsion to hide the facts about his early breakdown and calamitous first marriage was not seen in relation to his statements about impersonality. His desire for privacy was understandable. But his nervous collapse of 1921 and his wife's acute mental illness were fairly common knowledge among the

English departments: I heard references to both before I graduated. His poetry was often personal: his intimate crises were distilled in *The Waste Land*—as he admitted when he was almost seventy, when he wrote, "To her the marriage brought no happiness, to me, it brought the state of mind out of which came *The Waste Land*." But when he'd felt his privacy was menaced by what was written about him, he had conferred with lawyers, though he didn't sue the British newspaper which reported the breakdown.

Biographies by Peter Ackroyd and Lyndall Gordon have shown that Eliot was frightened by his own emotions, by sexuality and the threat of internal chaos, by his fantasies of violence (which resurfaced in *Sweeney Agonistes* and some of the poems). The guilt-stricken man who feared that he'd driven his wife deeper into madness, first by living with her and then by leaving her, who felt he deserved punishment for his sins, dreaded an exposure of his suffering and the contagion of sickness between them. His attempts to prevent anyone from writing his biography reveal an aspect of his character. Yet the poet's determination to conceal the sources of some of the anguish in *The Waste Land* and *The Family Reunion* would have been deemed irrelevant by critics who said that a writer's life has little to do with his work.

In his later years Eliot amended his theories of criticism. A poet's "lines," he wrote, could provide him with "a means of talking about himself without giving himself away." He confessed that his feelings had underlain poems which were metaphors for spiritual deprivation, for universal despair and (later) mystical renewal. Today we can see how his personal torments generated images of a "deranged" civilization. His marriage was hell on earth—which was also his vision of the age: "I think we are in rats' alley/Where the dead men lost their bones," living amid "stony rubbish" and "sterile thunder," in a void where "I can connect/Nothing with nothing." But the idea that parts of Eliot's writing were autobiographical would have been heresy in the Fifties.

And whether we read Stendhal or Lawrence, Woolf or Faulkner, we knew that a work of art must be timeless, not topical: a writer must transcend his period. Therefore, steeped in the glories of the past, armed against the "neuroses" or "excesses" of recent fiction by William Styron or Norman Mailer or Carson McCullers, cautioned that neither private life nor the issues of the present were worth exploring, many who were starting to write were more inhibited than stimulated by tradition. Pound as well as Eliot was cited to show that originality required rigorous scholarship. "Imagination" was enshrined—but not invited to run free; talent would not be fulfilled without erudition. So the notebooks rustled while the bibliographies were perused, and the libraries were filled with heads bowed in humility as well as concentration.

• • •

Central to much of the New Criticism (though not as practiced by Richards's adherents) was Eliot's belief that culture could not exist without a unified religious faith. Although he had studied Buddhism and the Indian scriptures when young, he thought that all civilization was rooted in Christianity. In *After Strange Gods* he announced that an exemplary society should have a "homogeneous" population: "What is still more important is unity of religious background; and reasons of race and religion combine to make any large number of free-thinking Jews undesirable." America, "worm-eaten with Liberalism," had been "invaded by foreign races" which had "almost effaced" tradition, at least in the Northern states. This was written in 1933, the year Hitler came to power. (Eliot became "dissatisfied" with these lectures and chose "to allow them to go out of print.") The New Critics didn't tangle with such subjects. But some of them gave the impression that Christianity was the only religion that need concern students of literature, and that a non-Christian might not be able to penetrate the works of Dante—or Eliot after his conversion to Anglo-Catholicism.

Those who had been raised outside the church, as I was, rapidly learned to spot the themes of original sin and expiation and absolution. No one ever asked us to be Christians. But there seemed to be an assumption that Christianity was our inborn heritage, that we looked at the world through the lens of Christianity. Neither an atheist nor an agnostic, I was moved by the inspiration for Chartres' spires and rose windows, by reading Donne and Herbert, by singing Bach's St. Matthew and St. John Passions, by Gerard Manley Hopkins: these were intense emotional experiences (indeed my emotions could have seemed pagan to a true Christian). Like many outsiders I was awed by the mysticism of Rome and I realized that Christianity could satisfy a craving for order. When some of my schoolmates became Catholics, I could see what attracted them, the exaltation and comfort in involvement with something so much vaster than the self. I could appreciate Nietzsche's observation that Christianity gave significance to every kind of suffering, that pain could never be pointless. But the divinity of Christ was as alien to me as it was to any Jew. I was at home with the Greek gods, not the Christian saints; I could never believe that all of us were guilty from birth and that Christ was our savior. Yet I wondered if I was deficient in perceiving all the "layers of meaning" in literature I loved. The church seemed pivotal for living authors as well as the dead; Auden had returned to the Christianity of his childhood, Tate and Robert Lowell were Catholic converts; Graham Greene soon became one of my favorite novelists.

Failing to fully understand a writer was a genuine cause for guilt, and in those days a non-Christian could feel like a flawed reader.

Yet we knew that the road to enlightenment was meant to be arduous. Because the works of Yeats, Pound, and Eliot were so complex, difficulty became a virtue of poetry. From the New Critics we learned to analyze each poem line by line, almost from punctuation point to punctuation point. And if you stared long enough at a passage by a poet like Robert Frost—whose work had seemed accessible at first—it would become difficult. The abstruseness of some of Faulkner's writing seemed to be prized almost as much as his talent, whereas Edith Wharton wasn't taught because she was much easier to read than Henry James. At Harvard there was a reluctance to teach Dryden and Shelley and Byron, who were also too easy. (Moreover Byron was "frivolous," which meant an excess of emotion, and Eliot had written that Byron's mind was "uninteresting.") Yet not everyone extolled opacity: Archibald MacLeish said he would give a bottle of Old Forester to anyone who could explain Yeats's *On a Picture of a Black Centaur by Edmund Dulac.*

Eliot thought "the variety and complexity" of our civilization required the poet to become "more allusive, more indirect, in order to force, to dislocate if necessary, language into his meaning." Ambiguity was the illustrious hand-maiden of difficulty. John Crowe Ransom had written that "the direct approach is perilous to the artist, and may be fatal . . . an art is usually, and probably of necessity, a kind of obliquity." (Howard Mumford Jones, who was cool to the New Critics, said the ideal title for any new book of criticism would be "The Ambiguous Arrow.") "Irony" was a partner to ambiguity, since irony confirmed that a piece of writing had "shades of meaning." Explanations of literature become "explications," perhaps in homage to the thoroughness of the French academicians. "Suggestions" and "indications" were admirable— because they weren't "definitions." Definition was despicable because it led to paraphrase, and the hallowed text must never be paraphrased. "Tone" was the kin of authenticity—an "authentic statement" rang true because of its tone—and "appropriateness" was related to tact, which was essential to the best writing.

But although the New Critics called for an objective approach to literature, the result was sometimes a highly subjective reading: if you studied an author without any regard for his life or his times, you could impose your own sensibility on his work. And when the New Critics were at the peak of their influence, their power could seem infectious: students who had dismantled a poem in order to elucidate it might feel that they had conquered it. This was intoxicating.

Meanwhile we hunted for symbols like road signs: peacocks screaming, cocks crowing, Christ figures, underground excursions or tunnels or caverns, phalli, scapegoats of all sorts, and waning moons. While Hawthorne and Conrad and Melville invited such inspection, we also probed for symbols in texts where they hardly existed. Here our coach was not a New Critic but Albert J. Guerard, who assumed that we were familiar with Freud—which very few were. (The New Critics rarely spoke of him.) For a professor like Guerard, we found or fabricated symbols on every page; no lamppost or hatrack or tower could be asexual.

Symbols—as opposed to allegory, which was all too overt—were prestigious because their meanings could be multiple, because they were hard to nail down. The mysterious "design" of the text would be discovered only after you had spent a long time in the labyrinth—led by a luminary who possessed the glittering key to each literary enigma. But some instructors were so avid for symbolism that chicanery became a huge temptation. A Harvard friend loaned me a sentence which both of us used in exams and papers on everything from Aeschylus to Willa Cather: "Unhampered by the denotative austerity of an allegory, these figures may move more freely as evocative symbols." It always won us high marks, no matter what the subject.

Then you teased the text until you came up with one of the reliable diagnoses, such as hubris. Knowing your limitations and not overstepping them (remember what happened to Achilles) was a moral for the time: "acceptance" was a groundnote of the period. Even Doris Day singing "Whatever will be, will be" seemed to echo the bland fatalism espoused by some professors of the humanities, who were enthusiastic about "redemption through suffering" and renunciation. The Christian concept of sacrifice often colored the interpretation of literature, and resignation suited an era when the young tended to be submissive.

Yet we were also hypercritical—of our education and our teachers. Harvard taught us to be so judgmental that we soon turned our judgments against the university itself. Henry Adams depicted his Harvard classmates of the 1850s as "distrustful of themselves, but little disposed to trust anyone else, . . . negative to a degree that in the long run became positive and triumphant"— which was true of my contemporaries a century later.

Harvard's legacy was doubt: of the self, of the validity of one's efforts. But though I often mocked the essays I wrote, as well as some teachers who assigned them, I had immense respect for certain professors. Perry Miller made Jonathan Edwards's *Sinners in the Hands of an Angry God* nearly as devastating as it was for Edwards's congregationalists, when the miscreant's soul dangled over the flames of hell as though it were hanging on a spider's thread. And much of our training in imagery was invaluable, especially in Harry Levin's Shakespeare course. Since Shakespeare was taught primarily as poetry, and almost all poetry was explained through its images, professors like Levin, William Alfred, John Kelleher, Walter Jackson Bate, Archibald MacLeish, and Kenneth Murdock endowed us with a sensitivity to language which outlasted the nonsense some of their colleagues asked us to write. Unquestionably the New Critics' fidelity to the text was excellent grounding for beginners. Robert O'Clair used to tell his students to read a poem as carefully as if it were a letter from someone they loved—and paying that kind of attention meant that the words could become a permanent part of your life.

We read as aspiring moralists, searching for "values," almost asking literature to teach us how to live. Some actually tried to learn from Achilles' over-reaching, or from Isabel Archer's punishment for "mistaking a part for a whole," or Hotspur's plight as "a just man in an unjust cause." Some of us saw literature as a ravine or gorge of warnings—an education in what to avoid. We looked to literature for transformation and salvation: an allegiance to great art would fortify us against corruption in language or thought, preserve us from sinking to lower levels of existence.

We also had lavish notions about self-expansion: in a Jamesian fashion, we felt it was "a task." Some Radcliffe students were charmed by James's sense of possibility: the fascination that led him to write again and again about "a certain young woman affronting her destiny." It was beguiling to think that destiny was waiting, and meeting it head-on would be essential to the task. Some young women I knew identified with Isabel Archer or Milly Theale, as I did; no one wished to suffer as they had, but one could be titillated by the experiences which seemed available to the intelligent American woman, the heiress of all the ages. Eager for adventures, we wanted to develop that "talent for life" and those "enrichments of consciousness" that James described. We had no idea that private incomes kept such consciousness afloat; fifteen months after graduation I was startled to find myself in a small dark London basement, writing synopses for MGM—which hardly chimed with destiny's intentions. Other Jamesians were frustrated by the confinements of the typing pool or the laundromat; foresight had not been part of the curriculum.

For me and a cluster of friends, aesthetics was a ruling passion, as compelling as an earlier generation's Marxism or the absorption of our juniors in the counterculture of the Sixties. Dependent on Keats and Melville and James and Yeats for nourishment and excitement, I could not imagine life without those touchstones, and I half-expected them to guide me in the choices I would have to make: in love, in work, about my future. My recordings of Bach and Palestrina and Purcell, the large photograph of a Byzantine mosaic—a hand extended on a sea of gold—taped to my wall, the postcard of a winged Venetian lion on the windowsill, sustained me in a world where ignorant armies sold each other harsh detergents and ugly cars, where slogans were heard oftener than sonnets. One might (I did) deride Harvard almost daily, ridiculing the constrictions of academia, the pretensions of section men. But throughout that education for malcontents, the place enabled one to believe that a few lines of Chaucer or a page of Joyce were more substantial than Dulles's latest pronouncement or whatever occurred on Wall Street. As Mozart's Requiem flooded my stereo, as I reread *Measure for Measure* or Chekhov, I could ignore almost anything beyond my threshold—except for a walled medieval town I hoped to visit, an epic not yet read, or the path of Odysseus on his journey home.

10

The Loyalty Oath at Berkeley

For decades Berkeley had been proud of its liberalism, and generations of its students felt free to pursue their interests ever since Lincoln Steffens cheated at cards, shot quail, experimented with hypnotism, wrote fiction, and graduated at the foot of his class in 1889. The flagship of the University of California attracted adventurous young persons from Jack London—who spent a term there before he joined the Klondike gold rush of 1897—to the cartoonist Rube Goldberg, the novelist Josephine Herbst, the conductor Antonia Brico, and Robert Merriman, a graduate student and teaching assistant in economics who fought and died in the Spanish Civil War and was a model for Robert Jordan in Hemingway's *For Whom the Bell Tolls*. But starting in 1934, political speeches and meetings were prohibited on the campus, hence many took place just outside its gates. Unorthodox students sometimes complained that they were surrounded by conformists, but they were hardly stifled by conventions. From the Thirties onward the university was teeming with all sorts of Left politics, and the future historian Leon Litwack, who became a Berkeley student in 1948, said he'd never realized that there were so many varieties of socialism.

Yet in 1940 the Regents of the University had decreed that Communists could not teach there and the Academic Senate accepted the ruling, which was the first of its kind in American academia. This action was taken because a teaching assistant in the mathematics department at Berkeley was a public Communist; his father was a dean. The young man was fired and forgotten by most outside the Party, which made him one of its two main officials in Alameda County.

But the case was remembered in 1949, when the Regents decided that all employees of the University of California—then the largest university in the country—must sign an oath which asserted that they weren't Communists. (Since 1942 they'd had to take an oath promising to uphold the United States Constitution and that of California, and no one had objected.) The University of Washington had recently dismissed two tenured professors because they were Communists; one then took part in a debate at UCLA, and the economist Harold Laski, a leader of the British Labour Party, was scheduled but disinvited to lecture at the University; the Regents were indignant that such figures could be permitted to speak in university buildings. The California legislature had adopted a resolution praising the Washington expulsions. It seemed possible that the legislature, prompted by State Senator Jack Tenney, chairman of the California Fact-Finding Committee on Un-American Activities, might begin a detailed investigation of the faculty (but none was undertaken). Tenney was soon discredited in the legislature when he stated that some of its members were fellow travelers. But by then the university had already tried to head off the state's interference by proclaiming its own anti-Communism.

University President Robert Sproul recommended the new oath to the Regents because he wished to emphasize the 1940 policy on Communists. But when he learned that many professors were appalled by the prospect of a political oath—the historian Dixon Wecter would compare it to "shooting alma mater to save her from rape"—Sproul gradually reversed himself and came out against the oath. Initially several hundred professors said they would not sign. The bulk of the resistance came from the Berkeley campus, though there were some dissenters on the Los Angeles faculty. Edward Tolman, the distinguished Berkeley psychologist who became the leader of the opposition, asked that the oath be dropped.

At Berkeley refugee scholars who had escaped from fascist regimes in wartime felt they were witnessing something all too familiar; some of them cited the oaths required at German universities in the early days of the Nazis—when each successive oath was more ominous than the last. Eventually the German professors had had to swear allegiance to Hitler and to admit if their relatives were Jews. Leonard Olschki, a renowned Romance philologist and expert in Oriental languages who had been hounded out of Germany by the Nazis and from Italy by Mussolini, said, "I have the impression that I am fighting the same foes."

In an academic Senate meeting, the Berkeley medievalist Ernst Kantorowicz dwelled on the probable consequences of the oath, and a listener remembered that his German accent grew stronger as his voice rose and fell: "A harmless oath formula which conceals the true issue is always the most dangerous one because it baits even the old and experienced fish. It is the harmless oath that hooks; it hooks *before* it has undergone those changes which will render it, bit by bit, less harmless. Mussolini Italy of 1931, Hitler Germany of 1933, are terrifying and warning examples for the harmless bit-by-bit procedure in connection with politically enforced oaths." Moreover, "The crude method of 'Take it or leave it'—'Take the oath or leave your job'—creates a condition of economic compulsion and duress close to blackmail. This impossible alternative which will make the official jobless or cynical, leads to another completely false alternative: 'If you do not sign, you are a Communist who has no claim to tenure.'" Like Kantorowicz, other emigrés thought it essential to resist at the very beginning; his impassioned speech and their statements had a tremendous impact on many of their hearers.

Not a single member of the faculty was charged with being a Communist. But Irving David Fox, a teaching assistant in the Berkeley physics department who had signed the oath, had invoked the Fifth Amendment during the September 1949 hearings of the House Committee on Un-American Activities in Washington, D.C., when he was asked about Party membership. The Committee was hunting for spies at the Radiation Laboratory at Berkeley, where Fox had worked on the atomic bomb project in 1942 and 1943. He told the Committee he knew of no espionage there; he'd reported "one case where I suspected that there might be espionage" to the security officer, adding that if he "had known of other cases I would have reported them and would not have approved or condoned it."

Later Fox told the Regents he had been drawn to the Party in those years and became involved, but on finding that he disagreed with many of its policies, he detached himself from it. He had taken the Fifth Amendment rather than answering the Subcommittee's questions about his left-wing friends. The Regents fired him. The Academic Senate didn't object, since a teaching assistant wasn't regarded as a member of the faculty. A few months afterward, another non-tenured university employee—a woman who played the piano for a gymnastics class in UCLA's department of physical education for women—was discharged after State Senator Jack Tenney wrote to President Sproul describing her as a former Communist, and the Hearst press kept running stories about her. She was ordered to abandon the keyboard in the middle of a class.

• • •

After about a year of altercations, the Regents ruled that those who didn't take the oath would be dismissed. A "sign-or-get-out" ultimatum was issued with a spring deadline in 1950. The deadline was extended while forty-nine Berkeley professors and three lecturers who chose not to sign were requested to reveal their politics and "attitude toward Communism" to the faculty Committee on Privilege and Tenure. (At UCLA twenty-one professors, five lecturers, and one supervisor were examined.) The Berkeley investigators were seven professors who'd already taken the oath—which was revised several times until a signer had to "state that I am not a member of the Communist Party or any other organization which advocates the overthrow of the Government by force or violence, and that I have no commitments in conflict with my responsibilities with respect to impartial scholarship and free pursuit of truth."

Radicals of any kind were very scarce on the faculty but plentiful among the teaching assistants and graduate students. Over two hundred of them refused to sign; probably a few were Communists. Meanwhile many angry professors protested the imposition of "a political test." But there were diverse reasons for contesting the oath. Many were offended that professors—alone among state employees—were singled out to prove they weren't "traitors" to their country. Membership in the Communist Party was not illegal. Many felt an obligatory oath was a violation of academic freedom, that the Regents' stance expressed a right-wing animosity toward intellectuals and was a fundamental attack on teaching. Others saw a much broader issue: an erosion of the civil liberties of all Americans, not only academics. In reply to outsiders who asked why they didn't sign and forget it, some answered that the issue was moral. Nevitt Sanford, a Berkeley psychologist who had just co-written *The Authoritarian Personality* with Theodor Adorno and two others, thought the implications of the oath were enormous, that it could be a step toward totalitarianism. As the tumult mounted, some professors came to believe not only that their university was threatened but that the traditions of American democracy were at stake.

The Los Angeles Times averred that "Communists, on or off the faculty, have cooked up a first class fuss over the 'academic freedom' issue." *The San Francisco Examiner* said some professors made "references" to the oath "in a sly and cunning manner while pretending to be lecturing about Plato, Socrates, and other ancients." Scores of editorials showed that higher learning was often associated with subversion; conservatives interpreted "academic freedom" to mean teaching Communism or concealing the activities of Communists on campus.

Because many Regents were businessmen and lawyers who attended to the financial administration of the university, some professors doubted whether they understood the nature of scholarship or a liberal arts education. The most vociferous Regent was John Francis Neylan, once the personal attorney and favorite advisor of William Randolph Hearst. As a public speaker Neylan was given to pounding his fist on the table and sometimes roaring at his audience. The faculty rebellion had inspired Neylan to say that barring teachers "for membership in the Communist movement would [not] set a bad precedent any more than the dismissal of members of Murder, Inc." Yet nearly half the Regents—including California Governor Earl Warren and Admiral Chester Nimitz—did not think the oath was desirable. But Neylan and L. M. Giannini, president of the Bank of America, said that the Regents and the oath provided "the last barrier" between the university and Communism. Giannini told the others, "I feel sincerely that if we rescind this oath, flags will fly from the Kremlin. . . . I want to organize twentieth century vigilantes, who will unearth Communists and Communism in all their sordid aspects, and I will if necessary."

• • •

Both moderates and conservatives said the oath would be ineffective because Communists would lie about party membership. Warren told the press, "Any Communist would take the oath and laugh." A much larger issue was the question of whether Communists had a right to teach. Many professors thought their colleagues should be judged only on the quality of their scholarship and teaching, that their politics were irrelevant. A small segment of the faculty felt that Communists ought not to be excluded because a university should offer a multiplicity of ideas. To these professors the oath seemed to authorize an ideological purge of the faculty. But perhaps a quarter of the faculty believed that Communists should not be allowed to teach, that they would be pledged to the Party line and incapable of presenting any subject without distorting its nature and history. Yet the American Association of University Professors had concluded that as long as a Communist didn't call for "the forcible overthrow of the government" or "use his classes as a forum for Communism," he should not be fired for Party membership.

More than eight thousand students crowded into the Greek Theater at Berkeley to hear professors deploring the oath. Some undergraduates felt the oath could intimidate teachers who explored alternative views, hence students would be exposed to "only one set" of perspectives in the classroom. The throng booed and hissed at a statement from the Regents. Berkeley economist Robert Gordon predicted that two hundred professors would resign if the oath were enforced, and "others will leave when they see their colleagues go." (Six months later he would apologize to his students for having signed the oath.)

Peter Odegard, head of the Berkeley political science department, told his listeners, "If [the University of] California yields to transitory fear and distress, how can we expect weaker institutions to resist?" Indeed others soon adopted anti-Communist resolutions.

• • •

Early in 1950 a vast majority of the faculty voted against the oath. Few had ever been in favor of it. Some who'd signed had changed their minds as the complexities of the situation developed. Almost as many voted for the ban on Communists—and a minority saw that vote as a surrender to the extreme Right. It was hoped that the anti-Communist platform would cause the Regents to shift on the oath. Neylan replied, "If we yield, every Communist in America will try to get on the faculty of this university." He was annoyed by the big anti-oath vote, and he thought the Regents should have a far more prominent role in running the university and in hiring or discharging academics—whereas the faculty was accustomed to autonomy. The faculty Steering and Policy committees stated that the Regents had "[violated] the principle of faculty self-government": an issue which would expand in the months ahead.

About fifty Berkeley professors still spurned the oath, and some of their colleagues accused them of jeopardizing the university, since it was feared that the California legislature would slash the budget if "radical troublemakers" remained on campus. The pressures to sign—already immense—increased after the Korean War began at the end of June in 1950; from then on the war pervaded discussions of the oath, especially when American troops were losing ground in southeast Korea. Non-signers were said to be unpatriotic, faithless to their country as it went to war. An editorial in Hearst's *San Francisco Examiner* said that "While American youth is being conscripted to die fighting Communistic barbarism in Korea and elsewhere," the state's professors didn't deserve "the privilege of defying a simple regulation to protect the institution which is engaged in research vital to the national defense." *The Los Angeles Examiner* declared, "The real question is whether educators, under the cloak of academic freedom, should be free to poison the minds of American youth with the fallacious doctrines of a foreign despotism."

The number of non-signers shrank. About twenty said the Korean War had impelled them to take the oath. Some who held out longest claimed it was more honorable to cooperate in August than in April or May—or that those who'd signed before them were cowards and those who signed later were irrational—and they reaped the scorn of both conservatives and dissidents. Within departments, trust evaporated when people who had said they would "never" sign did so—and then vowed to quit if non-signers were fired, but didn't. Tortured logic was occasionally employed: the economist Robert Brady, an independent Marxist who had exhorted the faculty to strike when the Regents resolved to fire the non-signers, signed with bitter flamboyance soon after that idea was discarded. He encouraged others to do the same, saying that the cause was hopeless and that it would be demoralizing to watch a slow deterioration of principles. To most non-signers he seemed to be a turncoat, and he was called both infantile and contradictory. Brady became an alcoholic; some thought him a casualty of the oath crisis as well as self-destructive.

After countless meetings and much lacerating debate, the majority signed the oath. Numerous liberals argued that the university would be strengthened if they stayed on to battle the Regents "from within," and some were wounded when non-signers retorted that they did more harm to free inquiry than the conservatives. Others signed because they thought further protest would be futile—especially because the university had compromised itself by barring Communists in 1940 and the faculty had not condemned that policy. Many professors felt they could not possibly support their families if they resisted: they were sure that no other institution would hire them in the midst of the Cold War. Others hated to think of leaving Berkeley: they prized their appointments there and their identities were rooted in the university and its prestige; they couldn't imagine a rewarding existence elsewhere. Some non-signers saw the oath as a test of character, though there was sympathy for elderly scholars who worried about losing their pensions and young couples with small children and meager incomes. But non-signers were infuriated by colleagues who were insensitive to the moral issue—when it seemed as if some signers were preoccupied with tenure while failing to perceive the menace to civil liberties.

Sidney Roger, a radio commentator and labor historian covering the controversy for his program in the Bay Area, recalled walking toward the campus with a professor who had morosely taken the oath. The latter was complaining that the classrooms were filthy because the janitors had been on strike for weeks. Then he and Roger saw two janitors in uniform picketing at Berkeley's North Gate. The professor remarked that if his colleagues had refused to teach classes for one day, they might have been able to defeat the oath. But, he said, they didn't have the courage that the janitors did.

Some late signers wanted their peers to follow their example because they were unhappy about capitulating after a long fight. If they felt they'd betrayed their principles, they became defensive—and then hostile toward their recent allies. Others appeared to be suffused with guilt; dignity was bruised and self-esteem receded. Several rose to their feet in the Senate and volunteered their reasons for signing and said they were ashamed. In their classes a few told their students how much they regretted having signed; the oath became a recurring theme in their lectures, a paradigm of problems in such fields as philosophy or government. But whatever a professor's position, few escaped the ravages of the experience: throughout the first three years of the oath, many lives were dominated by anxieties and confrontations. Some could not concentrate on their work and they felt their teaching suffered from all the hours and days spent in caucuses and Senate meetings. (Yet some former students told me that their best teachers continued to be exciting, while the bland continued to be bland.) The turmoil may have made professors doubtful of their performance; as scholars most had been confident of their judgment, but that assurance ebbed among clashes with respected colleagues.

Domestic life could be disrupted: some wives were pressed to persuade their husbands to sign; certain families were split in two and one signer's adolescent children were so angry at him that he was on poor terms with them for years. Recurring waves of agitation and apathy exhausted professors who longed to focus on their research. Insomnia and heavy drinking were common, and a lecturer remembered that the fatigue from combatting the oath resembled lingering pneumonia. One professor collapsed physically in the middle of a Senate meeting. A nurse at a large local hospital said the staff had treated "lots of oath cases."

The Academic Assembly, which represented nontenured junior teachers, announced that the Regents had used "misinformation" and "whispering campaigns," even "slander," to discredit opponents and to create confusion throughout the community. All but one of those who worked on a book, *The Year of the Oath*, did so anonymously; it was attributed to the novelist George Stewart "in collaboration with other professors of the University of California." The contributors organized themselves along the lines of the members of the French resistance during the Nazi occupation: no one knew the names of the other participants. Their caution had peaked on learning that a few professors had reported both private conversations and those which occurred in closed Senate meetings to the Regents. A standing order prohibited the faculty from communicating directly with the Regents, but plainly there were informers on both the Berkeley and Los Angeles campuses.

Joseph Adelson, a future psychologist who was a student at the time, wrote in 1962 about the undergraduates' observation of the evolving "morality play"—when the "compelling question" was whether the professors "would behave honorably. They did not, not most of them." Still, students knew of "a very few who behaved heroically," saw "that moral courage is possible . . .

and that is uncommon. All in all, it was a quick and unpleasant education. Perhaps it is just as well for all of us, teachers and students alike, that serious moral examinations occur so rarely."

• • •

Some non-signers were severely critical of the requirement to appear before the Committee on Privilege and Tenure; they thought its investigations all too similar to those of the congressional committees and that cooperation was equivalent to signing. The university, they felt, was functioning like the government in punishing political dissidents. Nevitt Sanford was one of five who explained why they rejected the oath but would not describe their politics to the committee. Sanford had been cleared by the FBI when he was in the OSS in wartime and yet again for a government job. But he thought the oath was a fertile issue on which to withstand the anti-Communist crusade and that the university had no right to inquire into an employee's beliefs. He and the other four were fired for not answering questions asked by the committee, which nonetheless found "no evidence of disloyalty" among them. A month later thirty-one non-signers—all cleared by the committee—were discharged: the Regents defied the committee's recommendations. Yet the Regents had been divided: almost half had voted to retain the thirty-one.

Among the twenty-four dismissed from Berkeley were Edward Tolman, Ernst Kantorowicz, Leonard Olschki, formerly of the University of Heidelberg, and the classicist Ludwig Edelstein (also of Heidelberg). One of the four ejected from UCLA was the physicist David Saxon, who would become president of the university in 1975. Two professors were fired from the San Francisco campus and one from Santa Barbara. The Regents repeated that none were suspected of being Communists. A New York Times editorial commented, "All that this famous oath has done has been to throw the University into an uproar, drive some scholars of integrity and distinction away from it and lower its prestige throughout the country."

In California the public's distrust of the faculty swelled as local headlines soared into fiction: SPROUL URGES U.C. FIRE 163 REDS (The Los Angeles Examiner); U.C. Board Split Develops on Communism Showdown (The San Francisco Examiner); U.C. Fires 157 in Communist Oath Row (The Sacramento Bee). Beneath a gleeful headline—Good Riddance of University Reds—The Los Angeles Evening Outlook alleged that 256 professors "would not say whether or not they are Communists." As more American soldiers headed for Korea, the Hearst papers identified non-signers as "foes" and "the untouchables."

Letters in support of the ousted professors were signed by scholars at Columbia, Princeton, Yale, Harvard, and over thirty-five other universities and colleges; statements of protest also came from Oxford and the University of Oslo. Albert Einstein and Reinhold Niebuhr wrote separately, urging opposition to the oath. Berkeley's Academic Senate moved immediately to collect funds for those deprived of their salaries: the money was donated by "sympathetic signers" and the faculty of other universities. The non-signers segregated themselves after their expulsion and they held seminars at a Benedictine monastery to raise their morale: Edelstein lectured on Plato, Charles Muscatine of the English department lectured on Chaucer, and others spoke about their specialties from mathematics to psychology. Some were out of work for a year or more. Tolman became a visiting professor at the University of Chicago; Kantorowicz went to the Institute for Advanced Study at Princeton, as did physicist Harold Lewis; Sanford was employed by Vassar and Muscatine by Wesleyan; Harvard hired mathematician Hans Lewy (who also taught at Stanford), psychologist Hubert Coffey, and political scientist Harold Winkler. Nuclear physicist Gian Carlo Wick went to the Carnegie Institute of Technology, then to Columbia. Some of the university's most eminent professors were dispersed throughout the country. Historian John Caughey wrote that it was painful "to be sent into exile" after twenty years of teaching at UCLA. The Berkeley psychology department had the heaviest losses: in addition to Tolman and Sanford, three professors and a lecturer were dismissed, and Erik Erikson resigned. (Later Erikson said he was proud to have done so.) The American Psychological Association advised its members not to accept jobs at the university. So did the Modern Language Association.

By March 1951 thirty-six more teachers—both tenured and nontenured— had resigned in response to the oath. Forty-seven professors who were offered appointments declined to teach at the University of California; among them were Robert Penn Warren of the University of Minnesota and Howard Mumford Jones of Harvard. Even before the warfare on campus was at its fiercest, Joel Hildebrand, dean of the College of Chemistry at Berkeley, had said, "No conceivable damage to the university at the hands of hypothetical Communists among us could possibly have equalled the damage resulting from the unrest and ill will and suspicion engendered by" the Regents' actions. Half of the Berkeley economics department hardly spoke to the other half: colleagues passed each other silently in the halls. Much of the faculty had come to loathe the subject of the oath, and President Sproul's standing was diminished among both liberals and conservatives because he failed to give clear guidance to either side. Long-term friendships had been shattered. Some likened the atmosphere to the aftermath of a civil war.

• • •

Twenty Berkeley non-signers sued the Regents—on the grounds that the constitution of California forbade such a loyalty oath. In the fall of 1952 the California Supreme Court ruled that the oath was invalid and the Regents had to reappoint the fired professors in the spring of 1953. But they were denied back pay. The result was another lawsuit, which was settled out of court in 1956, when the professors were reimbursed.

But California had established a new loyalty oath for all state employees, known as the Levering oath, in the fall of 1950. Earl Warren was then running for his third term as governor. While he hadn't backed the Regents' oath, some thought he proposed the Levering Act—which referred to "the present emergency in world affairs"—as a political gesture when the American army was faltering in Korea. In Tolman's words, the state oath was "even worse" than the one the faculty had fought: signers not only had to swear that they had not been in a party "that advocated the overthrow of the Government . . . by force or violence" in the last five years, but also to admit membership in any organization that might be considered subversive and to promise not to join one while working for the state. (No list of such groups was distributed with the Levering oath, so some unworldly academics confessed to belonging to organizations like the Berkeley Co-op—as if they were Communist fronts.) The Levering Act stated that failure to provide accurate information would bring a conviction of perjury, resulting in a jail sentence of one to fourteen years; joining certain left-wing groups would count as a felony to be punished by as many years in a state prison.

If someone did not sign the Levering oath, his salary would be suspended. But after swearing to "defend the Constitution of the United States and the Constitution of the State of California against all enemies, foreign and domestic," a signer had to affirm "that I take this obligation freely, without any mental reservation or purpose of evasion"—as though the oath were not compulsory. A handful of nontenured university employees and students with part-time campus jobs went to court to ask for an injunction to halt the Levering Act, but it was not withdrawn until 1967.

Nine rehired professors resigned soon after they were reinstated; some could not stomach the Levering oath, others had settled into jobs elsewhere. Thirteen signed the Levering oath and returned, including Tolman; he was given an honorary degree and a hall was named for him after his death in 1959. For the returnees the first oath was a six-year ordeal. As they rejoined their departments they saw the colossal expansion of an institution which had not been permanently injured, even though illustrious scholars like Kantorowicz and Edelstein would never come back to Berkeley. Amid the lavish budgets for new appointments and research, rising enrollments and the opening of more campuses, the oath wasn't often mentioned. When it was, non-signers still viewed it as a virus of the Cold War. Others tended to characterize the crisis as a "power struggle" between faculty and Regents, an undignified dispute about tenure. Those who hadn't been much involved were apt to say that principles were not central to the conflict. In most fields, professors and students were likely to shun controversy. Outside Berkeley's Sather Gate, where scores of political rallies had been held since the mid-Thirties, there was sometimes a lone man singing hymns while he played a barrel organ.

11

High and Low

Better that all the factories in Detroit should be destroyed than one El Greco: that pronouncement by a Harvard student mirrors the audacity of the youthful aesthetes of the Fifties. (Still the young man soon visited Toledo and discovered that he didn't even like El Greco.) Naturally most aesthetes were intellectual snobs. The concept of intelligence was partly based on what one knew. A student who knew that "shambles" derives from the Latin "scamnum"—meaning the leftovers around a butcher's bench—felt superior to those who lacked that information—as did others who knew what lines Auden had cut from which poem. I always felt inferior to anyone who had read Dante in Italian. But one French major deftly reversed this rule: when asked if he liked Mark Twain, he replied proudly that he knew "nothing about Americana." At *The Harvard Advocate*'s party for T. S. Eliot, the same student told the Shakespeare scholar Harry Levin, "The more I read Shakespeare, the better I like Racine."

We also judged intelligence by taste and vocabulary. Someone who loved Tchaikovsky or Dali or Thomas Wolfe, or failed to laugh at Amy Lowell, or used the word "creative," simply couldn't be bright. The standards were inflexible, since art was a quasi-religion. Yet when absolute beauty was the criterion, the young could quite airily deduce that George Bernard Shaw was "not an artist" but a pamphleteer, or that Dryden was too topical, or reject *Huckleberry Finn* because dialect was crass. The habit of judging others' minds—and finding them wanting—resulted in a sense of superiority that coexisted with a profound lack of confidence. Henry Adams's recollection of his Harvard classmates of the 1850s as "the most formidable critics one would care to meet, in a long life exposed to criticism," made them sound just like my own a hundred years later.

Meanwhile the uncouth society outside the aesthetes' cocoon did seem menacing in the Fifties: as though the squares of the nation really were going to clamp down and crush you. My friends and I feared that our most conventional schoolmates were going to be in charge of our lives, that they were our future employers or editors. (As it turned out, those I dreaded most disappeared rapidly into the suburbs.) But would-be writers were absurdly antagonistic to acquaintances with circle pins and Peter Pan collars or crewcuts and tie clips and white buck shoes, to young men who thought of going to business school or girls who collected sheets and silver even before they met the men they might marry. We were very hard on those we called the worthies: the guileless, conscientious students who led well-pruned lives. When they wore Bermuda shorts it was plain that they had no taste or imagination; wearing angora was almost a mark of perdition. We mocked their beige-colored righteousness, the discreet pearls, the cardigan sweaters neatly buttoned up the back, the earnest approach to *mal du siècle* or Chinese poetry (in translation). Even when beset by love or trouble, the worthies never seemed dishevelled: with clear voices they would discuss the sexual crisis they had just experienced. Like us, they might be racked with emotion, but not a hair slipped out of place. We were irked at them for cluttering up our literature courses, sneered at their comments on Homer or haiku—annoyed that they could tread on our territory. There was the expense of energy that sometimes appeared in Salinger: the scorn for rather blameless persons who happened to think that the culture belonged to them too.

Indeed Lane Coutell, who was pilloried in Salinger's *Franny and Zooey*, used the language we despised. Referring to "testicularity" (when he meant masculinity), or "the *mot juste*," describing a professor as "a big Flaubert man," stating that "none of the really good boys—Tolstoy, Dostoyevsky, *Shake*speare, for Chrissake—were such goddam word-squeezers. They just *wrote*"; eating frogs' legs and snails, he was compared to one of "those" section men who "completely *ruin* Turgenev" for their students. Elsewhere Buddy Glass declared, "I didn't want any degrees if all the ill-read literates . . . and pedagogical dummies I knew had them by the pack."

One could share Salinger's contempt for pretension while noticing that his heroine sounded just as foolish as Lane Coutell; invited to define "a *real* poet," Franny replied, "If you're a poet, you do something beautiful. I mean you're supposed to *leave* something beautiful after you get off the page and everything." So—despite enthusiasm for the most scathing passages in Salinger's earlier work, his empathy for misfits, and the furious humor of *The Catcher in the Rye* and *Nine Stories*—we couldn't embrace him wholeheartedly. Our own snobbery cut in two directions: few of us could accept his idea of salvation—which seemed to be restricted to Zen Buddhist converts who could perceive divinity in all persons and objects—and his later writing was too whimsical, and the Glass family too sentimental, to perch within our pantheon of art. I never did believe that the Glasses were capable of loving all humanity, in spite of Zooey's disclosure that the Fat Lady was Jesus Christ. Actually *Franny and Zooey* was known to some of my friends as "Zany and Phooey."

Moreover we didn't subscribe to Salinger's hatred of the ego: in the Fifties a young person needed all the ego that he or she could summon. Also, although adolescents of any era would understand why Holden Caulfield was "confused and frightened and even sickened by human behavior," we were critical of Salinger because many of our seniors presumed that we identified with his characters, and we were much too mulish to allow others to make such choices for us. Older people said we were "disaffiliated" (which was true) and that Salinger conveyed our distrust of the establishment. But we recoiled from the clichés that went with the simplicity of that analysis. And we heard the word "alienation" so often that I vowed at twenty that I would never use it in print.

And yet some of Salinger's preoccupations were our own: "phoney" and "fake" were two of the most damning adjectives of the period. There was little of the outrage about lies and liars which came later, after Lyndon Johnson and Richard Nixon lied to us about Vietnam and Watergate. The fakes of the Fifties were merely guilty of affectation, like one of Salinger's ogres: a woman who had "a finger in all the arts." Holden Caulfield's phonies were less obsessed with art than those the Glasses detested; Holden simply disapproved of people "who always clap at the wrong things," or wore tattersall vests, or carved their initials on doors. Given his capacity for indignation, his allergies were milder than the Glasses'. But Salinger did appear to express the values that timid rebels upheld: intelligence in defiance of stupidity, probity at war with fraudulence, the exceptional (almost the chosen) against the philistines.

According to the reverse snobbery of the age, a superior being had to be unaffected. In a similar vein, Lee Strasberg demanded that performers schooled in the Actors Studio should *really* feel what they were portraying. Actors who studied with Strasberg learned to draw on their own personalities and memories of their most intimate experiences in order to "live" their roles. Relying on techniques of "emotional recall," they refused to imitate behavior that wasn't natural to them. In the name of psychological realism they were urged to play themselves—while avoiding anything that was "false," which could mean diction or even the playwright's concept of his characters. Therefore many could not perform parts that required much imagination. But believing that we were seeing someone's authentic emotions on the stage or screen was a reassurance against phoniness. Whether or not we were witnessing Marlon Brando's or James Dean's actual feelings when they muttered or howled at their adversaries, the Studio's training did heighten the immediacy of males in revolt against the hypocrisies around them. And when they wore jeans or lumberjackets on the street as well as in the movies, Brando and Dean presented an image of incorruptibility in the midst of sham.

At the same time, I think many college students had a genuine fear of the uneducated: the multitudes out there for whom sonnets or sonatas had no worth, who might deface a culture they didn't share. And of course mass culture—like mass movements—was in disrepute among our seniors. The postwar intelligentsia lamented the proliferation of defective taste, and they railed against the vulgarities promoted by television and advertising. Even if one didn't read their irate essays in *Partisan Review*, some of them were professors and their revulsion filtered through the air; I remember very young persons using the word "barbarous."

In the late Fifties I came to know Dwight Macdonald, whose generous nature enabled you to feel comfortable when differing with him, even while he was shouting, "No! How can you say that? You *can't* mean it! How can you possibly . . ." (Later on, when we disagreed about anti-Communism, his yells grew fiercer but were still nonpunitive.) He was willing—at times even eager—to admit that he had changed his mind or been in error. He loathed inflated writing with the passion of one who loves good prose; his enthusiasms were as powerful as his aversions, and his spontaneous delight in something well-said almost outdistanced his horror at a botched metaphor or a Samuel Goldwyn movie. He didn't disdain all popular culture: he'd been "enchanted" by the 1939 World's Fair; he enjoyed Bob Hope, Red Skelton, and Jimmy Durante. But in the Eisenhower years he was distressed by the emergence of "a tepid, flaccid middlebrow culture that threatens to engulf everything in its spreading ooze." Deploring "Masscult"—*The Saturday Evening Post* and the products of Leon Uris, Erle Stanley Gardner, and Norman Rockwell—he was far more alarmed by "Midcult"; a "dangerous opponent of High Culture because it incorporates so much of the avant-garde."

Macdonald worried that "the values of Midcult" might "become a debased, permanent standard." Yet his examples of Midcult—among them, the hard-cover magazine *Horizon*, the novels of Irwin Shaw and J. P. Marquand, Ernest

Hemingway's *The Old Man and the Sea*, Thornton Wilder's *Our Town*, and Archibald MacLeish's *JB*—simply didn't have the impact he feared; they did not partake of the avant-garde and none was as influential as the early Hemingway or T. S. Eliot, Picasso or Stravinsky. And Norman Mailer's *The Naked and the Dead* (which Macdonald liked) and *The Catcher in the Rye* were widely imitated in a way that James Gould Cozzens's *By Love Possessed*— probably Macdonald's unfavorite novel of the decade—wasn't. Cozzens's style was alleged to be "Jamesian": "The successive, earthquake-like throwing-over of a counted-on years old stable state of things had opened fissures. Through one of them, Arthur Winner stared a giddying, horrifying moment down unplumbed, nameless abysses in himself." Because Cozzens's 1957 best-seller had many spectacular reviews, Macdonald felt that "the failure of literary judgement and simple common sense . . . indicates a general lowering of standards." His ardent assault on the novel's pretensions was most exhilarating. Yet he didn't make a strong case for the critical standards of the past; since the nineteenth century, pompous books had been overpraised by reviewers.

Macdonald was at his best when he assailed the manipulations of *Life*, which appeared "on the mahogany library tables of the rich, the glass cocktail tables of the middle class, and the oilcloth kitchen tables of the poor," all of whom could be numbed and misinformed by its juxtapositions. "The same issue will present a serious exposition of atomic energy followed by a disquisition on Rita Hayworth's love life," he wrote, "photos of starving children picking garbage in Calcutta and of sleek models wearing adhesive brassières; an editorial hailing Bertrand Russell's eightieth birthday (A GREAT MIND IS STILL ANNOYING AND ADORNING OUR AGE) across from a full-page photo of a matron arguing with a baseball umpire (MOM GETS THUMB); nine color pages of Renoir paintings followed by a picture of a rollerskating horse." As Macdonald noted, "the final impression is that both Renoir and the horse were talented." Showing how *Life* degraded culture by trivializing "the serious rather than elevating the frivolous," Macdonald illuminated the perils of packaging with greater skill than many critics. Yet he sometimes seemed surprised that millions were eager to ingest trash and to perpetuate it.

Perhaps some of the cultural critics like Macdonald, Irving Howe, and Theodor Adorno were still reacting to the schisms of the Thirties, when the Left hoped that working people would develop a "proletarian art" which would enrich the entire culture, and their opponents believed that high culture must be sheltered by an elite minority. By the Fifties liberals and conservatives were equally appalled by the public's appetite for rubbish: such bad taste could almost seem like an indictment of democracy or an emblem of totalitarianism.

Protecting high culture sometimes seemed to be a task for literary anti-Communists, a moral responsibility. Yet some of the targets of their disgust—Broadway musicals such as *Oklahoma!* and *South Pacific*—seemed harmless. Although it was easy to agree with the unhappy essayists that mediocrity and commercialism were everywhere, it was puzzling to find them incensed by "Hollywood" and the Book of the Month Club: institutions which were hardly about to pervert the arts. And they seemed baffled by those who could appreciate both high and low culture: a person who loved Proust and James Cagney, or Gregorian chant and Bing Crosby, made them a bit uneasy.

At a time when many Americans dwelled very much within their fiscal or educational classes, taste could be isolating. What people liked appeared to recommend or discredit them. In *The Immediate Experience*, the critic Robert Warshow sounded somewhat defensive when he wrote that popular culture should be analyzed because of its "pervasive and disturbing power." Admitting that it was influential might give a critic "a bad conscience" even though he was "aware of the superior claims of the higher arts," and Warshow felt impelled to tell his readers, "I hope I have shown that the man who goes to the movies is the same as the man who reads [Henry] James."

12

Deliver Me from the Days of Old

In the early Seventies I was startled to learn that students at several state universities were reviving the trappings of the pop culture of the Fifties: pony tails and Howdy Doody, Hula-Hoops, duck tails and sock hops and saddle shoes. This was disconcerting to some of us who hadn't participated in that culture, apart from going to all sorts of movies. There was also a cult of bad movies: we went out of our way to see items like *South Sea Woman* or *Killers from Space*. And one could be dazzled by James Dean while feeling that the obsessions of his schoolmates in *Rebel Without a Cause* were as unfamiliar as the rites of warring Aztecs.

Yet many who were in private schools or universities had little contact with other aspects of popular culture. The best Broadway musicals, from *Guys and Dolls* and *The Pajama Game* to *My Fair Lady* and *West Side Story*, and a few movies such as *Singin' in the Rain*, teemed with songs that would become classics for people of all ages. But prior to rock—or outside it—much of the pop music was insipid. (Frank Sinatra's career had sagged at the beginning of the decade; when it rebounded he sang many songs from previous eras.) The jukeboxes throbbed with slow, wailing, semi-operatic numbers about loving forever, really and truly, oozing with lines like "If you love me, really love me, let it happen, darling . . ." Love, which would never die, sounded dull as well as soggy, and freedom was something you eagerly abandoned for the One you loved. "If I knew you were comin', I'd've baked a cake": few lyrics were intoxicating. "I Saw Mommy Kissing Santa Claus," Patti Page's "How Much Is That Doggie in the Window?" Eddie Fisher singing "Oh, My Pa-Pa" ("To me he was so wonderful/To me he was so good"), the bland crooning of Perry Como, Johnnie Ray ("the Million Dollar Teardrop," "the Prince of Wails" who sobbed at every performance), Frankie Laine, Eddie Fisher—truly inescapable—pleading, "I Need You Now," and Debbie Reynolds announcing that "Tammy's in Love": no wonder some of us fled to Edith Piaf or folk music or Scarlatti.

Jazz belonged mainly to our seniors; my parents and their friends loved Dixieland and felt they owned it, but few of my contemporaries had an ear for it or for swing, and many were bored by the muted notes of the Modern Jazz Quartet, exalted for its respectability and its cool professionalism. So our elders sat in on jam sessions that we didn't attend, or listened to Ella Fitzgerald and Billie Holiday, just as they went to football games without us, while we immersed ourselves in baroque concertos and whispery tête-à-têtes.

I always envied the way that the middle-aged New Yorkers I knew could disport themselves in a group or joke freely around a table. Many of us could talk to only one person at a time. Perhaps our inability to enjoy groups, plus our habit of judging others for their tastes, resulted partly from a lack of popular culture. We had almost no forum for feeling free. Occasionally a few of us went to the Central Plaza in the East Village to watch young working people jitterbugging in the aisles, stamping and clapping as the Dixieland trumpets and trombones soared toward the highest notes, but that was rather like an archeological expedition, and we were only spectators.

Like ragtime in the 1890s, swing in the Thirties, and bebop in the Forties, doo-wop and the rock of the Fifties began as black music. Many radio stations which were programmed for whites were reluctant to play black rhythm-and-blues until 1955; some had banned black performers outright. But a few disc jockeys—in particular, Cleveland's Alan Freed—did put black singles on the air after learning that local white teenagers were purchasing the records. Freed renamed r & b "rock'n'roll" and in 1954 his "Rock and Roll Show" was on prime time radio in New York. By the mid-Fifties Fats Domino's "All By Myself" and Chuck Berry's "Maybelline," the swamp rhythms of Bo Diddley and the cries of Little Richard—"Awop bop a loo mop a lop bam boom! Tutti frutti! Aw rootie!"—resounded through white middle-class homes, to the horror of many parents. And when Elvis Presley mingled black blues with hillbilly cadences and lashings of gospel, the echoes of black sensuality continued to alarm the guardians of morality; after all, "rock and roll" was a ghetto term for sex as well as dancing. Presley's inspired raunchiness entranced radio listeners even before they saw his writhing pelvis on television, and it was often said that rock was "jungle music," that it was "tribal" or downright

"African." Yet many conventional white singers like Pat Boone and Ricky Nelson, who made rock seem more acceptable to adults, prospered by adapting and recording black hits; Boone copied Domino's "Ain't That a Shame" and Little Richard's "Long Tall Sally," Nelson made his debut with Domino's "I'm Walkin'," and Bill Haley rewrote the words to "Shake, Rattle, and Roll." Presley relied on numerous songs which had been introduced by black singers such as Joe Turner, Willie Mae Thornton, and Little Richard. But copyright laws did not protect composers as they do now, and only a few black musicians made much money—or received decent royalties.

Rock, however, was the property of the public high schools, and many Ivy League students or recent graduates ignored it, with the exception of Presley being sulky and very funny in the movies of *Love Me Tender* and *Jailhouse Rock*. For those who were past twenty, his immense comic talents were apt to be more appealing than his songs; at times his sneers and grins suggested that he was kidding the audience as well as himself. He even seemed to be making fun of his own legend: the poor boy from the country who triumphed in the big city, who reveled in stardom and owned a pink Cadillac. But for infinite teenagers his music was a liberation: they were hearing the call of the wild. Suddenly they had a beat and lyrics that others couldn't understand—and weren't meant to—a sexuality that frightened older people, a pathway to rebellion. (One younger friend of mine was sent out of her family's living room whenever Presley appeared on the screen, which of course made him irresistible.) Testifying before a congressional committee, Sinatra said rock was "the most brutal, ugly, desperate, vicious form of expression it has been my misfortune to hear," and that "by means of its almost imbecilic reiterations and sly—lewd—in plain fact dirty—lyrics . . . [it] manages to be the martial music of every sideburned delinquent on the face of the earth."

When Chuck Berry sang, "Hail hail rock and roll/Deliver me from the days of old" in 1957, rock had started to define a generation that wasn't yet in its teens. But the English majors I grew up with were hardly acquainted with the redneck rockabilly of Jerry Lee Lewis and the "western and bop" of Buddy Holly, or the "clean white boys": Frankie Avalon, Fabian, and Paul Anka. "See You Later, Alligator" and "Hound Dog" and "(Let Me Be Your) Teddy Bear" amused my friends as a form of camp, but none I knew danced to them or bought the records. Later some of the same persons owned every Beatles album and exulted in the sounds of the Sixties, wishing that they'd had such exciting or magical music earlier on.

• • •

There was not yet a highly developed youth culture that captivated a large diversity of Americans, as Bob Dylan and the Rolling Stones later did: their vast audiences would include many devotees over thirty. But some sociologists of the Fifties had begun to write as though "the young" were a cohesive group: a crowd of conformists who frothed in the presence of Presley. Sometimes they failed to distinguish between teenagers and people in their twenties. The pundits may have been misled because a number of their colleagues were being hired to do market research for companies which manufactured "youth products": the motorcycle boots, hot combs, pimple lotions, charm bracelets, Rory Calhoun jackets, hot rod magazines, and hi-fi sets sold to millions who had no particular connection with one another. The "youth industry" flourished, but consumers of dissimilar backgrounds weren't linked by many shared experiences. Yet sociologists who said that my generation was "alienated" also seemed to assume that all of us wanted the same things, from pedal pushers and "Tears on My Pillow" to early suburban marriages.

As Dwight Macdonald observed in his valuable 1958 *New Yorker* articles about Eugene Gilbert, the tycoon of youth marketing, there was "something artificial about the concept of the teenager": those in big Eastern and Midwestern cities behaved differently from adolescents in small towns, thirteen-year-olds had little in common with nineteen-year-olds, and the academic polling was unreliable (in reply to a questionnaire sent out by Purdue University's Opinion Panel, some teenage boys "answered yes to Problem No. 244—'I am bothered by menstrual disorders.'") Since Macdonald was mystified by rock, he was glad to report that a hundred thousand "I LIKE LUDWIG" buttons, displaying Beethoven's face, had been bought as a riposte to the "I LIKE ELVIS" buttons worn all over the country. Suspecting that "the very notion of the teenager" was partially "created by the businessmen" who exploited the market, Macdonald also remarked on "the weakness of the academic mind in dealing with teenagers." Reflecting on a professorial "tendency to substitute vocabulary for thought," he quoted some tortuous sentences from the Harvard sociologist Talcott Parsons, summarized by Macdonald as: "Teenagers are disobedient, group-minded, and unrealistic." Yet Parsons's abstruse works were consulted by entrepreneurs for clues to the nature of young consumers.

In the meantime sociology was abhorred by my Harvard friends—not only because it polluted the language, but because it was employed to bracket people: "inner-directed" and "other-directed" beings lost all singularity in their "upreach" for "selfhood" once they were categorized. The New Critics had taught us to hate "definitions" and sociology seemed like an enemy of the arts. In 1961, when Elizabeth Hardwick examined the "incoherence" of the sociologists' prose, she decided that there was "not merely an accidental relationship between bad writing and routine sociological research," but that "the awkwardness is necessary and inevitable. . . . It is the extreme fragility of the insights that leads to the debasement of the language." Hardwick thought "the need to turn merely interesting and temporary observations into general theory" created the problem: "By seeking a false significance, a tone of professionalism, perhaps it is natural that the 'affectionate person' will have to be called the 'warmth indulger.'" My friends and I had also been unnerved by the arrogance of the sociologists we encountered: they seemed to feel entitled to give directions, even to make decisions for the rest of us.

Yet the academic sociology of the Fifties avoided politics and was cautious about social criticism. Much of the homegrown socio-cultural research of the period was superficial because few scholars chose to look closely at American poverty or racial issues when their funding came from the government: dollars were unlikely to keep flowing to professors who were investigating the failings of our society. But most sociologists rationalized the social order, as Talcott Parsons did—while claiming that the field was "value-free" and socially impartial. And when C. Wright Mills infused cultural criticism with political comment, denounced the Cold War and "the power elite," and lambasted other sociologists for indifference to the crises of postwar America, many of his colleagues labeled him a mere left-wing polemicist. Defining their neutrality as objectivity, some of the reigning sociologists helped to perpetuate the reactionary elements of the era, even if that wasn't their intention.

Although the anti-Semitism of the European fascists was discussed in certain sociology courses at Harvard, racism in the United States was hardly explored. Sinuous reasoning was often apparent when racial topics were approached. David Riesman, whom Norman Mailer called "the professional liberal's liberal," wrote in his *Individualism Reconsidered* (1954) that "girl students at some of our liberal universities need occasionally to be told that they are not utterly damned if they discover within themselves anti-Negro or anti-Semitic reactions—else they may expatiate their guilt by trying to solve the race question in marriage. But even that judgement has to be made in terms of the wider social context—in this case, a judgement that the lot of Negroes, let alone Jews, in America is not always so utterly desperate as to call for the ruthless sacrifice of protective prejudices." It was respectable to shield the young from unnecessary "guilt," and in academia American anti-Semitism was usually handled with care. A Radcliffe classmate of mine heard a sociology professor say to a student, "Oh for God's sake, don't bring up the Jews again, they're the exception to everything." The professor was Jewish.

Sociologists did seem uncomfortable with exceptions, and when they were struggling to make sociology into a science, they tried not to sound like muck-rakers. But in 1965, throughout the sixtieth annual conference of the American Sociological Association, many delegates confessed that they had been "caught short" on "race relations." Self-criticism was abundant among those who pronounced their field "archaic." A consensus was reached among a gathering of more than two thousand scholars that their profession had "overlooked" crucial contemporary issues—in part because the "conservative" foundations were unwilling to support research into "potentially explosive topics." Some were chagrined because there was not a single workshop on the Watts ghetto, which had erupted a month before the meeting. The harshest strictures came from Professor Pitirim A. Sorokin of Harvard, the outgoing president of the association, who was also hopeful that sociology would soon advance due to "the pressures of the times."

Coming across an old article about that conference, I thought of Dorothy Dean, a Radcliffe friend of mine who was one of the angriest people I'd known. Raised in Westchester, the daughter of a minister, she had been told not to play with other black children. A brilliant student of philosophy at Harvard, she received a master's degree in art history. At college and thereafter she lived in an almost entirely white world, and she was hostile to most blacks she met. She became a fact-checker at *The New Yorker*, one of the magazine's first black employees. Then she had jobs she didn't like at *Vogue, Essence, Show,* Harper & Row, was a bouncer at Max's Kansas City—small and slight, she was paid to insult unwelcome guests until they hurried out the door—and acted in a couple of Andy Warhol's movies. A passionate grammarian who read Fowler's *Modern English Usage* for recreation, she was equally addicted to Mozart and cats. She wasn't involved with the civil rights movement, though she and I did team up to report the names of New York landlords who wouldn't rent to black tenants in the early Sixties. But she was a child of the Fifties in that she didn't want to confront the enormous scope of racism—any more than her white friends did at that time.

A vitriolic wit, a fierce critic of behavior who also savaged herself, she directed her rage and scorn at individuals of every stripe: "big black apes" (black men who went out with white women), "rug rats" (most children), "fourth-rate fruits." New York was "scum city." To a man who sublet an apartment one floor below someone who'd offended her, she said, "I hear you're living beneath contempt these days." Yet she was an utterly loyal friend: if a person she cared about was in trouble or in a hospital, she got on a bus or a train or a plane and went to see him; as a mutual friend said, that was her private morality. Many of her intimates were young gay white men; at moments she treated them as playmates to be mocked. She loved the way most of them looked while disliking what she saw in the mirror. She said she had "the soul of a white faggot trapped in the body of a black woman—and a short black woman at that."

Over the years there were breakdowns and she was sometimes suicidal. But her appreciation of the absurd increased as she grew older, and she made me laugh even when I was worried about her. While much of her life was circumscribed by pain—at twenty-three she had to give up an illegitimate baby for adoption and never stopped wondering what became of him; two of her closest friends killed themselves, she wrestled with alcoholism—I thought the deepest wounds were racial. I felt she feared others wouldn't like or respect her just because she was black. And it seemed as if she could not tolerate her own blackness: as though it were ugly, even hateful, to an educated Northerner dwelling among whites who admired her mind, quoted her lacerating jokes, and fondly called her "outrageous."

At her funeral in the Eighties some spoke of her as a figure of the Sixties, a sardonic reveler at Warhol's Factory. But to me she had seemed partly immured in a period when racial identity or suffering were hardly acknowledged. In *Partisan Review's* 1952 symposium, "Our Country and Our Culture," Max Lerner had written, "The Negro is entering into the full stream of our effort, helped by the great assimilative energies of an impersonal economy, a legal system which is ceaselessly being used on his side, and the conscience of decent men." Staring at that sentence I can hear the swoop of Dorothy's laughter.

• • •

A liberal arts education could be a garden of discrepancies. For example, although some of my fellow students hoped to be artists, they knew they shouldn't be ambitious. Actually "ambition" was such a repulsive noun that you rarely heard it around Harvard. We didn't perceive that our professors had had to be very ambitious to obtain tenure. But even the word "career" was scarcely uttered in Cambridge in the Fifties: the concept itself was vulgar.

Later I realized that the distaste for ambition was often buried anti-Semitism, although we would have been stunned if anyone had said so. Refined racism seemed to thrive within "liberal" families, where few adults would have referred

directly to Jews. Rather, they talked dryly about *"aggressive people"* or *"opera-*
tors." Anti-Semitism was apt to be expressed through an aesthetic response
to behavior: disparaging the "unattractive manner" of someone who hustled
to advance himself. Naturally that attitude was more noticeable in New England than New York. In fact "New York" was a Bostonian code word for Jewish.

In 1922 Harvard's President Abbott Lawrence Lowell had established a quota
on Jews: Lowell didn't think it desirable to educate too many offspring of
Eastern European immigrants. In the Fifties we heard denials that the quota
was still intact. But in the name of "geographic representation," Harvard had
reduced its admissions from urban public high schools in the Northeast, and
that policy diminished the number of Jewish students. In 1958, when the
university refused to permit several Jewish couples to be married in Memorial
Church and President Nathan Pusey wrote to *The Harvard Crimson* defending
the prohibition and defining Harvard as a Christian university, the ensuing
uproar bypassed the issue of racism. Instead professors who considered Pusey
a provincial of limited intellect who had over-expanded the role of religion at
Harvard used the controversy as an occasion to attack his presidency.

At any rate it was nicer not to "know" who was Jewish, unless a last name
made it obvious. A Radcliffe graduate told me that she'd been repelled by the
"pushy" young women in her tutorial group who kept raising their hands and
answering most of the questions—which she didn't, although she studied
diligently. Raised in Massachusetts, it didn't occur to her then that they were
Jews. Years afterward she reflected that the Jewish students were fulfilling their
upbringing: they'd been raised to succeed. Musing on the New England death
wish, which decrees that descendants can't be as accomplished as their forebears, she added, "Whereas I was brought up to fail." So when some of
Harvard's Jewish alumni changed their surnames, muted the impulse to tell
old friends that a new job was going well, or almost apologized for their
achievements, they were obeying the Wasp tradition of pretending that they
hadn't worked very hard. It was another contradiction: although the puritan
work ethic was still in evidence, effort was not supposed to show in public; it
was like being caught with an open fly or conspicuous bra-straps: slightly
embarrassing and surely accidental.

Nevertheless New England declared that work strengthened the character,
and discipline seemed to be valued as much as the love of learning. And
Harvard did encourage you to enjoy your work, even though some of its
brightest students could not be persuaded that labor was gratifying: one I
knew skipped most deadlines to spend hours on the floor with his Tinker Toy,
building a model of a peacock in heat. (It was, he has since admitted, a woman-

substitute.) "Man needs an image to live by!" he would shout, adding another piece to his construction. But most studied intensively; the fear of failure was as sharp a spur as pleasure. We would later be amazed when failure seemed insignificant to the students of the Sixties—and when visible success seemed essential to the young of the Eighties and Nineties.

13

Spiders' Threads

In the age of lowered voices and pale cashmere, some of the young were humble romantics—humble because our parents' youth had been far more adventurous than our own. And in middle age they preserved the lineaments of personal freedom in a way that seemed unfeasible for us. So we had a clumsy problem: how do you rebel against persons who are much more liberated than yourself? Some responded by becoming terribly proper, which was appalling to their parents.

Since there was then no style of behavior for those between eighteen and twenty-five, most of us tried to act like little grownups. We didn't know that we were young, nor that one might not be fully adult at twenty. Balanced on high heels or buttoned into tight vests, gasping in girdles, clutching a cigarette holder like a wand for one's own protection, we would make conversation at one another: about *Les Enfants du Paradis* or *Rashomon* or our last trip to Europe or Kafka or Joyce, wondering wildly what we would say next. There were terse verbal jokes with scrupulously delivered punch lines, or anecdotes: a Harvard luminary (sometimes said to be the dead President Lowell, sometimes the classicist John Finley), strolling along the Charles River, had seen a small boy fishing and exclaimed, "Hail, young piscatorian!" The child replied, "Same to you, old shithead." Not the world's worst two-liner, but I heard it retold for years. We thought we had to rely on props for conversation: brief stories that had been tested. Spontaneity seemed impossible, as did improvisation.

• • •

In those days we needed every ounce of private identity that we could muster: each small tic or trait that could define us to ourselves. I remember a hyper-rationalist making fun of a young man who had a breakdown "because he thought he didn't exist." Some of the young had an amorphous fear that they might disappear or evaporate. It wasn't quite like the fear of death. Instead there was a feeling that you could be engulfed by a culture that despised individuals: you might end up as a featureless, neutral being which simply functioned to earn a living and to occupy one narrow space. Best-sellers like William H. Whyte's *The Organization Man* warned that independence and originality were in jeopardy. When Norman Mailer wrote about the perils of being "trapped in the totalitarian tissues of American society," the image didn't seem extravagant.

Yet the severe angst was hard to dissect even then: there was merely an instinct that you must defend yourself, hold on tight, brace yourself against some kind of onslaught. The air seemed to be charged with indifferent powers that weren't directed at you—but which might blow you away. One young man I knew told another, "You're lashed to the mast when there isn't any storm!" We couldn't have located any storm; we only felt that we had to protect ourselves. Just when our society was being praised for its stability, existence could often seem precarious. There was also a foreboding that it might add up to nothing, that one's life might be a void. Hence a very young person could feel a kinship with the aging hero of *The Beast in the Jungle*, when he dreaded an event or force that might overwhelm him—and could understand his admission that he didn't know what he was afraid of: "I only know I'm exposed." Finally he realized that a vacuum had been in store for him: apprehension had prevented him from living at all.

The sense of helplessness engendered guilt, since helpless meant feeble. To counteract the guilt one clung to the idea of free will. And we really couldn't imagine how public events—short of a third world war—could affect our lives. Although zeitgeist had been mentioned in a few courses, we didn't believe in it. Especially to those who were reared in New England it seemed that each person ought to be in control of his or her own future. Eventually some of my friends were beguiled by the palmistry and planet-worship of the Sixties: by then fatalism was attractive to people who hadn't been able to govern their lives.

In the midst of all that malaise, freedom was an obsessive theme. Mainly it meant traveling, impulsive sex, eating dessert before soup, staying up late, sitting twice through a double feature. We thought we longed to be adult: actually we craved an extension of childhood pleasures. The compulsion to *be grown up* was partly due to a hazy notion of freedom, though the realm of jobs and marriages awaiting us was far from free.

The middle-class rebellions of the period took small, diffident forms: driving slightly over the speed limit, not wearing a hairnet while waiting on table in a dormitory (that meant breaking a Massachusetts law), squirting soda water on a dean, shouting "Let copulation thrive!" from open windows. Sex wasn't a rebellious act because most took it seriously, and eager volunteers are hardly rebels. Resistance to custom occurred largely because individualists disliked being told what to do: a friend of mine almost didn't graduate from Harvard because he balked at running a mile and pissing into a little glass bottle, rituals that were required to earn a degree. Each tame assertion of independence was applauded by those I knew: even impudence could seem like bravery.

A cape, wearing jeans on the street, sandals, a taste for solitude, even shyness: oddities were easily classified. Suspicion greeted many who quietly strayed from the status quo. Often we were oversensitive to that reaction. And yet, recalling the widespread loathing of those who were called hippies in the Sixties—the outraged responses to trailing hair, beads, a guitar or two—it's plain that the animosity which cautious dissidents of the Fifties anticipated was lurking in the landscape all along. We challenged no one and there weren't very many of us. But as soon as our successors raised their voices and gave the finger, they reaped the hostility that we had feared.

• • •

Although Erich Fromm and countless sociologists maintained that modern Americans shrank from freedom, a number of us ignored that thesis—mainly because of the mistrust of sociology. Meanwhile some of the young were enlivened by a zealous misreading of Sartre. Savoring his passages on liberty we deduced that existentialism meant absolute freedom: you could invent yourself anew each day. Because no principle could be taken for granted, you were free to make up principles as you went along. "Existentialism" seemed to enable you to reject all authority. And it entitled you to live for the moment, since the existentialists felt that the present obliterates the past and the future effaces the immediate present.

We also relished the stress on "authenticity" of emotion: you shouldn't pretend to traditional feelings that you didn't have, just as the hero of Camus's *The Stranger* refused to pretend to grieve for his mother's death. From there it was only a step to the mass market interpretation of existentialism: adven-

tures for anyone who desired them, Juliette Greco singing in a basement—
Greco did seem to symbolize sexual and artistic emancipation—espresso bars,
black stockings and white lipstick, the best of orgasms.

Mathieu, the key character in Sartre's *The Roads to Freedom*, was appealing
because he pursued "real liberty"; he didn't want to marry or to involve himself
in the Spanish Civil War at the risk of losing his personal freedom. But Sartre's
conviction that freedom demands responsibility and commitment wasn't what
his youthful American audience wanted to hear. When one of Mathieu's
friends asks why he's saving his freedom, if not to engage himself in something,
and adds that he will grow old while his "liberty" enslaves him, the implication
was distressing. There were echoes of *The Beast in the Jungle* when Mathieu
reflected that he had led "a toothless life. . . . I've never chewed, I preserved
myself for later—until I've come to realize that I no longer have any teeth."

In midlife Sartre had moved away from the tenets of *Being and Nothingness*,
where he'd suggested that all human activity was pointless, that our actions
could never be more than gestures without purpose. In truth he had evolved
two conflicting philosophies—which was perplexing to those who didn't read
him chronologically. Initially he argued that effort was fruitless; later he urged
his followers to bend their energies to restructuring society. American liberals
who derided activism and yet felt ineffective could appreciate Sartre's early
discussions of futility—as easily as they could dismiss his unorthodox Marxism.

Sartre's belief that human beings had created God—as a device for escaping
accountability for their existence—made sense to those who had no ties to
Christianity. But his insistence that no twentieth-century citizen could lead
a private life that wasn't influenced by global politics was disconcerting to
some readers of the Fifties. He cautioned that belonging to a political party
conferred no virtue on anyone. Yet his allegiance to working against oppression
and toward the evolution of a society of equals was alien to Americans who
were wary of all ideologies.

During the year after graduation I kept returning to a speech in *The Flies*
that moved me: early in the play, Orestes' tutor tells him that he's had all the
advantages of education and freedom and that he can do anything he wishes—
so what is he complaining about? Orestes replies, "No, I'm not complaining.
I can't complain: you have left me as free as those threads that the wind tears
from spiders' webs which float ten feet above the ground; I weigh no more
than a thread and I live in the air. I know I'm lucky and I appreciate it. . . ."

Throughout the play Sartre emphasized the most painful aspects of freedom.
Like many of my schoolmates I was feeling uncertain about how to use the

freedom I'd longed for. We were supposed to be the best educated of our
generation, unhampered by anything, qualified to excel at whatever we
attempted. The American economy was flourishing, we heard that opportunities abounded. But few of us could find a foothold. Solitude had been exalted
(in the name of artistic endeavor) by young aesthetes who weren't prepared
for isolation—in surroundings or jobs where their values were irrelevant.

So I reread Sartre and grappled with his analysis of freedom: the idea that
life was formless and senseless, that feeling free meant being guilty, that there
could be no guidance for any of the choices one had to make. In *The Flies*,
when Orestes decided to tell his countrymen that they were all free spirits,
Jupiter warned him: "You are going to make them a present of loneliness and
shame . . . you are going to show them their obscene and tasteless existence,
which is given to them for no purpose." Orestes retorted that everyone must
learn "that human life begins on the far side of despair." (The play's ending
was a subtle wartime exhortation to the French to join the Resistance during
the Nazi occupation, but that wasn't grasped by young postwar Americans
who knew little about the Vichy government.)

Sartre also declared that protecting one's liberty could mean paralysis, as
Mathieu discovered. And a spectrum of anxieties seemed to be confirmed on
reading in *Nausea* that "everything is made up of chance . . . and the present
comes like a thief in the night." Moreover Sartre's assertion that freedom required
commitment was disturbing because we couldn't conceive of attaching ourselves
to a social movement (even if one had existed). The only imaginable commitment would be a commitment to art, which was as yet untested. Still I seized
on the last few pages of *Nausea*—where the narrator envisions art as a form of
salvation—even though that theme did not appear elsewhere in Sartre's work,
and he had also written that literature was powerless. No doubt I often misunderstood him, but some of his writing expressed a lifelong struggle with contradictions—as well as a battle with his own cultural elitism.

Sartre's conviction that we were all defined by our acts—that a person
fashioned "his own being" through his actions—was discomforting to young
persons who had assumed that their behavior (when it was witless or destructive) didn't necessarily represent them. But in Sartre's philosophy, if your car
ran over a cat you were a cat-killer; if you failed an exam you were a failure:
there was no solace in thinking that you'd behaved "unlike yourself." The
great speech in Middleton and Rowley's Jacobean play, *The Changeling*—when
a woman who arranged but didn't actually commit a murder was called a
murderess—tugged at my memory as I steeped myself in Sartre:

Look but into your conscience . . . settle you
In what the act has made you; you're no more now . . .
You are the deed's creature.

That, it seemed, was existentialism: one's clothing gradually became one's skin, and the freedom we had cherished was illusory.

In the Fifties one could share Sartre's pessimism and even his sense of cosmic absurdity without heeding his call to action. And before long the American notion of existentialism was muddled with evocations of mystical catharsis and hipsters and beats, though that was hardly the audience for his contention that there are no adventures, that experience is always disappointing. Some of us felt we were floating like the torn spiders' webs; dispirited by that condition, berating ourselves for being insubstantial, it seemed reasonable to accept our lack of gravity.

14

The Autherine Lucy Case

Throughout the Fifties the Democratic ballot in the state of Alabama still bore the slogan WHITE SUPREMACY. In Birmingham a city ordinance forbade black citizens to ride in elevators or taxis with whites or to play checkers with them. Montgomery's ordinance banned interracial games including dominoes, cards, dice, baseball, and football. The signs on public toilets which read "Ladies," "Gentlemen," and "Colored" revealed that both sexes had to share the latter. Because many Southern whites considered blacks to be unclean, the races rarely ate at the same table, but most white meals were cooked and served by black hands. Whites in the South often said that blacks were riddled with venereal diseases, yet many white babies were tended by black women.

The Supreme Court's *Brown* decision of 1954, which outlawed segregation in public schools, revitalized the Ku Klux Klan, and Citizens' Councils were formed in direct response to the Court's ruling. Council members—mostly male—usually tried to dissociate themselves from the Klan: they wore neckties, not sheets, and they focused on educational institutions that faced desegregation. There were governors, congressmen, and judges in the Councils, whose members felt themselves to be of a higher social class than the Klansmen. But a number of them funded the Klan and some harbored a kindred violence. (In 1956 singer Nat King Cole was beaten up by six men who jumped on the stage while he was giving a concert for a white audience in Birmingham; his attackers were former Councilmen who had joined an offshoot of the Ku Klux Klan.) AFL-CIO President George Meany called the Councils "a new Klan without hoods." The Klan could sometimes be as intimidating for whites as for blacks: whites who betrayed "the Southern way of life" and befriended blacks or upheld their civil rights could be assaulted by the Klan as traitors to their race. Catholics as well as Jews were hounded by the Klansmen, who were often charged with "flogging while masked." Because anonymity seemed essential to terrorism, some states had laws which prohibited the wearing of masks in public.

Klansmen and Citizens' Council members were united in the belief that the National Association for the Advancement of Colored People was dominated by Communists, though the NAACP was aggressively anti-Communist. Of course the label was appropriate to the era, but some older segregationists remembered that Communists had organized groups of Alabama's black farmers and factory workers during the Depression, and that the Party had supported the Scottsboro defendants in Alabama in 1931. Hence "outsiders" who came South "to agitate the Negroes" were suspected of Soviet inspiration. Men who wished to join the Central Alabama Citizens' Council, the largest in the state, signed a membership application which asserted: "I pledge myself to help defeat the NAACP, integration, mongrelism, socialism, Communist ideologies, FEPC [the proposed Fair Employment Practices Commission], and one world government." Some pledges to other councils stated, "I do not want my child to marry a Negro."

Birmingham, a sooty town of iron and steel and coal, came to be known as "Bombingham" when Klansmen and their allies dynamited the homes and churches of blacks who participated in any attempts at desegregation. Martin Luther King called Birmingham "the most widely segregated city in the United States." In the Fifties, when Theophilus Eugene (Bull) Connor was the police commissioner, Birmingham had several dozen unsolved bombings and it was frequently said that the police department had "a working relationship" with the Klan.

• • •

Northerners could be slow to realize that the Southern abhorrence of "racially mixed" schools was partially fueled by sexual obsessions. Black male teenagers were expected to ravish young white girls after class; schoolmates would produce "mongrel" children. White supremacists were dedicated to the idea of protecting Southern women from black assailants just as the aristocratic Klansmen in *The Birth of a Nation* had. Alabama State Senator Walter Givhan said the NAACP aimed "to open the bedroom doors of our white women to Negro men." President Eisenhower, who'd been born in the South and had lived there for some years, disapproved of the Supreme Court's ruling on the schools and sympathized with many Southerners' emotions. Shortly before the Court's decision he told Chief Justice Earl Warren that segregationists were "not bad people. All they are concerned about is to see that their sweet little girls are not required to sit in schools alongside some big overgrown Negroes." He told Arthur Larson, director of the United States Information Agency, that equal opportunity did not mean "that a Negro should court my daughter."

In the mid-Fifties interracial marriages were still illegal in thirty states. The Citizens' Councils distributed thousands of copies of *Black Monday*, a book by Tom Brady, a Mississippi circuit judge, which analyzed the horrific consequences of miscegenation. Brady wrote, "Whenever and wherever the white man has drunk the cup of black hemlock, whenever and wherever his blood has been infused with the blood of the negro, the white man, his intellect, and his culture have died." Brady attributed the decline of ancient Egypt, Babylonia, Greece, and the Roman empire to "negroid blood like the jungle, steadily and completely swallowing up everything." A Council pamphlet quoted Mississippi Senator Theodore Bilbo: "If the blood of our white race should become corrupted and mingled with the blood of Africa, then the present greatness of the United States of America would be destroyed and all hope for the future would be forever gone." Council publications averred that cannibalism was central to the black heritage.

Some Southern politicians fanned the voters' fears with images of child molestation. In *The New Yorker*, A. J. Liebling described a campaign flyer for a gubernatorial candidate in Louisiana, a drawing which "showed two dainty female children, the puffed skirts of their crisp frocks midway up their plump thighs, picking flowers. . . . One little girl kneeled and culled, a frilly bit of the bottom of her panties innocently peeping from beneath the skirt, and turned a precociously provocative face toward her sister, who stood and held the basket. There was a carefully planted suggestion of eligibility for rape." Part of the copy read: "THIS IS A FIGHT FOR OUR CHILDREN! WE CANNOT . . . WE *MUST* NOT leave them a heritage of integration to struggle against!"

• • •

Before the Autherine Lucy case of 1956 I'd hardly looked at daily newspapers; then I bought several each day. Growing up in the Northeast, where racism wasn't openly acknowledged, I knew little about lethal racial passions until I read about the experiences of the first black student at the University of Alabama in Tuscaloosa. No other black had ever gone to a white school or college in that state.

Autherine Lucy, aged twenty-six, was admitted after a three-year lawsuit sponsored by the NAACP Legal Defense and Educational Fund Inc. The youngest of ten children of a tenant farmer, she had graduated from Miles Memorial College, a black Methodist college in Birmingham. She then taught high school English and Sunday school, and she was eager to earn a degree in library science; later she said she would like to be a librarian in the high school near her home. In 1952 her friend Pollie Anne Myers, who had been prominent in the student chapter of the NAACP at Miles, proposed that they apply to the state university to study subjects which black colleges did not provide. Myers, a mettlesome, enterprising young woman, was the initiator; Lucy, a very retiring and modest person, didn't see herself as an activist. It was not against the state law for blacks to attend the university, which had no written policy that denied admission on racial grounds, but black applicants were always advised to go elsewhere. The two consulted Arthur D. Shores, Birmingham's foremost black lawyer and the NAACP Fund's counsel in Alabama. Predictably Myers and Lucy were turned down by the university. Shores filed their suit in conjunction with Thurgood Marshall, chief counsel for the NAACP, and NAACP Fund attorney Constance Baker Motley.

In the wake of the *Brown* decision, Federal District Judge Hobart H. Grooms ruled that the university could not disobey the law as defined by the Supreme Court and that both women must be enrolled. (The Court had also established that the ban on segregation applied to tax-supported colleges and universities.) The case was brought as a class action suit, meaning that other blacks could enter the university in the future.

At that time the state retained detectives to investigate the personal backgrounds of plaintiffs in desegregation suits—in hopes of disqualifying them. (Such plaintiffs were apt to lose their jobs with white employers or to be deprived of their mortgages at local banks; this was known as "the economic lynch law.") Once the two women applied, the university hired detectives who learned that Pollie Anne Myers had been pregnant by a man convicted of burglary when she first applied to the university; her baby was born six months after her marriage. The university excluded her for her "conduct and marital record." But Autherine Lucy's dossier was impeccable and she became the sole candidate. It was hard to approach the university on her own; as she often said, she never chose to be a public figure nor to make history. Deeply religious, she prayed for guidance, then decided "it was my task" to proceed on behalf of those who had never been permitted to study at the university.

All throughout the summer of 1955 Lucy was advised by her friends in the NAACP and Birmingham on how to conduct herself on campus: she was to ignore all insults, to hold her head high. She expected to hear "snarls" and had prepared herself for those moments. She looked forward to her courses and hoped she might take piano lessons. A dress committee from the NAACP helped her select her clothing; her middle-aged mentors thought an elegant wardrobe would make her acceptable to professors and classmates, and she was dressed in her Sunday best for her first appearance at the university.

When she registered in February 1956, the black bus boycott in Montgomery, Alabama, was two months old. The boycott, which started after Rosa Parks was arrested for refusing to give her seat on a segregated bus to a white man, propelled twenty-six-year-old Martin Luther King into the national spotlight. The Montgomery City Lines bus company and the city's downtown stores were losing many thousands of dollars without black customers; the homes of boycott organizers were bombed and King was jailed for the first time. In Tuscaloosa some thought the fury that greeted Lucy was heightened by the boycott. Segregationists were discovering that black Southerners were ready to defy racist laws; Northern agitators weren't needed to animate them, and whites had begun to understand that they were confronting a social revolution. The Autherine Lucy case became a symbolic battlefield for those who were determined to maintain segregation and those who had resolved to eradicate it.

Right after Lucy's registration, papers such as *The Birmingham Post-Herald* claimed that her clothes were too "fashionable," that she was "hustled ahead" of white students in the registration line, and that she had paid for her tuition with "a crisp $100 bill." She was immediately denied a room in a dormitory and barred from the dining halls. She was informed that the board of trustees had specifically ordered that she should not be assigned a room because "it might endanger the safety or result in sociological disadvantage of the students." (University administrators had urged that she be given a room, but they were overruled by trustees who feared that young black men might call on her in the dormitory lounge.) So she had to commute to her classes from Birmingham every day, a distance of sixty miles in each direction.

Some whites surmised that blacks who weren't shabby must have acquired money by illicit means; if they appeared to be more than solvent, they might possess shady connections. Segregationists were often outraged by intimations of black prosperity. Lucy's carefully chosen wardrobe—a matching peach-colored sweater and skirt, a powder blue suit, a gray coat threaded with yellow and worn with a small yellow hat—the $100 bill, and the fact that she once arrived in Tuscaloosa in a Cadillac, excited so much angry comment and hostile press coverage that Constance Baker Motley compiled a "fact sheet," which explained that Lucy had a scholarship from a New York foundation; however, the university had returned the money because she was not yet registered. "A citizens' committee in Alabama had raised funds" for some of her expenses; "therefore, on the morning . . . when she needed money to pay her tuition until the scholarship matter could be straightened out, the chairman of the committee hurriedly withdrew $100 from a bank and handed it to [her], so that there would be no question of her having completed registration on time." (Members of the committee also doubted that the university would accept a check written by a black person.) She had been "escorted" to the front of the registration line "by anxious university personnel"—who hadn't foreseen how much that gesture would be resented. She was driven daily from Birmingham by black volunteers: on the first day she was delivered "by a man who happened to own a Buick"; on the second day in a Ford; on the third in an Oldsmobile; on the fourth "by a man who happened to own a Cadillac."

Later, when Thurgood Marshall asked university trustee John Caddell in court if Lucy had done "anything unlawful when she came to the university," Caddell replied that she "came in a Cadillac automobile, had a chauffeur, and walked in a way as to be obnoxious and objectionable and disagreeable." Caddell implied that the "actions" of Lucy and her companions had generated the ensuing violence: "All that publicity was calculated to cause rioting and they knew it."

• • •

There were twice as many whites as blacks in Tuscaloosa, but many whites said they were in a minority. Much of the national press emphasized that blacks and whites had enjoyed harmonious relations there—until the advent of Autherine Lucy. *The New York Times* reported that "Race relations in Tuscaloosa had been so happy that, as the Lucy affair was coming to a head, Negroes only gathered to watch and laugh when a fiery cross was burned on the edge of a Negro high school campus." But soon Lucy was labeled "the controversial colored girl" (*Newsweek*) who had infused a whole city with hatred. Many white Tuscaloosans bought guns.

The Klan took credit for numerous gasoline-soaked crosses set ablaze at and near the university. Bomb threats were plentiful. Racist leaflets—containing pictures of black men embracing white women—were distributed on campus by Robert Chambliss, an ex-Klansman called "Dynamite Bob" who belonged to a Klan offshoot; he would be convicted in 1977 of the 1963 bombing that killed four young black girls in a Baptist church in Birmingham. But Lucy went through two days of classes without incident, and some students told her they wished her well.

While she was away over the weekend, mobs assembled on the grounds; pistols and rifles were confiscated from their cars. After a rally they paraded through the neighborhood and vandalized a post office, where they splashed ink on the American flag—a symbol of the hated Supreme Court and its desegregation ruling. Leonard Wilson, a sophomore in the School of Commerce, exhorted the crowd to halt cars driven by blacks: "Make them roll down their windows. Ask them if they believe in segregation. If they say no, then make them believe in it." His listeners attacked the vehicles of several black townsmen: slashing tires and breaking taillights, they partly tore the door off one car and nearly overturned another. Amid the yells of "Keep 'Bama white!" and the waving of Confederate flags, University President O. C. Carmichael was showered with gravel and firecrackers when he tried to address the jeering demonstrators who surrounded his house.

Leonard Wilson had told the crowd that Lucy deserved "a greeting she would never forget." When she arrived on Monday, the car that took her to classes was stoned and the black man who drove it barely escaped injury. Many glass bottles were thrown. The university chaplain who tried to pacify the rioters was kneed in the groin. Several university officials would later testify that a mob of about two thousand seemed ready to murder Lucy: shouting, "There she goes!" they pursued her as she was driven from one class to another. J. Jefferson Bennett, assistant to the president, and Sarah Healy, dean of women, risked their lives in protecting her; the windows of Healy's car were shattered with rocks. As Lucy ran toward the library for a class on children's literature, the mob raced after her up the steps of the building, yelling "Let's *kill* her! Kill her!"

Twenty-eight years afterward, when I called on Autherine Lucy Foster in Opelika, Alabama, I asked what had sustained her at the time. She told me how she had sat and prayed inside a locked room in the library while the voices outside chanted, "Hey, hey, ho, were in the hell did Autherine go? Hey, hey, ho, where in the hell did that nigger go?" She recalled, "I asked the Lord to give me the strength—if I must give my life—to give it freely. And if I *were* to give my life, to let someone else take over where I left off. And that if it were mine to see it through, to give me the courage to go through with it." After she had "composed" herself, she noticed that a thick yellowish liquid was streaming from the shoulder of her new green coat to the hem—outdoors she'd felt an object hit her, but she was running too fast to see what it was.

Still in semi-shock, she realized that it was a rotten egg because the yolk and white were mingled. As she talked she appeared to relive that moment: it seemed as if the memory of the egg was even uglier than her recollection of the mob—the egg was a symbol of loathing and she had felt befouled.

Lucy was finally driven away from the bellowing throng, lying on the floor of the highway patrolman's car that rescued her. The next day the trustees suspended her "for her own safety." A student said, "Well, we won. It took her four years and the Supreme Court to get her in, and it took us only four days to get rid of her." In the Alabama Senate, Senator Albert Davis praised the crowd and said, "Yesterday was a great day for Alabama."

During the two weeks after Lucy's first day of classes, thousands of Alabamians joined Citizens' Councils throughout the state. In Montgomery a multitude attended what was said to be the century's biggest segregation rally to protest her admission to the university: rebel yells alternated with the singing of "Dixie" and Council leaders said the Lucy case had been splendid for recruitment. Tuscaloosa's first council was organized soon after her suspension; local businessmen as well as factory workers and farmers went to its opening meeting. Leonard Wilson, the temporary chairman, told a cheering, foot-stomping audience of more than a thousand, "We will control every public office from the lowest county peanut politician to the Governor's mansion." His hearers roared, "Hallelujah!" State Senator Walter Givhan declared that Communists were advocating desegregation "because they know the South is one of the few places in which pure Anglo-Saxon blood exists." At a subsequent meeting Givhan said the NAACP was scheming to elect a black vice president and then to take over the country after assassinating the President.

• • •

The Lucy case was the first occasion when a black student's admission to a Southern university was savagely opposed. Because other blacks had entered all-white Southern universities without encountering resistance, neither the university nor the NAACP had anticipated the turmoil at Tuscaloosa. The mobs which menaced Lucy had included undergraduates, but many of the men were rubber workers from the nearby Goodrich plant and others were employees of a steel foundry; the Klan's recruiters had been active at both companies. (News photographs showed that the crowds contained many men who looked about forty years old, as well as members of a nearby high school football team.) The NAACP heard that people from other parts of Alabama and from other states, especially Mississippi and Virginia, had come to swell the hordes. The national press did not refer to the Klan, but the local papers and university officials did—at length and often.

The case was featured in headlines all over the world and given detailed coverage in the Soviet press. Such columnists as Walter Lippmann upbraided the university for capitulating to the mob. One of the few white politicians who displayed a strong reaction was Governor Averell Harriman of New York, soon to be a candidate for the Democratic presidential nomination of 1956. He asked for "vigorous" federal action against those who were preventing Lucy from continuing her education; he charged Attorney General Herbert Brownell with failing to enforce the law, and he said President Eisenhower was taking the case too "lightly."

On the same day Adlai Stevenson observed that the "situation" merited "the prompt attention of the President," but that the topic of segregation should be avoided in the upcoming presidential campaign. When pressed he said segregation was a local matter and that 1965 might be a possible target date "for a gradual settlement of the school racial crisis." George Meany of the AFL-CIO retorted that Stevenson's plan was "nonsense," adding "Mr. Stevenson is running away from the issue." Eisenhower "deplored" the rioting and said federal "interference" was undesirable. Questioned about desegregation per se, he subsequently remarked, "Now let's don't try to think of this as a tremendous fight that is going to separate Americans and get ourselves into a nasty mess." He then managed to shun the subject until it was necessary to send twelve hundred army paratroopers to defend nine new black students from crowds who howled for their blood and promised to "lynch the niggers" at the Little Rock Central High School in Arkansas in 1957.

Some blamed Governor James Folsom of Alabama because the state National Guard was not summoned after President Carmichael sent a request through the mayor of Tuscaloosa. (Folsom was absent from his office and his staff didn't act on the request. It was rumored that the governor was in a clinic, receiving treatment for the alcoholism which would ruin his career by 1962.) Folsom, a populist who had been regarded as quite enlightened about civil rights—to the extent that some Citizens' Council members had demanded his impeachment—then made some ambiguous comments about desegregation. Throughout Lucy's ordeal, the university's trustees—mostly businessmen and lawyers who represented the "big mules" of Birmingham and the industrial powers of Alabama—had been at odds with the administration. (Almost none of the trustees had wanted to admit her, but they were not going to violate the law.) O. C. Carmichael and J. Jefferson Bennett hoped she would soon resume her studies because the university's integrity was at stake. The two made plans for her future safety there. The student president, Walter Flowers (later a congressman), denounced the behavior of the mob, and about two hundred students out of some seven thousand signed petitions supporting the readmission of Autherine Lucy.

Following her suspension she stayed with her sister in Birmingham; her brother-in-law and his cousin guarded the house with guns because the phone was throbbing with death threats. Although the last morning at the university had been terrifying, the butt of all that hatred continued to expect a more rational and humane world than the one she inhabited. But her relatives and friends remembered the murder of fourteen-year-old Emmett Till in Mississippi the year before: they were determined to shield her from the white violence which had killed the young black boy, who had chanted while he was thrashed before he was shot, "Mama, Lord have mercy, Lord have mercy."

When Lucy's lawyers brought a suit to reinstate her at the university, black men with shotguns stood on the top floors of buildings along the streets where she walked with Arthur Shores to the courthouse. She told me she didn't credit herself with bravery because she knew about so many people who had been flogged and bombed or had died for equal rights.

• • •

Pete Seeger wrote a song called "Autherine" which was released on his 1956 record, *Love Songs for Friends and Foes*. At an Authors League panel on "The Writer's Position in America," Langston Hughes said some major black writers chose to live in Europe "Because the stones thrown at Autherine Lucy at the University of Alabama are thrown at them, too. Because the shadow of Montgomery and the bombs under Rev. King's house, shadow them and shatter them, too." William Faulkner was terrifically upset by the Lucy case. Like many others, he was certain she would be murdered if she returned to the university: "If that girl dies, two or three white men will be killed, then eight or nine Negroes." Then, he believed, the government would send troops to Alabama, armed Southerners would fight back, and a new civil war would begin. As the challenge to the schools continued and rage inflamed the South, both liberal and conservative Southerners wondered if such a war lay ahead.

Faulkner had already made speeches and written an essay in an effort to persuade Americans to accept desegregation. He felt that rural and small-town Southern whites feared economic competition from blacks, that countrymen resembling his Snopes family thought racial equality would impoverish them. Desperate to forestall calamity after the riots in Tuscaloosa, he went on the radio, trying to explain the South to the North, dreading the violence that could erupt from mutual incomprehension. After *Life* published his "Letter to the North," he sent another missive to the magazine, characterizing his first letter as "the attempt of an individual to save the South and the whole United States too from the blot of Miss Autherine Lucy's death."

In the mid-Fifties Faulkner's statements about the races were sometimes contradictory. He was far more sensitive to the suffering of black Americans than most of his Mississippi friends and relatives. In *Harper's Magazine* he wrote, "To live anywhere in the world today and be against equality because of race or color, is like living in Alaska and being against snow." Elsewhere he paid cautious respects to the Montgomery bus boycott and rebuked the Citizens' Councils, yet he entreated the NAACP to "go slow." Drinking profusely as his alarm about the Lucy case accelerated, he repeated during an interview for the London *Sunday Times* and *The Reporter*, "The Negroes are right," adding, "I've always been on their side." He also said that the Southerners were wrong. Still, "if it came to fighting I'd fight for Mississippi against the United States even if it meant going out into the street and shooting Negroes." He soon retracted that remark, calling it "foolish" and "dangerous," indicating that he'd been drunk when he spoke. But it was quoted for years. (Langston Hughes was disgusted by Faulkner's words, but some years later he said at a PEN symposium, "Maybe he was a little drunk. Maybe we are all a little drunk, intoxicated on the moonshine of history.") When a student at the University of Alabama wrote to Faulkner asking how students might alleviate the crisis there, Faulkner replied that the South must "abolish" segregation rather than experiencing enforced desegregation—because whites would "stay on top" if they supported racial equality, whereas blacks would be "the victor" if the government supported them "against opposition." While trying to locate a "middle road" he infuriated racists as well as black leaders and a multitude of liberals.

Faulkner also asserted that whites "who believe in individual freedom" needed the allegiance of blacks: "Let us have them on our side, rather than on that of Russia." Many politicians worried that the Lucy case would discredit America abroad, that manifest racism undermined the country's role as "leader of the free world." (A few years earlier Attorney General J. Howard McGrath had written in a brief filed with the Supreme Court, "Racial discrimination furnishes grist for the Communist propaganda mills, and it raises doubt even among friendly nations as to the intensity of our devotion to the democratic faith.") The Associated Press reported that Averell Harriman told the United Parents Association of New York that "mob rule" at the University of Alabama had "hurt the United States in its fight against Communism." When the Soviet Union celebrated its annual Women's Day, articles in the Moscow press contrasted the "genuine freedom" of Soviet women with the oppression of Autherine Lucy.

At home Lucy was required to deny any ties with the Communist Party, and she was asked to speak on the Voice of America to disclaim a letter attributed to her which was addressed to the students of North Vietnam and broadcast on Hanoi radio. The letter, which was clearly a fake, said that Americans—while "despising" Negroes—were trying "to embrace the yellow-skinned Vietnamese" and "pretending to be charitable just to bring the people of South Vietnam under their yoke." Thurgood Marshall told *The New York Times* that the letter was spurious and that "Miss Lucy knows the Communist Party is as big an enemy of Negro rights as any other enemy." Her statement of disavowal—translated into many languages—was broadcast by the Voice of America to Southeast Asia and to countries around the globe.

●　●　●

On March 1, 1956, the university trustees found a legal excuse to expel Lucy permanently, because her lawyers filed an affidavit accusing them of conspiring with the mob. Trustees and administrators thought Constance Baker Motley had written the affidavit. A number of black people did believe that the trustees had "conspired" by omission—because Lucy had not been given adequate police protection. They deduced that the riots provided a pretext for postponing desegregation. The legal brief stated that she had been "punished . . . for having sought to secure her constitutional rights." But university officials who had been roughed up by the crowd which called them "nigger-lovers" were stunned by the notion that there had been collaboration with the men they'd been fighting. The charge of collusion was withdrawn by Thurgood Marshall, who told the court he had no evidence to sustain it. In the word-storm that surrounded Autherine Lucy, she read some of the lawyers' phrases about conspiracy aloud on television, so she was expelled "for libelous allegations against the board and the President." In the Fifties students were thought to have few rights—and certainly no right to criticize the authorities at a university. Leonard Wilson was expelled soon afterward for the same reason; not only had he "fomented" the crowds, but he'd called for a student boycott of classes attended by Lucy and for the dismissal of President Carmichael. Some of his schoolmates were suspended or reprimanded for rioting, and it was stressed that students of both races had been disciplined.

A month after her expulsion, Lucy married her longtime fiancé, Hugh Lawrence Foster, who soon became a Baptist minister. (They had planned to marry a year before but had decided to wait until she had her degree from the university.) Her husband was assigned to many different parishes; they moved often while she taught in public schools in Texas, Louisiana, and Alabama, and had four children. The publicity the case received apparently cost her some jobs in the early Sixties: one school superintendent said her association with the NAACP made her unacceptable. The NAACP arranged some lecture engagements; in the Seventies she was invited to address several American history classes at the University of Alabama.

But the case was only one chapter in a very full life, and she didn't want to be defined by it. An extremely private person, she had no desire to excavate the past, but she felt an obligation to share the history which had claimed her. In the mid-Eighties she was pleased that the university had the highest percentage of black students of any of the once-white Southern universities. But she spoke of "segregation within integration": the scarcity of black teachers in the schools she knew, the "isolation" in housing (she lived in an almost entirely black neighborhood), the gulf between black and white churches even though "we say that we worship the same God," the undergraduates who sat with their own races in the lecture halls and belonged to separate clubs. She still hoped that black and white students would profit from mutual exposure, but she saw them as dwelling far apart.

• • •

Immediately after the Lucy case, the zeal of the segregationists intensified: at a Citizens' Council meeting in Montgomery in 1956, Georgia's Attorney General Eugene Cook referred to desegregation as "racial suicide." The Councils boycotted products of firms which were said to have given money to the NAACP or the Urban League, or were believed to support integration: three targets were Philip Morris, Falstaff beer, and the Ford Motor Company. The Alabama House of Representatives passed a resolution to determine whether the NAACP was "directed or controlled by Communists" and a subpoena was issued to make Lucy appear as the first witness. (She had already left the state, and the hearings didn't take place.) The Councils sent questionnaires to candidates in Alabama's next Democratic primary, asking if they were committed to segregation and if they had told "the Negro that you do not want his vote"; it was understood that their replies would be publicized. Council members hardly ever endorsed candidates, but any Deep South office-seeker who wasn't a white supremacist was almost sure to lose.

A resolution in the Alabama Senate requested federal funds to relocate black

Alabamians in Northern and Western states, where they "are wanted and can be assimilated." Representative Charles McKay of Talladega said he thought "most white Southerners" would be "glad to cancel out any debts" owed by blacks "if they would leave the state"; he recommended that they be convicted of felony if they returned. Bills were introduced to terminate grants to black colleges such as the Tuskegee Institute if a single black student was allowed to enter a white college or a public school. Since 1945 black students had also been subsidized to attend universities outside the state when they wanted to study subjects like law or medicine, which weren't taught at Alabama's state-supported black colleges. In 1956 it was proposed in the legislature that all those scholarships be discontinued if desegregation persisted in Alabama.

A house resolution was also passed requiring President Carmichael to supply the names of students who had signed petitions in support of Autherine Lucy. The names were never submitted. Carmichael, formerly the chancellor of Vanderbilt University and ex-president of the Carnegie Foundation for the Advancement of Teaching, had expected the university to be desegregated without a court order during his tenure, which began in 1953. (Raised as an Alabama segregationist, he'd understood that change was inevitable but couldn't welcome it, nor had he provided any clear policy on the issue.) Resigning to join the Ford Foundation for the Advancement of Education in 1957, he denied that his departure was prompted by the Lucy case. But his closest colleagues said he was demoralized and humiliated. Censured by liberals, reviled by segregationists, and—most painful of all—congratulated on Lucy's expulsion, he left Tuscaloosa in waning health.

The NAACP was shut down in Alabama for eight years; some of its members thought the injunction issued against their organization was a direct consequence of the Lucy case, since many of the state's politicians and lawyers were alumni of the university. Gigantic fines were imposed on the NAACP when it declined to reveal its membership list to state authorities, and it was then enjoined from operation in the state. Convinced that the members would be in danger or even killed if their identities were known, unable to pay the fines and therefore certain to be imprisoned, the directors closed their offices, which were moved to Atlanta, Georgia, until a Supreme Court decision enabled them to function in Alabama once again.

Union leaders in Tuscaloosa said the Lucy case had damaged their locals: relations between black and white members degenerated right after the campus riots and many whites had rebelled against the desegregation policies of the AFL-CIO. Some members of the United Steel Workers in Birmingham threatened to form their own all-white union. Breakaway segregationist locals were founded in 1956 and soon thereafter; although they didn't prosper, anti-union propaganda from the Councils and the Klan slowed the development of the labor movement in Alabama. Tuscaloosa union officials told *The New York Times* that Northern "interference" in the case had weakened their authority and had "set organized labor back twenty years" in their region.

In the aftermath of the case, segregationists felt they had triumphed. About a hundred white-robed Klansmen drove a cavalcade of fifty-seven cars through Tuscaloosa and across the campus. Yet some of their opponents also had a sense of achievement: Lucy and her lawyers had opened the university to black students. But none went there until seven years later, when Governor George Wallace "stood in the schoolhouse door" in 1963 and performed his charade of resistance until he was instructed to step aside on the orders of President Kennedy. Wallace knew he could not legally prohibit the enrollment of two black students, but he was making a symbolic gesture to mollify his constituents; his actions did help to keep the Klan off campus before registration day and probably prevented bloodshed. Ample federal troops were on hand and the university had prepared for weeks for the arrival of the black students; even the soft drink machines in campus buildings were emptied or sealed up so that no one could use a bottle as a weapon. The next month the city of Birmingham repealed all its segregation laws. Two months later the Sixteenth Street Baptist church was bombed after a Bible class on its annual Youth Day and four black children were dead.

15

Rapture Unwrapped

Feel-ups in the front seat, the number of buttons that could be undone, articles in *Seventeen* with titles like "How to Say No—Nicely," the Nichols and May skit about two panting teenagers on the brink ("Would you respect me?" "Oh God, would I *respect* you!"), fingerfucking, "everything but"—so much has been written about the sexual restrictions of the Fifties. Yet I feel that the issue has been greatly exaggerated, in part because members of my small generation were obsessed with privacy, hence the public didn't know what they were up to. (One friend told me she had such an overdeveloped sense of privacy that she disliked the idea that anyone was even thinking about her.) Some cherished privacy as a form of freedom: a protection of the self from a stifling society.

As students our only real freedom was sexual and I think we had more liberty to discover sex for ourselves than some adolescents did later, since we could slide between the sheets without the glare of publicity which was focused on campuses in the Sixties. Kinsey's report on male sexuality had some lively side effects; several years after his statistics on teenage masturbation were published, the boys at my boarding school often chanted, "Ninety-two, ninety-two, ninety-two per cent of us do—Kinsey! Kinsey! Rah, rah, rah!" But the media didn't interview us about our favorite positions or how many abortions we'd had, or whether we coupled in airplanes or in washrooms. We weren't burdened by our seniors' curiosity about our sex lives, and fantasies weren't pasted onto us, as they were on the young of the Sixties. So it was still possible for novices to feel as though they had invented sex. And some who were very shy found it much easier to talk to one another in bed—in a way that seemed almost impossible outside it.

I think that sexual constraint was nourished mainly in all-male or -female schools and colleges, where the opposite sex maintained its mystery. Yet in coeducational institutions there was plenty of sexual enthusiasm—at a time when other enthusiasms had to be hidden, because they were uncool. But because of the rigor of parietal rules, it was difficult to find a place to shed your virginity. One of my friends first made it in a gravel pit, another in a fire-fighter's lookout tower, several in snowdrifts, one during a lesson in artificial respiration. You learned to spring up and dress rapidly when a relative's key turned in a lock or when a classmate wandered in to ask for your notes on *Lycidas*. In some dormitories certain long-playing records were used as signals: you didn't enter a room or even knock on a door when you heard Wanda Landowska playing Bach (harpsichords helped to disguise squeaking bed-springs). Most collegiate walls were thin: a Harvard friend of mine once heard a girl's remorseful voice from the next room: "Now you *see*: I have a flat chest and a pot belly." A young man muttered huskily, "Oh, that's all right." Learning to have a silent orgasm was part of an Ivy League education.

As soon as we had unloaded our shameful virginity, we became sexual snobs, derisive of those without experience, so virgins over nineteen tended to keep their condition a secret. As a sophomore I incorrectly assumed that everyone was having sex with everyone. But I should have recalled the melancholy I'd shared with a roommate when another young woman strolled into our room and commandeered the supply of vaginal foam that we'd bought months before: in anticipation of the event which hadn't yet occurred for either of us. Our visitor explained that she needed the birth control right away, adding cheerfully, "And nobody around here seems to be using it, do they?" Sadly we handed the stuff over; I wrote that down because I was keeping a notebook of things that depressed me. Soon our foam-swiping friend loaned us an ultra-literary sex book full of quotes from Balzac and Baudelaire and far too much Latin and German. We loftily claimed that we knew it all—from *Lady Chatterley's Lover*.

In truth the printed word was not very helpful: I never understood what Norman Mailer meant by a "bad orgasm" as distinct from a good one. Also it was puzzling when psychologists wrote in favor of female resistance to sex— when they weren't really recommending chastity. (Even then it was accepted wisdom that sexual frustration was damaging to both sexes.) But some male writers implied that sex had to be *imposed* on women by men—as an assertion of power, which women would appreciate once they submitted to it. Sexual reluctance was deemed to be an inherent characteristic of the female. However she was allotted her own species of power: while men strove to dominate, she could withhold. And it was said that men's pleasure in pursuit was equaled by women's pleasure in evasion. But the theorists of the Fifties didn't acknowledge that many women, including virgins, were just as eager and impatient as the men were. Randy young women could feel out of step with the culture, which throbbed with titillation but didn't quite sanction fulfillment.

Indeed our popular culture announced that men wanted sex but women didn't, and some movies—like Marlon Brando's—suggested that virile men were fairly brutal about the preliminaries: a woman might not unreasonably shrink from the first onslaught from a motorcycle. But none of that had any connection with the world (or the men) that I knew. Yet the young did accept the filmic assumption that sex meant love: supposedly you could not be thoroughly aroused without the possibility of loving the arouser. We were unprepared for sexual incidents, especially when they were enjoyable; among the very young, hit and run episodes were rather rare.

And of course young women learned to pretend to have orgasms when they didn't; not only was it rude to omit the appropriate sighs, but a woman who neglected that nicety could be condemned as frigid, an unspeakable condition. A reputation for frigidity was worse than being called promiscuous, even at a time when sexual restraint was urged on the young. The frigid woman was hateful because she made a man feel inadequate: her own failure might dim his potency. So if he kept asking, "Are you coming, did you come yet?" it would have been mortifying to say no.

Still none I knew worried about expertise (as many would in the Sixties, when beginners dreaded being unsplendid in the sack). But some young couples were diffident about sharing their imaginations: in saying where and how they liked to be touched. Perhaps the period nurtured the idea that the best sex was totally instinctive: each person ought to "know" what the other wanted, and it would be wrong to make suggestions. Few would have foreseen the technology that was introduced into the national sexuality a decade later; we hadn't heard about the varieties of vibrators for women, the men who penetrated the nozzles of vacuum cleaners, or the bundles of feathers and bowls of ice cubes, the joys of Jello in the bathtub.

But we still had far too little information about birth control: some believed that a Pepsi-Cola douche was sufficient. Philip Roth was correct in *Goodbye, Columbus*: I did read the excerpt from Mary McCarthy's *The Group* in *Partisan Review* in order to learn more about diaphragms, and women students told each other where to find the magazine in Widener Library. But literature and myth did not suffice, nor did the foam of the Fifties; among my private word association tests, when someone says "Radcliffe," I think "pregnant." And the secrecy imposed on illegal abortions yielded images which you had to hide from others: the sight of a doctor taping up the edges of a door frame so that no light would show through to alert anyone that the office was being used at night; the warnings against ever mentioning an abortion in a taxi (some cab drivers were known to blackmail doctors); awakening to find your cheeks rouged by the doctor, so the post-abortion pallor wouldn't be noticed by the doorman; the intricacies of paying in advance in cash. (My boyfriend and I kept our wad of money wrapped around a pencil, secured with a rubber band. Just before setting off for the operation, we saw that the $10 bills were so tightly curled up that not all of them could be crammed into one purse. So we spent five minutes—laughing rather hysterically—flattening them out with a hot iron: they were still warm upon delivery.)

The elderly Viennese doctor who charged a special low rate to students disliked the legal risk of performing abortions, but she disapproved of anyone's education being interrupted and she deplored shotgun weddings. In my last year at college I arranged several New York abortions for Radcliffe friends because it seemed hopeless to find a willing doctor in Catholic Boston. My own doctor insisted on a "personal introduction" to each couple before she would agree to operate, since she didn't trust the discretion of young strangers. Offering tea, cookies baked by the anesthetist (her husband), and reassuring words after the abortion, she was a rarity at a time when other doctors often punished unmarried pregnant women with abusive lectures or made passes at them. One friend of mine was called "an animal" by her family doctor after he'd pronounced her pregnant. Then he wanted her to have sex.

• • •

Social historians sometimes write as though communes were an invention of the Sixties. But there were pre-Aquarian communes in the Fifties. One I dwelled in during a New York summer became a spontaneous crash pad: fellow students were constantly arriving and departing, leaving suitcases in the hall to show that they would return, greeting strangers at breakfast. I was living with a young man, but there was another girl for cover: to make things look more respectable—a notion which convulsed our older friends. (No one's parents were deceived. But they pretended to be fooled: it was an exercise in good manners between generations.)

In those drugless days we were trying to learn how to drink: we made horrible concoctions—blueberries and cucumbers in the gin we didn't really like—and then dumped them down the sink. We preferred wine but gin seemed worldly, so we kept buying it and pouring it away. Soon we'd squandered the low salaries from our summer jobs and could hardly afford groceries. The other girl's father had said she could sign for dinner at the Yale Club, so we ate there quite often—enormous steaks and flambé desserts and liqueurs that smelled like bananas, flinging crumbs to the pigeons which clustered on the penthouse roof at sunset—and the young man's parents allowed him to use their charge account at S. S. Pierce in Boston. Every few weeks he rode the rails to bring back the frozen lobster tails and pears in crème de menthe which kept us alive.

Sex and exotic food and any drinks seemed like the badges of being grown up: at twenty I was outraged when anyone took me for less. The young woman who shared the apartment was eighteen, and she was still encumbered with the albatross of virginity. She looked and dressed much older than she was—tailored black silk cocktail frocks, an impeccable short permanent—and she went out with desirable older men who recoiled on discovering her age. One complained that her virginity made him impotent. Repeatedly she and I agreed that it was revolting to be young: if only we could skip the years between twenty and thirty-five. It was hard to forgive our seniors for treating us as though we were innocents.

Finally it looked as if she were going to ditch her virginity. A distinguished man of the arts had invited himself to lunch: roses and champagne arrived by messenger that morning. These old-fashioned tokens destroyed her nerve and made her feel the generation gap acutely. Although she longed for sexual initiation, she was alarmed by the social situation. So she begged me to stay for the beginning of the lunch and I reluctantly agreed.

Around noon the temperature hit 98 degrees; I later learned that it established the century's record for that date. The suffocating, bone-melting heat defied our two tired little electric fans. My friend prepared the one dish she knew how to make: a casserole of cornflakes, condensed cream of mushroom soup, and canned tuna. Reassured by my duenna's presence, she put on a plunging black dress. But it wouldn't stay off the shoulders: the elasticized fabric kept springing up around her neck. So we anchored the neckline down with lots of concealed Band-Aids and pieces of Scotch tape. Then, sweating fiercely, we greeted her guest as billows of smoke from the sizzling casserole streamed through the apartment.

As I'd feared, he was fairly appalled to see me—not only because he'd expected an intimate lunch, but also because he knew my parents. Gloom gathered in his eyes as we sat down with disgusting gin drinks and the Band-

Aids worked their way out of my friend's décolletage and bits of tape shot into the air and swooped to the floor, while the stink of boiling tuna intensified until it seemed identical with sweat. Where, he asked timidly, was the champagne he'd sent? We explained that we'd broken the bottle while trying to open it—in the midst of our apologies the casserole exploded.

I rushed to scrape the stove, but my friend soon ran in to hiss, "Don't leave me!" She was finding him terribly difficult to talk with. He didn't respond to her response to Dylan Thomas, nor to her anecdote about Gide rejecting *Swann's Way* at Gallimard. Fortunately she had some more tuna and mushroom soup and cornflakes, so she served them to him cold. One of the fans broke down, and the other began to emit small electric groans. By this time her age was written all over his face. He'd had no idea that she was still in college, let alone a freshman, and he was wretchedly embarrassed. But the heat rendered all of us immobile: although he'd thrown out his gin when we did, he sat as though stupefied, warily sipping iced water.

Suddenly my boyfriend returned from a visit to the country; at that stage in his life he looked about fifteen. He pointed and said loudly, "Who's *that?*" as he always did on sighting one of our friend's not-quite-seducers. The dejected figure sprang gratefully to its feet: "I know your parents too! How *are* they?" It sounded as though he yearned for them to join us. Then he rallied enough to swallow a spoonful of wet cold soupy corn flakes, and to ask us about our professors and what they were writing. We barely knew our teachers, let alone their works in progress, but he seemed slightly less despondent when he tottered out into the August streets.

Soon afterward we heard that he'd said we were nice kids, all of us, but he'd added that we did seem awfully young for our age. And perhaps that was a paradox of the Fifties: when the young tried so hard to appear older they grew far more awkward—so much so that their elders regarded them as children: raw beings with very little to contribute. So that deepened our suspicion that we hadn't much to offer anyway.

16

Excavations

S~ex~, we had discovered, did not confer worldliness, and although—for those I knew best—there was no guilt in sexual pleasure, there were other wellsprings of guilt. The dead puritans who still seemed to shape the New England sensibility had declared that pride was the worst of the seven sins. Almost everything we'd read, from Milton to Melville, echoed that principle. Most of us were proud, therefore queasy—because we'd been educated to know we had small cause for self-esteem. Feeling special and feeling worthless created a dichotomy (the section men's favorite word) that sent quite a few to psychiatrists. Naturally the contradiction took a variety of forms—paralyzing dejection or frenetic activity, gorging or not being able to face food—but many of my contemporaries were stricken with a towering sense of deficiency, which battled with the arrogance that was also a legacy of our schooling. Unlike some of our reckless parents, we lived cautiously, but that was no protection against turmoil.

While people turn to psychiatry for many different reasons, my friends who did so in their late teens or early twenties were apt to be depressed by feelings of inadequacy—which put them acutely at odds with what was expected of them: at college or in an upcoming marriage, within their families or in ordinary dealings with acquaintances. Some also felt they didn't "fit" anywhere: they must be at fault because there seemed to be no place for them.

The Fifties have often been called "the heyday" of psychiatric treatment of the middle class. (Before the war only acute mental illness seemed to justify therapy; otherwise the flight to the couch implied weakness or self-indulgence.)

The profession was far more confident than it has been since: many psychiatrists thought they could cure almost any sort of disorder. Frequently the doctor's role was to assist the patient to function within the existing social order: to achieve a "healthy adaptation." This was a very American vision; for Sigmund Freud such an adjustment had not been a goal of analysis. And in this country, the idea that there might be different kinds of normality wasn't widespread. In the postwar years psychiatry had become a mainstream profession; as the field rapidly expanded it had attracted newcomers who were less imaginative than their professors, whose ranks included adventurous European emigrés. The respectabilities of the era were reflected in the values of some new practitioners, who looked on almost any "misbehavior" or "deviation from the norm" as pathological.

In the culture at large, a prevailing notion seemed to be that happiness meant health and that unhappiness was an ailment—which had not been Freud's view. (Freud believed that "ordinary unhappiness" was intrinsic to the human condition, and that psychoanalysis could only lead a patient "from the depths of neurotic despair to the level of general unhappiness which is the lot of mankind.") But the public wasn't familiar with Freud's sense of tragedy or his pessimism about complete "curability." Given the psychiatric optimism of the Fifties, a layman's expectations could be immense: psychotherapy should be able to uproot pain, and if it didn't, ongoing misery could almost seem like transgression.

The virtues of the nuclear family weren't often questioned: social workers strove to strengthen the family unit, to spur its members to love one another more "effectively." While anyone could understand that children needed loving parents, the conviction that families should remain intact at all costs and that relatives or married adults owed each other love led to some confusion. Love was seen as the remedy for nearly everything from delinquency or being overweight to the rage of the potential suicide, hence some psychiatric patients could feel terribly guilty if they didn't love their parents or husbands or wives. One friend of mine was told to "go home and work on your marriage" when the relationship was literally sickening to the mismatched young couple, whose main affliction was being married to one another.

The concept of latent troubles also impelled many into treatment: the inkling that you might have a *hidden* problem filtered through the ether of the Fifties. If things were not what they seemed—if the stud was really a homosexual, if the ultraprotective mother was actually hostile toward her children—the diffuse anxieties mirrored the broad, impersonal apprehensions of the period: was the next-door neighbor a subversive, were the Russians pilfering our newest atomic secrets? In the years when we had little communication with our perceived enemy, the Soviet Union, the home front itself seemed to be riddled with inscrutable threats and ambiguous fears. Even our science fiction movies reflected this concern: since the Martian invaders could take possession of human bodies, a friend or your favorite relative might become a menace. And at a time when it was difficult to define the enemy, your foe might also turn out to be yourself. The image of the adversary within reappeared throughout our popular culture: anyone might harbor a mysterious force which only an expert could exorcise or explain.

The psychiatrist was often seen as a mentor; the patient should trust his judgment. And if a patient passed from therapy to full analysis, he or she ought not to make any major decisions—such as marrying or divorcing or changing jobs—during the treatment. (Within the profession, a lengthy analysis entailing four or five sessions a week was held to be far more productive than weekly therapy—that is, if the patient had enough money and time.) Three women of twenty, all friends of mine, were warned by their psychiatrists not to get married once they had decided to do so, and each was told that she should embark on several years of analysis instead. None did. In at least one case the doctor's counsel was a stimulant: the bride married in rebellion against his admonition. The fact that those three marriages were ravaging later prompted some rueful hindsight among the young wives. But each had shrunk from entering the long, airless tunnel—the limbo of inaction—that analysis could appear to be. Some psychiatrists of the Fifties made the procedure sound benumbing—as though the psyche would be diminished in the course of all the adjusting and accommodations—rather than an illuminating journey into the self. In theory analysis was meant to put you in touch with feelings that you didn't know you had, or that you'd been dodging. But it seemed to some youthful patients that the aim of analysis was to dilute the intensity of your emotions: to feel whatever animated you less strongly.

These were the themes that recurred among my friends between the ages of eighteen and twenty-five. Only a few challenged their doctors, although one did reduce an authoritarian to tears: when she went to see him a year after she'd had a breakdown he hadn't foreseen. He wept, I think, because he hadn't recognized the gravity of her symptoms—so her crackup seemed like evidence of his own inadequacies; as her despair had crested he had informed her that she was "just going through a phase."

Some of the young drifted away from their psychiatrists after about a year, due to an amorphous feeling that the treatment didn't "take." This happened especially when the doctors were orthodox Freudians who rarely spoke or reacted. (Patients who kept questioning the doctor could be considered unco-operative—and that meant they were being "resistant.") Some who dropped out of therapy felt vaguely culpable: perhaps they hadn't been "good patients," since the doctors scarcely responded and the patients gained no particular insights from exhausting their voices in the presence of apparently passive ears.

I came across little criticism of the process in print until I read Salinger's "Zooey" when it was published in *The New Yorker*. As his sister Franny suc-cumbs to a psychic collapse, Zooey Glass tells his mother: "You just call in some analyst who's experienced in adjusting people to the joys of television, and *Life* magazine every Wednesday, and European travel, and the H-bomb, and Presidential elections, and the front page of the *Times*, and the responsibili-ties of the Westport and Oyster Bay Parent-Teacher Association, and God knows what else that's gloriously normal"—and predicts that Franny will be made even sicker by the treatment. Although I knew from my friends that some kinds of therapy could be harmful, I relished Salinger's audacity: for much of his audience the idea that the doctor knows best was still an article of faith.

And yet my own experience of psychiatry was utterly unlike most that were described to me. At nineteen I had a year of once-a-week sessions with a doctor who may have been exceptional for the period. (I deduce that she had been trained in the Thirties, when many mavericks entered the field.) In her office, filled with large plants and small trees, where the shelves were lined with the Gallimard editions of French poetry and fiction (it was she who first urged me to read Alain Fournier's *Le Grand Meaulnes*) and an elderly black Scottie dozed in a wicker basket, I learned how to link images—above all, those that upset me. The year before, my mother had slashed the veins of her wrists, throat, and ankles in the bathtub, and I had always imagined that scene suffused with steam: from the hot water tap that was running. She was found just in time to preserve the life she didn't want, but she lost some fingertips to gangrene.

Six months after that tub had overflowed I was a chambermaid for a summer at a huge turn-of-the-century hotel on Monhegan Island, off the coast of Maine. It was my task to keep the bathtubs clean: a ritual that became obsessive after the hotel-owner scolded me for not scrubbing them thoroughly. Mean-while the island was cloaked in a thick, choking fog that rotted leaves and grasses and didn't lift for a month—very unusual in midsummer—while I grew frantic about failing to scour the enamel sufficiently: the rings and the stains seemed to reappear almost hourly. And everything was decaying within the dense, motionless vapor that surrounded us: mushrooms and fruit and birds' nests and wildflowers and the hotel's upholstery; everywhere one encountered slime that seemed like a foretaste of death.

The psychiatrist helped me to see that the Monhegan bathtubs and the fog had re-created my mother's nearly successful suicide, which I felt I should somehow have prevented. Moreover the doctor enabled me to understand that I could not expunge my mother's perennial death wish: it was not up to me to wash out the years of suffering that had spilt her blood; in fact no one could clean up the past. That comprehension dissolved the ferocious insomnia which had assailed the inept chambermaid, and freed me to sleep and eat as I hadn't in months. The treatment continued as a workshop where I could bring the unremitting troubles of my parents, hoping that I would not repeat their history.

Therefore, since I had profited enormously from therapy, I was appalled by the psychiatric ordeals of my friends—all the more so because my doctor had never suggested that I should live in accord with convention. (She occasionally remarked that my enthusiasm for simple forms of freedom might offend conservative persons, but she encouraged me not to be too disturbed by their reactions. And she seemed very cordial to exploration: after all she'd loaned me Le Grand Meaulnes.) So I burned with indignation at the accounts of those whose doctors had made them feel "maladjusted"—when their singularities seemed admirable to me.

In the meantime jokes about psychiatry were plentiful, especially from young men who hoped to elude the draft: should they wear earrings and make eyes at the army shrink in order to be declared unfit for service? Or perhaps they might concoct a few homicidal fantasies, or claim that Lizzie Borden was their favorite heroine. (Those who had never consulted a psychiatrist assumed that head doctors were gullible.) But the levity disappeared if someone mentioned Korea.

While the war was still on, a friend of mine said between his teeth that he couldn't and wouldn't kill anyone; convinced that he would fail his midyear exams, positive that he would then be drafted—and he was probably right on both counts—he had a severe breakdown at nineteen. The illness may have been inevitable, but the deadline of failure and the army seemed to have hastened it.

Earlier, when we were at boarding school together, he used to climb trees and swing lightly from branch to branch with a grace that's rare among primates. Earthbound by plumpness and clumsiness, I loved to watch him: that forthright celebration of the body was infectious even if one couldn't imitate it. He also had a gift for perceiving comedy in the habits of wild creatures or in the lines of a landscape: nature amused as well as sustained him, and his puns were the nimblest I'd heard. We shared a pagan delight in the Vermont mud season: in March we played in the melting ooze of snow and soil that preceded spring, running down hills and jumping over rocks from which he leaped to dangle from a bough against the sky.

Later, as his crisis approached, he struggled for sanity by reviving the rhythms of adolescence: he scaled the trees in Harvard Yard and in the January dusk of Mount Auburn Cemetery. Several months afterward, when I visited him at the hospital—Bloomingdale, in White Plains—I was asked to talk with his psychiatrist beforehand. That complacent doctor seemed to embody much that repelled me about the analysts of the period. One particular conversation with him seemed worth writing down at the time. "What," he enquired, "about all this tree climbing?"

"I'd do it too if I could," I said, "Only I'm not built that way." (Deadpan: I was hoping to get a rise out of him.)

He replied that my friend was trying to work his way back through evolution, that he wanted to be an ape. I protested that climbing just made him feel better, it was like dancing, and that it brought relief when he was deeply depressed. No, said the doctor, it was a sign of profound sickness: climbing couldn't be carefree.

The theory of evolution was belabored until the patient, who longed to get out of the hospital, learned to give all the right answers: it was quite easy, he told me. He also wove a number of baskets. Occupational therapy was in vogue in the Fifties: a patient could choose between ceramics and woodwork and weaving or making plastic wallets. It seemed to me that my friend was also taught self-loathing in that institution; in one letter he wrote that he hated the feelings induced by his illness so much that he hated the object that contained them: which happened to be himself.

After a year he was released, and—perhaps to dispel the symbolism with which his doctors had invested roots, trunks, limbs, and leaves—he took a job as a tree surgeon. Months later he fell from a branch that was some forty feet above the ground. No bones were broken, but he walked for a while like someone who has been dropped from a great height: shoulders hunched, knees bent. The playfulness—which had somehow survived the hospital—receded, and he no longer climbed for pleasure.

The psychiatrist's other preoccupation (at least when he questioned me) had been the abnormality of a young man who showed such resistance toward the army and to war. Healthy men wanted to serve, the doctor said.

17

On the Balcony

Perhaps each decade devises new ways for the sexes to fall out of step. In the Fifties many educated persons paid lip service to equality, but neither sex was ready to deal with it. While I wanted to believe in the sincerity of those who said the sexes were equal, I also wished to believe that the issue belonged to the past: that the suffragists of my grandmother's generation had won equal rights for all of us along with the vote. Although outspoken feminists were scarce, I was told they were chaining themselves to railings which were no longer there: fictitious barriers of their own invention. (It was also said that they were neurotics who were exaggerating their own very personal problems.) Like some other young women, I was fearful that if inequities were even discussed, the delicate balance between the sexes would be upset, then destroyed: that we would all suffer if anyone challenged the precarious equilibrium. So I dodged the whole subject, refusing to think about it—even when society signaled that I should rest on its lower rungs.

I was able to maintain the delusion that women could expect equal treatment because my family was quite liberated and I was always urged to think carefully about my choice of work. But since my parents and their friends would not talk about money, no one admitted that equal pay was a mirage. And almost no family background was strong enough to combat the attitudes of the world one entered at eighteen. When Sylvia Plath, aged nineteen, wrote in her diary, "Why can't I try on different lives, like dresses, to see which fits best and is most becoming?", she was uneasy with the consistency prescribed for women— when experimentation was for men.

Yet the young men I knew weren't raging chauvinists. In fact many have said they were daunted by the period's concept of virility. Measuring themselves against Marlon Brando or Paul Newman, male English majors could feel effete. Education was thought to be emasculating. Humbled by the image of a sweating hulk in a torn T-shirt or by memories of Brando smashing a bottle against a mirror before the rape in A *Streetcar Named Desire* and the triumphant scowl of *On the Waterfront*, some men seemed to suspect that truck drivers or lumberjacks must appear far more potent than they. And since the idea of "latent" homosexuality was a tremendous threat for them—some worried that they might wake up one morning and discover themselves to be gay—a few adopted a hyper-male persona in order to reassure themselves: riding a motorcycle without a helmet, cuffing one another in hallways, claiming that a little violence between the sexes was exciting. (Although *Tea and Sympathy* was a sentimental play, it did distill the anxieties of the time: an unathletic boy whose "artistic" interests inspired his peers to call him "sisterboy," an older man who behaved like a jock to mask his fatal predilection. The play implied that it would be catastrophic to be homosexual.) Young men who didn't attempt machismo worked on an aura of authority: a defense strategy of liberal arts graduates. The men vented their own uncertainties on their female classmates: the insecure tried to raise themselves above the insecure.

So when David Riesman wrote that "American men seem constantly pursued by the fear of unmanliness, and therefore feel the need to present themselves as hard and realistic," he was stating what many twenty-year-olds, male or female, could have told him. Meanwhile women were asked to be mysterious— which really meant suppressing or withholding a part of themselves. Another style was Audrey Hepburn's: sensitivity, the appeal of the high-class waif—a gamine who could romp a bit, but was very much a lady after all. Based on vestigial social snobbery, "being a lady" satisfied an aesthetic code of behavior while hinting at privileges in the wings.

A number of young women did fashion themselves on Hepburn: the downcast eyes, the wistful poise, the vulnerability worn like an expensive garment. But no one with sizable breasts could mimic her. Breasts were rather controversial: the culture extolled them, but large ones were a joke. It was hard to get them right. Needing a bosom, a skeletal schoolmate of mine stuffed her strapless gown with fresh Kotex, which worked its way out of the sides and back of her bodice during a Christmas dance: her partners' pockets were soon filled with sanitary napkins. But those with ample cleavage tended to slump, and tight sweaters stretched over full breasts belonged to the uncouth.

• • •

What was attractive or desirable, or how one "ought" to be: all these made the mind clang with confusion. Contradictions about the nature of womanhood were ferocious in the Fifties. We heard that we were more compassionate than men, but young women knew that was not true of one another. If women were praised for their fortitude—when they were supportive of men and children—they were frequently denounced as overbearing. They were said to be sensible and literal—in contrast to the imaginative male—but they were also accused of being irrational. It was stressed that women weren't competitive, but they were presumed to be in ceaseless competition with each other (over men) and with men. They were masochists, requiring pain to remind them that their greatest experience was childbirth, yet cruelty to others could titillate them. A woman was inherently dependent—but that very quality was oppressive to the men who had to look after her. She was passive, but she would have to "catch" a man: who would resist entrapment. She liked to wait on her husband, but then she made him pay for her services by becoming a spiteful servant, a hostile martyr. She'd been put on earth to comfort and invigorate those who thought her capable of smothering, shackling, and crippling them. She was practical, she was "a realist," but she should be gifted at casting spells.

Entering the ranks of ultra-femininity, some of us ditched our jeans for intricate costumes: stoles, crinolines, capes, fringes, layers of tulle, earrings made from enormous sprays of rhinestones, artificial flowers, heavy perfumes, as much fantasy as possible. While I'm still fond of fantasy I recall how much effort was needed to keep all the paraphernalia in place, and what my family called "stole control" took special concentration: the things often slipped or got snagged on furniture or other people. Much of the raiment was rather Pre-Raphaelite, and the brilliant colors—the purple, orange, and red—were also emblems of defiance: to disconcert the navy blue and brown tweed squares. (Young men had no such options, since male attire aimed at being both invisible and correct.) Some female aesthetes cherished the notion of personal deportment as a work of art: through one's gestures, even the way one picked up a glass or crossed a room, all a bit arduous for uncoordinated adolescents. The tulle and the stoles caught fire when you were learning to smoke, and some of the drapery got singed.

Later I realized that the super-feminine style was a statement—almost a plea—to men: it was a way of entreating them not to be alarmed by the fact that you had a mind and that you intended to use it. The manner was a device for hiding the intellect: wrapping it in organdy and feathers, wreathing it in fine French smells. Energy too was hidden: in a rather languid, formal demeanor, ornate sentences—the pace of thought was deliberately slowed down. The goal was an elegance that masked vitality. Throughout you were promising to be amusing and light in hopes that you wouldn't be spurned by men. So there was also an attempt to manipulate men: to charm them into thinking that you weren't too serious, that you didn't judge their abilities or their characters as they judged one another's.

But all sorts of women, charming or not, were being depicted as saboteurs. The American male's fear of women permeated the atmosphere of the Fifties; the legacy of Freud's popularizers—who had elaborated the theory of penis envy until almost any women could appear to be a potential castrator—was everywhere. In *Generation of Vipers*, a best-seller in the Forties, Philip Wylie announced that we dwelled in a matriarchy where "the women of America raped the men," and that "the destroying mother" was as dangerous to her husband as to her sons. *Modern Woman: The Lost Sex*, by psychoanalyst Maryania Farnham and sociologist Ferdinand Lundberg, published in 1947, not only pilloried independent women but warned that single females were a menace because many of them became teachers; since "all mature childless women" were "emotionally disturbed," they were likely to damage their students' psychic health and should "be barred by law" from teaching. As for feminists of previous eras, "when they came to perform the sexual act . . . they were frigid." Even those who hadn't read these books—as I had not—could hear the echoes of their influence throughout the culture. A woman could also be seen as an unclean temptress who distracted men from their work, then caused them to debase themselves. And trying to assuage the masculine fear of wives and mothers and unmarried women was central to a young girl's training. Because men were said to feel so vulnerable, you were supposed to treat them as though you thought they were superior—even when you didn't believe it for a moment. Yet you didn't have to play dumb: allusions to literature, or an appreciation of the arts, were part of being feminine.

At heart the style was similar to camping, since it could be an effort to disguise pain: at being classed as inferior. And it was a male habit to see intelligence in women as "bitchery": being bright or sharp meant that you might be mean, equipped with talons. A prominent writer told me that a magazine editor had eagerly asked her, "Can you be a bitch? I want a bitch!" He was hiring a critic, but it didn't occur to him to phrase it that way. She added that she often wore pastel colors to the office.

Philip Wylie had compared the evil mother to Medusa, the snake-haired gorgon whose face was so hideous that those who looked at her turned to stone. It was hardly common knowledge that Freud regarded the head of Medusa, which he called "a symbol of horror," as an image for the vagina. But even in the classroom, you could catch a hint of the revulsion. In the Fifties Harvard's best-known anthropologist used to start the first session of his survey course by asking the women students to cross their legs; after they did he said, "Now that the gates of hell are closed, the lecture can begin." Repeatedly we heard that we had magical powers; sometimes it wasn't a compliment.

Femininity was also equated with male homosexuality. Women and gay men were often thrust into the same category: since both were threatening to the standard of machismo, misogyny and homophobia were close kin. So while you labored to charm men, some of them made it plain that the trappings of femininity—the flowers, the abundance of pink and mauve—made them uncomfortable and suspicious. Many young men seemed unnerved when women expressed their sexuality through their behavior or their clothes. Sexiness was supposed to be subtle. One friend of mine called it "doing the Lorelei stunt." Since a woman couldn't take any sexual initiative, she ought to sit on a rock and sing to the air, beguiling men without making direct signals.

It simply wasn't acknowledged that men and women possess many of the same feelings: about work, about love, about the difficulties of survival. While I wasn't asked to be one of the boys—a complaint I heard from some older women who'd felt obliged to appear enthusiastic about football teams and poker games which didn't interest them—I sensed that quite a few of my Harvard classmates wanted me to be a man, or wanted to think of me as one. That was probably a rather friendly impulse on their part, because anyone who wished a young woman well for the future couldn't expect her to be welcome in the professions. Now and then someone would tell me that I had "a male mind," and I would feel vaguely insulted, even though I had no feminism. Later on some of my male friends approved when I worked hard for little money and lived in a basement: they seemed to think it was good for my character, that it would make a man of me.

Also if they could ignore the fact that I was a woman, they could feel more at ease in my company. I resented the young men's resentment of my female self. But I had no idea of what to do about that. Hence the allure, for some young women, of older foreign men. It was our hope that—just because they were older—they wouldn't be put off by enterprising women. And men of other nationalities were rumored to be more amorous than American men.

So one waded through a sluggish evening with a man over thirty whose accent might have come from Paris or Prague, listening to a soliloquy about synthetic fibers—waiting for the hidden music to begin and then pining for dessert, coffee, escape. Then there was a dinner with an eloquent Englishman whose monologue became a diatribe against American education, American architecture, American landscapes from Connecticut ("Too many trees") to Long Island ("All those fields wasted without cows"), American cooking, American barbers, the weather, nylon sheets, and chlorophyll dog food: one might find oneself held personally responsible for drum majorettes and John Foster Dulles. After a lecture on vulgarity, "massive retaliation," and the rudeness of all Americans, the charms of a BBC accent receded, and one dined with a melancholy Italian who had a great deal to say about his visa problems.

• • •

Back among one's compatriots it was clear that a woman could be penalized for projecting the feminine persona of the Fifties: what was praised was also mistrusted. You were either too womanly or you had too much in common with men. And the public role-playing that seemed to be necessary denied you much diversity of character—if you agreed to participate in a myth or to appear as stoical as a statue. The woman on the balcony felt hampered by the imagery of others. And if she belched or lost her car keys or spilled soup on the floor, her audience might be repelled. Bored and restless upon the balcony, she learned that some will not forgive the loss of an illusion. So she usually played her part with the knowledge that her nature, like her flaws, should be concealed—if she was to be thought attractive. At the same time men were pretending to be much stronger or more decisive than they felt. On each side deception seemed to be essential. Small wonder that many young persons hardly knew who they were marrying—when both sexes were performing skits for one another. Several years after the weddings, it would turn out that some marriages had been based on mistaken identities.

Although every era has its dishonesties, I think the Fifties demanded more masks and facades than others I've known. If a young man wished to see himself as a master, a woman had to bolster his fantasy. Reluctantly I realized that many men depended on us to make them feel invincible. (Yet that dependency could make them angry: when they relied on us to tell them that they were self-reliant.) Women also camouflaged their opinions and ambitions so that men could be infatuated with their own imaginations—about the devotion of the women they chose. Once when I was about to sneeze and my eyes watered, the man sitting across the table said tenderly that no one had ever wept for love of him before. Somehow I stifled the sneeze; since I did love him I managed not to laugh.

Deceit was almost a reflex for my contemporaries. A young man I knew used to tell his parents, "I'll be back in twenty minutes!" and then vanish for a whole day; they didn't notice how long he was gone because they believed he would soon return. The subterfuge was unnecessary when he was twenty-one: it was just how our generation tended to behave. Then he ridiculed those who were duped. Like many of us, he sensed that the young should hide their actions and their thoughts from older people and from the public at large: secrecy was self-protection for individuals who weren't in accord with the status quo. And having a secret makes you feel cleverer than anyone who seems to be more powerful than you are.

Mutineers knew how to feign submission: if you were scheming to break a rule, to play hooky from convention, you didn't do it by daylight. Dissembling was our way of appearing to be obedient, and dishonesty about our motives and emotions was probably even more universal among young women than men. Perhaps we had more practice than they did. Laughing politely at a feeble joke, shoving a can of beer or a diaphragm under a dormitory mattress, being deferential to a dull man at a party: all these prepared you for arranging an illegal abortion when almost everyone assumed you were a virgin. And if you were in love, you ought not to tell a new boyfriend too much about yourself, especially not about anxieties and depressions. But if he was glad to misunderstand you, it was easy to captivate him. So you perfected your sleight of hand: you learned how to make parts of yourself disappear.

In any period the unattainable has always seemed romantic. Still a person who appeared to be "aloof" or a situation that seemed "impossible" (a word often pronounced with relish) suited the taste of an era when the literary section men celebrated the themes of renunciation in Henry James's novels, the unlikelihood of satisfaction detailed by Proust, the utter hopelessness of Yeats's yearning for Maude Gonne, the pessimism about human relations in Eliot's *The Cocktail Party*. So the most desirable woman might be one who was known mainly at a distance—an acquaintance who could be admired because she was almost a stranger, not a venturesome, menstruating mortal.

• • •

You kept hearing that women wanted to get married and men didn't. But among those with whom I grew up, it was quite often the other way around— at least as far as early marriage was concerned. There was a rift between young women who wanted adventure and young men who wanted security. Adventure meant travel, self-development, and also a certain passivity: allowing the world to reveal you to yourself and just seeing *what would happen* if you left yourself open to anything that might occur. Of course that curiosity was literary. But some equally literary young men craved hot regular meals and tranquil evenings at home, a stable rhythm, sanctuary at twenty-two and twenty-three.

Naturally the romantic women and the very domestic men were perplexing to one another. Perhaps the acute male domesticity was a response to the ominous prospect of jobs and offices, where a degree in English was no recommendation and might be a liability. The men I knew best expected to be at odds with their jobs. So a beginner wanted someone at his side when he entered the fray. It was easier for young women to be romantics: even those who had to support themselves hadn't heard much about the debilitations of the marketplace, as the young men had.

Most of my friends, especially the women, went through severe contortions in making the decision to marry. After months of vacillation, some finally made the leap *because* they couldn't decide, because they were so uncertain. Our New England schooling decreed that indecision was disgusting: you must be a worm if you can't make up your mind. So a lot of the young took the plunge for that reason. Many also thought that marriage was inevitable. Moreover marriage seemed to offer freedom to those of twenty-one: getting away from your parents' home, becoming a grownup who could no longer be controlled by anyone. For some, marriage was an attempt at escape: a flight from experience rather than a way of starting a life. And a few married as an act of defiance: against the elders who beseeched the young to wait, to live a little, not to commit themselves just yet.

As for the inevitability of marriage: it was often said that when a young couple had been together for a while, they should "marry or quit"—that was a common phrase. Among those who had traveled or lived with each other for a summer, the issue was time: time spent, time invested. Certainly "investment" was an image of the age: you put money or months into acquiring a possession for the future: a home or a husband or a wife. Just like money, time should not be wasted: you were supposed to get something in return. Hence the dislike (and sometimes horror) of "a halfway house," another phrase I recall. A halfway house was a relationship which dragged on without turning into a marriage. And the supreme test of love was its permanence: what didn't last couldn't be considered worthwhile. A romantic like myself could feel that love had a better chance of surviving without marriage, but almost no one I knew held that view.

Some of us who were nervous about marriage tried to distinguish between our rational fears and irrational terrors. As a native of Manhattan, where so many marriages I'd known had been disastrous, I suspected that being married meant being unhappy, and that a miserable marriage could do abiding harm: I'd seen middle-aged casualties who seemed to be injured for life. When I admitted my apprehensions to a few seasoned New Yorkers, they were sympathetic, and they couldn't claim that marriage had agreed with many of their friends. Yet since each generation hopes that the next one will do better, some of those veterans talked as though the cure for fearing marriage was marriage itself: get married and the dread will evaporate—as though one's doubts were traditional but not valid. "Conquering" a distrust of marriage by going through with it was a familiar ritual of the period.

According to national statistics, young people in the Fifties married earlier than had any other generation in this century. By 1959 nearly 50 percent of all brides were under nineteen. Also a greater percentage of the population was married than ever before. But while the Fifties exalted marriage, some of us who weren't in tune with the period grew up with the feeling that divorce might be the norm—that is, when we looked at couples who had married in the Twenties and Thirties. Yet we were careful not to say this outside a small group of intimates, since women who questioned marriage would be branded as terribly neurotic. My friends and I had a cloudy impression that you probably ought to be faithful after marrying because we could see that our parents' polygamy had had its penalties. We were anxious not to make the same mistakes, but no one had an alternate recipe on hand.

As soon as an engagement was announced there was an avalanche of wedding gifts: a couple could feel they were being buried together. Though a number of us came from families that were unimpressed by belongings, many young people later found that they'd amassed a lot of objects which weighed them down and complicated their daily lives. There were sets of brandy snifters and spice racks and ice buckets made of soft red plastic foam or pseudo-silver, martini shakers and cake stands, enormous two-part stereos and infrared Rotiss-O-Mats and bamboo trolleys for dinner on the couch that unfolded into a bed. There were mint dishes, gigantic pepper mills, pâté molds, escargot plates. It was hard to avoid ownership, which showed that you were a responsible person. Before I was married, when older friends asked what presents I wanted—"Linen or flatware?"—some were disturbed when I said money for travel: for the many trips my future husband and I wished to take. That sounded sinister to several, and I got a lecture about furniture as a symbol of commitment. When I spoke of Greece, a sectional sofa was suggested, and I was told that skiing in the Alps would not be a good alternative to a rug.

• • •

Even though many American women had relinquished their wartime jobs soon after the GIs returned, more than ever before were working by the mid-Fifties, when twenty-two million women were employed in a third of the nation's jobs. But of course most were poorly paid and sparsely promoted. At the end of 1956 *Life* paid tribute to the working woman: "Household skills take her into the garment trades; neat and personable, she becomes office worker and saleslady; patient and dexterous, she does well on repetitive, detailed factory work; compassionate, she becomes teacher and nurse." The colossal resistance to women who wanted substantial careers caused some with recent degrees to reevaluate their concept of work. They no longer heard about self-enrichment. Instead the female spirit was alleged to thrive on drudgery. And many employers seemed to typecast women by their looks: a very short, round-faced mathematician I knew was urged to apply for a job in a kindergarten—when she was qualified to teach calculus to the twelfth grade. As for those who hoped to write or paint, such pursuits were thought harmless if they were confined to a few years: before the children were born. I once heard the desire to write compared to a childhood disease: like mumps or measles it would run its course—a healthy life would not be disrupted for too long.

From the suburbs there were reports of bake sales. Some of my schoolmates had husbands whose professions had moved them all over the country, often to communities where the wives' credentials from previous jobs were inapplicable. Those who were self-employed or studying medicine were viewed with suspicion—as though they were unbalanced cranks who didn't like children—and other women pressured them quite grimly to participate in the local bake sales. When they politely replied that they didn't have time to make droves of pies and cookies for the Girl Scouts or the church supper, and volunteered to contribute money they'd earned to the fund-raising drive, they were chided for withholding their "home skills" and their work was called "a hobby."

However, in a city like New York, dilettantes were damned to a degree that disoriented some young women: those who loved reading and going to concerts but didn't aspire to a career in the arts. The brides whose priority had been marriage, who wished to raise children while continuing to enjoy literature and to play the piano, were sometimes hurt and bewildered. In theory they should have earned the public's approval: for putting marriage and family first.

But many were scorned as triflers and dabblers: Manhattan, like Harvard, found such women uninteresting, and they were snubbed if they tried to join a conversation about God or Gropius, Verdi or Auden.

So the crossed signals of the culture persisted in keeping bright young women in a double bind: whether they designed buildings or wheeled their babies to the park or subscribed to the new season at the opera or served up a fine salmon mousse, they were always lacking in some dimension that a satisfactory woman ought to have.

18

*The Poets' Theatre
and the Beats*

"Can I have the bacon out of your BLT?"

It seemed like cause for justifiable homicide, that question, which Gregory Corso asked nearly every day. What was the point of a lettuce and tomato sandwich on toast—bereft of bacon? Lounging at the cafeteria steam table, lulled with postadolescent greed after hearing the pleasing yell to the kitchen— "B-L-T—*down*! Mayo!"—I would brace myself for Corso's punctual request: "Like can I have the bacon—"

"No!"

I couldn't then recognize a small cultural collision—between insubordinate persons who were incapable of sharing anything, even a sandwich. Both Corso and I were spending a summer at the Poets' Theatre, near Harvard Square. Friends of mine had rented the theater: a small loft decorated in what we were told was "the taste of Léger" (terra cotta walls, black and white details), which had superseded plans for "the taste of Cecil Beaton." There was almost no backstage space; in warm weather the actors waited for their entrances outside the theater in the fallout zone of a restaurant whose garbage sometimes spattered their doublets or veils.

The original Poets' Theatre, founded in 1950, was a loose affiliation of poets living in Cambridge; the senior members included Richard Eberhardt, John Ciardi, and Richard Wilbur, and among the fairly recent Harvard graduates were Lyon Phelps (who initiated the concept of the theater), Alison Lurie, Edward Gorey, Donald Hall, John Ashbery, and Frank O'Hara. The objective was to generate work by poets who would act, administrate, direct, and sell tickets—while retaining total control of their own writing. There would be workshops where playwrights could refine unfinished scenes, and the goal was the emergence of an American verse theater. But none of its members could agree on a precise definition of the new sensibility they sought to forge. Wilbur said the Poets' Theatre was like the Communist Party: everyone belonged to it, but no one wanted to admit it.

A galvanizing force was Molly Howe, also known as Mary Manning: the Irish playwright and novelist who was trained at the Abbey Theatre in the Twenties, where she was rehearsed by Yeats in his *Countess Cathleen*. (She said Yeats was an "appalling" director: he sat at the back of the theater, "vaguely" waving his hands to indicate where and how the actors should move.) Her first plays had been performed at the Gate Theatre in Ireland. Sometimes called the Lady Gregory of the Poets' Theatre, she was its theatrical conscience: she knew better than any of her young colleagues what was playable, what would or wouldn't work onstage. And since Yeats and Synge had been able to revolutionize the theater in Dublin early in the century and in equally threadbare circumstances, she felt that something similar should be possible in Cambridge, Massachusetts, in the Fifties.

The results of reviving poetic drama were more than catholic: the productions I saw there ranged from William Alfred's moving *Agamemnon*—which dwelled on the private angers that persist after a war ends—to an ingenious spoof of a Japanese Noh play and a lumbering skit in which the cast capered about in pink union suits, exclaiming, "*Is* this it?" "Is *this* it?" and (finally) "This is *indeed* it." Noh plays—which required little scenery and few actors—were cheap to produce, and a number of them were done in earnest. Incest was a favorite topic among the fledgling dramatists. There was also a Salem witch play that predated *The Crucible*: its most memorable moment occurred when the actor cast as Giles Corey—who was being slowly crushed to death beneath a mound of stones offstage—loudly grunted "*Pile . . . on . . . more . . . rocks*" in tones of agonized constipation.

Some of the plays that the Poets wrote were shot with old-fashioned surrealism, and there were strong echoes of Cocteau or whiffs of Ionesco, rather than distinctly American voices. But the group seethed with confidence. After all there had been an upsurge of verse drama in the Forties, stemming from Eliot's plays and the success of Christopher Fry's; in the early Fifties Auden and Isherwood's *The Dog Beneath the Skin* was produced at Harvard, where the plays of William Carlos Wiliams were also admired, and Dylan Thomas came to give *Under Milk Wood* its first reading in America at the invitation of the Poets' Theatre—on all sides there seemed to be evidence that poetic drama was worthy of a life commitment. Some of the Poets were elated by doing readings of Wilbur's translation of *The Misanthrope*: they felt he was turning pure couplets for the first time since Pope and perfecting a modern verse voice for Molière. Senior poets like Archibald MacLeish affirmed that the lyric would never die. It seemed that a new Elizabethan age of playwriting was at hand, and the Poets' Theatre was the institution which would unite prophecy and literature with performance. In that heady atmosphere, poets who'd had little interest in dramatic forms began to write plays.

A few who were involved with the theatre even invoked Shakespeare—"This music crept by me upon the waters"—as a source of their inspiration. Also Jacobean plays were expected to transform the content of verse drama, which would elevate domestic tragedy. (Thomas had recited soliloquies from the Jacobeans when he was in Cambridge, and his zeal was contagious.) But the theater always abounded with conflicting aspirations. Others in the group were kindled primarily by Cocteau's movies: they saw *La Belle et La Bête* repeatedly and would have been enraptured to produce *The Blood of a Poet* on the stage. Several wrote plays about Orpheus, locally known as "Orpheus things." Arnold Weinstein said that a line from *Les Enfants Terribles*—"Les privilèges de la beauté sont immenses!"—ought to have been emblazoned over their doorway, since that was all anyone needed to get into the Poets' Theatre.

The quasi-surrealists immersed themselves in "anti-books"—Salvador Dali's autobiographical novel, Raymond Queneau's *The Skin of Dreams*—while Gorey reread Djuana Barnes's *Nightwood*. Several explained Ronald Firbank to one another. But not everyone had a sense of mission about revitalizing poetic drama, and the theater answered a galaxy of appetites. Some had an acute hunger for European culture and European life. In those days Cambridge and Boston had almost no foreign movie theaters or decent restaurants, and those who had a romantic craving for other places and other times—prewar Paris or the St. Germain of the existentialists—were drawn to the Poets' Theatre because it seemed to evoke what they had never known: the European past. Most were middle-class provincials, and even those who didn't pine for the Left Bank found that joining the theater helped them to make a break with their own pasts: to discard the orthodoxies of the Midwest or the strictures of small New England towns.

And still other elements fertilized the Poets' soil. Gorey's late Victorian taste dominated the first productions: he designed most of the sets, and his frowning cherubs and somber fantasies recurred in the Poets' backdrops and posters. He also wrote the kind of short non-play they esteemed: in one of his creations a murderous teddy bear was attached to a string on which it was gradually pulled offstage while a husband and wife argued with one another. (They didn't know that the bear was on its way to strangle their baby in the nursery.) And although Frank O'Hara and John Ashbery were gone from Cambridge while the theater was developing, the conversational, anecdotal style of their early poetry influenced some of the playwrights who wrote in a formless fashion—which was the fashion of the time. Meanwhile performing in one another's plays increased the mutual involvement; Weinstein observed that he went onstage as if he were very carefully carrying a chalice full of words he didn't want to spill, which would be served up to the audience. "And if they didn't like the fare, we'd throw it at them!"

During the Poets' very first evening in 1951, the spectators laughed freely at the comic juxtaposition of images in O'Hara's one-act play, *Try! Try!* Thornton Wilder, who was a visiting lecturer that year, leaped to his feet at intermission and scolded them: how dared they laugh? How could they fail to recognize the vitality of the new "creative dramatic poetry in America"? Pacing to and fro while shaking his finger, he lectured his listeners until even the smiles were suppressed. Then he asked for contributions for the theater. The whole production had cost about a dollar—for a window shade that had been painted by Gorey, who compared Wilder's fervent performance to that of an irascible bee. The reviewers—such as Daniel Ellsberg of *The Harvard Crimson*—complained that some of the Poets' lines were difficult to follow, and William Alfred thought they were inclined toward "symbolic beanfeasts." But they were rarely troubled by the notion that parts of their work might be inaccessible; their attitude resembled the young Henry Adams's when he realized that Beethoven was "intelligible"—if a composer's music was so easily understood, then it must be overrated.

Naturally the group was charged with many aversions. Some detested the preciousness of Christopher Fry—although their own productions were sometimes precious. They were disturbed by Fry's popularity because his work seemed to fulfill a public need in a philistine era—to assuage the audience's feelings of guilt for not reading poetry: a guilt that could be dissolved by the penance of seeing Fry's *The Dark Is Light Enough*. And quite a few of the Poets disliked blank verse (even though some of them wrote it), because it could be a vehicle for "easy dualities," such as "honor versus dishonor" or "fame versus oblivion." They shrank from "meaningful statements" and they hated to be caught in the act of *"saying something,"* so they were embarrassed when a colleague's play included a poet's wand. There was also an antipathy to poetry that could be declaimed; instead they preferred the lowered, unauthoritative voice, and they loathed professionalism: Broadway and even Off-

Broadway were reviled. (Their program notes announced that "broad public appeal is not a factor in the selections.") Experiment or self-expression did not seem possible in the professional theater of the Fifties—not to those who were entranced by their revolt against the corporate and the commercial. Eschewing publicity was part of the mystique: people were welcome to come and see the plays—if they could find the theater. In their first years, before they had the loft, they performed on porches and in living rooms and churches, and were proud to feel like strolling players.

But unity was never an aim of the Poets' Theatre. Right from the start there were "bigwig walkout evenings," when exasperated dignitaries like Ciardi would exit from a meeting because the group would not support their projects. There were also fractious debates about whether to produce plays written in "poetic prose." Some of the fiercest battles erupted over the choices of performers: everyone wanted to act, but there weren't enough roles for all the poets. William Alfred said, "They fought like wet cats." There would often be a flurry of telegrams of resignation, citing "artistic differences"—these would arrive just before the dress rehearsals, so that the opposition had to capitulate at once. Some were trying to work out their personal destinies through the theater, and it was gratifying to reject others' verse or their habits of performance: "I won't direct this play if she's going to hold a candle like that!" Aesthetic dicta could also be used as bargaining chips among sexual rivals. The fabric of the Poets' Theatre was woven out of sex, poetry, and internal politics, and the feuds sometimes reflected the psychosexual competitions or the shifting arrangements for living. A perennial statement was: "I cannot go through this again. I've got to go home and *decide*"—whether to quit the theater or leave Cambridge or commit suicide.

The Poets' Theatre also had a congregational purpose: it was home for poets and performers in a period when artists were often seen as freaks, when homosexuality was regarded with horrified fascination. (There were a number of openly gay men in the group, and some of the heterosexuals savored the audacity that mocked the conventional world. Still the homosexuals took some teasing from those who had not left all of Topeka or White River Junction behind them.) Above all the company had an exciting aura of a counterculture, which was very hard to locate in the Fifties. As I watched their plays I seemed to share in their intentional delinquency—the delinquency of aesthetes who exulted in irreverence. Even though some of the plays were underwhelming, I was constantly impressed by the acting, since their productions featured some of the most talented performers in the Boston area.

The sense of community was heightened by the theater's indigence: Gorey called it the theater of poverty, and Molly Howe struggled valiantly to raise money whenever an oil bill or the Massachusetts Amusement Tax seemed likely to wipe out the institution, infuriated that no angels ever materialized to sustain what she felt could be a national verse theater. (During one financial emergency, many invitations were sent out for a fund-raising evening: $2 to attend, $5 to stay away, $6 to bring someone who hadn't been invited. Once again the theater was saved.) But some were charmed by the necessities of invention: making curtains for a proscenium that didn't exist, sewing their costumes while learning their lines, concocting lights out of big pineapple juice cans, lending each other jewelry for tomorrow's performance—there was a thrill in prevailing over penury. The theater could seat only forty-nine in its folding chairs; when a production was sold out, one or two people could perch on a sink at the back which always dripped a little; from there Felicia Lamport, a dedicated member of the board, saw an opening night "with a very wet colon."

This was the setting where Corso tried to plunder my sandwich, where I defended my bacon. He had been steered to the theater by V. R. Lang (known as Bunny), the poet, the playwright, and actress who was one of its key founders. Corso was already a good friend of Allen Ginsberg, whom Corso had met soon after serving a jail sentence for theft. Finding him destitute in New York, Bunny brought him to Cambridge and passed the hat among the cast and crew. Some of the young men lived in a boardinghouse they called O'Sullivan's Jungle, where the landlord's ancient father peed without remorse on the hall carpets; O'Sullivan explained, "He just doesn't care anymore." Bunny made the group shelter Corso—O'Sullivan's father would later appear in one of his poems—and she insisted that Corso be hired to sweep the theater.

Corso also had a walk-on (more of a spring-on) as a Jacobean madman in our production of Middleton and Rowley's *The Changeling*. One of his fellow maniacs was a sad-faced postal worker named Jerry Gellison, who should have been one of the century's great clowns. Bemused—like many others—by Yeats's Women of the Sidhe, who had drifted through our first production, Gellison enquired mournfully, "What in hell is a shape-changer?" The poet Allen Grossman embarked on a lengthy explanation of the Yeatsian vision of fairyland and the people of the wind, plus Yeats's theories of the imagination, while Gellison's narrow concave face grew almost tragic with regret: it was the living mask of anyone who was sorry he'd asked a particular question.

While it was almost impossible to wring a smile from Gellison, Corso's antics occasionally raised the corners of the drooping mouth. Corso was an amiable adjunct to the theater: he shouted and snarled with gusto when the mad people had to spring out of the shadows, and he did a bit of sweeping. But no one except Bunny could appreciate what would soon be a voice of the immediate future. We were still buried in the past; a modern poet meant Dylan Thomas, who was dead and therefore safe in the past too. Absorbed in reviving plays by Yeats and Lorca and the Jacobeans, we would never have guessed that Corso was about to prance out onto a much larger stage than the little stretch of uneven boards where we performed as courtiers and lunatics. At that time the most resonant name on our program belonged to the musician who made the drums for our Yeats plays: Kahlil Gibran, Jr.

One of our producers sometimes referred to Corso as "the black poet"— due to the blackness of his hair, his periodic scowl and his disdain for detergents, also his black garments. (Years afterward it was recalled that Corso wore Vietnamese guerilla clothes before we knew there were any: he did prefigure many things.) So the epithet wasn't intended as a compliment. But when Corso overheard it he was delighted: "Yes! I am! I am . . . the black poet." Before long *I.E., The Cambridge Review* published a poem in which Corso confronted the stygian state of his soul and the blackness of his perceptions while he rode the subway to Boston:

> . . . And I could hear
> The steel say to the steam
> and the steam to the roar: a black ahead
> A black ahead a black and nothing more.

After several years of Harvard's literary decorum I relished an exposure to Bunny, a superb comedian as well as a former Boston debutante who'd joined the chorus line in a Scollay Square burlesque house called the Old Howard when she needed to pay some debts; she either wrote, acted in, or directed each of the theater's early productions. A formidable presence, she had harsh blond hair, heavy jaws, and wide, expressive nostrils; her whispery, gutteral voice could coil from a sexy growl to a parody of prudery. Elegance and a whimsical reserve enhanced the lustiness of her performances, and her varied vocal range convulsed audiences nightly when she played a bawdy chambermaid in *The Changeling*. To me her poetry seemed arch and sententious and so did her plays, which were peopled with mythic figures but displayed the manner- isms of drawing room comedy. Yet for many who saw her act, she became a legend—and that nourished the reputation of her writing. To her public she appeared as a witty outlaw whose passions overflowed the confines of New

England gentility. Intent on killing the conventions, she seemed to think that whatever was *un*Bostonian was enlightened.

She was also gifted with authority: she could bully or beguile others into doing what she wanted. Those who knew her well cherished a temperament that seemed to thrive on challenges, while her colleagues were often awed by her aptitude for seizing control of situations. One day we had some trouble with the Cambridge fire inspectors: they suspected that the electricians' lightboard was a fire hazard in the tindery little loft, and no doubt it was. (The theater had previously been a sign painter's office, so decades of paint were embedded in the floors, and it did burn down a few years later.) The inspectors were about to slap us with a violation—which could have meant closing down indefinitely—when one of them sternly asked, "Do you have AC or DC?" Bunny swelled up and breathed, "Oh, we have *everything*." Jolted by the atmosphere of a sexual soup kitchen, the men fled, and we heard no more from them. Long silences during phone conversations were also a strategy for getting her way; Molly Howe's husband described Bunny's telephonic muteness as "extrasensory deception."

When she summoned friends to her court, they could anticipate a ritual. Bunny's parties in her family's Boston house were apt to be structured around a central event, which she directed: on one occasion the guests were bidden to reduce rose petals boiling in oil to some kind of essence, and the party revolved around a vast bubbling cauldron. There was usually a rich diversity of people: taxi drivers and policemen she'd encountered as well as poets. Her many admirers loved her apparent heedlessness—she wrote plays which had no professional future, and she ruined a couple of productions because it amused her to dress the cast in ludicrous costumes or to make them dance to preposterous music. Bunny embodied a crucial aspect of the Poets' Theatre: the anti-professionalism that exalted the enjoyment of the act itself with small regard for the results. The personal statement was far more important than its consequences. For some the nature of the theater was distilled in memories of driving in Bunny's jalopy after a badly received performance to a beach and plunging into the ocean when there was raging thunder but the lightning hadn't yet arrived, and then plunging back into the car in time for the last call at Cronin's, a beer joint where the Poets had a regular pew. Amid the high solemnities of Cambridge, where so many sat in judgment on one another, it was exhilarating to seem carefree, even careless.

Wherever she operated Bunny seemed to personify a world of cultural rebellions; her intimates fondly called her a subversive. For example, planting Corso in Cambridge was probably a deliberate act of sedition. No one at

Harvard—not even the New Yorkers—had met anyone like him, and she took him to starchy gatherings and urged him to be insolent. (She liked to scatter people in haphazard directions, to see how they would line up on return— the better to know them: her active form of knowledge was ongoing drama.) Corso then spent a year camping out in a couple of Harvard houses; to most of the New Critical section men he appeared as a symbolic threat to Harvard's traditions, an explosive device that might fragment custom and usage: the hipster language he imported was utterly new to Harvard Square.

Bunny soon injected lines like "Live it up and have a ball" and "You bug me" and "He flipped" into her verse plays—phrases that came from black jazz musicians via the incipient beats. Peter Sourian, a young Harvard novelist who acted in Bunny's *I Too Have Lived in Arcadia*, likened her to Marco Polo bringing back the gunpowder from Cathay: as an impeccably reared Bostonian as well as an explorer, she foresaw Corso's impact on the community—where his style and idiom became contagious for some restive undergraduates.

Certainly when Ginsberg subsequently lauded Corso as "a great word-slinger . . . a scientific master of mad mouthfuls of language," he was celebrating a form of poetry that was anathema to much of Harvard. Diverted by Corso's insurrectionary nature, Sourian constructed a tent of dyed sheets and metal poles in his room at Eliot House, where Corso slept and wrote; in the dining hall he once informed Archibald MacLeish, "You're not a poet!" Corso gave different reasons for having been in jail: sometimes he said he'd been sentenced for starting a bookstore with stolen books. And Sourian was sure that Bunny had plucked Corso from Greenwich Village to flout the Cantabridgian principles that she herself was eager to derail.

The Poets' Theatre continued to gyrate in many directions. Bunny was close to Frank O'Hara, and although he was in New York they traded their aesthetic discoveries: whatever stimulated him was funnelled through Bunny into the theater. (There was a sporadic linkage with the beats: Ginsberg was anxious to have O'Hara read a draft of *Howl* because O'Hara had introduced him to the work of Mayakovsky, whose public voice gave Ginsberg a direction for *Howl*.) The naturalistic intrusions of the beats' language tilted a few of the Poets toward the notion of an essentially American theater—and away from the re-creation of an imaginary Europe. Bunny's last (unfinished) play was about a pilot flying meat from Miami to the Caribbean, and she used proletarian speech for poetic effect. But the theater was also an Irish showcase. Molly Howe's excellent adaptation of *Finnegans Wake* was produced there in 1955, and it was praised by her old friend Samuel Beckett when it was later performed in Paris. (Beckett gave the Poets' Theatre permission to mount the first American production of *All That Fall*.) The group put on Denis Johnston's *The Dreaming Dust* and *The Scythe and the Sunset*, and Johnston directed Donagh MacDonagh's *Happy as Larry*. Tom and Liam Clancy appeared in a few of the Irish plays, long before they were acclaimed as folksingers. Eventually some deduced that the theater was becoming a mausoleum for Yeats.

In the midst of all these currents the Poets' Theatre became respectable, which was unsettling for some of its members; the Rockefeller Foundation bestowed small grants for poets in residence such as W. S. Merwin. Over the years a number of playwrights did fulfill the original concept of developing a natural speaking voice for poetry that emphasized American themes and speech patterns. Within little more than a decade of its existence, the Poets did plays by Paul Goodman, Archibald MacLeish, Robert Penn Warren, James Merrill, Howard Moss, Kenneth Koch, Peter Viereck, and several by Richard Eberhardt. They also produced works by Louis Simpson, Lawrence Durrell, and Ted Hughes. The group was exceedingly fluid, some of the founders were dispersed, there were always monetary crises, and yet a gallant merriment endured: everyone in the troupe worked very hard, but they didn't feel like drudges.

By the mid-Fifties the works of Brecht had magnetized some who had worshipped Yeats's plays, and they turned to a highly dissimilar form of verse drama. But the Poets' Theatre had yielded a premonition of the Off-Off-Broadway movement to come. As a small organization with a small audience, they'd maintained the freedom to experiment—feeling themselves at liberty to make mistakes, to try absolutely anything. In the Sixties phases of the Living Theatre and the Theatre of the Ridiculous sometimes reminded me of the Poets at their most provocative, and when the American Place Theatre produced Robert Lowell's plays and William Alfred's *Hogan's Goat*, I felt that company was perpetuating the Poets' intentions. Some evenings at the La Mama Theatre Club suggested that the more anarchistic dreams of the Poets' Theatre had come to pass, transmuted into improvisation and nudity. Their allegiance to the fantastic and to personal utterance had left a legacy, even though their commitment to literature was replaced by the gleeful anti-verbalism of their successors. In the late Sixties the spontaneity that some Poets had prized was triumphant—although the verse plays they had promoted were largely forgotten.

A year after our *Changeling* summer I ran into Bunny at the opening night of *Waiting for Godot* at the Arts Theatre in London: we were so enthralled by the play that we barely spoke of the Poets' Theatre. She was traveling with her new husband; in one more year she would be dead of cancer at the age of thirty-two. Later I was told that her extremely formal wedding was jammed with Bostonians remarking that it was "brave of her" to marry when she knew she was going to die. Some felt she got married because only a year was left to her. Many said that the theater changed greatly after her death in 1956; it lasted into the Sixties, but the sorcery it owed to Bunny was never quite regained. And I often thought of her when poets she had championed in their obscurity became familiar even to those who hardly read them.

• • •

Ambivalence toward the beat writers was inevitable for my generation. Their energies and their exuberance were appealing as they sought to atomize the constrictions of our culture. They suggested that existence was bristling with possibilities: the rucksack which could be packed at once, the bus or the car or the freight train that might speed one off to a new chapter of life at any moment, the random encounter that could blossom into an adventure. They restored passion to the landscape. And they helped to ventilate the concepts of literature which had been codified by the New Critics, especially when they maintained that their own experiences were valid subjects for poetry or fiction. The beats regarded T. S. Eliot's criticism, the Southern Agrarians, and *Partisan Review* as reactionary influences which had intimidated some who hoped to find new voices for a new mythology.

We'd been told that American innovations had ended with the Twenties and that there could not be another avant-garde. But Ginsberg and Kerouac and their disciples were dancing on untrodden ground, and one could savor their drastic brand of comedy along with the gleeful defiance of authority. Moreover their assumption that our society was destructive—at a time when the young were instructed that American values were the finest in the world— was most refreshing. A friend of mine who hadn't even tackled *On the Road* said that the example of the beats prevented him from taking a couple of bad highly paid jobs. Since they were immediately denounced by the literary establishment—in *Partisan Review* Norman Podhoretz was incensed by Ginsberg's enthusiasm for "spontaneous bop prosody"—they could be welcomed as disturbers of the peace.

But no one I knew could identify with their movement. For one thing, they were too old to represent those who came of age in the Fifties; the postwar fatigue of the "beat" that was supposed to make them receptive to enlightenment was alien to us, and so was their ecstatic approach to drugs. Some of my Harvard friends earned money as guinea pigs for drug research programs at the Massachusetts General and Boston Psychopathic hospitals; they received five dollars an hour for taking "regular drugs" and twenty-five dollars an hour for LSD. The projects mainly attracted young men who needed cash. (Years later they would learn that some of these programs were funded by the CIA or the army.) Although a few confessed that their participation made them feel rather special, they described their brief derangements without enthusiasm and some also became very depressed; there was no hint of the cult of acid soon to come.

An even larger barrier between us and the beats was a horror of chaos and madness shared by some who had mentally ill or alcoholic parents. When the beats romanticized psychosis we couldn't follow them—not after visiting a relative in Bellevue or attending a suicide's funeral. To me it seemed that a crackup like Holden Caulfield's was a commonplace of the middle class, not a badge of beatitude. Others, who shunned convention yet longed for psychic safety, didn't wish to find themselves drained or burned out, hence the beats' exalted exhaustion wasn't enticing. Much later I was humbled on learning that Ginsberg's mother had been even sicker than mine; he'd been devoted to the woman who believed that wires in the ceiling were attached to her head, that her family was trying to poison her, who saw Hitler's moustache in the sink, and he was drawn to outcasts, addicts, and the wounded who weren't as sane as he was. But I didn't expect the sick to be visionaries, and the road to Bellevue did not look like the path to insight.

I also recoiled from Kerouac's insistence on the holiness of everything and everyone; at times all that affirmation seemed asphyxiating. And when he wrote, "I knew, I knew like mad that everything I had ever known and ever would know was One," his version of Buddhism sounded sentimental. His mysticism was undoubtedly sincere, but Ginsberg was more gifted at expressing metaphysical emotions and the experience of satori (awakening). After they had studied Zen and Hinduism, Kerouac, a lifelong Catholic, found comfort in the Buddhist doctrine "All life is suffering." While I could appreciate Ginsberg's spiritual quest, I couldn't follow Kerouac when he claimed that he and his friends were saints. In New York in the late Fifties one kept meeting overnight Buddhists who said they'd found the Word—either in a paperback by D. T. Suzuki or Alan Watts or through their drugs of choice—but most seemed short on the serenity which Zen discipline can provide.

Black jazz, for those who loved Thelonious Monk, Charlie Parker, and Bud Powell, was a link to the beats, but most of my friends were unmoved by bebop, which had developed during World War II and seemed to be the property of older generations. And although many individuals who were at odds with the ethos of the Fifties were rather proud of being misfits—after all the outsider was a romantic figure—the transports and commotions of

Ginsberg and Kerouac often seemed uncool to the young, who were striving for self-control. Besides those men were public performers: a role that was distasteful to their juniors, who didn't want to be conspicuous; our own mutinies were very private indeed.

And there was certainly no place for women in Kerouac's universe, where chicks were seen as servants and bedwarmers. Kerouac's vision of women as emasculators, combined with Burroughs's extreme misogyny and Ginsberg's celebration of homosexuality, suffused the inscape of their writing. Kerouac's wrathful dependence on his mother—he lived with her for many of his adult years, and she took over his finances and forbade him to sleep with women in his own house—was perhaps responsible for the stunted female characters in his novels. His books gave little sense of sexual pleasure, merely sexual compulsion and scorekeeping.

William Burroughs's *Junkie* (published under the pseudonym "William Lee") seemed to me the most compelling narrative that the group produced in the Fifties; the book submerged the reader in the mid-Forties heroin culture: the scenes in scarred railroad flats and Times Square bars and subway tunnels were lit with a savage authenticity that made one feel almost at home in realms that were both foreign and frightening. And passages of Ginsberg's Whitmanesque *Howl* were mesmerizing, as when he wrote about his friends "who jumped off the Brooklyn Bridge this actually happened and walked away unknown and forgotten into the ghostly daze of Chinatown soup alleyways & firetrucks, not even one free beer . . . who demanded sanity trials accusing the radio of hypnotism & were left with their insanity & their hands & a hung jury, who threw potato salad at CCNY lecturers on Dadaism . . ." In 1959 Ginsberg was reading drafts of his *Kaddish* aloud in Lower East Side lofts: one of his finest works was born when the decade died.

But while spurts of Kerouac's frankness had charm— "I like too many things and get all confused and hung-up running from one falling star to another until I drop"—I had to start *On the Road* several times before I could finish it. Since he embraced Thomas Wolfe as his model and then imitated the worst of Wolfe, since the benzedrine rhythms of his prose accentuated the naiveté of his personae, it appeared that "writing in accordance . . . with the laws of orgasm" could be an invitation to blather. Admittedly the portrait of Burroughs—intentionally patronizing the dullest bars in New Orleans, jabbing heroin into his tired veins, reading Kafka, shooting at amphetamine tubes with an air gun, building a shelf meant to last for a thousand years, throwing knives, and disappearing into his orgone box—was hilarious. Yet I squirmed at the novel's pretensions to prophecy and "the wild yea-saying overburst of American joy." And even before the civil rights movement was under way, it was dumbfounding to learn that Kerouac envied the black inhabitants of the Denver ghetto: "the happy, true-hearted ecstatic Negroes of America," blessed with a "really joyous life that knows nothing of disappointment and 'white sorrows.'"

Kerouac's headlong hero, the male naif, appeared to be an inflated child. Buttressed by the Blakean image of the celestial innocent, the thirty-five-year-old dropped his pants, dug his arm into a vat of chocolate ice cream and licked the drippings from his paw, played cowboys or leap-frog, giggled while the grownups frowned. The frolics sometimes seemed like amusing retaliations to the "maturity" and gentility that the Fifties extolled. But the winsomeness could pall when the games seemed tinged with contempt—toward those who didn't belong to the select team. And women were the male child's enemies, since they were expected to order him to pack his toys away, to call for a curfew, to obstruct his revels and destroy his dreams.

I felt that the ideas of Kerouac and his emulators had more significance than much of their prose, that their lives were more intriguing than their books. But it was troubling to see how their work was steadily attacked on moral grounds: they were assailed for preaching "degeneracy" and criminality— themes that belonged to Norman Mailer more than Kerouac. The critics also punished Kerouac for his romanticism about writing: proclaiming his genius, he sounded fatuous, which made his work all the easier to dismiss. Throughout the late Fifties he helped to diminish his own reputation by boasting that he didn't revise his manuscripts (although he had rewritten *On the Road*), and by pretending to be anti-literary—when he was immersed in Melville and Proust and Céline.

While the talents of Ginsberg and Burroughs would carry them far beyond the context of beatness, the writing of many of Kerouac's acolytes had dated before Eisenhower left the White House. And publicity weakened their impact: the press—particularly the Luce magazines—created caricatures that made the originals seem like synthetics. Suddenly there were scores of "Beatniks" who aped the way of life that the media ascribed to artists: mattresses on the floor, bongo drums, grass, leotards, mugs of espresso, shirtless dancing to flamenco on the hi-fi, temporary beards: props and gestures which conveyed little that the beat writers had tried to express. But even before *On the Road* was published, Nelson Algren had observed that "It is better to be out than in. It is better to be on the lam than on the cover of *Time* magazine"—a prescient epitaph for writers whose fame brought ridicule. I tended to think of the beats as victims of self-promotion: when they advertised themselves along with their work, their convictions were dispersed among headlines and talk shows. Outside a few neighborhoods in San Francisco and New York, it looked as if they were giving ammunition to those who would not tolerate dissent and were hostile to invention.

• • •

That was how it seemed at the time. Years later at a memorial service for John Clellon Holmes at St. Mark's-in-the-Bowery, where Ginsberg read the dead man's poems and the composer David Amram sang a tribute to him, I felt that the beats were touchingly demystified. Holmes's *Go*, published in 1952, was the first novel of the beat generation and he was the first writer to define it in print. Among his other books were *The Horn, Get Home Free*, and *Nothing More to Declare*. I hadn't met him, but he and his wife Shirley had once stayed in my apartment while I was abroad, and the notes and gifts and surprises they left behind were so delightful that it seemed as if I knew them.

Amram—once a revered senior at my boarding school, where we sang a Handel chorus for his birthday: "Hallelujah, Amram, Amram!"—stressed that although there hadn't been many beats to begin with, they had truly been "each other's fans," and I recalled how much support they'd given one another before their writing was published, how Ginsberg had circulated the manuscripts of Burroughs and Kerouac and Corso. Jay Landesman, founder of the magazine *Neurotica*, remembered how Holmes had encouraged other writers, "sharing their early successes and later disappointments." Seymour Krim spoke of the "cyclonic and beneficial energy" and productivity of the late Fifties, when he'd gone to the Cedar Tavern—"that great outpatient ward"—night after night. He became involved with the beats after having a breakdown, a time when "you needed friends and hot chicken soup of the soul." Acknowledging that there had been "a great deal of waste and self-indulgence" among the beats, Krim still thought of them as "the most fertilizing artistic factor" of the Fifties.

Later Krim told me that the fraternity was fortified not only by a sense of "a common enemy"—the middle-class and the literary conventions of the period—but by the fact that many of the initial beats, like Ginsberg, had been in psychiatric hospitals: "Almost everyone had done time in a nut farm, it kind of took the sting out of craziness." Referring to the electric shock treatments he'd had, Krim said the beats were "an electroshock generation. We didn't want to be electroshocked, didn't want to be told what sanity or insanity was." While Ginsberg frequently used "madness" as a poetic term, the rest—rejecting the vocabulary and attitudes of psychiatrists who made snap-diagnoses of "psychotic episodes"—talked about "going bananas" and "flipping," "laughing academies" and "bug-houses" and "funny farms"; the words freed them from feeling stigmatized for having lost control. Nothing, they were saying, was abnormal, nothing should be forbidden; it was rewarding to be deviant. As the beats' views were heard across the country, Krim's friends could feel that other Americans were being liberated from petty definitions of normality.

At Holmes's memorial, Herbert Huncke—ex-convict, mystic and memoirist, once a heroin addict, hustler, and thief, now a little hunched-over figure with a pinched childlike face—read the last paragraph of *On the Road*: "So in America when the sun goes down and I sit on the old broken-down river pier watching the long, long skies over New Jersey ..." Twice there were loud groans from the back of the church hall; on the third groan, Corso surged up the aisle and told us how Holmes had praised his poetry and gotten him a doorbell-ringing job in market research. The essayist Carl Solomon, who'd arranged for the publication of *Junkie* and to whom *Howl* was dedicated (it was he who had thrown the potato salad at City College), read a letter that Holmes had written when he was dying.

While Holmes and Kerouac were fondly quoted and several speakers briskly mentioned being over sixty—Ginsberg said that some of the writers there might "never see each other in the same room again"—it was plain that although the genuine beat movement had been fairly small, its formulators had had an ongoing influence, perhaps especially on those who grew up after the Fifties. In the decades that followed, students kept telling me what *On the Road* had meant to them as teenagers in provincial high schools. Kerouac's capacity for taking risks enabled some young people to feel that they could do the same. Being called stupid or crazy hadn't deterred him from portraying life as he saw it—at a time when many would-be novelists were crippled by inhibition. And readers both older and younger than I had found that Kerouac's perceptions had altered their own.

As I listened to Ginsberg and Krim in St. Mark's-in-the-Bowery, heard Amram's flute rise plaintively to accompany Holmes's poetry, and saw how the friendships had endured, I also saw how the former beats—dead or alive— had survived the New Critics, *Time* and *Life*, the sojourns in Bellevue, foolish publicity, and an era they had depicted while it was receding. Whether one admired their writing or not was unimportant: they had loosened the bonds of propriety, had honored heresies which had invigorated the culture. In the small church a handful of aging men were jovial and rueful, humorous and sometimes still rebellious; they missed their dead friends and rejoiced in having known them. Most of the living appeared to be at ease—and still open to the unpredictable.

Joel Sayre (Garrison-Sayre)

Gertrude Lynahan Sayre, early 1930s

(Garrison-Sayre)

Edmund Wilson, early 1950s

(Sylvia Salmi)

S. J. Perelman and
Joseph Mitchell on Sixth
Avenue and 42nd Street
in the 1950s   (COURTESY OF

NORA SANBORN)

James Thurber, early 1930s

Nunnally Johnson (COURTESY OF NORA JOHNSON)

Walker Evans, *Main Street, Saratoga Springs, New York, 1931*

(WALKER EVANS ARCHIVE, THE METROPOLITAN MUSEUM OF ART)

Walker Evans, Douglas Glass, Lily Emmet West,
at the Mystic Seaport Museum, 1953

Walker Evans, *Billboards and Frame Houses, Atlanta, Georgia
March 1932*

August 1950: Marines marching along Eighth Avenue to Penn Station, Manhattan; from there they will go to Camp Lejeune, North Carolina, for ten days training, then probably to Korea

Whittaker Chambers testifying before the House Committee on Un-American Activities, Alger Hiss listening (*left center*), August 1948.   (UPI/Bettmann News Photos)

President Dwight Eisenhower and John Foster Dulles, 1952.

J. Edgar Hoover testifying before the Senate Internal Subcommittee, 1953

Senator Joseph McCarthy at the Army–McCarthy hearings, 1954

V. R. Lang (COURTESY OF FLETCHER DuBois)

The Poets' Theatre: program cover by
Edward Gorey (HARVARD THEATRE COLLECTION)

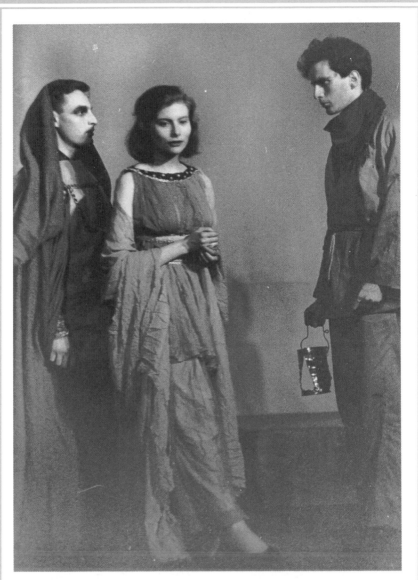

The Poets' Theatre: Yeats's *The Dreaming of the Bones*, with Robert Layzer, Nora Sayre, Peter Judd   (Will Rappaport)

Autherine Lucy, after she was suspended, February 1956

(UPI/Bettmann)

Little Rock, September 1957: On the first day of classes, crowds jeered at fifteen-year-old Elizabeth Eckford as she tried to enter the Central High School; some called for a lynching   (UPI/BETTMANN)

Donald Ogden Stewart at Frognal, 1955

(W. Suschitzky)

Ella Winter   (W. Suschitzky)

Cedric Belfrage, Charlie Chaplin, Josephine Martin, 1956

(COURTESY OF JOSEPHINE MARTIN)

Sally Belfrage, 1956

(COURTESY OF JOSEPHINE MARTIN)

Abraham Polonsky

Leonard Boudin at a Smith Act rally in Carnegie Hall; W.E.B. DuBois on the stage behind him, March 1956   (COURTESY OF EDITH TIGER)

19

Invading The New York Times

Harvey Matusow joined the Communist Party in the Bronx in 1947 when he was twenty-one. During his four years as a member he took part in a campaign to end the draft, worked for the reelection of New York Representative Vito Marcantonio, helped to start a youth group which called for a ban on atomic weapons, participated in several unions' efforts to improve employees' wages and job conditions, and sold many subscriptions to the *Daily Worker*. He was expelled from the Party in 1951, a year after he contacted the FBI and started sending reports to the bureau for seventy dollars a month.

Soon Matusow became a much better paid professional informer, working with the House Committee on Un-American Activities, the Ohio Un-American Activities Commission, the Subversive Activities Control Board, and the Senate Internal Security Subcommittee, among others. He named two hundred and forty-four persons as Communists; later he said he had "probably" testified falsely about "every one" of them. Many had lost their jobs, some had gone to prison. Having undergone "a deep religious conversion" on joining the Church of Latter Day Saints, Matusow chose to make his public confession at a press conference on Washington's Birthday, 1955. He asserted that he had been coached in several of his fictions by Roy Cohn when the latter was an assistant United States attorney. Cohn indignantly denied that he had ever given such instructions to Matusow, who served almost four years in jail for perjury—not because of his lies about alleged Communists but because of what he'd said about Cohn.

Before he fell from grace, Matusow testified against the East Asia scholar

Owen Lattimore and was a key witness in the 1952 trial of thirteen second-echelon Communist leaders. He was also instrumental in the conviction of Clinton Jencks, an official of the Mine, Mill, and Smelter Workers Union. "The happiest day" of Matusow's "blacklisting career" was when he was hired by *Counterattack*, the newsletter which circulated the names of supposed Communists to television and radio networks, sponsors, and employers at large; Matusow was thrilled because the job enabled him "to rub elbows with the really successful people" in show business. The Weavers were blacklisted after he told the FBI that the singers were Communists. The New York City Board of Education paid for Matusow's guidance in the dismissal of many public school teachers, and he wrote a lucrative piece about "Reds in Khaki" for *The American Legion Magazine*. One of his specialties was the Communist threat to youth: he swore that there was a Communist plot to infiltrate the Boy Scouts, that innocents were seduced at wild parties given by Communist youth clubs, and that Communists rewrote *Mother Goose* with the aim of indoctrinating small children.

When the comedian Jack Gilford was contracted to perform on a popular television program, Yogi Berra, the star catcher of the New York Yankees, was to be on the same show. In order to blacklist Gilford, Matusow kept phoning the Yankees' office, using different voices to protest the baseball player's upcoming appearance with "a known Communist fronter"; after Matusow made seventeen calls Gilford was dropped from the program. An occasional puppeteer and stand-up comic in small nightclubs, Matusow had learned a variety of accents. As he wrote, "I loved play acting." Informing had earned him a comfortable living; no one could be certain why he recanted. Still, doing so brought him as much media attention as his previous role. He was frank in admitting that it was exciting to make "revelations," that he adored the limelight and "the narcotic of newsprint." Two former undercover operators for the FBI testified that he'd expected a movie to be made about his life in which he would star.

After Matusow contradicted his original testimony, some of his adversaries on both right and left portrayed him as "unstable," even psychopathic. Senator James Eastland suggested that Matusow had had a breakdown due to the "pressure brought by Communists" to rescind his story. But the witness seemed sane enough even when his testimony was surrealistic—as when he did comedy routines on the stand, discussed his back problems, and talked about having invented the stringless yo-yo: "an entertaining non-destructive toy." He changed his first name to Job and told the press he'd written a poem about the hydrogen bomb: "For Whom the Boom Dooms." Murray Kempton, who covered his perjury trial for *The New York Post*, wrote, "Harvey Matusow's brain is a bubbling mass of jelly. That doesn't mean that the government which used him hasn't got much to explain."

More than a year before Matusow reversed himself, FBI memos sent from New York to Washington showed that the bureau distrusted him, knowing that he'd frequently made "irresponsible public statements." Moreover what he said in court often differed from his FBI reports. Yet the Justice Department went on employing him as a witness as long as he agreed to testify. After he said he'd fabricated most of his "evidence," he kept repeating that many of the government's foremost informers—especially Paul Crouch, Elizabeth Bentley, Matthew Cvetic, and Louis Budenz—had also lied under oath, and that all of them should be tried and jailed along with him. Now that he was "pregnant with the truth," as he put it, he insisted that the investigating committees "forced" their witnesses to lie: out of "fear, greed, and need." Attorney General Herbert Brownell said Matusow was "part of a concerted drive to discredit government witnesses, the security program, and ultimately our sense of justice." Carey McWilliams, editor of *The Nation*, observed that Matusow "was prosecuted because he finally told the truth."

In October 1952, while testifying against the Mine, Mill, and Smelter Workers Union, Matusow said there were "well over a hundred dues-paying" Communists on *The New York Times*; later he declared that there were a hundred and twenty-six on the Sunday staff alone. (Less than a hundred people worked on the Sunday sections, as the columnists Joseph and Stewart Alsop were quick to point out.) In *False Witness*, Matusow's autobiography, he explained that placing his allegations about *The Times* in the record of the Senate Internal Security Subcommittee's hearings was helpful to Joseph McCarthy, who could then demand an investigation of the press. One of McCarthy's favorite informers, Matusow was glad to do the Senator a favor, "and we would both make headlines." But *The Times* did not report or refute Matusow's claim—even though he often repeated it in speeches while he campaigned for McCarthy and other Republican candidates in the fall elections of 1952.

In answer to queries from *The Times'* publisher, Arthur Hays Sulzberger, an official of the Justice Department said he had no information about "Communist influence" at the paper. But Walter Winchell quoted Matusow about *The Times* in his *Daily Mirror* column in January 1953. *The Times* was slow to pursue Matusow himself, but on September 28, 1953, he was interviewed by the West Coast correspondent Gladwin Hill, and gave *The Times* a sworn affidavit in which he retracted his statements of 1952, saying he knew of just six Communists on the paper. (When he was later examined by the Senate

Internal Security Subcommittee, he named only one person.) Julius Ochs Adler, general manager of *The Times*, asked J. Edgar Hoover if the individuals Matusow named were in fact Communists. Hoover replied that Matusow was unreliable and that the bureau could not furnish such information to outsiders. (In truth the FBI often leaked material to state governments, school or university administrations, congressional committees, and sometimes to the press, but the bureau always denied it.)

The Times published nothing about the affidavit for more than two years, nor was it used as a springboard for investigating cases where Matusow could be suspected of lying and his victims had been imprisoned. He gave a similar affidavit to Time Inc. in 1954, conceding that he was wrong to have said there were seventy-six Communists on the staffs of *Time* and *Life*. Like *The Times*, the Luce magazines didn't unearth the lies in Matusow's other testimony. Perhaps the managements of both publications were anxious about the political dossiers of a few employees. Winchell continued to quote Matusow about Communists on *The Times*. In September 1954 Winchell also featured a story from the informer Louis Budenz: "A former editor of the Red *Daily Worker* in New York has named a *New York Times* reporter as a Communist—still covering Washington and Senator McCarthy." The reporter, Clayton Knowles, had left the Party in 1939. But *The Times'* hierarchy was terribly distressed at having unwittingly assigned an ex-Communist to write about hearings on Communism.

On February 5, 1955, the paper ran an editorial which said that Matusow's confession "requires the Justice Department to reexamine all the cases in which this man's testimony did play a part. It is essential in the interests of elementary fairness that the effect of Matusow's worthless testimony be erased from every case in which he was seriously involved. . . . The Matusow case ought to spur the Department of Justice to act in defense of its own integrity." These points could have been made when Matusow gave his affidavit to *The Times* some eighteen months earlier. Naturally the government's investigators did not want to reopen cases where he'd been a stellar witness. They argued that Matusow had been truthful until he "fell into the hands of the Communists," who must have bribed him to say he had lied. Of course new trials for everyone named by Matusow would have weakened the Justice Department's campaign against the Communist conspiracy, a crusade which had furthered many careers.

• • •

The Times of the Fifties was called "moderately conservative" by such papers as the Quincy *Patriot-Ledger* and "mildly liberal" by reporters I met years later.

Still, tales of Communist perfidy at *The Times* were not unusual: in the late Forties Arthur Krock, the profoundly conservative Washington bureau chief, complained steadily to Sulzberger about the "pinkos" being published in *The Times Book Review*. Krock kept writing Sulzberger to give examples: Henry Steele Commager had reviewed John Gunther's *Inside U.S.A.* and Robert Sherwood's *Roosevelt and Hopkins*; John Kenneth Galbraith had written about a Twentieth Century Fund study of American resources; Arthur Schlesinger, Jr., had reviewed a book by the Republican Harold Stassen. Krock's charges against his own paper were not quite as crude as those which filled the FBI's files, but the spirit was similar. Under the heading of COMINFIL INTO THE "NEW YORK TIMES" a 1955 memo referred to the Sunday editor Lester Markel as the "Number one pro-Communist" on the paper; other memos reported that Louis Budenz had said that the music critic Olin Downes and the dance critic John Martin were Communists, a notion which would have dumbfounded their colleagues. Yet both critics were in the Security Index: the FBI's list of people who would be arrested and sent to detention camps if an "internal security emergency" occurred.

The FBI files contained material offered by a couple of informers on *The Times* and their "suspicions of Communist sympathies" on the part of members of the staff. It was noted that "against the orders of his superiors," a young man on the makeup desk "ordered a larger headline for the obituary notice of Mrs. Earl Browder, the wife of the former Communist Party leader." A "strong pro-HISS attitude," a college friendship with "a campus Red," a group of printers "whispering among themselves," "suspicions [based] upon snatches of conversation . . . overheard at adjoining tables in the cafeteria"—all were duly recorded and preserved in the files. In July 1953 Hoover was informed that fifty-two people who'd worked for *The Times* had been "subjects of security investigations."

Despite many memos warning that Matusow could well be a perjurer, the FBI thoroughly investigated the six *Times* employees he called Communists. Some FBI reports specified whether an individual—and his or her parents— was American-born or foreign-born. A memo about the reporter Peter Kihss commented that he was "Latvian by descent, but is believed to be Jewish." (Kihss was said to be "sympathetic toward those suspected as security risks.") The files also contained book reviews and Sunday *Magazine* articles which displeased the bureau. (Yet the agents must have approved of a short review of Matusow's *False Witness* by a *Times* court reporter who wrote that "a renegade and admitted liar" could not be believed on any count; nothing was said of Matusow's lies about *The Times*, which were described in the book—

as was the affidavit.) The Senate Internal Security Subcommittee had close ties with the FBI, and raw data from the bureau's files were the principal source of the subcommittee's "information" during its investigation of the press in 1955 and 1956.

• • •

Democratic Senator James O. Eastland of Sunflower County, Mississippi, chairman of the subcommittee, was one of the nation's most impassioned segregationists. He had announced on the floor of the Senate, "The Negro race is an inferior race." As a candidate he'd promised to prevent blacks and whites from eating together in Washington if he were elected. He stated that the Supreme Court's 1954 ruling on integration of the schools was "an illegal, immoral, and sinful doctrine," that the Court's justices were "brainwashed victims of Red plotting," and once said that the entire Court should be impeached for "pro-Communist decisions." Urging white Southerners to fight desegregation "every step of the way," he hoped the school policy would be reversed if millions rose up against it. Vowing that the South would "protect and maintain white supremacy throughout eternity," Eastland was a spokesman for the Citizens' Councils, which Mississippi newspaper editor Hodding Carter referred to as "the uptown Ku Klux Klan." Exhorting his audience at a Council rally to "organize and be militant," he was accused of preaching violence. As chairman of the Senate Judiciary Committee, which dealt with most bills concerning civil rights and civil liberties, he was able to stall or bury potential laws that he opposed.

Mississippi had more black residents than any state in the country—and fewer who were registered to vote than any other state. Beatings and death threats kept many from registering, and in 1955 Eastland boasted that "due largely to the Citizens' Councils" the number of black voters was shrinking rapidly in Mississippi. To him blacks were suited only for cheap labor. On Eastland's vast plantation, blacks earned less than thirty cents an hour. Some black men on parole from the state prison worked in the millionaire's cotton fields without any pay at all. Each year he received federal crop subsidies of one hundred thousand dollars from the U.S. Department of Agriculture. Because he was a member of the Senate Agricultural Committee, he could help to keep the subsidy program afloat. And as a white supremacist he won the votes of rednecks as well as Mississippi's wealthy planters. Senator Herbert Lehman of New York said Eastland was "a symbol of racism in America." *Time* called him "the nation's most dangerous demagogue."

McCarthy had said he was going to investigate the press, but he lost his power before the opportunity arose. In the summer of 1955, when the Senate Internal Security Subcommittee began its "Inquiry into Communist Party Influence in the Press," Eastland had already presided over weeks of hearings about Harvey Matusow's lies. Although the latter's affidavit about *The Times* was put in the record, Eastland and Julien G. Sourwine, the subcommittee's counsel, disregarded Matusow's recantations. Sourwine, known for his abusive style of questioning, and the senator kept trying to restore Matusow's credibility while the informer was destroying it.

Eastland denied that *The Times* was the target of the investigation, but thirty out of thirty-eight subpoenas to closed hearings went to current or former *Times* employees, and fourteen out of eighteen witnesses at the last round of public hearings were or had been on the paper. When *Times* writers speculated about Eastland's motives, some thought the paper might have been looking into the legality of the cotton subsidies he'd received. Perhaps he thought *The Times* would investigate him—and decided to take the offensive? But many believed he assailed the paper because of its editorials supporting school desegregation and the liberalization of the immigration laws; like Senator Pat McCarran of Nevada, Eastland aimed to "keep America white" by reducing immigration quotas from countries with large black populations. And Eastland was undoubtedly angered by the editorials criticizing his mentor Joseph McCarthy, most of them written by John Oakes.

It was also rumored that Eastland was animated by anti-Semitism. (Yet Sulzberger, who was wary of Zionism and would never visit Israel, had tried to keep *The Times* from being regarded as "a Jewish newspaper": writers whose first name was Abraham used initials in their bylines.) Many doubted that Eastland was seriously pursuing dangerous subversives, as he claimed; he also claimed that the subcommittee had learned that the Russians were trying to recruit spies from the news business. (Here Eastland cited the foggy testimony of Winston Burdett, a CBS correspondent who talked about spying for the Soviets abroad, where his contacts seemed to have had little use for him: they rarely assigned him any tasks and often failed to show up for appointments.) The investigators said they were not interested in the content of *The Times* and whether it was "slanted" by Communists. Hence many reporters were certain that Eastland and Sourwine simply wanted to smear the paper and tarnish the groups the two thought it represented, above all the Northeastern establishment and powerful Jews. Eastland seemed to enjoy the publicity he reaped from the investigation, and Southerners who hated desegregation appeared to relish the assaults on Northern institutions.

Most of *The Times'* handful of subpoenaed ex-Communists had resigned from the Party before they came to the paper. The investigators told the *Times* executives whom they were going to examine, so the employers knew who would be called before the suspects did. At first the subcommittee was allowed to deliver the subpoenas in the *Times* building: the process servers were even directed to the right offices. This practice eventually ceased, perhaps because of protests from some of the staff. But the subcommittee was still free to use the paper's files. Meanwhile the management went through months of internal debate to determine its policy toward its employees.

Sulzberger loathed all manifestations of Communism; years later I was told that he couldn't understand how an American could possibly become a Communist. His initial instinct was to discharge all former Communists who would not reveal their political histories to *The Times* and to the subcommittee. But Sulzberger was also extremely paternalistic: he thought of the staff as part of his family and disliked firing anyone for any reason—which he hardly ever had. Still the *Times* employees were expected to be good sons and daughters, and to Sulzberger the ex-Communists among them seemed unfilial. He would not have permitted someone who was still a Communist to work for him. After the subpoenas arrived, caution pervaded the city room; few discussed the case in public. Most didn't fear the subcommittee, but many feared their own employers: how would *The Times* behave toward those who were called to testify? Two of them told me they'd been treated kindly by their colleagues—in the midst of racking suspense about what action the management would take.

• • •

In the context of the Matusow case, Murray Kempton wrote in 1955, "As an organized political group, the Communists have done nothing to damage our society a fraction as much as what their enemies have done in the name of defending us against subversion." Reflecting on the Justice Department's "techniques" for sending the Communist leaders to prison, Kempton added that their "trials rested on the proposition that the writings and speeches of Communist Party leaders were dangerous to our national safety because they could inflame the populace to armed revolution. This was nonsense on its face; and, to convict them, we had to substitute a malignant fantasy for reality."

Surrounded by fantasies, much of the public didn't comprehend the legal situation of left-wingers who wouldn't answer "the $64 question." Anyone who conceded past or present membership in the Communist Party in front of a governmental investigating committee would then have to name other members he had known; the Supreme Court did not protect people who talked about their activities as Communists and then refused to identify former colleagues. But the role of informer was intolerable to witnesses who wanted to protect their associates from being fired. Throughout the Fifties those who were summoned before a committee were likely to recall the prosecution of the Hollywood Ten in 1947; many lawyers believed that it raised the largest questions about civil liberties of any case of that era. When the witnesses— seven screenwriters, two directors, and a writer-producer, all past or present Communists—were asked by the House Committee on Un-American Activities if they were or ever had been Party members, they at first avoided answering by lambasting the Committee; they called that "answering in our own words." At their trials for contempt of Congress they took the First Amendment. The screenwriter Albert Maltz told me that by doing so they aimed to make a political statement: declaring that the First Amendment forbade Congress to pass any law that could curtail the freedom of speech or opinion, that the government had no right to investigate a citizens's beliefs or associations. (In that interpretation, the First guarantees the right to remain silent as well as the right to speak.) By challenging the power of the Committee to legislate in the field of political associations, the Ten hoped to destroy it in the courts and to rid the United States of political inquisitions. Some of the Ten also invoked the entire Bill of Rights.

Lawyers who had radical clients constantly discussed the choice between the First and the Fifth Amendments; the First was considered preferable because it challenged the legality of the existence of the Committee and defended the tradition of free speech in this country. The Fifth—which affirmed that no one could be "compelled in any criminal case to be a witness against himself"—merely shielded the individual against self-incrimination. Many Communists and ex-Communists were proud of their political past, and they did not want their anti-fascist or pro-union activities of the Thirties to be classified as "criminal." But the Hollywood Ten lost their case in 1950. Their experience showed that taking the First usually resulted in a jail sentence for contempt of Congress or in years of crippling legal costs; lawyers often warned that you needed to be rich to plead the First Amendment. The Fifth did keep many out of prison—although they were dismissed from their jobs because the Committee had deprived the Fifth of its legitimacy, and most Americans assumed that anyone who took the Fifth was a Communist.

At *The Times* the editorial writer John Oakes, the managing editor Turner Catledge, and a few others thought the witnesses should be able to take the Fifth Amendment when they chose not to name Communists they had known. But Sulzberger felt that the use of the Fifth suggested that a witness had something to hide, and the publisher was convinced that the paper's reputation would be severely damaged if it retained reporters or editors thought to be Communists. So he and *Times* lawyer Louis Loeb insisted on the First Amendment for everyone involved in writing or editing the news. Loeb told the witnesses-to-be that if they also conducted themselves with dignity on the stand, they could probably stay at *The Times*. But the paper declined to help with legal fees.

Each subpoenaed *Times* employee was required to tell Catledge and Loeb whether or not he had been a Communist; all but two did. When the witnesses met with the subcommittee in private hearings, a few gave names; but they did not repeat some of them in their public testimony. Reluctant witnesses were urged to name dead Communists when they felt it was dishonorable to name live ones. Several Linotype operators who took the Fifth in the open hearings were allowed to keep their jobs in the composing room. But Melvin Barnet, a financial copy editor who said he had not been a Communist since 1940 and invoked the Fifth when asked about membership before that date, had had a telegram from Sulzberger dismissing him even before he'd finished testifying.

The public hearings were supposed to be completed in 1955, but when Sourwine discovered that the final sessions would coincide with Freedom of the Press Week in November, they were rescheduled for January 1956. It's often been said that the proceedings resembled show trials: the subcommittee had heard all the witnesses' answers in the secret hearings, but now the investigators received media coverage that would benefit their careers. Four *Times* witnesses cooperated with the subcommittee: the reporters Charles Grutzner, Ira Henry Freeman, and Clayton Knowles, and the education editor, Benjamin Fine. Knowles had already told the FBI as well as the subcommittee the names of alleged Communists on *The Long Island Daily Press* and in the New York Newspaper Guild; he wasn't asked to utter all of them again in public. Jack Shafer, a copy editor on the foreign desk, and Nathan Aleskovsky, an assistant editor at *The Book Review*, were fired for taking the Fifth. A police reporter on *The New York Daily News* and an editor on *The New York Daily Mirror* were also discharged right after they refused to tell the subcommittee if they'd been Communists.

Seymour Peck and Alden Whitman, who had left the Party before they went to *The Times*, were willing to talk about their years as members, but they would not name others. Peck was an editor at the Sunday *Magazine* and a cultural reporter; long afterward he told me that his professional life had not been harmed by the investigations (in 1965 he became the editor of the Sunday

Arts and Leisure section.) But Whitman, who was editor of the night city copy desk, was moved to a humbler position as a daytime copy editor. (In 1965 he was assigned to obituaries, where no one had ever had a byline; however his pieces were so widely praised that his name appeared on them after two years of anonymity.) Although Knowles had been helpful to the subcommittee, he was demoted to assembling the daily news index and his byline vanished for over a year.

The New York Newspaper Guild gave the group almost no support at all, though it did briefly contest the dismissal of Jack Shafer. Communists had been powerful in the Guild during the Thirties. But an anti-Communist spasm occurred in 1941, and in 1948 the organization became very conservative, partly due to the influence of the Association of Catholic Trade Unionists. In 1954 the Guild voted to bar Communists from membership. (Even so, the FBI's files were full of reports about Guild activities in the Fifties; merely belonging to the union aroused the bureau's interest.) Under the strict terms of the Guild contract, no one could be fired if he was performing his job satisfactorily. But the Guild condoned the firings and turned down the witnesses' appeals to join their case as amicus curiae.

The Times published editorials and columns upholding the constitutional rights of Americans to take the Fifth Amendment—even Arthur Krock wrote one in 1955—but the paper did not sanction that right for its own employees. Other *Times* editorials stated that the political interrogations were necessary; they did not challenge the government's right to investigate a citizen's associations and beliefs, although they objected to McCarthy's methods and the browbeating tactics of some congressional committees.

On the last day of the subcommittee's hearings in 1956 *The Times* ran an editorial by Charles Merz, titled "The Voice of a Free Press," restating Sulzberger's conviction that a Communist could have no place in the news or editing departments. The editorial then announced that the *Times* executives would decide whom they wanted to employ: "We do not propose to hand that function over to the Eastland subcommittee." Furthermore: "This newspaper will continue to determine its own policies. It will continue to condemn discrimination, whether in the South or the North. It will continue to defend civil liberties. It will continue to challenge the unbridled power of government authority. It will continue to enlist goodwill against prejudice and confidence against fear." Yet *The Times* had actually capitulated to the subcommittee: by firing three of its employees who took the Fifth Amendment. Had those individuals not been subpoenaed, they would have kept their jobs—since they had given no dissatisfaction except in being singled out by Eastland and

Sourwine. I heard about one ex-Communist who was never summoned, perhaps because no informer happened to know him. Hence his right to write for *The Times* was never questioned.

Those who invoked the First Amendment were convicted of contempt of Congress and all but one received prison sentences. (Seymour Peck's conviction was reversed in 1957 on the grounds that the subcommittee had not adequately informed him of the purpose for which he was asked about others in the Communist Party.) For several of the witnesses, including Alden Whitman, taking the First resulted in ten years of litigation and titanic expenses. Their cases went to the Supreme Court and the defendants won on a technicality, due to the vagueness of the charge, which was classified as "a non-specific indictment." But in 1962 Attorney General Robert Kennedy's Justice Department reindicted four of them—even though Justice William O. Douglas had said that all the indictments should be barred because the investigation violated the freedom of the press. The defendants were not jailed; they received suspended sentences and the government finally dismissed the indictments in 1965.

Toward the end of 1956, students at Solvey High School in upstate New York took out a subscription to *The Times*, which was to be read in social studies classes. Then the town's Board of Education ruled that the subscription must be canceled because of the paper's "Communist slant."

20

Coda

In the fall of 1951 President James Bryant Conant of Harvard had addressed the freshman class of 1955 and told them that their generation would live to see a man on the moon, universal military training, and "oral contraception." Mystified and titillated by the last reference, some eighteen-year-olds wondered how birth control could be oral: it seemed improbable that Conant was talking about blow jobs, and few had heard of the Pill.

A disbelief in change was common among my contemporaries. When we were in our teens, the prevailing illusion was that there would be no change: the patterns of society and private life would endure, should endure. Accepting the norm was a rondo theme of our education, and the future was expected to perpetuate the past. Nor was there much anticipation of progress; machines would speed up traveling or dishwashing, the zipper might be perfected, but civilization wasn't likely to advance; "a better tomorrow" was a phrase which had died with the Thirties.

Hence the wider implications of footprints on the moon didn't capture the imaginations of the young. One of my Harvard friends made a graduation speech about waiting: we would sit back and wait until the world declared itself to us, showed what it had to offer. We'd been specifically advised by adults to hold still and to allow things to come to us. Also Freud's popularizers had led the public to confuse his definition of aggression with hostility; therefore we were raised to be unaggressive and were apt to feel guilty about almost any kind of assertion. Endowed with caution and skepticism, we knew it was an error to obtrude.

As a result we were a generation of inept job-hunters: in interviews we'd wait for the employer to draw us out, to be impressed with the subterranean gifts that he was going to spot and reveal to us. We didn't know we had ten minutes to make an impact: to lean forward and prove how bright we were. It took some years to realize that New York corporations valued a vivid persona far more than the qualifications we had on paper or the record of previous jobs. (And a Harvard degree could be a handicap: there was a suspicion that we were over-privileged, over-educated, unlikely to be useful.) But since we'd been schooled in self-criticism, we could hardly recommend ourselves. One Harvard classmate, who urgently needed a salary, told me he could never respect anyone who hired him, because they ought to know he wasn't any good. Sincere in his self-doubt, he was also obeying a creed of the Fifties: if you were serious, you shouldn't be too easily absorbed by the marketplace— it might mean that your integrity was flawed, that there was a streak of gray flannel in your soul.

Our seniors stressed our great fortune in graduating when there was no war, no depression, no reason to be desperate for dollars. A *Life* editorial of 1955 called us "The Luckiest Generation." Because so few Americans had been born in the Thirties, "the Depression babies of today have the pick of the high-paying jobs . . . each, in the most prosperous time in U.S. history, gets a bigger piece of the nation's economic pie than any previous generation ever got." We might be appalled by *Life*'s syntax, but we managed to bypass the pie, and some of the best minds I knew in New York were cataloguing newsreels for NBC or checking facts for *Time*, where they had to put red dots over every word, including "and" and "the"—to show that everything had been double-checked. One was at the *Book of Knowledge*, working her way from B to E, provided with a list of forbidden words that children weren't expected to understand. (There was a compulsory office party for a detested supervisor, who was presented with a cake in the shape of the *Book of Knowledge*; she wore a button reading, "Kick Me, It's My Birthday.") Another wrote fashion copy for *Gentleman's Quarterly*, which was campaigning for brown flannel suits instead of gray: the key line was "Back to Brownstone!" A third tried but failed to be hired as a tour guide in Radio City: the personnel department found his suit too shabby and it was the only one he had. Others were scattered throughout the publishing industry, treading time like water, waiting for opportunities but not creating them.

Naturally some humble work is inevitable for all beginners. (Although corporate recruiters visited the campuses each year, they weren't looking for aesthetes—or vice versa.) But outside of business and the law, the young were unwelcome in the organizations of the decade: ignorance and a dearth of "expertise" were all that was expected of them. And some older employers associated youth itself with hedonism or the political fervors of their early days: they thought we would be unreliable or disruptive, as they now felt their own age-group had been. But they didn't notice that many of us were behaving as soberly as the middle-aged. Most of my friends had very demanding as well as stifling jobs. Years passed without notable improvement: nearing thirty, a number were still trudging off to offices they loathed or laboring to produce what they couldn't respect—a mediocre magazine or a series of second-rate textbooks. For some the lingering appetite for freedom was quite debilitating: when they perceived that little liberty was available to anyone in the professions of the Fifties.

In the Twenties our parents had found their feet far more quickly, and so did those who graduated in the mid-Sixties, when many companies sought to profit from the "Youthquake." But we plodded on, saddled with an awareness that a liberal arts education—especially if it was a fairly good one—was almost guaranteed to make you hate what you did for a living. (I was told that the liberal arts programs of the nineteenth century had been designed for Christian gentlemen of leisure. Those who were neither gentlemen nor Christians, and were unfamiliar with leisure, were mutants in limbo.) So the effort to earn decently coexisted with a gloomy revulsion toward the firm and its products— among those who seemed unable to summon a shred of ambition. The absence of aspiration was an honest response to the dreariness of many jobs, along with an antipathy to Madison Avenue and the dawning dislike of corporations. But the Cantabridgian contempt for hustling hobbled some who should have been able to generate work that was more congenial to them.

We knew that people our age—especially from Yale, Columbia, and the City College of New York—were adept at promoting themselves and were succeeding in their careers. But we didn't want what they did: a senior editing job at Random House or *Harper's Magazine* or to be on night rewrite at *The New York Times*. We didn't want to run anything. Instead we wanted to be in charge of our lives, as few of us felt we were. And for those who still hoped to live in accord with the principles of their education, necessity was harsher than the images of affluence implied. Few I knew yearned for riches, but many hungered for time: to try out their capabilities. A weary air of self-protection was apparent: armored against a world which seemed quite likely to grind them down or use them up, some deduced that the self could be easily diminished. Self-preservation preoccupied many I knew: conversations that began with literature would shift to the question of staying intact. Some suspected that our ongoing education meant unlearning much that we'd ingested. Aesthetes also discovered that "living apart from one's time" was almost impossible. So a band of intelligent persons functioned rather feebly within the system—longing to escape from it, scanning a pale horizon for alternatives.

• • •

Nobody went dancing: until the Beatles' first American tour, our feet were still. But certainly there were good times: spontaneous picnics in Central Park or on tarred rooftops or fire escapes, listening to guitars and folksingers around the fountain in Washington Square, excursions to hear baroque music in the countryside, fine foreign films or gloriously bad movies—Fellini or Tab Hunter and Jayne Mansfield were sure to refresh the soul—laughter around tables heaped from the delicatessen. Private as always, we shared our pleasures with very small clusters of intimates. Some lived in railroad flats within the tenements of Second and Third Avenues, where the bathtub was in the kitchen: topped with a broad wooden board, it became the dining table. Large clamshells became ashtrays. The couch was a foam rubber slab: encased in denim, it lay on a flush door mounted on iron legs. There were woven grass tatami mats on the floors and bookcases made from bricks and planks. Many railroads had no inside toilet, so you made a trip down the hall. Bright bolts of Indian cotton covered the cracks in the walls, mobiles or white Japanese lanterns dangled from slanting tin ceilings. Between those walls, beneath the ceilings, a little Chianti went a long way, and jokes were like presents or trophies you collected and brought to your friends.

Yet even rather simple ways of living reflected impalpable anxieties. For young couples who had some money and dwelled in new apartment buildings, acquiring objects seemed to be an obligation: the Noguchi lamps and Danish teak, the canvas butterfly chairs, the scarlet or yellow enameled casseroles, the molded fiberglass bucket seats that Frank Lloyd Wright called "ass trays." Some had monograms on the towels. Objects expressed you: they were almost a necessary proof of your existence. And that proof was crucial to the young of the Fifties, when institutions already appeared to be overpowering, when many were infused with a nebulous fear of being engulfed by nameless forces; there was a sense that psychic survival could be very difficult. Objects also seemed essential to announce that a marriage had taken place, would continue: the Design Research fabrics, Eero Saarinen's tulip chairs, the wide striped Mexican rugs and the café curtains on small brass rings, were like pledges of cohesion.

When both husbands and wives were looking for jobs or working in equally unpleasant offices, it was assumed that men and women were on equal footing. But in the year or two before the babies began, there was a ritual that seemed intrinsic to the period. Many young wives went in for intensely competitive, wrathful gourmet cooking. Your hostess would tell you angrily that it took three days to make the pâté, or that she'd been up all night with the aspic, or that stuffing those deviled eggs had nearly driven her insane. As far as I could see, their husbands weren't pressuring them into this: the frenzy seemed self-imposed. But except for a few who truly loved cooking, the fixation on complex recipes appeared to make women defensive and resentful; the succulent food turned ashy in your mouth while the cook detailed her exhaustion in slicing, straining, basting, and whipping it. Some were savagely critical of each other's meals: the botched osso bucco, the rancid cassoulet, the curdled béchamel sauce. You heard that beef stroganoff was passé and so was coq au vin. Sweet desserts— apart from zabaglione—were sneered at; sophisticates who'd been to Europe knew that a civilized dinner should end with cheese and fruit.

Food was meant to be an extension of happy sensuality and an emblem of enlightened taste. But why did it beget so much tension? Most of the young gourmets weren't full-time employees: they did translations or research or freelance editing. Some typed administrative reports and letters for professors to help their husbands pay for graduate school. (In the lingo of the era, a woman who earned her husband's tuition was said to be entitled to a Ph.T.: "Putting Hubby Through.") And perhaps all the hours in the kitchen were an effort to create something of quality: to say that they too were gifted—as much as those who were embarking on a doctoral thesis on Proust, Joyce, and Mann or a first novel. Hence the indignation at watching the creation disappear: down the throats of guests who enjoyed the gnocchi or the blanquette de veau but promptly forgot it. All that remained was a mess to be cleaned up.

Most educated women were eager to perform a wifely role. Yet what they toiled to produce didn't reap any real respect: coquilles St. Jacques were hardly on a par with a poem, the best ratatouille couldn't rank with an essay on Kafka. Although the young cooks knew better than to compare food with literature, their dazzling banquets seemed to make some feel inconsequential. For them—as for those who processed grant applications for obscure founda- tions or proofread copy for trade magazines devoted to hotel management— "life as a work of art" was no help either.

• • •

The babies came: chuckling and crowing and howling and farting, they absorbed almost all the love and time that anyone had. They took over the cramped New

York apartments, the bedrooms (if there was more than one), the bathroom, the kitchen; closets overflowed with Port-a-Cribs and strollers and squashy toys. Talcum powder was everywhere. Some new parents thrived on having such total dependents: whatever a baby needed—milk, warmth, cradling, washing— was gladly provided, and it was gratifying that every requirement could be fulfilled. The books said that "pre-Oedipal" children ought to spend time with men as well as women, and most young husbands I knew were involved with colic and toilet-training and diaper rash as their own fathers never were. Many couples were proud of raising children with almost no household help: nothing should come between them and their offspring. Vowing to be better parents than their forebears, they felt their lives should revolve around the children— short of moving to the suburbs with the squares. And their children would be stronger and happier than any born before them: they would not suffer emotional deprivation, and whenever a baby cried, it would be fed and comforted.

The American birthrate had declined steadily since 1810; the only exception was the postwar baby boom, when it was nearly on a par with India's. I'd been living in London in the late Fifties; on visits home I was somewhat startled to see how swiftly each baby followed the last. But whether they were conceived on purpose or not, they seemed truly welcome. Although my friends hooted at *McCall's* crusade for "togetherness," having more babies was expected to increase the parents' intimacy, to strengthen the ties between them. At the start I saw a new kind of confidence among individuals who'd lacked it: they *knew* how to have children, knew how to bring them up, they were certain that they would be good at it.

Making babies also enabled some young couples to feel rather powerful: creating big families helped them to displace the elders who had governed them, and—in the supermarkets and on the airwaves and in research labs— they and their babies were changing the tone of the culture. Our very small generation was producing legions: their enormous presence was making us important, along with our values and priorities. Homes and parks were being designed to please us, at least in theory; department stores teemed with loose A-line shifts which made a woman look pregnant even when she wasn't; television comedies swarmed with the lovable emergencies of family life: spilt cereal, the first day at nursery school, the rare but voluptuous babysitter. Few foresaw that the children were going to dominate their households and the economy: when they learned to talk, that was the end of adult conversation; when they clamored for products shown on the tube, parents rushed to buy more Sugar Pops and space helmets—that appeared to be the only way to purchase peace.

Benjamin Spock was my doctor until I was thirteen; no other has ever suited me so well. I was always grateful when he told me he would reassure my mother that my ailments were entirely normal—when most of my classmates had measles or chickenpox, it would be unusual not to have them—and it was heartening to hear that one adult would pacify others. Now he was reassuring a whole nation, urging parents to trust their instincts. But I've never believed that he unleashed "permissiveness"; instead I think that occurred because young mothers were utterly overworked; when the six-week-old baby was being nursed and the two-year-old was throwing up, it was merciful that the three-year-old twins were watching *Gunsmoke* or *Dragnet*. Men returned from the office to find the apartment glittering with broken glass, streaming with tears and blood and upchuck; while they searched for Band-Aids and sponges as the sobs reached a crescendo, neither parent had the energy to insist on toothbrushing and punctual bedtimes.

Those who couldn't afford part-time help or a weekly cleaning woman might nonetheless discuss it now and then, but like the well-heeled they were apt to recoil from the idea; hiring outsiders to care for their children or homes seemed altogether wrong; the very thought made young wives feel guilty. Women were supposed to be wonderful at coping. A woman who wasn't could feel that her sexual identity was at stake. So she continued to function as though she were a large staff of servants—while being a mother, a wife, a partial wage-earner, a hostess. This was said to be her natural way of life: any other would be abnormal.

A sensation of failure threatened to join the stunning fatigue that descended on a wife who shoveled macaroni onto paper plates while the strained apricots oozed over the formica. When the couple needed money, she did some copy-editing at home, but the printer's symbols blurred before her eyes after she'd been up all night with flu-stricken babies, and when she attempted a dinner party, the sole aux crevettes might be imperfect. Several of my friends wrote their first books while their new babies slept, but they worried that neither would turn out well. Meanwhile sex was curtailed: couples learned to perform quickly and quietly, rehearsing what to say if a small child walked in—"No, Daddy isn't killing Mummy, she *likes* it, we're having fun"—so the children wouldn't grow up frigid or impotent.

The confidence bestowed by early parenthood could begin to recede. Although many men did change diapers and scrub greasy pans at night and on weekends, their wives would remind them that they were away all day, far from the wails and the whine of the vacuum cleaner. The husbands would retort that hours of nerve-rending meetings with employers topped by domestic chaos was more punishing than afternoons with babies at the laundromat when all the machines were full. Then there would be a terrific fight. The men were angry because buttons hadn't been sewn on their shirts: "Who pays the bills around here!" The women replied that the men didn't have to iron or to be walled up with shrieking children on a daily basis, that no one asked men to be selfless. Feminism was far in the future, nobody spoke of it. Within my hearing, nobody said that women existed to serve men. But the billboards said it, the social workers and psychologists said it, the novelists and the jingle-writers. And the fighting would subside between young people who genuinely wanted to be responsible: to each other, for their children, throughout a marriage meant to nourish all of them. It was childish to yell just because they were so tired, and being juvenile was shameful—in a culture which demanded maturity from those who'd never felt very young. Marital exhaustion was like the metal stress that afflicts airplanes: gradual but relentless. None of my friends' children was more than four when the Fifties ended, and sometimes it seemed as if crawlers might never learn to walk, that toddlers wouldn't ever manage to dress themselves or cross a street alone or read.

• • •

Resignation was conspicuous among the young, who worked hard to accept the circumstances (domestic or professional) in which they found themselves. Years afterward a Harvard friend of mine wrote, "Perhaps growing up for me simply meant learning to inhabit without complaint the landscape you were condemned to live in." He cut that sentence from his memoirs but I remembered it.

As I listened to my former schoolmates, *The Beast in the Jungle* seemed appropriate once more: "It wouldn't have been failure to be bankrupt, pilloried, hanged: it was failure not to be anything." Some I knew were feeling this at twenty-six—as though they were forty-eight or sixty. They didn't think in terms of success, but the jobs and marriages which defined them did not seem to be developing in any direction. In Warren Miller's *The Way We Live Now*— a novel of 1958 which distills the period more forcibly for me than any other— a man said, "It used to be that Americans never grew up—now it seems we marry too young and grow old too soon." Aging quickly was a phenomenon of the time, but it had nothing to do with risks, nothing in common with the excesses—booze in the Twenties, drugs in the Sixties—of other generations. And many recent college graduates tended to fear that life would "pass them by"—or that it would never begin. Whether they trundled children to the swings and sandboxes in the park or rewrote jacket copy for a publishing house, they saw that each week or month was much like the last, that next year would be a replay of this one. Yet nothing tangible was happening to them. Perhaps it never would.

New Englanders had warned us that existence was mainly struggle and procedure. We were respectful of routine, we got to the office on time, and few expected to be rewarded for merely meeting their obligations. But there was a powerful conviction that options were shriveling, that very little could change if you were halfway through your twenties. Commitment to employers and spouses and children seemed to mean no further surprises, no more beginnings. I kept hearing that it was "too late"—for love or excitement in one's work, for experiment and renewal. At twenty-five Sylvia Plath wrote in her diary, "I am afraid. Of what? Life without having lived, chiefly." She had already published poems in *The New Yorker*, *The Nation*, and several English literary magazines; she'd been married to Ted Hughes for two years, but— exceptional as she was in her talent and her despair—she shared my friends' dread of not being able to make something out of life, of not knowing how to use one's energy or imagination.

Soon after my twenty-second birthday, a friend who was twenty-three had told me he felt as if he was standing in a room lined with electric sockets: he had various plugs in his hands, but he couldn't guess where to attach them— where to connect with the circuit or how to make the current flow—even though he had plenty of extension cords.

The image seems valid for many who came of age in the Fifties: for all the talk of American power and productivity, there was an atmosphere of futility. "Other people" were in charge, and few of them had any use for the young or the arts or for aesthetes. My friend with his hands full of plugs knew he was privileged: he'd been raised with the assurance that he could make all sorts of choices. And yet he felt guilty for lacking a sense of possibilities.

• • •

Of course we were wrong: the Sixties offered us a wealth of astonishments. And the intellectual snobbery developed at Harvard and kindred institutions crumbled away because the culture was teeming with challenges: you couldn't afford to limit your perceptions. Around thirty we had a chance to be young— as we hadn't been at twenty. Many of the changes were very painful indeed, and there were countless divorces. Security turned out to be a sham and "maturity" was a joke. But we discovered that Scott Fitzgerald had been mistaken when he wrote that there were no second acts in American lives; we found it wasn't too late to explore the world and ourselves. Yet before the landscape around us began to alter—before mountains and valleys shifted, craters disappeared and new planets were seen in the sky—some certainties seemed immutable. On New Year's Eve in 1959, I told a friend that I was sure of just two things about the year (and probably the decade) which lay ahead: hemlines wouldn't rise far and Richard Nixon would never be my president.

SEQUELS

TO THE

THIRTIES

On the one hand America considers itself the
strongest nation, the first and only nuclear
nation, the wealthiest, the most powerful
nation in the world. On the other hand
it must live in fear of the Russian.
—E. L. Doctorow,
THE BOOK OF DANIEL

History's always a *mess*. But it's our mess.
—*Abraham Lincoln Polonsky*

21

Snakes or Tigers

At Chasen's restaurant in Beverly Hills, amid the prime ribs and the chili con carne, a dress designer I later knew overheard a pronouncement from the next table, where Ginger Rogers's mother was explaining that Communist armies were waiting in Mexico and Canada to engulf the United States in a giant pincer movement. (Lela Rogers was employed by RKO to scrutinize scripts for hidden Communist propaganda; in 1947 a member of the House Committee on Un-American Activities called her an "outstanding" expert on Communism.) The designer said that the foolish remarks of an ignorant woman would have been amusing—had it not been that J. Edgar Hoover and the editors of the Hearst newspapers and some CIA functionaries were behaving as if such things were true.

• • •

By the time I came to know a number of people who had been blacklisted, they had traveled far from the ideological wars of the Thirties; by the mid-Fifties many had already devoted about five years to their legal problems and to finding temporary work. I first met American radicals in England, where quite a few had settled in hopes of employment in the British film industry and the universities. Since neither my background nor my teachers had exposed me to the experiences of those who had been punished for their politics, I found I needed to examine the recent history of my country—as I had not before. It would take some years to fill many gaps, especially since no one I encountered in the Fifties ever told me that he or she had been a Communist. But although some expatriates of the Left had never joined the Party, they had lost their jobs. Meanwhile I sought to understand why the writers and film makers I often saw in London had been vilified and feared.

And why did the putative victors—the anti-Communists—still detest those who had been fired, ostracized, even jailed or deported? As I saw them having tea together on Sundays, or went with them to new American movies like *Marty* and *The Man with the Golden Arm*, or heard them describing the feuds between Louis B. Mayer and Irving Thalberg in the Thirties or discussing Harvey Matusow's conviction for perjury in 1956, it was difficult to imagine how they could be considered a menace to their country.

Certainly some of the New York writers I'd known had been exasperated by the smugness and militancy of the Left in the Thirties. (While most of those writers were non-political, they would have identified themselves as liberals—or liberal skeptics.) Some had been alienated by the internal factionalism, the cultural meetings disrupted by people who were supposed to be working on the same side as the speakers they shouted down, the tendency of Communists to regard socialists and admirers of the New Deal as enemies because their reforms would obstruct the birth of a classless society. And certainly writers had disliked the notion that "revolutionary literature" almost had to be written in jargon if it was to be comprehensible to "the masses"; Malcolm Cowley observed that the reader of a proletarian poem often "stumbled over a party slogan left standing like a baby carriage in his path." After 1936 the dedication to proletarian art declined. But until then, complaints that Communists no longer spoke English and were "talking Borscht"—sounding like an inept translation from Russian—were frequent. However, the writers I knew never thought the radicals dangerous.

Still, authentic liberals of the past had had a further cause for aggravation: sometimes finding themselves outmaneuvered in such organizations as the Screen Writers Guild, they had been called "social fascists" by individuals who later said that accounts of purges in the Soviet Union were lies. Naturally those who abhorred Hitler were contemptuous of the Communists' defense of the Nazi-Soviet pact—and of the rapid switches of the Party line right after the Germans invaded Russia. Having differed so profoundly with the Communists, many liberals had always disassociated themselves from the Left of the Thirties. The two groups could share a hatred of fascism and an allegiance to the social programs of the Depression, and liberals muted their aversion to Stalin while he was our ally during World War II. Along the way, writers like Edmund Wilson had simply (albeit severely) disagreed with the Communists,

while repudiating the cold warriors' view that political nonconformists deserved
the retributions of the Fifties.

Newly acquainted with some casualties of the period, I kept thinking about
the animosity and fear which had deprived many of them of their constitutional
rights. How had they lost what millions took for granted?

• • •

After the war, various expectations had clashed. Americans had never been
given an indication of what our postwar society might be. Liberals had hoped
for a resumption of the New Deal. And since there had been predictions that
the economy would sag once the war was over, repeating the fiscal slump that
followed World War I, the Left thought that a revival of the Depression would
encourage the public to accept radical leadership. Instead the voluptuous
economic expansion of the Fifties astounded many who had braced themselves
for fierce austerity. But if liberals wished to pick up the threads of the Thirties,
so did conservatives who aimed to recapture the White House from those
whose prewar commitment to the poor had dismayed many of the comfortable
and the rich. Republicans blamed the heritage of the New Deal and the Left
for the postwar aggressiveness and widespread strikes of many labor unions,
whose members were determined to raise the salaries which had been frozen
during the war. Hostility toward the labor movement was central to domestic
anti-Communism.

Roosevelt's confidence that he could handle Stalin had been shared by few.
The assumption that the Soviet Union would soon be our adversary dilated
as the large Soviet military presence in Eastern Europe fed fears that a victorious
Soviet army was going to sweep through Western Europe—although some
Kremlinologists argued that Russia was mainly intent on protecting her borders
from invasion and solidifying her "spheres of influence." But in George Kennan's famous *Foreign Affairs* article, "The Sources of Soviet Conduct," signed
"X" and published in 1947, the author advised that "Soviet pressure against
the free institutions of the Western world" could "be contained by the adroit
and vigilant application of a counter-force at a series of constantly shifting
geographical and political points." Although Kennan later claimed that he
wished to combat Soviet expansionism through political and economic strategies rather than a vast military build-up, he had written that only "unanswerable
force" could halt Moscow's pursuit of world power. Secretary of Defense
James Forrestal and others thought he was recommending an enlarged defense
establishment.

In his *Herald Tribune* columns, Walter Lippmann warned against the perils of Kennan's doctrine of containment, calling it "a strategic monstrosity" that would fail because it would require supporting an "array" of anti-Communist regimes—which might demand that we defend them against local insurrections. (Years afterward Kennan said he hadn't favored military action, but he didn't make that clear in 1947.) Those at the most influential levels of government such as John J. McCloy, former Assistant Secretary of War and soon-to-be High Commissioner of Germany, did not think the Soviets intended to overwhelm Western Europe. Yet the heightened rhetoric of Kennan, Truman, and Dean Acheson persuaded many Americans that worldwide revolution—and even direct aggression—was the Soviets' goal, although a country which had lost more than twenty million people was hardly fit to launch a major war. But Russia's presumed threat to Western Europe was confirmed in many minds by the tightening of the Soviet grip in Eastern Europe, culminating in the Communist coup in Czechoslovakia in 1948 and the Berlin blockade of the same year.

In 1946 Winston Churchill had delivered his momentous Iron Curtain speech in Fulton, Missouri, in which he said that Communist parties throughout the world constituted "a growing challenge and peril to Christian civilization." A year later the British asked for our help in defending Western interests in Greece and Turkey. In March 1947 the Truman Doctrine was unfurled, whereby we promised to assist any nation resisting Communism—therefore we provided financial and military aid to destroy the Communist forces in Greece and to maintain a royalist regime there, while protecting a conservative nationalist government in Turkey from the Russians. Although Stalin declined to give direct aid to the Greek Communists after he and Churchill agreed that Greece was a British zone of influence—just as part of Central Europe and much of the Balkans were Russia's—our leaders were sure that the Soviets would support Communists in every country. To convince Congress that intervention in Greece was necessary, Senator Arthur Vandenberg urged Truman to "scare hell out of the country." Only ten days after Truman asked Congress for four million dollars on behalf of Greece and Turkey, Truman's federal loyalty program was issued, which resulted in the investigation of the political beliefs and associations of all federal employees; some were ousted from their jobs on fragile evidence of "disloyalty"—in a pattern that would soon be repeated throughout a galaxy of professions, even though the far-flung loyalty checks did not unmask any spies.

Not many voices challenged the loyalty order: already most guessed that if they protested, the finger might be pointed at them. Thereafter the actions of the Italian and French Communist parties in their own countries, the defeat of Chiang Kai-Shek by the Chinese Communists in 1949, and the arrest and conviction of atom spy Klaus Fuchs in England gave further momentum to the investigating committees, as did the timing of the Korean War. A vision of a world split in half, where every country would have to side with the Communists or fight them, existed among many who never expected that enmity would one day develop between the Soviet Union and China—and when the two nations diverged in the late Fifties, John Foster Dulles refused to believe it.

Looming throughout the political investigations was the Republican loathing of the New Deal (which Alger Hiss seemed to personify), encouraging the allegation that many New Dealers were Communists or fellow travelers—a device that was zealously employed in the elections of 1946 and 1952. (Even before the war had ended, Representative Clare Booth Luce had said that "the Communist Party had gone underground, after the fashion of termites, into the Democratic Party." In the House and Senate elections of 1946 the GOP urged voters to choose between "Communism and Republicanism.") Truman, accused by many Republicans of being "soft on Communism," had said that his loyalty program "should take the Communist smear off the Democratic Party." He did not seem to be concerned about left-wingers; at times he said the issue was synthetic. But he was yielding to political pressures and the demands of J. Edgar Hoover, who was greatly enlarging the FBI along with the range of his own powers, while contending that Truman was weak on domestic security.

As the "smear" spread instead of contracting, the Catholic church sustained it and Francis Cardinal Spellman reproached Truman for "appeasing" the American Communist Party. Catholic leaders often announced that the Communists were going to destroy Christianity and morality: the two were identical in the minds of many Christians. Church attendance had declined right after the war, but then the heresy hunt helped to unify the Catholic church. The Protestants also needed a revival in their church and most of their dignitaries endorsed the creed of anti-Communism. As a Fundamentalist Billy Graham was more succinct: in 1953 he said on his radio program, "Either Communism must die, or Christianity must die."

The consternation—even panic—generated by the first Soviet atom bomb test in September 1949 mounted in the decade that followed. No country but ours was meant to have atomic or nuclear weapons, and our monopoly was supposed to guarantee peace—on the grounds that those weapons would never be used after Hiroshima. Since our scientists were proclaimed as the best in the world, it was thought that the Russians would be incapable of producing such marvels, and the Rosenberg case indicated that the Russians' espionage had been successful.

Due to the charges leveled against their party, many Democrats thought they had to surpass the Republicans in the war on American Communism. Hubert Humphrey, then Senator from Minnesota, proposed a bill that would outlaw the Communist Party and he supported a plan to send Communists to detention camps—which he regretted when it was too late. In 1952 some voters mistook Adlai Stevenson's literacy and wit for ultra-liberalism, even though he sometimes outdid the Republicans in chastising Communists. At the start of his first presidential campaign Stevenson addressed a national convention of the American Legion, defining Communism as "the death of the soul." But when he added, "We must take care not to burn down the barn to kill the rats," his rivals responded gleefully; Richard Nixon said Stevenson had "made light of the menace of Communism." Hence Stevenson's staff felt he should not offer to seek an end to the Korean War, as Eisenhower did. Toward the end of the campaign, Stevenson declared that the goal of our Communist enemies was "total conquest, not merely of the earth but of the human mind . . . [and] to destroy . . . the concept of God Himself."

The Democratic candidates continued to dwell in a double bind. Stevenson had called Joseph McCarthy's tactics "an hysterical form of putrid slander" and had vetoed several "anti-subversive" bills in Illinois. But like many governors Stevenson received confidential FBI reports about alleged radicals among state employees—whom he then fired. (The FBI called this the Responsibility Program; it was initiated at the request of Stevenson and some of his fellow governors.) Stevenson also said that Communists should be "excluded" from the educational system and he praised the FBI as "a magnificent instrument" for "catching real Communist agents," a task he likened to "killing poisonous snakes or tigers."

• • •

Soon after the postwar investigations began, numerous Americans began to denounce those for whom they feared to be mistaken. Some liberals had belonged to organizations run by Communists, such as the League Against War and Fascism; when those groups appeared on the Attorney General's list of "subversive" organizations in 1947, former participants were nearly always dismissed from their jobs. Many Americans found themselves unemployable if they had ever signed a petition, gone to a meeting, or contributed money to one of the anti-fascist groups of the Thirties. In the entertainment industry, rumor or innuendo could land someone on the blacklist if he or she was said to have kept the wrong company—or openly deplored segregation. Understandably those who had never had any respect for the Communist Party did not want to be identified with it. But not many liberals had the personal or public self-assurance of the director and critic Harold Clurman, whom I later heard asserting with impatience (while he waved his arms), "Being on the Left is *not* the same thing as loving the Soviet Union!"

The sociologist Nathan Glazer wrote long afterward that the "political stances" of New York intellectuals were "treated as matters of guilt and innocence, not simply of right or wrong." The notion that all American left-wingers revered Soviet totalitarianism was one of the pervasive myths of the Fifties, and was reflected in Leslie Fiedler's *An End to Innocence*, published in 1955. Fiedler's leading question was: "Who that calls himself a liberal is exempt?"— from "illusions" that made one guilty of "complicity." Intending to speak for all liberals Fiedler stated, "We have desired good, and we have done some; but we have also done great evil," and he flogged himself along with everyone who had upheld "trade unionism, social security, and the rights of Negroes, Jews, and other minorities, including socialists and even Communists." (Elsewhere in the book his reference to "the blatant ghettos in which the Negro conspicuously creates the gaudiness and stench that offend him" made his support for racial equality seemed ephemeral.) The culpable "liberal-intellectuals" were also "those who believe or believed that Sacco was innocent, who considered the recognition of the Soviet Union not merely wise strategically but a 'progressive' step, and who identified themselves with the Loyalist side in the Spanish Civil War." Fiedler did not directly link an adherence to civil liberties to furthering the global power of the Soviets, but he gave the impression that being in favor of unemployment insurance or public housing was almost equivalent to condoning the crimes of Stalin. Reviewing Fiedler's book, the critic Harold Rosenberg, a passionate anti-Communist, retorted, "Fiedler's line is, 'We have been guilty of being innocent.'"

Fiedler's reasoning seemed to echo that of Whittaker Chambers, who had written in *Witness* that New Dealers "who sincerely abhorred the word Communism, in the pursuit of common ends found that they were unable to distinguish Communists from themselves." Chambers stressed the vulnerability of such persons: "For men who could not see what they firmly believed was liberalism added up to socialism could scarcely be expected to see what added up to Communism." In other words, a person might be contaminated without knowing it, or he might undergo an appalling change without fully choosing to do so. The concept of "latency" was sometimes cited in relation to politics as well as sex. Just as some young men feared they might be latent homosexuals, there was a dread of intangible political forces. When Nixon called former Vice President Henry Wallace "an unconscious follower of the Party line," the phrase indicated the preoccupation with latency: you could be infected by an ideology that took you unawares—just as you might harbor a tumor which had not been detected.

At a time when some anti-Communists insisted on their liberalism to a degree that confused their readers or students, it was worth wondering why they wanted to be known as liberals. It should be remembered that the United States had no tradition of a conservative intelligentsia, as many European countries did; although books by Peter Viereck, William Buckley, and Russell Kirk received favorable attention in the Fifties, there was as yet no solid conservative movement. (Buckley's *National Review*, which began publication at the end of 1955, had a slender audience.) "Conservative" not only meant reactionary—it made one think of Senator James Eastland or Representative Martin Dies—it was associated with backwaters where the intellect was dim. Because "liberal" seemed to mean well-educated, almost anyone who considered himself intelligent was likely to regard himself as a liberal. In academic circles or the community of *Partisan Review*, historians, critics, and editors would have recoiled from being classed with the fairly mindless figures known as conservatives. And since some of the key reactionaries—like Representative John Rankin—were anti-Semitic white supremacists, they were despised by Northern Democrats as well as Jewish intellectuals. Yet the right-wing politicians' influence was discounted by many liberals. The critic Lionel Trilling sounded completely confident when he wrote in 1949—when countless Americans had already been fired because of their politics—"In the United States at this time liberalism is not only the dominant but even the sole intellectual tradition. For it is plain that nowadays there are no conservative or reactionary ideas in circulation."

The Cold War liberals' view of Stalin and the Soviet Union couldn't be faulted. (And they were useful in reminding left-wingers who were romantic about the Spanish Civil War that Soviet agents and Spanish Communists had murdered anarchists and independent Marxists who didn't follow the Kremlin's directives during that war.) But as these liberals hastened to distance themselves from radical acquaintances, they tended to demonize the American Left. And although many Americans who had joined the Communist Party in the Thirties had resigned before 1950, the small and steadily dwindling organization was evoked by demagogues like McCarthy and Eastland as though it were enormous—while some liberals talked as if it threatened American democracy. Throughout our history intellectuals had been suspected of disloyalty and subversion. When the postwar anti-Communist crusade put them on the defensive, some went on the offensive.

The leading Cold War liberals were mainly writers and academics, and most were nimble polemicists. Among them were the nominal Trotskyists of *Partisan Review*, including its first editors, Philip Rahv and William Phillips, who were eager to bring European authors to American readers. In the late Thirties the magazine had featured what their colleague William Barrett called "the two M's . . . Marxism in politics and Modernism in art," and they "were attacking Stalin and the Soviet Union from the point of view of a purer Marxism." They published André Gide on his disillusionment with the Soviet Union, the first two of T. S. Eliot's *Four Quartets*, George Orwell, Albert Camus, Jean-Paul Sartre, Saul Bellow, Robert Lowell, Delmore Schwartz, Mary McCarthy, and championed the works of Dostoyevsky, Proust, Joyce, Pound, and Kafka. (Dwight Macdonald had been a key editor and writer at *Partisan Review* until 1945 and again in the Fifties, but he had fierce and frequent fights with his colleagues there.) Before the war several of the editors saw themselves as socialists, but their brand of socialism wasn't clearly defined, and it evaporated early in the Cold War. Other influential anti-Communist liberals were the philosopher Sidney Hook, *Commentary*'s Irving Kristol (who moved to *Encounter* in 1953), the historian Arthur Schlesinger, Jr., and the sociologists Nathan Glazer, David Riesman, and Daniel Bell. By the late Seventies, Kristol, Barrett, Glazer, and Bell would be neo-conservatives.

Most had criticized McCarthy for his personal excesses—to Barrett he seemed "a seedy and unpleasant character"—and he had disparaged several of them. But not many had objected strongly to the government's prosecution of American leftists, and when the right-wing investigators clashed with the witnesses, these liberals were apt to remark that the antagonists deserved one another. Some said the investigations were necessary in order to remove Communists from unions or schools and universities. Kristol wrote that the New Deal reformers "were stained with the guilt of having lent aid and comfort to Stalinist tyranny." Schlesinger has written that "a liberal must by definition be both anti-Stalin and anti-McCarthy," which oversimplified the issue by tying it to those individuals. Yet few liberals acknowledged the damage that the inquisitions were doing to the freedom of expression and debate. An exception was the Committee for the First Amendment, organized in 1947 by the screenwriter Philip Dunne and a couple of colleagues "to protest the procedures of the House Committee on Un-American Activities and to head off blacklisting and censorship." But that group had few counterparts around the country.

Young Marxists of the Thirties had feared that fascism might dominate the world; they hadn't guessed that hostility between the United States and the Soviet Union would replace the battle against fascism. (Soon after Hitler's ascendency in 1933, many leftists thought European governments would "choose" either Communism or fascism—just as postwar American conservatives and liberals felt that there must be a "choice" between Communism and "freedom.") For the ex-Marxist liberals, capitalism was no longer an enemy, and they came to believe that only American armies and dollars could protect other nations from Moscow's plans to seize universal power. According to Barrett, a year after the war Rahv felt that certain Americans were facilitating Soviet expansion: " 'Those goddam [leftists]' he fumed, 'They'll end by giving away the whole of Western Europe to Stalin. He won't even have to push for it, they'll make a present of it to him.' " (Murray Kempton later mused on the mentality of "those ready to imagine a *Nation* and a *New Republic* capable of giving away whole continents to anybody.") In 1951 the philosopher Hannah Arendt's *The Origins of Totalitarianism* persuaded many readers that Nazism and Communism were "essentially identical," even though the two ideologies were rooted in entirely different economic systems, and Nazism was designed to elevate a pure-blooded master race. But such distinctions didn't seem significant to many members of the Congress for Cultural Freedom, founded in 1950 to show that intellectuals of "the free world" were staunch anti-Communists who would uphold the superiority of Western culture and deflect assaults by the Kremlin's propagandists who said that American society was racist and conformist.

At the first meeting of the Congress the philosopher Sidney Hook of the American delegation anticipated an "era when references to 'right,' 'left,' and 'center' will vanish from common usage as meaningless." It was declared that "ideology" (which meant Communism or socialism and sometimes liberalism) could no longer appeal to Western societies or younger generations. The American Committee for Cultural Freedom, established in 1951, mingled such right-wingers as Whittaker Chambers, James Burnham, and Ralph de Toledano with the Cold War liberals Schlesinger, Kristol, Bell, and Hook; many of their views were similar even though Hook was still a "democratic socialist." The group's goal, Hook told the executive committee, was "to expose Stalinism and Stalinist liberals wherever you may find them"—which meant they would be fired. He and kindred liberals kept complaining that "anti-anti-Communism" hindered the work of investigating committees not headed by McCarthy and harmed our reputation abroad. Some felt McCarthy was bungling his duties, and a report by the American Committee said his anti-Communism was neither "authentic" nor "responsible." In 1952 the American Committee was fragmented over the issue of whether opposing McCarthy was more important than combating Communism; bitter fights erupted. In the meantime Americans for Democratic Action, which was supposed to uphold postwar liberalism, was denouncing leftists as fervidly as the American Committee.

Christopher Lasch later wrote that "the anti-Communist liberals cannot claim to have defended cultural freedom in the United States with the same vigor with which they defended it in Russia." In the Sixties, when it was revealed that the Congress for Cultural Freedom and one of its magazines, *Encounter*, had been secretly funded by the CIA for sixteen years, *The Sunday Times* of London asked what course a "free thinker" should follow "when he finds out that his free thought has been subsidized by a ruthlessly aggressive intelligence agency as part of the international cold war?" Many New York intellectuals were skillful infighters who loved having the last word; after the news about the CIA spread through the city, some were unusually silent.

In his study of the Congress, Lasch concluded that "cultural freedom has been consistently confused with American propaganda." It was true that the genuine horror with which informed Americans viewed the Soviet Union's labor camps and liquidations seemed to preclude much criticism of the United States; the liberals' praise for their nation supplanted the social critiques of an earlier time. Although they attacked the banalities of middlebrow culture and mocked the aspirations of corporate conformists, many paid compliments to the government and the capitalist system. In a prelude to *Partisan Review's* 1952 symposium, "Our Country and Our Culture," the editors stated, "most writers no longer accept alienation as the artist's fate in America; on the contrary, they want very much to be a part of American life." The literary historian Newton Arvin wrote that a negative attitude toward American culture was "simply sterile, even psychopathic, and ought to give way, as it has done here in the last decade, to the positive relation." The acclaim for our heritage and achievements prompted the expansion of many American studies courses and departments, which had been rather scarce in universities before the war. Soon there were fellowships and teaching posts for specialists in American subjects, who were becoming cultural leaders. The growing enthusiasm for American literature and history greatly enriched the culture itself. But an avalanche of "national self-congratulation" was disturbing to the historian Richard Hofstader, who saw that a tendency to advertise rather than analyze American values sometimes made the past appear too idyllic and could make the present seem bland.

It was often said that there were few problems in the United States, that poverty had almost been eliminated, that "race relations" were rapidly improving, that only a handful of malcontents would find fault with the status quo. Dwight Macdonald was puzzled when his 1958 essay "America! America!" was rejected by *Encounter*, where he had just spent a year as a visiting editor; the piece examined the materialism and violence he noticed in his homeland after living abroad. Years later Macdonald wrote that it "seemed odd" that the directors of the Congress for Cultural Freedom "should have felt so strongly about my little un-American raspberry: one would have thought the CIA more sophisticated." But in 1958 Macdonald hadn't known that his censors were the kind of bureaucrats who functioned as though freedom should be sacrificed to safeguard freedom, as if dissent must be quashed if American democracy was to endure.

• • •

Harold Rosenberg called the New York intellectuals "the herd of independent minds." But independence was rare when the Hiss trials were mentioned. Because of the lurid charges against Alger Hiss, he was pegged as a Communist even before he was heard in court. Conservatives who assailed the legacy of the New Deal by stating that there had been Communist spies in Roosevelt's administration, and Cold War liberals who wanted to publicize their anti-Communism, sounded much alike when they insisted that Hiss was guilty of perjury in denying that he had stolen classified documents and passed them to Whittaker Chambers, who said he was the Soviets' courier, between 1934 and 1938. Just as some Jewish intellectuals were alarmed by the Rosenberg case because it strengthened the reactionaries' belief that most Communists were Jews, the Hiss case made many Ivy League liberals wish to disown ideas that appeared to resemble his—when right-wingers were defining people who defended Hiss as Communists. To support Chambers or to say that Hiss should "confess" his guilt were ways of announcing that you shouldn't be accused of subversion, not even if you went to Harvard.

The year 1948, when Chambers's claims were made public, was a presidential election year. If an eminent Democrat like Hiss were identified as a Communist, that might be useful to the Republicans in defeating Truman. *Time* indicated that all Democrats were on trial in the Hiss case; Henry Luce's biographer W. A. Swanberg wrote that for Luce the case "was divinely constructed to please God and help the Republicans." Richard Nixon, a little-known first-term Congressman and a member of the House Committee on Un-American Activities, used the case to boost his career. J. Edgar Hoover, who detested Truman, hoped to see the President unseated; moreover Hiss had been one of the young New Dealers who had criticized FBI procedures in the Thirties and felt that Hoover should be removed from office. Through a Catholic priest who acted as a conduit, an FBI agent leaked Chambers's ongoing allegations about Hiss to Nixon. (Although Nixon complained that the bureau wasn't cooperative and preferred to give credit to the Committee's staff, the Committee later issued official thanks to the FBI for its work on the case.) Every member of the Committee was up for reelection that year.

During the Committee's hearings and Hiss's indictment for perjury before a grand jury in Manhattan and his two trials in 1949, Americans—perhaps especially New Yorkers—argued about the possibility of "forgery by typewriter," about the expensive oriental rug presented to Hiss by Chambers, who said it was a gift from the Soviets in return for purloined documents (Hiss replied that it was a partial payment for rent owed on a sublet apartment), and about the old Ford roadster Hiss gave to Chambers, who said it was transferred to a Communist organizer. There was also the question of whether Hiss was "shielding" someone: either his wife, who was said to be more radical than he (Nixon wrote that Chambers told him Priscilla Hiss was "the 'red hot' of the two") or his stepson, who'd been discharged from a naval cadet program in 1945 on grounds of homosexuality. (FBI agents kept calling on the young man's gay friends; it was plain that his private life would be exposed if he testified that Chambers had lied when he said he was often at the Hisses' home—or if Hiss's lawyers alluded to Chambers's own sexual history.) Hiss would not allow his stepson to go on the stand.

Although Hiss steadily repeated that Chambers had never been a close friend, many were impressed by the details Chambers provided about the Hisses' lives: for example, that they were "amateur ornithologists," once excited by seeing a rare prothonotary warbler. But the public and the jurors didn't know that the couple had been under FBI surveillance for more than two years, that everything Chambers described could have been furnished to him by the bureau—including the false information that Hiss was deaf in one ear and that the Hisses were teetotalers. It was rumored that Chambers was homosexual; some thought he'd been spurned by Hiss and was acting in vengeance. (Hiss said Chambers hadn't made "advances," but it did appear that Chambers was emotionally obsessed with Hiss.) Others thought Chambers's espionage story was true because he seemed passionately remorseful about depicting a man who'd been "perhaps my closest friend" as a powerful revolutionary. Spectators and the press noted the dramatic contrast between the accused and the accuser: calm, well-groomed, handsome Alger Hiss and agitated, messy, fat Whittaker Chambers.

During his trials Hiss and his lawyers believed he would be acquitted. In his professional life he was accustomed to success; after excelling at Harvard Law School, the clerk for Supreme Court Justice Oliver Wendell Holmes had risen from working in the New Deal's Agricultural Adjustment Administration to a high position in the State Department, then was one of the main architects of the United Nations and headed the Carnegie Endowment for International Peace. And his confidence was conspicuous when he faced the Committee in 1948. According to Robert Stripling, the Committee's chief investigator, Nixon took a vehement dislike to Hiss on their very first meeting. Nearly forty years afterward Nixon's resentment still seemed fresh when he wrote that Hiss was "a striking representative of the fashionable Eastern establishment" with "impeccable social and intellectual qualifications," and that the media were "dazzled by [his] background." But Hiss's elegant, imperious manner did not serve him well at the Committee's hearings; politely, he appeared to be treating Nixon as an inferior. After his first trial, two jurors who voted for conviction told *The New York Journal-American* they had been antagonized by the series of stellar character witnesses for Hiss; Supreme Court Justices Felix Frankfurter and Stanley Reed, Governor Adlai Stevenson of Illinois, John W. Davis (the Democrats' presidential candidate for 1924), the president of Johns Hopkins University, a retired admiral, two judges, and two diplomats all paid tribute to the defendant, making him seem more privileged than ordinary mortals.

Over the years Hiss's associates and friends noticed that although he usually sounded very sure of himself, his memory was uneven. There were contradictions between his testimony before the Committee about his dealings with Chambers and what he said in court the following year. There had been errors in his initial statements; he later explained that he'd corrected himself after going over his records. Some observers thought his self-assurance was arrogance, and the corrections were regarded as carefully calculated lies.

In the years before Vietnam and Watergate, few Americans suspected the federal government of deceit or illegalities, or that the FBI might falsify evidence. (The dishonesty and corruption of Warren Harding's administration in the early Twenties had long receded in the national memory.) What took place inside a courtroom was supposed to elucidate what had occurred outside it; the prosecution (or the defense) was expected to solve a mystery: the truth was to be unveiled. That "facts" could be manufactured within the law was not widely understood in the postwar era. It seemed that many citizens accepted the guilty verdict in the Hiss case because the government produced an array of documents. But the famous pumpkin papers, five rolls of film which Nixon said were "conclusive proof of the greatest treason conspiracy in this nation's history," were largely routine State Department cables, plus some Navy documents concerning fire extinguishers, life rafts, and parachutes; the latter had been kept on open shelves in the Bureau of Standards library. Two rolls containing material about proposed trade agreements with Germany were made public at Hiss's trials; those rolls also included speculations about the Japanese military presence in China in 1938 and three incoming telegrams initialed by Hiss (what kind of spy would initial stolen material before passing it to another?). The fifth roll was blank. Photographs of Nixon gazing sternly at a strip of film—sometimes without a magnifying glass—were featured on front pages across the country while he staked his career on a conviction.

Throughout the first of the two trials, eleven Communist leaders were being prosecuted for conspiracy in the same New York courthouse; each day the Hiss jurors had to walk past the Communist Party picket lines encircling the building: the scarlet menace appeared to be everywhere. When the first Hiss trial ended in a hung jury, Nixon wanted the judge to be impeached and to subpoena the four pro-acquittal jurors for examination by the Committee. (A. J. Liebling wrote that if Hiss were not convicted, "Nixon would be wiped out, and the old foxes of [Nixon's] party . . . would put a black mark against him as a young man who went too far out on a limb without testing it.") In the next trial a juror would have needed great courage to reject the government's case. Some who were selected for that trial "asked to be excused" because—as one of them wrote to *The New York Post*—they feared being "branded" as Communists or harassed at work if they voted for acquittal. In 1976 the Freedom of Information Act revealed that two jurors in the second trial had relatives employed by the FBI. During the trial, the prosecution asked the bureau that this "be kept quiet," which it was.

A substantial number of people thought Hiss was innocent—first, because he'd volunteered to come before the Committee and refute Chambers under oath, then when Chambers called him a Communist, challenged him to repeat the charge outside the protection of a governmental hearing. Chambers did so on *Meet the Press*; Hiss sued him for libel. Second, many believed Hiss because Chambers emerged as a pathological liar. As Chambers kept changing his tale, he admitted that he'd perjured himself; he denied sixteen times that he'd ever participated in spying. When Chambers first told the Committee that Hiss was a Communist, he didn't say Hiss was involved in espionage; then he repeated under oath that Hiss had never been a spy—and then that he'd always been one. Twice Chambers informed the FBI that he would not testify that he had received documents from Hiss. Chambers spoke of espionage only after Truman was reelected; when the administration which was expected to lose was returned to the White House, Nixon warned Chambers that Truman's Justice Department was planning to indict him for perjury. Nixon and Chambers reasoned that the Democrats wanted to silence Chambers and "save" Hiss for the sake of their party's reputation.

Known as Bob and Karl (or Carl) and Eugene and Charles as he worked his way through at least ten aliases, Chambers's gift for fantasy was so immense that students of the case wondered if aspects of his past might have been exaggerated to make him seem like an expert on Communism, which enhanced his career at *Time*; Henry Luce esteemed right-wing ex-Communists. Becoming *Time*'s foreign news editor in 1944, Chambers rewrote all the dispatches from correspondents abroad, inserting an anti-Communist perspective despite the wartime alliance with the Russians; in *Witness* he boasted that he had "reversed the magazine's news policy," maintaining that Russia "was actively using World War II to prepare World War III." Before long, prominent correspondents called for his removal as editor, among them John Hersey in Moscow, Charles Wertenbaker in Paris, and Theodore White in Chungking. Hersey found parts of his cables had been "torn from the context" in keeping with "an editorial bias" which was "grossly unfair" and "actually vicious." Chambers's disdain for facts and his mangling of the news caused a furor at *Time*'s New York office, but when researchers protested the untruths, Chambers told them that truth didn't matter. Although Luce was pleased with Chambers's work, he shifted him to slightly different duties.

Well before the Hiss case, Chambers's Time Inc. colleagues were frequently amazed by his remarks and behavior, and some called him a fanatic. Chambers said he feared he would be murdered by Stalin's agents because he knew many secrets of the Communist Party's underground apparatus, and he even imagined that his new assistant at the magazine might try to poison him during their first lunch together. In restaurants he sat facing the door with his back against the wall. On the eve of Hiss's libel suit, when Chambers thought the Party might eliminate him "as the one dangerous witness against the conspiracy" or kidnap one of his children, he and his wife "distributed bullets for handy use" in all the rooms of their house. Chambers often let acquaintances know that fate had a great role in store for him, that he was directed by "God's purpose." He told a *Time* researcher, "I cannot really be beaten because on my side is a Power." At the end of the first trial, he said to a Washington reporter that he was "destroying [myself] that this country and the faith by which it lives may continue to exist." By "destroying" he meant confessing "to every crime, every sin, every evil" in his past. (When Chambers informed the FBI in 1949 about his homosexual experiences, that was part of the confession.) Often suicidal, he tried to kill himself soon after the pumpkin papers were unearthed. Given his emotional infirmity, some who followed the case felt that it would have been quite easy for Nixon and the FBI to manipulate him.

For years after the trials Hiss's supporters wrestled with overlapping theories about the Woodstock typewriter which Chambers stated that Priscilla Hiss had used to copy sixty-five pages of stolen State Department documents. (Known as the Baltimore documents, this material was separate from the pumpkin papers; Chambers had given neither to the Russians but kept them as proof of a Communist spy network.) The Hisses said they had given their typewriter away in 1937; the documents were dated 1938. Some thought the FBI's experts had erred in identifying the Woodstock among the hundreds of secondhand machines the bureau had rounded up. Others thought the FBI had built a new machine or that Chambers had arranged to have one made. Yet others wondered if Chambers had stolen the Hisses' typewriter from their home and put another Woodstock in its place, or had obtained the machine after it was no longer in their possession. More than two decades later, Hiss and his lawyers concluded that FBI agents had planted an old Woodstock where his 1949 defense team would find it and mistake it for the original; the serial number showed that it had been constructed more than a year after the Hiss typewriter.

Security was loose in Washington in the Thirties, when papers of all sorts were left on desktops or shelves in unlocked government offices. Of the typed pages in Chambers's possession, almost a third were devoted to economic conditions in Manchuria; others described the hopes of France's Foreign Minister for a reconciliation with Hitler's Germany in 1938 and his disbelief in a potential Nazi-Soviet pact. There were hazy reports of Japanese troop movements in China, accounts of conversations between ambassadors in Europe about Hitler's conquest of Austria, and telegrams from the Far East about a Japanese decision to use Tsinhua University's buildings for military barracks and then a reversal of that decision.

In short, the content of Chambers's pages did not put the nation's safety at risk. But the fact that he had copies of official documents was more important in convicting Hiss than the nature of the documents themselves, and the public had been persuaded that vital government secrets had been betrayed to the Soviets. Other State Department employees could have given those particular papers to Chambers; in the past Henry Julian Wadleigh, Franklin Victor Reno, and others Chambers didn't publicly name had supplied him with material. Also someone could have fished Hiss's four handwritten memos out of a wastebasket or filched them from his desk. Chambers could also have helped himself from some open sources, such as the Bureau of Standards. The prosecution did not disclose that an FBI laboratory report said "it would be impossible for an expert to testify to the fact that because of the similar or common errors it followed that PRISCILLA HISS actually typed the documents."

Finally it was Chambers's word against Hiss's. Along the way, as Chambers replaced one lie with another, both Hoover and Nixon worried about his credibility. But in the midst of the domestic Cold War, Chambers's saga seemed to confirm a host of nightmares. Although the charges of espionage could not be proven, Hiss was convicted of perjury and sentenced on January 25, 1950. Two weeks later Joseph McCarthy made his speech in Wheeling, West Virginia, claiming that the State Department was full of Communists and launching his career. In *Six Crises* Nixon made the same statement twice on one page—"The Hiss case brought me national fame"—and he felt he owed his vice presidency to the case. Supreme Court Justice William O. Douglas wrote in his memoirs that the case "gave agencies of the federal government unparalleled power over the private lives of citizens." The FBI kept files on Hiss's most active supporters, including those who wrote about the case. And in Lewisburg Penitentiary Alger Hiss lost the lofty manner which had alienated some observers; long afterward he told his son, "Forty-four months in jail is a good corrective to three years at Harvard."

Because some Cold War liberals had been anti-Communists since the Thirties, they felt the case justified their long-held views. But there were others who became emotional and defensive when anyone brought up the case: repeating that Hiss was guilty, they seemed to cling to the idea of his guilt. To think that he might be innocent was to call their own conduct into question—and could rob them of the right to see themselves as liberals. If his innocence were ever established, they would feel guilty for defiling him. As the years passed they seemed grateful whenever a new article or book said that he had been a Communist spy, and many of them became very angry if the case was called a miscarriage of justice.

22

Assaulting the Left

Diana Trilling wrote in *The New Leader* in 1952 that "the idea that America is a terror-stricken country in the grip of hysteria is a Communist-inspired idea." But her logic was not sustained by history. By the beginning of the Fifties many Americans were afraid of one another: the Right feared the Left, the Left feared the Right, and the apolitical feared contact with either side. People of conflicting views felt they were living through a terribly dangerous time: some on the Left thought fascism could soon be realized in the United States, whereas segments of the Right thought that American Communists would undermine their society while the Soviet Union would gain control of the globe.

But apart from Trotskyists who had clashed with Communist classmates at the City College of New York during the Depression, or those who had opposed their Communist colleagues in unions such as the United Auto Workers or the Newspaper Guild, millions of Americans who feared Communists had never met one. The foe was almost faceless. What was unknown was all the easier to fear, especially for the uninformed. Commentators like Claude Bourdet, editor of *France Observateur*, noted that the scarcity and obscurity of American Communists made them seem particularly threatening. Europeans who detested Communism and the Soviet Union were usually acquainted with Communists: they could argue with them in person. But in the United States the Communist was hardly a familiar figure. Presumed to be working "underground" or behind the scenes, he seemed to have almost magical powers: to be invincible because he was imperceptible—as well as ubiquitous.

Even Leslie Fiedler admitted that there was "a certain incapacity to believe in Communists as people. . . . When counter-pickets to the Rosenberg defenders carried placards demanding 'Death to the Communist rats!' there was involved, beyond the old American metaphor for spies, a wish to believe that the enemy is subhuman, an animal to exterminate rather than a man to confront." At a time when there was no possibility of an American revolution, demonology could develop because the friends were both invisible and bestial.

• • •

In the late Forties American policy makers had not believed the Soviet Union would initiate a war against us; in 1949 John Foster Dulles said that no "responsible official" he knew thought "the Soviet government now plans conquest by open military aggression." But although our leaders never felt there was any danger of a Soviet invasion of the United States, they were alarmed by the spread of socialism as well as Communism in Europe. They were mistrustful of the British Labour Party while it was in power. (That John Strachey, who'd been a Communist in the Thirties, was Clement Attlee's Secretary of State for War, caused agitation in the Pentagon.) On our side the Cold War was not only a response to Stalin's despotism, it was a reaction against social change all over the world.

By midsummer of 1950 all sorts of citizens felt that a world war was imminent. Edward R. Murrow of CBS, a pragmatic pessimist, thought war with Russia was almost inevitable, though he did not favor "preventive war." The fact that the Soviet Union had been our ally in World War II was totally erased by the Korean War, which was portrayed as one of the first steps in the global Communist conspiracy. By 1952 George Kennan, newly reappointed Ambassador to Moscow, found that "People on both sides expect [Korea] soon to develop into a real Soviet-American war."

Just as the Soviet expansion in Eastern Europe had increased the strength of our investigating committees, the Korean War gave further substance to the fear of an enemy at home. And memories of the recent world war inspired an abhorrence of any nation—like North Korea—which might prepare the way for another one. On our own turf, many were persuaded that American Communists were as menacing as those in Asia or Europe because Lenin had adopted Trotsky's theory of "permanent revolution"—hence all Communists must be committed to the concept of perpetual war. So Representative Harold Velde, a member of the Committee from 1949 to 1956, could be confident of ample support when he said, "It's a lot better to wrongly accuse one person of being a Communist than to allow so many to get away with such Communist acts as those that have brought us to the brink of World War III."

By the Fifties our country had become a national security state, ready for military action at any moment. John Kenneth Galbraith wrote that while Dulles was Secretary of State, "American foreign policy was dominated by a single ruling passion, which was to defeat Communism." Yet despite Eisenhower's 1952 campaign pledge to "roll back" the Iron Curtain and "liberate" the "captive peoples" of Eastern Europe, in spite of Dulles's "brinkmanship," the White House did not interfere when the Russians crushed the Hungarian revolution of 1956. Some Hungarians had hoped for American aid, but that would have meant risking a major war. Far from using "massive retaliation"— the nuclear bombardments sometimes threatened by Dulles—Eisenhower increasingly relied on covert operations to implement part of his policies, as when the CIA overthrew Iran's premier Mohammed Mossadegh in 1953, returning the Shah to his throne, and ousted Guatemala's elected socialist government in 1954. In each case the public was informed that pernicious leftists had been foiled, although Mossadegh, a keen nationalist, had made the Soviets leave Iran soon after World War II and had outlawed the Iranian Communist Party. The rationale for both coups was questionable because Mossadegh had nationalized the oil fields vital to British and American companies, and Guatemala's president had nationalized plantation lands owned by the United Fruit company—while seeking to eliminate the company's tax exemptions.

Impoverished countries were thought to nourish Communists if they were not governed by right-wingers. The historian Arnold Toynbee observed that the United States had become the new Roman Empire, opposing "revolutions of the poor against the rich" in faraway nations which were not going to attack us. Helping to install or perpetuate dictatorships in the name of democracy was hardly questioned by voters who were told that we lived in constant peril from the Marxists or anti-capitalists of even small countries. The "domino theory" was invoked so frequently that it sounded as if Communism could easily be exported from Southeast Asia to Brooklyn. Stalin's death and Khrushchev's exposure of Stalin's crimes helped to decrease our politicians' expectations of world war, but the fear remained vibrant in the public mind.

• • •

Almost anything seemed justified in combating Communism: at home or abroad. Soon after World War II American military intelligence agents recruited and paid many fascist collaborators and Nazi war criminals—among them the Gestapo chief Klaus Barbie—to help spy on European Communists and the Soviets, then arranged their escape to South America so that their knowledge of American espionage techniques would not be revealed. And while the United States was employing and sheltering mass murderers, the CIA—convinced that foreign Communists were expert brainwashers—embarked on thirteen years of experiments in thought control, which lasted until 1966. Some CIA executives believed that drugs and hypnosis had elicited the confessions of Joseph Cardinal Mindszenty during his trial for treason in Hungary in 1949. Hence research in behavior manipulation seemed imperative to CIA directors Allen Dulles and Richard Helms. Yet in 1953 a high-level military study group reported that neither the Russians nor other Communist nations had mastered the art of mindbending, and that there was "little threat, if any, to [our] national security." But the intelligence community reasoned that it should proceed with its experiments because the Communists might one day excel in that field.

Eminent professors of psychiatry, neurologists, behavioral scientists, chemists, and physiologists were soon on the CIA payroll in pursuit of techniques that could convert an individual into a vegetable or propel him into treason. Through a couple of conduits, specialists at such institutions as Columbia, the University of Illinois Medical School, the University of Oklahoma, the University of California, and the University of Rochester, received CIA grants for clandestine research on LSD. Some of the scientists knew where the funding came from. Others were deliberately deceived about the source of the money.

Meanwhile, since none of the seven thousand American prisoners in Korea had escaped from captivity and few had attempted to do so, and because subsequent State investigations suggested that about seventy per cent of them had cooperated with the Koreans to some extent—mainly by making "confessions" or signing petitions that urged an end to the war—it was tempting to think they had been brainwashed. It also seemed essential to protect the public from evidence of collaboration—and therefore to protect the ex-prisoners from the public: at home they were shielded from the press, instructed to sign statements that bound them to silence, and plunged into "rehabilitation" courses.

With millions of dollars being spent by the National Institute of Mental Health on experimenting with LSD and other psychochemicals, CIA officials decided that testing on "unwitting" people was necessary—in direct contradiction of the Nuremburg Code, which stated that those tested in medical research must be made aware of the risks involved and must consent to undergoing them. In 1953 the Code was adopted by our government. The CIA's mind control experiments began in the same year, some in coordination with the Army in a project code-named "Often Chickwit."

Many of the human guinea pigs were prisoners and mental patients. At the New York State Psychiatric Institute, Army-sponsored researchers gave injections of several mescaline derivatives to a forty-two-year-old professional tennis player named Harold Blauer, who had admitted himself when he was despondent after a divorce. His daughter later testified that he'd had devastating reactions to the medication: following the fourth shot he had suffered hallucinations as well as "violent tremors" and feared he might be going mad. Blauer, who had not volunteered to participate in any kind of diagnostic testing, resisted another injection, protesting that he was to be discharged from the hospital the next day. But a resident physician told him that his doctor had ordered it. Seventy-three minutes after the fifth shot, he went into a coma and then died in about an hour. To avoid "adverse publicity" the Army listed his death as a heart attack. Thirty-four years later a federal judge in Manhattan ruled that the government must pay seven hundred thousand dollars to Blauer's daughters as damages for his "wrongful death."

One of the CIA's early LSD experiments climaxed in the suicide of Dr. Frank Olson, a civilian biochemist working on covert germ warfare for both the Army and the CIA. Nine days of acute depression and recurrent paranoia after he was given a surreptitious dose of LSD in a glass of Cointreau caused him to leap from the tenth story of the Statler Hotel in Manhattan. The liqueur was spiked by Dr. Sidney Gottlieb, who directed many of the CIA's behavioral investigations for more than twenty years. The doctors and professors who explored the impact of LSD had already been warned that it might induce temporary psychosis. After Olson killed himself some CIA officials privately agreed that the drug had "triggered" his suicide. But the CIA cover-up was so thorough that twenty-two years passed before his family discovered that he had been dosed without his knowledge. The case had been classified for the sake of patriotism—which was often identified as the impetus for illegal drug-testing. The experts involved in similar projects referred to "national survival," their "sense of mission," and their "patriotic vision" as they dispensed chemicals that could alter a person's concepts of truth and falsehood and right and wrong.

Both Blauer and Olson died in 1953. But the CIA's experiments increased thereafter. In 1955 some patrons of New York and San Francisco bars became violently ill and were hospitalized after they unknowingly imbibed LSD in their cocktails. Unsuspecting men in San Francisco were also lured by a narcotics agent from bars to a CIA "field laboratory": an apartment garnished with red drapes, black velveteen, and pictures of handcuffed women, and equipped with two-way mirrors, where "parties" were under way; in that "safehouse" prostitutes were often available. The CIA called the project "Operation Midnight Climax." Some of the parties were filmed so that the CIA could study the use of prostitutes as information-gatherers. The guests were unaware that they'd ingested LSD and other drugs; some fell sick but doctors were rarely present to "observe" them, and most of the witnesses concealed behind the mirrors were CIA employees.

Due to the "urgent need" (cited in a CIA report) to learn how to "render an individual subservient to an imposed will or control," random Americans continued to vomit and hallucinate in the service of their country, uninformed of their role in scientific research. But the CIA's testing grounds were not limited to the United States. In 1957 fifty-three patients in the Allan Memorial Institute at McGill University in Montreal received megadoses of LSD—plus powerful electric shocks that were administered two or three times a day—as part of a "behavior modification" program financed by a CIA front called the Society for the Investigation of Human Ecology. Some were plagued with amnesia which lasted months or even years after the treatment.

The experiments were conducted by Dr. D. Ewen Cameron of McGill University, a well-known psychiatrist. His patients also submitted to "psychic driving"—listening to recorded messages for up to sixteen hours per session for days or weeks—and periods of drug-induced sleep which sometimes went on for sixty days. The aftereffects could include panic and incontinence. Neither the patients nor their relatives were told that they were functioning as subjects. Twenty-seven years later, nine Canadians sued the United States for compensation. One of them—the wife of a member of the Canadian Parliament—revealed that her ability to concentrate had been permanently destroyed. Another former patient said that after the experiments she was unable to remember giving birth to her four children. The case was settled out of court in 1988, when the Justice Department agreed to pay seven hundred and fifty thousand dollars to the plaintiffs.

Throughout the Fifties the CIA worked on "controlled production" of personality changes, also headaches, earaches, twitches, staggers, and diarrhea, all with the goal of reducing a person to a condition where it would be possible to "subvert his principles," as a CIA document explained. "Stress-producing" drugs and hallucinogenic Mexican mushrooms and hypnosis and amphetamines and sensory deprivation and "simulated schizophrenia" were employed with the aim of creating foreign spies for the CIA. Could extreme disorientation steer an unwilling subject into divulging information that would betray his country—or to assassinate one of its leaders? Many of the projects were eventually abandoned after years of testing showed that brainwashing did not produce reliable agents or force people to tell the truth.

In the late Seventies, when CIA advisors and staff members were called to testify before Senate committees and subcommittees about the mind control experiments, a few defended the procedures on the grounds that the public had been terrified of Communism in the Fifties. In other words, top secret research was described as a tranquilizer for the national nervous system, although almost no one but Allen Dulles, Richard Helms, and a handful of their colleagues knew anything about it.

• • •

At a time when the United Nations was sometimes characterized as a conduit for Communism, when *Collier's* magazine devoted a special issue to World War III (which the United States won after dropping an atom bomb on Moscow), when anxieties about fallout near an atomic testing site in Nevada were dismissed by Senator George Malone as "Communist-inspired scare stories" even after small children began to die of leukemia, when *Ferdinand the Bull* was denounced as left-wing propaganda because the bull refused to fight the matador, fictions were a staple of the national diet.

It was an age of investigations, but investigative reporting was fairly sparse. Banner headlines often outweighed flimsy stories: "McCarthy Has New Evidence" (*The Baltimore Sun*) and "Knows Names of 57 Reds" (*The Kansas City Star*) turned out be charges without substance. It was a time when liars flourished even more easily than usual, partly because much of the press didn't ferret out the facts behind their statements. In 1950 quite a few Washington journalists still thought McCarthy was a joke, but their papers gave him lavish attention because he was "colorful," the stories were lively. On occasion he was intentionally confusing—waving documents and jumbling allegations so that no one could follow him—which gave the impression that his mind worked more quickly than anyone else's, and the press allowed him to sound like an expert.

After 1952 there were papers that criticized McCarthy; some, like *The Capitol Times* of Madison, Wisconsin, and *The Washington Post*, investigated and refuted his charges in detail. But many had previously quoted his giddiest fabrications without questioning them. The quotes were correct; only the content was not. But often the inflammatory headlines seemed to proclaim his veracity: "Purge State Department Reds, Senator Urges" (*The Atlanta*

Constitution) and "Harvard Ties to Red Groups Upset Alumni" (*The Chicago Tribune*) led readers to believe that Communists already controlled large portions of the establishment. In the first five years of McCarthy's triumphs, many papers avoided challenging him. Some editors felt that no American politician would accuse others of treason unless he had substantial evidence of their guilt. The concept of "objectivity" also demanded that a public figure be quoted without interpretation. Years afterward *The New York Times'* columnist James Reston wrote, "Putting quotation marks around McCarthy's false charges did not relieve us of complicity in McCarthy's campaign." And when McCarthy tried to instigate advertisers' boycotts against papers that enraged him, many publishers and editors suffered what the columnist I. F. Stone called "a prolonged attack of *laryngitis intimidatus.*" Objectivity became passivity—which resulted in superficial reporting.

So the coverage of McCarthy was copious but bewildering. Later, when such papers as *The Milwaukee Journal* documented the spuriousness of his statements, their work had little effect because many subscribers thought he had been successful in sweeping numerous Communists out of the government—even though he had never identified a single one in office. (*The Journal* balanced McCarthy's lies with factual corrections inserted in brackets: a technique that some other papers used toward the end of his reign.)

Every decade has its fantasists, but some may have prospered in the Fifties because "truth" seemed relative to many followers of McCarthy. It was quite widely known that he had falsified his military record: he had forged a letter from his commanding officer in order to award himself a citation from Admiral Chester Nimitz. McCarthy had injured his leg during a shipboard party of marines who were celebrating the crossing of the equator. But the fact that he was never a tailgunner and had no combat wounds—even the shrapnel in his leg was imaginary—did not seem to diminish his credibility nor his gift for exploiting the media.

After McCarthy's search for spies in the Army Signal Corps at Fort Monmouth, New Jersey, in 1953 proved fruitless, *The New York Times* obliquely acknowledged that it had misled its readers in its initial accounts of the investigation. A *Times* editorial stated, "The reading public should understand that it is difficult, if not impossible, to ignore charges by Senator McCarthy just because they are usually proved exaggerated or false. The remedy lies with the reader." Richard Rovere wrote in response, "To many people, this was rather like saying that if a restaurant serves poisoned food, it is up to the diner to refuse it." Most newspapers—even those that deplored McCarthy's tactics—had approved of his crusade. But when he assailed Eisenhower's administration at the beginning of 1954—claiming that the CIA and the Department of Defense were full of Communists, that "twenty years of treason" under the Democrats had become "twenty-one years" under the GOP—many editors felt he was damaging the cause of anti-Communism as well as the Republican Party. Therefore it was no longer controversial to impugn him. While he was sabotaging his own career as recklessly as he had ruined others', the press assisted in his self-destruction. Some commentators waxed so righteous that it sounded as if McCarthy was almost the only politician who had ever twisted the truth.

• • •

Political leaders lied about the perils of nuclear testing and most Americans didn't know it. (In 1953 Eisenhower advised the Atomic Energy Commission to "keep [the public] confused as to fission and fusion" and to omit words like "thermonuclear" and "hydrogen" from their speeches and press conferences.) But most Americans were sure that Communists had to lie: a Communist would say "sofa" when he meant "chair," or "land" if he meant "sea," or "cigar" if he meant "opium." The concept of "Aesopian language"—which was analyzed by Herbert Philbrick, the FBI's "Red underground" columnist for *The Herald Tribune*, and Louis Budenz, ex-editor of the *Daily Worker* and paid professional witness against Communists—probably derived from Lenin's preface to *Imperialism*, where he referred to "that cursed Aesopian language" which he and other exiled revolutionaries had used during the period of Czarist censorship, when they could not publish their work without disguising some of their ideas. Some conservatives assumed that since every American Communist must be a disciple of Lenin, no Communist could say what he really meant: he had to speak or write in code. And leftists who thought their phones were bugged realized that when they rang each other and arranged to go to the movies, the FBI might well deduce that they were exchanging covert information.

Allan E. Sloane, a television writer who cooperated with the Committee, testified about Aesopian language when he explained how strangers were described to Party members: "a terrific guy" was a Communist; "a good guy" was a sympathizer; "a bastard" was "an active anti-Communist." Aesopian language was also featured by the prosecution in the New York trial of eleven Communist leaders; the defendants were convicted in 1949 of conspiracy to teach and advocate the overthrow of the government by force and violence— but not of attempting to "overthrow" anything. (The Smith Act of 1940 made it a crime to "advocate" overthrowing the government—and "advocating" meant belonging to the Communist Party.) The prosecutors could find no proof that the defendants had instructed others in the use of explosives, nor had they organized "armed insurrection." But since they did *not* advocate violence, the jury was told that they must have intended to do so; what they had not said was used as evidence against them. Years afterward Supreme Court Justice William O. Douglas—who had voted against upholding the defendants' conviction—said they "were not plotting revolution, handing out grenades. . . . They were teachers only—men teaching Marxism." In effect the Communist leaders were judged guilty not for their actions but for their ideas, and all but one were sentenced to five years in jail.

Communists were often credited with a diabolical cleverness. Producer Jack Warner told the Committee that you had to be almost "superhuman" in order to spot some of the propaganda injected into film scripts by left-wing writers: the dialogue they wrote was so "subtle" that, Warner said, "You have to take eight or ten Harvard law courses to find out what they mean." It was widely believed that a college education was an exercise in deceit and that professors might be skilled at masking Communist dogma in artful trappings. In the early Fifties FBI agents sat in on classes in government and political science taught by the civil libertarian H. H. Wilson and his colleagues at Princeton: to check on the subtleties that might be dispensed. The FBI also conducted an elaborate "cryptanalysis" of Walt Kelly's "Pogo" strip—which had lampooned McCarthy and J. Edgar Hoover—to determine if they contained coded messages of further disrespect for anti-Communists. After two weeks of testing, none were found.

• • •

The air raid drills of the period seemed to highlight the futility of any defense against the enemy. While children were being trained to hide beneath their school desks from the atomic bomb, McCarthy told a vast audience at a communion breakfast of the New York Police Department's Holy Name Society, "Ten thousand agents in Moscow can do very little to hurt us, but one Communist agent with a razor blade poised over the jugular vein of this nation in an atomic energy plant or in a policy-making post can mean the death of America."

When the keenest of Cold War politicians sought to convince the public of the dangers from the Soviet Union, the tactic was to suggest that danger existed in everyone's community—among teachers, within trade unions, on movie screens: whatever was close to home. Since our country was so vulnerable, it seemed that subversion must be fought in every field. Because Aaron Copland had attended the 1949 Cultural and Scientific Conference for World Peace at the Waldorf-Astoria Hotel—where American leftists and liberals met with Soviet intellectuals in hopes of a cultural dialogue—his *Lincoln Portrait*, scheduled for performance at the Eisenhower inauguration of January 1953, was banned from the program. The press had depicted the Waldorf Conference as an orgy of Stalinism, and Representative Fred Busbey of Illinois said that the GOP "would have been ridiculed from one end of the United States to the other if Copland's music had been played" in honor of "a President elected to fight Communism." Copland was questioned by McCarthy about the United States Information Agency, which had sent the composer abroad to give lectures. At the hearing McCarthy was not at his fiercest, but Copland's concerts and appearances were canceled by universities from Alabama to Colorado, also by the Hollywood Bowl Committee and the Borough of Brooklyn. Just before a music festival in Pittsburgh, the mayor of that city announced that none of Copland's compositions could be played there.

In 1956 several television stations—pressured by their sponsors—declined to run the movie of James Thurber and Elliott Nugent's *The Male Animal* because the leading man read a letter from Bartolomeo Vanzetti aloud. Sponsors had a history of timidity: conservative consumers boycotted products advertised on programs which seemed too liberal or where individuals of questionable "loyalty" appeared. In 1950 Campbell Soup had ceased to sponsor *Edward R. Murrow With the News* when the program was considered insufficiently anti-Communist. (Murrow had defended the China scholar Owen Lattimore, baselessly accused by McCarthy of being Russia's foremost American spy.) Murrow acquired other sponsors, but that year CBS introduced a loyalty oath, asking its employees if they belonged to the Communist Party or any organization that the Attorney General had designated as subversive.

Counterattack, a fiercely anti-Communist newsletter, hatched by three former FBI men, had called CBS "a particularly Red network." Perhaps that was why its executives were easily cowed. CBS did sanction Murrow's *See It Now* exposé of McCarthy in March 1954, which many felt was crucial to the Senator's downfall. But the program came late in McCarthy's tenure: he had already wrecked himself by defaming Eisenhower as well as the Army (even Hoover had withdrawn his support for McCarthy some months before). And CBS's own blacklist would endure for at least a decade. In 1956 Aware, Inc., a powerful pressure group which monitored the airwaves, distributed lists of alleged Communists within the industry, and bullied sponsors, attacked the broadcaster John Henry Faulk. The liberal Democrat had incensed the directors of Aware because he'd organized an anti-blacklist slate in the American Federation of

Television and Radio (AFTRA), also because he'd gone to a dinner party for Andrei Gromyko, the Soviet foreign minister, at the United Nations. Libby's Frozen Foods dropped Faulk's humorous radio show, *Johnny's Front Porch.* CBS fired him. Faulk finally won a lawsuit for libel against Aware, and in 1975 the network did penance by producing a docudrama about his ordeal. But he was never again hired by a major network.

Death of a Salesman was closed in Illinois after the American Legion picketed it there; the Legionnaires were infuriated not only by Miller's politics, but by the content of the play, which they saw as an insult to American business. (When *Salesman* was filmed by Columbia, the producers worried that the movie "might be construed as an attack on free employment," so they prefaced it with a short documentary which stated that being a salesman was a splendid career. After Miller spoke of suing, the preface was expunged.) During the Fifties Linus Pauling's name could not be uttered on the Voice of America— even after he won the Nobel Prize in chemistry—because he had opposed nuclear testing. In 1954 Thoreau's *Walden* was removed from USIA libraries because it was deemed "downright socialistic."

• • •

Some leftists were old enough to remember the Palmer raids of 1919 and 1920, which occurred after Attorney General A. Mitchell Palmer's house in Washington was bombed. The bomber died in the explosion and was never identified, but a radical leaflet was found near his scattered limbs. Packaged bombs had also been mailed or addressed to about three dozen public officials and businessmen (most were intercepted but two people were badly injured; the case wasn't solved). Palmer had presidential ambitions; steelworkers and coal miners were striking all over the country and there was a general strike in Seattle; Socialists and anarchists and Communists were suspected of planning a revolution like Russia's. Many conservatives saw labor's revolt against management as a prelude to a dictatorship of the proletariat, probably instigated by Moscow. Palmer said that ninety per cent of the "Red agitators" were immigrants. A drive against radicals seemed likely to win popular support and valuable publicity for Palmer. The raids were organized by twenty-four-year-old J. Edgar Hoover, head of the Radical Division of the Justice Department.

Hoover's division spread rumors of Bolshevik plots to overthrow the American government. Approximately ten thousand foreign-born persons were arrested and imprisoned in thirty-three cities; over five hundred of them were deported, including Emma Goldman. Some were radicals, some were Communists, some were members of the Industrial Workers of the World, some were merely visitors to immigrants' social clubs, pool rooms, or union halls; some had no connection to any political group. H. L. Mencken, who had no use for "so-called Reds," wrote about the "*pogrom* against" them, noting that "the machinery" involved "would have almost sufficed to repel an invasion by the united powers of Europe. They were hunted out of their sweat-shops and coffee-houses ... dragged to jail to the tooting of horns, arraigned before quaking judges on unintelligible charges, condemned to deportation without the slightest chance to defend themselves, torn from their dependent families, herded into prison-ships, and then finally dumped in a snow waste, to be rescued and fed by the Bolsheviki. ... All the constitutional guarantees of the citizen were suspended, [and] ... the country was handed over to a frenzied mob of detectives, informers, and *agents provocateurs*."

When the prisoners' friends went to see them in jail, the visitors were often arrested (Palmer said that radicals could have no friends but radicals). Many of the prisoners had to be released because they were American citizens and could not be deported—or because the raiders had no evidence against them. Arrests without warrants, Communist Party meetings arranged by Hoover's agents for nights when the raids would take place, unlawful searches, illegal detentions, and reports of violence by policemen and agents, discredited Hoover and Palmer's venture. *The New York Times* reported in January 1920, "Agents quietly infiltrated into the radical ranks ... and went to work, sometimes as cooks in remote mining colonies, sometimes as miners, again as steel workers, and where the opportunity presented itself, as 'agitators' of the wildest type." Palmer defended his campaign on the grounds that "There could be no nice distinction drawn between the theoretical ideas of the radicals and their actual violation of any national laws"; furthermore the "alien filth" possessed a "misshapen cast of mind and indecencies of character." Twelve distinguished lawyers signed a petition defining the raids as "the continued violation of the Constitution ... by the Department of Justice of the United States Government"; Hoover opened files on all of them. Labor Secretary William B. Wilson called for an end to the "gigantic and cruel hoax" of the "deportation delirium." At Senate hearings on the raids early in 1921, Senator Thomas Walsh of Montana referred to the sweeping arrests as "the lawless acts of a mob." Palmer's reputation was permanently damaged.

The bombings and assassinations that Hoover predicted for May 1, 1920, did not take place, and the Red Scare faded in the spring of that year. But much of the public had been manipulated into fearing the labor movement, which lost about a million members. By the Fifties Hoover and his staff were far better prepared for a crusade against the Left, and he would be careful to avoid the bureaucratic errors of the past.

• • •

Organizations, like individuals, found it necessary to brandish their credentials of Americanism. Between 1951 and 1959 the American Civil Liberties Union not only refused to defend Communists at the trial level, but a couple of its key officers donated informations about some of its own members to the FBI—and also asked the bureau to help identify Communists who might try to reach prominence on the boards of the ACLU's state affiliates.

A few ACLU officials, including Morris Ernst, its general counsel until 1955, told the FBI the names of their colleagues who had been critical of the bureau. Since it was hoped that friendly intercourse with the FBI would armor the ACLU against those who called it a Communist organization—in 1952 the American Legion had asked the government to investigate its members— ACLU personnel handed over minutes of their meetings to the FBI, along with confidential memoranda, private correspondence, and position papers. Among memos in the bureau's files, the ACLU was described as "nothing but a front for the Communists" even though Hoover himself had said it was not a subversive organization. Nonetheless the FBI monitored the ACLU for some fifty years.

Ernst and Hoover had maintained a cordial relationship that dated back to the early Forties. In November 1948 Ernst wrote to Hoover, "You are a grand guy and I am in your army." Eager to do favors for Hoover, Ernst tried to mute I. F. Stone's and Edward R. Murrow's criticism of the FBI. Between 1948 and 1952 Ernst wrote many articles extolling the bureau, among them a 1950 essay for *Reader's Digest* titled "Why I No Longer Fear the FBI"— which had given him the material for that piece of public relations, helped him to compose it, and persuaded the *Digest* to publish it.

The ACLU also eschewed involvement in the 1951 trial of W.E.B. Du Bois, the radical black historian and philosopher who had been a founder of the NAACP in 1910, when he was charged at the age of eighty-three with being "an unregistered agent" of the Soviet Union. (He was acquitted.) He had already been expelled from the NAACP because he'd protested the organization's allegiance to "the reactionary, war-mongering" Truman administration in 1948 and because he supported Henry Wallace's presidential candidacy. Du Bois, who had often disagreed with the Communists, did not apply for Party membership until 1961, when he was ninety-three. But his situation in the Fifties was analogous to Paul Robeson's: admired abroad and defiled at home.

Robeson, one the most eloquent dissidents of the postwar era—until the invitations to speak waned and so did his health—was called "one of the most dangerous men in the world" by the federal district attorney representing the State Department when the singer tried to regain his passport after it was revoked. Robeson's ongoing tributes to the Soviet Union and his contention that it was a society free of racism, plus his public friendships with leaders of the American Communist Party, were regarded as more significant than his art. His long sojourns in Russia and the American Communists' efforts on behalf of racial justice in the Thirties had given him hope when he saw that his own government was largely indifferent to inequality. So the press kept featuring him as Moscow's dupe. Unable to perform overseas for eight years, he had fewer and fewer chances to sing in his own country after 1952. The NAACP had removed his name from the list of those who had been awarded its annual Spingarn medal. Langston Hughes had deleted references to Robeson from his children's book, *Famous Negro Music Makers*, at the editors' insistence—so that schools and libraries would be willing to buy it. Nor had Du Bois been mentioned in Hughes's *Famous American Negroes*.

A radical socialist, Hughes had been hounded by right-wing groups, smeared by Hoover, and grilled by McCarthy and Roy Cohn, all of which cost him many speaking engagements vital to the poet's livelihood. The FBI, which identified him as a "Negro pornographic poet," also as an "alleged poet," kept him on the Security Index. After an immersion in the Committee's "warm manure," Hughes distanced himself from the Left though never from the cause of civil rights. Black Americans who challenged the government were often seen as even more disloyal than their white counterparts: if they had excelled in their professions, they were expected to be grateful. But if they talked about racism, it was felt that they blighted the nation's image abroad. (The attorney who called Robeson "dangerous" also told the judge, "During concert tours of foreign countries [Robeson] repeatedly criticized the condition of Negroes in the United States.") Like Hoover, our investigators of the Fifties kept linking civil rights to subversion: Albert Canwell, chairman of the Washington State Legislative Fact-Finding Committee on Un-American Activities, said, "If someone insists that there is discrimination against Negroes in this country, or that there is inequality of wealth, there is every reason to believe that person is a Communist."

But even if many Americans had never met a Communist, suspects were treated as if they might start an epidemic: I heard about a blacklisted man who had already written two movies which were ranked as American classics; later, working under a pseudonym for one of Hollywood's leading directors, the writer was smuggled in and out of a studio's screening room for almost a decade when the rushes of his films were shown. His colleagues needed his advice, but they didn't want anyone to see him. So he was sneaked in after the lights went down and hastened out before they were turned on again.

23

Withstanding the Right

Few who feared or scorned the Left knew anything about the fears which permeated that community. Although many liberals and independent radicals lost their jobs while being watched by the FBI, not a lot of them were subpoenaed to appear before the Committee after 1950. But former and current Communists faced litigation that could permanently change their lives. The histories of the ex-Communists I later came to know were similar: having joined the Party in the Thirties, they had resigned in the Forties and were punished in the Fifties. Years afterward some would tell me that their apprehensions had often seemed preposterous. But so did the events of the domestic Cold War: what they'd believed to be impossible was taking place. The Hollywood Ten had initially thought they would win their case and they had gone to jail for contempt of court. The Rosenbergs had been sentenced to death. When McCarthy referred to former British Prime Minister Clement Attlee as "Comrade Attlee" in the Senate and described him as an instrument of the Communists, even absurdities could not be dismissed as inconsequent.

The Internal Security Act of 1950 (also known as the McCarran Act) entitled the Attorney General to order that "dangerous or potentially dangerous" Americans be rounded up and imprisoned without trial during "internal security emergencies" or if the country became "involved in war." Well before the Act was passed, organizing the Security Index—a list of candidates for detention— was one of Hoover's major projects in the Truman years; the plans were further refined under the Eisenhower administration. Determined not to repeat the chaos of the Palmer raids, Hoover made detailed preparations for the arrest of citizens expected to be traitors, spies, or saboteurs at a time of national crisis or if we were at war with the Soviet Union. Along with Communists and ex-Communists, individuals qualified for the Security Index because of "formal or informal leadership in a front group," "anarchistical revolutionary beliefs," "willingness to interfere with a war," invoking the Fifth Amendment before a governmental committee, belonging to organizations "that have been declared subversive or may hereafter be declared subversive by the Attorney General," and possessing "propaganda material which fosters, encourages, or promotes the policies, programs, or objectives of the enemy or insurgents." In July 1950 the FBI reported to the Justice Department that eleven thousand, nine hundred and thirty persons were on the Security Index; by the end of 1954 the list had swelled to twenty-six thousand, one hundred and seventy-four.

Even an anti-Communist stance did not deflect the bureau's suspicion. The FBI files of Democratic Senator Paul Douglas of Illinois reveal that he was one of those "whose arrest might be considered necessary" in wartime. As an officer in the Marines in World War II, Douglas won a Bronze Star for bravery in combat; with Senator Hubert Humphrey he promoted the custodial detention legislation of the Fifties. Yet his files—which the bureau maintained from the early Forties until 1964—warned that he was "believed to be engaged in espionage for the Russian government." He'd once belonged to the Socialist Party; informers said he had associated with Communists in the Forties, and one report noted that he was "particularly active among the Negro population . . . and as such has participated actively in meetings with the National Assn. for the Advancement of Colored People."

Of course no one could guess if or when sudden arrests might occur. Some present and former Party members had savings stored away in cash, in case they needed to vanish quickly. In 1951, after the Supreme Court upheld the convictions of the first eleven Communist leaders who had been jailed, many on the Left thought they could end up in the internment camps which had been filled with Japanese-Americans during the war. The phrase was "Five minutes to midnight"; meaning that fascism was looming, that it might soon be time to leave the country or to live in hiding. Two decades later some discovered through the Freedom of Information Act that they had indeed been on the Security Index: their forebodings had not been irrational after all.

To some Jewish emigrés what was happening here seemed similar to what they had known in Germany: they felt they had seen it all before. (So did Thomas Mann, who left the United States in 1952.) A film maker who had fled the Nazis kept a hundred dollars in single bills—prepared if necessary to depart from Los Angeles as swiftly as he had left Berlin. One woman told me that her blacklisted husband had urged her to buy a heavy winter coat which they really couldn't afford, because the camps would be poorly heated.

Those who had been born abroad anticipated deportation under the McCarran-Walter Act. Some—like Cedric Belfrage, editor of the independent left-wing weekly, the *National Guardian*—were classified as "dangerous aliens" before they were forced to emigrate. Belfrage, born in London, had lived in the United States for twenty-nine years. He was a member of the Communist Party for three months in 1937. In 1955 he was escorted by federal guards from jail to the ship which took him back to England in 1955, and he wasn't permitted to enter his former homeland for more than fifteen years. (After 1973, when he was allowed to revisit, he had to petition the State Department for a waiver of his exclusion and to provide a meticulous itinerary, giving the addresses where he stayed each night.) As another exile reflected, deportation was a life sentence with no parole. A prison term, at least, had a definite conclusion.

Belfrage later wrote that "the U.S. government didn't give a whoop whether one was a Communist or not. The word encompassed anyone said to 'advocate force and violence,' which was interpreted to mean any resister of the Cold War." He noted that under a clause of the McCarran-Walter Act, one could be prosecuted for owning or circulating "any printed or written matter . . . advocating . . . violence"—which meant any text that discussed revolution, such as Lenin's *The State and Revolution*. Most radicals owned Marxist books or pamphlets, and it was not unusual to lend them to friends.

The volumes on certain Americans' shelves were used as evidence against them in court when they were prosecuted for their politics—as in the 1949 trial of the eleven Communist leaders, when Judge Harold Medina compared the Marxist texts introduced by the prosecution as "exhibits" to a bank robber's tool kit. Books belonging to Carl Braden helped to convict him in Kentucky in 1954 when he, a white who had sold a house in an all-white neighborhood to a black couple in Louisville, was imprisoned under the state's sedition laws. When Steve Nelson and two other prominent Communists were tried for sedition in Pittsburgh, three thousand books were transported from their office to the courtroom: to show what the defendants were "advocating." The books were wheeled into court on trolleys—to demonstrate the sheer bulk of the literature, since the jurors were hardly expected to read them. At Nelson's second trial a prosecutor said the Party's office was "filled with weapons," declaring, "I regard these books as weapons."

A script editor told me that when the Committee turned its spotlight on Hollywood, she and her husband drove to the Mojave desert on a windy day with all their Marxist-Leninist publications. (In the Thirties the husband's apartment in Germany had been searched by the Nazis, who questioned him at length when they found Marxist books.) In the desert they burned the cover of the Marxist theory of self-determination and they tore out the pages and fed them to the wind. "And the wind blew the pages away . . . and we felt like absolute idiots." She paused, and then explained that fear can have an electroid taste: "There's a metallic flavor in your mouth and your bladder is always leaking just a little." Waiting to be subpoenaed and then investigated and sentenced "wasn't like going into battle, where there are grenades and explosions and bullets flying. The fear was not only intangible, it was unreasonable—perhaps that's why it was so devastating."

Many told me that it was also degrading. A former Communist who was moving from Brooklyn to Manhattan—for him a significant rite of passage—had about half a dozen Marxist books; he spent two weeks disposing of them before he settled into his new home. Early in the morning he would furtively drop a volume into a different public trash can, fearful that the police were following him. But some are constitutionally incapable of throwing books away: they hid them in obscure corners, in attics or in cellars. Books were also shoved into the incinerators of apartment buildings. And some leftists removed a series of prints by a Spanish artist called Sim—which depicted the Abraham Lincoln Brigade during Spain's Civil War—from their walls. Reproductions of paintings by William Gropper, whose cartoons had appeared in *The New Masses* and the *Daily Worker* and who had been lambasted by McCarthy, disappeared from certain living rooms.

A number of liberals canceled their subscriptions to *The Nation* and *The New Republic* because the FBI was checking on the lists of regular readers. *The Nation* (closely watched by the bureau since the Twenties) was singled out partly because of its long-term criticism of Hoover's methods, its editorials favoring coexistence, also for its pungent criticism of the Catholic church— which resulted in its being banned by the New York City Board of Education from the libraries of the city's public schools between 1948 and 1963. (Harold Clurman, who became *The Nation's* drama critic in 1953, was warned by his nephew at *Time* that in some circles the magazine was regarded as politically impure, which didn't deter Clurman from writing for it for twenty-seven years.) Agents who gathered information about Americans living in England kept track of their subscriptions to the *New Statesman* and *The Manchester Guardian*. In New York there were building superintendents who told the FBI which of their tenants received the tabloid *PM*. J. Edgar Hoover sent a memo to his deputy, Clyde Tolson: "Let me have a memo on *The Progressive* & its staff of whelps"; the bureau then kept files on the monthly for nearly four decades. And the FBI visited some of the *National Guardian*'s subscribers; in small towns the local post offices gave the bureau their names. In rural mailboxes the paper was often delivered torn in half. Naturally its circulation sank.

At the University of Michigan the FBI asked students and professors to report each other's radical statements to the bureau. At Princeton several professors of government began to tape their own lectures—so that they could not be misquoted on foreign affairs. Some would commence by repeating that they detested Stalin and the Soviet Union, to put that on the record. H. H. Wilson, whose FBI file conceded that he was "a non-Communist civil libertarian," wrote in the Princeton alumni magazine in 1954 that FBI agents had asked to see some of his students' papers. Hoover sent him a letter denying the charge, adding that the FBI was "totally dedicated to academic freedom." Wilson replied to Hoover by citing the case of a Princeton student who was writing a thesis on proletarian literature; the young man was picked up and questioned by the FBI on leaving Michael Gold's apartment at two in the morning. He was carrying some old copies of *The New Masses* and the agents did not believe his concern was literary. Hoover wrote back to Wilson at once: to request the name of the student.

• • •

During the years when McCarthy often implied that Communists were homosexuals and vice versa, the Washington, D.C., police created a special unit of the vice squad "to investigate links between homosexuality and Communism." Many government employees who were fired during the loyalty probes were identified in their files as "perverts" rather than as left-wingers. Senator Kenneth Wherry of Nebraska declared in 1950, "I would not say that every homosexual is a subversive, and I would not say that every subversive is a homosexual. But a man of low morality is a menace in government, whatever he is, and they are all tied up together." Wherry also suggested that Owen Lattimore was homosexual.

In June 1950 the Senate established an Appropriation subcommittee to conduct an investigation into the presence of "sexual deviates" in the Executive branch of the government. The subcommittee's report, published six months later, deduced that even "one sex pervert in a government agency tends to have a corrosive effect on his fellow employees. These perverts will frequently attempt to entice normal individuals to engage in perverted practices. This is particularly true in the case of young and impressionable people. . . . One homosexual can pervert a government office." At the same time the FBI was using quite a few homosexuals as informers within government departments; when an FBI agent discovered that a man was gay, he could be asked to report on his colleagues—rather than lose his job.

When Joseph and Stewart Alsop wrote a column in *The Saturday Evening Post* that criticized Wherry's efforts "to elevate the subject of homosexuality in the State Department to the level of a serious political issue on the ground that sexual perversion presents a clear and present danger to the security of the United States," McCarthy replied with an impassioned letter to the *Post*'s editors. Defending Wherry, McCarthy stressed that the Roman Empire had crumbled when its rulers became "degenerate." He also hinted that Joseph Alsop, who was unmarried, was homosexual. In a second letter McCarthy promised, "I might also add that Alsop or anyone else who gets in the way of cleaning the Communists out of government may well get injured." During the four years that followed that warning, the Alsops wanted to write more pieces opposing McCarthy for the *Post*. But the magazine ran no subsequent articles about him by anyone.

While the first Kinsey Report was reassuring to male homosexuals—since it revealed that there were far more of them than had been realized—the figures were horrifying to much of the public. Theories concerning the nature of "deviance" proliferated. Representative A. L. Miller of Nebraska, who developed the federal legislation against homosexuals, said, "The cycle of these individuals' homosexual desires follows the cycle closely patterned to the menstrual period of women." Miller, who was also a physician, explained, "There may be three or four days in each month that the homosexual's instincts break down and drive the individual into abnormal fields of sexual practice. Under large doses of sedatives during this sensitive cycle, he may escape such acts."

When Adlai Stevenson was campaigning for President in 1952, it was rumored that he was gay—and that was why his wife had divorced him. He was already listed in the FBI's "Sex Deviate" file; an earlier report from the bureau's New York office said he was "well known as 'Adeline'" and that "he would not run for President" because of his homosexuality. It is not certain that the FBI gave material of this kind to Eisenhower's staff, but it was leaked to McCarthy, Nixon, and some news reporters. And in 1961 Hoover told John Seigenthaler, a special assistant to Attorney General Robert Kennedy, that Stevenson was a "notorious homosexual."

Although seventeen hundred federal job applicants had been rejected between 1947 and 1950 because of their alleged "tendencies," Eisenhower signed an executive order in 1953 which legalized the exclusion of homosexuals from government posts. By then more than four hundred and twenty-five people had been discharged from the State Department alone because of their "proclivities," and the pace of the dismissals accelerated. The American Civil Liberties Union upheld the constitutionality of the government's sanctions against homosexuals. In 1948 the Communist leadership told homosexual members they must leave the Party because they were likely targets for the police and could be pressured to testify against other Communists—as Jerome Robbins did in 1953. (The choreographer denied that he was trying to shield his private life when he gave names to the Committee, but many thought that was the reason for his testimony.) To gain a gay man's cooperation the police could produce a couple of juveniles and talk about statutory rape. Therefore left-wing homosexuals were threatened with exposure and imprisonment on morals charges as well as with blacklisting.

• • •

In the meantime fear flooded through many homes. The publicity that ensued from anyone's being summoned by the Committee ravaged many families. Their phones raged with obscene calls after midnight and household help evaporated; young women were cautioned not to babysit for couples under investigation. Being followed or accosted on the street by FBI agents seemed to strip the nerves of protective sheathing. At times it appeared that the pursuers wanted their prey to know that they were being tailed: that was part of the strategy. It was easy to recognize the agents: they were said to have gray gabardine suits, gray fedoras, gray faces. When agents questioned the suspects' neighbors, colleagues, and church groups, countless Americans were pitted against each other; when one person was subpoenaed, many others were alarmed.

The bureau usually checked radicals' addresses twice a year: spurious "salesmen" would telephone to ask if they wanted to buy a vacuum cleaner, calling them by their names. The FBI might tell the superintendent of their apartment building that they were wanted on a drug charge—hence the necessity of interviewing the other tenants about them. The phone of someone under such scrutiny would not stop ringing. But sometimes the midnight telephoners were speechless: when there was no sound at the other end of the line—not even breathing—the calls seemed like a symptom of the period: silence from those who seethed with fear and hatred, silence from those who were afraid.

The numbers actually ordered to testify were only a fraction of those who feared they might be called. So many were anticipating the day, the knock on the door; even if the subpoena never came, waiting lacerated their lives. They wrestled with the spectre of uncertainty: because the anti-Communists cast a such a wide net and attacked from all directions, there was no way of knowing how far the retributions might extend—or how extreme they might be. Many were also intimidated by court costs, which would exceed their earnings and savings. Those with modest salaries could not afford to take the First Amendment, because that route resulted in lengthy and therefore very expensive litigation. But someone who needed to keep a job could not afford to take the Fifth Amendment: since the Committee had damaged the reputation of the Fifth, most Americans believed that anyone who invoked it was a Communist, and he or she would be dismissed and subsequently turned down for future employment.

Being fired held a particular horror for the generation which had come through the Depression, when a job was the most crucial aspect of your life, when losing a job was the worst thing that could happen to you. Without a regular salary, personal life also seemed precarious; marriages and family ties might well deteriorate. Even in the prosperous Fifties, most were terribly grateful to be earning steadily. So their fear was not only contagious, it was progressive.

Sometimes it was hard to get up in the morning and start the day. Health ebbed; for some it never returned. For those awaiting subpoenas and for many who received them, there were ulcers and hypertension, migraines and shingles, colitis and heart attacks—or accidents: broken arms or ribs, burns from boiling water that was spilled, cars that crashed. And as the years of blacklisting continued, there were some suicides: depressions which could not be dissolved by an act of will.

Often the Committee helped to fan the anxiety by announcing who would be subpoenaed well before the investigators arrived in their town. Parents would keep their children home from school while staying away from their own offices. Humiliation—in private or in public—was almost inevitable. The screenwriter Maurice Rapf was subpoenaed at dinner in front of his children. The offspring of Alvah Bessie, one of the Hollywood Ten, were embroiled in fistfights at school, where other students told them their father was a traitor to his country.

Only the most resilient families were likely to weather the ongoing indignities. One survivor concluded that a good marriage could grow stronger under that kind of adversity, but a marriage which was vulnerable usually disintegrated. A blacklisted man, thinking of his wife, said to me, "How long can you live with someone who has a cloud over his head? You get wet along with him, you get drenched, you drown in his sorrows." And when there were fissures in a marriage, it was standard procedure for the FBI to try to persuade one spouse to give evidence against the other. Quite a few who were separated did cooperate, as did some of the divorced.

The screenwriter Richard Collins, a friendly witness who had quit the Party just before the 1947 hearings began, sued his ex-wife, the actress Dorothy Comingore—whom he had recruited into the Party—for child custody. Accusing her of associations with the Hollywood Ten and of taking their children to "Red swimming pools," he won the custody suit because she had invoked the Fifth Amendment. During the hearings she was also charged with prostitution, and many believed she had been framed. Comingore, who'd been castigated by the Hearst papers ever since she had been selected to play a character based on Hearst's mistress Marion Davies in *Citizen Kane*, was never reemployed after 1951. She became an alcoholic and died twenty years later at the age of fifty-eight.

Among the couples who remained together, there could be eruptions of reproach. Bitterness toward the Committee and its actions was sometimes directed at a husband or wife, especially if one had been radicalized before the other. Whether either or both or neither had been Communists, one might blame the Party for everything that had happened to them—the loss of work and income and friends—while the other still felt impelled to defend it, or at least to defend its intentions. So the policies of the Party could enter the battles at breakfast or in the bedroom, one person denouncing the Communists' initial rationale for the Nazi-Soviet pact and the other arguing that the committees to aid refugees from Hitler and Franco had been commendable. At times whatever problems the family had might be traced to associations with the Communists: if a child failed a test at school or was stricken with stuttering, and teachers or doctors suggested that the atmosphere at home was responsible, the parents' guilt might become entangled with their politics, past or present, which were now under assault. Or else, since they could not punish the Committee, they punished one another.

Even a devoted couple might undergo a species of stress that cut them off from lifelong intimates—until it seemed as if they were each other's sole support. The actor John Randolph, who was barred from Hollywood but able to find roles in touring theatrical companies, maintained a cheerful public manner although his confidence was impaired as he accepted smaller and smaller parts than he'd had ten years before. Playing waiters—serving soup and water and beer—and butlers, he asked himself if his enfeebled career was really due to the blacklist or if he was simply a third-rate actor. But he concealed the inner erosions, knowing they could wreck his ability to perform any role at all. He knew how to appear optimistic and he did enjoy "peripatetic theater":

giving staged readings of literature directed by a left-wing professor fired from Brooklyn College, or acting in synagogues on Long Island and in union halls.

When the blacklist ended and he was offered his first movie in thirteen years, his Hollywood colleagues gave parties in his honor and praised him for remaining intact, for not being wounded by the years of exclusion. Outraged by their insensitivity, his wife, the actress Sarah Cunningham, cried out that he had suffered greatly and that only she had seen the bleeding—"And I don't know what to do to *stop the bleeding.*" A decade later, when she told me about that moment, her voice soared in anger at those who had understood nothing about the hidden damage. Then she added quietly that her husband had never complained.

• • •

Often the wives of blacklisted men were not only the family wage-earners; they also spent many days and nights on committees to raise money for the husbands' legal costs. After the Hollywood Ten went to prison, women whose own husbands weren't in jail felt they must make speeches and organize financial aid for the prisoners. Several later said they had neglected their children at that time; one spoke of "Iphigenia in Hollywood," as if the children had almost been sacrificed in a war. Many film makers' wives had not had full-time jobs in years: now they became underpaid salesclerks and reception-ists. Some of the husbands were helpless at coping with money: without the business managers who had handled their studio salaries, the men didn't know what was in the bank or how to apply for a loan. For certain writers, fiscal ignorance had been intentional: insisting that they must approach their type-writers with unclouded minds, they had rarely written a check or paid a bill. (After one renowned screenwriter was fired, bonds were found scattered throughout his desk drawers at the office: the radical had forgotten all about them.) Although wives learned how to stretch the shrinking funds, there were husbands who still disdained addition and subtraction.

When Zero Mostel was blacklisted, Kate Mostel, who had been a dancer, fed her family by conducting a women's exercise class in Manhattan: it became a vital support group for the wives of blacklistees in the Fifties. They always paid her in cash so that she could buy groceries on the way home. Following a strenuous workout, the group lunched as cheaply as possible at the nearby Carnegie Delicatessen. Some shared sandwiches, cutting them into halves or quarters, others had Jello and coffee; the second cup of coffee was free. The waiters were unhappy to see them because they had to have separate checks. At their table everything which wasn't mentioned to outsiders was aired: the difficulties that radicals' children were apt to face at school, how to find emergency employment, where to obtain a piece of fabric to reupholster an old couch, and above all how to live with a blacklisted man.

What they told each other was sealed in secrecy, since they would never have criticized their husbands to anyone else—aware of what each man had been through, of how one was struggling to hold on to a temporary job he hated or that another had not worked for a year. But alcohol and anger surged through many households, and some fathers hardly talked to the children at all. Over lunch Kate Mostel led the spirited discussions and didn't permit interruption: each woman must be allowed to finish what she was saying, and they were encouraged to unleash the feelings that could not be released elsewhere. Indignation and then laughter welled up over the Jello as the women found ways to assist one another, and when they exchanged frugal recipes or traded cots for high chairs, they knew that few husbands could understand how food or furniture were provided: those subjects were still alien to men who expected wives to shoulder all practicalities. The women felt that Kate Mostel and the group had sustained them throughout the domestic Cold War, that they would hardly have survived those years without each other, and almost all the marriages endured. One participant who was the co-founder of a leather business gave her friends small billfolds inscribed "Katie's Class." More than two decades afterward I was shown a worn gray wallet, carefully preserved in tribute to the strength that had been generated by Kate Mostel.

● ● ●

The children of the Left grew accustomed to seeing the cars of FBI agents stationed outside their homes; sometimes they could hear the engines running at night. In country towns agents might stage a show for the neighborhood, banging loudly on a front door and then racing around the house to pound on the back door—before anyone had time to come to the front. The children also saw agents searching through the house, peering at the shelves of books about Russian history and the Spanish Civil War. Then there were the amiable guests who were eventually revealed to be informers for the bureau: they were attentive to the names of other visitors and often introduced political topics for debate—all of which would turn up in the files in Washington. The son of blacklisted writer Gordon Kahn learned that a guest had described his father's fiftieth birthday party as "a Red cell meeting."

Some children were instructed to be very polite to the agents, which was perplexing: why should they be on their best behavior with men their relatives didn't seem to like? And some were harassed even in kindergarten: when their parents were evading subpoenas, they were quizzed about their families' whereabouts by the agents, who also questioned their teachers. (Once a subpoena was delivered, the recipient was legally obliged to appear before the Committee. Those who planned to take the Fifth Amendment could remain employable a bit longer if they delayed being subpoenaed.) Some parents who disappeared were not seen again for months, and their children could feel unloved. The family might be reunited in another state, where it would be necessary to enter a new school in the middle of the term, where the taunts of classmates rose once more.

In certain families it appeared that the prosecution of the parents had a withering effect on the children's emotional lives. Some learned to suppress their feelings about almost everything: their parents, intent on stoicism, had trained them to be impassive. Others had aged too quickly: their demoralized parents became dependents who wanted to be comforted. But certain parents didn't explain why they were under surveillance, or why an adult wept suddenly in the middle of a meal. Their children knew next to nothing about the politics involved—only that the household was brimming with fear. Seeking to protect the young from matters that were thought too complex for them, these parents succeeded mainly in mystifying them. Home was full of secrets. If they asked what a Communist was, or why it was bad to be called a Red, some were told that they weren't old enough to understand such things. When a red rubber rat was found hanging on the front door of one of the Communist leaders, his six-year-old son was told that someone had left a toy for him.

A former Communist of eighty—who had left the Party nearly five decades before—said to me, "*Of course* you didn't tell the children!": because of what they might repeat without guessing the harm it could do. She sometimes spoke to me about her long-distant participation—but only at moments when her son was absent from the dinner table or making the coffee. Her timing did not seem calculated, and since the two were close and candid with each other I assumed that he knew about her past membership, which he did. Yet I saw that she still had habits which derived from his childhood: she never brought up the subject unless he (aged forty-eight) was out of the room.

In many homes, bewildered children and evasive parents grew further apart. Some small children didn't know why fathers and mothers no longer went out to work but stayed in typing resumés and job proposals, anxiously waiting for the mailman, who didn't seem to deliver what they wanted. Vigorous persons bereft of their regular occupations could be difficult to live with. Either their unused vitality disrupted others' daily rhythms—they became overly involved with a twelve-year-old's homework or demanded attention for hours at a stretch—or else their dejection and fatigue sapped the energies of everyone around them. And if a blacklistee was in therapy, the patient might feel it wasn't safe to talk about his or her political situation to the psychiatrist—which could skew the treatment and further unbalance relationships at home.

Labor Day parades, union picnics, square dances, parties where everyone knew the refrain to songs by Leadbelly, Paul Robeson, Woody Guthrie, and Pete Seeger, potluck dinners for Progressive Party candidates: the Left had been gregarious, the children were used to crowds and festivities. But now the conviviality was fading: there were fewer gatherings and strangers weren't welcome in their parents' homes. Any stranger, it seemed, might be an informer. Children could be sent to bed earlier than usual when a lawyer came to discuss strategies. And if the parents had cause to think their house was bugged, they might converse about their case in whispers or go into the bathroom and keep flushing the toilet, or else they went out at night and walked around the block. The whispering and the running water could make it hard to interrupt or confide in them—if something went wrong at school or if a friend said he'd been warned to not play with classmates whose families were called un-American.

Some of the children spent their summers at camps with names like Seeds of Tomorrow or Wo-chi-ca (Workers' Children's Camp). They had already been taught that racism must be fought in every arena. Their parents had taken them to demonstrations protesting segregated hotels and restaurants and public swimming pools; they'd passed out fliers demanding police protection for black homeowners threatened by vigilantes in white neighborhoods. On marches they had sung, "And before I'll be a slave, I'll be buried in my grave," and chanted, "Jim Crow/Must go!" The principles never changed, but it was no longer clear which actions were the right ones. An eighteen-year-old—whose parents hadn't yet told him they were being investigated—was asked to join the NAACP during his first week at college and he did. His soon-to-be blacklisted father was furious: how could the son be so stupid, why had he invited all the troubles that such an association would bring? That was the son's introduction to his parents' political problems.

In left-wing families there were adolescents who became skilled at keeping secrets, including the pseudonyms of blacklisted screenwriters; when Dalton Trumbo's phone rang with a message for an unknown person, his children didn't hang up because the caller might be asking for their father under his newest name. But when there was trust within a home, it seldom extended beyond the threshold: Trumbo's son said there was no "place" where he could feel comfortable "outside of the family."

From Brooklyn to Santa Monica, children who were jeered at on the playground displayed a rainbow of responses: some became withdrawn, others turned on their parents and shouted accusations at them, and others drifted toward delinquency: stealing from supermarkets and smashing windows, prone to violent outbursts, they seemed impervious to all authority. Long afterward some would say that they had never fully understood their parents—even if they'd been fond of them and respectful of their courage. Those who remained close to their parents were likely to have been told a good deal about their politics, also about the Committee and the blacklist. Though very few ever joined the Party, some were active in the civil rights and antiwar movements of the Sixties. But many grew up to be apolitical. Some became conservative. Others never quite digested the early diet of confusions—even after the facts were clarified by the Freedom of Information Act. Their own FBI files would include snapshots of themselves at three or four, along with lists of subversive play groups and Marxist summer camps.

•   •   •

The Committee nearly always knew the names that witnesses uttered at its hearings; making a former Communist do penance before a congressional audience was the main point of the exercise, and the witness's condemnation of Communism also helped to advertise the potency of the investigators.

The informer who first mentioned your name to the FBI or the Committee had the power to alter your life overnight—perhaps forever. So the fear of informers was common among liberals as well as prevalent on the Left. To criticize the Committee in public, to give a job recommendation to someone fired for his politics, or to sign an amicus curiae brief for the Hollywood Ten, meant that even a moderate Democrat could attract the FBI's attention. An informer did not need to prove that you were a Communist—it was enough to suggest it or to say that you had been seen by candlelight at a Party meeting in a cellar in Pittsburgh in 1938. Once you had been named, you were guilty. It didn't matter if the informer was in error (or habitually drunk) or if he had mistaken you for someone else. If you were named, you were a malefactor—in the past and for years to come.

But often people did not know who their accusers were: it was impossible to challenge or refute them. Over the years Hoover repeated that the FBI would lose its sources on Communism if they were known: he did not want many of them to appear in court or at the hearings. So the names of numerous informers remained secret while their reports or remarks thickened the bureau's files. In the Fifties no one seemed aware that Ronald Reagan, president of the Screen Actors Guild, had been an FBI informer since the early Forties. When he was a cooperative witness before the Committee in 1947, he did not give names in his public testimony—only in a private executive session.

The question of who might be listening and where—at a Sunday brunch or in an office cafeteria—increased the anxiety about the identity and location of the informer, who might be an old friend or a total stranger and who seemed to be everywhere. Some were ex-Communists whose jobs were in jeopardy unless they provided the names of current or former members. Some, like Matthew Cvetic, an undercover FBI agent who said that American Communists "plan to liquidate one-third of the American population, mostly the oldsters," earned a living as "experts" on Communism. Indeed so many agents infiltrated the Party with such ease that one blacklistee observed that the FBI could penetrate the organization "just by sneezing." But some informers had only tenuous connections with the bureau: they were rabid patriots who reported to the American Legion, which filled its dossiers with insinuations and some outright inventions—before delivering them to employers, such as the heads of film studios.

There were also figures who could not quite be called informers. These were either ardent and sincere conservatives who volunteered to help the Committee, like the actor Adolphe Menjou, who, when asked if the liberal director John Cromwell behaved "like" a Communist, replied, "He acts an awful lot like one," or non-politicals like Robert Taylor, who—embarrassed at having starred in the pro-Soviet *Song of Russia*—said that a certain writer was "reputedly a Communist. I would not know personally." But although these friendly witnesses could not be positive about anyone's membership, their testimony was ruinous to reputations.

In Hollywood many tried not to be paranoid. But since the 1947 hearings, informing had become a profession. Moreover, some cooperative witnesses were individuals whom no one had expected to comply. Alvah Bessie told me that Lee J. Cobb, extolled by the Party's instructors as a brilliant student of Marxism, had indignantly declined an offer to perform in an anti-Soviet movie at Twentieth Century Fox. Cobb proudly showed his letter of refusal to Bessie: writing to Darryl F. Zanuck, Cobb declared that he would be no more willing to appear in such a film than in an anti-Semitic picture. The actor dwelled on the fact that he was a Jew, that the Russians, our recent allies, had helped to rescue Europe from Hitler—adding that the studio could suspend him or break his contract, but nothing could force him to accept the role.

During the May hearings of 1953 there were rumors that Cobb had given private testimony to a member of the Committee. Few were able to believe it because Cobb had steadily refused to cooperate ever since he'd been named by Larry Parks in 1951. A writer I knew went to George Tabori's play, *The Emperor's Clothes*, in which Cobb was a radical Austrian professor who would not give the Nazis any information when they tortured him; in the third act, when Cobb entered bleeding but triumphant in his intransigence, the audience burst into applause. After the final curtain the writer went backstage to visit another actor. He planned to avoid Cobb—who surged toward him with out-stretched hands, exclaiming that it was marvelous that, despite the Committee, a play with this theme could still be produced.

Soon thereafter Cobb's testimony was made public. The writer asked a friend how Cobb could unfurl such passionate conviction on the stage when he was already an informer, and he was told that he simply didn't understand actors—who can never resist a good part. Among the twenty people Cobb named was his close friend Shimen Ruskin, a Yiddish actor and an expert on Sholem Aleichem. Just before Ruskin died in 1976 he said that—with his luck—Cobb would be the first person he would see in hell.

Some in Hollywood deduced that Cobb was helpful to the Committee because he desperately yearned to reappear as Willy Loman—his best role on Broadway—when *Death of a Salesman* was made into a movie. Fredric March was cast instead. Ever since Parks had referred to him as a Communist, almost no one had hired Cobb; his savings were gone, he had two small children to support, and his wife—distraught over their situation—was hospitalized as an alcoholic. His friends thought that even if Cobb had not been a compulsive gambler, his past earnings could not have sustained his family throughout the blacklist. After two years his capacity for resistance was exhausted. Quite soon after he gave in he had a severe heart attack. Fine roles followed, such as the perfidious union boss in *On the Waterfront*. But it was said that he continued to be equally bitter about his experiences with the Committee—and toward the colleagues who had shunned him, some after Parks's testimony and others after his own.

In the meantime some non-Communists found themselves on lists that could damage their standing at the studios. For example, the identities of liberals who would not cross the picket lines during the long strike of the radical Conference of Studio Unions had been well documented. And those who patronized a couple of small Hollywood theaters which showed foreign movies often saw Howard Emmett Rogers—a vehement antagonist of the Left since the mid-Thirties—standing outside the theaters and writing down the names of studio personnel buying tickets; he then reported their transgression to their employers. Rogers gave special attention to audiences at Russian movies, such as *Potemkin*. In 1944 he was one of the founders of the Motion Picture Alliance for the Preservation of American Ideals: the group that urged the Committee to investigate the film industry.

Rogers—who had even called himself "a reactionary"—was a familiar figure to his adversaries. (He was on the MGM payroll as a writer, but he wrote more memos to the authorities than scripts.) Once the film community realized that almost anyone could turn out to be an informer, many precautions were taken. Radicals who worked in the story department at Paramount acquired the habit of tapping pencils on their desks to cover the sound of conversation when they conferred about union meetings or any kind of politics whatsoever. They knew how thin the walls were. Years before, a young organizer of the Screen Writers Guild had listened to a discussion among its opponents by holding a glass against the wall of his office at MGM. Who might be overhearing them now?

At home the telephone could no longer be a lifeline between relatives and friends: casual conversations became colorless, intimate exchanges ceased. And while discretion on the phone may not have been essential for all radicals, Bertolt Brecht's FBI files later proved that he'd been correct in assuming his own instrument was wired. To confuse the eavesdroppers, Brecht's wife Helene Weigel sometimes read recipes from a Polish cookbook over the phone to a friend who didn't know the language. Although the FBI kept Brecht under surveillance for thirteen years, the phone taps were discontinued after two.

Some informers seemed to be invisible. A blacklisted screenwriter met to talk with his former employer at an obscure spot in Santa Monica; both men had arrived in Hollywood as refugees from the Nazis and the bonds between them persisted. The next day the employer received a call from an official of the American Legion, who asked why he was seeing that writer. So they knew they were being watched by someone who had contacted the Legion—if not by Legionnaires themselves. And if a remote coffee shop or a bench on a boardwalk by the beach could afford no privacy to old acquaintances, not many living rooms or offices seemed secure. Pleasant new acquaintances might have concealed motives for cordiality, long-term associates could be preparing to testify in order to rehabilitate their careers. Even those who despised suspicion and ridiculed the small rituals of caution could begin to mistrust their own instincts—to feel they were inept at judging character. Some were also angry at themselves for allowing fear to render life abnormal. Then that anger could be infused with shame: for being frightened.

• • •

During nearly two decades of the blacklist, some screenwriters acquired new Social Security numbers for their pseudonyms: so much hope rode on those names and numbers. At the office the blacklistees continually feared meeting someone they'd known from the past—who might innocently call them by their own names and thus cost them the jobs which had been so difficult to obtain. Hastening down corridors, dodging into men's rooms or elevators, they were afraid to expose what they'd worn all their lives: a face, a name.

Throughout the Cold War it could even seem imprudent to have the wrong address. In the northeast Bronx two apartment buildings called the Workers Cooperative Colony—organized in the late Twenties by Communist factory workers—had resounded with the activities of the Left during the Depression. May Day parades, classes in Russian folk dancing, and campaigns to save the Scottsboro Boys had united many residents, just as the Moscow trials and the Nazi-Soviet pact had divided others. But although the buildings had been sold to private owners in 1945, some tenants decamped in the Fifties because they or their neighbors had been involved with organizations (such as the International Workers Order) that were on the Attorney General's list, and it no longer seemed safe to dwell at 2700 Bronx Park East. And when locations could be linked with ideology, institutional affiliations seemed all the more ominous. At Brooklyn College, which many considered a haven for Communists, undergraduates often feared that their reputations would be tarnished simply because they had studied there; an alumnus told me that some dreaded the label of subversion far more than they feared the Soviet Union. A tenant, at least, could move out of an apartment, but no one could disown a college degree.

And fear could even be rooted in a landscape. In California a law was passed in 1950 that required any Communist who entered the county of Los Angeles to register as a subversive. (No one is known to have registered and the law was later overturned as unconstitutional.) A small piece of the Sunset Strip— some five or six blocks of county property which did not belong to the city— came under that sanction, and some Party members were assailed by acute anxiety whenever they drove through it. Worrying that a policeman might stop them for a moment's inadvertent speeding or a dead headlight—and that someone might recently have named them to the FBI without their knowledge—they would ask themselves each time they approached the neighborhood if they ought to take a long detour. The local law seemed more immediately threatening than the Internal Security Act (which required registration with the Subversive Activities Control Board but was mainly aimed at those who were prominent in unions or were leaders of the Communist Party). So a parent who was driving to pick up children after school would think of being jailed for having failed to register—and of not having enough money for bail. European emigrés also thought of deportation: might they be sent back to Austria or Greece? They wondered how their American families would fare in an unknown country with an alien language—as they drove to work or to keep an appointment, fearing that crossing that perilous terrain might lead to events which would devastate their lives. Similar legislation was enacted in other states throughout the country. So the pathways of ordinary life were laced with risk: when owning a book or driving through a neighborhood could have drastic consequences.

• • •

Once someone had been investigated, he was quite likely to be examined again—if not at a hearing, at least by FBI agents. The Committee's staff kept changing: its members were retired or promoted while the leadership passed from J. Parnell Thomas to John S. Wood to Harold Velde and Francis E. Walter. New inquiries would arise because material had been overlooked in the files or updating was desired, or if a state committee decided to question a person who'd previously appeared before a congressional committee. Since the administration of paperwork and filing systems was often inefficient, some investigators duplicated one another's research. Also some cooperative witnesses—who rationalized that there was no harm in naming individuals who had already been called Communists—would recite their names anew. But the repetition of a name meant that the owner's reputation would deteriorate even further—or that he would receive a fresh subpoena.

For more than a decade before his death, the magazine writer Kyle Crichton, who had contributed pieces to *The New Masses* during the Thirties under the name of Robert Forsythe, was constantly "rediscovered" as a subject for scrutiny. His son Robert Crichton later wrote that each time a different congressman took over the Committee, "the humiliation of inquisition by incompetents began once more. It is a peculiar fact of our system that a person can be judged just once for a crime, but if his crime is not wrongdoing but wrong thinking, he can be judged forever, right to the lid of his coffin."

• • •

As the years passed some unwavering radicals found the period almost too painful to discuss, partly because they discovered that they felt irrationally guilty—when they were still very proud of all they'd done: working for the Home Relief bureaus and the Unemployed Councils during the Depression, forming anti-fascist committees, helping to organize the CIO, campaigning against lynching and for desegregation, trying to eliminate the poll tax, lobbying for unemployment insurance and old age pensions, exhorting local welfare offices to deliver the coal that hadn't arrived, gathering support and money (as well as groceries and clothing) for miners on strike in the Southwest and textile strikers in the East, pressuring state governments to provide housing for the homeless veterans of World War II. For quite a few participants, those had been the most rewarding years of their lives—and then it became necessary to keep quiet about them, to muffle their sense of achievement. And some realized that whatever the debilitated Left endorsed in the Fifties—an end to the war in Korea or clemency for the Rosenbergs—might be discredited by the fact of their support.

Some told me that their previous admiration for the Soviet Union and their inability to acknowledge Stalin's crimes had been only a component of the burden—because, when they were viewed as reprobates, they also began to wonder if they had done something wrong. Even though they were absolutely certain that none of their actions had been harmful to their country, feeling defensive fed a subterranean sense of remorse. A woman who'd been blacklisted said to me, "Somehow, faintly, you accepted the fact of being a pariah. You accepted that status. We were trying to protect who we were and what we were as though we were really guilty of something. Now that does something to you: it's corrosive to the soul."

In the aftermath some felt they ought to preface even the mildest of political observations with an affirmative remark about the United States. At the same time those who wished to explain why they had not cooperated with the Committee and also why they were no longer Communists had no outlets: they would not publish an article or give a talk on that subject without inviting a sentence for contempt. Unable to say that they still believed in many of the Party's principles but not in its recent policies, they knew that there was no way to speak for themselves—without contributing to the crusade against the Left.

In *An American Testament*, written in the mid-Thirties, Joseph Freeman had referred to socialism as "the utmost imaginable freedom for the mass of humanity." One of the most powerful attractions of Marxism was the promise that after socialism had triumphed the state would "wither away." Intent on their vision of a free society, American Communists and unaffiliated radicals were confident that their efforts on behalf of justice would benefit their country—and then it was said that they were working to ruin it. Their adversaries claimed that they only pretended to "advocate" freedom—when they were actually scheming to destroy freedom of every sort. Leftists had seen themselves as liberators, yet they were defined as engineers of oppression. So the gulf between their aspirations and their reputation widened. Although Party members had studied the Russian Constitution, one told me that while Earl Browder was the national chairman, "We thought of American Communism as the apotheosis of the Declaration of Independence. If there was a confusion, it was shared by many!" Alleged to be "always serving Moscow" when they thought they were advancing the rights of their compatriots, some agonized in private about the disparity between their aims and their collective image. How could they disentangle their intentions from the myths of their corruption—when they could have no forum of any kind?

• • •

Relations with others grew more and more constrained. The earliest days of the subpoenas had taught them that long-term acquaintances might shrink from sitting next to them in public. Many on the Left feared contaminating their friends: merely by bidding them good morning or good evening. They ceased to be surprised when people they knew well walked by them without nodding.

Soon after John Randolph testified, he and Sarah Cunningham learned that a close friend of theirs had said he did not know them. Then he came to their house at midnight to admit that "denying" them had made him feel like Simon Peter; he offered thirty-three dollars to help with legal expenses. They realized that if their friendship with him had been widely known, he could have lost the first substantial job he'd had: as an actor on the *Howdy Doody* show.

The broadcaster Sidney Roger, an independent radical who worked for decades with the International Longshoremen's and Warehousemen's Union, recalled a scene that distilled the Fifties for him. Walking down a sunlit street in San Francisco, he saw an old friend duck into a doorway in order not to say hello to him. Roger himself hurried into a vestibule, since he didn't want to embarrass someone of whom he was fond. (Some years before, he had persuaded the other not to join the Communist Party. But as he stood in the shadows, he thought the man might have remembered that he was a friend of Paul Robeson's.) Then Roger saw his friend peering about in hopes that he'd walked on. "And there we were, two middle-aged men on a main street at high noon in a large city, hiding in doorways from one another."

• • •

Civil libertarians hoped that the Senate's repudiation of McCarthy would help to wind down the domestic Cold War. But the fortunes of many Americans were not reversed by the disgrace of one politician. Between 1951 and 1957 about three hundred teachers were dismissed from the New York City public schools after the New York City Board of Education and the Senate Internal Security Subcommittee delved into "subversive influences" in the schools. At their trials the teachers were not charged with "indoctrination" in the class-room. They had already been queried about their political affiliations and pressured to identify other teachers "who may be or may have been" Commu-nists; they could keep their jobs only if they supplied names. The majority refused to do so and they were suspended, then fired for "insubordination and conduct unbecoming to a teacher." Most had taught for at least fifteen years; their careers had commenced during the Depression, when employment in the public schools had been prized as a form of job security.

Numerous testimonials to the teaching skills of individuals were heard in court, even from principals who (sometimes reluctantly) admitted that their work was "outstanding." Witnesses also testified that there was no evidence that the teachers had dispensed "Communist ideology." But William Jansen, the Superintendent of Schools, said their exemplary teaching records were "irrelevant." Arthur Levitt, a member of the Board of Education who acted as a trial examiner, concluded, "Their high qualities as teachers and their extraordinary records in the profession constitute no defense whatever to the charge of insubordination." In short they were pronounced to be fine teach-ers—who were not fit to teach.

The first eight to be discharged were leaders of the Teachers Union (founded in 1916, it was the city's first teachers' union). The second batch of eight was especially active in their local schools. For years these teachers had publicized the overcrowded classes where poorly paid, understaffed faculties struggled with the learning problems of low income students. They had sought to increase the percentage of black teachers in the public schools and to eliminate or revise textbooks which included "biased material," such as one that called the Ku Klux Klan "patriotic" and another, Herbert Townsend's *Our America*, which claimed that slaves in the South had been "happy" and "did not want to be free. The people in the North did not understand this." They had worked with black and Puerto Rican parents to improve conditions in the schools—at a time when community involvement was rare. Some had even managed to provide the children with shoes and clothing. The union had initiated a Negro

History Week more than three decades before black studies were introduced on college campuses. Union members had also protested the American role in the Korean War and the possibility that atomic weapons might be used. The Teachers Union was often said to be led by Communists and it had been expelled from the American Federation of Teachers in 1941.

All of the sixteen who were fired first were Jews. Like the ACLU and the Anti-Defamation League of B'nai B'rith, they had vigorously opposed "released time" for "religious instruction," which enabled Christian students to leave school for one afternoon every week, a privilege greatly resented by other students. Some Jewish teachers also objected to the reading of certain passages in the New Testament—such as those referring to "Our Savior, Christ the Lord"—in morning assemblies. There were many Catholics on the Board of Education and the Jewish teachers were often at odds with their Catholic colleagues, who tended to receive the choicest teaching assignments.

The first group of teachers who were fired had long fought anti-Semitism in the schoolrooms. They had documented the practices of particular teachers. There was one at P.S. 80 in the Bronx who scolded a Jewish student for bringing an absence-excuse note written in Yiddish, asserting that Yiddish was not a language. After complaints from parents, the teacher was ordered by Superintendent Jansen to teach a "corrective" lesson on "the evils of name-calling." But when the parents inspected their children's notebooks, they found lists of racial epithets which she had dictated to her pupils—some of whom had never heard the words before.

Another teacher told her students in a Williamsburg high school that the immigrants who arrived in the United States after 1880 were "the scum of Europe," also "garbage." At a school in Washington Heights a teacher called her sixth grade pupils "un-American" and "Communist" after they played records by Paul Robeson during an historical play they had written; the teacher advised them that "a plane leaves the airport every hour" and that they had "better go back where they came from." (She had approved of both the play and the music until she learned the name of the singer.) Punitive actions were not taken against these teachers.

In 1946 a teacher in Brooklyn named May Quinn—who had praised Hitler and Mussolini, distributed an anti-Semitic leaflet to her class, recommended segregation for black Americans, often called Italian children "greasy foreigners," and instructed her students to copy racist statements from the blackboard—had eventually been found guilty of "discrimination" by the Board of Education. *The Tablet*, published by the Catholic Diocese of Brooklyn, came to her defense. After paying a fine she was allowed to return to her job. In

1949 parents and Quinn's colleagues reported that she was still making abusive remarks about "colored people" in the classroom. Superintendent Jansen said she would not be penalized because of her "past good record." Since the Thirties the Teachers Union had upbraided the Board for condoning the conduct of teachers like Quinn, and for permitting most of New York's schools to remain segregated. (While the separation of the races was not an enunciated policy, it was common throughout the city until the *Brown* decision of 1954.) *New York Teacher News* frequently quoted union members on the "racial and religious bias" in the schools; one teacher publicly declared that there was "a cesspool of bigotry at the Board of Education."

The Board felt that teachers were not entitled to any sort of union. But the union kept dwelling on issues that aggravated the Board: deteriorating school buildings—many had leaky roofs or filthy toilets, some had rats—the low teacher salaries, the severe teacher shortage, and the possibility of graft in the purchase of school supplies. As the union campaigned aggressively for the rights of black citizens, opposition to such efforts swelled. By the early Fifties the union was also calling for the removal of George Timone, a powerful member of the Board with close ties to the Brooklyn Diocese of the Catholic church. An admirer of Franco and a disciple of Father Charles Coughlin, the anti-Semitic radio priest who called Roosevelt's administration "the Jew Deal," Timone was equally eager for the removal of the union's activists from the schools. Some teachers were certain that the Board acted in retaliation against those who challenged its policies and that the Board's intention was to destroy the union.

In 1952, when Superintendent Jansen's investigators interviewed the suspended teachers, they were not only asked about Party membership, but also such questions as "Do you know the following people?"; "What did your father do?"; "Did you ever recommend the reading of these books?"; "Have you ever been to the home of . . ."; "Have you discussed foreign policy with people during the last two years?" and "Did you ever say that the United States was imperialistic?" A few were also asked, "How long have you worn your hair like that?" Some of the suspended teachers' colleagues were supportive, but many were afraid to have any contact with them; one found that others raised newspapers before their faces when she walked into the faculty lounge. In the months before their trial, the defendants' own fears intensified because they didn't know who could be trusted in the age of informers. Some teachers weren't even sure if they could trust their own lawyers.

One of the key informers was Bella Dodd, ex-Catholic and ex-Communist, who was guided back to the church by Bishop Fulton J. Sheen after she was expelled from the Party. Another was Harvey Matusow, who received a guarantee of ten days' "consulting" work from Superintendent Jansen; Matusow earned twenty-five dollars a day. Hired to "uncover" former Communists, Matusow wrote in *False Witness*, "I contributed much to the intimidation of the teachers" while proffering "insubstantial evidence" against about a dozen of them.

Of the Feinberg Law, which forbade the state of New York to employ anyone belonging to what was deemed to be a subversive organization, Justice William O. Douglas wrote, "The law inevitably turns the school system into a spying project. . . . Ears are cocked for telltale signs of disloyalty. This is not the usual type of supervision which checks a teacher's competency; it is a system which seeks for hidden meanings in a teacher's utterance." The Supreme Court ruled in 1967 that the Feinberg Law was unconstitutional.

The World-Telegram and Sun published the names and addresses and ages of those who were suspended. Waves of hate mail ensued; long afterward the sight of an envelope with no return address could be a sickening reminder of the ferocious letters that had jammed the mailbox. Once the teachers were fired, many found it difficult to relinquish a calling they loved and which had required so much training. Few had any acquaintance with the professional world outside the schools. As they searched for new occupations in middle age, there was reason to envy the blacklisted screenwriters who could work under pseudonyms—whereas a teacher must present a detailed record of experience and explain the cause for dismissal. Although each received several thousand dollars from the pension fund, that could not support them for long. For some there were years without employment; they lived on welfare. Some were ill with no income. One ex-teacher sold dental supplies. Another repaired television sets. A colleague sold clothing. A fourth became a salesman of truck bodies and insurance policies. A fifth worked in a bookstore—until the FBI called on the shop's owner. Several became clerks. Some ended up in private schools that paid far less than the city schools. Others taught where academic standards were low. Some tutored children who were behind in reading and arithmetic; the schools would not pay for the tutorials and the parents could afford only small sums. The yeshivas hired a number of the discharged teachers, asking only if they were currently members of the Communist Party, not if they'd belonged in the past.

A handful made rewarding transitions: one became a children's psychoanalyst, another was a photographer, another wrote many highly successful mathematics textbooks and taught at Columbia. One prospered in Wall Street: he caustically told a former colleague that he was now "a captain of industry."

Others sustained themselves on "meaningless tasks." One committed suicide. In addition to those who were fired, some three hundred more had swiftly resigned or taken early retirement—either because they had been summoned for questioning and didn't dare to fight the case or because they feared investigation in the near future. Some immediately moved out of New York state.

In 1973 thirty-three former teachers, represented by the National Emergency Civil Liberties Committee, sued for reinstatement by the Board of Education. Their dismissals of twenty years before were declared unconstitutional and they won the case. The condition of their reinstatement was that they would be rehired for one day and would then resign. Still unwelcome in the school system, they were awarded damage rights for life (for far less than their pensions would have paid). They agreed not to sue for back pay because that might bankrupt the city. One remarked that they would be able to die with dignity.

In 1976 ten more were reinstated, one posthumously. Another journeyed to New York from his home in Israel to hear the Board vote in their favor. Newspaper editorials referred to "justice at last" and the "wrongs" they had "suffered." *The New York Times* deplored the "vindictive and unlawful" actions of the "shameful" past and hailed "a moral victory." But as two of the teachers later told me, scores had not participated in the lawsuits because they were still too frightened to be identified with the issues—even though the Feinberg Law had been overturned.

24

Flashbacks

Since those who had become radicals in the Thirties spent much of the Fifties in litigation while looking for stopgap employment, I sometimes found it hard to picture those anxious people in their youth—when they had been so sure that they could change their own society. Weary from coping with legalities, some appeared to be temporarily disconnected from their political history. By the beginning of Eisenhower's second term, it seemed as if the congressional investigations and the blacklist could go on for years and years— one could hardly see how (or why) the wind would shift.

Not until the late Seventies—when I consulted them about their formative years—did I gain a vivid sense of the enormous energies that had kindled them. And by then most who had been Communists were ready to say so. Moreover independent radicals felt more comfortable about criticizing the Communist Party than they had in the Fifties, when they hadn't wanted to give ammunition to the anti-Communists. For the independents, defending the rights of Communists while disagreeing with them had been central to the experience of the era. But the disagreements had been expressed mainly in private. (However when the *National Guardian* had rebuked the Communists for trying to dismantle the New York branch of the American Labor Party, and protested the Soviet invasion of Hungary, cold warriors gave the paper no credit for taking positions that incensed the *Daily Worker*.)

Pursuing the themes of the Fifties from a distance of more than two decades, I found that many of the Left insisted on first recounting their activities during the Depression: they could not discuss anti-Communism or loyalty oaths without depicting what had led up to them. They talked very freely, yet some asked me not to use their names: mainly because they feared that their past might be injurious to their children's professional lives, especially in fields like law or medicine. (In the Seventies and thereafter security clearances for federal employment were denied to some descendants of blacklistees. The FBI didn't show much interest in the political tropisms of the younger generation; instead they were quizzed about their parents, even when the latter had been dead for years.) Several of my sources said they had never shared their history with their adult offspring, who, in turn, had been careful not ask about it. So the legacy of the period was still constricting for some who were close to one another.

And as those who had been shaped by the Thirties looked back at the Fifties, pride and pain and some chagrin competed among their memories. But when they journeyed even further back—to the days of organizing unions or tenants' groups—most became lively, even vivacious: their circulation appeared to quicken. Seeming to relive the past as they described it, they stared out of windows or across rooms, as though almost forgetting that there was a listener or a tape recorder. Some said they had not spoken of these things for a long time—in a few cases, never.

• • •

There was a sentence that I heard more than once: "I became a Communist because I am a Jew." Since the Soviet Constitution of 1936 declared anti-Semitism to be illegal, and because the Soviet Union appeared to be an implacable enemy of the Nazis, some who hated Hitler felt that joining the Party meant taking a stand against the killing of the Jews. In the Thirties New York Jews had watched the German-American Bund marching in full dress parade through the streets of Astoria and Yorkville, singing the Horst Wessel song while doing the goose-step. Thousands of Americans entered the Bund, and in the German movie theater in Yorkville, audiences cheered when they saw Hitler in newsreels. Mussolini also had many admirers in the United States—not only among Italian-Americans but on Wall Street—and Hitler's diatribes were being echoed by the followers of Father Charles Coughlin throughout the country. While homegrown fascism was expanding, fear of the Nazis was an overwhelming emotion, as was the fear of a world war—which so many felt was coming. Hence for some Jews, the Nazis' abhorrence of Russia and all Jews could instill an identification with the Soviets.

Once the war was under way, many left-wingers believed that the Soviet Union was more effective than any other nation in trying to protect the lives of European Jews. The Left and some liberals thought we were at war with racism as much as fascism: that our mission was to defeat worldwide anti-Semitism as well as Hitler. When Jerome Robbins was a cooperative witness before the Committee in 1953, he said he'd been drawn to the Communist Party because "Fascism and anti-Semitism were synonymous to me." And some Americans—including non-Communists—hoped that socialism could eventually destroy racism.

Many future radicals had received early lessons in racial hatred. When the writer Albert Maltz was a small child, his family had moved from a battered section of Brooklyn to a better street in Flatbush. On their first day in their new home, groups of boys gathered in the backyard, yelling "Kikes!"; they threw stones and broke windows. Maltz remembered that a piece of shattered glass had cut his lip. Later those boys became his friends. But he never forgot the initial greeting. In Baltimore the embryo musician Larry Adler was told by his parents that he mustn't play with black children, while young gentiles were beating him up and saying he'd killed Christ. A revulsion against racism had propelled many toward the Left well before they encountered Marxism. After the Wall Street crash they'd heard figures like Coughlin and Reverend Gerald L. K. Smith—founder of the Christian Nationalist Crusade, which supported Mussolini and Hitler—announcing that Jewish international bankers were responsible for the Depression, and they knew that the paucity of jobs made it all the easier not to employ Jews and black Americans. Many advertisements in the "Help Wanted" sections of the newspapers were addressed to "White" or "Christian" job applicants.

Of course many non-Jews had been animated by the experience of or an exposure to poverty. They knew people who were evicted when they couldn't pay the rent, who waited with their furniture on the street for friends or relatives to take them in. They had seen children gnawing their fingers when there was nothing to eat. Often a rash appeared around the mouths of those who kept licking their lips when they were hungry. Then there was the man who had lost his job in a meat market; soon afterward he was arrested for breaking into the market at night and stealing a side of beef to feed his family of nine. In the first years of the Depression, when millions were close to starvation, some farmers' families ate mule feed. Others ate boiled thistles. Famished babies died of dysentery. As more factories closed, thousands of migrants hitchhiked or rode in boxcars all over the country in search of construction work or crops to pick. Outside automobile plants, men stood in line throughout the night in case there might be some work in the morning. Young men with law degrees but no hope of employment used to long for colossal blizzards in winter because they might earn a bit of money from shoveling snow.

Economic boundaries were dissolving. Those who'd been accustomed to moderate salaries competed with the longtime poor for opportunities to wait on tables or do laundry, to deliver milk and eggs to people who could pay for them. Arthur Miller recalled "the constant visits" of middle-class men "who knocked on our door pleading for a chance to wash the windows, and then some of them fainted on the back porch from hunger. In Brooklyn, New York. In the light of weekday afternoons." Miller also remembered the ravaging guilt of fathers who could no longer provide for their dependents: they blamed themselves for being poor during the Depression. Coroners' reports on suicides often listed the cause of death as "no work or money" or "no work" or "despondency over finances." Some could not face the shame of going on public relief. Others turned on the gas or drowned or shot themselves so that their wives and children could receive the life insurance.

Debilitation from hunger made it impossible for some people to support themselves: when a limited number of jobs became available in the Pittsburgh steel mills, quite a few of the steelworkers were too weak to perform them. As malnutrition and therefore infectious diseases spread, many could not afford to go to a doctor. Unfilled teeth rotted and were not replaced: dentistry was a luxury. And since many people were understandably depressed, they were all the more vulnerable to illness. In West Virginia hospitals would not admit patients who couldn't guarantee that bills would be paid. Doctors who'd been unable to collect their fees refused treatment to the poorest among the sick. And while the health of the population was declining, merely keeping warm could be a challenge: some stayed in bed in the daytime to conserve fuel; others burned their furniture piece by piece to heat their homes—just as farmers burned the crops they couldn't sell for the same purpose. Those with nothing left slept in doorways or under the boardwalks on beaches.

Watching hunger marchers being clubbed by policemen in Manhattan's Union Square, learning that the Bonus Army of 1932 had been driven out of Washington by armed troops who burned the flimsy shacks where the jobless veterans had camped while petitioning Congress for their bonuses, seeing elderly people digging through garbage cans for anything edible, hearing about ten persons who were killed in Chicago when police fired into a crowd which was picketing Republic Steel for the right to unionize, many Americans' sense of helplessness about the Depression coexisted with a belief that something could and would be done about it. The dread of unending poverty fueled a confidence in impending change: monumental changes in our society seemed possible because they seemed imperative, and many thought life would improve—because it had to. Despite the economic anguish (in part, because of it) the decade was also tinged with hope: that the worst inequities would not remain unaltered.

• • •

To me the assurance that the Thirties radicals had once possessed seemed staggering, since that quality was totally absent among my contemporaries, who felt incapable of changing anything larger than a comma. Amazed by a particular sentence from a leftist who was enumerating the errors rampant throughout Henry Wallace's presidential campaign of 1948—"But people mustn't be *afraid* of making mistakes"—I thought of what had fettered my classmates at twenty, what had drained youth from the young: the terror of making a mistake.

But many who were on the Left during the Depression had enormous confidence in the future, and also, if they were Communists, in their organization. While few believed that an actual revolution would occur, some were positive that socialism would come—soon and peacefully—to the United States. Marx and Engels were quoted: both had quite often said that the shift from capitalism to socialism might be achieved in America and England by parliamentary methods. Some radicals had even felt infallible: history was on their side and they were going to sculpt the future. Yet they said that the drudgery involved was not oppressive. Even humble tasks—running mimeograph machines, distributing leaflets, lettering picket signs—could seem endowed with historical significance.

Between 1933 and 1938 the national disarray was so immense that capitalism was thought to be destroying itself. Because no experts on Wall Street had been able to prevent the demise of the stock market, the business community seemed as frightened as the middle class. In 1931 leftists referred to the new Empire State building as "capitalism's last erection." Before the New Deal programs were implemented, some felt the climate was growing downright anarchistic, when even temperate citizens were saying that they would break into bakeries or grocery stores before they would let their children go without meals. But in 1935 the establishment of Social Security was interpreted as a signal that the country was moving to the left, and when the CIO was organized (also in 1935) many assumed that the labor movement was winning its primary goals.

During the Depression some of the radicals I later knew had been more absorbed in the crises of the United States than in "the Soviet myth." Yet many of them had been impressed by accounts of Soviet economic policies. George Charney, who became a Communist in 1933, wrote that in 1935, "Reports from the Soviet Union on its spectacular successes of industrialization, the abolition of illiteracy in a decade, the [metamorphosis] from a poor peasant country to a mighty world power, gave wings to our imagination." But for the majority of Americans the Soviet Union was much too remote to serve as a model. And left-wing writers who couldn't embrace dialectical materialism manufactured their own brands of radicalism: Lewis Mumford, who felt that the Communists' ideology was "as unsound as it is cocky" and that their tactics were "transparently opportunistic," explored the idea of "basic communism," Max Lerner pondered "planned collectivism," and Dwight Macdonald—anti-capitalist and anti-Communist—blended Trotskyism with aestheticism.

But neither the independent radicals nor the Communists had a blueprint for American socialism: much of the theorizing was nebulous. Little thought was given to the transition between capitalism and socialism—such as the "takeover" of factories. Instead a wave of nationwide conversion was anticipated. Some expected that banks, airlines and railroads, mines, public utilities, telephones and radio stations, and all other major industries would be nationalized. Working people would own the means of production and farmers would be allowed to produce as much as they could. Briefly there would be a "mixed economy," but it wouldn't last long. Centralization and decentralization would increase at the same time; the role of the federal government would be strengthened, but the municipal, state, and county levels would be run by democratically elected groups. Once the poor were no longer exploited, crime would dwindle, perhaps even disappear. Some radicals deduced that there was no point in saving money for their old age, since the state would surely take care of them. There were even some who thought that human nature might be bettered by a humane society. A lifelong Marxist conceded that their views had sometimes been Utopian—and yet it seemed as if they were doing the impossible every day: in organizing the labor unions.

Dorothy Healey, once the chairman of the Communist Party in Southern California, had joined the Young Communist League when she was fourteen; she told me that Marxism had made growing up so much easier, that there had been no identity problems. "We knew who we were . . . we weren't subject to any doubts or hesitations. Not only would we triumph, we would triumph soon." While deriding the concept of Marxism as a religion, she added, "Yet it is the kind of faith that 'moves mountains': you can stand enormous persecution, you're not subject to moods: the euphoria one day, the deep despair the next. You are motivated by the long range vision that, come what may, no matter what the momentary obstacle may be, it is *only* momentary."

In the early Thirties some Marxists felt that Hitler's power would be fleeting, since the horrors of his regime would invigorate the opposition and hasten his downfall. In 1933 the Swiss-German Communist Willi Münzenberg told an audience at Madison Square Garden that Hitler would not last ten years, not five, not one year, not six months. His listeners stood on their chairs and cheered and cheered. Four decades later Arthur Miller wrote that to be a Marxist "was to feel contempt for all irrationality. It was capitalism that was irrational, religious . . . and Hitler was its screaming archangel. Pride lay not in what one felt but what one was capable of analyzing into class components. The story went around that Wall Street stockbrokers were calling Earl Browder, head of the Communist Party, for his analysis of the economy. A Communist *knew*, had glimpsed the inevitable."

Another radical reflected, "What were we confident about? That if Spain could hold, that fascism could be defeated. That if enough strength could be brought against the Nazis, that Germany might crumble." Committed to demolishing segregation and to trying to resolve the plight of the farmworkers, many were also galvanized by confidence in sustained effort: if enough people worked hard, equality could be achieved and suffering would be alleviated. There is (and was) no reason to suppose that Americans were more compassionate during the Depression, but economic catastrophe made many feel they must act in unison because no individual could make a dent in the system. To spread the word, to persuade others that change glimmered on the horizon, was part of the enterprise—which reinforced the exhilaration: several told me that they had never felt tired in those years when "there were no idle moments." Some had even thought that "if we could raise enough money for one more ambulance, we might turn the tide in Spain. In our own way, we believed in the domino theory."

Non-Communists like Arthur Miller and Malcolm Cowley had savored a sense of communion along with a pride in their intentions: to transform the nature of their society. Cowley wrote almost fifty years after Wall Street collapsed that the radical movement "made everything else seem unimportant, including one's pride, one's comfort, one's personal success or failure, and one's private relations. There wasn't much time for any of these. . . . All one's energies turned outward, and they seemed to be vastly increased by being directed toward purposes shared with others. One borrowed strength from the others and gave it back twofold." Fortified by mutual support, imagining that all kinds of Americans would collaborate to uproot the injustices of class and wealth, numerous radicals of the Thirties had also known the excitements of adventure, as if they were voyaging into a new terrain that no one had been privileged to see before.

Still, as a former Communist Party theorist said to me, international socialism was "mainly an intellectual obsession" which never appealed to many working people in this country. He and others also said that it took the Left years to perceive that American workers thought of themselves as middle class. Those who had seemed radicalized by unemployment would be in favor of capitalism once they found new jobs; most workers would prefer to buy a car or own a home than to seize "the means of production" and they were certainly not inclined to "smash the bourgeois state." Many were immigrants, and while right-wingers suspected that immigrants imported radicalism, the foreign-born often longed for assimilation. Yet he had believed that socialism was "a practical possibility" for the United States: "For the future, for another generation. And I thought you could talk about it without getting shot in the neck the next morning!"

25

Blacklist in Exile

Around the time of Quemoy and Matsu, the Salk vaccine, and *Gunsmoke*, I wandered across a threshold without being quite aware that I was doing so: I encountered some of the men and women whose politics had repelled and mystified millions of my compatriots. I happened to be living in London, where the spectrum of American political exiles included the family of a college friend. Delighted to see other Americans in an unfamiliar city, I was soon spending most of my Sunday afternoons at 103 Frognal. That vast Georgian house high on a hill in Hampstead echoed with the activities of the screenwriter and playwright Donald Ogden Stewart and journalist Ella Winter, who had been married to Lincoln Steffens before DOS, as Stewart was often called. Blacklisted writers and film makers who, like DOS, had been deprived of their passports by the State Department, joined the British socialists and artists who flocked to Frognal every week.

The house had once been the home of British Prime Minister Ramsay MacDonald. From the mid-Fifties onward, numerous Americans gathered at Frognal to reminisce about a lifetime on the Left, to compare their experiences with the FBI or the American Legion, to whoop in DOS's gentle deadpan presence at his stinging jokes, to yell when Ella—refilling teacups from a great height—poured hot water into the laps or crotches of her seated guests.

Amid the shouts of laughter and the cries of the scalded, between bursts of music from records just arrived from New York, such as *Damn Yankees*, and the barks of Ella's frantic miniature poodle or the sobs of small children bewildered by the commotion, the ideas of those who had been called un-

American did emerge. The Sundays were festive, often hilarious: you didn't hear the issues analyzed over each teapot. Sometimes you could hardly hear anything: while early recordings of "Joe Hill" or tapes of animal noises— brought from Africa by one of Ella's young protégés—were playing at full volume. Yet the sense of community was the strongest I'd seen. (Although some of my parents' friends were very close as individuals, they had no particular adherence as a group.) At Frognal I gradually realized that the old American Left was an intimate extended family: over the decades, most had not only worked together, they'd spent their free time with one another, rented rooms to each other, raised their children together, and—by the time I met them— suffered together. They had had their differences—about how to aid the San Francisco longshoremen during the strike of 1934, about whether it was best to take the First or Fifth Amendment—but cohesion was based on an assumption that commitments were still shared. That gave them a continuity which seemed to be heartening in their worst years.

Among the Frognal visitors were independent radicals, ex-Communists, and genuine liberals; naturally they couldn't agree on every point. But in that house I was first exposed to those who felt a responsibility for the character of their society. Their government or their former employers had asked them to disown their beliefs or to apologize for them; they had not cooperated. But some were still sorting out the accusations leveled against them, still amazed at the notion of their alleged guilt. As many historians have noted, the themes of the Cold War sprang to national attention through the investigations of the film industry, and the 1947 firings in Hollywood set a pattern that would be followed in professions throughout the country. At Frognal the recent survivors were reassessing the upheavals which had marooned them on a safe but remote reef.

• • •

During the New Deal there had been a handful of movies about "progressive" subjects, such as poverty or tenant farming, while businessmen and landlords often appeared as villains. In the Thirties most of the Hollywood moguls had worried about losing their German and Italian markets if they made films that could offend Hitler or Mussolini, but a wave of anti-fascist pictures went into production right after Pearl Harbor was bombed. Immediately after World War II some producers encouraged films that explored current social questions, such as the anti-Semitism examined in *Crossfire* and *Gentleman's Agreement* or the predicaments of returning veterans in *The Best Years of Our Lives*. With an eye on best-selling books, the producers were correct in expecting the topical to be profitable. Therefore until late in 1947, the screenwriters of the Left— including some successful social realist playwrights of the Thirties whose work had developed out of the New Playwrights' Theatre, the Group Theatre, the New Theatre League, and the Workers Laboratory Theatre—were able to incorporate mild versions of their views into their scripts. But opportunities were limited because the studio executives felt that the public disliked "messages" and because writers weren't in charge of content: the producers were totally in control of the final screenplays.

Writers had been considered alien and suspect beings in Hollywood since the Thirties, partly because many of them came from the East. The structure of the industry kept them in quarantine: isolated in their offices, unwelcome on the set. Jack Warner defined writers as "schmucks with Underwoods." At Columbia all the lights were switched off at 7:30 because Harry Cohn thought writers who worked late were either drunk or lazy, so there was no point in wasting electricity. Cecil B. De Mille, convinced that "Pretty writing can ruin a picture," had also declared, "God protect me from the writer who wants to write." Irving Thalberg was said to have described the writer as "a necessary evil." (S. J. Perelman, once employed by Thalberg, claimed that was a misquote: probably the word was "weevil.") Screenwriters were constantly replaced: often a whole series of them worked on the same script, and frequently a writer would discover that several others had been secretly assigned to the same project at the same time. Until 1939 the contract stipulated that the studio was "the author" of the work. Most screenplays were adaptations of books or plays: producers wanted "properties" instead of "originals" because outsiders might claim that their ideas had been stolen and sue for plagiarism. Yet although writers were treated as near-irrelevancies, the executives feared their influence. The issue was economic rather than political: writers were thought to be poor judges of what would be commercial.

Contrary to the insistence of the Committee that postwar movies were seething with Communist propaganda, even writers who were Communists knew it was impossible to make left-wing films. Still, some were excited by the idea of writing egalitarian material which would be seen by a large audience. But at most they could advance "democratic" themes: they wrote pictures upholding equality and peace or opposing oppression—in a tone that was tailored to the realities of the movie business, where entertainment was always the priority. So the aims of the Left were usually modest: to portray an intelligent black character or the erosions of unemployment, or even (although rarely) a woman who earned her own living. For Walt Disney the young screenwriter Maurice Rapf created a rebellious Uncle Remus and a liberated Cinderella, but his scripts were heavily rewritten.

Some conveyed sympathy for the labor movement, others depicted the bravery of those who battled fascism abroad; now and then they were able to eliminate some anti-Soviet implications from a few scenarios. Occasionally one of the Marxists wrote a script that seemed to condemn the American way of life or the corruptions of our government, but it was revised by the producers to deflect any controversy. Very few films were as radical as *Body and Soul* (written by Abraham Polonsky and directed by Robert Rossen) or Polonsky's *Force of Evil*, which dissected the consequences of craving much more money than one needs—in a culture that stimulates an appetite for opulence. Before he was blacklisted, Polonsky wrote brilliantly pessimistic movies charged with sufficient violence to appeal to popular tastes, and they were concerned with working people at a time when Hollywood concentrated on the middle class.

The content of movie scripts was a pivotal issue in the Committee's hearings of 1947. *Mission to Moscow* (1943) and *Song of Russia* (1944) were gargantuan mash notes to our wartime ally; both were considered patriotic during the war and branded as subversive a few years afterward. Committee members suspected that the Roosevelt administration had pressured the studios to make them, though the producers denied it and tried to blame screenwriters for the pro-Soviet nature of the films. *Mission to Moscow*, based on the memoirs of Joseph Davies, ambassador to Russia from 1936 to 1938, was written by Howard Koch, a non-Communist who was blacklisted mainly because of producer Jack Warner's testimony. The movie claimed that the defendants in the Moscow trials were guilty (which Davies believed), showed Stalin as a benign figure, and neglected to mention Communism.

Song of Russia, initially intended as a tribute to the Russian resistance, was a semi-musical which suggested that scorching the earth was a tuneful procedure: happy peasants sang and danced when they weren't fighting the Germans and the film bypassed the Nazi-Soviet pact. The movie was written by two Communists—Richard Collins, who later gave twenty-three names to the Committee, and Paul Jarrico, who was blacklisted after Collins and others named him—but they were not allowed to show that the joyful peasants worked on a collective farm, and they had to cut the word "community" from their script.

Both movies were unintentionally comic, but the Committee cited them as evidence that Roosevelt and Hollywood were Stalin's dupes. The Committee also heard friendly witnesses describing un-American moments in *The Best*

Years of Our Lives, where a bank was reluctant to give a veteran a G.I. loan; *Tender Comrade* (directed in 1944 by Edward Dmytryk and written by Dalton Trumbo, who would be two of the Hollywood Ten), concerning women who shared a house while their husbands fought overseas; *None But the Lonely Heart*, written by Clifford Odets, which displeased Ginger Rogers's mother— she quoted *The Hollywood Reporter*'s remark that the musical score by Hanns Eisler was "moody and somber throughout in the Russian manner"; and Odets's script for *Deadline at Dawn*, where Lela Rogers detected Communist inspiration in a joke which implied that it was a crime not to be a success. Toward the end of the hearings, Committee chairman J. Parnell Thomas said the Committee would produce "an extensive study" of Communist propaganda in motion pictures, but that document never appeared.

In truth Hollywood's overwhelming attraction for the Committee was its celebrities: the investigators had a fixation on the famous. Although the public hardly knew the names of writers or directors, the word "Hollywood" conferred a kind of royalty—which meant dazzling publicity for the Committee. For Mississippi Congressman John Rankin, who had reactivated the Committee in 1945, Jews and Communists were barely distinguishable—and much of the power in Hollywood was Jewish. (Although the percentage of Jews in the American Communist Party is uncertain, some historians have estimated that during the Thirties and Forties about half the membership was Jewish.) But the Congressman may not have realized that most of the Jews who owned the studios were staunch anti-Communists, as was Louis B. Mayer. Rankin—who said in 1945 that those who were plotting to "overthrow" the government had their "headquarters in Hollywood," which was "the greatest hotbed of subversive activities in the United States"—explained to the Congress that "Communism is older than Christianity. . . . It hounded and persecuted the Savior during his earthly ministry, inspired his crucifixion, derided him in his dying agony, and then gambled for his garments at the foot of the cross." He added that "alien-minded Communistic enemies of Christianity and their stooges" were trying to seize control of the media, including "the radio. Listen to their lying broadcasts in broken English and you can almost smell them."

J. Parnell Thomas, who became chairman of the Committee in 1946, did not share the Mississippian's obsession with Jews, though the anti-Communist crusade continued to resound with anti-Semitism. Like his colleagues, Thomas was intent on equating the New Deal with Communism and on persuading voters that Truman was perpetuating the New Deal (when he was actually retreating from its policies). And Hollywood was as rich in admirers of the New Deal as it was in Jews. By 1951—after Thomas had been jailed for payroll padding—the Committee members were also stimulated by the knowledge that the Hollywood Left had collected large sums for such causes as Russian War Relief, refugees from fascist countries, and the more radical unions. Some left-wingers were such expert fund-raisers that Hollywood was known as "the Moscow of the West." And the investigators were well aware that contributions to some front groups benefitted the American Communist Party. By that time, although film content was barely an issue, many citizens had been convinced that our movies were riddled with Communist doctrine.

· · ·

At Frognal the excesses of the California Right were recalled with laughter as well as revulsion. In the Thirties the actor Victor McLaglen had organized a brigade of uniformed horsemen who paraded in military fashion, promising to rid Hollywood of subversives. The Light Horse Cavalry Troop, as it was called, was determined to "save America." William Randolph Hearst prevailed on Gary Cooper to be the co-founder of a similar group, the Hollywood Hussars, and George Brent headed the California Esquadrille. Schooled by army officers, these vigilantes offered their services to local authorities "in case of trouble." But their posturings had been greeted with no more gravity than Robert Taylor's proposal—soon after the 1947 hearings—that members of the Beverly Hills Tennis Club be required to sign a loyalty oath. And the Hollywood Left had been amused when arch-conservative Sam Wood boasted that the movie of *For Whom the Bell Tolls*, which he directed, took no sides in the Spanish Civil war.

But amid all the levity of Frognal, some were still pasting themselves together. Quite a few of the exiles had been savaged by their intimates, before the Committee or in private, and time was needed to mend the dignity which had been mutilated. Over the years I heard them say that when they were younger, most had been animated by hating Hitler—more than by loving Stalin—and that the distinction wasn't understood (or was deliberately distorted) after the war. Yet the crimes of Stalin had been hung around their necks—and astounding as that was to them, it was an extremely painful weight to bear.

And it was characteristic of the Fifties that the exiles' legal position was thoroughly misunderstood by many Americans. Some liberals thought the blacklistees ought to have stayed at home to battle against the expansion of the domestic Cold War—disregarding the fact that most of them simply could not earn a living in the United States. Their detractors also felt that people who were or had been Communists should have said so on the witness stand.

But many observers didn't realize that those who admitted that they'd belonged to the Party would then have to give the names of other Communists or go to prison for contempt: there was no other option. If someone conceded membership, he then lost the legal right to remain silent and would be asked to inform on others—a role that was unacceptable to anyone who came to tea at Frognal.

Passport renewals were denied to exiles who had been uncooperative witnesses and to those who had left-wing "associations"—even if they had not been summoned by the Committee. Some passports were revoked while their owners were abroad. Starting in 1951 leftists could not obtain passports because the State Department claimed that their "conduct abroad is likely to be contrary to the best interests of the United States." It was expected that such radicals as Paul Robeson would "engage in activities which [would] advance the Communist movement" if they went to Europe. (In Robeson's case, the State Department had acted to prevent him from speaking out on American racism in other countries; as he said, he was under "a sort of domestic house arrest.") Moreover it became a felony to apply for a passport if the applicant had been a Communist in the last five years. Ruth Shipley, the Director of the Passport Office in the early Fifties, indicated that people who had criticized our foreign policy would not be permitted to travel. Linus Pauling, who'd opposed the Smith and McCarran Acts and nuclear testing, was refused a passport to participate in a conference on the structure of proteins in London in 1952; he was refused again when Nehru invited him to India in 1954 and also when he was asked to lecture at the University of Athens, even though the Soviets had attacked his work as "vicious" and "hostile to the Marxist view." And under the 1952 McCarran-Walter Immigration Act, foreign "undesirables" such as Pablo Picasso, Yves Montand, Graham Greene, and Alberto Moravia were not allowed to enter the United States. In the meantime most of the exiles I knew could not leave England because other countries would not have admitted them or would have deported them.

At least England did not eject them. But when the blacklisted screenwriters first settled there, the British studios—which were then dominated by American interests—were wary of them. If their names were on the credits, their pictures couldn't be shown in the United States because the American Legion and kindred groups would picket those movies—hence American distributors wouldn't handle them. The power of the Legion was colossal: in the early Fifties, when Hollywood was already losing much of its audience to television and scores of movie theaters were closing, the producers feared that the Legion's pickets could ruin the entire movie business: millions would shun the films they condemned because it would be un-American to cross that picket line. Studio officials promised the Legion not to hire anyone who took the Fifth Amendment and they asked the Legion for its own files on suspects. The "loyalty" of the employees of all the major studios was checked against the Legion's carelessly compiled dossiers; the producers were afraid to retain anyone of whom the Legionnaires disapproved.

The Legion's influence extended all the way to England, where the Ealing Studios had at first seemed eager to commission DOS to write comedies; then they recoiled from his political history. Yet some of the American movie executives based in London admired those who had defied the Committee and wanted to employ them. Gradually the blacklisted began to work in Britain under pseudonyms. But writing anonymously meant they could not rely on their previous credits: it was as though they'd achieved nothing in the past and were starting their careers anew each time. As a result some earned about fifteen to twenty per cent of their former fees.

Since some of the Frognal guests had substantial savings from the days before the blacklist, they were privileged in comparison to teachers who could no longer teach or factory workers expelled from conservative unions. But quite a few exiles were economic refugees: they were in London because they couldn't possibly support their families at home. And all of them chafed at their anonymity. DOS wrote as Gilbert Holland, using the first and middle names of his dead brother. (Others chose pseudonyms that were all too penetrable: some wouldn't relinquish their own initials.) Larry Adler's name was expunged from the American prints of the British comedy, *Genevieve*, for which he wrote the music; the credit for composition went to the conductor Muir Mathieson. Hy Kraft couldn't have a credit for the movie of his musical, *Top Banana*. When Joseph Losey and Carl Foreman made films under fictitious names, they hired or collaborated with blacklistees whenever possible. Foreman, who wrote most of *The Bridge on the River Kwai*, did not receive the Oscar for the script; the award was given to the French novelist Pierre Boulle— who could not then read or write English. When the exiles' old movies were shown on television, their names were blacked out of the credits. So there was momentary elation among them when *Marty*, featuring the blacklisted actress Betsy Blair, and *Rififi*, made in France by blacklistee Jules Dassin, won prizes at the Cannes Festival.

At home there was ample gossip about the authorship of certain screenplays. Many scripts were ascribed to Dalton Trumbo, who worked steadily under a host of names. Ring Lardner, Jr., later wrote, "To the frustration of the actual writers, some of the best work in Hollywood was being assigned by rumor to

Trumbo, and the more outstanding the picture, the broader the leer with which he declined to comment."

Books by the blacklisted were plucked out of American libraries and the State Department ordered their work removed from USIA libraries in Europe. Their prose couldn't be adapted for film or radio or television: all their earlier writing was banned as well as their latest efforts. Though their books could be published in England and their plays were produced abroad, they reached very few American readers or theatergoers, which distressed those who felt that a writer's home country contains his most important audience.

Meanwhile Hannah Weinstein, a New Yorker who produced the British television series, *The Adventures of Robin Hood,* hired over twenty blacklisted writers, including Ring Lardner, Jr., Ian Mclellan Hunter, and Waldo Salt. The serial boomed away on the TV set at Frognal; against its surging theme song—"Feared by the bad/Loved by the good/Robin Hood, Robin Hood, Robin Hood"—the exiles would speak of dead or distant figures like Tom Mooney (framed on a bombing charge and imprisoned in California from 1916 to 1939), China expert Agnes Smedley, and labor leader Harry Bridges. The conference on thought control held in Hollywood in 1947 (where it was concluded that "no progressive citizen is safe") and the violence at Peekskill, New York, in 1949—when over a hundred people were injured by stones hurled by Legionnaires after Paul Robeson gave a concert and some policemen joined the assailants—were often mentioned by those who worked namelessly in London.

At Frognal I also heard about Upton Sinclair's EPIC campaign of 1934, when the novelist won the Democratic nomination for governor after he vowed to End Poverty in California. Because he had written an exposé of the movie business and planned to impose special taxes on the studios, the alarmed executives promptly backed the Republican candidate, Frank Merriam, and the film industry rapidly united with *The Los Angeles Times* to portray Sinclair as a Bolshevik menace. At MGM—where DOS was co-writing *Marie Antoinette* for Norma Shearer—everyone who earned over a hundred dollars a week was pressured to donate a day's wages to Merriam's campaign. Some other studios withheld "gifts" to Merriam from staff paychecks. MGM also produced three sham newsreels, which pretended to represent the California voters' attitudes toward Sinclair. Sinister men with beards and foreign accents championed his candidacy, as did vagrants who were supposedly heading for California to enjoy the welfare that Sinclair would dispense; it was said that EPIC would ignite a local revolution. The "documentaries"—which were given free to movie houses throughout the state—were originated by Irving Thalberg: this was reputed to be his only political act since his adolescence, when he had made street corner speeches for the Socialist Party in Brooklyn. Other studios concocted similar footage and their employees were instructed to work on the films without pay. When Sinclair lost the election, *The New York Times* reported that "political leaders attribute Sinclair's defeat to the splendid work on the part of the screen."

Frognal was a warehouse for the American past: memories of DOS's dead friends, like Robert Benchley and Scott Fitzgerald, stayed fresh around the lunch table while Ella would recall visiting unionist J. B. McNamara in San Quentin and Folsom prisons, or revive the question of whether Clarence Darrow had been involved in jury tampering during the McNamara trial. (The McNamara brothers, officials of the A. F. of L. Structural Iron Workers, dynamited the building of *The Los Angeles Times* in 1910 while the union was on strike.) She also told me that Whittaker Chambers—whom she'd met while she was married to Lincoln Steffens—had asked her to take some papers from the Washington desk of her old friend William Bullitt, the first ambassador to the Soviet Union. (She wouldn't comply, but Chambers had nettled her: "He gave me the feeling that if I couldn't do that, then I wasn't much good. And I didn't *want* him to think I wasn't much good!" She swore that she and Steffens had known nothing about Chambers's underground activities.) And Ella kept reminding others that DOS had helped the young Hemingway to find a New York publisher and that he'd given Hemingway money to live on before *In Our Time* was sold. Legendary one-liners of the Twenties were also preserved at Frognal. After a famous lesbian murderer of the Twenties sent her victim's uterus in a suitcase to her new lover, Dorothy Parker was asked to define the carrier which held such an object. She decided that it was a snatch-all. Her opinion of Lawrence Stallings, the co-author of *What Price Glory?* who had tried to break up the Screen Writers Guild, was quoted: "I wouldn't like him if he had no legs." (He did have one.)

During five years of Sundays at Frognal, I came to feel that the strength of the Left was probably more familial than religious. Outsiders who compared the American radical movement to a church had, I think, misunderstood the power of the bonds between those who had relished working together, even though they also fought each other. Hymns to "fraternity" would have embarrassed them. But after at least two decades, these people did behave like relatives; bound by affection and exasperation throughout their common history, they appeared to be utterly at home with one another. I had been raised to believe that it would be a mistake to depend on others because no one wants a dependent, but the Frognal regulars seemed comfortable with mutual reliance. And although radicals of the Thirties had often been depicted as unsmiling drudges, toiling grimly to create a socialist paradise, neither their opponents nor the Marxist historians had acknowledged that American leftists could enjoy each other's company. Academics of the Left and pundits of the Right might have been disoriented by the waves of laughter rising from the garden or in the living room at Frognal, which could be heard even when you stood outside the front door.

· · ·

In his last decade Donald Ogden Stewart called himself the luckiest and happiest of men—and on his best days there was a gaiety that was contagious, an exuberance that seemed enviable. The style was faintly self-deprecating: he invited you to join him in mocking himself. Hemingway caught some of that essence in *The Sun Also Rises*, where DOS appeared as Bill Gorton, the successful writer who longed to buy stuffed dogs when he was drunk. (Gorton was also partially based on Bill Smith, Hemingway's boyhood friend and fishing companion.) With Hemingway DOS ran with the bulls during the fiesta in Pamplona in 1924—he was soon tossed and cracked a rib or two—and he later vouched for the accuracy of the novelist's account of their disastrous week in Spain in 1925. Their friendship ended after DOS protested the cruelty of "a viciously unfair and unfunny poem" Hemingway wrote about Dorothy Parker; Hemingway couldn't bear to be rebuked. But DOS still had fond memories of the first "male festival" in Pamplona and he told me he would like to see another bull fight before he died—if only he could find the right bull.

Mild but persistent raspberries were a mark of his affection. He was proud of his lethal martinis; when I asked for a glass of wine instead, he said, "I suppose you'd order scrambled eggs at Tiffany's!" (When he was a guest, he usually behaved like a host: at others' parties he would take someone's half-empty glass, murmuring politely, "May I deal with this?" Then he would drink it.) In his seventies he was told by a stern young doctor that he must have prostate surgery, adding, "We'll operate through the penis, of course." DOS replied, "Mine or yours?"

When I first knew him in the mid-Fifties he was still angry at his government, at being excluded from his profession, at being treated like a traitor—a formidable bitterness tinged the sweetness of his manner. I always thought him a partial depressive, as many satirists are. Years after his death I was reminded of him when I read a letter Chekhov wrote to his wife, the actress Olga Knipper, during rehearsals of *The Three Sisters*, warning her not to look sad in her role:

"Angry, yes, but not sad. People who have long carried a grief within them and grown used to it merely whistle a bit and brood a lot." Yet as DOS aged he insisted on his felicity: "My story is about a kid from Columbus, Ohio, who has the American dream dumped into his lap, who has it all come true. He has the Whitneys, the Vanderbilts, the Racquet Club, big salaries, success on the stage—and that guy becomes Marxist. Give a man in America every-thing, and he'll turn out to fight for socialism. Now I think that's a happy story."

Once he told me how his politics had evolved. Born in 1894, the son of a Republican judge, DOS was taught that "Work was a thing called success. It was connected with society and belonging to the right clubs." Moreover, "Society *was* security. And security was somehow connected with knowing the Whitneys and the Vanderbilts," although it was acceptable to know an occasional outsider, such as what Columbus called "a darn nice Jew." When he was about to graduate from Exeter and was on his way to Yale, his family lost most of their modest income, and he waited on tables, dug holes for telephone poles, and sold corsages before college proms: "I would knock on doors and hope to Christ no one was in." (Ella interrupted to exclaim that it must have been humiliating to sell objects on doorsteps—"It's the lower classes who go from door to door"—but DOS said he hadn't felt humbled: "I was a hero to myself.") Before discovering that he wanted to write, he imagined himself as "the cultured vice president of a bank: I learned the first and second movements of various symphonies." Nonetheless he had an early sense of social obligation, which he felt he'd inherited from his grandfather, the first president of Fisk University, founded after the Civil War to educate the freed slaves.

In the Navy during World War I—he had never been on a ship or touched a gun—he taught classes in seamanship and gunnery, where he learned how to make his students laugh at his attempts to tie a bowline. In 1921, fired from the bond business when he was broke and had to support his widowed mother, he began writing parodies for *Vanity Fair* at the suggestion of Edmund Wilson—"And the kid was off. Honestly, toots, it was as lucky as that." Planning to be the Mark Twain of his generation, he also wanted to be the life of the party—"It was a profession in those days"—and he was. And yet "I felt that you ought to use humor as a weapon. I *always* felt that." Later he would be stimulated by Voltaire and Swift. But he wasn't yet political; when Robert Benchley went to Boston to testify against the judge in the Sacco and Vanzetti case, or when Dorothy Parker and Edna St. Vincent Millay picketed the statehouse, he did not accompany them: "That was none of my business."

Yet in the early Twenties he'd experienced an indignation that was common among his contemporaries; he'd believed in the war: "I really wanted to go over the top, really believed that America was fighting for a better world. Then suddenly we had Warren G. Harding and the First National Bank and the return to normalcy: *normalcy* was the word that made us angry. We were angry that we'd gone to war and it hadn't worked—the idealism with which we went to war was later betrayed. The outcome of the war was meant to be a peaceful and just society. But that wasn't what Warren G. Harding was elected for!"

In that mood he wrote *Aunt Polly's Story of Mankind*—"A very bitter book: I thought it was the *Candide* of 1923. Everybody was doing outlines of history then: Hank Van Loon and others as well as H. G. Wells. Mine had a self-satisfied pompous woman telling her young nephews and nieces how the amoeba developed into a monkey and then into a man, and then came Uncle Frederick, the vice president of the First National Bank. And that's the wonder-ful story of how the world is getting better, that was progress. I was angry at the Uncle Fredericks of this world: the lying hypocrites who might make another war."

During his first marriage he had "ten marvelous years of fun and dancing and Hollywood and plays and success." Two of his comedies did well on Broadway. Between 1930 and 1949 he worked on some twenty-eight movies, including *Laughter, Tarnished Lady, Smilin' Through, Going Hollywood, The Barretts of Wimpole Street, Kitty Foyle* (co-scripted with Dalton Trumbo), *That Uncertain Feeling, A Woman's Face, Edward, My Son,* and the screen versions of Philip Barry's *Holiday, The Philadelphia Story,* and *Without Love.* Like most major screenwriters he had collaborators in the Thirties because producers thought two writers would be more productive than one, and he usually adapted plays or novels. But he was known for elegant dialogue and often he wrote the final version of the screenplay—that is, the shooting script itself. He also made "uncredited contributions" to *The Women* and wrote the last scene of *Red Dust.*

Early on, pleasure seemed limitless. I asked him what his definition of freedom had been then. He answered, "Freedom was knowing the right person to get into a speakeasy. But there were a few things you weren't allowed to do. You couldn't spit in certain places. And you couldn't sit in reserved seats." But almost everything he wanted seemed attainable: "If you start on your ass, there's no place to go but off it. I very bravely accepted happiness. I never fought it."

In 1933, when Louis B. Mayer tearfully asked him to take a pay cut because the movie business had been devastated by the Depression, DOS agreed to a 50 percent reduction of his salary. At first he thought Mayer was crying about the plight of the nation, but soon he realized that the tears were for MGM. (He may not have known that Mayer was an easy weeper, especially when he planned to manipulate others.) Since DOS earned more than almost any writer in Hollywood, he didn't then see the need for protection against cuts that the new Screen Writers Guild sought to ensure, nor did he perceive the importance of the Guild in safeguarding the salaries of those who were paid far less than he.

In 1935 DOS was writing a play called *Insurance* in which a wealthy man became a Communist, "But I had no idea what Communists were like." He told me he'd consulted the doorman of Claridge's Hotel while he was visiting London, and the man sent him to a bookstore which recommended John Strachey's *The Coming Struggle for Power*. During the same trip he bought twenty-four dress shirts: twelve of them were stiff-bosomed and the rest were soft.

The Strachey book had an enormous impact: he felt it committed him to Marxism and to the Soviet Union. He also read André Malraux's *Man's Fate* and *The New Masses*, a periodical unfamiliar to him. In that magazine an article by Kyle Crichton (signed Robert Forsythe) reminded DOS of the anger that had impelled him to write *Aunt Polly's Story of Mankind*. The contradictions between the bread lines and his own life was inescapable. Having been quite poor when young, having sported with the rich, DOS was shaken by the Marxist view that the rich were corrupt due to the position of their class: however decently some might behave, they were inevitably the exploiters of working people. And since his paychecks put him in that category, he didn't want to be identified with evil. He wrote in his memoirs, "It suddenly came over me that I was on the wrong side." If a "class war" was underway, "I had somehow got into the enemy's army." Years later he would comment on his ignorance about the Soviet Union—with no regrets for anything he did on behalf of his new convictions.

While outsiders joked about the dawning social consciousness of screenwriters who were prospering as they never had before, many people in Hollywood were sincere in feeling that they owed something to the destitute while malnutrition was ravaging the country. I don't think they felt guilty for earning well. But some didn't feel entitled to hang on to all that money. It seemed imperative to donate time as well as dollars to the homeless and the hungry. And many middle-class radicals of the Thirties gained self-respect from activism. When an exposure to misery shocked them into political involvement, they were obliged to examine their past indifference to millions whose lives had no connection to their own. The sight of people dwelling in vacant lots or eating garbage dissolved indifference and quickened a reflex of concern.

Forty years after the British novelist and critic Philip Toynbee had left the Party, he told a lecture audience that he "had always wanted to be a great writer and a good man." The latter meant "being a good Communist," and "to be a good Communist—dutiful, hard-working, loyal and obedient—was to be a good man." (Since the witty Toynbee was also an uproarious drunk, his friends had not discerned the lust for virtue.) Naturally the goal of goodness could breed arrogance: the loftiness of the Left which often irritated outsiders. But some nascent American radicals found that their endeavors gave them a sense of worth. And DOS—who wrote that he'd "wanted to be well liked by everyone"—was on better terms with himself after he was immersed in the radical movement.

For him it was insufficient to write a check for the migrant workers on strike in the Salinas Valley. In 1936 he was one of the founders of the Hollywood Anti-Nazi League and became its first president. He was also president of the League of American Writers, created by the Communist Party. Both leagues attracted many liberals and radicals as well as Communists. As DOS described those years to me, he added, "And the thing is, toots, I still have those dress shirts, because people stopped asking me to parties. I've got the shirts upstairs, they're very yellow now."

At the Conference of Western Writers in San Francisco he heard Ella Winter give a lecture. He had expected Lincoln Steffens's widow to be "a little old lady in purple and lace, and then out comes Aimée Semple McPherson! She talked politics, but it was sex, sex, sex all the way." (Ella told me that when she was a student, she never kissed anyone: "I was an intellectual and you just didn't. Kissing led to prostitution and marriage.") She and DOS met in 1936 and were married in 1939.

From 1933 onward, thousands of European Jews settled in and near Los Angeles, so the Hollywood Left was on the front line for news about the killings of Jews abroad, well before most Americans knew about them. Hollywood radicals also received information from Otto Katz—sometimes known as Rudolph Breda—a Communist leader of the German underground. Katz helped to start the Anti-Nazi League when he visited Los Angeles and distributed copies of *The Brown Book of the Hitler Terror*, and he was a model for the anti-fascist in Lillian Hellman's *Watch on the Rhine*. Throughout the Thirties DOS gave abundant energies to the League, raising money for refugees from Spain as well as Germany, organizing committees and meetings, sponsoring delegations, making innumerable speeches about the responsibility of

Americans to combat fascism and to aid its victims. In the mid-Thirties, a time of isolationist fervors, not many Americans seemed to feel that what happened in Europe had any significance in the United States.

The League was an extraordinary recruiting device: new members might begin by protesting a studio dinner given by the producer Hal Roach in honor of Vittorio Mussolini, the dictator's son; then they joined the League's campaign to buy ambulances for the Spanish Loyalists; and—after Japan invaded China—widened the League's boycott of Japanese products, especially silk stockings. Soon they could be involved with the problems of itinerant workers: the Okies in the San Joaquin Valley or the Madera County cotton pickers.

DOS was also very active in the Screen Writers Guild. Supporting civil liberties groups and labor militants, he lost some friends and he lost a cordial relationship with his employer Irving Thalberg, who wanted him to withdraw from politics long before Hollywood was investigated. (Among all the producers, Thalberg was the most fiercely opposed to the Guild, and he once threatened to shut down MGM if the writers persisted in trying to form a union.) But nothing diminished DOS's efforts to increase the public's awareness of the atrocities abroad and injustice at home. There were many Nazi sympathizers in Los Angeles, where the German-American Bund kept handing out anti-Semitic leaflets. Like most on the Left, DOS felt the United States was nurturing its own brand of fascism, disguised as patriotism—the theme of his script for *Keeper of the Flame*, released in 1942.

At first the Hollywood producers backed the Anti-Nazi League "because most of them were Jewish. Then they got worried about Communists." After a Carnegie Hall benefit for the Spanish Loyalists, DOS found Harry Warner waiting outside with a check. (In the Thirties and early Forties Warner Brothers was ranked as the most liberal studio in Hollywood; *The New York Times* had praised Warner's for its "good citizenship" and it had even been complimented by the Communist press.) Later Jack Warner would tell the Committee, "Subversive germs breed in dark corners" and that "My brothers and I will be happy to subscribe generously to a pest-removal fund."

While granting that he'd been "a romantic Marxist," DOS never told me if he had belonged to the Communist Party. (Nor did I ask: a child of the Fifties hated to do that.) But I eventually deduced that he'd been a member from about 1936 until April 1941—because he would not deny membership before that date when he sought to regain his passport in 1956. He had left the League of American Writers when that organization defended the Nazi-

Soviet pact and urged the United States to stay out of World War II; he could not "go along with the American Peace Mobilization campaign of the Communist Party." A couple of his letters to Ella (reproduced in his FBI file) show that he'd become critical of the Soviet Union: "I do not think that the present success of the Soviet armies proves necessarily that their brand of Socialism is leading toward a world" of equals. He no longer saw Russia as "a Magic Helper," deciding that "in future, I shall work with Communist Party members but I shall not front for them blindly."

While the pact had given him great pain, it had not destroyed his belief in socialism, and he wept with "relief" when Hitler invaded the Soviet Union, grateful that the forces of anti-fascism could be reunited. A year or two later he wrote to Ella that for him a "connection" with Russia was "a decided handicap" in "the fight against American fascism ... and I want to stay in that fight." He also wanted his critics to understand that he was acting from no "source other than my deepest American convictions."

The film industry's radicals and some liberals were attacked in the late Thirties and again in 1940 by Representative Martin Dies of Texas, who chaired the new House Special Committee on Un-American Activities from 1938 to 1944, and who had helped to kill the funding for the Federal Theatre Project. In Dies's book, *The Trojan Horse in America*, he made several scathing references to DOS's "record." DOS was also cited seventy-four times by California's Joint Fact-Finding Committee on Un-American Activities, regarding statements he'd made and petitions he'd signed, as well as the organizations he had joined. But the Hollywood Left presumed that it could withstand its opponents until the hearings of 1947, which led to the jailing of the Hollywood Ten.

DOS may not have guessed that his FBI file, begun in 1936, would one day be nine hundred and fifteen pages long. It included Ella's file, which was started in 1927 and contained copies of some of her letters to Lincoln Steffens. Once she and DOS were married their own correspondence was monitored. (When DOS wrote to her praising John Dewey's early book on Russia, an agent commented, "this [was] noteworthy because of the well-known anti-Communist views of Dewey.") The bureau faithfully listed Ella's prewar articles for *The New York Times Magazine* ("The Soviet Way with the Child," "Our Engineers Find Romance in Russia"), also her 1944 articles from the Soviet Union for *The New York Post*, and kept track of DOS's affiliations, among them the Joint Anti-Fascist Refugee Committee, the Greenwich Village Salute to the Red Army, the Citizens United to Abolish the Wood-Rankin Committee, the Friends of the Abraham Lincoln Brigade, the American Committee for Spanish Freedom, the American Council for Democratic Greece, and the Harry Bridges Defense Committee.

DOS and Ella were on the Security Index, candidates for custodial detention. Some FBI memoranda indicate that both—but especially Ella—were seen as potential spies for the Soviets. (As Ella sailed for Russia in wartime, an agent "examined" her luggage for "possible espionage material with negative results.") The bureau began to watch them on a daily basis before she left. Agents copied Ella's engagement book ("Dinner Hacketts, *People's World* party at Laura Perelman's"). They also noted when the lights in the Stewart home were turned off at night, that DOS sometimes called his wife Fidget or Muffet and referred to the Communist Party as the Railroad or the R.R., and that the couple went to see Alfred Hitchcock's *Lifeboat*. By then they realized that they were under surveillance.

DOS was blacklisted in 1950. MGM had ordered him to "clear" himself: to say he regretted having been "duped" and to name names. He refused without hesitation—"I was terribly proud of everything I'd done"—and his contract was canceled. He and Ella moved to England, where the American embassy in London kept the FBI abreast of their activities, and DOS wrote English dialogue for Roberto Rossellini's *Europa '51*, additional dialogue for Lewis Milestone's *Melba*, and the screenplay for *Escapade*; his name could not appear on any of them. His passport was revoked in 1952, so he couldn't go to Germany to see a production of his play, *The Kidders*, nor to Venice to finish his draft of the shooting script for David Lean's *Summertime*, which another writer completed. And so he both festered and flourished in Hampstead, digesting his disgust with the recent past while savoring the rewards of the earlier years, and welcoming those who remembered them.

• • •

The genial anarchy of Frognal sprang primarily from the temperament of Ella, who had been born in Australia and raised in England. When she could pause in an orbit that seemed to demand her presence in sixteen places at once, it was engrossing to hear her reminisce about her Fabian youth at the London School of Economics or about Lincoln Steffens, who seemed like a resident of the household—not a ghost, but a part of the menage. Sometimes I felt he had left Frognal for only an hour or so: as if he were out conducting a seminar or taking the dog for a long walk.

Steffens wrote in his *Autobiography* that when he first met Ella—a twenty-one-year-old employed by Felix Frankfurter at the Versailles Conference—"It seemed to me that she was one of the happiest things I had ever seen" as he watched her "dancing about among the delegates, lobbyists, and correspondents." (For those who knew her decades later, when she was periodically stricken with clinical depressions, there was a poignancy in that description.) But Steffens recalled her as "joyous. . . . This girl danced. Her eyes danced, her mind, her hands, her feet danced as she ran—she literally trotted about on her errands." Since she was thirty-two years his junior, Steffens was "fascinated by this personification of the younger generation." He soon became the tutor of the "young genius." "Forced . . . to clear my own mind while I was clearing hers," eager to "disillusion" her of liberal ideas and to endow her with more radical "illusions," to saturate her with "the facts" he thought she neglected, he chided her for "excessive quickness" and "impatience," and was proud of her development under his aegis.

But some years after he embarked on Ella's education, he felt she had enriched his own: that she revealed America to him when she saw it for the first time. Indeed some historians concluded that in the long run, she influenced him—particularly in furthering his enthusiasm for the Soviet Union after she went there in 1930 and 1931, although his perspective remained more sophisticated than hers. (Max Eastman, after he'd renounced the Left, claimed that Ella—"unmellowed by experience" and "born to be a zealot"— had converted Steffens "from a sentimental rebel . . . to a hard-cut propagandist of the party line.") Bruce Bliven of *The New Republic* credited Ella with "bullying" Steffens into writing his autobiography: Bliven wrote, "It had to be snatched from him almost page by page and rushed to the publisher, to keep him from destroying the manuscript."

In Steffens's final years, as Ella lectured and wrote about Russia, organized support for the migrant lettuce, cherry, and cotton pickers in California, covered the great 1934 waterfront strike in San Francisco for *The New Masses*, and headed the John Reed Club in Carmel, the couple was a target of American Legionnaires. After a local paper stated that Ella had had sex with twenty-nine black men, Steffens said, "Why not thirty?" The U.S. immigration authorities considered deporting her because of "her alleged activities in connection with San Joaquin Valley labor troubles," but although she was foreign-born her American citizenship was unassailable.

At Frognal she described how Steffens used to tease her for being a reformer: You put a good man in when a dike is broken, he told her, and then he's swept away; "Then, he said, you keep putting in other good men and they keep being swept away. You reformers will never learn that it's not a question of good men or bad men, but of *forces*—it's forces that corrupt." Ella told me Steffens had not read Marx when he said that, but she stressed that he was arguing from a Marxist point of view.

Although some of her declarations sounded simple, she left a trail of complexities behind her: you could puzzle over one of her pronouncements for days. While she never acquired the reflective intellect that Steffens envisioned, ardor propelled her through the anti-nuclear protests which began in England in the Fifties, with some detours for the promotion of African crafts and Yugoslavian toys. As an activist she seemed almost capable of cloning herself— you might meet her on the stairs and then suddenly sight her in the garden— and she gleefully recalled how she and the film distributor Thomas Brandon used to infiltrate German-American Bund rallies during the Thirties to shout anti-fascist slogans from opposite sides of the hall, so that the audience would assume that dozens were present: "They would call out, 'They're here!' 'No, they're there!' and they never knew that there were only two of us!" Activism could also make her inaccessible: in Hollywood, when DOS asked his MGM secretary to phone her and the line was busy for hours, he finally said, "Oh hell, get me my first wife!" Sometimes I received postcards from her with nothing written on them: the invitation or the command had been forgotten after the card was hastily addressed.

Amid the constant drama of changing au pairs—the young women quit Frognal because they couldn't possibly keep pace with Ella—the past and present could be scrambled: in the late Seventies, when I told her that *The Los Angeles Times* had improved, she cried, "I *spit* on *The L.A. Times!*"— because of its anti-union policies of 1910. Change, for which she had labored, could be overlooked: wicked institutions or individuals were not expected to redeem themselves. Yet she had no respect for obstacles, nor could she be deterred in any quest: in pursuit of some elusive information, she told me to ring a film scholar she'd known; I objected that he was dead. Ella barked, "Then call someone who isn't!"

I heard her say that the Hollywood Left had made many errors, especially in their misunderstanding of the Soviet Union: "Some of what we believed wasn't true. But that doesn't matter, because we *worked* for what we believed in." Functioning rather like a cyclone, she could be criticized for rashness, for inaccuracy, for running off the road, but not for indecision—while others pondered, she hurtled forward: she was a generator, as unjudging as a dynamo.

Somewhat surprised by the rebirth of feminism, she—although an early suffragist—had been persuaded by her Fabian friends that inequality was a social condition unrelated to gender, and that socialism would give women the same rights as men. But she had always led an unrestricted life. Frognal used to razz her because her small son had had to stand waiting for her outside men's rooms—because she rarely bothered to read the signs on public toilets. Yet she did acknowledge a few differences between the sexes. The novelist Ira Wolfert said Ella thought men were created to run errands and carry heavy objects, and he was one of many she encumbered with large items to lug through customs.

Alternating with her depressions, there were manic periods when her instincts seemed frantic beyond focus. Then she would whirl into pressuring a Member of Parliament to raise questions in the House of Commons about a licorice candy called Nigger Babies, or berating the young Italian maid for not wearing socks while serving meals, or trying to arrange London concerts for Paul Robeson in hopes that the State Department would be embarrassed into returning his passport (the Let Robeson Sing committee did achieve a concert via amplified transatlantic telephone, attended by a big audience), hurling fruit rinds from the iced tea pitcher over the garden wall until the neighbors' solicitor arrived to remonstrate, organizing a children's party, ringing up a new acquaintance who was said to be ironic and witty: "Why aren't you ironic and witty with *me?*" scrubbing her rubber plant with steel wool until it collapsed with a hiss, and harassing her lemur. She found that nocturnal animal bad company because it slept in the daytime, so she banged on its cage or placed it next to a bellowing television set to keep it awake. Since it couldn't sleep at night, the rings beneath its sunken eyes grew even deeper, and it had no relief until she went away for a week; then it keeled over. On her return it fled squawking from her arms up the chimney and was not seen again. Some of us thought she should have been more sympathetic to its habits because she too was given to sudden naps—especially at the movies, where she would doze, then jerk violently awake, exclaiming, "Needs some Stewart dialogue!" and then plunge into slumber again.

Sexual curiosity was still a powerful stimulant for Ella when she was over seventy: at times it took the form of recollection. As a girl she spent years trying to find out what Oscar Wilde's crime was. Since her parents provided no sex education, she'd thought that babies were born from the anus and she wondered how they were kept clean of shit. Her mother had told her that men were after only one thing; therefore when Steffens first touched her hand, she said, "So you're a rotter, like all the other men." Steffens dropped her hand. Much later, when she was dining with him at the Russell Hotel in Bloomsbury and was racked with menstrual cramps, he took her to his room and offered some gin. Before long the hotel manager walked in on them: Ella was in bed, the bottle of gin was nearby—"If you were Toulouse Lautrec, you couldn't do it better," DOS reflected. The manager ordered her to leave and Ella, who was mortified, confessed that she was "unwell." The man asked how she could have been well downstairs in the dining room and unwell in the bedroom, and she was ousted after rejoining that "A woman is sometimes well *and* unwell." That tale, often repeated, was part of the lore at Frognal.

Ella could display a beguiling frankness about matters which were unflattering to her. She recalled asking Joseph Losey, "Why is it that I like you so much and you don't like me?" He replied, "Maybe that's the reason." After the Thurbers visited Frognal, they reported that "the hollow laughter began immediately"; afterward Ella said of Jim, "He thinks I'm a Thurber woman!" When she and DOS began to write their separate memoirs, his work room was directly over hers and when there was a lull in his typing, she pounded on the ceiling with a broom handle. One day he sweetly informed her that he had switched to a ballpoint pen; thereafter she wouldn't be able to know if he was writing or just checking out the cricket scores in a newspaper. Ella was infuriated; she felt his wit should be employed to wring the withers of history every day—and besides (as she often said) she couldn't make jokes herself. Yet she wasn't always as invincible as she seemed: once while sitting in a waiting room, she saw that all the other women's skirts were longer than hers— the fashion had changed without her knowing it. Ella swiftly ripped out her own hem and pulled it down to her shins. Daily life was a series of challenges: crossing a street, she would charge into heavy traffic with her head lowered and a broadbrimmed hat tilted over her eyes: brakes screamed and drivers yelled but she wouldn't look at them.

Initially I thought her ruthless, possibly destructive, even though DOS was clearly devoted to her. (After they had a lively quarrel about whether to be cremated or buried, he said, "Let's dissolve together, dear." He meant it and ultimately they did—dying less than three days apart.) Many adored him but disliked her, although a few of their intimates felt he used her as a shield, making her shoulder the unpleasant tasks or play the ogre when he wanted to evade others—so that he could continue to appear angelic while Ella was regarded as a scoundrel. Sometimes he gracefully undercut her: when she named a cat Kim Il Sung, he told everyone to call it Pussy. Ella often behaved outrageously, even abominably—hence it was striking that she was much loved: by both husbands, by some lifelong friends, who flew forward to defend her when she was denounced. One day when she made a scene at lunch and then dashed into the kitchen to browbeat the maid, DOS told Sally Belfrage what he would inscribe on Ella's tombstone: "She was awful but she was worth it."

And over the years it became plain that it was she who had made this community congeal, who made Frognal an indispensable refuge for emigrés and dissidents, especially those who had no passports and were locked into England. Many of them might have remained isolated—rootless or rudderless—had it not been for the energies Ella brought to reuniting them: she did realize how much they needed that coherence. The English assumed that the exiles were overjoyed to have left the repulsive country which had abused them. But few of their English acquaintances understood that these Americans missed their own culture—or that they sometimes felt like amputated limbs.

At moments the British used the blacklisted as exhibits: to prove that Britain was a great democracy. So Frognal was a haven where the exiles could escape the strains of diplomacy; one recalled, "We could go to Frognal and say, 'This fucking country! The toilets don't work—' without being insulting to the English." The commonwealth of Frognal may also have protected the blacklisted from the spasms of guilt that punished persons can feel—simply because they have been punished. (Elsewhere I encountered various penitents of the Thirties. But although mistakes were admitted, self-flagellation seemed scarce at Frognal.) And like many others who were at first alarmed by Ella's tendency to pounce and scatter, I became fond of her and grateful for the confederacy she had created, the sanctuary she had made.

• • •

When you entered Frognal, as the heavy front door slowly swung open on its hinges, you were almost overwhelmed with objects: Picasso's sketches and Lissitzky's paintings and a magnificent Mondrian portrait of a chrysanthemum and a large wooden sphinx's head over the fireplace competed for your dazed attention: the house itself was an event. (It was also a zoo: parrots, a monkey, mynah birds, cats and dogs, all gibbering or wailing between their sporadic feedings.) Within the walls stacked with numerous Klees, Chagall drawings, and ancient African carvings, there were glass cabinets crowded with small pre-Columbian sculptures and Asante gold weights; Peruvian puppets and embroideries from Eastern Europe could distract the eye from drawings by George Grosz. As guests inspected the Marini horseman rearing up in the living room and the Jo Davidson statue in the terraced garden, they were apt to carry their teacups and ashtrays around with them, since there were few bare surfaces at Frognal. New acquisitions appeared while old ones vanished, as evidence of Ella's fiscal talents: in Hollywood she'd invested DOS's salary in works of art, and after he was blacklisted they lived comfortably by selling one painting or sculpture at a time. Some of the Klees commuted between Frognal and the Tate Gallery, where they joined exhibitions which undoubtedly increased their value.

Among the frequent visitors were Cedric Belfrage, editor of the *National Guardian* until he was deported, his daughter Sally Belfrage, author of *A Room in Moscow* and later, books on Mississippi and India and Northern Ireland; psychiatrist Josephine Martin; the British writer John Collier, who was particularly helpful to the blacklisted; playwright Benn Levy and the actress Constance Cummings; Eileen and Shivaun O'Casey; Dina and James Aldridge, the Australian novelist; the actor Sam Wanamaker, Ingrid Bergman, Dr. Patrick Woodcock, Kenneth Tynan and Elaine Dundy, folklorist Alan Lomax, who occasionally brought his guitar, and Larry Adler minus his harmonica.

Bergman—expansive and unstarlike—loved to talk, and she had an engaging tendency to rush into subjects that intrigued everyone, such as the expectation that *Casablanca* would be a catastrophe. She hardly became acquainted with Bogart because he was off fighting with the producer and the director about the chaotic state of the film. Bergman said the script was in such disarray that the action was invented from day to day, and no one knew how the movie would end. She told us that two conclusions were planned: in one of them, she would have stayed with Bogart for good. But the renunciation scene was shot first and the film makers decided to use it. Ella said she loathed that ending.

At Frognal Larry Adler was called "the bush baby": his small triangular face with deepset eyes looked like Ella's lemur. Adler had taken a very public stand against the Committee and had raised money for Henry Wallace. Igor Cassini, the Hearst gossip columnist, had accused Adler and the tap dancer Paul Draper, who often performed together, of peddling "Red propaganda." That inspired a woman from Greenwich, Connecticut, to write letters to the press, saying that they were "pro-Communists" and should not be allowed to give a recital in her town because their earnings would be sent to Moscow. Adler and Draper sued her for libel. Filing the suit required them to swear in preliminary affidavits that they had never been Communists. But the attacks from Walter Winchell and Westbrook Pegler (known to the Left as Pestbrook Wiggler) continued, Cassini called for their deportation, many bookings were canceled, and Adler and Draper lost their suit. Adler settled in London. The State Department almost rescinded his passport—until it was discovered that a Leonard Adler of *The Brooklyn Daily Eagle*, allegedly a Communist, had been mistaken for the musician. Yet Larry Adler remained on the blacklist. But he gave concerts through Europe, and in London you could hear him playing Bach and Gershwin and Ravel and music from his own bar mitzvah all over the city.

As a radical, Adler seemed glad to be unaffiliated. He told me that DOS—grown tearful on champagne on a New Year's Eve in the mid-Fifties—had said he worried about Adler because he had "no philosophy, no faith," that he didn't know what held Adler together. DOS volunteered that Marxism sustained him, but that some of his friends had cracked up because they had nothing to fortify them. Adler replied that he was better off without a faith: the Nazi-Soviet pact had not traumatized him, and "If Henry Wallace is less than perfect, I can live with it." But he was touched by DOS's concern for those who lived without a framework.

Abraham and Sylvia Polonsky, Harold Clurman, the lawyer Leonard Boudin, and the lyricist E. Y. Harburg checked in at Frognal whenever they passed through London. Salka Viertel, the former actress who wrote several of Garbo's movies, came from her home in Klosters, Switzerland; the Frognal gatherings were rather like sequels to her Sundays in Santa Monica, where the Hollywood Left had mingled with emigré artists from the late Thirties until the early Fifties. Katharine Hepburn—whom DOS had known since 1928 and who'd starred in four of his screenplays—strode to and fro between the house and the flowerbeds for brisk bouts of weeding; equally imperious and cordial, she was critical of the condition of the garden tools and showed no tolerance for rust.

While Carl Foreman's *The Mouse that Roared* was being filmed in England, Jean Seberg came to tea: after the disasters of *St. Joan* and *Bonjour Tristesse*, she seemed relieved to be in a small movie. She spoke angrily to me about her experiences with Otto Preminger, who had launched her career—which already appeared to be fading. (She had not yet been discovered by the French directors.) Working with Preminger at seventeen, she'd expected an adult to provide her with some guidance, but she said he had mainly dispensed humiliation and had given her little direction on her first two films. Whenever we met at Frognal she talked about her upbringing in Marshalltown, Iowa; like me, she seemed to crave the company of other Americans. And she enjoyed shocking me by repeating that she and her high school classmates had believed that you could get pregnant from necking. Because anxiety delayed their periods, the girls thought they were pregnant almost all the time. Since my reaction amused her, I did not say that she'd told me that story before.

The Berliner Ensemble visited Frognal only a few weeks after Brecht's death, when the group was performing in London. His widow Helene Weigel had been a friend of Ella's since the Thirties, when the Los Angeles community of German refugees included Fritz Lang, Hanns Eisler, and Thomas Mann, who wrote *Dr. Faustus* in Hollywood; Brecht had written *Galileo* there. Despite their immense loss, the Brecht troupe joked about the playwright's idiosyncrasies. They referred to their arguments with him about props and described how Brecht had wanted a character to wear a giant ear as a symbol for spying: finally the actor had rebelled against that huge organ and battled with Brecht until it was eliminated.

As such disparate persons sat in the large living room, crumbling chunks of Ella's stale fruitcake rather than trying to chew them, dodging paper gliders flung by the smallest guests, memories of the best aspects of the past sometimes rose with the steam from the electric kettle. The massive Popular Front of 1935 to 1939, when liberals and radicals had collaborated to strengthen the forces of anti-fascism and unionism, had seemed to show that all sorts of Americans could perceive a kinship between international and domestic issues when democracy was at stake.

The excitement of building the guilds in Hollywood—above all the Screen Writers Guild—had been heightened by the knowledge that Los Angeles had long been a violently anti-labor town. The film industry had hated unions ever since the advent of sound had precipitated the organizing of technicians, and Hollywood's anti-Communism was closely allied to the animosity toward labor. A couple of Frognal visitors had worked for trade unions before they arrived in Hollywood, and they relished their recollections of "practical victories"— as when the National Labor Relations Act of 1935 had legalized the right of workers to organize. Abraham Polonsky, who'd been involved with the United Auto Workers and was the CIO's educational director in Westchester County from 1939 to 1941, spoke of the formation of the CIO as an historic moment "when the practical and the prophetic come together."

Those who had worked hard to uphold the legitimacy of the Screen Writers Guild while the producers kept trying to destroy it, reminisced about its foremost achievements, such as establishing a credit system which prevented producers from putting the names of their friends, relatives, and in-laws on scripts. (Until 1939 the studios could assign any credit they wished. Some producers put their dependents on the payroll by giving them credits for screenplays they never wrote.) Screenwriters had been on the forefront of the Hollywood Left and their union—despite all the internal fighting—was the most effective of the talent guilds.

In the early Forties the Hollywood Democratic Committee (which later became the Hollywood Independent Citizens Committee of the Arts, Sciences, and Professions) reunited the broad coalitions of the Popular Front. The "headiness" of that diversity was recalled, along with the liaisons with such figures as Harold Ickes, Roosevelt's Secretary of the Interior. In 1944 the Left appeared to be an influential wing of the Democratic Party, as the HDC toiled for the reelection of Democratic congressmen and to ensure Roosevelt's fourth term. But a few years after the Left's enthusiastic immersion in electoral politics, HICCASP would be fragmented over the question of initiating a third party and supporting Henry Wallace; there were lasting schisms among those who did or did not want to withdraw from the Democratic Party. And the deterioration of the labor movement continued to sadden many of its early allies; for them it was still painful to acknowledge that some trade unions could become reactionary or corrupt, or both. But all the defeats of the postwar era could not erase the memory of what it had been like to win—when a union contract was signed, when the Nazis were vanquished.

• • •

Sometimes there were disagreements at Frognal about whether anyone had had an excuse to be surprised by the torrents of anti-Communism which had flooded the country right after World War II. Some stressed that the fear of international socialism had long been intrinsic to the United States, that Americans had recoiled from it as an alien concept—especially because most Communists of the Twenties were foreign-born—and that this emotion was only temporarily muted by our wartime alliance with the Russians. As soon as the war ended, the fear grew "when you took the heel off it," Polonsky observed.

The Palmer raids of 1919 and 1920 and the execution of Sacco and Vanzetti were cited as examples of the long-term dread of "Bolsheviks within the gates." Prior to World War I, as millions of immigrants were arriving from Europe, the nationwide repugnance toward foreigners—seen as sly, shabby people who were believed to import and spread diseases like bubonic plague—was thought to have fueled the fear of anarchists and syndicalists and other precursors of the American Communist Party.

Since such sentiments had been rabid in the early Twenties—even after the Red Scare had abated because public figures had condemned its excesses— some at Frognal felt that the Left should not have expected to have a role in the "mainstream," not even during the Depression. It was said that many Americans had feared Communism more than fascism: because most patriots believed that ours was the finest democracy in the world, hence fascism could never develop in the United States—whereas the New Deal seemed to threaten the nation with socialism. And the anti-labor campaign of the Right, augmented immediately after World War II, appeared almost inevitable in response to the gains that unions had made during the Roosevelt years.

But others felt that the expansion of public hostility to the Left in the late Forties had been so rapid that they couldn't have foreseen it: someone used the word "flashfire." Their attitude had been: "We'd just fought a war against oppression—how could that happen in *our* country?" The atmosphere of "Big Three Unity" was recalled. So was General Douglas MacArthur's 1942 tribute to the Soviet Union—when he urged the Allies to "unite in salute to that great Army and that great Nation which so nobly strives with us for the victory of liberty and freedom"—and the hopes roused by the first United Nations conference in San Francisco in 1945. It was also thought that the United States, by defeating the fascist countries, had actually abetted the Communist countries—therefore some left-wingers had imagined that Washington might be sympathetic to the enemies of fascism.

Other misapprehensions about the past were exhumed at Frognal. For example, the Left had at first expected the Hollywood Ten to win their case. Although the Ten knew they would be cited for contempt—for declining to confirm or deny Party membership—and that they would lose in the trial court and the appellate court, and that they risked a year in jail, they did think they would be vindicated in the Supreme Court. By contesting the power of the Committee to legislate in the field of political associations, they aimed to destroy it in the courts, to halt the inquisitions. Their lawyers had anticipated at least a five-to-four ruling and they had moved to postpone the case until after the 1948 elections, reasoning that the Supreme Court would be affected if Henry Wallace did well: if he received five to seven million votes. (He got slightly over one million, even less than the segregationist candidate Strom Thurmond.) But the two most liberal members of the Court, Frank Murphy and Wiley B. Rutledge, died in the summer of 1949, before the second round of hearings—and that changed the composition of the Court, which turned down the Ten's petition to be heard. In 1950 they all went to jail.

It was also repeated that in 1947 leftists did not foresee blacklisting. They hadn't guessed that individuals on the Committee would tell producers like Jack Warner that the studios should expel "ideological termites," and they had accepted the assurance of Eric Johnston, the president of the Motion Picture Association, that there would never be a blacklist. As the blacklist lengthened in the early Fifties, so did the graylist: non-Communists who had radical associations weren't always fired outright, but they were moved to innocuous positions and barred from promotion, and many had great difficulties in finding new jobs.

Radicals all over the country were stunned when the Ten were jailed. And the film community was indignant that the Hollywood executives refused for years to admit that there was a blacklist. The fact that the blacklist was unofficial made it all the harder to challenge. Hopes that the Supreme Court would rule that blacklisting was illegal were defunct by 1951, when the practice accelerated.

The reasons given for not employing the undesirables were nonpolitical: actors were informed that they were too short or too tall, too old, "not the right type" for a particular role; John Randolph later told me, "Suddenly you heard that the part had been rewritten for a midget." Since they couldn't work anonymously, as writers did—Lee J. Cobb said, "It's the only face I have"— some actors lost at least fifteen years out of their professional lives. This was especially true for character actors whose early careers had been interrupted by wartime military service, then disrupted by the blacklist when they were already middle-aged.

Few agents would handle blacklistees. When one agent considered representing the actress Karen Morley, he learned that Paramount wouldn't hire any of his clients if he took her on. (Morley then applied to a prominent New York theatrical agent, who offered her an anti-Communist script full of lines like "She went from underdog to overbitch." When Morley turned down the script, the agent turned her down: that was one tactic for disposing of left-wing performers.) Writers were almost as easily rejected: it was said that when Waldo Salt was fired by RKO, he was told it had nothing to do with his politics—that he just wasn't writing well. Naturally those who were notified that their talents were dwindling sometimes came to think that it was true: they could no longer feel confident of their calling. An actor who knew that the studios didn't dare to cast him would wonder if, after all, he was a mediocre performer. Directors and writers grappled with work blocks and the debilitations of self-doubt. Albert Maltz told me he became dubious of what he produced after being blacklisted; remembering how demoralized he'd been, he drew on an image from baseball: "As pitchers say, I lost my rhythm."

●　●　●

At Frognal informers were lampooned as well as despised: references to Larry Parks's testimony elicited "Al Jolson sings again!" (Parks had played the lead in *The Jolson Story*.) Contempt for those who had betrayed their principles out of fear—or who apparently had no principles at all—filtered through the smoky dusk at teatime. And Frognal was intrigued by Arthur Miller's A *View from the Bridge* when it opened in London in 1958. Some saw the play as a reply to *On the Waterfront*—that impassioned defense of the informer directed by Elia Kazan and written by Budd Schulberg; both ex-Communists had been highly cooperative witnesses. In his own waterfront drama, Miller, a non-Communist who'd refused to give names to the Committee, had portrayed the informer as a disgrace to his community: the man was not presented as a villain, but his unforgivable act ruined his life. Yet when Miller expanded and reworked the play for its London production, he hoped that audiences might sympathize with the protagonist.

Long afterward Miller told me the play wasn't conceived as an answer to Kazan's film, but that it was "an attempt to throw a different light on the whole informing theme," which he felt had been "terribly misused" in *On the Waterfront*. Still, many leftists thought the two works must be closely related, especially since the press reported that Miller had withdrawn his friendship from Kazan (his former director) for years after Kazan named sixteen persons.

Throughout the 1951 investigations of the movie industry the Hollywood Left listened to the hearings on the radio every day, to learn whose names were being uttered. Most informers named John Howard Lawson, the first president and founder of the Screen Writers Guild and head of the Hollywood Communist Party: it was like saying "Amen" at the end of a prayer. Some radicals found their reactions weren't always rational: a writer who expected the screenwriter Leo Townsend to name her listened apprehensively to his testimony—and then was momentarily outraged when he didn't: "My first thought was, 'Doesn't he think I'm important?' " There was a good deal of rumination about the personalities of the informers. Carl Foreman told me that some who had been extra-militant—extremists who "tended to jump for the barricades when there was no need to"—became informers. Foreman thought they had once had fantasies of heroism or martyrdom—displaying "a desire to be burned at the stake *until* the fire is lit"—and that an inherent volatility had enabled them to swing wildly from Left to Right.

In Hollywood "A man has to eat" was a recurrent statement from friendly witnesses which particularly disgusted the Left; I was told it was the cliché of the era. That justification for informing came from some for whom luxuries had become necessities, when deprivation might have meant parting with the Beverly Hills mansion, the pool, the staff of servants. Protecting a lush way of life was also rationalized with "My first responsibility is to my family." There was eventual sympathy among radicals for informers with waning careers and inadequate salaries—and certainly for those with sick children or disabled relatives to provide for. But responsibilities which included yachting won no compassion from the blacklisted. Theirs was the traditional American scorn for the betrayal of the childhood password or the schoolyard confidence, the vows of brotherhood taken on the playground. In the ethics of Twain and Tarkington, you don't tell: not even if the Indians light a fire underneath you, not when the rival cowboys uncoil the rope to string you up. And you never collaborate with people whom you know to be despicable, such as Joseph McCarthy and J. Edgar Hoover.

At the beginning of *The Crucible* Arthur Miller had written, "Old scores could be settled on a plane of heavenly combat between Lucifer and the Lord," and that "the envy of the miserable toward the [fortunate] could and did burst out in the general revenge." In Hollywood those who had long disliked individual leftists could be complimented by Committee members for denouncing them, while radicals thought that certain informers also wanted the jobs of the best-paid writers of the Left. Dalton Trumbo earned more than any writer in the industry, whereas Martin Berkeley—who named one hundred and sixty-one people—was usually assigned to second-rate animal pictures; his foremost credit was *My Friend Flicka*. (Ring Lardner, Jr., observed that Berkeley was unable to write dialogue for humans.) Berkeley named some of the producers' favorite writers, DOS and Trumbo among them.

Several other unprosperous informers also named colleagues whose careers had far outdistanced their own. But not every informer was rewarded: after the hearings Larry Parks was cast in only three movie roles, none of them substantial, before his death twenty-eight years later. (He had been a most unwilling witness, and a blacklistee who knew Parks well rather sadly referred to him as a Kansas cornflower who should never have been involved in any political movement.) But most informers were soon hired by the studios—although some were dropped before long, since their work was no better after they had aided the Committee than it had been beforehand.

Since no informer was going to proclaim that his motives were sordid or that he was terrified of the Committee, many proffered an ideology to support their actions: Communism was as much of a menace at home as in Russia. Their critics replied that the informers' positions on Stalin and the Soviet Union were perfectly understandable, but some doubted their sincerity— because most had discovered that they detested Communism only when they were summoned by the Committee. As for those who claimed that the Left had ensnared and defiled them at an early age, DOS said he still believed that "the Thirties were Hollywood's finest hour" and that he could never quite forgive people who disowned their past convictions and called themselves dupes.

The naming of intimates had set off shock waves because the Hollywood Left was such a family: it was as though some informers had done violence to their closest kin. (Richard Collins named Waldo Salt; Collins had been best man at Salt's first wedding.) Years later Betsy Blair, who'd been blacklisted soon after she appeared in *Marty*, said to me that she had not been especially disillusioned by the behavior of the informers—but that she had been thrilled by the conduct of the non-cooperators. That probably meant, she added, that everyone must harbor an expectation of corruption: due to the ambitions which ignite almost any career. No one at Frognal had been unambitious. Many continued to suffer from the loss of their vocations. But when laughter rose in protest as Ella waved her large knife and threatened to cut more slices of inedible cake (DOS said she looked like Lady Macbeth) or when Bronx cheers greeted a botched pun, I sensed a special kind of loyalty among those who were entitled to mock one another—since they had sustained each other's dignity when it was assaulted from all sides.

• • •

There were warm words for Franklin Roosevelt at Frognal, particularly from DOS. Perhaps the over-assurance of the Thirties radicals—which had left them unprepared for the Cold War—was partially due to their reliance on Roosevelt: his presence in the White House had made them feel more powerful than they were. Yet some were still objecting that he had "saved capitalism": that the seeds of socialist principles embedded in the New Deal had actually been smothered by his administration, that the resulting compromises prevented the development of socialism. (In the Fifties the conservative Peter Viereck praised the New Deal's "revolution-preventing social reforms"— thereby concurring with radicals who felt that FDR had undermined their goals.) But many left on the Left had been proud to work for Roosevelt's reelection in 1944, and they had mourned his death well before it was clear that a whole era had died with him.

Frognal was engrossed by the news bulletins when Bulganin and Khrushchev visited England in April 1956 and amused when the Queen invited them to tea. In those days it wasn't easy for someone of my generation to see why some American leftists still seemed to feel a linkage with what happened in Russia, even though the ties had weakened. Technically one could understand what the Soviet Union had meant to them in the Thirties, when the first socialist country in the world had been the experiment which they so eagerly hoped would succeed—when so much emotion had been poured into upholding the Soviet Union's right to exist, to survive. I also knew that many hoped Russia would change enormously in the Khrushchev years, hoped that repression would not recur there, and that it would at last become a socialist democracy. And Khrushchev's repudiation of Stalin made some hopeful that the Soviet Union was beginning to transcend its past.

So there was still an appreciation of the concept: an old tropism that hadn't expired. In the late Fifties I found this puzzling, since I was becoming acquainted with the British Left, which showed no interest in Russia. But later I caught a clue to some American radicals' feelings when I heard an elderly trade unionist quoted on the Soviet Union: "It's my mother. She may be a whore, she may be a thief, she may be a junkie. But she's my mother. I'm not going to throw her out or leave her on the streets. . . ."

I wasn't present when Frognal discussed Khrushchev's revelations at the Twentieth Congress in detail, though I could see that DOS was tremendously upset. But I was on hand when the Russians invaded Hungary in the fall. International attention had been centered on the Middle East when Britain, France, and Israel attacked Egypt because President Gamal Abd al-Nasser had nationalized the Suez Canal. But then the Soviet tanks rolled into Budapest, and I heard DOS express his revulsion with the Soviet Union. The Soviet leaders of 1956 were hardly mentioned by the Frognal guests: it was Stalin they blamed. (It didn't sound as if he'd been a hero to them, as Trotsky had been for his adherents, but they had worked hard to accept his decisions and to believe he had been maligned.) Now they were appalled that the new— and supposedly more enlightened—Soviet regime had behaved just as murderously as its predecessor. DOS bitterly recalled the contortions that had seemed necessary to defend many of Stalin's actions. Respect for the principles of Marxism was reaffirmed, but Stalin's betrayals of Marxism were gloomily explored by those over fifty or sixty.

Only a couple of voices demurred, arguing that John Foster Dulles and the CIA must be partially responsible for manipulating the rebellion of the Hungarians, and that Imre Nagy's appeal to the United States and Britain for aid meant that counter-revolution and war were possible—hence the necessity of bringing in Soviet troops. But others replied that the CIA could have had no entré if Moscow had not maintained a dictatorship for eleven years, that the groundwork had been laid by the Soviet Union.

• • •

Charlie and Oona Chaplin were often at Frognal during the filming of A King in New York. For the Sunday tribe, Chaplin's recent history was as significant as his dimensions as an artist. The lurid fallout from his 1944 paternity trial— Representative John Rankin later referred to him as "the perverted subject of Great Britain who has become notorious for his forcible seduction of white girls" and urged that he be deported—the invective from right-wingers when he called for a Western second front early in World War II, the pickets organized by American Legionnaires who marched outside movie theaters showing *Monsieur Verdoux* until it was withdrawn from circulation, plus the success of the Legion and the Catholic War Veterans in dissuading many theater-owners and some television stations from reviving his silent films, had all climaxed in the Attorney General's decision in 1952 that Chaplin (who was en route to England for the premiere of *Limelight*) could not return to the United States without a hearing on charges of "moral turpitude and Communist sympathies." The Immigration Service was forbidden to admit him unless his "beliefs and associations" were thoroughly investigated.

Chaplin stayed away, repeating that he wasn't a Communist but "a peacemonger." When the Legion promised to picket *Limelight*, the movie was canceled by Twentieth Century Fox's west coast theater chains—in keeping with Rankin's recommendation that Chaplin's "loathsome pictures be kept from the eyes of American youth." Loew's and RKO's theaters canceled too, and *Limelight* did not play in Hollywood for twenty years. The fact that the American government demanded a million dollars in back taxes from him was deemed as punishment at Frognal. Sometimes the issues seemed fused: one couldn't tell if the accusations concerning his "moral worth" or his politics or his taxes made him angriest. As an exile of several years, he seemed thoroughly out of touch with the United States. Yet although he sounded muddled, no one could fault his rage. He had been used as an example, exhibited as a warning to others—as though his work as well as his opinions should be a source of shame.

Chaplin needed a dedicated audience and it was one's duty as a guest to respond as a spectator, even if only three people were present. (The critic Robert Warshow wrote that all Chaplin's performances contained "one insistent personal message": a demand to be loved, and I think that was what we were seeing at Frognal.) Leaping to his feet to snap his fingers and warble the theme song from A King in New York—"Mister, won't you hurry/And get out your money/Put a nickel in the slot, I'm getting hot"—or acting out an interview he'd just given to a reporter from *Time*: "I said to that young man, you can tell them that the only thing Charlie Chaplin likes about America is Mounds candy bars! They can put it in an ad if they want to, put it on a billboard, [louder] the ONLY thing Charlie Chaplin likes about America is MOUNDS"—his fury at the country which had discarded him was as urgent as the impulses that suddenly turned him into a cat or a tree or a cocktail hostess in mid-conversation.

One could applaud his anger and be captivated by the spurts of pantomime while remaining skeptical about how much money a millionaire needs. Since he obviously adored wealth and property, it was ironic that he was ever called a Communist. (Harold Clurman once told Chaplin that Clifford Odets thought he ought to make a movie "about the 'little man' of *The Gold Rush* after he strikes it rich," about the miseries he would then endure. " 'It's not true,' Charlie snapped, 'I like being rich.' The point was that Chaplin had fulfilled himself through money and Odets hadn't.") At times he behaved with some of the winsomeness and bathos which marred the weaker scenes in his movies. A ten-year-old remarked, "Yesterday we saw Charlie in *The Gold Rush*. He was funny. Today we saw him at Frognal. He wasn't funny."

Naturally it was disturbing to feel ambivalence toward a genius who had been castigated for his politics. Yet it was instructive to realize that a great artist could be a naif and a despot. Chaplin often spoke of himself in the third person and he loved to repeat that traffic had stopped on Broadway during his visit to New York in 1916, when a newspaper headline simply announced "HE'S HERE!" Frognal listened politely to that story, which most had heard several times before, while Chaplin kept asking others if they could imagine how exciting that acclaim had been—"Have you ever known anything like it? Have you? Have you?"—and a few celebrities would murmur tactful denials.

If anyone made a joke he was unlikely to laugh; Thurber wrote in a letter that Chaplin was "one of the worst appreciators of comedy outside of himself and his own genius." As he rambled away, he sounded more like an anarchist than a socialist; I remember him talking about an ideal society where people would walk into stores and help themselves to anything they wanted; they wouldn't need money because everything would be free. Graham Greene once fled Frognal early in the afternoon "because I couldn't bear to hear Chaplin talking such rot about politics." But most of his hearers were indulgent, since they knew what he had suffered in virtual expulsion.

A former story editor at Paramount subsequently told me about a Hollywood benefit in 1950 where Chaplin had paid tribute to Harry Bridges, president of the International Longshoremen's and Warehousemen's union, for his courage in facing a prison sentence. Chaplin said that if he was ever threatened with jail, he would leave the United States, that he could not remain in prison for a single night, that he would die the minute the cell door closed on him, that he would not be able to breathe, that he would suffocate, that he would not be able to live. He became so agitated that he uttered the same phrases over and over again.

In the summer of 1956 friends of mine arranged a small dinner for the Chaplins to celebrate the completion of the filming of A King in New York. But the evening was premature: one short take was still required, a shot of Chaplin walking out of a movie theater. It would be quick work, so Oona Chaplin invited the guests to come to Leicester Square and be extras, standing in line to form a ticket queue. We piled into cars—and arrived in time for a ferocious scene.

The movie camera had been hidden in a taxi just outside the cinema: elaborate precautions had been taken so that no one would guess that filming was about to occur. But the sheet fell off the camera. It was a warm Saturday night and a huge crowd suddenly gathered: word spread rapidly that Chaplin was inside the theater and soon several hundred people were massed around the entrance. We found Chaplin having a tantrum in the lobby: he screamed at everyone in sight and vowed to fire the technicians he held responsible. He also refused to shoot the scene that night.

Oona pleaded gently that all he needed to do was to ask the spectators to move back, stressing that they'd be glad to do him any kind of favor—while he sneered at the "fools" and "bastards" outside, expressing his contempt for those plebeian moviegoers who now jammed the street and much of Leicester Square. It was a very friendly throng, full of Cockney accents; waving and tapping on the glass doors—"Hello, Charlie," "Hey there, tramp!"—they thought he was one of their own: as his movies and public statements had always told them. But he stamped out scowling and shoved his way to his car: it was beneath him to acknowledge or even nod at his beaming audience.

And they got the message. Separated from my friends, I was trapped among the bodies on the pavement, and it was the first time I'd witnessed that moment when an amiable crowd turns angry: muttering about his haughtiness, "His Highness," they knew they'd been insulted. The mood was hostile and briefly I was rather nervous. Hypocrisy wears many garments, but I could never again hear Chaplin talk tenderly about "the Little Fellow" or "the little people" without recalling how he had disowned the class from which he came, for which he claimed to be a spokesman.

Dinner afterward was bleak; everyone had been upset by Chaplin's behavior and few were skillful at hiding it. Conscious of his exhaustion and his age, we stared at our food while he ranted on about the alleged inefficiency of his staff, the stupidity of film fans. The evening crawled along until it was finally rescued by the poet Laurie Lee, who dissolved the constraint by singing ballads with his guitar. That inspired Chaplin to parody a Kabuki dancer and we all cheered up a bit.

When *A King in New York* was released in 1957 it proved to be a clumsy attempt to spoof the Committee; between some bewitching passages of mime, Chaplin managed to scramble his arguments and to caricature his own convictions. As the king of a nameless country who loses his throne because he opposes nuclear weapons and plans to use atomic energy for peaceful purposes, he escapes to Manhattan only to discover that America is insane. He's shocked to learn that Americans have to perform debasing tasks in order to make money. Yet the movie oozes with Chaplin's awe of the rich: the camera ogles opulence. His son Michael, aged ten, was cast as a radical prodigy, spouting Marx while the indignant king tries to reason with him, and the child's rhetoric becomes a diatribe against all forms of government.

Chaplin crammed his own views between the boy's jaws—and deliberately made them sound foolish. Characterizing the child—who informs against Communists so that his parents will be released from jail—as a pathetic monster hardly struck a blow for liberalism. The result seemed oddly reactionary, since the king who defied the Committee was presented as a ridiculous ineffective figure. But the fact that even Chaplin couldn't make guilt by association comic was essential to the history of the Fifties.

For years the film industry called *A King in New York* "the forbidden comedy"; no major American distributor wanted to handle it, and there were cautious references to its "controversial" content. Chaplin didn't allow the movie to be shown in the United States until 1973; he said that earlier offers from independent distributors would merely have earned "peanuts."

Only once did I see Chaplin looking like Chaplin. I was walking along Piccadilly with Don Stewart, the son of DOS, while dense traffic was stalled to a standstill, when we noticed a long limousine that was parallel to us; in the back, huddled on the gleaming seat, was a small bunched solitary figure with its cheek resting on one hand—within that elegant vehicle, his pose distilled all the moments of dejection that trickle through his movies. He did seem to be the Tramp: isolated in unlikely grandeur. Then he saw us and sprang into wild animation, grinning and waving violently. The next day he explained that he'd had an agonizing toothache and was on his way to the dentist. He seemed defensive about having been seen when he looked so despondent. So I felt it would be wrong to say that glimpse of him had moved me.

• • •

At Frognal the attitudes of prosperous radicals were sometimes perplexing. Surrounded by archeological treasures and Paul Klee's paintings, one didn't detect many echoes of the Marxist conviction that the capitalist system degrades all humanity—even though DOS had attacked and burlesqued the capitalist mentality in several of his plays. I didn't doubt his esteem for social-ism. But Frognal scolded no one for being wealthy.

DOS recalled leaving a Hollywood benefit with another screenwriter of the Left; walking out of a sumptuous mansion they agreed that "We have nothing to lose but our shekels." (Deaf to the Marxist imagery, Ella interrupted: "You know what killed the American Left? They never, *ever* did anything without charging for it! They asked people to benefits who couldn't afford them.") I also remember Ella extolling the Chinese for "digging dams with teaspoons," praising their austerity and then breaking off to rebuke a child for helping herself to a pear from a vast centerpiece. Yet the Stewarts continued to arrange fund-raising events for the international Left, just as they had in Hollywood, where parties for the Anti-Nazi League or the North American Committee to Aid Spanish Democracy were central to the radical social calendar.

The food at Frognal could be terrible: old shepherd's pie, dank moussaka, reboiled corn on the cob, gray pâté. Confronted by a dish of moldy beans, some children cried, "But we had that two weeks ago!" Peering into the refrigerator and seeing slime on the leftovers, Eileen O'Casey "thought we'd all be poisoned." Wine from half-empty bottles was often poured into one decanter and served anew; Ella rarely drank, so she didn't think others would notice. Frugality or indifference? One couldn't be sure. But a few guests used to bring gifts of cheese and smoked fish, in case nothing else was edible. "Living well"—in the tradition of DOS's friends Gerald and Sara Murphy— didn't seem to mean eating decently.

I once heard Dalton Trumbo quoted on the theory that when radical writers were employed within the system, they should reap all they could from it— the best contracts and highest wages—even though they were trying to change that system. Someone objected that this was only a rationalization for being as acquisitive as most Americans. The reply was that the writers of the Left had inserted some social content into their scripts, which would not have been there if others had written them. One left-wing writer said that making movies meant "You could be rich and holy at the same time."

Most of the screenwriters I saw at Frognal had really liked working in movies; they were impatient with New York writers who were snobbish about the film industry. And no screenwriter would deny that earning amply had been exhilarating. But Hollywood had also taught them more than anyone wanted to know about greed. A woman who'd been active in the 1945 strike of the Conference of Studio Unions for better working conditions at Warner Brothers told me she and her colleagues had been certain that if just one Sinatra or Dietrich had refused to cross the picket lines, then the strike would have been settled in the union's favor. And yet some picketers perceived that stars would find it much harder to give up five thousand dollars a week than to relinquish fifty-two dollars and forty cents. So she and her friends among the strikers began to understand "the fear of losing a *maniacal* amount of money."

• • •

Some years would pass before I digested all that I heard at Frognal. Meanwhile I had started to learn a few things about the British welfare state. When I came down with a mild case of viral hepatitis, I didn't go to a doctor because I thought I couldn't afford to; at home my parents were deeply in debt because of my mother's ongoing illness. Then a London friend persuaded me to see his physician, who explained the National Health Service. Walking away from the doctor's office through a thick tawny fog, I was amazed to realize that medical care could be considered a right, not a privilege. And my relief on receiving affordable treatment released all my stored anger at the American medical system.

Throughout my mother's breakdowns and accidents, ambulances kept taking her to Bellevue Hospital during the final years of her life. She was once in the violent ward, then in the psychiatric ward, usually in a general ward. Bellevue became my university as much as Harvard: a large part of my education took place there. I had seen the contempt with which the poor were treated—and how middle-income families became poor when medical costs devoured all their earnings and savings. I saw how patients became objects. On entering Bellevue you passed a huge sign: CASUALTIES SORTED HERE; often I wondered when a bus or a train wreck would require the disentangling of limbs and torsos beneath the sign. I came to recognize the stink of different wards: through a long maze of corridors I learned to turn right or left at an odor— ether or ammonia or some mysterious reek—though the smell of pea soup and old urine was pervasive. Sometimes I rode in elevators with moaning inmates strapped down on trolleys—had they just had electroshock?—who seemed semi-conscious of pain but not of the orderlies joking and giggling above their heads. In certain other hospitals the patients' cries and wounds were their own business, but in a Bellevue ward the stumps of thighs or arms were as public as the groans; you heard desperate pleas for painkillers that seemed long overdue. When a patient suddenly vomited, the orderlies were apt to fight about whose job it was to clean up—depending on whether the bed or the floor had been soiled. A friend once said to me that privacy was the only luxury of the poor. At Bellevue the patients' misery appeared to be increased by all the suffering around them.

There were some fine doctors and a few were sensitive as well as skilled. But others resented a relative's questions and their irritation indicated that people who ended up in Bellevue did not merit much thought: they were rubble—casualties perhaps, but they didn't deserve much more than sorting. The poor were guilty—and so was anyone without enough money for private care. In the Fifties poverty was supposed to belong to the past, to the Depression. Those who had mismanaged their lives or lost control of them had also lost the right to dignity—or even health (or maybe existence): that was one of the lessons of Bellevue.

My mother and I were not close: the span and the violence of her illness had built barriers that we could rarely cross. But affection or intimacy hardly mattered in the context of Bellevue. Someone you loved, or someone you barely knew, or someone you didn't love: all assumed an equal weight within those wards. The emergencies that brought patients to Bellevue and the punishments dispensed by the hospital overwhelmed the nature of any relationship. Friend or stranger, favorite sibling or family albatross: they were all humiliated there, reduced to breathing or dying debris. I didn't expect my mother to be cured. But as she journeyed back to Bellevue between long stays in other hospitals—Columbia Presbyterian and Bloomingdale in White Plains and Goldwater Memorial Hospital on Welfare Island—until her "remains" were delivered to the Bellevue morgue for an autopsy, I learned that there were no solutions for the sick unless they had limitless funds.

I didn't know then that my anger had any relation to politics or social systems; no one had yet said that the personal could be political. But in England I saw how certain kinds of equality had been legislated. Occasionally I heard a Frognal guest say that Britain's welfare state was merely an exercise in reform, that the Labour Party hadn't advanced socialism. But those remarks couldn't diminish my respect for a program designed for anyone who was ill.

The contrast between Bellevue and a national health plan showed me that an aesthete could not dwell apart from politics, that what happened to one's body had a lot to do with the mind and soul. My perspective wouldn't jell until the Sixties, but what I listened to at Frognal would give me a background for the future as well as the past.

• • •

When the exiles were together there were fond references to Tim Costello's saloon on Third Avenue and hearing jazz at Eddie Condon's, and DOS was excited by the prospect of following the World Series on special broadcasts at the American embassy. And I thought they were probably as homesick as I was—since the need to be with other Americans drew us back to Frognal every week. I was keen to hear further tales of Columbus, Ohio, where my father and DOS had been raised, along with the familiar lore of Manhattan and Hollywood; at Frognal I touched based with tangibilities that I missed more and more.

I liked London: one could easily be charmed by a leafy city of verbal wit where no one was an eccentric. But like many generations of my compatriots, I first discovered my native identity by living abroad: I became more American each month. After two years I pined for New York until my hunger for its physical details was almost absurd. I longed to see great ugly chocolate rabbits in Fifth Avenue windows at Easter. From a distance I tried to visualize the view of the Con Edison smokestacks that appears when you sit on the steps of the Public Library, and I wondered what insults or poems or bawdy messages were being pounded out on the little typewriter mounted on a pedestal in front of the Olivetti office building. The infectious energy that seems to leap from the sidewalks, the scents of my Yorkville block where—halfway between the brewery and the Necco wafer factory—you could sniff the switch from beer to candy when the wind changed, the whole scope of incongruities that characterize the city, and many friends: memories of these could suddenly tighten the throat of an infrequent weeper. Dreaming again and again of sauntering beneath the Third Avenue El in summer, watching the soot swirl down through the sunlight when a train passed overhead, I grieved for a landscape already demolished and grew possessive of that grief because the English couldn't share it.

Craving a glimpse of the Triborough Bridge or a flock of bright yellow taxis, I went to third-rate American movies just because they were shot in New York. And I kept returning to revivals of the best ones. When I needed to hear the voices of my town, I was gratified when Marlon Brando sighed, "I coulda been a contender" in *On the Waterfront* or when Tony Curtis snarled, "I'm nice to people when it pays me to be nice!" in *Sweet Smell of Success*. Hankering for American landscapes I'd never seen, I also sat through many Westerns, which used to bore me. One evening I found the poet and playwright William Alfred—who was on a sabbatical from Harvard—standing alone in a line for the movie of *Oklahoma!*: he'd been in London barely a month, but he was feeling as misplaced as I was. I writhed when British actors mangled the accents in the plays of Eugene O'Neill and Tennessee Williams, trying to mimic Americans by whining through their noses or using imbecilic drawls. I guarded my own accent: nothing could induce me to pronounce the "h" in herb or to ignore the "c" in schedule. Nor would I call an elevator a lift or a dessert a sweet: stubborn in fidelity to my language, I was ashamed of visiting Americans who said "Cheerio" instead of "Good-bye." And I was perversely pleased that the English appeared to have little understanding of Emerson and Thoreau and Whitman and Melville: if parts of my literature were inaccessible to them, the independence of my heritage seemed all the more valuable.

Toward the end of five years in London I lived on Cheyne Walk in an apartment where the Thames was reflected in the mirrors on the walls. My desk faced the river. But the waters seemed dead: only a few houseboats and some listless swans rocked slowly on the gray tides below me, and I yearned for the turbulent life of the East River, where steamers and tugs and cargo ships and garbage scows churn past the John Finley Walk. Between the moments when my mind raced along that river or exulted in the bridges that swing between Manhattan and Queens, I reread *The Waste Land* and felt I had a fresh insight into Eliot's choice of the Thames as a symbol for the moribund nature of England: "Unreal City/Under the brown fog of a winter dawn/A crowd flowed over London Bridge, so many/I had not thought death had undone so many . . ." Of course Eliot chose London and the Thames as images of sterility in all contemporary culture. But unfairly enough I saw that dull water as a metaphor for what the English criticized in their own society, especially the mossy conventions which some thought were paralyzing the nation. The late Fifties was actually a time of vitality in England: the arts and the economy were thriving and there was an agreeable delusion that the class system was fading. But in my appetite for my country and my city, I felt that London had little to offer anyone who wasn't English.

Missing the immigrant culture of New York, I found it strange not to hear Yiddish; the English didn't know what was meant by kvetching or schmoozing; there seemed to be no equivalent to the drive that carried emigrés from the Lower East Side and Brooklyn to Carnegie Hall or Tin Pan Alley, to City

College and Columbia, to the pages of *Partisan Review*. New York was a Jewish city—to the extent that a non-Jew could assimilate traditions that weren't instilled from birth. Although London welcomed intellects from many countries, most of its districts from Pimlico to Hampstead seemed almost entirely British, even though you could see yarmulkes or turbans in a few of them. But I was accustomed to ethnicity of all sorts, to bagels and gefilte fish, tamales and tostadas, the dumplings of Mott Street. The Poles and Russians and Hispanics and Italians of my city—whose idiom enlivened the speech heard all over town—were part of its mainstream, whereas the Indians, Jamaicans, and Cypriots living in London in the Fifties didn't have much influence on its language or its customs.

I was hardly an irretrievable expatriate; only the fact that I had married an Englishman prevented me from walking down York Avenue or across 86th Street. But as I learned more about exiles throughout history, I allied myself with those who had had to leave their countries—either because they were thrust out or had needed to escape. From the German Jews to Americans who had been stripped of their passports, I identified with people who couldn't see or smell their own neighborhoods, couldn't visit the local delicatessen or trade jokes at the newsstand or hear their own vernacular. A character in *The Caucasian Chalk Circle*—which Brecht wrote while he was an emigré in America—says, "Why does a man love his home country? Because the bread tastes better, the sky is higher, the air is spicier, voices ring out more clearly, the ground is softer to walk on."

Most of my British friends thought such emotions ludicrous. But it is difficult for the expatriate to convey the intensity of those feelings or to legitimize the sadness that accompanies them. Years later I was told that wartime refugees from Berlin and Prague and Budapest used to weep over their desserts at Yaddo, the artists' colony in Saratoga, when the Bavarian pastry chef made the tortes or soufflés of their hometowns. The spectacle of middle-aged writers and composers in tears over the whipped cream was astonishing to onlookers who'd been impressed by their self-control in larger spheres. But often it is the most prosaic item which triggers a sense memory—releasing a gust of deprivation that runs beyond the rational.

The Frognal community was more fortunate than some: their affinities had moved to London when they did, their luggage included shared pain and slang. Yet I noticed that while they dwelled on the past and lived very much in the present, they seemed to have little sense of the future—perhaps because they didn't know if they would ever be able to see their own country again: in the mid-Fifties there could be no certainty of that, and some of them were approaching sixty. When Arthur Miller's adaptation of Ibsen's *An Enemy of the People* was performed on British television in 1957 and the besieged "revolutionist" said, "We'll go to America"—where life would be freer than in his neofascist town—the Frognal guests whooped and slapped their thighs. At the same time most felt they were "the *real* Americans": proud of their participation in the Thirties, proud of their refusal to tolerate the Cold War inquisitions, they asserted that an American had the right to hold any opinion, to vote as he wished or to express unpopular views. For them the Committee was un-American, even treasonous, since it betrayed the country's best legacies—and they were the patriots.

• • •

"Have you got the little green book?": in 1958 the exiles began to ask each other that eager question, and then to brandish the passports which had been restored at last—usually after prolonged legal exertions. When Leonard Boudin won back the passport of the artist Rockwell Kent in a 1957 landmark case and the Supreme Court ruled that passports could not be withheld for political reasons, many others then regained theirs through similar litigation. DOS happily showed me the passport he received just before his sixty-third birthday. At the bar of the American embassy he held a small wake for his blacklist pseudonym, toasting the death of Gilbert Holland. Once again it was possible to revisit or even live in the United States. All over London the elation was contagious. Rarely have passport photographs displayed such a range of triumphant smiles.

In the Frognal garden Paul Robeson was embraced by jubilant blacklistees soon after his passport was returned, and W.E.B. Du Bois called on DOS and Ella when he was permitted to travel. But few foresaw that blacklisting would persist well into the Sixties. Although Otto Preminger openly hired Dalton Trumbo to write *Exodus* in 1960, almost no one else fared as well. Albert Maltz did not receive a screen credit until 1964—after sixteen years on the blacklist. Abraham Polonsky had to write anonymously for nearly two decades; twenty-two years passed between the first film he directed and the second. Ring Lardner's name didn't appear on the screen until 1965. In that same year Lester Cole had to use a pseudonym for *Born Free*: even so, Columbia had balked at retaining any part of his script when the executives realized who had written it. (They did so only at Carl Foreman's insistence.) Cole had worked as a waiter, a short order cook, and in a warehouse while he was blacklisted; Nedrick Young, an actor and occasional screenwriter, became a bartender; George Willner, a blacklisted agent, became a salesman of cheesecloth in downtown Los Angeles. Anne Revere and Elliott Sullivan were barred from movies until 1969. Pete Seeger was not allowed on a sponsored television network between 1950 and 1967, and Larry Adler still could not perform on any sponsored show in the Seventies. Many others were too old or too far out of touch to reenter the industry; some careers could never be recovered.

Hence quite a few exiles, like DOS and Ella Winter, continued to reside abroad; they would return briefly to the United States only when a grandchild was born or if a book of memoirs was published. But the pain and fear and fury that had governed the Fifties had also destroyed many intimate friendships, which could never be resumed: in that realm few of the exiles could regain the lives they had known before the blacklist. And an abhorrence of the Left lingered on among countless American liberals, who kept deploring the dead McCarthy as a phenomenon, an aberrant personality, but were equally contemptuous of those who had been reviled. So the little green book provided an entré only to carefully chosen company, to some altering landscapes—but it was not valid for travel to Hungary or Bulgaria or to some ruined chapters of the American past.

26

Thinking of Stalin?

From long-term radicals I heard about a woman named Helen Black, born in 1890, who was reared in a conservative family in the Richmond Hill section of Queens, graduated from Barnard, and became the secretary of a pacifist Protestant clergyman in Brooklyn. She joined the Communist Party soon after it was founded in 1919. Leaving home in the early Twenties to live in Greenwich Village, she rented a room in the St. Luke's Place apartment of the poet and future novelist Genevieve Taggard, as did the writer Josephine Herbst. Letters between the three adventurous young women showed a preoccupation with love and birth control ("being babyproof") and adequate earnings. They served jasmine tea every day after coming home from their jobs; friends dropped in to talk about everything that mattered to them until late at night; Herbst recalled the ongoing excitement and the "magnetic currents of common interests" that pervaded their "small world." The apartment was "a gay place" and the guests were "young going-to-do-its who were just beginning to . . . get into real work. . . . Young men hovered around; love was in the air." Among the regular visitors were the writers Joseph Freeman, Max Eastman and his sister Crystal Eastman, and Alexander Gumberg, a New Yorker born in Russia who had provided a nonpartisan liaison between the new Bolshevik government and the United States; he teased his hostesses about their romances.

Helen Black worked briefly for *The Freeman* and several publishing houses; in 1926 she was listed as the business manager of *The New Masses*. With Margaret Larkin, a *New Masses* contributor and poet, she published a collection of Western ballads, *Singing Cowboy*. For the rest of her life Black represented Soviet authors and composers at the American-Russian Literary and Music Agency, therefore she was registered with the U.S. Department of Justice as a foreign agent. She also managed Sovfoto, which sold Soviet news photographs to American publications. Her brother was the president of Doubleday; he told his family he didn't know if she was a Communist and that he wasn't going to ask her, adding that he didn't care if she was. She often went to the Soviet Union to confer with her clients: among them were the writers Konstantin Simonov and Ilya Ehrenberg and the composer Reinhold Glière. Music was central to her life, and a niece heard that she brought a Shostakovich symphony back to the United States after her first postwar trip to Russia. I saw a photograph of her standing on a Moscow street: a tall round-faced woman with glasses, a wistful smile.

In 1922 she fell deeply in love with Michael Gold; they were together while he wrote *Jews Without Money*, published in 1930, and they lived sometimes with each other, sometimes apart, torn between a need for independence and a craving for stability. For a while they were in San Francisco, where they spent their weekends on a beached houseboat and fed bits of bacon to the sea gulls; Upton Sinclair took them to visit San Quentin prison; Sherwood Anderson warned them that most writers could not make enough money from their "own" work.

Dedicated to the development of Gold's writing career, Black wouldn't marry him because marriage was a bourgeois institution which might hamper him as an artist. She broke with Gold in the Thirties when she found him with another woman, who became his wife. Helen Black then sought psychiatric treatment; she told a friend that she might not have weathered the break with Gold without the therapy. Yet the Golds were frequent guests at her small Village apartment a decade later. A quiet self-effacing person, she was so immersed in her work with Russian authors that few of her many acquaintances knew her well. One remembered that when he wrote a negative review of John Howard Lawson's play, *International*, for the *Daily Worker* in 1928 and she made a special trip to his office to protest, she chided him so gently that he barely felt reproved; although she was often called fearless, it was not her nature to assault.

In her fifties when the Cold War began, Helen Black suddenly grew very hard of hearing. A cousin of hers told me that the deafness seemed to stem from her emotions: she couldn't bear to hear the voices which were making her doubt the Soviet Union. After she died of cancer in 1951 her Communist friends gave her a memorial service in a hall hung with large portraits of Marx and Lenin; the organist played Russian music. There her death was blamed on the American government: it was said that she might have lived if federal funds had been spent on cancer research instead of the arms race. To her cousin it seemed that the mourners were grieving for the cause as much as for her.

• • •

At Frognal in the late Fifties, it had been evident that the Soviet Union had lost most of its lustre. But if there were discussions of the Left's most consequential errors, I didn't hear them. In a period when radicals were recuperating from lacerations made by the Right, they weren't likely to probe self-made wounds. Twenty years would pass before activists of the Thirties would tell me how it had felt to realize that their organizations and their conduct had sometimes injured their objectives. Our conversations did not begin in this arena. But the theme evolved as they described the best and worst years they had known. Most said that they still valued their participation, and there were few defensive moments. But they made distinctions between fine intentions and poor judgment; many took the initiative in criticizing actions of the past.

When we spoke of the Moscow trials of 1936–1938, some recalled the Communists' official explanation: the executions were unavoidable because Stalin had had to eliminate Trotskyist conspirators who aimed to overthrow the Soviet regime with the aid of Germany and Japan. As for the purges of millions, the ground-note was utter disbelief: many had been certain that our newspapers' reports were deliberate falsifications, that the editors were implementing the desire of our government to disgrace the Soviet Union. Malcolm Cowley wrote that the Hearst press "had told so many lies about Russia in the past that we didn't believe it when it told the truth." Extensive accounts of terrorism and mass murders were taken as proof that reactionaries were trying to destroy the first socialist state. Albert Maltz said to me, "The Soviet Union was the *last* place where you would look for contradictions or deceit. As for Bolsheviks framing and torturing other Bolsheviks—that was as *incomprehensible* as torturing someone with whom you'd marched in a May Day parade."

Often citing the long analysis of *The New York Times'* distorted reporting of the Russian Revolution—written for *The New Republic* in 1920 by Walter Lippmann and Charles Merz—many radicals reasoned that the American press resorted to monstrous fabrications on any aspect of Soviet affairs. Nor was the Soviet persecution of Jews imaginable: three decades afterward Arthur Miller told *The Paris Review*: "In the Thirties, it was, to me, inconceivable that a socialist government could be really anti-Semitic. It just could not happen"— not when the Soviet Constitution had outlawed anti-Semitism.

Yet some young California Communists had been acutely upset by the liquidations of Russian writers. Having admired Bukharin in particular, they inquired what the writers' crimes were—and the answers from Party leaders were far from satisfactory. Asked to regard men who had made the Revolution as traitors, some youthful Communists expressed their misgivings in private. But they knew they should not publicly criticize the Soviet Union for any reason whatsoever, on pain of expulsion by the Party leaders. And distress about the executions of old Bolsheviks was put into suspension when the Spanish Civil War began in 1936; a screenwriter said, "Hitler and Mussolini were on Franco's side and the Russians were on the Loyalist side. So you stilled your doubts about the trials."

Since the Communists of the Thirties would never admit to others that they could be mistaken, some of their critics—including those who would later defend their constitutional rights—were fascinated by the swift reversals of the Party line. The political scientist H. H. Wilson told me that when there were speculations in 1939 that Germany and the Soviet Union might make some kind of treaty, Communists assured him that such conjectures were strictly "capitalist propaganda." Soon thereafter he happened to be in a lawyers's office with a group of Communists on Staten Island, when a man just off the ferry from Manhattan came in with a batch of newspapers and held up the enormous headlines announcing the Nazi-Soviet pact. Within fifteen minutes Wilson heard the others rationalizing the Soviet decision, and he was informed that anyone who had read Lenin would know that the pact was a logical proceeding.

Some liberals agreed that the Allies' failure to join Russia in a policy of collective security against Hitler had driven Stalin into the pact after the Soviets had entreated England and France to side with them against the Nazis. But those liberals also felt that the Russians' tactics of self-defense could never justify condoning any kind of alliance with Hitler. After the pact and the Russian invasion of Finland had demolished the credibility of the American Communist Party for outsiders, its members continued to infer that Stalin was only buying time to prepare for war with Hitler. There were wishful rumors that the pact contained a subtle "escape clause," also that it was a device to compel the Allies to confront Hitler. Some even said the pact would create "a zone of peace." But while they were excoriating liberals, radicals who hated the Nazis were disoriented when World War II was depicted solely as a collision between "imperialists" (Germany, England, and France) which were competing to acquire colonies. Among Communists, years of commitment to combatting fascism could not be forgotten.

During the long Battle of Britain, when sixty thousand British civilians were killed and some leftists felt that our government should aid England, the Communist leaders' insistence that the United States should not fight Germany grew harder to live with. A former Communist, who told me he'd had nightmares about the bombing of Britain, even went to pro-British rallies— where he felt disloyal both to England and to the Party. In their opposition to entering the war and to a third term for Roosevelt, the Communists were taking the same position as the right-wing isolationists of the America First Committee. And the *Daily Worker* denounced the British and the French (especially the British) for appeasement at Munich more often than it impugned the Nazis. Britain was portrayed as the arch-enemy of the Jews, and *People's World* labeled the British rulers "the greatest danger to Europe and all mankind."

Not that the Communist leaders paid compliments to Hitler. But during the twenty-two months of the pact they downplayed the nature of fascism. Peggy Dennis, who belonged to the Party for fifty years, wrote, "We had accepted in 1939 the Soviet view that the Nazi beast had changed its spots." The Party halted its campaign to boycott Nazi goods. The Hollywood Anti-Nazi League was renamed the Hollywood League for Democratic Action. An ex-Communist couple told me that they'd been accustomed to the concept of temporary coalitions, where one might briefly join forces with an associate without sharing most of his beliefs: "If you're moving in the same direction, you walk half a block with him. Then you can part company." But they had never expected to find themselves "walking with Hitler."

A New York Jew, a former Communist who had spent more than four years organizing the union of the Pennsylvania Railroad workers in Queens, recalled "the fissures and fractures that were taking place in one's spine" because of the purges and the pact: "How can a Communist who's been working like a dog believe what he's reading?" Ten days after the pact the Germans invaded Poland. Seventeen days later, when the Red Army occupied Eastern Poland, the organizer led a group of Communists to Union Square, where they demonstrated in support of the Soviet "defense" of Poland, since they thought the Russians intended to rescue the Polish Jews from the Nazis; that is, they assumed that the pact had been dissolved in less than a month—"So we feel better: we're fighting the Nazis now." Then they learned that Germany and Russia were in collusion to divide Poland between them: "I can't tell you what that did to us," he said. Yet he, like numerous American Communists, didn't want to desert the Party while it was under siege, not even when the press was calling them "Communazis."

On June 22, 1941, when the organizer went to his newsstand and found the owner in tears, he asked her what was the matter and she gestured at a headline: HITLER BEGINS WAR ON RUSSIA. Admitting that "One had a complicated reaction—this was terrible and this was wonderful," he added softly, "Hooray." The colossal relief that most American Communists felt was compounded with their fears for the Soviet Union, since military experts were predicting that Moscow would fall in six weeks. It was clear that some American politicians would be grateful if the Soviet Union and Germany dismembered one another. The day after Nazi troops crossed the Russian border, Senator Harry Truman had said, "If we see that Germany is winning we ought to help Russia and if Russia is winning we ought to help Germany and that way let them kill as many as possible."

• • •

As I sat listening in different living rooms and kitchens and backyards, on porches, in offices and coffee shops, I asked what it had meant to be a Communist, or to work closely with Party members. While I was growing up, most of my schoolmates and I had heard Communism discussed only by anti-Communists. Naturally the replies were as varied as the background of librarians and film makers and teachers who had been heartened by the Party's influence on labor, frustrated by its inflexibility, buoyed by a sense of community, infuriated by factionalism. But quite a few said they had been drawn to the Party in the Thirties primarily because of the American crises of poverty and racism, more than by a devotion to Russia. Here I encountered disparities between generations. Most (though not all) of the older radicals—born before about 1916—had certainly "looked toward Moscow"; although their illusions had died long before I met them, embroidered Russian shawls or a few peasant carvings still decked some homes, like mementoes of an early love which wasn't denied simply because it had ended. But their juniors, who had entered the Party in the late Thirties or during the war, seemed far less interested in Russian history than concerned with American problems. A blacklisted actress, referring to her years of working for civil rights, suddenly laughed and said, "Whatever I did, I didn't help Stalin that much!"

Repeatedly I was struck by the diversity within the American Left, by the range of experiences and opinions among those who had been part of it. Daniel Aaron observed in *Writers on the Left* that the word "Communist" had different

meanings for different individuals. The radical literary critic Joseph Freeman
had advised Aaron that "an accurate history of the literary left ... ought to
define 'Communism' at every 'crucial *point of change* in at least three ways.
It should show what Moscow meant by 'communism,' what the Party meant
by it and what various WRITERS meant by it.'" For some ex-Communists I
knew, the wages and working conditions of black dining car waiters across the
nation or dressmakers in Manhattan or granite-cutters in New Hampshire had
more immediacy than the mystique of the Bolshevik revolution. And there
were those who thought that leaflets which "linked up" demands for decent
pay in American industry to the marvels of the Soviet economy could disaffect
American workers, who would probably be cool to such phrases as "For a
Soviet America."

A lawyer told me about a New York friend of his who had gone to Alabama
in 1931 to investigate the Scottsboro case months before the public was familiar
with the plight of eight black youths sentenced to death for rapes they didn't
commit. The New Yorker's efforts on the defendants' behalf enraged a crowd
of Southern men who pursued him with pitchforks. Running away from them,
he dashed into a laundry and hid beneath a huge pile of dirty clothes. Soon
the pitchforks plunged into the heap of garments, scattering the top layers
but not penetrating far enough to pierce his body. The lawyer paused. "As he
lay there, under the clothing, was he thinking of Stalin?" Did I think the man
had risked his life because of Stalin? Remembering those who'd been beaten
on the picket lines or imprisoned, or both, he sighed and said that Stalin had
not moved them to undergo such pain and danger in the streets of American
towns and cities, outside steel mills or coal mines.

But Communists—instructed by the Party leadership to keep defending the
actions of the Soviet Union—had few avenues of escape from what occurred
in Russia, even while they were immersed in union negotiations or tenant's
rights in their own country. Members who concentrated on American issues
could not be disconnected from Russian affairs, even if they felt that what
took place in the Kremlin was hardly relevant to the days they spent in meetings
with the Brotherhood of Sleeping Car Porters or at the Sunshine Biscuit
factory in Queens. In 1943 a woman I later knew—she had raised funds for
impoverished California farmers and organized office workers in the movie
industry—was assigned by the Hollywood Writers Mobilization and the Committee for Russian War Relief to accompany Ivy Litvinov, wife of the Soviet
Ambassador to Washington, on her lecture tour of the United States. During
their travels the two became friendly, and the American was given detailed
descriptions of Stalin's atrocities by her companion. "I said to her, 'You must

be very careful not to tell anyone else.' But I couldn't sleep, I knew she wasn't lying to me. The only person I could trust with this information was my social democrat husband. I called him up at ten in the morning, sobbing my head off, I told him what she'd told me. He said that if you believe in a philosophy, it has got to hold up regardless of who espouses it, because men are corruptible and you can't judge a philosophy by people who [violate] it. And my loyalty and my sense of discipline were such that I told no one in the Party." Having ceased to be a Communist well before the Khrushchev report of 1956, she was prepared for the chronicles of horror which stunned her former colleagues.

Blindness toward the Soviet Union could overlap with misunderstanding the United States. The early vision of American workers as noble peasants could complicate dealings with urban machinists or municipal streetcleaners. And the habit of calling liberals "social fascists" (which was supposed to be abandoned after 1935, but wasn't) hardly strengthened the alliances that the Communists needed to build. Several independent radicals told me about attending introductory Party sessions in the Thirties; one disliked the rigid definition of class struggle, another was allergic to "the catechism," and a third walked out after being called "a stupid bourgeois." All three agreed with the Communists about major foreign and domestic matters, but they never again considered membership. Malcolm Cowley wrote that he couldn't accept the Party's demand for "utter obedience." And he felt that Communist writers like Michael Gold were "declining into Party hacks," that their prose was rapidly deteriorating. "It was these literary reservations, rather than caution or good sense, that kept me from applying for membership in 1932." But no one I met hesitated about joining the Party because it might be detrimental to their careers. When I asked about that, most said the notion had not occurred to them.

• • •

Since Communists often antagonized outsiders who thought as they did—about desegregation, about subsidized housing—it seems amazing that they were sometimes able to manipulate them. In the meetings of many organization, Communists employed the system of fractions. Having planned which points to bring up, when (and whom) to interrupt, and when to call for a vote, a minority could dominate a debate and eventually prevail over a majority. And since they were willing to spend more hours in meetings than anyone else, they could carry a vote by outstaying their weary opponents. Although the use of fractions was officially revoked in 1938, some Communist units continued to caucus.

An ex-Communist who had been instrumental in starting many childcare centers for working women in Los Angeles during the Forties, who had also formed a committee to improve the city's public schools and worked with the League of Women Voters, told me she came to regret the patronizing and disingenuous treatment of liberals—as when Communists pretended that their only interests were children's welfare or the quality of teaching. She later felt they could have attained their goals without "Party guidance." A Marxist perspective hadn't been necessary to set up a retirement home for actors or to run a black candidate for the Los Angeles Board of Education. Before long, non-Communists would be angered on discovering that they had been working with Communists without knowing it: either because Communists had entered their organizations or because groups such as the League of American Writers had been created by the Party. Liberals felt they'd been used—by people who had outwitted them and therefore did not respect them.

• • •

Decades after they had left the Party, its former adherents were still disputing the policy of covert membership and the harm it did to the entire Left. Before World War I the Socialist Party and the Industrial Workers of the World (the Wobblies) had functioned openly. But after the passage of the Espionage Act of 1917, the Sedition Act of 1918, the Immigration Act of 1920, various Criminal Syndicalist Acts, and the violence of the Palmer raids, radicals who aimed to stay out of jail felt they must act in secret—especially if they were foreign-born and subject to deportation. And since the United States government did not give diplomatic recognition to the Soviet Union until 1933, the Communist leaders' ties to the Comintern were deemed illegal. Yet some of the ex-members I consulted thought that if American Communists had acknowledged their allegiance in the Thirties, there might not have been investigations twenty years later. Secrecy was partly responsible for the lethal atmosphere of the Fifties, because the Party's emphasis on "security" had given the impression of a sinister fraternity which did not dare to reveal its nature to other Americans. And if membership had been public, liberals and independent radicals could not have been accused of being Communists.

A few open Communists, like Dorothy Healey, operated far more easily than the rest: they could make speeches and widen their constituency. Since Healey's salary was paid by the Party, she didn't need to worry about being discharged by a hostile employer. But recruiting would have been much simpler if belonging to the Party hadn't meant that most members were hiding their affiliation from relatives and friends. Some American Communists envied their counterparts in Britain and France, who were not handicapped by secrecy.

Yet the secret wasn't airtight: in such unions as the Mine, Mill, and Smelter Workers and the Fur and Leather Workers, it was possible to guess who the Communists were. When John Howard Lawson joined the Party in 1934 he wrote in *New Theatre* magazine, "As for myself, I do not hesitate to say that it is my aim to present the Communist position and to do so in a most specific manner." Dalton Trumbo usually let his producers know that he was a Communist—when he signed a contract. In the MGM commissary there was even a Communist lunch table. (But secrecy in the film industry went to such lengths that it was thought unwise for Communist screenwriters and directors to mingle with the technicians on the back lot.) At the end of the Thirties a group of Pittsburgh steelworkers openly announced that they were Communists. In Brooklyn during the Forties some branches of the Party were almost public: a new member could meet twenty others the day after he joined, and discussions of internal Party crises took place on many street corners. Moreover the Party held huge wartime rallies in Madison Square Garden.

Recruitment entailed long debates about each candidate before anyone could be invited to an introductory session. Was that person given to "loose talk"? Was her brother-in-law an enemy of progress? Married couples could be a problem: would a spouse guard the secret? But if a wife didn't know that her husband was in the Party, where did she think he went on Wednesday nights? Would she fear he was seeing another woman—and hire a detective to follow him? In Hollywood the Screen Writers Guild was a convenient cover: Communists could say they had been at Guild meetings when they were actually teaching Marxist classes or collecting dues. But what if their small children complained about their regular absences to playmates next door? And what if a marriage seemed shaky: if there was a separation, might a vindictive partner report the other to the FBI?

Most branches were very strict about security. In the Cold War era a Communist who moved to a new town was sometimes given half a dollar bill and told to match it with the other half, which was held by his Party contact there; the ritual was supposed to verify his membership and to prove that he wasn't working for the FBI. But even in the Fifties these tactics seemed juvenile to those who couldn't believe that Americans needed to behave like revolutionaries in Czarist Russia.

Yet in the Thirties secrecy had seemed indispensable in certain professions. In many factories workers were fired if they were recognized as Communists, and few could risk losing their livelihood during the Depression. Some radicals I met were sure that the fledgling CIO would have been destroyed if the Communists who helped to begin it had been detected early on. It appeared that all union organizing had to be surreptitious to start with—whether or not Communists were involved—until many employees were ready to join. After all Irving Thalberg had warned MGM's staff that anyone who participated in the Screen Writers Guild would be persona non grata at his studio. Only after President Roosevelt signed the Wagner Act of 1936—which gave all employees the legal right to organize and bargain collectively through their representatives—could union members feel their jobs were safe. Yet even before the Cold War, there was no job security for leftists. The 1940–1941 investigations of the Rapp-Coudert Committee, which was searching for Party members on the faculties of Brooklyn College and the City College of New York, led to the firing of about twenty professors.

But in the early Forties, when Earl Browder was the Party's national chairman, many wished to abolish secrecy. Since Browder was trying to "Americanize" the organization, they argued in favor of "raising the face of the Party" (a phrase that made several laugh when they recalled it). In Los Angeles some also felt that the names of prestigious Hollywood members might make the Party appealing to possible recruits. But the leaders did not permit the membership to be overt. As a result Communists could find themselves in the position of advancing views which contradicted their own. When it was thought that working people weren't yet "ready" for socialism, Communists presented themselves as New Dealers—although they still believed Roosevelt was "saving capitalism."

All in all the policy of subterranean membership made liberals and unionists think of Communists as deceivers, bent on disguising their ideas as well as their identity. And as one ex-Communist told me rather wryly, "Secrecy was a precaution that did not afford much protection": years after she was investigated and blacklisted, she still suspected that the man who matched her half of the dollar bill was the person who gave her name to the Committee.

• • •

Always correct about facts, never mistaken in their interpretations, many Communists would not tolerate anyone who didn't accept their wisdom. As I listened to men and women who no longer held cast-iron opinions, it seemed to me that the early certainty of their own moral superiority—and their aptitude for invective—might have kindled their contemporaries' anti-Communism almost as much as the dictatorship of Stalin. Many of their detractors would remember scathing lectures in a living room, or charges of "political illiteracy" around a punch bowl, with an aversion that lasted for a lifetime. No compromises were permitted in Communist thinking, and even some of their sympathizers lost sight of "a middle ground." Malcolm Cowley wrote, "Like the Russians . . . and like many American intellectuals at the time, I insisted on thinking in terms of either-or: either peace in a world that was ruled by the workers or war between rival imperialisms. I differed from the Communists in being mildly attracted to Roosevelt . . . but still he was defending capitalism; therefore his social experiments were directed toward the wrong goal and they would fail."

In the Thirties some Communists had suppressed the memory of their own middle-class origins, along with the experiences which had radicalized them. So they wanted others to take shortcuts to enlightenment: there was no patience with those who couldn't grasp the truth at once. Peggy Dennis explained in *The Autobiography of an American Communist*, "We alone were tapped by history to fulfill its mission for humanity's liberation from exploitation and oppression. We alone had the answer as to how this could be done." George Charney, who had been the chairman of the New York Communist Party, later wrote, "We believed we were the chosen people." Socialists, like the first New Deal Democrats, were erecting barriers in the path of progress, since they were delaying the necessary struggle between capitalism or fascism and "the worker's republic." In the early Thirties it seemed crucial to defeat the "reformers" who were perpetuating "bourgeois democracy" and deterring the proletariat from waging revolution. And personal abuse in the name of dialectical purity became a habit for some Communists who would one day reproach themselves for their conduct.

In the Twenties and Thirties only an apostate could have doubted that the workers would lead the revolution—after the Party had "mobilized" them. But many working people appeared keen to join the middle classes rather than to depose them, as the radical economist and pacifist Scott Nearing pointed out in 1925 when he applied for Party membership. According to Joseph Freeman, Nearing was turned down because he didn't think American steel workers or railway crewmen could be inspired to hate capitalism. For many years Party leaders echoed Marx's idea that the middle class was a fleeting phenomenon—which would vanish as the capitalist system disintegrated.

Nearing was allowed to join the Party in 1927 and he remained in it for three years. Freeman wrote that Nearing was also rejected for the first time because his views on "the proletarian dictatorship" were defective. On that particular issue, Party leaders alienated generations of liberal-leftists who could never swallow the theory that a temporary dictatorship would be required for the triumph of social justice. Even if the revolution were to be nonviolent, liberals were repelled by the supposition that "repressive measures" might be taken against the former "rulers" of society, and that civil liberties and free speech could be limited or suspended during the years of transition; even in the abstract, the idea that repression might be essential to achieve "a society without bosses" was too vast a contradiction for non-Communists.

In hindsight the former Communists I met were adept at enumerating the Party's fallacies. Because the Trotskyists had asserted that Stalin had betrayed socialism, they were called everything from "foes of the working class" to "the fleabites of the universe," and they were said to be "in the pay of the enemy"— that is, the fascists. Since Communists were told not to read Trotsky's books they were hardly familiar with his theories, but they reviled his followers for believing in "world revolution" rather than the development of socialism in one country. So when eighteen members of the Trotskyist Socialist Workers Party in Minneapolis were tried and jailed under the Smith Act in 1941, Communists applauded the government's prosecution of their antagonists, not foreseeing that the same legal procedures would send about fifty of their own leaders to prison in less than a decade.

• • •

The Trotskyists' ideology was unimportant to the White House. But Dan Tobin, president of the Teamsters and a supporter of Roosevelt, had asked the President for help when Tobin's authority was undermined by an affiliate of the Teamsters which cast its union votes on instructions from the Socialist Workers Party. Two weeks after Tobin's request to Roosevelt the SWP's offices were raided by federal marshals.

Although the Communists had praised the government's actions in that case, their own attitudes toward Roosevelt had altered so often that his staff was skeptical when they backed any of his policies. In the early Thirties, when Communists repeated that no kind of democracy was possible under capitalism, they had called Roosevelt "a demagogue" and "an enemy of the people." But they embraced the New Deal immediately after the United Front Against Fascism was established at the Seventh World Congress of the Comintern in 1935. Soon the Hearst newspapers decried

> The Red New Deal with a Soviet Seal
> Endorsed by a Moscow hand,
> The strange result of an alien cult
> In a liberty-loving land.

In 1936 leftists of all sorts were outraged by Roosevelt's policy of non-involvement in the Spanish Civil War, when they felt that defeating Franco could deprive Hitler of a useful ally and might forestall a world war. During the years of the Nazi-Soviet pact, Communists identified Roosevelt as "a warmonger"; one of their cartoons showed him as Salomé, shedding veils of neutrality as he enticed his country into war. But after the Germans invaded the Soviet Union and Pearl Harbor was bombed, Roosevelt had the Party's total support in fighting Hitler. Overnight the Communists' slogan changed from "The Yanks Are Not Coming" to "The Yanks Are Not Coming Too Late," and they accepted the incarceration of the Nisei as a "necessary" wartime measure because Roosevelt's decisions should not be challenged while the Axis was undefeated. The Party also backed a no-strike pledge for unions throughout the duration—which factory workers resented when war profits soared but their wages didn't. Communists worked zealously throughout Roosevelt's campaign in 1944, especially in New York, Michigan, and California, industrial states which were vital to his reelection. And as one unaffiliated radical remembered, "When Roosevelt died, nobody cried as much as the Communists."

• • •

Since the Twenties Communists had excelled at combating one another: accusations of "sectarian leanings" and "reformist tendencies" hurtled through the air at meetings which could have been devoted to plans for foiling "the common class enemy." The Party had a taste for swamp imagery: "falling into the swamp of left sectarianism" or into "the swamp of right opportunism" were equally abysmal. In theory Communists espoused fraternity; in fact they were often fratricidal. When anti-Communists described the Party as a conspiracy of robots programmed to think and act identically, they were ignorant of the feuds that were intrinsic to the organization. Binges of obligatory self-criticism were supposed to be beneficial to those who were humiliated by their comrades when they apologized for their transgressions. But those exercises in degradation were hardly conducive to the "unity" that Party leaders desired.

At moments it seemed as if Communists could fight about almost anything. For example, although several men I consulted cautiously commended the Party's record on "the woman question," I heard a different view from some California feminists who had labored to define "surplus value" in terms of the American household. The issue was whether a woman who ran a home that gave priority to her husband's work was contributing to what he produced, known as "the product." After a while these women were called "deviationists" by their male colleagues for giving so much time to the topic, and they were

informed that a wife did not contribute to the product. The women also told
me about arranging poker games to raise money for Party projects, such as
the strike fund for coal miners in Harlan County, Kentucky. There had been
"dreadful" arguments as to whether they would be allowed to play poker with
the men. But Communist women could not say that men were "oppressors"
because the oppressor was the capitalist system. And though some male Communists seemed willing to wash dishes after supper, the subject of sharing
equally in housework or tending children was hardly explored. There were few
women in the Party's leadership; apart from questions of equal pay and job
opportunities within the unions, the Party was phlegmatic about women's
rights. At Communist symposia, where the reports were usually too long, a
speaker would address himself to the international situation, then the national
situation, then the labor situation, the farmers' situation, "the minority struggle
situation," and the youth situation; finally, when his listeners were exhausted,
there would be "a word on women."

Perhaps the most destructive internal warfare exploded after the Duclos
letter of 1945. Jacques Duclos, the second highest official in the French Communist Party, published an article in *Cahiers du Communisme*, assailing Earl
Browder's commitment to "class collaboration"—specifically, the alliance with
non-Communists on behalf of the war effort—and charging that the American
Party had forsaken class struggle. Moreover Browder had erred in assuming that
Soviet-American cooperation would endure after the 1943 Teheran Conference
and into the postwar era. Many believed that Stalin had ordered Duclos to
discredit Browder—that in effect, Stalin was telling American Communists
to renew the attack on capitalists and the liberals who abetted them.

It was true that in the Browder period the Communists had ceased to talk
about revolution and were detaching themselves from traditional Bolshevism.
(In wartime—when the Party was at its largest—even "the struggle for socialism" was in abeyance.) Castigated by his colleagues, Browder clung to his
belief that his party should not "be a reflection of the Communist movement in
Europe," and declared that American Communists must remain independent.
Following two months of passionate infighting about Browder's "social imperi-
alist" reasoning, his delusion that Communists could work peacefully and
productively with Democratic politicians, and his concept of "enlightened
capitalism," Browder was removed from the leadership and replaced with
William Z. Foster, his rival since the early Thirties. In 1946 Browder was
expelled from the Party altogether.

Thereafter "Browderism" meant "uncritical cooperation" with liberals. Some
considered Foster's record as a labor leader to be unchallengeable: he had

organized the meat-packing industry during World War I, led the great steel strike of 1919, and had worked on the railroads and as a migrant laborer in agriculture, lumber, and metal mining. Joseph Freeman had written in *An American Testament* that Foster was "an outstanding Party leader . . . the product of stockyard, street-car, factory, and ship." To Foster's admirers Browder seemed a weakling and a dreamer. (In private Foster often spoke of Browder as "that schoolboy.") But Browder's partisans saw Foster as a doctrinaire authoritarian whose ideas were out of date. The clashes within the leadership estranged many members, who left the Party because it no longer seemed viable. Quite a few I later met had lost confidence in the organization then—just before the anti-Communist campaign was launched against them.

• • •

"Democratic centralism" supposedly involved the ordinary members of the Party in developing its policies. But the most prominent leaders never relinquished their sovereignty, and major decisions were often made in secret, unknown even to the second rank of leaders. Dorothy Healey characterized the proceedings as "all centralism and no democracy." Allegedly the top leaders were "of the masses"; actually they were an elite. Foster and his closest associates, who had become Communists in the early Twenties, would not stray from the Marxist-Leninist analyses of nineteenth-century capitalism—hence their habitual misreading of the United States in the middle of the twentieth century. As the Cold War commenced they misled the membership, especially because of their inability to comprehend the needs of the labor movement and the non-Communists who were expected to follow the vanguard party as the state "withered away."

Jessica Mitford wrote that the National Committee, located in New York, was "largely dominated by European immigrants and their immediate descendants, giving it something of the character of an ideological old folks' home with strong allegiance to the European Communist Parties." Foster, one of the few native-born leaders, seemed remote from American working people despite his impeccably "proletarian origins." And he was ill-equipped to enlighten them about economics: while he promised that capitalism would soon be derailed, American workers witnessed the expansion of postwar prosperity.

I was told that until the memoirs of such prominent former Communists as George Charney, Al Richmond, Joseph Starobin, Peggy Dennis, and Steve Nelson were published between 1968 and 1982, many members had not fully realized how thoroughly the national leadership had relied on orders from the Soviets. But why hadn't they known it? There seemed to be several reasons.

One was that the anti-Communists had always called them Stalin's slaves—so they had ridiculed the notion. Moreover, although they understood that elements of the Party line were imported from Moscow, the American leaders didn't tell them that instructions for specific actions—such as the drive to oppose the Marshall Plan—came from the Comintern; the sources of policy were kept secret. Occasionally members heard rumors that an emissary from the Comintern was visiting their city, but he or she was rarely introduced to them. Still some in Hollywood suspected that an organizer called Stanley Lawrence was a representative of the Comintern. Lawrence had breakfast with the young writer Maurice Rapf every week, delivering Party literature to be distributed; Rapf described Lawrence to Scott Fitzgerald, who used him as a model for the Communist named Brimmer in *The Last Tycoon*.

But while the American functionaries tried to be faithful to the Kremlin, they didn't succeed in ruling the loose-knit units all over the country; often the control was exceedingly weak. The California branches were especially independent. When Party leader Steve Nelson settled in California in 1939, he found it "the healthiest Party district" he'd worked in: there was more open discussion and less "leftist jargon" than he'd encountered elsewhere. Numerous Communists in Los Angeles and San Francisco were attuned to the radical heritage of their state, where Wobblies of an earlier generation had joined the local units. Also as Dorothy Healey had said to me, "We were three thousand *lovely* miles away" from the directives of the national leadership in New York. While the Californians' disobedience angered Foster, their maverick spirit was privately admired by at least one middle-echelon leader on the National Committee.

• • •

Tactical errors continued to be plentiful in the postwar period. When the Hollywood Ten took the First Amendment, they thought others would understand that they were exercising their constitutional rights, since the First grants the right to be silent as well as the right to freedom of speech. But neither the Ten nor their lawyers explained this point clearly to the public. Albert Maltz told me that they had also confused their audience during the first hearings by claiming to "answer the question" about Party membership when they were actually refusing to—because the government had no legal grounds for inquiring into any citizens' beliefs. Blustering and sometimes hollering, the Ten traded insults with the Committee in a fashion that embarrassed civil libertarians. And their replies made them sound dishonest. Herbert Biberman said, "I have not refused to answer the question. I have told you that I will answer this question fully." Declining to do so, Lester Cole said, "I have to answer the question in my own way." Albert Maltz said to Robert Stripling, "I *have* answered the question, Mr. Quisling." (The traitor Vidkun Quisling had led a pro-Nazi party in Norway during the war.) The producer Sam Zimbalist remarked that only a deaf-mute Alaskan could have believed they were trying to answer the question.

Carl Foreman told me about watching newsreel footage from the first day of the hearings in a Los Angeles movie theater. In the row just ahead of him, a middle-aged couple was reacting violently to John Howard Lawson's testimony. Lawson, known as an adroit and graceful parliamentarian, shouted and fumed in a manner that wasn't natural to him. Foreman, who was extremely fond of Lawson, realized that he looked devious on the stand: "Jack seemed sly, cunning, shady. Suddenly the woman in front of me yelled, 'Kill him, kill him!' She thought he was a man who wouldn't tell the truth." And Foreman had never forgotten a stranger's ferocity toward his old friend.

• • •

Steered by William Z. Foster, Communists in the trade unions voted against the Marshall Plan when the AFL and the CIO were strongly in favor of it. George Charney remembered the Communist leaders asserting that "the real aim" of the Marshall Plan was to rebuild "the tottering capitalist structure of Western Europe and above all [to restore] Germany as the main power on the continent vis-à-vis the U.S.S.R."

As Party policy grew more militant and dogmatic in the late Forties, Communist officials also demanded that all union leaders back the Progressive Party and Henry Wallace in 1948. By making the Wallace candidacy a priority within the unions, the Left splintered its constituency. Wallace's campaign was built on the themes of diplomatic relations with Russia and economic policies that would raise the rate of employment, and was waged in response to the growing conservatism of the Truman administration. Many on the Left thought the Progressive Party would capture the votes of the "mainstream" and become a fixture in the political landscape. If Wallace had merely run against Truman in the Democratic primaries, his Communist adherents might not have shattered their relations with the CIO. But the creation of a third party, just when Thomas E. Dewey appeared likely to win the election, seemed suicidal to millions who didn't want a Republican president. Having followed a line that was directly antagonistic to the CIO leadership, Communist-led and radical unions were expelled from the CIO in 1949 and 1950, and they would never recover power within the labor movement.

By the end of 1948 the Party's leaders failed to see that they had lost not only the momentum of the Thirties but also the gains made during the war. As Stalin's animosity toward the West intensified, American Communist leaders maintained their unwavering fidelity to Moscow—just when it seemed clear that Stalin no longer believed in coexistence. Some independent radicals who had criticized Truman for bellicosity toward the Soviet Union began to think that the Russian and American governments were equally responsible for enlarging the Cold War. But naturally the theme of joint responsibility was as indefensible to the American Party leaders as it was to the White House.

"Liberal-baiting," which had been rampant among Communists until the mid-Thirties, diminished after Pearl Harbor but was briskly revived in the Foster period. In 1950, when Representative Helen Gahagan Douglas ran for the Senate against Richard Nixon, his staff called her "the Pink Lady" and Reverend Gerald L. K. Smith was eager to "help Richard Nixon get rid of the Jew-Communists." The Democrat's husband, Melvyn Douglas, was once Melvyn Hesselberg, and anonymous telephone callers kept reminding California voters of his "real name." (Homeowners were also offered free silverware if they answered the phone with "Vote for Nixon!" instead of "Hello" just before the election.) Helen Gahagan Douglas had voted to terminate all funding for the Committee and against a contempt citation for the Hollywood Ten. Although Ronald Reagan campaigned for her, Nixon said she was "pink right down to her underwear" and that she had "often followed the Communist line." But because she—like almost all liberals—endorsed the American intervention in Korea, Communist leaders announced that Douglas must be opposed as forcefully as Nixon, that no distinctions existed between them. Yet there was fervent disagreement within the Party leadership in California: Dorothy Healey and some of her Los Angeles colleagues said that Douglas should be criticized but not equated with her opponent. But they made no inroads on the state leadership's policy, and the Party ran its own candidate. Nixon won by a landslide. The Communist candidates took few votes away from Douglas, but once again Communists had neglected to make even a partial alliance against the Right.

That Senate race was described to me as an example of the Party's inattention to history. In 1932 the German Social Democrats were said to be no better than the Nazis. A few years later Britain's government was compared to Hitler's. Prior to the United Front Against Fascism, Communists had declared that there was no difference between Democrats and Republicans. Yet this style of reasoning had already been employed against the Left itself: ever since the Nazi-Soviet pact, many Americans had been persuaded that there was no difference between Communism and fascism. And some who said so were former Marxists like Sidney Hook and ex-Communists like Budd Schulberg.

• • •

Given all the setbacks of the American Communist Party, while the leadership provided torturous explanations of Stalin's excommunication of Tito and the executions of Eastern European Communist leaders, some members would later ask themselves why they had remained in the organization after 1948—when Foster's policies were completely at odds with the mood and character of their country, where "class struggle" meant little to working people. Perhaps one answer was the continuity that the Party gave to their lives. George Charney—who did not resign until 1958—wrote that some were sustained by imperishable memories: "The picket lines, a new CIO Union, the fight for jobs in Harlem, the activity and interest that extended from [one's own neighborhood] to faraway Ethiopia [linked us] with peoples all over the world and with each other and our own families. We followed the long march in Yemen. We joined the International Brigade and sang its songs. . . . Our daily activity brought the future closer as our visions of it inspired fresh bursts of energy even in the darkest hours—Munich, the death watch for the Rosenbergs in Union Square, the fall of Madrid." Concerning his colleagues within the leadership, Charney reflected, "Perhaps we stayed too long, but who can ever know at which point he crosses the line between the positive and the futile? And are all futile endeavors unworthy?"

• • •

When people were expelled from the Party—for a "breach of discipline" or "bohemianism" or for constant criticism of the leaders—the ejection wasn't always formal; others were told to have no contact with them, not even to say hello in the supermarket. If members stayed in touch with someone who had been "put on non-association," they too could be expelled. After the war, campaigns to purge the Party of impure influences—such as "infantilism" and "white chauvinism" or obscure symptoms of Trotskyism—made some Communists fear that their own integrity might be questioned. (In any period, disagreeing with the authorities could bring charges of "obstructionism.") Because the Party was such an intimate community, those who were ousted could feel that they'd been banished from a nurturing tribe. Some had almost no ties outside the Party; since they'd given it all their free time for many years, they were acquainted with no other circle and they could hardly imagine living apart from it.

Joseph Freeman stressed that loyalty to the Party extended equally to its members, who were bound together by "a common goal that is also your personal goal," who were also "your personal friends." Freeman's memoir, *An American Testament: A Narrative of Rebels and Romantics*, received many fine reviews when it was published in 1936 and it seemed likely to be a best-seller. But it was denounced by Moscow because it was considered disrespectful to Stalin and did not present Trotsky as a total fiend. Earl Browder told Freeman to sabotage his own book and the writer obeyed, instructing bookstores to withdraw their orders and cancelling his book tour. Three years afterward he was edged out of the Party and ostracized by the friends of decades. He had lost confidence in the Soviet Union, where many of his early associates had vanished or died. But he still believed in socialism and he wrote fiction about the painful dilemmas that beseiged some of his Communist contemporaries. Freeman never assailed the Party in his publications, but I heard his name pronounced with scorn by a couple of ex-Communists more than fifty years after his departure from their ranks.

Because many American Communists felt the Party had given them a home, that it rescued individuals from isolation and a sense of helplessness, they dreaded being disowned by the family. When Albert Maltz was savaged by Party leaders in 1946 for his *New Masses* article—which had challenged the concept of "art as a weapon" and stated that books should not be judged "*primarily* by their formal ideology"—the accusations of "Browderism" hurled him into "an emotional crisis." Thirty years later his voice rose when he told me that "to be cut off from the movement" at that time would have been "terrible." Hence, he said, he was "emotionally overwrought" when he wrote his next *New Masses* piece, which retracted his original thesis.

Sam Moore, who wrote *The Great Gildersleeve* and was president of the Radio Writers Guild, said to me, "You didn't have to be very bad before they'd shut the iron door." Just before Lester Cole flew East to begin his prison sentence in 1950, Moore and Cole spent an evening with their close friends Leo and Pauline Townsend. Cole brought his ukulele and they all sang old songs to cheer him before his departure. After Cole went home Pauline Townsend volunteered that she and her husband, who was no longer in the Party, were now in accord with "the political position" of the *Monthly Review*. Moore exclaimed, "She might as well have said 'the position of a rattlesnake!'" (Communist leaders had called the independent socialist *Review* "an agent of imperialism" when it criticized Stalin.) The Townsends continued to recommend the magazine to Party members, and "the iron door clanged shut." Most of the Townsends' friends stopped speaking to them. Some months later Leo

Townsend phoned the FBI and offered to provide information about the Party. In 1951, when he gave thirty-seven names to the Committee, he referred briefly to "Soviet fascism." But some of his old associates wondered if he was taking vengeance on the men and women who'd behaved as though he didn't exist when he entered a room.

• • •

Apart from Budd Schulberg and Elia Kazan, the former Communists I met were not bitter about their experiences with the Party. Schulberg was still upset by the Communists' assaults on his first novel, *What Makes Sammy Run?*, in 1940, and he spoke of Communists who had not protested Stalin's purges as "accessories to murder." Kazan's autobiography shows that he never forgot the evening in 1935 when a Party organizer attacked his character and the Communists in the Group Theatre didn't defend him; after that, Kazan wrote, he "understood the police state" and he angrily resigned from the membership. Kazan avoided discussing his year and a half in the Party with me, but of course I knew he'd gone to greater extremes than most American ex-Communists. Having paid for a long announcement in *The New York Times* in 1952, in which he advertised his "abiding hatred of Communist philosophy," he had advised other former Communists to follow his example and become informers. It was widely believed that he'd given names mainly to safeguard his film career—which he subsequently denied but partially admitted in his book. (If he had not appeased the Committee he could have continued to direct plays, since Broadway did not maintain a blacklist. But by then movie work was apparently more important to him than the stage.) Kazan and Schulberg had prospered more than most cooperative witnesses. Some of the less fortunate informers grew all the more resentful over the years: still disparaged by right-wingers for having once been Communists, despised and insulted by the Left, they were angry to find themselves in limbo.

• • •

In the summer of 1951, after the Supreme Court upheld the convictions of the eleven Communist leaders tried in New York, while McCarthy's triumphs multiplied, Party officials assumed that the nation was on the threshold of fascism. They also expected war with the Soviet Union, since the prospect of a prolonged Cold War was inconceivable to them. An ex-Communist said to me, "The reactionary forces did have dire intentions. But we underestimated the resiliency of democracy in this country. McCarthy could not mobilize the

American people as Hitler did the Germans. But that kind of misunderstanding makes you go into a storm cellar and cut yourself off."

The Party had already sapped its own waning vigor by drastically reducing its membership. Those who were thought to lack the fortitude to withstand an onrush of domestic fascism were dropped because it was felt that they might yield to the federal pressures to name names. Not all were expelled outright; some were told that they could still be considered "sympathizers." Psychiatric patients were also asked to leave the Party, either because they were judged to be unsteady or because they might reveal their membership to therapists who could become informers. Following the example of the French Communists in the Resistance movement in Nazi-occupied France, the Americans decreased their numbers for the sake of security. With some asperity Dorothy Healey said, "We were cleansing our own ranks for the future."

Older Communists remembered how the leadership of the Industrial Workers of the World had been imprisoned during the Palmer raids. In 1951 hundreds of seasoned Communists were ordered to go underground—not for their personal safety but to keep the organization from collapsing if all its leaders were arrested. After they disappeared their friends were told not to mention their names. But many still attended secret meetings to formulate policy and some wrote under pseudonyms for *Political Affairs*, the Party's theoretical journal. One of these was Sam Kushner, a former lathe operator who had been the business agent of the United Electrical Workers Union at his local in Chicago. Reflecting on the decision to send the leadership into hiding, he told me, "We did too much too soon." Living under another name from 1951 to 1955, he worked in and near Chicago as a trade union secretary of the Party, also as organizational secretary. Kushner said the Party "spent a fortune" on cars, homes, and new identities for those who were dwelling out of sight. The network of couriers who took messages from the underground leaders to their colleagues had many different drivers' licenses. Some went through two or three cars a year: as soon as the FBI spotted a vehicle, another immediately replaced it. The fugitives moved into new quarters whenever they discovered they were under surveillance.

From the start they were instructed to stay away from their "natural habitats": Kushner, a pipe-smoker who enjoyed saloon life, was told not to go to pipe stores or bars, and book lovers were warned to keep out of libraries. Kushner quite often knew that the FBI's agents were on his heels; since they didn't arrest him, he was sure that they hoped he might inadvertently lead them to the Party's contacts in the labor movement or to any of the four key leaders who had jumped bail after their trials. The strategy of bail jumping shocked much of the membership, even though it was explained that their flight had been designed to perpetuate the Party's existence.

Kushner saw his family once every six months; he said the years of separation "laid the seeds" for his divorce. A gregarious man, he found that living in solitude heightened the temptation to talk with strangers, who might later describe him to the FBI. On one occasion he succumbed to loneliness and passed a night chatting with a baggage handler on a train—where he was unnerved to learn that the box he was sitting on was one of a batch of coffins filled with corpses. Traveling or simply navigating though a city required leaving a confusing trail: changing buses and subways, getting lifts between towns, never taking a direct route. The Party had a list of FBI license plate numbers which was useful for checking cars that were idling through any neighborhood he visited. The agents who pursued quarry like Kushner frequently chose to be conspicuous: on both sides part of the maneuver was to wear out the adversary.

Dorothy Healey compared the underground to "a bad spy movie.... We were turning ourselves into a caricature of the conspiracy that the Hearst papers" and the investigating committees "had always accused us of being." After all the dodging into alleys and shuttling from house to house, while commuting between message centers and contacts, several hundred Communists were released from a harrowing way of life when the Party canceled the underground program in 1955. Surfacing wasn't difficult; Kushner said, "It was like walking back through a door." He resumed writing for the *Daily Worker* and the FBI did not close in. (Inevitably, concealed Communists had attracted the attention of J. Edgar Hoover more than others, and the groups that the bureau infiltrated most successfully were the closed branches.) By devoting so much effort and ingenuity to security, the already depleted organization had squandered the energies of some of its abler members. Their "unavailability," as well as the Party's policies, had merely increased its isolation.

• • •

The thirty-second anniversary of the *Daily Worker* was celebrated in Carnegie Hall in January 1956. Most of the Smith Act defendants had finished their prison terms and the evening reunited them with friends who had recently been underground. Some wept as they embraced; it was the first time they had seen one another in almost five years. By then only about twenty thousand Americans belonged to the Communist Party. But optimism was in the air that night: since the Korean War was over and the Supreme Court had ruled that segregation in the schools was illegal, the leadership thought it might be a propitious moment for the Left to rebuild itself—if the battered survivors could manage to work together. Especially in periods of crisis, Party leaders had turned on each other, as they did throughout the Cold War. Proud of their resistance to the investigations, they were nevertheless aware that their shrunken organization was still fragmented.

Eugene Dennis, the general secretary, was one of the two main speakers on the stage of Carnegie Hall. When he said, "We Communists respect the rights of others to disagree with us," he was shattering the traditions of the Party's lifetime. He also told his listeners, "We admit we have not had all the correct answers to every problem in the past, nor do we have a monopoly on wisdom today. We have, like many others, made not a few mistakes"—and vowed that the Party was going to learn from its "wrong judgements" and "theoretical errors"—whereupon the audience burst into "thunderous applause and cheers." His widow, Peggy Dennis, later wrote that his statement was "a bombshell." Eugene Dennis's desire to "engage in friendly debate" with Party opponents, to create new coalitions with outsiders and to permit dissent within the Party, was "a daringly new concept." George Charney recalled that "the response was tumultuous . . . as though we had come to the end of an era of misfortune and were about to enter a new era of achievement and progress."

But as Peggy Dennis observed, William Z. Foster and his supporters were "horrified" by such "heresy." The aging leaders displayed the inexorable rigidity that had blighted the Party for much of three decades. Some Communists had long argued in favor of an indigenous American movement. But after the Browder period, the main leadership was deaf to such "deviationism" until the *Daily Worker* editor John Gates, Eugene Dennis, Steve Nelson, and others declared that the Party's policies should be redesigned in keeping with American experience and American culture. Nelson already realized that adult children of the immigrants who'd shaped the Party were not inclined toward Communism—in part because they didn't regard the Soviet system as superior to an American way of life.

In April 1956, as the fights about "public candor" and "revisionism" accelerated, a copy of Khrushchev's report to the Twentieth Congress reached the American Communist leaders—just when some were hoping to "reconstruct" the Party. In the wake of the disclosures, the reformers still struggled to assess the disastrous tactics of some thirty years. As Dennis had said in Carnegie Hall, "We too often treated criticism from sincere trade unionists and liberals as though it came from the professional anti-Communist and anti-Soviet baiter." He and several of his colleagues wanted to encourage "an atmosphere in our Party where individuals feel free" to disagree with "the majority and to submit alternative and unorthodox . . . proposals." Soon the *Daily Worker* was calling for "an American road" to socialism departing from the Soviet model, and some leaders hoped to liberate their organization from stifling conventions. But Dennis—reprimanded by Moscow and violently opposed by Foster—retreated from some of his "innovations" in 1958. (He was often referred to as "a vacilator," even by associates who respected him.) John Gates resigned, announcing that the Party "has ceased to be an effective force for democracy, peace, and socialism in the United States." At that point the Party had less than five thousand members. Foster's response to the ongoing avalanche of resignations was "good riddance." According to Peggy Dennis, Foster—then seventy-eight—"demanded punitive organizational action against those who remained and did not agree with him."

• • •

For those who had been convinced that the Soviet state was the most humane in history, the revelations of 1956 caused even more pain than the blacklist. Finally they knew that they had revered a regime while it was slaughtering its own citizens, that anti-fascists who'd fought Hitler had also been terrorists. Albert Maltz had been out of touch with the Party for about six years before Khrushchev's speech, which shocked him so profoundly that he had to stop working: in order to return to the classic texts of Marxism, which he thought "the noblest body of literature" ever written. From rereading Lenin's *The State and Revolution* he deduced that the first Russian Marxists "had been too busy analyzing capitalism and how to overthrow it" to tackle the practical questions of how a socialist republic would function. Maltz said that Lenin had provided just "half a page of lyric assumptions" about the future: there would be a transient bureaucracy, but it need not stay in power for long—"And that was all he had to say." (Lenin had half-jokingly explained that he did not complete the book because the October Revolution had "interfered.") The blacklisted writer, then living in Mexico, still admired much of the literature—above all because the authors had promised "an end to all exploitations": among nations, among the economic classes, between the races and the sexes. But as he told me many years afterward, he came to think that the lyric assumptions were "utter nonsense."

Bewilderment about the nature of Soviet society was not dispelled by statements from American or European Communist leaders or the Soviet officials. Al Richmond, who had been the executive editor of *People's World*, wrote that he and his associates felt "that Khrushchev offered no explanation for the evils he revealed, that placing the total burden of them upon Stalin's personal defects was no more valid than prior attribution of all Soviet successes to Stalin's personal genius, that it was still necessary to explore what it was in Soviet society that permitted these evils to develop and to achieve the magnitude they did." Many leftists acknowledged the courage of Khrushchev and his colleagues in unveiling the vileness of Stalin, and in admitting that millions of Russians had been executed to divert attention from the gigantic errors in Stalin's economic policies. But some long-term American radicals were troubled because the Soviets did not resolve the question of how Marxism and the Revolution itself could have been corrupted. And if the Russians were preparing to dismantle Stalinism, why didn't they expose the flaws in their antiquated doctrines?

When they looked back to 1956, the anguish which some American ex-Communists conveyed seemed to me to demonstrate what had once been a genuine inability to believe the facts about Russia. Frenzied anti-Soviet propaganda, coupled with McCarthy's fictions, had enabled certain leftists to reject "facts" cited by their opponents: whatever they said must be false. As Dorothy Healey said to me, the Khrushchev speech made the Fifties "a decade of great tragedy" for her Communist contemporaries; she emphasized that even the persistent victories of the anti-Communists were not as devastating as learning the truth about Stalin's tyranny.

Steve Nelson, who had fought in the Spanish civil war, chaired the New York meeting of the National Committee where the speech was read to some hundred and twenty people, "the collective backbone of the Party." The reading took several hours. He watched tears pouring down the faces of Americans who had been Communists for forty years or more, for their entire adult lives; some had been beaten and imprisoned along with him. Nelson broke the long silence following the speech with one stunned sentence: "This is not why I joined the Party." Then he was driven in a car across the city with old friends: "not one of us could bring him or herself to speak."

• • •

After an evening of recalling middle-aged friends who had depended on typing or selling hats or running laundromats to pay the rent throughout the Cold War, a screenwriter said to me, "The blacklist was a howling success. It destroyed the left-wing movement." His wife replied quietly, "Was that the only thing that destroyed it?" And I felt that those brief sentences distilled certain discussions among radicals which had outlasted the Fifties. Many thought the triumph of the Right was almost inevitable, since American conservatives were so well organized and so thoroughly united with Wall Street. The Palmer raids had shown that it was perilous to be a leftist even in 1920; long before the Cold War began, Hoover had convinced the public that the Left endangered the security of the whole nation. And because the persecution of all kinds of political dissidents had benefitted the careers of countless politicians, the Truman and Eisenhower years could never have been auspicious for the Left. It was difficult to guess how any group could have stayed robust throughout the overwhelming assaults by the government. Yet as Steve Nelson wrote—looking back on nearly a decade of his own state and federal prosecutions—the Communist leadership had "made the reactionaries' job easier by following policies that didn't fit American realities," such as the acceptance of the Nazi-Soviet pact as well as the attacks on the Marshall Plan.

Some unaffiliated radicals argued that if the Party's leaders had not made so many catastrophic decisions—just when they were treating potential allies like enemies—there might have been an enduring non-Communist Left, as there was in England and France. But the barbarities of our domestic Cold War had not been equalled in European countries; British and French leftists had not been suppressed. At the same time some of the older radicals I knew felt that the Communist hierarchy had hindered the development of an American form of socialism, that they had disfigured the concept of the Left by maintaining an undemocratic organization.

• • •

In the Fifties most of the shriveling number of people who were still in the Party had little time for anything apart from legal self-defense, though some units kept trying to further the desegregation of schools and housing. The Party's branch of the Civil Rights Congress in Oakland, California, effectively tackled ongoing police brutality as well as judicial discrimination against blacks, and protected those who bought houses in white neighborhoods from rock-throwing mobs encircling their homes. Early in 1951 Party members also mounted on international campaign for executive clemency for Willie McGee, a black Mississippi truck driver unjustly accused of rape by a white woman. McGee was executed after five years in jail. Like much of the press, *Time* charged the Communists with "whipping up racial tensions at home and giving U.S. justice a black eye abroad." Jessica Mitford later wrote, "Communism, not racism or injustice, [became] the issue." Thereafter most Communists had to focus on constitutional rights rather than violations of civil rights or the advancement of socialism.

Some ex-Communists who received subpoenas were invited to meetings where legal tactics were explored, but they weren't pressed to rejoin the Party. And members who found the organization ineffective and ingrown could see no compelling reason for staying in it. It was already clear that involvement with the Party decreased the opportunity to work with "mainstream" Americans—not only because of repression by the Right but also because of the autocratic behavior of many Communist leaders. For those who had joined in a period when the Party appeared to be an instrument for social change, there was no point in remaining after its purpose was defused.

But no matter when they had resigned, quite a few told me they had done so rather sadly—and without rancor. Many simply ceased going to meetings. Leaving the Party wasn't always a momentous decision: some said they had just "drifted away" once they perceived it as a cul-de-sac. Others thought they should explain their grounds for departure to old friends and there were small gatherings in private homes. No one I knew encountered the contempt directed at individuals who had quit in the years before Pearl Harbor, when they had been scorned for weakness and cowardice, chastised for listening to criticism from liberals, even called traitors.

Yet after most of the former Communists had described the depth and width of the Party's failings, they said they had no regrets about having been members. Knowing the price they had paid in wrecked careers, in the sufferings of their families, I was occasionally a bit startled to hear this. But then they talked once more about the rewards of the work they had done: among longshoremen or transit workers, in the writers' guilds, in the ghetto. Some said they were grateful for the practical training they'd had in the Party: in running conferences and meeting deadlines, dispensing information at short notice, alerting a neighborhood to the need for a traffic light or a policeman on a dangerous street corner. And they cited the Party's achievements: the organizing of Unemployed Councils which called for unemployment insurance and protected jobless citizens from eviction during the Depression, the hunger marches outside city halls, its role in the inception of the CIO, the exertions for the rights of black Americans, the benefits gained for workers in both Communist-led and non-Communist unions, the fruitful participation in Roosevelt's campaign of 1944. Most still thought capitalism exploited the nonrich and that people were deformed by poverty, and they still believed that socialism was desirable in the United States.

As our conversations sent them roving through the decades, the Thirties radicals kept returning to the question of whether an American Left might one day be more than diffuse or episodic. In the Sixties they had been pleased by the advent of the New Left, but they'd disapproved of the stress on spontaneity and the consequent disorganization; hearing that "the blueprint will grow out of the struggle," they predicted that it wouldn't and were hardly surprised when it didn't. In the Eighties and Nineties most I knew were still active: in the War Resisters League or the National Emergency Civil Liberties Committee, working on programs for the homeless, giving legal guidance in First Amendment cases, battling the crusades to outlaw abortion, lobbying for a moratorium on nuclear testing, organizing support for local candidates with strong records in representing black constituents. Rivetted by the revolutions of 1989 in Eastern Europe, they wondered if reactionary governments would replace some of the crumbling or corrupt regimes overthrown by outraged citizens, and they were as stunned as everyone else by the collapse of the Soviet Union. Most had long ceased to regard Russia as any kind of model. But great sadness was tinged with memories of what they had once believed: that Marxist economics, properly administered, could create a just society, and that the goals of the earliest socialists might be reached before the century ended. Instead they soon heard about the new Moscow millionaires who cruised the city in their Mercedeses, dispensing bribes and dodging taxes. At home, dwelling with foreign and domestic policies they abhorred, they sustained a determination to redress the inequities around them.

• • •

A few months after Donald Ogden Stewart and Ella Winter died less than three days apart in 1980, their New York friends assembled in a large Upper West Side apartment to honor their memory. We stood throughout a series of short spoken tributes, and then everyone sat around quoting the dead and exchanging stories from thirty and forty years before. For a couple of hours I felt as though we were all back at Frognal: I almost expected Ella to stride into the room with her kettle and pour hot water into our laps. When DOS was eighty-four and parts of his past were eluding him, he had told me that he was rereading his autobiography—in order to recapture his life. And while his friends talked about what he had said and done, we retrieved some of what he'd forgotten before his death. Long afterward Sally Belfrage and I remembered how Frognal had provided a forum for the Left: Ella's energies combined with DOS's wit had enabled dissidents to explore their concerns in a context that forbade rhetoric.

In the midst of the tales about Frognal, I also thought of what Edward Albee had said at the beginning of the afternoon: that DOS and Ella had been "betrayed by history." For the radicals of their generation that had happened twice: as the monstrosities of Stalin's Russia became apparent and when their own government called them un-American. DOS and Ella had had no taste for sacrifice; early on they had not guessed that punishments awaited them. But knowing that they had been proud of their efforts and recalling how they had survived the bleakest chapters of their lives, I hoped that the satisfactions had outweighed the tribulations.

HINDSIGHT FROM THE NINETIES

The past is never dead. It's not even past.
—*William Faulkner,*
INTRUDER IN THE DUST

27

Voyage to Columbus

In the Eighties I spent a long spring in the attic of an 1870s house in Columbus, Ohio, which had been the home of James Thurber and his family from 1913 to 1917. I had never been to Columbus, although my father had grown up there; he and Thurber and Donald Ogden Stewart had imbued it with the legends I'd heard all my life: a town of deep conservatism and wayward fantasists, where staunch middle-class proprieties collided with the bizarre. To enter the landscape of these myths as a writer-in-residence seemed like a most personal adventure. My aunt said that those men would have been amused if they had known I would one day be eager to go to the very place which they'd been keen to leave.

As a national landmark the Thurber House was wired with the most complex security system I'd ever seen. On unlocking the door one had to punch a code number into a series of buttons within thirty seconds in order to forestall the alarm. During my first evening there a professor accidentally set it off—whereupon sirens wailed, policemen with drawn guns surrounded the house, and a helicopter descended amid flashing lights and kept circling the building. I felt that Thurber would have relished the uproar, which was in the tradition of "More Alarms at Night." But since electronic eyes had been installed on the ground floor—if a visitor wandered into certain rooms, the sirens screamed—the image of a blind man's home under so much surveillance was rather poignant.

Beneath a gabled roof covered with fish-scale tiles, the large top floor—remodeled into an admirably secluded apartment for a writer—retained the erratic angles and half-moon windows of the attic where Thurber's father had sometimes slept, where his bed had once collapsed. Dwelling at the site of inspiration for many of the events in *My Life and Hard Times*, I thought of the grandmother who was positive that electricity was leaking all over the house from the empty light sockets, and the aunt who threw her shoes down the hall each night to frighten off imaginary burglars. Those obsessions had been genuine; some of what Thurber had written was true. The dog that bit people had been fed on a table in the kitchen, and "The Night the Ghost Got In" was not a total fabrication; in middle age Thurber had met a previous tenant of the house who had also heard feet pacing rapidly around the dining room and then running up the stairs, as Thurber and his brother William had in 1913. (In a somber letter to Edmund Wilson in 1959 Thurber admitted his reluctant belief in the supernatural, and he wrote to an Ohio friend that there really was a ghost: "A Columbus jeweler is said to have shot himself in the house after running up those steps.")

I had assumed that "The Day the Dam Broke" was fiction. But I learned that more than a hundred people had drowned in Columbus during the vast Ohio floods of 1913, when the west side of the town was under thirty feet of water and the main bridge was swept downstream; on the east side, where my family and the Thurbers lived, terrifying rumors that the dam on the Scioto River had disintegrated sent residents racing down the central streets. Robert Thurber, the last surviving brother, gave me postcards made from photographs of the flood, and those bleak scenes of rooftops rising from the waters indicated why Thurber had waited twenty years to infuse a tragedy with comedy.

I kept hearing that Columbus was the wellspring of Ohio Republicanism, a rigidly conventional community controlled by reactionaries. Yet in my first weeks there I encountered open minds and diverse opinions. I went to a flamenco party where some of the guests were Vietnamese and watched an angry crowd of bank depositors demonstrating on the steps of the State Capitol, protesting the delay in reopening the seventy failed Ohio banks where their savings were frozen. I was steadily warned that Columbus was intolerant of exceptions, even of mild digressions from the norm. But I rode on a city bus full of young black men dressed like Prince in *Purple Rain*, ate scrod with macadamia nuts in a restaurant decorated with fire hydrants and empty bathtubs, listened on the radio to a local rock band called the Shifty Christians, and met gay men who seemed thoroughly at ease when they took their lovers to supper at their parents' homes. I'd heard that Columbus was once the heartland of isolationism, and some inhabitants said it was still spiritually landlocked, distrustful of ideas or individuals that came from either coast—

or even from Cleveland. But some of the best new soccer players were young Cambodians and Laotians. For decades Columbus blamed "outside interests" for altering its customs and invading its industries, although about five old families continued to reign over the banks, the local media, and the department stores. I was told that Columbus abhorred controversy and resented any criticism of its institutions. Yet the censorship of textbooks was a heated issue while I was on hand, and so was the battle between evolutionists and creationists in the public schools. (The city's Board of Education ruled that both subjects should be part of the curriculum: evolution would be taught in biology courses and creationism in social studies or literature classes, which sounded like a recipe for confusion.) When a young reporter at *The Columbus Dispatch* complained that the paper was very stuffy and I asked for an example, he replied that a big diagram of a testicle in the Health/Science section had been cut from the second edition on the orders of the publisher, and I tried to imagine a testicle in any edition of *The New York Times*.

Perhaps my favorite Sunday columnist was the religion editor of *The Columbus Citizen-Journal*, who reviewed and scored the city's churches as though they were restaurants. Each week a different church received several (or few) stars for its sermon, atmosphere, music, and "friendliness." I only wished that the critic would use crosses instead of stars. Everyone stressed that he—an ordained Unitarian minister—was utterly serious about his mission. And I looked for the enigmatic weekly messages posted outside a United Methodist church, such as "Beauty Without Grace is the Hook Without the Bait," a statement which seemed downright Thurberish. As I walked on Broad Street past a store called Zacchaeus—" Clothier for Men Five Foot Eight and Under"—my companion recalled that Zacchaeus was the short man in the New Testament who climbed a sycamore tree in order to see Jesus, adding, "Now you know you're in the Bible Belt." I was gratified to find that the Columbus Yellow Pages had a listing under "Religious Goods" for "Pagan Commodities."

In the elegant Columbus Club, built in the 1860s, in a paneled room at the top of the curving red-carpeted staircase, a woman in her sixties who avoided vulgarisms—she had just referred to the liberal Democratic Governor Richard Celeste as "a horse's you-know-what"—repeated a joke told by her hairdresser: "Do you know what happened to the cow in the abortion clinic?— She was decaffeinated." Then the conversation shifted to plans for the next church benefit. Soon thereafter I learned that the Ohio Penitentiary, where O. Henry had served time, might be converted into luxury condominiums; a rock concert had just been held within its grim turreted limestone walls to raise money for a rehabilitation program for ex-inmates. And I was charmed to hear that when a member of one prominent family dies, the corpse rides around the town sitting up in the back of a car: to take a last look at Columbus. So I wondered if the young Sayres and Thurbers and Stewarts had seen the corpses of previous generations propped erect in their carriages.

My father had said that Columbus was always surrealistic. And as the weeks passed I suspected that what Thurber had written was still accurate, that it continued to be a town of upright eccentrics who did not consider themselves eccentric. Touring the statues on the State House lawn—where some of Ohio's Civil War heroes and Presidents are grouped below a Roman matron with outstretched arms, whose pedestal proclaims, "These Are My Jewels"—I circled the likeness of Governor James A. Rhodes, commissioned by him in 1982 and engraved with his sayings, such as "'Profit' is not a dirty word in Ohio." (Natives often speculate about the contents of the effigy's bronze briefcase: perhaps the legal briefs for the Kent State University case—in which Rhodes was sued by the parents of the four students killed by National Guardsmen in 1970.) Next I visited the Peace statue, commemorating "the heroic sacrifices of Ohio's soldiers of the Civil War and the loyal women of the period." Peace herself seems militant: she brandishes her olive branch as if it were a club. Her bronze body is framed to the waist in stone; from behind she looks as though she is struggling to get through a doorway, because her voluminous skirts are much too wide for the frame.

As I was inspecting the problems of Peace, I heard voices over a loudspeaker urging the public to throw pies. I proceeded to an open plaza, where I saw a wet white figure in a suit and tie slumped in a sopping upholstered chair: drenched with cream, he resembled a liquefying statue. Dozens of people were hurling pies at him from a range of about four feet, while he kept mopping his streaming features and gasping for breath. A sign announced that on behalf of the American Cancer Society, Columbus celebrities and citizens were competing for the Guinness World Record for the number of pies received in the face. Over two thousand had already been flung at this man, who taught government at a select prep school. Hoping he looked less miserable in the classroom, I walked on to the McKinley monument, constructed in 1906. The murdered President, shown delivering his last speech, is flanked at a respectful distance by a few allegorical figures, including a blacksmith whose long bronze apron is split up the back to reveal half of a gleaming bare buttock. While I was peering at his garments, a young man in a blazing orange punk costume strolled up to me and asked what "vouchsafe" meant, pointing to the sentence inscribed below McKinley's feet: "Our earnest prayer is that God will vouchsafe prosperity . . ." After I told him, he exclaimed *"Weird word!"* Then he informed me that McKinley had been shot because he was an anarchist—and strode away before I could explain that McKinley had been assassinated by an anarchist. I thought my hour in the State House park would have been pleasing to Thurber, since the inhabitants of Columbus were still behaving as if he had invented them.

• • •

To a stranger, parts of the city's past seemed almost as remarkable as its legends. I read that Indians had named the river "scioto," meaning hairy: when multitudes of deer gathered to drink from its currents, the water was covered with a film of their brown hair. The tale may have been apocryphal, but the notion of a shaggy river was beguiling, as were the many incongruities of Columbus itself. I was told that Samuel Gompers chose to found the American Federation of Labor there in 1886—not because the town was cordial to unions, but because no strong reaction was expected from the community, hence the AFL could be hatched in peace. The United Mine Workers of America was organized in Columbus in 1890. George Bellows, ridiculed by schoolmates of the Nineties for his enthusiasm for drawing and painting, resolved to play baseball better than any of them; soon the artist was tolerated because the infielder was revered. As an adult Bellows became a socialist partly because of the contrast between the middle-class pieties of Columbus and the miserable slums he saw and depicted after moving to Manhattan.

By 1910 Ohio was one of the most heavily unionized states in the country. That year, during a long streetcar conductors' strike in Columbus, two dozen cars operated by strikebreakers were dynamited, hundreds of people were arrested, and a third of the police force mutinied while the Columbus Railway and Light Company refused to arbitrate; as a result of the strike a chapter of the Socialist Party was formed in Columbus, attracting about ten thousand voters. Yet as I glanced through faded Chamber of Commerce brochures and other pamphlets which beckoned entrepreneurs to "the Retailers' Paradise" between 1910 and 1919, I saw claims that Columbus had few "labor troubles." (The habit of ignoring or denying a problem was frequently described to me as a trait of modern Columbus.) But in 1917, in that town which cherished the status quo, the local branch of the National Women's Party had won women the right to vote in municipal elections—three years before nationwide suffrage was achieved. And I heard that Republican Warren G. Harding and Democrat James M. Cox used to dine and relax together at the Columbus Club—after a day of campaigning against each other in the presidential race of 1920. Perhaps a town which prized its normality enabled rivals, even incompatibles, to coexist without outright enmity? That is if they were Anglo-Saxons.

Occasionally I saw vestiges of a complacency which colors the city's reputation. Listening to those who still loathed Franklin Roosevelt forty years after his death—they said it was "no wonder" he'd been unfaithful to his wife, since she was even more detestable than he was—I realized that they assumed I shared their views, because any sensible person would. Also I detected a certain smugness among some of the richer citizens: as if their milieu were the only one in existence, which made them appear more insular than their counterparts elsewhere. But they and others seemed quite astonished that a newcomer enjoyed their town as much as I did, or when I admired the range of its cultural life. Ohioans expected Easterners in particular to be condescending, even disdainful, toward the Midwest. A witty octogenarian teased me for my efforts to learn all I could about Columbus, exclaiming, "And when you get home, no one will be interested!" (She was right. On my return to New York, a voice on my answering machine said, "Welcome back from the middle of nowhere," and other messages implied that I'd been exiled to a wasteland.) The self-satisfactions of Columbus seemed to overlap with a belief that the city would not be appreciated by strangers—as though civic pride was mixed with a sense of inadequacy.

• • •

Enthralled by Columbus, I was also exposed to its hereditary failings. My father and DOS had prepared me for a world of homespun anti-Semitism, and I noticed how often the natives mentioned that someone was Jewish when the identification was irrelevant, as in "a Jewish librarian" or "one of those Jewish baritones." Allusions to "jewing" somebody "down" in price were not uncommon. They didn't use language like Harry Truman's when he called New York "a kike town" in 1918 and referred to it as "the U.S. Capital of Israel" in 1957, but I sensed that many Midwesterners had reflexes like his. And I knew some of the history. In 1922 the novelist and critic Ludwig Lewisohn, who had taught German at Ohio State University, wrote in his autobiography *Up Stream* that the end of World War I had left the country "in an uproar of reaction and nationalism" which led to "a revival of the Ku Klux Klan, outbreaks of smoldering race animosities and the apparently inevitable recrudescence of Jew-baiting." To Lewisohn Columbus seemed dominated by the national demand for "one hundred per cent Americanism." In the Eighties I heard that a young woman who was dating a Jewish classmate at Ohio State had recently been waylaid and held down by a group of students who etched a swastika on her belly with a key, pressing just hard enough to break the skin. Swastikas had also been painted on the office door of a Jewish professor whose politics were perceived as radical. No gentile I met in Columbus seemed to know what a schmuck was; the word was used as though it meant schlemiel. Yet I also heard praise for the Lazarus family, which had desegregated the sales staff of its department store years before its chief competitors were willing to hire blacks to serve whites.

Even Columbus loyalists kept telling me that their city lacked ethnicity, that it was still wary of any culture that seemed less than ultra-American. The old brochures were forthright on that score: in 1910 the Chamber of Commerce boasted that about 94 per cent of Columbus residents were "of American parentage," and another pamphlet of that year declared that Columbus "is the composite of all the races which have lifted Ohio to her high rank of leadership in the sisterhood of states. No state is more typical of American life at its best and in none has there been a nobler blending of all the great peoples who have settled and mastered the New World"—specifically, "a virile stock of Yankees" and the "proud descendants" of the Virginia colonies. A guidebook of 1919 bragged that there were very few "foreign born people in Columbus." Still "the farsighted men of the city are now bending every effort toward the Americanization of these foreigners," attempting to make them "law-abiding" and to rid them of "ignorance." Here was a theme of Theodore Roosevelt's World War I "Americanization" campaign against "hyphenated Americans"; Roosevelt argued that German-Americans, Irish-Americans, and others should forget their origins, relinquish their languages, and become pure Americans without links to their former cultures. He said that those who hadn't learned English after five years should be forcibly repatriated.

The Columbus booklets did not mention the waves of German immigrants who had brought music and beer to Ohio, starting around 1830: the stone-masons, brewery workers, carpenters, blacksmiths, and vegetable farmers who founded choral societies, bands, and song festivals. By 1852 a third of Columbus's population was German. Throughout the next six decades they enlarged the school system and built one of the city's handsomest neighborhoods, donating a statue of Schiller to their fellow citizens. Grape arbors rose in the walled gardens between their stone cottages and Queen Anne houses, and the very first American kindergarten was in Columbus. As the United States entered World War I, they became objects of hatred. Accused of pacifism—some still had relatives in Germany and dreaded combat between the two countries—they were investigated for "unpatriotic actions," and they saw piles of German books being burned by armed guards on the sidewalks of Columbus. The Board of Education punished "disloyal acts and utterances" by German teachers, and the Germans' neighbors were urged to monitor their actions. "Seditious" remarks were reported to the District Attorney's office: any German might be a spy, just as any foreigner might be a radical or a unionist. The teaching of German was banned in the public schools and the Board of Education pulped its German texts and sold them at fifty cents per hundred pounds. Streets were hastily renamed: Germania became Stewart, Bismarck became Lansing, Mozart became Fourth Street. Dachshunds were slaughtered at Schiller's feet and their corpses were heaped around the pedestal. During and right after the war, the German-Americans fled Columbus. Countless Germans had been persecuted all over the country, but their pain was particularly vivid to me in that city—because the patterned bricks, wrought iron, and hand-blown glass windows of their abandoned village displayed the care and pride with which they had built it.

In contemporary Columbus I heard many references to blacks living or just walking in neighborhoods "where they shouldn't be." The city seemed even more socially segregated than others I'd known: during my season there I went to only one party where there were black guests. Columbus has had a substantial black population since the beginning of the century. Because thousands of escaped slaves had passed through Ohio on the Underground Railroad during the Civil War, black Americans had hoped that the state would provide them with opportunities, but they merely meant underpaid labor to Ohio employers. And many whites in Columbus had sympathized with the Confederacy. In my father's childhood the hotels refused all black guests, restaurants and bars discouraged them from entering, and one restaurant put salt in the coffee and eggshells in the food of any black who did eat there.

Yet my father's first school—like most in northern Ohio—was integrated, and he had fond recollections of a black classmate who was the fastest runner and best ballplayer, marble shooter, whistler, and fighter in their elementary school; the boy also excelled at patting his head and rotating a hand on his stomach at the same time. (Fifteen years later, when my father was sent by a newspaper to attend executions at the Ohio Penitentiary, he met his friend from fourth grade in the death chamber: the man smiled and winked at him as he was strapped into the electric chair.) As a cub reporter Thurber had covered the first open air meeting of the local Ku Klux Klan in the summer of 1922, when its members "used to stand, in full bedsheet regalia, on street corners, with lighted cigars protruding from the mouth-holes in their robes." Thirty years afterward Thurber was still indignant that his two columns about the Klan were reduced to one "emasculated" paragraph because his editor decided to "wait and see" how readers felt about the Klan. There were no lynchings in Columbus, but Ohio's Klan was the second largest in the country and the Columbus chapter was ample. In the Twenties foes of segregation regarded Columbus as one of the most racist cities in the United States.

The Vanguard League, a radical black and white organization, was founded by Ohio State students and alumni in 1941: they held sit-ins at lunch counters near the university, sought to integrate the movie theaters, and went to the railroad station to try to desegregate the taxicabs. They brought lawsuits against restaurants, which usually received fines of five hundred dollars, and a reprimand for "discrimination" instead of a guilty verdict. The restaurant owners grew weary of paying fees to the attorneys who defended them, so they began to admit blacks. At its peak in the mid-Forties the League had about fifteen hundred members; it expired in the Fifties but was thought to have helped prepare the way for some of the civil rights litigation of the Sixties.

The city's public schools had been resegregated in the early Twenties. In the years following the *Brown* decision of 1954, many whites moved to the suburbs of Columbus when the black population could not afford to leave the inner city. In violation of the Fair Housing Act of 1968, the patterns of residential segregation perpetuated the segregation of the schools, and black schools grew blacker as white ones became whiter. But a 1977 lawsuit—*Penick versus the Columbus Board of Education*, which was fiercely contested by the Board—resulted in school desegregation in 1979. After the extensive legal efforts to prevent busing were overruled, community leaders, including the president of Buckeye Steel Castings, rallied to ensure that Columbus would respect the law, that there would be no violence: it was explained to me that the town's innate conservatism helped to enforce desegregation. Nevertheless a few prosperous suburbs, such as Bexley, remained white citadels, and a teacher in Upper Arlington described her school to me as "all blond."

Before the fall term of 1979 Ohio Klan members passed out leaflets and called for demonstrations against busing. But white parents shunned them and concentrated on sending their children to school without disruption. Robert Duncan, the black district judge who wrote the court order on desegregation, told me he'd been apprehensive on that first September day when the buses rolled. But then he discovered that far more civilian volunteers had turned out to maintain peace than had been asked for or were needed. No rocks were thrown, no buses were blocked. (The small American Nazi Party had threatened to bomb the school where Duncan's daughter was a pupil, but the would-be bombers were arrested on their way to buy explosives.) Duncan reflected that the smooth transition to busing was heartening for Columbus as a whole: the city had succeeded where many others had not. In the mid-Eighties Duncan observed that Columbus had the most racially balanced school system in the United States. But there could be no certainty that it would stay that way—if whites kept moving out of the city or if the school board voted to eliminate busing, as some of its members wished to.

• • •

Exploring Columbus and its history and its contradictions showed me what my father and Thurber and DOS had gained from it and why they had chosen to leave it. Meanwhile I roamed through the streets where they were raised, searching for taproots and touchstones. On Rich Street there was a parking lot where my family's large Victorian house had been, where my grandmother had shocked the neighbors by painting her mahogany dining table white. Widowed soon after she was forty, she would become a photographer and an interior designer, an expert in gold leaf stencilling and a creator of shadow boxes, but all that was in the future when she lived on Rich Street. Across from the site of her former home there was an empty field of tall grass, but I knew that wealthy beer brewers had erected an enormous mansion there; from Germany they had imported a spectacular fountain festooned with Rhine maidens whose breasts spouted jets of water. Otherwise the neighborhood belonged to the middle of the middle class: no one was rich and no one was poor. Tossing balls in the alleys outside the livery stables or hanging out with the black grooms who would later become chauffeurs, my father and his younger brother were on a team called the Rich Street Sluggers. Sports were almost a religion in Columbus: athletes were demi-gods and children yearned to be champions.

A few blocks away I found the fields where the Sayre brothers and Robert Thurber and DOS had played baseball and football. The baseball diamond was behind the gigantic Blind Asylum, known as the Blinky, and the football field was in front of the colossal Deaf and Dumb Asylum (the Dummy). From the 1870s until 1953, both state institutions had housed hundreds of sightless or speechless children. To James Thurber, who had lost an eye in a childhood accident but could see with the other until his fifties, the Blinky was a "brooding monster" which "was to become one of the landscapes of my nightmares," and he recalled the infrequent sounds that drifted out of the building: "a tray falling, a sharp voice protesting, a melancholy hand running scales on a piano lost in the wilderness of stone." But for others that field was scene of ecstatic memories: my nine-year-old father had exulted in carrying buckets of water to the teams before he was old enough to join the game. (Thurber, then fifteen, often made him laugh so much that the water spilled.) Two decades earlier George Bellows had played in the shadow of the Blind Asylum before he became one of the finest shortstops at Ohio State.

Each day as I set out from the Thurber House on a borrowed bicycle, riding past the Blinky and the Dummy, I came across more landmarks of their youth: the site of the movie theater named the Bijou Dream (because the owners were Jewish it was known as the Big Jew Dream), the yards where they made and flew their kites, and the street where Boy Scouts like my father used to pick up drunken Senator Warren Harding from the sidewalk and escort him to his lodgings (they would remember those good deeds after he moved to the White House, and when historians judged him to be the country's worst President). Near the Deaf Asylum there had been a gleaming castle which fascinated my father because the marble walls around it had portholes; it was built for Dr. Samuel Hartman, who had made a fortune in the 1880s by mixing alcohol with a tinted liquid and selling it as a patented medicine called Peruna. During Prohibition Peruna was more popular than ever. The castle was gone but I kept picturing other traces of vanished Columbus, like the metal arches studded with hundreds of light bulbs that had sparkled throughout the city early in the century; Thomas A. Edison had sent a telegram of congratulations on their installation. Recalling Thurber's drawing of an uncle who succumbed to the blight that was killing off the chestnut trees, I was amazed to see two surviving chestnuts in flower as I cycled past the football field. And I rode where the boys of the neighborhood had practiced riding their own bicycles without touching the handlebars or with the saddles turned backward and downward. As my wheels spun and my lungs filled with the spring breezes, I realized how my father and his team mates had revelled in an outdoor American boyhood—in a community that would seem oppressive after they turned twenty.

In my first weeks on the bicycle I rode into their past. Through their eyes I saw Olentangy Park and the Scioto River, and I knew what they had felt and thought while they were growing up in those solid brick houses which seemed constructed to last forever. In their day huge campaign posters of Republican candidates had hung in almost every window of their neighborhood; when the rare face of a Democrat was displayed, children threw eggs at it. Pedalling toward the German Village I followed the route my grandmother and taken when she drove her two sons in her horse-drawn trap (and later in her electric coupé) on their excursions into an exciting maze of cobbled streets and small rust-colored houses and the tantalizing smells of wurst and sauerbraten. As I rode through leafy alleys, past scalloped iron fences, etched glass door panels, and clay chimney pots on slate roofs, or sampled the tortes and hasenpfeffer, I realized how exotic the Germans' little sanctuary must have seemed to young Midwesterners. Years afterward my father said that his passion for foreign travel and languages was kindled by those expeditions into the German Village.

He also said his childhood in Columbus had seemed like a series of adventures. Houdini had challenged the town's breweries to build a barrel from which he couldn't escape, and he soon emerged from it, dripping with beer. My father had also seen the climax of a murder when he was playing ball in Rich Street: a man who shot his wife and then himself had reeled out of a house—when he fell, the derby hat that tumbled from his head continued to roll on its brim in circles which grew smaller and smaller, an image retained by witnesses long after they forgot the motive for the murder.

As the bicycle carried me further into my predecessors' lives, I had more flashbacks to eras before I ever existed. When my adolescent father told his father (the treasurer of a window glass firm) that he wished to write, the admission was badly received; my grandfather's impression of writers derived from only two of that unsavory tribe: Walt Whitman and O. Henry. He admired Whitman's poetry and could recite "A Woman Waits for Me." In 1865, when he had been a shy fourteen-year-old errand boy in the Office of Indian Affairs in Washington, Whitman—then a clerk in the same section of the Interior Department—had been kind to him and had described his own experiences in a similar job in Brooklyn. A senior bookkeeper warned my grandfather that no boy should accept horse car rides or candy from Mr. Whitman—indeed a boy should avoid him—and the poet was soon discharged by Secretary of the Interior James Harlan because *Leaves of Grass* was said to be a filthy book. My grandfather felt that Whitman had been shamefully treated. (In mid-life he and some tipsy friends resolved to topple the statue of Harlan in the Capitol to avenge the firing of Whitman, but a guard ejected them from the building before they could locate the statue.) Yet my grandfather could not bring himself to mention Whitman's homosexuality to his son. As for O. Henry, many did not think he was guilty of embezzling about a thousand dollars from a bank in Texas. But since he had been incarcerated for nearly three years in the Ohio Penitentiary, his conviction strengthened my grandfather's belief that writing was a disreputable trade.

Too young to participate in World War I but "eager to strangle the Kaiser," my father falsified the date on his birth certificate and enlisted in the Canadian Expeditionary Force, which transported him to Siberia as he was turning eighteen. (Some Allied troops were aiding the White Russian Government against the Germans, with whom the Bolsheviks had made a separate peace.

The British and the French also hoped to overthrow the Bolsheviks.) Stationed in Vladivostok, the Canadian infantry did not fight the Bolsheviks, as the Americans eventually did; instead they guarded stores of munitions and food. My father was a messenger, so he was able to range all over the port city, which had once been a part of China and retained strong Asiatic overtones. Having saturated himself in Chekhov, Turgenev, and Gogol before he left Columbus, he was enraptured to be on their continent, where he studied Russian, found companions among the French, British, Czech, Cossack, and Australian soldiers, drank sake with the Japanese allies, bought vodka from the Manchurian coolies (whom he once saw entranced by a YMCA screening of Charlie Chaplin's *Shoulder Arms*), rode in three-horse droshkies whose drivers roused their steeds with piercing falsetto shrieks, visited Japanese and Russian "singsong girls," made night tours of the Chinese bazaars with a pharmacist from Hong Kong, ate gargantuan Pacific crabs whose legs were almost six feet long, and discovered that if he approached a Christian woman during Easter Week and said "Christ is risen" in Russian, she would reply "Verily risen" and kisses would be exchanged on both sets of cheeks. For a couple of months he was coached in Russian grammar by the British High Commissioner to Siberia, who was also a marine biologist and the world's foremost authority on sea slugs. My father watched his fellow infantryman Raymond Massey dancing in a grass skirt to entertain the troops, had many glimpses of Admiral Alexander Vasilievich Kolchak—the counter-revolutionist and Supreme Ruler of the Supreme All-Russian Government, who was supposed to lead the country once the Bolsheviks were vanquished—and was regretful to board the ship that took him home seven months after the Armistice.

Following a season at the Harvard Summer School, he spent one term at Williams, dropped out, and went to Oxford. Back in Columbus, aged twenty-one, he was employed by *The Ohio State Journal* at ten dollars a week. (The paper had paid the same salary to the young William Dean Howells when he was a junior editor in 1859.) The publisher who hired my father asked if he knew the motto of the state of Alabama, which he did: it was "Here We Rest." The question was meant to discourage a young writer from rushing off to New York. It was then that he and Thurber, who was working for *The Columbus Dispatch*, became close friends, the gap between their ages canceled out. Together they chafed at the constrictions of Columbus. After my father's sojourns in Siberia and Oxford, many trips to France and a summer in Germany, their hometown seemed provincial—even stifling—as it did to Thurber, who had been in Paris for over a year as a State Department code clerk. (The narrator of *The Great Gatsby* expressed a similar restlessness: "Instead of being the warm center of the world, the Middle West now seemed like the ragged edge of the universe.") Columbus, the ultra-confident capital of the state which made presidents—between 1868 and 1920 Ohio sent seven Republicans to the White House—appeared to be populated by men and women who prided themselves on being average, just as Warren Harding did when he promised to represent the ordinary man. In fact the city seemed to be addicted to the average.

Still Thurber envied the editorial flexibility of *The Ohio State Journal*, where my father managed to insert a reference to "a pregnant mule" into a feature story about a gifted hog caller. Thurber wrote, "It was the first time the word 'pregnant,' an obscene synonym for 'expectant,' ever got into a Columbus newspaper, and many readers were shocked." (Howells's employer at *The Journal* had told him, "Never, never write anything that you would be ashamed to read to a woman.") Feeling themselves surrounded by prudes and philistines, exasperated by the forces of Methodism and Republicanism, both of them often quoted Dean Joseph Villiers Denney of Ohio State—a Shakespeare professor who struggled to expand the university's arts budget when the Ohio legislature preferred to fund the School of Agriculture—"Millions for manure, but not one cent for literature."

Thurber sometimes characterized Ohio State—from which he didn't graduate—as a purveyor of degrees in Sanitary Engineering. As his discontent with Columbus intensified, he extolled Lewisohn's *Up Stream*, which contained an indictment of the university and "the appalling mental vacuity" of the citizens of Columbus. Lewisohn wrote that his students had no interests but "football and fudge," that "any stirring of the mind" was "considered 'highbrow,' queer," and therefore "undemocratic," and that they harbored "a blind terror of nonconformity." The graduating seniors were "uncontaminated by wisdom and understanding"; as adults they would "go to foolish plays, read silly magazines, and fight for every poisonous fallacy in politics, religion, and conduct." Since they believed that "the aim and end of life" was "happiness in terms of a blameless prosperity," Lewisohn concluded that "the hardware man and the undertaker [had] triumphed" in imposing mediocrity on Midwestern culture. After dining at a men's club whose members talked exclusively about "the price of real estate, of stocks and bonds and sugar," Lewisohn observed: "Well-fed, well-groomed, they sat in their impenetrable stolidity, taking liberties with everything but their minds." Thurber rejoiced in the "cruel truthfulness" of *Up Stream* and remarked that Columbus was reading it "avidly."

The commercialism of Columbus, which repelled my father and his friends—and before them, the young George Bellows—was partly generated by its location: encompassed by fertile farmlands, near the Appalachian coal-fields and close to iron, oil, and gas resources, the city had flourished as a center for industry and agriculture and banking in the nineteenth century. Caleb Atwater, who wrote the first history of Ohio in 1838, declared, "Our position in the Nation is peculiarly felicitous, as to soil, climate, and productions, and it will be our own fault if we are not the happiest people in the Union." During the 1870s Columbus was publicized as a town where new arrivals could get rich quickly, and the kinship between wealth and happiness seemed indisputable. By 1919 the residents were said to buy and spend with more gusto than those in most American cities. Education and the arts, Lewisohn noted, were seen as "luxuries for women" in a city where the manufacture of automobiles and oil cloth and beer were far more significant than literature. (In Columbus in the late 1850s Howells had discovered that while men talked to him about politics and finance, only with women could he discuss books and music; in those same years Henry James had found a similar imbalance in Manhattan.) In 1922 Thurber complained to Elliott Nugent that few of his fellow citizens could focus on anything but business. And while I lived in Thurber's attic I understood his impatience when I heard some repetitious boasting about Columbus's national importance to market research: disposable diapers had first been tested there, so had interactive cable television and King-size Coca-Cola. Milk in plastic bags and turkey burgers had failed because Columbus had spurned them. Shopping was still said to be the favorite recreation of most inhabitants. Yet I also heard echoes of the vitality which had built the city: a sense that Americans can do anything they want to, that there need be no limits to attainment. And it seemed to me that this species of assurance was inherited by venturesome young natives like my father, who had no respect for money and were contemptuous of the money culture—but felt free to follow any path in the world.

• • •

As I bicycled through the decades, immersed in the early lives of several dead men, I found that their memories became mine. But after a month of coasting through Columbus, I also rode into their future. I knew what was coming—all the innovations and disasters that were in store for this country and for the boys who had raced their sleds through the main streets of their town before many people owned cars. Yet the rewards and punishments awaiting them seemed nearly inconceivable in the heart of their old neighborhood, full of Methodist churches and neat beds of geraniums and day lilies planted beside immaculate lawns. I foresaw what they didn't know at eighteen or twenty: Lindbergh's flight across the Atlantic, talking pictures, penicillin, Stalin and Mussolini and Hitler, the towers of Rockefeller Center, breadlines and shantytowns throughout the nation, Social Security, the Trylon and the Perisphere, Pearl Harbor, jitterbugging, Hiroshima, television, Israel, nuclear power, credit cards, the birth control pill. I knew what was yet to be invented or suffered or celebrated. Cures would be found for tuberculosis and polio, millions would die hideously in World War II and in Indochina and in the Middle East, the Supreme Court would outlaw segregation, human beings would walk on the moon. Life expectancy would soar in the richest countries and genocides would multiply in others whose names were hardly known in Ohio. And all of these things lay ahead when the young men from Columbus began their journey to New York.

In Manhattan, reunited in the speakeasies, they might remember the football songs of Columbus. For my father and my uncle there would be early success, suicidal first wives, a daughter apiece, multiple pleasures, financial crises because of long family illnesses, admiration from those they admired. My father would write for *The Herald Tribune* and *The New Yorker* and Hollywood; the war would immerse him in the ruins of Germany. Later he would live with the Hopi Indians in Arizona, mesmerized by their ceremonial dances and driving carloads of their corn to trade with the Navajos in New Mexico; he would hurtle through the Grand Canyon in a rubber boat, shooting seventy-two rapids in the Colorado River; join a deep sea search for sunken treasure in Bermuda; penetrate the mysteries of Scotland Yard; seek out Mexican Indians dwelling in the caves of Chihuahua; and savor a return visit to Columbus two years before his death. My uncle would earn his pilot's license in the rebuilt planes of World War I and would make the first extensive study of American air masses; he would run a division of the Civil Aeronautics Authority in Washington and then become the first chairman of the department of aeronautics at Princeton. He would direct Princeton's Forrestal Research Center, where jet propulsion, thermonuclear energy, and atomic fission were explored. His first marriage would wither but his second would be envied by relatives and friends. My father would be frustrated whenever a fiscal emergency tied him to a desk job, and his writing block would worsen while he was assailed with guilt over my mother's breakdowns during a marriage that was calamitous for both of them. Yet his energies appeared to be restored each time he embarked on a new writing project: research renewed his hopes and appetites. No one I've known seemed quite so open to the exhilarations of discovery, or to have taken such delight in the moment. Thurber, anguished by blindness, often racked with rage, disgusted by the changes in his culture, also felt that he had been responsible for an American classic or two. DOS would bask in the munificence of his screen career—regarding himself as a skilled craftsman rather than the incisive writer he might have been—would try and fail to affect the policies of his government, and would live long enough to hear his persecutors discredited and to be respected for his intentions.

As I rose on the pedals of the bicycle, clattering over the uneven brick streets of the German Village, whirling past Schiller's statue at its center, I was still passing through chapters of history that weren't mine. Others' experiences and emotions kept flowing through me. I knew the elation of being published and praised in the Twenties and Thirties and Forties, and I grappled with the reversals that came later. I knew what it was like to watch the construction of the Chrysler Building from a nearby office window, while feeling that I owned New York—or to dance all night in Harlem, to sail on the *Ile de France*, or to have a hit on Broadway and then be fired in the middle of a movie, or to gaze with disbelief at headlines about spies in the State Department. And I knew how it felt to lose control of one's life. To go blind or be blacklisted, to dwell with mental illness and chaos: I knew what it was to reach that point where possibilities seemed to dwindle every year.

But despite all the setbacks and errors of the men who had met on the baseball fields of Columbus, their achievements had been tangible—no less so than their pain. Some of their intimates would attribute their losses to their flaws: my father's freewheeling irresponsibility, Thurber's volatile furies, DOS's spells of political myopia. Yet I felt they had been reared in a world which made everything look much simpler than it was—and which promised its offspring more security than anyone ever attains. Indeed one of the charms of Columbus may have been the implication that life could be conducted without turmoil or complexity, that decent American values could protect one from misfortune. Columbus seemed to suggest that respectable citizens had the right to expect comfort and stability—and to deny that uncertainty is a natural condition, that almost any success is temporary. As far as I could see, there had been no education for tragedy, perhaps not even for hardship. That most of us live with fragmentation—or that few decisions can have lasting results—seemed to be alien ideas at the crossroads of the country. Flux was rarely acknowledged there; also I suspected that a person besieged by conflicts would be regarded as a weakling. And how would Columbus have responded to the highs and lows of these former inhabitants? I thought I knew that too. At their wildest or their saddest, they would probably have embarrassed the town where they began, appeared as threats to equilibrium, as agents of excess.

In the Eighties Columbus continued to be proud of George Bellows (some of whose paintings had once scandalized the city's art committee); and of Tod Galloway, who co-wrote the Whiffenpoof Song; the football star Chic Harley; Billy Ireland, a widely syndicated cartoonist who married one of my aunts; Jesse Owens, the black runner who won four gold medals in the 1936 Olympics in Berlin; the aviator and war hero Captain Eddie Rickenbacker; Milton Caniff, creator of *Terry and the Pirates*; and General Curtis LeMay, who said we should bomb Vietnam back to the Stone Age. But only one person I knew in Columbus had heard of Donald Ogden Stewart. No one I met had heard of Ruth McKenney, who wrote *My Sister Eileen* and was expelled from the Communist Party for "left deviationism"—although many were familiar with the song, "Why Did I Ever Leave Ohio?" from Leonard Bernstein's *Wonderful Town*, adapted from McKenney's books. It seemed that Marxists who'd once lived in Columbus had left no traces behind them.

And I was aware of other buried histories within the middle class of the Middle West. When Warren Harding was a state senator, he had gone five different times to an Ohio sanitarium, where he was treated for nervous prostration and melancholia. Chic Harley, the great halfback who had inspired Thurber's portrait of an athlete whose professors helped him to pass exams, had a breakdown in his last year at Ohio State and never fully recovered. My father's older half-brother had shot himself in his bedroom, which was full of Horatio Alger novels, when he was twenty-five (no one quite knew why). My cousin's great-uncle, aged nineteen, had waded into a river and killed himself with a new pistol after falling in love with a young prostitute. Severe depressions had descended on Thurber's father and each of the three sons. But life in or near the shadows was thought too unwholesome for much discussion. And when Thurber treated lunacy as a joke, that was perhaps the only way it could have been broached among the civil servants and Rotarians of Columbus.

While the city now pays abundant tribute to Thurber, many there had resented his work for decades because it was considered disrespectful of the town and its citizens. Thurber had refused to return for several years after the 1951 speakers rule was introduced at Ohio State University, requiring that the politics of all visiting lecturers be screened before they were allowed to talk on campus. Thurber denounced the university for suppressing "freedom of speech and freedom of research." He felt that its president, Howard Bevis, should be replaced, and he declined to accept an honorary degree. A few years later, when a right-wing reviewer asserted that Thurber and his relatives must be conservative by nature and that Thurber ought to support Joseph McCarthy instead of attacking him, Thurber wrote to *The Nation*'s editor, Carey McWilliams,

"Columbus is the heart of evasion and [the] fatty degeneration of criticism," adding, "My unfond memories would fill a bucket."

• • •

When I asked middle-aged citizens of Columbus about their memories of the Fifties, many talked about Senator John Bricker, a feverish proponent of states' rights who opposed censuring McCarthy in 1954, kept trying to amend the Constitution in order to curtail the treaty power of the president and the Senate, and saw left-wing conspiracies everywhere. When two Ohio State professors wrote a history of Ohio and their chapter on the Depression described unemployment and breadlines, Bricker insisted that such things had never existed in his state. When the Ohio Historical Society planned to issue an illustrated version of the book, Bricker tried to prevent its publication.

The "gag rule" that had incensed Thurber was established soon after Harold Rugg, professor emeritus from Columbia Teachers College, gave a lecture at Ohio State in 1951. Because Rugg was identified as a socialist, the Columbus newspapers demanded that the university's College of Education be investigated by the newly formed Ohio Un-American Activities Commission; Bricker, a university trustee, urged that "subversive" visiting speakers be banned from the premises. Little attention was given to the content of Rugg's speech; no detailed notes were preserved. (It seemed that he had criticized American schools for inadequate teaching of current affairs and that he'd predicted "increased public control of the economy.") But his fleeting appearance in Columbus inflamed the passions of the town's arch-conservatives, including the American Legion. Despite strenuous opposition from much of the faculty, the board of trustees passed the speakers rule, whereupon a Quaker pacifist was barred from lecturing even though he was an anti-Communist.

The university was castigated by educators all over the country and by the Ohio Council of Churches. Columbus's hotel and restaurant trade dwindled when numerous professional and conference groups took their business to other cities. Perhaps because of the loss of revenues, the trustees agreed to a slight alteration in the procedural minutiae of the screening rule. But it remained in effect until the mid-Sixties.

Although many professors had campaigned against the rule, few raised the issue of academic freedom when Byron Darling, a distinguished professor of physics, was suspended for taking the Fifth Amendment before the House Committee in 1953. In a private session with President Bevis, Darling declared that he had never been a Communist, that he hadn't violated the university's loyalty oath, and that he knew of no Communists on the faculty. Darling offered to answer any questions put to him by the president and the trustees. He explained that he had not cooperated with the Committee because he thought its investigations were unconstitutional and because he feared being indicted for perjury—since paid informers were saying that non-Communists were Party members and the Committee wasn't rigorous about facts. On Bevis's recommendation Darling was hastily discharged, although Bevis had also told the trustees that the physicist was "an outstanding research man in his field" who had behaved with "scrupulous propriety" throughout his tenure. Editorials in the Ohio press congratulated Bevis and the trustees for the speed with which Darling was fired.

The Columbus newspapers were among the most zealous in the nation in chastising subversives. In 1948 Frank Hashmall, a district organizer for the Communist Party sent to revitalize the small branch in Columbus, visited the Timken Roller Bearing plant with a few colleagues. They tried to distribute leaflets criticizing the Truman administration; a couple of steelworkers assaulted them and the leaflets were flung into the gutter. The police were called in and Hashmall's address was published in *The Columbus Dispatch*; *The Columbus Citizen* printed pictures of the home he had rented, also his unlisted phone number. Two weeks later, when Hashmall was away, the house was stoned and the windows smashed, the doors were battered down, Venetian blinds were ripped from their frames, and the furniture was broken to bits by some thirty men while a mob of about a thousand cheered from the street outside. Hashmall's books were thrown all over the yard. A police captain ordered the raiders to disperse, but no one was arrested. Hashmall had appealed to the police department for protection after the incidents at Timken; the police chief told him there would be "no special police for this anti-religious group." A photographer I met in Columbus spoke of his boyhood memories of the recurring pictures of the Hashmall residence in the local papers; one showed a group of men smiling as they stood on the book-strewn lawn, and he recalled that some were wearing American Legion caps.

The Ohio Un-American Activities Commission, organized in 1951 and located in the Capitol building in Columbus, had "three primary fields of inquiry": industry, schools and universities, and the groups listed by the Attorney General as Communist fronts. The Columbus lawyers I consulted were doubtful that the Commission was seriously concerned with left-wing unions, since its members' main interest seemed to be publicity that could advance their careers. The group hired Harvey Matusow, who was instructed to tour the state's industrial plants in search of Communists, also to name Party members in the Dayton Women for Peace, the National Negro Labor Council, the Young Progressives of America and the Labor Youth League, many schools, and Antioch College. Matusow wrote in *False Witness*, "I had a big job on my hands in Ohio," where, as he later admitted, he "manufactured baseless charges of subversion." But Matusow was so garrulous about the enticement of young Americans through folk music, square dances, and radical summer camps that his testimony was somewhat neglectful of labor. King George VI of England died while Matusow was on leave from the Ohio Commission to appear before the House Committee, and he was upset because the dead monarch got larger headlines in Washington than he did. But in Columbus, Matusow was able to "knock King George off the front page."

Folk singing on picket lines and as a stimulant for recruitment, fund-raising, and "political agitation" was lengthily discussed by Matusow in his public hearing before the Commission. He testified that the Communists had altered "the legitimate words" of old American songs such as "Clementine," where the refrain became "Oh my darling Clementine, be a shrewd one, join the union, be a smart one, Clementine." "Casey Jones" was rewritten so that Jones was a scab expelled from heaven by the angels. The "political implications" of hootenannies received close scrutiny: Matusow cited the "Smash the Indictment of the Twelve Communist Leaders Hootenanny," the "Repeal the Taft-Hartley Hootenanny," and the "Stop the Work of the Un-American Committee Hootenanny."

Ohio's Governor Frank Lausche had banned the Weavers from the Ohio State Fair a year before Matusow went on the stand in Columbus. (The FBI had shared its "confidential" files on the Weavers with Lausche and with the press.) The singers had offered to give a benefit concert for the Heart Fund in Cleveland, but the American Legion and the Knights of Columbus objected. Someone broke into the Heart Fund's offices and scattered the files and wrecked the typewriters. Pete Seeger's name was repeated in the Commission's questioning of uncooperative witnesses: "Did you ever attend a meeting at which Pete Seeger provided the entertainment? Do you know Pete Seeger? . . . Do you know what a hootenanny is? Is it not a fact that you attended a Communist Party hootenanny at the home of Anna Morgan in Columbus, Ohio?" These were some of the queries which prompted witnesses to take the Fifth Amendment.

Anna Morgan was a nurse and a public Communist; she had a small bookstore stocked with black literature and books on labor history as well as poetry, current fiction, and the Bible. It was said that her house was the headquarters of the Communist Party of Franklin County, that she was its finance director and executive secretary. When she was fined five hundred dollars for contempt after invoking the Fifth Amendment before the Commission, her husband had been without a salary for six years.

Richard Morgan, an extremely talented archeologist who specialized in the prehistoric culture of the Adena and Hopewell Indians of Ohio, became Curator of the Ohio State Museum, which was funded by the state legislature, in 1938. He excavated sites of Indian burial mounds, earthworks, and villages in the Midwest, co-authored *The Bibliography of Ohio Archeology*, and published scholarly articles on the Ohio prehistoric peoples. In 1947 he married Anna Rubio, whom he'd met while working on his doctorate at the University of Chicago; she had several grown children from a previous marriage. Her son Alfred Rubio, a machinist and an open Communist in Chicago, owned the house which was attacked because Frank Hashmall lived there. In 1948, one day after the Columbus press revealed that Morgan's stepson was a Communist, Morgan ceased to be curator. Driving to his office he heard on his car radio that he had been fired.

I was told that Morgan was a reticent man, devoted to his work and to his dynamic wife, whose boundless energies were balanced by his diffidence. Widely perceived as apolitical, Morgan battled to regain his job. The museum's board of trustees decided that he must tell them if he or his wife were Communists, though no one thought he was. Since he didn't answer his employer's questions, the firing was upheld. The American Anthropological Association investigated Morgan's case, concluding that "his rights as a citizen" had been violated, especially because his "professional competence was not in question." Morgan asked distinguished archeologists and anthropologists for letters of support; at least fifty wrote on his behalf, among them Margaret Mead. The president of the Ohio State Archeological and Historical Society agreed that Morgan's work was not at issue, but stated that the museum would not retain anyone who had "a close or continued or sympathetic association with a Communist." By then the Hashmall residence had been ravaged by the mob, and the press coverage horrified the Society's directors.

Morgan was never subpoenaed by the Ohio Commission nor by any congressional committee. His name was not uttered during the Commission's examination of his wife. In fact Morgan was a Communist, but he was in no position to say so at the time. Since no institution would hire him as an archeologist, the couple operated a chicken farm and sold eggs on the outskirts of Columbus. Whenever Anna Morgan found a nursing job she was fired once her political history was discovered. Eventually they moved to Chicago, where he worked for an insurance firm and served as honorary curator at a museum of Afro-American history. But he was never able to return to this field. In 1968 the Morgans went to Oaxaca and he wrote to a friend about his excitement on seeing the pre-

Hispanic Mesoamerican burial grounds for the first time in his life. He died suddenly of a ruptured aorta when they were about to leave Mexico.

Morgan's successor at the museum, Raymond Baby, had no degrees in archeology or anthropology; because he wasn't qualified for the job, some suspected that Baby had facilitated Morgan's firing so as to replace him. Long afterward Baby told a young professor that Morgan had been tutoring black children "after hours" at the museum. Baby sometimes referred to blacks as "Mau Maus." Morgan, who had grown up in Klan territory in Middletown, Ohio, was powerfully concerned with civil rights. The professor wondered if racism in Columbus was partly responsible for Morgan's dismissal, as well as his wife and stepson's Party membership. The archeologist James B. Griffin, who had known Morgan since they were graduate students, told me that Morgan was the best archeologist the Ohio State Museum ever employed. More than two decades after Morgan's death, another scholar said that Morgan's exit from the museum was a catastrophe for Ohio archeology, not only because of the quality of his work, but because Baby was incompetent. Ohio is central to an understanding of prehistoric developments east of the Mississippi, and at that time the state had more known earthworks than any other. But research lagged in the thirty years that Baby held his post.

Anna Morgan had been judged guilty of contempt on the same day as Oscar Smilack had: the two shared a headline in *The Columbus Dispatch*. Smilack belonged to the Unitarian Fellowship for Social Justice, the American Civil Liberties Union, and the NAACP. With his father he owned a small and profitable scrap metal company; most of the employees were black. They participated in a profit-sharing plan and received health insurance and pensions: benefits which were rarely available to black people in Columbus in the Fifties. Smilack also put some five black students through college and graduate school. Accused of being a benefactor of the Communist Party of Franklin County—also of taking part in Marxist study groups at Anna Morgan's house and of paying for a jeep used by Columbus Communists—Smilack finally took the Fifth Amendment, though he had answered some questions. Thereafter he was thoroughly ostracized by the small Jewish community of Columbus while being shunned by the gentiles he knew, and the town's rabbis gave no sustenance to the Smilack family.

Eight weeks after his testimony, a judge in the local Court of Common Pleas ordered a sheriff to take Smilack to the Lima State Hospital for the Criminal Insane for a month of tests. The county prosecutor had hinted that only a demented person would give money to left-wing causes. In 1948 an intruder had stabbed Smilack's mother to death in her home. In the wake of her death Smilack became depressed and sometimes saw a psychiatrist. The prosecutor said Smilack had never recovered from the shock of the murder. Smilack's lawyer told the judge that his client was "just as sane" as either of them. But Smilack was led from the courtroom in shackles as well as handcuffs and driven away to Lima. Committed to the "custody and control" of the hospital without a hearing, Smilack spent two weeks in Lima before his lawyers were able to win his release on a writ of habeas corpus. A year passed before the prosecutor's efforts to have Smilack returned to the hospital were defeated in the Ohio Supreme Court.

Like Richard Morgan, Smilack had long been active in the movement to desegregate the city's housing. Restrictive racial covenants—deeds which forbade whites in some neighborhoods to sell or rent their homes or land to blacks—were declared unenforceable by the Supreme Court in 1948. But the practice of excluding "non-Caucasians" from restricted property continued in most states throughout the Fifties. In Columbus, when a black or interracial couple was threatened with violence after moving into a white neighborhood, groups of civil rights advocates would call on them each night in hopes that their presence would shield the newcomers from danger. Many of the nightly visitors were Quakers. Some of the blacks' irate neighbors wrote down the visitors' license plate numbers and sent them to the Ohio Commission. No one knew how or if that information was used, but it seemed prudent to walk to the homes of black householders rather than drive to them.

The Commission did not function after the mid-Fifties because the House Committee preempted its work. But the Commission's influence persisted in the lives it had invaded: the pacifists in church groups whose homes were damaged by vigilantes, or the naturalized citizens facing deportation (sometimes garbage was dumped in their driveways). As I listened to semi-retired lawyers and heard their voices tighten with anger at cases of some thirty-five years before—when the Commission had been applauded in Columbus—I was struck by the resilience of liberals, now over seventy, who had not been intimidated by the era or their community. One lawyer, a Quaker, said he had lost "a whole stack" of clients and several years' income not only because he represented Oscar Smilack but also because he had black clients who bought homes in white neighborhoods. But he wasn't muzzled: when the Commission proposed legislation which would require signing a loyalty oath to obtain a driver's license or a marriage license, he was the ACLU's spokesman in forestalling that legislation.

Another lawyer who took on many clients rejected by other attorneys because their "political chastity was in question," recalled the years when civil liberties was "anathema" in Columbus. At a time when almost anyone who was "against hunger" could be called a Communist, he denounced the investigating committees in lectures all over Ohio, and was praised by many listeners who said they weren't free to speak out as he did. Independence, a loathing of injustice, a refusal to compromise on a principle: these were values which our school texts claimed as inherently American—and which the demagogues of the Fifties didn't manage to destroy. Not even in Columbus, where the director of the Ohio Civil Defense was also a professor of Industrial Arts Education at the university and sold secret files on "subversives" throughout the country.

• • •

No matter what happened in Moscow or in Eastern Europe, I wondered if the domestic Cold War had ever fully ended in Columbus. So I asked various residents if they thought it had—and received a host of conflicting answers. A few talked about the Free Speech Movement at the university, which developed after 1961, when a group called Students for Liberal Action began to invite speakers who had criticized the House Committee. Because such visitors were still forbidden to lecture on campus, protests against the gag rule swelled. The trustees vehemently resisted any change in policy and John Bricker urged dissident undergraduates and professors to leave the university for good. Pickets, bitter antagonisms, a two-year lawsuit filed by the ACLU, and orderly sit-ins—where male students wore neckties and women wore skirts—peaked in the spring of 1965, when a *Columbus Dispatch* editorial warned that "students, like automatons, parade mechanically to the cadence of Communism's drum." But some members of the faculty picketed a trustees' meeting, students who marched to the State House were addressed by several legislators who supported the campaign for constitutional rights, and Ohio Senator Stephen Young upbraided the "McKinley era" trustees in a speech to Congress.

In accordance with the speakers rule, the historian Herbert Aptheker, a guest of Students for Liberal Action and an open Communist, sat silently backstage in the University Hall Chapel while an audience of nine hundred heard a graduate student read excerpts from his books aloud, along with the books' call numbers at the Ohio State library. The gag rule was not totally abolished. But the trustees did vote to "liberalize" it in the fall of 1965, and Aptheker returned to speak in public.

• • •

Pedalling my bicycle across the campus, noticing that the administration building had been named Bricker Hall, I allowed my thoughts to linger in the

Sixties. I recalled some of the signals that the national mood was shifting: the favorable responses to the idea of the Limited Test Ban Treaty of 1963, which was warmly received in mainly Republican states where President Kennedy talked about it; the Voting Rights Act of 1964; the Civil Rights Act of 1965. Among voters the Cold War mentality had ebbed in the years after Kennedy's assassination—not because of his death, but because the errors in his foreign policy were gradually perceived. I remembered how I'd watched the rebellion against the Vietnam War spreading from lofts in Greenwich Village to the working-class suburbs of Philadelphia, where I heard middle-aged women with rollers in their hair announcing that they did not want their sons to fight in that dirty war. On Wall Street I had seen businessmen in three-piece suits making antiwar speeches at lunchtime rallies. Near Fort Bragg in North Carolina I had listened to GIs just back from Vietnam—mostly blue collar enlistees—saying they no longer believed in the war and deriding the domino theory; on the black wall of their coffeehouse, someone had written in chalk, "My country right or wrong, but right the wrong in my country."

In those years, civil rights workers and peace activists could still be called Communists, but the word seemed to be losing its magic. When hard hats yelled their scorn at long-haried demonstrators on parade, or when aging members of the Committee awkwardly asked young radicals if they hoped to overthrow the government and received affirmative answers, the label of "Communism" was unthreatening to youthful Americans who knew little about Marx and had no secret affiliations. . . . Now I had ridden far away from my father's and Thurber's past, musing on the decade when their generation was waning—and which was already a memory for mine. On the sedate campuses of the Eighties, few might guess that death—in an Asian jungle or in the ghetto—had once been a more compelling subject than careers.

• • •

As the Sixties ended, black students were scarce at Ohio State and so were black professors. Black undergraduates—who'd felt like Martians amid all the beer blasts, hay rides, fraternity pranks, proms, and bridge games of Midwestern student culture—presented a list of priorities to the administration: more scholarships to increase black enrollment, the hiring of black faculty, and a Black Studies department. Late in April 1970 students who were against the war and the draft began to hold joint rallies with the blacks. The university replied that all the demands were unacceptable.

On April 29 a huge crowd of marchers closed the tall iron gates at the south end of the campus: a ritual that was common after football games. (Photographs subsequently showed that two undercover policemen helped to shut the gates.) The atmosphere was rather festive: some male students carried young women on their shoulders. But suddenly dozens of Ohio highway patrolmen arrived to open the gates. Columbus Mayor M. E. Sensenbrunner and Governor James Rhodes—who was running for the Republican nomination for Senator against Robert Taft, Jr.—reacted to a peaceful demonstration by declaring "a state of emergency" and imposing martial law. Twelve hundred Ohio National Guardsmen were sent to occupy the campus, and the stadium parking lot overflowed with troop carriers and jeeps. Guardsmen with fixed bayonets stood shoulder to shoulder around the administration building. Army trucks chased fleeing students through the streets.

Soon professors canceled their classes to protest the overwhelming presence of the military and a majority of students voted to strike. Some Guardsmen put tape over their name tags and it was dangerous to heckle a man in uniform: there were several hundred arrests and many injuries while tear gas billowed through the dormitories. Sometimes policemen ran into a crowd and collared black students, including Africans, at random. Students also fought with students, especially in front of the Business School, where fraternity members and antiwarriors belted one another with rolled-up cardboard posters as well as fists. Woody Hayes, the renowned football coach, was booed off an outdoor podium when he tried to give a speech—larded with sports metaphors—about hanging together, and he had to be escorted through the jeering throng by athletes acting as bodyguards.

Three days after the May 4th killing of four students at Kent State, Ohio State's president Novice Fawcett closed the university for ten days. (On May 5th Rhodes lost the Senate race. Early on his ratings in the polls had risen when he assailed student "agitators," but it appeared that the dead defeated him.) Understandably many Ohio students identified with the victims at Kent, who had hardly been seasoned radicals. In Columbus it was easy to imagine being shot by National Guardsmen while walking to class, or if one was merely a bystander watching the action. A woman who had been a student in 1970 told me that her college friends had not been very political, but their anger had flared when their campus became an armed camp. Then their opposition to the war began to evolve. Because many of their public high school classmates had gone straight into the Army at seventeen or eighteen, most had a concrete connection with a death or a casualty—if not a friend, then a friend's cousin or a neighbor's nephew. So they were closer to young men who had been killed or disabled than most Ivy League students were. For many male students, she said, dying in Vietnam was tangible, and the official explanations for the war sounded "foolish" to the friends with whom she played cards and watched the news at Ohio State.

Columbus had long been accustomed to youthful uproar, but in the context of sports, not politics, and "anarchists" made little sense to a town where football generated passions that outdistanced almost all others. (In the mid-Sixties, when the faculty had voted against the Ohio State team going to the Rose Bowl and a Columbus paper printed all their names and addresses, some found garbage and turds in their mailboxes.) A lawyer told me that the community's feelings about the student strike were probably reflected on the front pages of *The Dispatch*. In the spring of 1970 the theme was "Radicals Riot on Campus." That November, when Ohio State beat Michigan, the Columbus Police Department and the student government gave a street party together: not only were the campus gates closed, but dozens of store windows were shattered, cars were overturned, bonfires blazed on the sidewalks, and the damage was estimated at seventy-four thousand dollars. The headline then was "Victory Celebration Bubbles Over."

• • •

I'd been informed that Columbus offered equal opportunities for optimists and pessimists. Although one didn't need to take a loyalty oath to get a job in a Dairy Queen, there was a sense that the country was safe from "Communism" mainly because it was governed by Ronald Reagan and George Bush. Yet Columbus natives who believed that most of their fellow citizens were deeply conservative also felt the community had become far more elastic than it once was. In the early Eighties Ohio's Governor Richard Celeste had invited Pete Seeger to perform in Columbus; he and another former Weaver stayed at the Governor's residence and Celeste appeared on the stage with them. Seeger sang "The Internationale" in French; the audience didn't seem to recognize the anthem and the local press did not acknowledge that his presence in Columbus was a reversal of history.

Christian fundamentalists were plentiful there; nonetheless the city had passed a limited gay rights ordinance. When some two thousand homosexuals and lesbians turned out for the annual Gay Pride parade, I heard a speaker give thanks for "the wonderful protection by the state police," who had guarded the marchers from hordes of "Bible-bangers" along their route. As pink and mauve balloons drifted up toward the dome of the State House and the civil rights record of the Reagan-Bush White House was attacked over the microphones, I wished that the members of the Ohio Commission could have been present.

Some residents who thought the city's capacity for tolerance had expanded also remarked that tolerance had a price—that an amiable acceptance of the unorthodox was possible because nothing could be as important as football. A man who was fond of Columbus said that progress was sluggish there, and he compared working for change to clawing one's way through pillows, through feathers, which open up and close behind one. Then he pondered the ahistorical nature of Americans at large. Outside the universities, who would know that the Spanish Civil War had once captured the concern of men and women throughout the United States, or what the issues in that war had been? Would many remember that people in the South had died for the right to vote? Before a recent civil rights demonstration, he'd sat next to a white teenager on a bus who had never heard of the Confederacy—and yet was certain that he must participate in a protest against racism.

• • •

Bicycling past buildings where the small Columbus Left had gathered before 1950—a hall on the edge of the German Village, the basement of a Unitarian church—I thought about Richard Morgan's banishment from archeology, Oscar Smilack's weeks among the criminally insane, and the dead dachshunds and burning German books of 1917. The city had furthered my education about the loathing of those who were considered unpatriotic. But I'd also met some of the stubbornest civil libertarians I had encountered anywhere. Although Columbus punished many kinds of non-conformists, it had had room for others who appeared to thrive on dissent. The contradictions of Columbus had heightened my perceptions of Americanism at its best and worst. A Chamber of Commerce pamphlet of 1961 had urged readers to "Come to Columbus and Discover America!" and the city did seem to be a microcosm of this country: a conservative entity with some liberated zones.

Nearing the white marble Carnegie Library I dismounted and chained up the bicycle because I wanted to check a half-remembered passage in Edmund Wilson's essay "Auden in America." Wilson wrote in 1956 that Auden was "dealing with the whole modern world: its discomforts, its disquiets, its crimes, its myths—'the city and the lion's den'; with the problem of how to live in it . . . to avoid being paralysed or bought by it." Wilson thought this theme of Auden's might be more "intelligible" to American readers than to the British, because "feeling oneself to be a member of a determined resistant minority has been now for nearly a hundred years a typical situation in America." Observing that Auden "must have had some desolating" moments in this country, Wilson quoted from *New Year Letter* of 1940:

> Some think they're strong, some think they're smart,
> Like butterflies they're pulled apart,
> America can break your heart,
> *You don't know all, sir, you don't know all.*

To me it seemed that the "determined resistant minority" had sturdy roots in Columbus, even though I also knew the record of lives ruined in and by that city.

I'd been told that the young and the adventurous were likely to leave Columbus—and to resettle there after a decade or so. But for my father and my uncle, for Thurber and DOS, the departure had been final. Like a number of their contemporaries who had joined "the revolt from the village," as Carl Van Doren called it, they needed the fecundity of much larger cities, to which they brought a Midwesterner's assumption that doors would open to them. Their voyage out of Columbus—through the sprees of the Twenties, the anguish of the Depression, global war, and the fears of the Fifties—had mirrored the experiences of many middle-class Americans who had been brought up to enter a world that was not expected to change drastically.

Some Ohioans still seemed impervious to mutations. I had talked with people in Columbus who appeared confident that their culture and its legacy would endure—which was astounding to someone raised in Manhattan. New Yorkers know that nothing stays the same: as miles of our skyline are resculpted or demolished, natives realize that life is precarious. Just as real estate developers may cause the Empire State building to disappear within my lifetime, a megablast—accidental or deliberate—could eliminate my whole city. But Columbus seemed sure of continuity, as though the Methodist churches and the State House statues and the bridges over the Scioto River might be permanent. I envied those who thought that what they knew would be perpetuated. They also made me somewhat anxious—if they felt so secure, was nuclear winter inconceivable to them? And I was grateful to have known them: because their community was as unpredictable as the United States itself.

Riding back toward the Thurber House, I made a detour and coasted slowly along East Town Street, past the brick house designed by George Bellows, Sr., the architect who had not wanted his son to go to art school; past the Greek Revival house where William Dean Howells was said to have proposed to his future wife on a staircase in 1862 (she was so talkative that long afterward Mark Twain informed his own wife that when Elinor Howells came into a room, "dialogue died" and "monologue inherited its assets"); past the lacy cast-iron portico of the mansion where the governor of Ohio resided during the Civil War; past the dark red chateau of Harry Daugherty, Attorney General under President Harding but forced to resign under charges of conspiring to defraud the government (Daugherty claimed that all the scandals of the Harding administration were part of a Communist plot to destroy him); and past the apartment building which Robert Thurber, a recluse of eighty-eight, had not left for thirteen years.

A botched thyroid operation at nineteen had robbed the former athlete of the strength to play professional baseball; later he had owned a bookstore specializing in first and rare editions; now he dwelled at the mercy of a relentless memory: it seemed that whatever he'd witnessed or heard or read remained with him. When I referred to Chillicothe he was distressed and became short of breath—because he recalled that over a thousand young recruits of World War I had died there in an epidemic of Spanish influenza at Camp Sherman. When I mentioned my father, he exclaimed, "How he loved life!" adding that my father had "played rough but fair, always fair" during baseball practice. When he talked about "my brother," he never said his name, but I knew he didn't mean William, who had worked at the Ohio Bureau of Weights and Measures. When I spoke of George Bellows, Robert Thurber said that Bellows was far better at catching balls than hitting them: "A wonderful painter and catcher but not a good hitter." From Thurber's apartment it was only a short ride to the Columbus Museum of Art, where I'd seen how Bellows had portrayed New York's turbulence along with its pastoral nature, as in the midnight blue 1909 *Riverside Park at Night*, where courting couples stroll under hazy street lights and the city looks as safe as a village field.

As I locked the bicycle in a carriage house at dusk on my last evening in Columbus, it seemed like the end of a journey: through the generations, through the finest and ugliest chapters of this century. Mutineers and reactionaries, mavericks and conformists, they had all come from Columbus—not a metropolis, not even (in their youth) a large town. By the back door of the Thurber House there was an old mulberry tree which shed its fruit in early summer: if one trod on the berries, they left purple stains on the carpets. I stepped carefully that last night, avoiding the newly sown grass as well as the berries. The next day scores of birds clustered on the lawn, devouring the grass seeds: none of them rose in flight as I trundled my suitcases past them. If I was temporarily invisible, or if I cast no shadow, that was appropriate to the time I had spent among the dead. They had not haunted me in any harmful way; instead they had rewarded me. But now I was ready to let them rest— at least until I reached my home in a city where the future had awaited them.

Notes

The books listed were published in New York, except where noted.

PRELUDE

1. Stalin and nuclear weapons: David Holloway, *Stalin and the Bomb: The Soviet Union and Atomic Energy, 1939–1956* (New Haven and London: Yale University Press, 1994), pp. 193–195, p. 413.

1. retired agents: *The New York Times*, Nov. 17, 1990; Jonathan Kwitny, "The CIA's Secret Armies in Europe," *The Nation*, April 6, 1992.

2. Why People Are Poor: John Kenneth Galbraith, *The Affluent Society*, 3d rev. ed., (Boston: Houghton Mifflin, 1976), p. xiii.

3. a thirty-five-hundred-dollar model: Douglas T. Miller and Marion Nowak, *The Fifties* (Doubleday, 1977), p. 51.

3. one of Plymouth's 1959 advertisements: Thomas Hine, *Populuxe* (Knopf, 1986), p. 11.

3. *Life* editorial, Dec. 28, 1959.

7. Comintern archives: Harvey Klehr, John Earl Haynes, and Fredrikh Igorevich Firsov, *The Secret World of American Communism* (New Haven and London: Yale University Press, 1995). The Russians' atomic bomb: Holloway, *Stalin and the Bomb*. Decoded cables and the Rosenbergs: Walter Schneir and Miriam Schneir, "Cryptic Answers," *The Nation*, August 14, 1995; *The New York Times*, July 12, 1995.

8. "Red mouthpiece": Edwin R. Bayley, *Joe McCarthy and the Press* (Madison: University of Wisconsin Press, 1981), p. 128.

8. "always and invariably": Richard Rovere, *Senator Joe McCarthy* (Harcourt, Brace, 1959) p. 15.

8. "the Pied Pipers": Editors of *Time-Life* Books, *This Fabulous Century*, vol. 6 (Alexandria, Va.: *Time-Life* Books, 1970), p. 118.

8. "debased, degraded": Rovere, *McCarthy*, p. 73.

9. "a political speculator": Ibid., p. 72.

9. "born under other": Robert Justin Goldstein, *Political Repression in Modern America* (Cambridge, Mass.: Schenkman Publishing Company, 1978), p. 100.

9. "In the long run": Theodore Roosevelt, *The Foes of Our Own Household* (Doran, 1917), p. ix.

9. "all was righteousness": George Kennan, *The Decision to Intervene* (Princeton: Princeton University Press, 1956), p. 7; see also pp. 6, 8–9.

10. "100 per cent": William O. Douglas, *Go East, Young Man* (Random House, 1974), p. 121.

10. "all anti-American": Ibid., p. 120.

10. "wildly socialistic": *Photoplay Journal*, Kevin Brownlow, *Behind the Mask of Innocence* (Knopf, 1990), p. 442.

10. "The chief evil": Nat Hentoff, *The First Freedom: The Tumultuous History of Free Speech in America* (Dell, 1981), p. 112.

10. "a reign of terror": Ronald Steel, *Walter Lippmann and the American Century* (Boston: Atlantic-Little Brown, 1980), p. 167.

10. "dishonored our Constitution": Douglas, *Go East*, p. 121.

11. "a moral disaster": *Newsweek*, Oct. 16, 1972.

13. "good fiction": Raymond Carver, interviewed in *The Paris Review*, Number 88, Summer 1983.

1. BLAME IT ON THE MOON

18. "There is a time": John Dos Passos, *The Best Times* (New American Library, 1966), p. 84.

18. "the only dignity": *The Letters of F. Scott Fitzgerald*, edited by Andrew Turnbull (Dell, 1966), p. 46.

20. "everywhere in my section": Herbert Asbury, *Up From Methodism* (Knopf, 1926), pp. 159–160.

21. "the scarlet career": Ibid., pp. 145–146.

21. "in deference to": Ibid., p. 147.

21. "Nowadays we do not": Lincoln Steffens, letter to Jane Hollister, Dec. 10, 1925, Bancroft Library, University of California, Berkeley.

21. "The only catch": Joel Sayre, letter to Gertrude Sayre, April 7, 1938.

22. "because they knew": Joseph Mitchell to author.

23. "mortal enemy": *Life*, March 14, 1960.

23. "Not long ago": James Thurber, letter to Malcolm Cowley, May 20, 1954 (James Thurber Collection, Ohio State University Library).

23. "the free-lance writer": James Thurber, "Ave Atque Vale," *The Bermudian*, November 1950 (Thurber Collection).

24. "I suppose I incline": *Don't Tread On Me, The Selected Letters of S. J. Perelman*, edited by Prudence Crowther (Viking, 1987), p. 222.

24. "People whose youth": A. J. Liebling, *Between Meals* (Simon and Schuster, 1962), pp. 181–182.

25. "places where you whispered": Dos Passos, *The Best Times*, pp. 37–38

25.–26. Much of the material on speakeasies comes from an unpublished article by Joel Sayre and conversations with Ann Honeycutt.

26. "We weren't lost": *The Selected Letters of James Thurber*, edited by Helen Thurber and Edward Weeks (Atlantic-Little Brown, 1981), p. 121.

26. *Rackety Rax* (Alfred A. Knopf, 1932).

26. "Voltarian masterpiece": *The Times Literary Supplement*, Nov. 25, 1965.

26. *Hizzoner the Mayor* (John Day, 1933).

26. "underground Swift": *The New York Herald Tribune*, Book Review, March 12, 1933.

27. Details on *Gunga Din* are from an unfinished piece by Joel Sayre, mid-1970s. For the script he did extensive research on the history of the Thugs and the worship of Kali.

27. Details from Joel Sayre, *The Persian Gulf Command* (Random House, 1945).

28. Sword of Stalingrad: Joel Sayre, interview with Wendell Shackleford, Feb. 20, 1974.

28.–29. details on Germany from Joel Sayre's articles in *The New Yorker*: "Letter from Germany," May 12, 1945; "Letter from Heidelberg," July 21, 1945; "Letter from Berlin," August 4, 1945; "Letter from Munich," August 11, 1945; and Sayre, *The House*

Without a Roof (Farrar, Straus and Company, 1948); Percy Knauth, *Germany in Defeat* (Knopf, 1946); and Knauth's "Berlin Summer," unpublished manuscript. Knauth was a foreign correspondent for *Time* who travelled with Sayre in Germany.

29. Joel Sayre, "The Man on the Ledge," *The New Yorker*, April 16, 1949; reprinted in *The Aspirin Age*, edited by Isabel Leighton (Simon and Schuster, 1949).

29.–30. "the wandering behemoth": Stanley Walker, *City Editor* (Stokes, 1934), p. 42.

31. "bleak travail": Joel Sayre, letter to Jeannette Lowe, Dec. 1, 1958.

31. "counting my feet": Ibid, May 8, 1956.

31. "You be an ant": Joel Sayre, letter to author, August 2, 1949.

32. "Milton's poetry": T. S. Eliot, *Selected Prose*, edited by John Hayward (Penguin Books, 1953), pp. 123–124.

32. "done damage": Ibid., p. 131.

32. "You don't need to be": *Letters of E. B. White*, collected and edited by Dorothy Lobrano Guth (Harper and Row, 1976), pp. 169–170.

32. map of his heart: collection of Ann Honeycutt.

33. "If Cain makes": James M. Cain, letter to author, March 8, 1973.

34. "cold and soft and horrible": Ibid.

35. "They expect so little": Dorothy Parker, introduction to *The Seal in the Bedroom* (Harper, 1932), p. viii.

35. "general feeling": Edmund Wilson, *Letters on Literature and Politics, 1912–1972*, edited by Elena Wilson (Farrar, Straus, and Giroux, 1977), p. 406.

35. "The little wheels": James Thurber, "Preface to a Life," *My Life and Hard Times*; reprinted in *The Thurber Carnival* (Delta, 1964), p. 174.

35. "The man who falls": *Graham Greene on Film* (Simon and Schuster, 1972), p. 162.

35.–36. a story E. B. White used to tell: I heard this repeated over the years. White also wrote about it in *The New Yorker*'s "Notes and Comment": Sept. 26, 1931; April 7, 1945; July 18, 1953. Also described in Scott Elledge's *E. B. White* (Norton, 1984), p. 161.

2. HANGING GARDENS

38. "A pox": S. J. Perelman, letter to author, April 9, 1968.

38. "It is like": A. J. Liebling, *The Press*, 2d rev. ed. (Ballantine, 1975), p. 522.

38. "We were eager": Ibid., p. 528

38. "a truly alarming condition": Edmund Wilson, *Letters*, p. 410.

39. "Money is something": Gene Fowler, comment for the jacket of Lucius Beebe's *The Big Spenders*, quoted in H. Allen Smith's *The Life and Legend of Gene Fowler* (Morrow, 1977), p. 165.

39. "food, shelter, heat": William Faulkner, quoted in Tom Dardis's *Some Time in the Sun* (Scribner's, 1976), p. 115.

39. "sad in the pocketbook": James M. Cain, "Camera Obscura," *The American Mercury*, October 1933.

39. William Faulkner and Joel Sayre: Joseph Blotner, *Faulkner, A Biography*, 2d rev. ed. (Random House, 1972), pp. 362–363; also Wendell Shackleford interview with JS: Dec. 23, 1973. My father told me that Nunnally Johnson wrote most of *The Road to Glory*, and NJ confirmed it.

39. "Afternoon of a Cow": inscribed "To Joel Sayre/Xmas 1935." In possession of the Brodsky Collection, Center for Faulkner Studies, Southeast Missouri State University. Published in Faulkner, *Uncollected Stories*, edited by Joseph Blotner (Random House, 1979), p. 424 ff.

40. "There is hardly an actor": Cain, "Camera Obscura."

40. Metro-Goldwyn-Merde: Marion Meade, *Dorothy Parker* (Villard Books, 1988), p. 287.

40. "still flailing": Crowther, *Letters of S. J. Perelman*, p. 47.

40. Much of the material on Hollywood comes from remarks made by Joel Sayre.

40. "Please be careful": interview with Joel Sayre, *The Baltimore Sun*, March 19, 1939.

40. *Love Affair*: Pat McGilligan, *Backstory, Interviews With Screenwriters of Hollywood's Golden Age* (Berkeley/Los Angeles: University of California Press, 1986), p. 343.

40. the only kind of "infidelity": Aaron Latham, *Crazy Sundays: F. Scott Fitzgerald in Hollywood* (Viking, 1971), p. 152.

40. "I like restraint": *The New York Times*, June 9, 1935.

40. "Omit the action": Leonard T. Leff and Jerold L. Simmons, *The Dame in the Kimono* (Grove Weidenfeld, 1990), p. 91.

40. "Please eliminate" Gerald Gardner, *The Censorship Papers* (Dodd, Mead, 1987), p. 134.

40. When John Ford was directing: adapted from Joel Sayre, "John Ford, 1895–1973," *The Washington Post*, Sept. 23, 1973.

41. Walter Wanger: Joel Sayre, letter to author, July 27, 1956.

41. "For God's sake": Frances Goodrich and Albert Hackett, conversation with author.

43. "Your godfather's": Joel Sayre, letter to author, Feb. 11, 1956.

44. Much of the material on New York newspapers comes from interviews with Joel Sayre, Nunnally Johnson, and Joseph Mitchell; some details are adapted from Joel Sayre's "Newspaper Town," *New York*, Dec. 30, 1974.

44. "revels de luxe": *The New York Herald Tribune*, August 16, 1924, and Richard Kluger's *The Paper* (Knopf, 1986), pp. 216–217.

45. "A spider": Emily Hahn to author.

46. "iconoclastic young men": Joel Sayre, *The New York Times Book Review*, June 26, 1977.

47. "Up the dark staircase": Nunnally Johnson to author.

48. "the paradise" and "Its hanging gardens": Stanley Walker, *City Editor*, pp. 64 and 51.

3 . CHURCH AND STATE

49. "The only thing": Edmund Wilson, *The Twenties* (Bantam, 1976), p. 114.

49. "All this concern": James Thurber, letter to E. B. White, Oct. 6, 1937 (Thurber Collection).

49. "liberals by acquiescence": Alfred Kazin, *On Native Grounds* (Harcourt, Brace, and World), 1942, pp. 270, 271.

50. "The business of America": Calvin Coolidge in a speech before the Society of American Newspaper Editors, Washington, Jan. 17, 1925.

50. "a world dominated": Edmund Wilson, *The Shores of Light* (Farrar, Straus, and Young), 1952, pp. 493, 498.

50. "a hateful society": "Walker Evans on Himself," *The New Republic*, Nov. 13, 1976.

50. "One couldn't help": Wilson, *The Shores of Light*, p. 498.

50. "jumping out": interview with Evans by Bill Ferris in *Images of the South, Visits With Eudora Welty and Walker Evans*, Southern Folklore Reports, no. 1 (Memphis, Tenn.: Center for Southern Folklore, 1977), p. 35.

51. "the most powerful personal": Walter Lippmann in *The Saturday Review of Literature*, Dec. 11, 1926.

51. "ransom": *The Vintage Mencken*, gathered by Alistair Cooke (Vintage Books, 1956), p. 232.

51. "The plutocracy": *The Vintage Mencken*, p. 176.

51. "a string of wet": H. L. Mencken, *A Carnival of Buncombe: Writings on Politics* (Chicago: University of Chicago Press, 1984), p. 39.

51. "a pathetic mud turtle": Sara Mayfield, *The Constant Circle: H. L. Mencken and His Friends* (Delacorte, 1968), p. 194.

51. "the preposterous Truman": *The Diary of H. L. Mencken*, edited by Charles A. Fecher (Knopf, 1989), p. 389.

51. "a demagogue": *The New Mencken Letters*, edited by Carl Bode (Dial, 1977), p. 396.

51. "a chartered": Justin Kaplan, "Mencken at 100," *The New York Times Book Review*, Sept. 7, 1980.

51. "maneuvered the country": *The Diary of H. L. Mencken*, p. 328.

51. "Roosevelt's itch": Ibid., p. 356.

51. "Obviously, the human race": *New Mencken Letters*, pp. 514–515.

51. "the great failure": Ibid., p. 527.

51. "the good ones": Mencken, *The Baltimore Evening Sun*, July 6, 1925.

51. "the philosopher": Kazin, *On Native Grounds*, p. 200.

51. "The simple truth": Robert Brustein, "The W. C. Fields of American Journalism," *The New York Times Book Review*, Dec. 19, 1976.

52. "the vast majority": Douglas C. Stenerson, *H. L. Mencken: The Iconoclast From Baltimore* (Chicago: University of Chicago Press, 1971), p. 23.

52. "It is high time": *The Vintage Mencken*, p. 229.

52. "unable to make": "H. L. Mencken," by H. L. Mencken, in *One Hundred Years of The Nation* (Macmillan, 1965), *p.* 138.

52. "the great curse": *New Mencken Letters*, p. 514.

52. "the so-called Reds": *The Vintage Mencken*, p. 102.

52. anti-Semite: Since Mencken's diaries were published in 1989, some critics have argued that—despite the references to "kikes" and "low-grade Jews"—he was not really anti-Semitic because he had Jewish friends such as George Jean Nathan and Alfred Knopf. But Charles A. Fecher wrote in his introduction to the *Diaries*, p. xix, "Let it be said at once, clearly and unequivocally, Mencken was an anti-Semite."

52. "My belief": Richard Lingeman, "Prejudices: Last Series," *The Nation*, Feb. 19, 1990.

52. "My motto": *New Mencken Letters*, p. 137.

53. "nothing more than a hangover": Mayfield, *The Constant Circle*, p. 192.

53. "a milch cow": Justin Kaplan, "Mencken at 100," *The New York Times Book Review*, Sept. 7, 1980.

53. Some of the attitudes toward religion were described in Herbert Asbury's *Up From Methodism* (Knopf, 1926).

53. "One of the most irrational" quoted by Edmund Wilson, *The Devils and Canon Barham* (Farrar, Straus, and Giroux, 1973), p. 103.

54. "malicious": Edmund Wilson, *Letters*, p. 496.

54. "By making certain": Heywood Hale Broun, *Whose Little Boy Are You?* (St. Martin's/Marek, 1983), pp. 93, 94.

54. "No sane man": *New Mencken Letters*, pp. 141–142.

55. "how the Vatican": Joel Sayre, letter to Jeannette Lowe, spring 1960.

55. "without question": Edmund Wilson, *The Bit Between My Teeth* (Farrar, Straus, and Giroux, 1965), p. 31.

55. "to speak of politics": Wilson, *The Shores of Light*, p. 435.

55. "The German scheme": *New Mencken Letters*, p. 494.

55. "We never expected": Wilson, *The Devils and Canon Barham*, p. 104.

55. "the greatest invention": *Letters of H. L. Mencken*, selected and annotated by Guy J. Forgue (Knopf, 1961), p. 501.

55. "We were born": F. Scott Fitzgerald, "My Generation," *Esquire*, October 1973.

57. Thurber's two long undated letters to Malcolm Cowley were probably written late in 1934 and early in 1935 (Thurber Collection).

58. "hysterical and": James Thurber, "Voices of Revolution," *The New Republic*, March 25, 1936.

58. "a diversionist Trotskyite": Sam Moore to author.

58. "Next year": Joel Sayre, letter to Gertrude Sayre, April 14, 1938.

59. the FBI kept files: see Herbert Mitgang, *Dangerous Dossiers, Exposing the Secret War Against America's Greatest Authors* (Donald I. Fine, 1988), pp. 20–23, 235; and Natalie Robins, *Alien Ink, The FBI's War on Freedom of Expression* (Morrow, 1992), pp. 442–444, 447.

59. "no obligation": E. B. White, interviewed in *The Paris Review*, Fall 1969.

59. "Security, for me": *Letters of E. B. White*, pp. 285–287.

60. "We grow tyrannical": Ibid., p. 358.

60. "people are daily": Perelman, *Don't Tread on Me*, p. 129.

4. "I AM STILL EXPECTING SOMETHING EXCITING"

62. "Both peace and fighting": quoted in James Thurber's letter to Malcolm Cowley, May 21, 1954 (Thurber Collection).

64. the publisher's advance: Edmund Wilson, *The Forties* (Farrar, Straus, and Giroux, 1983), p. xvi.

65. "Marxism never": Wilson, *Letters*, p. 568.

65. "transformations" and "were really": Wilson, *The Forties*, pp. 10, 16.

65. "He wants to conserve": Ibid., pp. 66–67.

65. "continuity": Edmund Wilson, *A Piece of My Mind* (Farrar, Straus, and Cudahy, 1956), p. 212.

65. "I reflected": Wilson, *The Forties*, p. 289.

66. "panics and depressions": Wilson, *The Twenties*, p. 415.

67. "the passion for": Edmund Wilson, *Europe Without Baedeker* (London: Secker and Warburg, 1948), pp. 21–22. Wilson cut this passage from his revised American edition.

67. "nationalistic propaganda": Wilson, *Letters*, p. 428.

68. a speech of Eisenhower's: Edmund Wilson, *The Fifties* (Farrar, Straus, and Giroux, 1986) p. 263.

68. "Am immersed": Wilson, *Letters*, p. 573.

68. "spending billions": Ibid., p. 621.

68. "an awful feeling": Ibid., p. 506.

68. "the periodical American panic": Edmund Wilson, *The Cold War and the Income Tax* (Farrar, Straus, and Company, 1963), p. 62.

68. "gigantic taxes": Edmund Wilson, *Upstate* (Farrar, Straus, and Giroux, 1971), p. 165.

68. "our pretensions": Wilson, *The Bit Between My Teeth*, p. 504.

68. "Our recent security": Wilson, *A Piece of My Mind*, p. 70.

68. "to take Communism": Wilson, "An Appeal to Progressive," *The New Republic*, Jan. 14, 1931.

69. "the government of oafs": Wilson, *The Fifties*, p. 434.

69. "The Russians emulating": Wilson, *Patriotic Gore*, introduction (Oxford University Press, 1962), p. xxviii.

69. "the general cross-fertilization": Wilson, *The Bit Between My Teeth*, p. 5.

69. "for an American": Ibid., p.3.

69. "several cultures": Ibid.

69. "seemed inaccessible": Ibid., p. 5.

69. "explaining the world": *The Times Literary Supplement*, May 19, 1972.

70. "not moral battles": Wilson, *Letters*, p. 619.

70. "self-justificatory": Ibid., p. 566.

70. "ought, I think": Ibid., p. 567.

70. "train ourselves": Ibid., p. 620.

70. "a vanishing type": Van Wyck Brooks, quoted by Harry Levin, *The Times Literary Supplement*, Oct. 11, 1974.

70. "inhibitions" and "I am much more": Wilson, *Letters*, p. 413.

70. "whole point of view": Wilson, *The Bit Between My Teeth*, p. 2.

70. "the vast academic": Ibid., p. 576.

70. "The sole function": Wilson, *Upstate*, p. 284.

71. "I am fascinated": Wilson to author.

72. "a great ritual": Wilson, *Letters*, p. 607.

73. "As a character": *Upstate*, p. 218.

73. "severe strain" and "Still, we have to": Wilson, *Letters*, pp. 205–206.

5. "A FLASH OF THE MIND"

75. "the swaying sweatbox": John Szarkowski, introduction to *Walker Evans* (The Museum of Modern Art, 1971), p. 18.

76. "a weapon": James Agee and Walker Evans, *Let Us Now Praise Famous Men: Three Tenant Families* (Boston: Houghton Mifflin, 1941), pp. 361–362.

76. drafts for the text: Evans, "People Anonymous" in *Walker Evans at Work*, edited by John T. Hill, Frances Lindley, and Edward Grazda, with an essay by Jerry L. Thompson (Harper and Row, 1982), p. 161.

76. "penitent spy": Evans, "The Unposed Portrait," *Evans at Work*, p. 160.

76. "The thing itself": *Yale Alumni Magazine*, February 1971.

77. "I'm just having": James Stern to author.

77. "I turn away": W. B. Yeats, "Meditations in Time of Civil War" *The Collected Poems of W. B. Yeats* (Macmillan, 1933), p. 204.

78. "an impure thing": James Mellow, "Walker Evans Captures the Unvarnished Truth," *The New York Times*, Dec. 1, 1974.

78. "I am not": "Walker Evans on Himself," *The New Republic*, Nov. 13, 1976.

78."When I was": Ibid.

78. "Nature rather bores": Ibid.

79. "the American novel": John Hohenberg, *The Pulitzer Prizes* (Columbia University Press, 1974), p. 55.

79. "to work against": Leslie Katz, "Interview With Walker Evans," *Art in America*, March–April 1971.

79. "the painterly": taped interview with Evans by Sedat Pakay, June 1968, Museum of Modern Art Archives.

79. "I got a lot": *Yale Alumni Magazine*, February 1971.

79. "I lean": Ibid.

79. "an honest medium": Ibid.

80. "the transcendent": Katz interview.

80. "*the* material": *The New Republic*, Nov. 13, 1976.

80. "I wanted so much": "Talk of the Town," *The New Yorker*, Dec. 24, 1966.

80. "Writing's a very": Katz interview.

80. "the incandescent center": "Walker Evans, Visiting Artist: A Transcript of His Discussion with Students of the University of Michigan," in Beaumont Newhall, *Photography: Essays & Images* (Museum of Modern Art, 1980), p. 315.

81. "the keen historic": *Let Us Now Praise Famous Men*, p. 39.
81. "with a flash": Katz interview.
81. "To be nostalgic": Ibid.
81. "the actuality": *Fortune*, January 1962.
81. "Any venture": *Yale Alumni Magazine*, February 1971.
82. "the street becomes" and "the American vernacular": Katz interview.
82. "slighted": interview, MOMA tape.
82. A former student: the architect William McDonough.
82. "witticism": Hank O'Neal, interview with Walker Evans, Feb. 17, 1975.
82. "I *want*": Jane Mayhall to author.
83. "the torn flower-designs": Walker Evans, "The Wreckers," *Fortune*, May 1951.
83. "ground-leavings": Ibid.
83. "honest" edifice: Katz interview.
83. "the worst thing": "Brother, Can You Spare a Line?", *The Village Voice*, Dec. 2, 1974.
84. "thought (most of the": John Szarkowski, *Walker Evans*, p. 15.
85. "Agee's rebellion": Walker Evans, foreword to new edition of *Let Us Now Praise Famous Men* (Houghton Mifflin, 1960), xii.
85. "kept out": Hank O'Neal interview.
85. "The wonder": Carl Sandburg, prologue to The *Family of Man* (Museum of Modern Art/Maco, 1955).
85. "made no sense . . . rubbish": O'Neal interview.
85. "cheap feelings": Evans used the phrase in his Yale class.
85. an outdoor lunch: Elizabeth Shaw to author.
86. "It was his": Calvert Coggeshall to author.
86. "diffident dandy": James Stern, "Walker Evans (1903–75) A Memoir," *London Magazine*, August/September 1977.
89. when they were young: Paul Grotz to author.

6. DERAILMENTS

90. "flecks of dust": Thurber, *Letters*, p. 31.
90. "That's not a diagnosis": unsent letter to Ernest Hemingway, Jan. 11, 1961 (Thurber Collection).
90. "There is too much": Thurber, *Letters*, p. 187.
91. "golden sparks," "retinal disturbances," and "their glory": Ibid., p. 84.
91. "I am a believer": Ibid., p. 85.
91. "He would go": Ibid., p. 109.
91. "The bundle": Peter DeVries, introduction to Thurber's *Lanterns and Lances* (Time, Inc., 1962).
92. St. Clair McKelway, *The New Yorker*, June 14, 1953, and McKelway, *The Edinburgh Caper* (Holt, Rinehart, and Winston, 1962).
93. Edward Paramore: see *The New York Times*, Feb. 27, 1927, and Edmund Wilson, *The Twenties*.
94. "white with passion": Joel Sayre, letter to Gertrude Sayre, April 7, 1938.
95. "We had vastly": Elliott Nugent, *Events Leading Up to the Comedy* (Trident Press, 1965), p. 71.
95. "head trouble": *Letters of E. B. White*, pp. 245–247.
95. "There isn't anything": Ibid., p. 374.
98. "To get rid": James Boswell, *The Life of Samuel Johnson*, vol. 2, 3d ed. (London: Oxford University Press, 1938), p. 246.

7. ENVOI

104. "a certain satisfaction": Edmund Wilson, *The Fifties*, p. 438.

8. MATURITY

112. "It wouldn't be too bad": J. D. Salinger, *The Catcher in the Rye* (Bantam, 1964), p. 140.

113. "the smelly mess": *The New York Times*, June 6, 1954.

For material on Sigmund Diamond and Henry Kissinger and the FBI, also Harvard's Russian Research Center, see Diamond, *Compromised Campus: The Collaboration of Universities With the Intelligence Community* (Oxford University Press, 1992), chapters 2–6, also chapter 10; Ellen Schrecker, *No Ivory Tower, McCarthyism and the Universities* (Oxford University Press, 1986).

113. "a most friendly and cooperative": Diamond, *Compromised Campus*, p. 147; FBI memo, August 23, 1951.

114. "bartered what they": Diamond, *Compromised Campus*, p. 243.

114. "stood like fortresses": Ellen Schrecker, "Academic Freedom and the Cold War," *The Antioch Review* (Summer 1980), p. 38.

9. TOUCHSTONES

115. "In a desperate effort": Alfred Kazin, *On Native Grounds*, pp. 441–442.

116. "from a definite ethical": T. S. Eliot, "Religion and Literature," in *Selected Prose*, edited by John Hayward (London: Penguin, 1953), p. 32.

116. "The whole of modern": Ibid., p. 41.

116. "any moral or": T. S. Eliot, *After Strange Gods, A Primer of Modern Heresy*, the Page-Barbour Lectures at the University of Virginia (Harcourt, Brace and Co., 1934), p. 39.

116. "the deplorable": Ibid., p. 63.

116. "the benign godfather:" Walter Jackson Bate, "The Crisis in English Studies," *Harvard Magazine*, September–October 1982.

116. "the impelling motive": Ibid.

116. Edwin Honig: conversation with author.

117. "The progress of": Eliot, *Selected Prose*, p. 26.

117. "The more perfect": Ibid., p. 27.

117. "Poetry is not": Ibid., p. 30.

118. "To her": *The Letters of T. S. Eliot, Volume I, 1898–1922*, edited by Valerie Eliot (Harcourt Brace Jovanovich, 1988), p. xvii.

118. "lines . . . a means of talking": Eliot, *On Poetry and Poets* (Faber and Faber, 1957), p. 137.

119. "homogeneous": Eliot, *After Strange Gods*, p. 20.

119. "worm-eaten": Ibid., p. 12.

119. "invaded": Ibid., p. 17.

119. "almost effaced": Ibid., p. 12.

119. "dissatisfied": John Hayward, introduction to Eliot's *Selected Prose*.

120. "variety and complexity": Ibid., pp. 118–119.

120. "the direct approach": John Crowe Ransom, "Glossary of the New Criticism," *Poetry*, February 1951.

121. "distrustful": Henry Adams, *The Education of Henry Adams* (Random House/Modern Library, 1931), p. 56.

122. "a certain young woman": James, preface to *The Portrait of a Lady*, in *The Art of the Novel* (Scribner's, 1934).

122. "talent for life": Henry James, *The Wings of the Dove* (1902; reprint, Modern Library, 1937), p. 193.

10. DOCUMENTARY ONE: THE LOYALTY OATH AT BERKELEY

125. "shooting alma mater": Dixon Wecter, "Commissars of Loyalty," *The Saturday Review of Literature*, May 13, 1950.

125. "I have the impression": *Life*, Oct. 2, 1950.

125. "A harmless oath": Read before the Academic Senate, Northern Section, June 14, 1949; later privately published as a pamphlet: "The Fundamental Issue: Documents and Marginal Notes on the University of California Loyalty Oath."

126. "one case where": Irving David Fox, testimony, House Committee on Un-American Activities, Sept. 27, 1949, 81st Congress, 1st session, 815, 827. Quoted in Schrecker, *No Ivory Tower*, p. 126.

127. "attitude toward Communism": Report to the Academic Senate from the Committee on Privilege and Tenure, Fall 1950.

127. loyalty oath printed in pamphlet, "To Bring You the Facts, A Message for all Officers and Council Members of the Alumni Associations of the University of California."

127. "a political test": Erik Erikson, 1950 statement to the Board of Regents, excerpted in *Harvard Magazine*, November–December 1984.

128. "for membership in": Minutes of a meeting of a Special Committee of the Regents of the University of California and the Advisory Committees of the Academic Senate, Sept. 29, 1949.

128. "the last barrier": minutes from Regents' meeting of April 21, 1950.

128. "I feel sincerely": *The San Francisco Chronicle*, April 22, 1950.

128. "Any Communist": Press release statement, Governor Earl Warren, Feb. 28, 1950.

128. AAUP position on Communists published in the *AAUP Bulletin*, Spring 1949, vol. 35, no. 1.

128. "others will leave": *The San Francisco Chronicle*, March 7, 1950.

129. "If [the University of] California": Ibid.

129. "If we yield": Notes from meeting of Board of Regents, March 31, 1950, quoted in Wecter, "Commissars of Loyalty."

129. "While American youth": *The San Francisco Examiner*, August 1, 1950.

129. "The real question": *The Los Angeles Examiner*, August 24, 1950.

131. "lots of oath cases": George Stewart, in collaboration with other professors of the University of California, *The Year of the Oath* (Doubleday, 1950), p. 68.

131. "misinformation," "whispering campaigns," "slander": Statement from the Academic Assembly (a group of nontenured lecturers, teaching fellows, and research assistants).

131. "morality play": Joseph Adelson, "The Teacher as Model," from *The American College*, edited by Nevitt Sanford (John Wiley, 1962), pp. 416–417.

132. "no evidence": Committee on Privilege and Tenure (Northern Section), Report to the President of the University, June 15, 1950.

132. "All that this famous": *The New York Times*, April 6, 1951.

132. SPROUL URGES: *The Los Angeles Examiner*, June 24, 1950.

132. U.C. Board: *The San Francisco Examiner*, June 24, 1950.

132. U.C. Fires 157: *The Sacramento Bee*, June 24, 1950.

132. Good Riddance: *The Los Angeles Evening Outlook*, June 26, 1950.

132. "the untouchables": *The Los Angeles Examiner*, August 19, 1950.

133. "to be sent": John Caughey, "A University in Jeopardy," *Harper's Magazine*, November 1950.

133. Later Erikson: *The New York Times*, May 13, 1994.

133. The American Psychological Association: Report of the Committee on Academic Freedom, University of California, Sept. 26, 1950.

133. "No conceivable": Carey McWilliams, *Witch Hunt* (Boston: Little, Brown, 1950), p. 113.

134. "the present emergency": David P. Gardner, *The California Oath Controversy*, (Berkeley and Los Angeles: University of California Press, 1967), p. 219.

134. "even worse": letter from Tolman to Benjamin Fine of *The New York Times*, in files of the Group for Academic Freedom, University Archives, University of California, Berkeley.

134. the Levering oath: Loyalty Oath Archives, Bancroft Library, University of California at Berkeley.

134. "defend the Constitution": Ibid.

11. HIGH AND LOW

137. quotes from Lane Coutell: J. D. Salinger, *Franny and Zooey* (Bantam Books, 1964), pp. 11–15.

137. "I didn't want": *Franny and Zooey*, p. 58.

137. "a *real* poet": Ibid., p. 19.

138. "confused and frightened": Salinger, *The Catcher in the Rye*, p. 289.

138. "a finger in": Salinger, *Raise High the Roof Beam, Carpenters and Seymour: An Introduction* (Bantam Books, 1965), p. 9.

138. "who always clap": *The Catcher in the Rye*, p. 84.

138. "emotional recall": Elia Kazan, *A Life* (Knopf, 1988), pp. 143–144.

139. "a tepid, flaccid": Dwight Macdonald, "A Theory of Mass Culture," *Diogenes*, Summer 1953.

139. "a dangerous opponent": Macdonald, "Masscult and Midcult," reprinted in *Against the American Grain* (Random House, 1962), p. 51.

139. "become a debased": Ibid.

140. "The successive": James Gould Cozzens, quoted in *Against the American Grain*, p. 202.

140. "the failure of": Ibid., p. 207.

140. Macdonald on *Life*: Ibid., pp. 12–13.

141. "pervasive and disturbing:" Robert Warshow, *The Immediate Experience* (Doubleday, 1962), p. 24.

141. "I hope": Ibid., p. 28.

12. DELIVER ME FROM THE DAYS OF OLD

142. reviving the trappings: *The New York Times*, May 17, 1971.

144. "the most brutal": Steve Chapple and Reebee Garofalo, *Rock 'n' Roll is Here to Pay, The History and Politics of the Music Industry* (Chicago: Nelson/Hall, 1977), p. 46.

145. "something artificial" and subsequent quotes: Dwight Macdonald, "A Caste, a Culture, a Market," *The New Yorker*, Nov. 22 and 29, 1958.

146. "not merely" and subsequent quotes: Elizabeth Hardwick, "Riesman Considered," in *A View of My Own* (Farrar, Straus, and Cudahy, 1962), pp. 132–133.

146. "the professional liberal's": Norman Mailer, *Advertisements For Myself* (Signet, 1960), p. 173.

146. "girl students": David Riesman, *Individualism Reconsidered* (Glencoe, Ill.: The Free Press, 1954), p. 22.

147. Quotes from conference of the American Sociological Association: *The New York Times*, Sept. 25, 1965.

148. "The Negro is": Max Lerner, *Partisan Review*, September–October 1952.
149. "geographic representation": *Radcliffe Quarterly*, September 1986, and *Harvard Magazine*, September–October 1986.

13. SPIDERS' THREADS

152. "trapped in": Mailer, "The White Negro," *Dissent*, Summer 1957.
152. "I only know": *The Beast in the Jungle* in *The Great Short Novels of Henry James* (Dial, 1944), p. 772.
153. The translations of Sartre are largely my own.
154. "a toothless life": Jean-Paul Sartre, *L'Âge de Raison* (Paris: Gallimard, 1945), p. 191.
154. "No, I'm not": Sartre, *Théâtre, Les Mouches* (Paris: Gallimard, 1947), p. 21.
155. "You are going": *Les Mouches*, p. 102.
156. "Look but into": Thomas Middleton and William Rowley, *The Changeling* (1653) (London: T. Fisher Unwin, n.d.), p. 131.

14. DOCUMENTARY TWO: THE AUTHERINE LUCY CASE

157. "a new Klan": *The Birmingham Post-Herald*, Feb. 11, 1956.
158. "flogging while masked": Patsy Sims, *The Klan* (Stein and Day, 1978), p. 144.
158. "I pledge": *The New York Times*, Feb. 18, 1956.
158. "the most widely segregated": James A. Colaiaco, *Martin Luther King, Jr.* (St. Martin's, 1988), p. 54.
158. "working relationship": Sims, *The Klan*, p. 143.
158. "to open the": Juan Williams with the *Eyes on the Prize* Production Team, *Eyes on the Prize* (Penguin, 1987), p. 38.
159. "not bad people": Earl Warren, *The Memoirs of Earl Warren* (Doubleday, 1977), p. 291.
159. "that a Negro": Arthur Larson, *Eisenhower, The President Nobody Knew* (Scribner's, 1968), p. 127.
159. "Whenever and wherever": Tom Brady, quoted in John Barlow Martin, *The Deep South Says Never* (Ballantine, 1957), p. 16.
159. "If the blood": Ibid., p. 24.
159. "showed two dainty": A. J. Liebling, *The Earl of Louisiana* (Simon and Schuster, 1961), p. 177.
160. "the economic lynch law": *The New York Times*, Feb. 1, 1956.
160. "conduct and marital record": *The New York Times*, Feb. 1, 1956.
160. "it was my task": Autherine Lucy Foster to author.
161. "fashionable": *The Birmingham Post-Herald*, February 1956.
161. "it might endanger": *The New York Times*, Feb. 12, 1956.
161. Autherine Lucy "fact sheet": all quotes from the Inc-Fund files on the Autherine Lucy case, drawn up in the fall of 1956 (no exact date).
162. "came in a": *The Birmingham News*, March 1, 1956.
162. "Race relations": *The New York Times Magazine*, Feb. 26, 1956.
162. "the controversial": *Newsweek*, Feb. 27, 1956.
163. "Make them roll": Anne Mitchell, *Keep 'Bama White*, thesis for an M.A. in history, Georgia Southern College, June 1971, p. 52.
163. "a greeting": J. Jefferson Bennett, "Autherine Lucy," manuscript/lecture.
163. "Let's *kill*": Autherine Lucy Foster to author.
163. "I asked the Lord": Ibid.
164. "for her own safety": *Newsweek*, March 12, 1956.
164. "Well, we won": *The Birmingham News*, Feb. 7, 1956.
164. "Yesterday was": *The Birmingham Post-Herald*, Feb. 7, 1956.

164. "We will control": Ibid.

164. "because they know": *The New York Times*, Feb. 18, 1956.

165. "vigorous": *The New York Times*, Feb. 13, 1956.

165. "the prompt attention": Feb. 1956, clipping in the Autherine Lucy files in the Alabama Room, University of Alabama at Tuscaloosa.

165. "for a gradual": *The Birmingham Post-Herald*, Feb. 13, 1956.

165. "nonsense . . . Mr. Stevenson": AP wire service, n.d.

165. "deplored . . . interference": *The Birmingham World*, Feb. 10, 1956.

165. "Now let's don't": presidential press conference, March 21, 1956.

166. "Mama, Lord have": *Eyes on the Prize*, p. 48.

166. "Because the stones": Arnold Rampersad, *The Life of Langston Hughes*, vol. 2 (Oxford University Press, 1988), p. 270.

166. "If that girl dies": Russell Warren Howe, "A Talk with William Faulkner," *The Sunday Times* (London), March 4, 1956, and *The Reporter*, March 22, 1956.

167. "the attempt": Faulkner, letter to the editor of *Life*, quoted in Blotner, *Faulkner*, p. 1598.

167. "To live anywhere": William Faulkner, "On Fear: the South in Labor," *Harper's Magazine*, June 1956.

167. "go slow": Faulkner, "A Letter to the North," *Life*, March 5, 1956.

167. "The Negroes are": Howe, "A Talk with William Faulkner."

167. "if it came": Ibid.

167. "foolish . . . dangerous": Faulkner, statement to press, quoted in Blotner, *Faulkner*, p. 1599.

167. "Maybe he was": Rampersad, *The Life of Langston Hughes*, p. 359.

167. "abolish": Faulkner, letter to *Crimson-White* (the University of Alabama student newspaper), March 8, 1956, published June 9, 1963.

167. "stay on top": Ibid.

167. "who believe in individual freedom": Ibid.

167. "Racial discrimination": C. Vann Woodward, *The Strange Career of Jim Crow* (Oxford University Press, 1966), p. 132.

167. "mob rule": *The Birmingham Post-Herald* (undated clip).

168. "genuine freedom": *The New York Times*, March 9, 1956.

168. "despising . . . to embrace": *The New York Times*, March 8, 1956.

168. "Miss Lucy knows": Ibid.

168. "punished": legal brief of the NAACP Legal Defense and Educational Fund Inc., folders 1328–1344, New York.

168. "nigger-lovers": Bennett, "Autherine Lucy."

168. "for libelous allegations": Ibid.

169. "segregation within" and subsequent quotes: Autherine Lucy Foster to author.

169. "racial suicide": *The Birmingham Post-Herald*, Feb. 11, 1956.

169. "directed or controlled": *Time*, March 12, 1956.

169. "the Negro that": *The Tuscaloosa News*, March 21, 1956.

170. "are wanted": *The Birmingham Post-Herald*, March 1, 1956.

170. "most white": Ibid.

171. "interference": *The New York Times*, Feb. 26, 1956.

Postscript: In 1988 the Board overturned Autherine Lucy Foster's expulsion and she reenrolled at the University in 1989. She graduated with an M.A. in education in 1992, along with her daughter Grazia Foster. Ten per cent of her fellow students were black. During the commencement ceremonies, she received a standing ovation, and the university established an endowed scholarship in her name (*The New York Times*, April 26, 1992, and E. Culpepper Clark, *The Schoolhouse Door* [Oxford University Press, 1993], p. 260).

15. RAPTURE UNWRAPPED

173. "bad orgasm": Norman Mailer, "The White Negro," *Dissent*, Summer 1957.

16. EXCAVATIONS

179. "ordinary unhappiness": Sigmund Freud, *Studies in Hysteria* (1893–95). Standard Edition, vol. 2 (London: Hogarth Press, 1955), p. 305.

181. "You just call": Salinger, "Zooey," *The New Yorker*, May 4, 1957; reprinted in *Franny and Zooey*, p. 108.

17. ON THE BALCONY

184. "Why can't I": *The Journals of Sylvia Plath* (Dial, 1982), p. 38.

185. "American men seem": David Riesman, quoted by Elizabeth Hardwick in *A View of My Own*, p. 128.

187. "the woman of America raped": Philip Wylie, *Generation of Vipers* (Rinehart, 1942), pp. 200, 215.

187. "all mature childless women": Maryania Farnham and Ferdinand Lundberg, *Modern Woman: The Lost Sex* (Harper, 1947), pp. 364–365.

187. "when they came to perform": Ibid, p. 245.

188. "a symbol of horror": Stephen Salisbury, "In Dr. Freud's Collection, Objects of Desire," *The New York Times*, Sept. 3, 1989.

192. national statistics on marriage: Eric Foner and John A. Garraty, editors, *The Reader's Companion to American History* (Boston: Houghton Mifflin, 1991), p. 701.

193. twenty-two million women: *Life*, Dec. 24, 1956.

193. "Household skills": Ibid.

18. THE POETS' THEATRE AND THE BEATS

198. The reviewers: Daniel Ellsberg, *The Harvard Crimson*, March 1, 1951.

198. "symbolic beanfests": William Alfred to author.

199. "They fought": Ibid.

200. "with a very wet": Felicia Lamport to author.

203. "a great": Allen Ginsberg, introduction to Gregory Corso, *Gasoline* (San Francisco: City Lights Books, 1958), p. 7.

205. "spontanous bop": Allen Ginsberg, dedication to *Howl and Other Poems* (San Francisco: City Lights Books), 1956.

206. "I knew, I knew": Jack Kerouac, *On the Road* (Viking, 1957), p. 123.

206. "All life is": Ann Charters, *Kerouac, A Biography* (San Francisco: Straight Arrow Books, 1973), p. 199.

207. "who jumped off": Ginsberg, *Howl*, pp. 14, 15.

207. "I like too many": Kerouac, *On the Road*, p. 104.

207. "writing in accordance": Kerouac, "The Essentials of Spontaneous Prose," quoted in John Tytell, *Naked Angels: The Lives and Literature of the Beat Generation* (McGraw-Hill, 1976), p. 142.

207. "the wild yea-saying": Kerouac, *On the Road*, p. 11.

208. "the happy, true-hearted": Ibid., p. 149.

208. "It is better": Nelson Algren, quoted in Kenneth Rexroth, "Disengagement: The Art of the Beat Generation," reprinted in *The Beat Generation and the Angry Young Men*, edited by Gene Feldman and Max Gartenberg (Dell, 1959), p. 360.

209. Quotes from John Clellon Holmes memorial, October 12, 1988.

209. "a common enemy" and other quotes: Seymour Krim to author.

210. "So in America": Kerouac, *On the Road*, p. 253.

19. DOCUMENTARY THREE: INVADING *THE NEW YORK TIMES*

211. Material on and quotes from Harvey Matusow, *False Witness* (Cameron & Kahn, 1955).

211. "every one": *The New York Times*, Sept. 20, 1981.

212. "pressure brought": Hearings, Subcommittee to investigate the administration of the Internal Security Act and other internal security laws, 84th Congress, 1st sess., Feb. 21, 1955 (Washington, D.C,: U.S. Government Printing Office, 1955).

212. "an entertaining" and "For Whom the Boom": *Time*, March 14, 1955.

213. "Harvey Matusow's brain": Nicholas Von Hoffman, *Citizen Cohn* (Doubleday, 1988), p. 90.

213. "irresponsible public": Albert Kahn, *The Matusow Affair* (Mount Kisco, N.Y.: Meyer Bell Limited, 1987), pp. 302–303.

213. "pregnant with": "Strategy and Tactics of World Communism," Hearings, U.S. Judiciary Committee (Senate), 84th Congress, 2d sess., p. 370.

213. "fear, greed": Ibid., p. 257.

213. "part of a concerted": "*The Nation* and Mr. Brownell," *The Nation*, July 23, 1955.

213. "was prosecuted": Carey McWilliams, *The Education of Carey McWilliams* (Simon and Schuster, 1979), p. 189.

213. "well over a hundred": Matusow, *False Witness*, p. 155.

213. "and we would both": Ibid.

213. "Communist influence": Turner Catledge, *My Life and The Times* (Harper & Row, 1971), p. 228.

213. Material on the Matusow affidavit in "Strategy and Tactics of World Communism." See also Catledge, *My Life and The Times*, pp. 229–230, and James Aronson, *The Press and the Cold War* (Bobbs-Merrill, 1970), pp. 129–130.

214. "A former editor": Catledge, *My Life and The Times*, p. 230.

214. "fell into": Eastland subcommittee's report on Matusow's reversals, released Dec. 30, 1955, quoted in Aronson, *The Press and the Cold War*, p. 130.

214. "moderately conservative": quoted in *The New York Times*, Jan. 8, 1956.

215. Krock on "pinkos": Harrison Salisbury, *Without Fear or Favor* (Times Books, 1980), p. 469.

215. COMINFIL: FBI File No. 100–113352.

215. "Number one pro-Communist": Ibid. All subsequent quotes are from the same file. Many of the page numbers are illegible, except where noted.

215. Security Index: FBI "CONFIDENTIAL" memo, no date, pp. 10 and 11.

215. "against the orders": Letter to Director from SAC, New York, May 2, 1955.

215. "a campus Red": Ibid., p. 5.

215. "subjects of": FBI memo from D. M. Ladd, July 23, 1953.

215. "Latvian": File 100–113352.

215. "sympathetic toward": Ibid.

215. "a renegade": *The New York Times*, March 27, 1955.

216. close ties with the FBI: Salisbury, *Without Fear or Favor*, p. 473.

216. "The Negro race": *Time*, March 26, 1956.

216. "an illegal": Neil R. McMillen, *The Citizens' Council: Organized Resistance to the Second Reconstruction 1954–1964* (Urbana: University of Illinois Press, 1971), p. 117.

216. "pro-Communist": Robert Sherrill, *Gothic Politics in the Deep South* (Grossman, 1968), p. 187.

216. "every step": *Time*, March 26, 1956.

216. "protect and maintain": Ibid.

216. "the uptown": Ibid.

216. "due largely": McMillen, *The Citizens' Council*, p. 219.

216. "a symbol of racism": *Time*, March 26, 1956.

216. "the nation's most": Sherrill, *Gothic Politics*, p. 187.

217. "a Jewish": Catledge, *My Life and The Times*, p. 214.

217. "slanted": *The New York Times*, March 23, 1956.

218. "As an organized": Murray Kempton, *The New York Post*, March 9, 1955; reprinted in *America Comes of Middle Age* (Boston: Little, Brown, 1963), p. 324.

218. "techniques" and "trials rested": Ibid., p. 325.

219. "answering": Philip Dunne, "The Constitution Up Close and Personal," *Constitution*, Fall 1992.

220. Senate Internal Security Subcommittee/Senate Judiciary Committee, "Inquiry Into Communist Party Influence in the Press," Dec. 5, 1955, and Jan. 3–5, 1956.

220. Clayton Knowles and the FBI: Section 7, Internal Security, 1956 Report, "Communists in Mass Communications and in Political Activity," Dec. 31, 1956, p. 106.

221. even Arthur Krock: "In the Nation," *The New York Times*, July 5, 1955.

221. "We do not propose": *The New York Times*, Jan. 5, 1956.

222. "a non-specific": Alden Whitman to author.

222. "Communist slant": Aronson, *The Press and the Cold War*, p. 152.

20. CODA

224. "The Luckiest Generation": *Life*, Jan. 4, 1954.

230. "It wouldn't have": *The Great Short Novels of Henry James*, p. 778.

230. "It used to be": Warren Miller, *The Way We Live Now* (Boston: Little, Brown, 1958), p. 64.

231. "I am afraid": *The Journals of Sylvia Plath*, p. 260.

21. SNAKES OR TIGERS

235. "outstanding": Hearings on "Communist Infiltration of the Motion Picture Industry," House Committee on Un-American Activities, 80th Congress, 1st sess., p. 237.

236. "stumbled over": Malcolm Cowley, *The Dream of the Golden Mountains* (Viking, 1980), p. 252.

237. "Soviet pressure": X [George Kennan], "The Sources of Soviet Conduct," *Foreign Affairs*, July 1947.

238. "a strategic monstrosity": *Walter Lippmann and the American Century*, p. 444.

238. "a growing": Ibid., p. 428.

238. "scare the hell": David Caute, *The Great Fear: The Anti-Communist Purge Under Truman and Eisenhower* (Simon and Schuster, 1978), p. 30.

239. "the Communist Party": Ibid., p. 19.

239. "should take the Communist smear": Marquis Childs, *The New York Post*, April 20, 1947.

239. "Either Communism": William Martin, *A Prophet With Honor: The Billy Graham Story* (Morrow, 1991), p. 165.

240. "the death of the soul": John Barlow Martin, *Adlai Stevenson of Illinois* (Anchor Press/Doubleday, 1977), p. 655.

240. "made light": Ibid.

240. "total conquest": *Major Campaign Speeches of Adlai Stevenson 1952* (Random House, 1953), p. 262.

240. "an hysterical": Martin, *Adlai Stevenson*, I. p. 481.

240. Stevenson and the FBI reports, and firing of state employees: Sigmund Diamond, *Compromised Campus*, pp. 244–246, 265–266.

240. "magnificent" and "catching": *Major Campaign Speeches*, p. 217.

241. "Being on": Harold Clurman to author.

241. "political stances": Nathan Glazer, "New York Intellectuals—Up From Revolution," *The New York Times Book Review*, Feb. 26, 1984.

241. "Who that calls himself": Leslie Fiedler, *An End to Innocence* (Boston: Beacon Press, 1955), p. 23.

241. "illusions" and "complicity": Ibid.

241. "the blatant ghettos": Ibid., p. 142.

241. "those who believe": Ibid., p. 68.

241. "Fiedler's line": Harold Rosenberg, "Couch Liberalism and the Guilty Past," in *The Tradition of the New* (London: Thames and Hudson, 1962), p. 229.

241. "who sincerely": Whittaker Chambers, *Witness* (Random House, 1952), p. 472.

241. "For men who": Ibid., p. 473.

242. "an unconscious": Richard J. Walton, *Henry Wallace, Harry Truman, and the Cold War* (Viking, 1976), p. 221.

242. "In the United States": Lionel Trilling, *The Liberal Imagination* (Doubleday, 1953), p. vii.

243. "the two M's": William Barrett, *The Truants* (Anchor Press/Doubleday, 1982), p. 11.

243. "were attacking": Ibid., p. 8.

243. "a seedy": Ibid., p. 94.

243. "a conspiracy": Daniel Bell, *The End of Ideology*, rev. ed. (Glencoe, Ill.: The Free Press, 1962), p. 123.

243. "were stained with": Irving Kristol, "Civil Liberties—A Study in Confusion," *Commentary*, March 1952.

243. "a liberal must": Schlesinger, "Liberals, Stalinists, and HUAC," *The New Leader*, Dec. 15, 1980.

243. "to protest": Philip Dunne, *Take Two, A Life in Movies and Politics* (McGraw-Hill, 1980), p. 193.

244. " 'Those goddam": Barrett, *The Truants*, pp. 78–79.

244. "those ready to": Murray Kempton, "Dishonoring *Partisan Review*," *Grand Street*, Summer 1982.

244. "essentially identical": Hannah Arendt, *The Origins of Totalitarianism* (Harcourt Brace, 1951), pp. 221, 429.

244. "an era when": *The New York Times*, June 27, 1950.

244. "to expose": American Committee for Cultural Freedom executive committee minutes, April 16, 1952, quoted in Mary Sperling McAuliffe's *Crisis on the Left: Cold War Politics and American Liberals, 1947–1954* (Amherst: University of Massachusetts Press, 1978), p. 116.

245. "the anti-Communist": Christopher Lasch, *The Agony of the American Left* (Knopf, 1969), p. 93.

245. "free thinker": *The Sunday Times*, May 14, 1967.

245. "cultural freedom": Lasch, *The Agony of the American Left*, p. 104.

245. "most writers": *Partisan Review*, May–June 1952.

245. "simply sterile": Ibid.

245. "national self-congratulation": Richard Hofstader, *The American Political Tradition* (Knopf, 1948), p. xi.

246. "seemed odd . . . should have felt": Dwight Macdonald, *Discriminations* (Grossman/Viking, 1974), p. 58.

246. "the herd": Harold Rosenberg, *Commentary*, September 1949.

246. "was divinely": W. A. Swanberg, *Luce and His Empire* (Dell, 1973), p. 403.

247. "the 'red hot' ": Richard Nixon, "Lessons on the Alger Hiss Case," *The New York Times*, Jan. 8, 1986.

247. "amateur ornithologists": Chambers, *Witness*, p. 564.

247. "advances": Allen Weinstein, *Perjury: The Hiss-Chambers Case* (Knopf, 1978), pp. 582–583. Source: C. Vann Woodward's May 1, 1959, notes, which became a memo on his meeting with Hiss.

247. "perhaps my closest": from a newsreel excerpt in *The Trials of Alger Hiss*, documentary produced, written, and directed by John Lowenthal, 1980.

248. "a striking representative": Nixon, *The New York Times*, Jan. 8, 1986.

248. "conclusive proof": quoted in I. F. Stone, "The 'Flimflam' in the Pumpkin Papers," *The New York Times*, April 1, 1976.

249. "Nixon would be": A. J. Liebling, *The Press*, 2d rev. ed. (Ballantine Books, 1975), p. 215.

249. "branded": *The New York Post*, March 21, 1950; quoted in Alger Hiss, *In the Court of Public Opinion* (Knopf, 1957), pp. 289–290.

249. "be kept quiet": FBI file, quoted in Curt Gentry, *J. Edgar Hoover, The Man and the Secrets* (Norton, 1991), p. 366.

250. "save": Chambers, *Witness*, p. 618.

250. "reversed . . . was actively": Ibid., p. 87.

250. "torn from . . ." "editorial bias.": Swanberg, *Luce*, pp. 317–318.

250. truth didn't matter: Dorothy Sterling, "Letters to the Editor," *The New York Times*, Feb. 28, 1984.

250. "as the one dangerous witness": Chambers, *Witness*, p. 721.

250. "God's purpose": Ibid., p. 769.

250. "I cannot really be": Ibid., p. 479.

250. "destroying": Ibid., p. 715.

250. "to every crime": Ibid., p. 762.

252. "it would be impossible": FBI laboratory report (CNX83), July 21, 1949, quoted in William Reuben, *Footnote on an Historic Case, In Re Alger Hiss*, No. 78 Civ. 3433, A Publication of The Nation Institute, 1983, p. 64.

252. "The Hiss case": Richard Nixon, *Six Crises* (Pyramid, 1968), p. 74.

252. "gave agencies": William O. Douglas, *Go East, Young Man*, p. 380.

252. "Forty-four months": Tony Hiss, *Laughing Last* (Boston: Houghton Mifflin, 1977), p. 3.

22. ASSAULTING THE LEFT

253. "the idea that": Diana Trilling, *The New Leader*, August 25, 1952.

254. "a certain incapacity": Fiedler, *An End to Innocence*, pp. 34–35.

254. "no 'responsible official' ": Sidney Lens and George Ott, "The Wrong Debate: America Is Losing The Real War," *The Progressive*, October 1979.

254. "People on both sides": George Kennan, "Flashbacks," *The New Yorker*, Feb. 25, 1985.

254. "It's a lot better": *The New York Times*, Feb. 9, 1953.

255. "American foreign": John Kenneth Galbraith, *A Life in Our Times* (Boston: Houghton Mifflin, 1981), p. 328.

255. "revolutions of": Arnold Toynbee, quoted in a letter from Professor Edward Pessen, *The New York Times*, April 23, 1989.

255. U.S. intelligence agencies recruiting Nazi war criminals: *Hotel Terminus*, directed by Marcel Ophuls, 1988; Christopher Simpson, *Blowback: America's Recruitment of Nazis and its Effects on the Cold War* (Weidenfeld and Nicholson, 1988); *The New York Times*, August 17, 1983, and June 28, 1985.

256. "confessions" and material on American POWs in Korea: Phillip Knightley, *The*

First Casualty: From Crimea to Vietnam: The War Correspondent as Hero, Propagandist, and Myth Maker (Harcourt Brace Jovanovich, 1975), p. 351.

256. Material on the CIA and drugs comes from *The New York Times* and John Marks, *The Search for the 'Manchurian Candidate,' the CIA and Mind Control* (McGraw-Hill, 1980). *The Times'* coverage of the hearings held jointly by the Senate Select Committee on Intelligence and the Subcommittee on Health and Scientific Research ran from August through October 1977, although earlier hearings were also held in 1975.

256. "unwitting": *The New York Times*, August 1, 1977.

257. "Often Chickwit": Ibid., August 4, 1977.

257. "adverse publicity" and "wrongful death": the cases of Blauer and Olson described in *The New York Times*, August 13, 1975, and May 6, 1987.

257. "triggered": Ibid., July 12, 1975, and Marks, *Search*, p. 83.

257. "sense of mission" and "patriotic vision": Marks, *Search*, pp. 28, 32.

258. "field laboratory," "safehouse," "Operation Midnight Climax": *The New York Times*, August 4, 1977; Marks, p. 99.

258. "urgent need": *The New York Times*, August 1, 1977.

258. "behavior modification": Marks, p. 177.

258. "psychic driving": *The New York Times*, Jan. 28, 1984, Oct. 6, 1988, and Nov. 18, 1992; Marks, *Search*, pp. 136–137.

258. "controlled production" and "subvert his": *The New York Times*, August 1, 1977.

258. "simulated schizophrenia": *New York Times*, August 3, 1976. "Stress-producing": Marks, *Search*, p. 150.

259. "Communist-inspired scare": *The New York Times*, May 13, 1979.

259. The families of those who died of leukemia after living near atomic test sites in Nevada began to receive apologies and promises of money from the Radiation Exposure Compensation Act in the Nineties. Commenting on the cancer deaths of Navajo miners in Arizona, who were employed by the government to gather uranium for atomic bombs, *The New York Times* noted on May 3, 1993, that "the greatest irony of the cold war was that the principal victims of the United States' development of a nuclear arsenal were Americans, not Russians."

259. *"Ferdinand"*: obituary of Munro Leaf, *The New York Times*, Dec. 22, 1976.

259. headlines quoted in Edwin R. Bayley's *Joe McCarthy and the Press* (Madison: University of Wisconsin Press, 1981), p. 64.

260. "Putting quotation": James Reston, *Deadline: A Memoir* (Random House, 1991), p. 216.

260. "a prolonged attack": William McCann, "Red Scare," *The Progressive*, November 1981.

260. "The reading public": "Fort Monmouth Case," *The New York Times*, Jan. 14, 1954.

260. "To many people": Richard Rovere, *Senator Joe McCarthy*, p. 166.

261. "keep [the public] confused": May 27, 1953, diary of Gordon Dean, Chairman of the Atomic Energy Commission, vol. 1 of *Health Effects of Low-Level Radiation*, a Congressional hearing in Salt Lake City, April 19, 1979. See also Peter Pringle and James Spigelman, *The Nuclear Barons* (Holt, Rinehart, and Winston, 1981).

261. "that cursed Aesopian": Cedric Belfrage, *The American Inquisition* (Indianapolis: Bobbs-Merrill, 1973), p. 106n.

261. "a terrific guy": Robert Vaughn, *Only Victims* (Putnam's, 1972), p. 194.

262. "were not plotting": Nat Hentoff, *The First Freedom: The Tumultuous History of Free Speech in America* (Dell, 1981), p. 144.

262. "superhuman": Jack Warner's testimony, hearings on "Communism in Motion Picture Industry," Oct. 20, 1947, p. 15.

262. "cryptanalysis": *New Times*, June 12, 1978.

262. "Ten thousand agents": Associated Press, April 4, 1954.

263. "would have been ridiculed": Proceedings and Debates of the 83d Congress, 1st session, Appendix, vol. 99 (3 Jan. 1953–23 March 1953), pp. 169–171.

264. "might be construed": *The New York Times*, June 26, 1975.

264. "downright socialistic": *The Nation*, Oct. 30, 1954.

264. "Red agitators": Richard Gid Powers, *Secrecy and Power:The Life of J. Edgar Hoover* (The Free Press, 1987), p. 72.

265. "so-called Reds": *The Vintage Mencken*, p. 102.

265. "Agents quietly": *The New York Times*, Jan. 3, 1920.

265. "There could be": Frank Donner, *The Age of Survelliance* (Knopf, 1980), p. 20.

265. "alien filth" and "misshapen cast": Ibid.

265. "the continued violation": Curt Gentry, *J. Edgar Hoover: The Man and the Secrets* (Norton, 1991), p. 98.

265. "gigantic and cruel": Athan Theoharis and John Stuart Cox, *The Boss: J. Edgar Hoover and the American Inquisition* (Philadelphia: Temple University Press, 1988), p. 67.

265. "the lawless acts": Ibid., p. 70.

266. Material on the ACLU and the FBI: *The New York Times*, August 4, 1977; Harrison E. Salisbury, "The Strange Correspondence of Morris Ernst and J. Edgar Hoover," *The Nation*, Dec. 1, 1984; Gentry, *Hoover: The Man*, pp. 233–237, 386–387, and 438–440; *Rights*, September–October 1977, July–August 1989.

266. "nothing but a front": Donner, *The Age of Survelliance*, pp. 144–145.

266. "You are a grand guy": Salisbury, "The Strange Correspondence."

266. "the reactionary": Manning Marable, *W.E.B. Du Bois: Black Radical Democrat* (Boston: Twayne, 1986), p. 175.

267. "one of the most dangerous": Duberman, *Paul Robeson*, p. 433.

267. "Negro pornographic" and "alleged poet": Robins, *Alien Ink*, pp. 63, 64, 283.

267. "warm manure": Rampersad, *The Life of Langston Hughes*, p. 220.

267. "During concert tours": Duberman, *Paul Robeson*, p. 434.

267. "If someone insists": Carey McWilliams, *Witch Hunt* (Boston: Little, Brown, 1950), p. 141.

23. WITHSTANDING THE RIGHT

269. "Comrade Attlee": *The New York Times*, May 15, 1953.

269. "dangerous or potentially": Theoharis and Cox, *The Boss*, p. 174.

269. the Security Index: originally called the Custodial Detention Program.

270. "formal or informal" and other qualifications for the Security Index: Donner, *The Age of Surveillance*, p. 164.

270. the FBI reported: Robert Justin Goldstein, "Internment Camp for Citizens, The FBI's Forty-Year Plot," *The Nation*, July 1, 1978; Theoharis, *The Boss*, pp. 172–174.

270. "whose arrest . . . believed to be . . . particularly active": Gary Wills, "File it Under 'Vicious,'" *The New York Post*, Nov. 21, 1978, and Donner, *The Age of Surveillance*, pp. 163–164.

271. "the U.S. government": Cedric Belfrage, "On Political Exile," *The Progressive*, August 1977.

271. "filled with": Steve Nelson, James R. Barrett, Rob Ruck, *Steve Nelson, American Radical* (Pittsburgh: University of Pittsburgh Press, 1981), p. 331.

272. "Let me have a . . .": Erwin Knoll, "But Not Forgotten," *The Progressive*, October 1986.

273. At the University of Michigan: Arthur Miller, *Timebends* (Grove Press, 1987), p. 227.

273. "a non-Communist": *The New York Times*, March 26, 1976.

273. Hoover's letter: H. H. Wilson to author.

273. "to investigate links"; Rovere, *Senator Joe McCarthy*, p. 154.

273. "I would not": Taylor Branch, "Closets of Power," *Harper's Magazine*, October 1982.

273. "one sex pervert": Committee on Expenditures in Executive Departments, "Employment of Homosexuals and Other Sex Perverts in Government," U.S. Senate, 81st Congress, 2d sess., Washington, D.C., 1950, pp. 3–5.

274. FBI using homosexuals as informers: Gentry, *Hoover: The Man*, pp. 412–413.

274. "to elevate": Bayley, *Joe McCarthy and the Press*, pp. 161–162.

274. "I might also": Ibid., p. 163.

274. "The cycle of": "The Feverish Fifties," Brooks Egerton, *The Progressive*, May 1985.

274. "well-known as": *The Secret Files of J. Edgar Hoover*, edited with commentary by Athan Theoharis (Chicago: Ivan R. Dee 1991), pp. 283–297; Theoharis, "How the FBI Gaybaited Stevenson," *The Nation*, May 7, 1990; Martin, *Adlai Stevenson of Illinois*, pp. 646–647; Gentry, *Hoover: The Man*, pp. 402–403.

274. seventeen hundred: John D'Emilio, *Sexual Politics, Sexual Communities: The Making of a Homosexual Minority in the United States, 1940–1970* (Chicago: University of Chicago Press, 1983), p. 44.

274. four hundred and twenty-five: "U.S. Ousted 425 on Morals," *The New York Times*, April 13, 1953.

275. The American Civil Liberties Committee upheld: Ibid., p. 48.

278. "And I don't know": Sarah Cunningham to author.

279. "a Red cell": Tony Kahn, "Growing Up on the Blacklist," *The Real Paper*, Dec. 18, 1976.

281. Dalton Trumbo's phone and "outside of": "The Legacy of the Hollywood Blacklist," film directed and produced by Judy Chaikin, co-written with Eve Goldberg, 1987.

282. Ronald Reagan as FBI informer: Theoharis, *From the Secret Files of J. Edgar Hoover*, pp. 115–117; Gary Wills, *Reagan's America: Innocents at Home* (Doubleday, 1981), pp. 249–250.

283. "plan to liquidate": *The New York Times*, March 15, 1950.

283. "He acts": Eric Bentley, *Thirty Years of Treason: Excerpts From the House Committee on Un-American Activities, 1938–1968* (Viking, 1971), pp. 122–123.

283. "reputedly": Ibid., p. 139.

285. "a reactionary": Larry Ceplair and Steven Englund, *The Inquisition in Hollywood: Politics in the Film Community 1930–1960* (Anchor Press/Doubleday, 1980), p. 172.

285. Brecht's telephone: *The New York Times*, March 31, 1979.

286. Workers Cooperative Colony: Calvin Trillin, "U.S. Journal: The Bronx, The Coops," *The New Yorker*, Aug. 1, 1977; *The New York Times*, Nov. 13, 1994.

287. "the humiliation": Robert Crichton, "My Father the Un-American," *New York*, March 10, 1975.

288. "the utmost imaginable": Joseph Freeman, *An American Testament: A Narrative of Rebels and Romantics* (London: Victor Gollancz, 1938), p. 576.

289. "And there we were": Sidney Roger to author.

290. "indoctrination": I. F. Stone, *The Daily Compass*, Oct. 3, 1952.

290. "who may be": Alistair Cooke, "Informers Wanted, Must Be Able to Teach," *The Manchester Guardian*, March 19, 1952.

290. "insubordination and": *The New York Times*, Dec. 8, 1976.

290. "irrelevant": from a 1950 statement by the Teachers Union, presented to the New York City Board of Education.

290. "Their high qualities": Celia Lewis Zitron, *The New York City Teachers Union, 1916–1964* (Humanities Press, 1968), p. 240.

290. "biased material": "A Message to Parents From the Eight Suspended Teachers," February 1952.

290. "patriotic" and "happy": Zitron, *Teachers Union*, pp. 102–103. *Our America* was still assigned in Harlem schools in 1964.

291. "the scum": "Keep Freedom in the Schools," pamphlet published by the Teachers Union, 1952.

291. "un-American" and "a plane": *New York Teacher News*.

291. "greasy foreigners": Zitron, *Teachers Union*, p. 96.

292. "past good record": Ibid.

292. "racial and": *The Daily Compass*, Feb. 8, 1952.

292. "a cesspool": *The Daily Compass*, Feb. 1, 1950.

292. "Do you know": *New York Teacher News*, Feb. 16, 1952.

293. "I contributed": Matusow, *False Witness*, p. 92.

293. "The law inevitably": Zitron, *Teachers Union*, p. 216.

294. "vindictive": *The New York Times*, Dec. 8, 1976.

24. FLASHBACKS

297. "Fascism and": Bentley, *Thirty Years of Treason*, p. 630.

297. "Kikes!": Albert Maltz to author.

297. Some of the material on the Depression comes from Cowley, *The Dream of the Golden Mountains*, and Caroline Bird, *The Invisible Scar* (David McKay, 1966).

298. "the constant visits": Arthur Miller, "Miracles," *Esquire*, September 1973.

298. "no work": Edmund Wilson, *The American Earthquake* (Doubleday, 1958), p. 419.

300. "Reports from": George Charney, *A Long Journey* (Chicago: Quadrangle, 1968), p. 49.

300. "unsound as": Lewis Mumford, quoted in Daniel Aaron, *Writers on the Left* (Oxford University Press, 1977), p. 258.

300. "basic communism": Bird, *The Invisible Scar*, p. 144.

300. "planned collectivism": Ibid.

300. "We knew . . . *only* momentary": Dorothy Healey to author.

301. "was to feel": Arthur Miller, "The Shadows of the Gods," *The Theater Essays of Arthur Miller* (Viking, 1978), p. 177.

301. "made everything else": Cowley, *The Dream of the Golden Mountains*, p. 118.

25. BLACKLIST IN EXILE

305. "schmucks with": Tom Dardis, *Some Time in the Sun* (Scribner's, 1976), p. 8.

305. "Pretty writing" Phil Koury, *Yes, Mr. De Mille* (Putnam's, 1959), p. 233.

305. "God protect": Ibid., p. 234.

305. "necessary evil" and "weevil": *Writers at Work: The Paris Review Interviews*, Second Series (Viking, 1963), p. 253.

307. "moody and": Alvah Bessie, *Inquisition in Eden* (Macmillan, 1965), p. 202.

307. "overthrow . . . the greatest hotbed": *The New York Times*, July 1, 1945.

307. "Communism is older": *Congressional Record*, July 18, 1945, p. 7737.

307. "alien-minded": Ibid.

308. "save America": Carey McWilliams, "Hollywood Plays With Facism," *The Nation*, May 29, 1935.

308. "in case of": Ibid.

309. "conduct abroad": Caute, *The Great Fear*, p. 245.

309. "engage in activities": Ibid.

309. "a sort of domestic": Duberman, *Paul Robeson*, p. 399.

309. "vicious" and "hostile": *The New York Times*, August 21, 1994.

310. "To the frustration": Ring Lardner, Jr., "My Life on the Blacklist," *The Saturday Evening Post*, Oct. 14, 1961.

312. "political leaders attribute": Bosley Crowther, *The Hollywood Rajah, The Life and Times of Louis B. Mayer* (Henry Holt, 1960), p. 199.

312. "He gave me": Ella Winter to author.

312. "I wouldn't like": Donald Ogden Stewart to author.

313. "a viciously unfair": Donald Ogden Stewart, *By a Stroke of Luck!* (London: Paddington Press, 1975), p. 157.

313. "male festival": Ibid., p. 133.

314. "Angry, yes": Anton Chekhov to O. L. Knipper, Jan. 2, 1901.

314. "My story is": Donald Ogden Stewart to author—as are the quotes that follow through page 320, except where noted.

316. "It suddenly came over": Stewart, *By a Stroke of Luck!*, p. 216.

317. "had always wanted": Jessica Mitford, *Faces of Philip* (Knopf, 1984), p. 5.

317. "being a good": Ibid., p. 29.

317. "wanted to be": Stewart, *By a Stroke of Luck!*, p. 269.

317. "a little old": Ella Winter was usually referred to as Steffens's widow. But they were actually divorced in 1931, due to Steffens's theory (stated when they married in 1924) that they should be secretly divorced after a while so that they would continue to be together voluntarily, not from obligation. Justin Kaplan, Steffens's biographer, describes the divorce as "a form of self-protection against being hurt" on Steffens's part. They lived together until he died.

317. "I was an": Ella Winter to author.

318. "Subversive germs": Hearings on "Communist Infiltration of the Motion Picture Industry," House Committee on Un-American Activities, 80th Congress, 1st sess., Oct. 20, 1947, p. 11.

318. "My brothers and I": Ibid., p. 10.

319. "go along with": Stewart, *By a Stroke of Luck!*, p. 252.

319. "I do not think," "a Magic Helper," and "in future, I": FBI file AL 100–3009, p. 116.

319. "connection . . . American convictions": Ibid., p. 115.

319. "record": Martin Dies, *The Trojan Horse in America* (Dodd, Mead, 1940), p. 71.

319. "this [was] noteworthy": agent's comment, FBI file.

320. on the Security Index: FBI memo, Oct. 16, 1950, Security Matter—C, Special Section of the Security Index, Bufile 100–18610.

320. "examined . . . possible espionage": FBI: NY 100–16983.

320. "It seemed to me": *The Autobiography of Lincoln Steffens*, vol. 2 (Harcourt, Brace, 1931), p. 812.

321. "joyous": Ibid.

321. "young genius": Justin Kaplan, *Lincoln Steffens* (Simon and Schuster, 1974), p. 274.

321. "Forced . . . to clear": *The Autobiography of Lincoln Steffens*, p. 813.

321. "excessive quickness": *The Letters of Lincoln Steffens*, edited by Ella Winter and Granville Hicks (Harcourt, Brace, 1938), p. 859.

321. "unmellowed by": Kaplan, *Lincoln Steffens*, p. 322.

321. "Why not thirty?" Ella Winter to author—as are all quotes through page 324, except where noted.

321. "her alleged activities": FBI File AL 100–3009 (64182).

324. "Let's dissolve" and "She was awful": Sally Belfrage, letters to author, Aug. 4, 1980, and Sept. 23, 1987.

326. "Red propaganda" and "pro-Communists": Larry Adler, *It Ain't Necessarily So* (London: Collins, 1984), p. 155.

327. "no philosophy" and "If Henry Wallace": Larry Adler to author.

328. "when the practical": Abraham Polonsky to author.

329. "headiness": Alice Hunter to author.

329. "when you took": Polonsky to author.

330. "unite in salute": D. Clayton James, *The Years of MacArthur, 1941–1945* (Boston: Houghton Mifflin, 1975), p. 641.

330. "ideological termites": Jack Warner's testimony, Hearings on "Communism in the Motion Picture Industry," p. 10.

331. "It's the only": Victor Navasky, *Naming Names* (Viking, 1980), p. 178.

331. "She went from": Karen Morley to author.

332. "an attempt to throw": Arthur Miller to author.

332. "tended to jump": Carl Foreman to author.

333. "Old scores": Arthur Miller, "Overture" to *The Crucible* (Penguin Books, 1976), p. 8.

334. "the Thirties were Hollywood's": *Hollywood on Trial*, BBC television film, written and directed by Tristam Powell, research by Ann Blaber.

334. "revolution-preventing": Peter Viereck, *Shame and Glory of the Intellectuals*, quoted in Douglas T. Miller and Marion Nowak, *The Fifties: The Way We Really Were* (Doubleday, 1977), p. 240.

335. Dulles and the CIA: In 1976 James Angleton disclosed that Eastern European units, including some from Hungary, had been secretly trained by the CIA for intervention in possible uprisings in Eastern Europe in 1956. But he said these groups were not ready to act in time for the Hungarian crisis: *The New York Times*, Nov. 30, 1976.

336. "the perverted subject": *Congressional Record*, July 19, 1945, p. 7738.

336. "a peacemonger": David Robinson, *Chaplin: His Life and Art* (McGraw-Hill, 1985), p. 545.

336. "loathsome pictures": *The New York Times*, Dec. 26, 1977.

336. "moral worth": Ibid.

336. "one insistent": Warshow, *The Immediate Experience*, p. 223.

337. "I said to": Charlie Chaplin to author.

337. "about the 'little'": Harold Clurman, *All People Are Famous* (Harcourt Brace Jovanovich, 1974), p. 126.

337. "one of the worst": *Selected Letters of James Thurber*, p. 115.

337. "because I couldn't": Nora Sayre, notebook, summer 1956.

340. "thought we'd all": Eileen O'Casey to author.

345. "Why does a man": Bertolt Brecht, *The Caucasian Chalk Circle*, translated by Michael Hamburger, *Collected Plays*, Volume 7; quoted in Anthony Heilbut, *Exiled In Paradise* (Viking, 1983), p. 197.

346. "We'll go to": Arthur Miller's adaptation of Ibsen's *An Enemy of the People* (Penguin Books, 1979), p. 101.

26. THINKING OF STALIN?

348. Material on Helen Black came from Victor Chapin, Rose Rubin, Bernard Koten, and Virginia Black; the papers of Genevieve Taggard in the Berg Collection in the New York Public Library; Elinor Langer; The Beinecke Rare Book and Manuscript Collection, Josephine Herbst Papers, in the Collection of American Literature, Yale University;

unpublished letter from Josephine Herbst to Genevieve Taggard, May 25, 1921, courtesy of Marcia Liles.

348. "magnetic currents . . . love was in the air": Josephine Herbst, an informal unpublished memoir of Genevieve Taggard, written for Kenneth Durant, 1949.

350. "had told so many": Cowley, *The Dream of the Golden Mountains*, p. 163.

350. "The Soviet Union": Albert Maltz to author.

351. "In the Thirties": *Writers at Work, The Paris Review Interviews*, Third Series (Viking, 1967), p. 229.

352. "the greatest danger": *People's World*, April 10, 1940.

352. "We had accepted": Peggy Dennis, *The Autobiography of an American Communist* (Westport/Berkeley: Lawrence Hill and Creative Arts, 1977), p. 160.

353. "If we see": Maurice Isserman, *Which Side Were You On?, The American Communist Party During the Second World War* (Middletown, Conn.: Wesleyan University Press, 1982), p. 105.

354. "an accurate history": Aaron, *Writers on the Left*, p. xv.

354. "For a Soviet": George Charney, *A Long Journey* (Quadrangle Books, 1968), p. 43.

355. "declining into" and "It was": Cowley, *The Dream of the Golden Mountains*, p. 117.

357. "As for myself": Otto Friedrich, *City of Nets* (Harper and Row, 1986), p. 73.

357. Dalton Trumbo usually: *Additional Dialogue, Letters of Dalton Trumbo, 1942–1962* (M. Evans, 1970), p. 391.

359. "Like the Russians": Cowley, *The Dream of the Golden Mountains*, p. 218.

359. "We alone": Dennis, *The Autobiography of an American Communist*, p. 26.

359. "We believed": Charney, *A Long Journey*, p. 103.

360. "the fleabites of": Sam Moore to author.

360. Socialist Workers Party and the Teamsters: Navasky, *Naming Names*, p. 30.

360. "The Red New Deal": Thomas A. Bailey and David M. Kennedy, *The American Pageant*, 7th Edition (Lexington, Mass.: D.C. Heath, 1983), p. 770.

361. "necessary": Dennis, *The Autobiography of an American Communist*, p. 157.

361. "sectarian leanings" and "reformist tendencies": Ibid., p. 124.

361. swamp imagery: Sam Moore to author.

362. "be a reflection": Joseph Starobin, *American Communism in Crisis* (Cambridge: Harvard University Press, 1972), p. 86.

363. "an outstanding Party": Freeman, *An American Testament*, p. 259.

363. "that schoolboy": Starobin, *American Communism in Crisis*, p. 262.

363. "The Party": Steve Nelson, James R. Barrett, Rob Ruck, *Steve Nelson, American Radical* (Pittsburgh: University of Pittsburgh Press, 1981), p. 275.

363. "all centralism": Dorothy Healey and Maurice Isserman, *Dorothy Healey Remembers: A Life in the American Communist Party* (Oxford University Press, 1990), p. 163.

363. "largely dominated": Jessica Mitford, *A Fine Old Conflict* (Knopf, 1977), p. 276.

364. "the healthiest": *Steve Nelson, American Radical*, p. 255.

364. privately admired: Charney, *A Long Journey*, p. 215.

364. "I have not": quotes from newsreel footage included in *Hollywood on Trial*, directed by Tristam Powell.

365. "Jack seemed": Carl Foreman to author.

365. "the real aim": Charney, *A Long Journey*, p. 160.

366. "the Pink Lady": Helen Gahagan Douglas, *A Full Life* (Doubleday, 1982), p. 316.

366. "help Richard Nixon": Ibid., p. 326.

366. "Vote for Nixon!": Ibid., p. 333.

366. "pink right down": Ibid., p. 327.

367. "The picket lines": Charney, *A Long Journey*, p. 254.

367. "Perhaps we stayed": Ibid., p. 263.

368. "a common goal": Aaron, *Writers on the Left*, p. 311.

368. Freeman's book and his departure from the Party: Ibid., pp. 368–371.

368. "*primarily* by": Navasky, *Naming Names*, p. 288.

368. "an emotional crisis": Albert Maltz to author.

368. "the iron door" and the Townsends: Sam Moore to author.

369. "accessories to": Budd Schulberg to author.

369. "understand the police": Elia Kazan, *A Life* (Anchor Books, 1989), p. 131.

369. "abiding hatred": *The New York Times*, April 12, 1952.

370. "We were cleansing": Dorothy Healey to author.

370. "We did too": Sam Kushner to author, also the Kushner quotes through p. 370.

371. "a bad spy": *Dorothy Healey Remembers*, p. 125.

372. "We Communists" and other Eugene Dennis quotes: Dennis, *The Autobiography of an American Communist*, pp. 221–223, 229.

372. "the response was": Charney, *A Long View*, p. 264.

373. "has ceased": John Gates, *The Story of an American Communist* (Nelson, 1958), p. 191.

373. less than five thousand: Maurice Isserman, *If I Had a Hammer. . ., The Death of the Old Left and the Birth of the New Left*, (Basic Books, 1987), p. 32.

373. "good riddance" and "demanded": Dennis, *The Autobiography of an American Communist*, p. 232.

373. "the noblest body" and other quotes: Albert Maltz to author.

373. "that Khrushchev offered": Al Richmond, *A Long View From the Left* (Delta Books, 1975), p. 373.

374. "a decade of": Dorothy Healey to author.

374. "the collective": *Steve Nelson, American Radical*, p. 386.

374. "This is not why": Ibid., p. 387.

375. "made the reactionaries' ": Ibid., p. 381.

375. "whipping up": *Time*, May 14, 1951.

375. "Communism, not racism": Mitford, *A Fine Old Conflict*, p. 193.

27. VOYAGE TO COLUMBUS

386. "a kike town": David McCullough, *Truman* (Simon & Schuster, 1992), p. 110.

386. "in an uproar": Ludwig Lewisohn, *Up Stream, An American Chronicle* (Boni and Liveright, 1922), p. 231.

387. "is the composite": Walter J. Sears, "Moving to Columbus," 1910.

388. salt . . . and eggshells: Curtina Malissa Breta Moreland, "The Black Community of Columbus: A Study of the Structure and Patterns of Power in a Midwestern City" (Ph.D. diss., University of Illinois at Urbana-Champaign, 1977).

388. "used to stand": James Thurber, *The Thurber Album* (Simon and Schuster, 1952), p. 250.

388. "emasculated": Ibid, pp. 314–315.

389. Sources on Vanguard League: Stanley and Louise Robinson; Moreland, "The Black Community of Columbus"; Vibert Leslie White, "Developing a School of Civil Rights Lawyers: From The New Deal to the . . ." (undergraduate thesis, Ohio State University, 1988).

390. "brooding monster . . . of stone": *The Thurber Album*, p. 231.

392. Material on Russia comes from Joel Sayre, "Homage to Vladivostock," an unpublished memoir.

393. "Here We Rest": Thurber, letter to James E. Pollard, Feb. 9, 1952 (Thurber Collection).

394. "Instead of being": F. Scott Fitzgerald, *The Great Gatsby* (Scribner's, 1925), p. 3.

394. "It was the first time": *The Thurber Album*, p. 284.

394. "Never, never": Kenneth. S. Lynn, *William Dean Howells* (Harcourt Brace Jovanovich, 1971), p. 81.

394. "Millions for": *The Thurber Album*, p. 207.

394. "the appalling mental": Lewisohn, *Up Stream*, p. 188.

394. "football and fudge" and other quotes from Ibid., pp. 156, 157, 161, 162, 167, 190.

394. "cruel truthfulness": Thurber, letter to Elliott Nugent, September (n.d.) 1922 (Thurber Collection).

395. "Our position in": *The Ohio Guide*, Federal Writers Project (Oxford University Press, 1940), p. 37.

395. "luxuries for": Lewisohn, *Up Stream*, p. 191.

398. "freedom of speech": Thurber, letter to President Howard Bevis of Ohio State University, Dec. 6, 1951 (Thurber Collection).

399. "Columbus is": Thurber, letter to Carey McWilliams, August 13, 1952 (Thurber Collection).

399. Harold Rugg: Stephen Philips Gietscher, "Limited War and the Home Front: Ohio During the Korean War," chapters on "Academic Freedom at Ohio State University" (Ph.D. diss., Ohio State University, 1977). Courtesy Professor Robert Bremner.

399. "gag rule" and Byron Darling: author interviews with Robert Bremner, Jack Grant Day; *The Thurber Album*, pp. 209–210; Ellen Schrecker, *No Ivory Tower*, pp. 90, 207–209; *The Columbus Citizen*, March 26, April 5, 1948.

400. Frank Hashmall: author interviews with Allen Zak; Olaf Prufer; James Murphy; *The Columbus Citizen*, March 19, 21, 23, 24, 26, 27, 28, April 5, 1948; *The Columbus Dispatch*, March 21, 27, 31, 1948; Hearings of the Ohio Un-American Activities Commission.

400. "three primary fields": Report of the Ohio Un-American Activities Commission, 1951–1952.

401. "I had a big": Matusow, *False Witness*, p. 78.

401. "knock King George": Ibid., p. 77.

401. "Did you ever": Hearings of the Ohio Un-American Activities Commission, May 1952.

402. Richard Morgan: author interviews with James B. Griffin, Olaf Prufer, James Murphy, William S. Dancey; James B. Griffin, "Richard G. Morgan, 1903–1968," *The Columbus Citizen*, March 25, 1948; Report of the Special Committee Of the American Anthropological Association on the Dismissal of Richard G. Morgan From the Ohio State Museum and Supplement to Report of Special Committee of the AAA on the Dismissal of Richard G. Morgan; *The Columbus Dispatch*, March 25, 26, 1948, April 1, 1952; *The Columbus Citizen*, March 26, 27, 1948; *The American Anthropological Association News Bulletin*, vol. 2, no. 3, June 1948, and no. 4, September 1948: vol. 3, no. 1, February 1949; vol. 14, no. 1, January 1950; Confidential Report, The National Detective Bureau Co., Columbus, Ohio, July 1, 1948.

403. Oscar Smilack: author interviews with Edith Smilack, Benson Wolman, Jack Grant Day, Mario De Sapio; Hearings of Ohio Un-American Activities Commission, April 1, 1952; "just as sane": No. 33197, Supreme Court of Ohio, State of Ohio, Ex. Rel. Oscar Smilack, Plaintiff-Appellee . . . Appeal from the Court of Appeals of Allen County, Supplemental Record; *The Columbus Dispatch*, April 22, 1953, May 3, 1954;

Warren P. Hill, "A Critique of Anti-Subversive Legislation," *Ohio State Law Journal*, vol. 14, no. 4, Autumn 1953.

404. "political chastity . . . against hunger": Jack Grant Day to author.

405. The Free Speech Movement and Herbert Aptheker: Benson Wolman; Emily Foster, "The Free Speech Movement at Ohio State," *Columbus Monthly*, December 1984.

405. "students, like automatons": *The Columbus Dispatch*, May 23, 1965.

405. "McKinley era": Foster, "The Free Speech Movement at Ohio State."

406. The Limited Test Ban Treaty did not prevent underground testing, hence many anti-nuclear activists found it unsatisfactory.

406. Ohio State University strike: Megan Mountain to author; Martha Brian and Mary Carran Webster, "The Campus Radicals: Where Are They Now?" *Columbus Monthly*, February 1977; *The Columbus Dispatch*, April 29 and 30, May 4, 1970.

409. "dealing with": Edmund Wilson, "Auden in America," *The Bit Between My Teeth*, p. 359.

410. "the revolt from" : quoted in Alfred Kazin, *On Native Grounds* (Harcourt Brace Jovanovich, 1942, 1970), p. 205.

410. "dialogue died": Lynn, *William Dean Howells*, p. 103.

411. "How he loved": Robert Thurber to author.

Selected Bibliography

The books listed were published in New York, except where noted.

LEGACIES FROM THE TWENTIES

Agee, James, and Walker Evans, *Let Us Now Praise Famous Men*. Boston: Houghton Mifflin, 1941. Foreword to the new edition by Walker Evans (Houghton Mifflin, 1960).

Allen, Frederick Lewis. *Only Yesterday*. Harper, 1931.

Asbury, Herbert. *Up From Methodism*. Knopf, 1926.

Behrman, S. N. *People in a Diary*. Boston: Little, Brown, 1972.

Blotner, Joseph. *Faulkner, A Biography*. Second revised edition. Random House, 1972.

Bode, Carl. *Mencken*. Carbondale and Edwardsville: Southern Illinois University Press/ Arcturus Books, 1973.

Cowley, Malcolm. *Exile's Return*. Viking, 1951.

———. *A Second Flowering: Work and Days of the Lost Generation*. Viking, 1973.

Dos Passos, John. *The Best Times*. New American Library, 1966.

Evans, Walker. Foreword to 1960 edition of *Let Us Now Praise Famous Men* by James Agee and Walker Evans. Boston: Houghton Mifflin, 1960.

———. "Walker Evans on Himself," *The New Republic*, Nov. 13, 1976.

———. *Walker Evans*. Introduction by John Szarkowski. Museum of Modern Art, 1971.

———. *Walker Evans at Work*. Edited by John T. Hill, Frances Lindley, and Edward Grazda. With an essay by Jerry L. Thompson. Harper and Row, 1982.

Fitzgerald, Scott F. *The Crack-Up*. Edited by Edmund Wilson. New Directions, 1956.

———. *The Letters of F. Scott Fitzgerald*. Edited by Andrew Turnball. Dell, 1966.

Johnson, Nora. *Flashback: Nora Johnson on Nunnally Johnson*. Doubleday, 1979.

Johnson, Nunnally. *The Letters of Nunnally Johnson*. Edited by Dorris Johnson and Ellen Leventhal. Knopf, 1981.

Katz, Leslie. "Interview With Walker Evans." *Art in America*, March–April 1971.

Kazin, Alfred. *On Native Grounds*. Harcourt, Brace, and World, 1942.

Leighton, Isabel, ed. *The Aspirin Age*. Simon and Schuster, 1949.

McGilligan, Pat. *Backstory: Interviews With Screenwriters of Hollywood's Golden Age*. Berkeley/Los Angeles: University of California Press, 1985.

MacShane, Frank. *The Life of John O'Hara*. Dutton, 1980.

Mayfield, Sara. *The Constant Circle: H. L. Mencken and His Friends*. Delacorte, 1968.

Mencken, H. L. *The Diary of H. L. Mencken*. Edited by Charles A. Fecher. Knopf, 1989.

———. *The New Mencken Letters*. Edited by Carl Bode. Dial, 1979.

———. *The Vintage Mencken*. Gathered by Alistair Cooke. Vintage, 1956.

Mitchell, Joseph. *My Ears Are Bent*. Sheridan House, 1938.

O'Neal, Hank. A *Vision Shared: A Classic Portrait of America and Its People, 1935–1943*. St. Martin's, 1976.

Parrott, Ursula. *Ex-wife*. 1929. Plume/New American Library, 1989.

Perelman, S. J. *Don't Tread On Me, Letters of S. J. Perelman*. Edited by Prudence Crowther. Viking Penguin, 1987.

Sayre, Joel. *The House Without a Roof*. Farrar, Straus, 1948.

———. *The Persian Gulf Command*. Random House, 1945.

Stern, James. "Walker Evans (1903–75) A Memoir." *London Magazine*, August/September 1977.

Sullivan, Mark. *Our Times: The Twenties*. Scribner's, 1935.

Thurber, James. *My Life and Hard Times*. Harper, 1933.

———. *Selected Letters of James Thurber*. Edited by Helen Thurber and Edward Weeks. Boston: Atlantic Monthly Press/Little, Brown, 1981.

Walker, Stanley. *City Editor*. Frederick A. Stokes, 1934.

White, E. B. *Letters of E. B. White*. Collected and edited by Dorothy Lobrano Guth. Harper and Row, 1976.

Wilson, Edmund. *The Bit Between My Teeth*. Farrar, Straus, and Giroux, 1965.

———. *The Fifties*. Edited by Leon Edel. Farrar, Straus, and Giroux, 1986.

———. *The Forties*. Edited by Leon Edel. Farrar, Straus, and Giroux, 1983.

———. *Letters on Literature and Politics*. Edited by Elena Wilson. Introduction by Daniel Aaron. Foreword by Leon Edel. Farrar, Straus, and Giroux, 1977.

———. *A Piece of My Mind*. Farrar, Straus, and Cudahy, 1956.

———. *The Shores of Light*. Farrar, Straus, and Young, 1952.

———. *The Twenties*. Edited by Leon Edel. Bantam, 1976.

———. *Upstate*. Farrar, Straus, and Giroux, 1971.

ADMONITIONS OF THE FIFTIES

Ackroyd, Peter. *T. S. Eliot: A Life*. Simon and Schuster, 1984.

Aronson, James. *The Press and the Cold War*. Indianapolis: Bobbs-Merrill, 1970.

Bartley, Numan V. *The Rise of Massive Resistance: Race and Politics in the South During the 1950s*. Baton Rouge: Louisiana State University Press, 1969.

Branch, Taylor. *Parting the Waters: America in the King Years, 1954–1963*. Simon and Schuster, 1988.

Charters, Ann. *Kerouac*. San Francisco: Straight Arrow Books, 1973.

Clark, E. Culpepper. *The Schoolhouse Door: Segregation's Last Stand at the University of Alabama*. Oxford University Press, 1993.

Durr, Virginia. *Outside the Magic Circle*. Edited by Hollinger F. Barnard. Tuscaloosa: University of Alabama Press, 1985.

Farnham, Maryania, and Ferdinand Lundberg. *Modern Woman: The Lost Sex*. Harper, 1947.

FBI File No. 100–1133352. Hearings on "Communism in Mass Communications," 1955. Hearings on "Strategy and Tactics of World Communism," 1955. Hearings before the Subcommittee to Investigate the Administration of Internal Security Act and Other Internal Security Laws of the Committee of the Judiciary, 1956.

Gardner, David P. *The California Oath Controversy*. Berkeley/Los Angeles: University of California Press, 1967.

Garfield, David. *A Player's Place: The Story of the Actors Studio*. Macmillan, 1980.

Gordon, Lyndall. *Eliot's New Life*. Farrar, Straus, and Giroux, 1988.

Halberstam, David. *The Fifties*. Villard Books, 1993.

Hardwick, Elizabeth. *A View of My Own*. Farrar, Straus, and Cudahy, 1962.

Hine, Thomas. *Populuxe*. Knopf, 1986.

Kahn, Albert. *The Matusow Affair*. Mount Kisco, N.Y.: Meyer Bell Limited, 1987.

Kazin, Alfred. *Contemporaries*. Boston: Little, Brown, 1962.

Kerouac, Jack. *On the Road*. Viking, 1957.

Kluger, Richard. *Simple Justice: The History of Brown vs. the Board of Education and Black America's Struggle for Equality*. Knopf, 1975.

Liebling, A. J. *The Earl of Louisiana*. Simon and Schuster, 1961.

Macdonald, Dwight. *Against the American Grain*. Random House, 1962.

————. *Discriminations*. Grossman/Viking, 1974.

McMillen, Neil R. *The Citizens' Council: Organized Resistance to the Second Reconstruction, 1954–1964*. Urbana: University of Illinois Press, 1971.

McWilliams, Carey. *The Education of Carey McWilliams*. Simon and Schuster, 1979.

Mailer, Norman. *Advertisements For Myself*. Signet, 1960.

Martin, John Barlow. *The Deep South Says Never*. Ballantine Books, 1957.

Matusow, Harvey. *False Witness*. Cameron and Kahn, 1955.

Miller, Douglas T., and Marion Nowak. *The Fifties: The Way We Really Were*. Doubleday, 1977.

Miller, Warren. *The Way We Live Now*. Boston: Little, Brown, 1958.

Mitchell, Ann. *Keep 'Bama White*. Master's thesis, Georgia Southern College, 1971.

Plath, Sylvia. *The Journals of Sylvia Plath*. Dial, 1982.

Raines, Howell. *My Soul is Rested: Movement Days in the Deep South Remembered*. Putnam's, 1977.

Rampersad, Arnold. *The Life of Langston Hughes*. Vol. 2. Oxford University Press, 1988.

Salinger, J. D. *The Catcher in the Rye*. Bantam, 1964.

————. *Franny and Zooey*. Bantam, 1964.

————. *Raise High the Roof Beam, Carpenter and Seymour: An Introduction*. Bantam, 1965.

Sartre, Jean-Paul. *Les Chemins de la Liberté*. Paris: Gallimard, 1949.

————. *Les Mouches*. Paris: Gallimard, 1947.

————. *La Nausée*. Paris: Gallimard, 1938.

Schrecker, Ellen. *No Ivory Tower: McCarthyism and the Universities*. Oxford University Press, 1986.

Sherrill, Robert. *Gothic Politics in the Deep South*. Grossman, 1968.

Stewart, George R. in Collaboration With Other Professors at the University of California. *The Year of the Oath*. Doubleday, 1950.

Tytell, John. *Naked Angels: The Lives and Literature of the Beat Generation*. McGraw-Hill, 1976.

U.S. Congress. Senate. Internal Security Subcommittee/Senate Judiciary Committee. "Inquiry Into Communist Party Influence in the Press." Dec. 5, 1955, and Jan. 3, 1956.

Williams, Juan, with the *Eyes on the Prize* Production Team. *Eyes on the Prize*. Penguin, 1987.

Woodward, C. Vann. *The Strange Career of Jim Crow*. Oxford University Press, 1966.

Wylie, Philip. *Generation of Vipers*. Rinehart and Company, 1942.

SEQUELS TO THE THIRTIES

Aaron, Daniel. *Writers on the Left*. Oxford University Press, 1977.

Barrett, William. *The Truants*. Anchor Press/Doubleday, 1982.

Bayley, Edwin R. *Joe McCarthy and the Press*. Madison: University of Wisconsin Press, 1981.

Belfrage, Cedric. *The American Inquisition*. Indianapolis: Bobbs-Merrill, 1973.

————. *The Frightened Giant*. London: Secker and Warburg, 1957.

Belfrage, Cedric, and James Aronson. *Something to Guard: The Stormy Life of the National Guardian, 1948–1967*. Columbia University Press, 1978.

Belfrage, Sally. *Un-American Activities*. HarperCollins, 1994.

Bell, Daniel. *The End of Ideology*. Revised Edition. Free Press, 1962.

Bentley, Eric. *Are You Now or Have You Ever Been*. Harper Colophon, 1972.

———, ed. *Thirty Years of Treason*. Viking, 1971.

Bernstein, Carl. *Loyalties*. Simon and Schuster, 1989.

Bessie, Alvah. *Inquisition in Eden*. Macmillan, 1965.

Bird, Caroline. *The Invisible Scar*. David McKay, 1966.

Caute, David. *The Great Fear: The Anti-Communist Purge Under Truman and Eisenhower*. Simon and Schuster, 1978.

———. *Joseph Losey: A Revenge on Life*. Oxford University Press, 1994.

Ceplair, Larry, and Steven Englund. *The Inquisition in Hollywood*. Anchor Press/Doubleday, 1980.

Chambers, Whittaker. *Witness*. Random House, 1952.

Charney, George. *A Long Journey*. Chicago: Quadrangle, 1968.

Ciment, Michel. *Conversations With Losey*. Methuen, 1985.

———. *Kazan on Kazan*. Viking, 1974.

Clurman, Harold. *All People Are Famous*. Harcourt Brace Jovanovich, 1974.

———. *The Fervent Years*. Harcourt Brace Jovanovich, 1975.

Cogley, John. *Report on Blacklisting*. 2 vols. The Fund For the Republic, 1956.

Crossman, Richard, ed. *The God That Failed*. Harper, 1950.

D'Emilio, John. *Sexual Politics, Sexual Communities: The Making of a Homosexual Minority in the United States, 1940–1970*. Chicago: University of Chicago Press, 1983.

Dennis, Peggy. *The Autobiography of an American Communist*. Westport/Berkeley: Lawrence Hill/Creative Arts, 1977.

Diamond, Sigmund. *Compromised Campus: The Collaboration of Universities With the Intelligence Community*. Oxford University Press, 1992.

Donner, Frank. *The Age of Surveillance*. Knopf, 1980.

———. *The Un-Americans*. Ballantine, 1961.

Duberman, Martin Bauml. *Paul Robeson*. Knopf, 1988.

Dunne, Philip. *Take Two: A Life in Movies and Politics*. McGraw-Hill, 1980.

Fariello, Griffin. *Red Scare: Memories of the American Inquisition, An Oral History*. W. W. Norton, 1995.

Fiedler, Leslie. *An End to Innocence*. Boston: Beacon Press, 1955.

Film Culture, ed. Gordon Hitchens. Fall and Winter, 1970.

Freeman, Joseph. *An American Testament: A Narrative of Rebels and Romantics*. London: Victor Gollancz, 1938.

Friedrich, Otto. *City of Nets: A Portrait of Hollywood in the 1940s*. Harper and Row, 1986.

Gabler, Neal. *An Empire of Their Own: How the Jews Invented Hollywood*. Crown, 1988.

Gentry, Curt, *J. Edgar Hoover, The Man and the Secrets*. Norton, 1991.

Goodman, Walter. *The Committee*. Farrar, Straus, and Giroux, 1968.

Healey, Dorothy, and Maurice Isserman. *Dorothy Healey Remembers*. Oxford University Press, 1990.

Hellman, Lillian. *Scoundrel Time*. Foreward by Garry Wills. Boston: Little, Brown, 1976.

Hiss, Alger, *In the Court of Public Opinion*. Knopf, 1957.

———. *Recollections of A Life*. Seaver Books, Henry Holt, 1988.

Hiss, Tony. "My Father's Honor." *The New Yorker*, Nov. 16, 1992.

Howe, Irving. *Decline of the New*. Harcourt, Brace, and World, 1970.

———. *A Margin of Hope: An Intellectual Autobiography*. Harcourt Brace Jovanovich, 1982.

Isserman, Maurice. *Which Side Were You On? The American Communist Party During the Second World War*. Middletown, Conn.: Wesleyan University Press, 1982.

Kanfer, Stefan. *A Journal of the Plague Years*. Atheneum, 1973.

Kaplan, Justin. *Lincoln Steffens*. Simon and Schuster, 1974.

Kazan, Elia. *A Life*. Knopf, 1988.

Kempton, Murray. *America Comes of Middle Age*. Boston: Little, Brown, 1963.

———. *Part of Our Time: Some Monuments and Ruins of the Thirties*. Delta Books, 1967.

Kennan, George F. "Flashbacks," *The New Yorker*, Feb. 25, 1985.

———. *Memoirs: 1925–1950*. Boston: Little, Brown, 1967.

Kimball, Penn. *The File*. Harcourt Brace Jovanovich, 1983.

Klehr, Harvey, John Earle Haynes, and Fredrich Igorevich Firgov. *The Secret World of American Communism*. New Haven: Yale University Press, 1995.

Kraft, Hy. *On My Way to the Theater*. Macmillan, 1971.

Kristol, Irving. "Civil Liberties—A Study in Confusion." *Commentary*, March 1952.

Kwitney, Jonathan. *Endless Enemies*. Congdon & Weed, 1984.

Lardner, Ring, Jr. *The Lardners: My Family Remembered*. Harper and Row, 1976.

———. "My Life on the Blacklist." *The Saturday Evening Post*, Oct. 14, 1961.

Lasch, Christopher. *The Agony of the American Left*. Knopf, 1969.

———. *The New Radicalism in America*. Knopf, 1965.

Littleton, Taylor D., and Maltby Sykes. *Advancing American Art: Painting, Politics, and Cultural Confrontation at Mid-Century*. Introduction by Leon F. Litwack. Tuscaloosa: University of Alabama Press, 1989.

McAuliffe, Mary Sperling. *Crisis on the Left: Cold War Politics and American Liberals, 1947–1954*. Amherst: University of Massachusetts Press, 1978.

McWilliams, Carey. *Witch Hunt*. Boston: Little, Brown, 1950.

Marks, John. *The Search for the 'Manchurian Candidate,' the CIA and Mind Control*. McGraw-Hill, 1980.

May, Henry. *Coming to Terms: A Study in Memory and History*. Berkeley and Los Angeles: University of California Press, 1987.

Miller, Arthur. *After the Fall*. Bantam, 1965.

———. *The Crucible*. Viking, 1953.

———. *The Theater Essays of Arthur Miller*. Viking, 1978.

———. *Timebends*. Grove Press, 1987.

———. *A View from the Bridge*. Viking, 1955.

Mitford, Jessica. *A Fine Old Conflict*. Knopf, 1977.

Mitgang, Herbert. *Dangerous Dossiers: Exposing the Secret War Against America's Greatest Authors*. Donald I. Fine, 1988.

Navasky, Victor. "Allen Weinstein's 'Perjury': The Case Not Proved Against Alger Hiss." *The Nation*, April 8, 1978.

———. *Naming Names*. Viking, 1980.

Nelson, Steve, James R. Barrett, and Rob Ruck. *Steve Nelson: American Radical*. Pittsburgh: University of Pittsburgh Press, 1981.

Nixon, Richard. *Six Crises*. Pyramid Books, 1968.

Ophuls, Marcel. *Hotel Terminus*. 1988. Film documentary.

Oshinsky, David. *A Conspiracy So Immense*. Free Press, 1983.

Pells, Richard. *The Liberal Mind in a Conservative Age: Intellectuals in the 1940s and 1950s*. Harper and Row, 1985.

———. *Radical Visions and American Dreams*. Harper and Row, 1973.

Podhoretz, Norman. *Making It*. Random House, 1967.

Point of Order! A Documentary of the Army-McCarthy Hearings. Produced by Emile de Antonio and Daniel Talbot. Norton, 1964.

Powers, Richard Gid. *Secrecy and Power: The Life of J. Edgar Hoover*. Free Press, 1987.

Radosh, Ronald, and Joyce Milton. *The Rosenberg File: A Search for the Truth*. Holt, Rinehart and Winston, 1983.

Reuben, William. *Footnote on an Historic Case, In Re Alger Hiss*. A Publication of The Nation Institute, 1983.

Reeves, Thomas. *The Life and Times of Joe McCarthy*. Stein and Day, 1982.

Richmond, Al. *A Long View From the Left*. Boston: Houghton Mifflin, 1973.

Robins, Natalie. *Alien Ink: The FBI's War on Freedom of Expression*. Morrow, 1992.

Rosenberg, Harold. *The Tradition of the New*. London: Thames and Hudson, 1962.

Ross, Lillian. "Onward and Upward With the Arts: Come In, Lassie!" *The New Yorker*, Feb. 21, 1948.

Rovere, Richard. *Senator Joe McCarthy*. Harcourt, Brace, and World, 1959.

Sarason, Bertram D. *Hemingway and the Sun Set*. Washington, D.C.: Microcard Editions, 1972.

Schlesinger, Arthur. *The Vital Center: The Politics of Freedom*. Boston: Houghton Mifflin, 1949.

Schneir, Walter, and Miriam Schneir. *Invitation to an Inquest*. Penguin, 1973.

———. "Cryptic Answers." *The Nation*, August 14, 1995.

Schulberg, Budd. *What Makes Sammy Run?* Random House, 1941.

Schultz, Bud, and Ruth Schultz. *It Did Happen Here: Recollections of Political Repression in America*. Berkeley and Los Angeles: University of California Press, 1989.

Smith, John Chabot. *Alger Hiss*. Holt, Rinehart, and Winston, 1976.

Starobin, Joseph. *American Communism in Crisis*. Cambridge: Harvard University Press, 1972.

Steffens, Lincoln. *The Autobiography of Lincoln Steffens*. Harcourt, Brace, 1931.

Stewart, Donald Ogden. *By a Stroke of Luck!* Paddington Press, 1975.

———. "The Dies Committee." *The Bulletin of the League of America Writers*, Fall 1938.

Stone, I. F. *The Haunted Fifties*. Random House, 1963.

Talbot, David, and Barbara Zheutlin. *Creative Differences*. Boston: South End Press, 1978.

Taylor, Telford. *Grand Inquest: The Story of Congressional Investigations*. Simon and Schuster, 1955.

Theoharis, Athan, and John Stuart Cox. *The Boss: J. Edgar Hoover and the American Inquisition*. Philadelphia: Temple University Press, 1988.

Tiger, Edith, ed. *In Re Alger Hiss: Petition for a Writ of Error Coram Nobis*. Hill and Wang, 1979.

Trumbo, Dalton. *Additional Dialogue: The Letters of Dalton Trumbo*. M. Evans, 1970.

U.S. 80th Congress, 1st Session, October 1947. *Hearings Regarding the Communist Infiltration of the Motion Picture Industry*. Washington, D.C.: U.S. Government Printing Office, 1947.

Vaughn, Robert. *Only Victims*. G. P. Putnam's Sons, 1972.

Viertel, Salka. *The Kindness of Strangers*. Holt, Rinehart, and Winston, 1969.

Weinstein, Allen. *Perjury: The Hiss-Chambers Case*. Knopf, 1978.

Walton, Richard J. *Henry Wallace, Harry Truman, and the Cold War*. Viking, 1976.

Wilson, Edmund. *The American Earthquake*. Doubleday, 1958.

Winter, Ella. *And Not to Yield*. Harcourt, Brace, and World, 1963.

"Writers Take Sides: Letters About the War in Spain From 418 American Authors." Undated pamphlet published by the League of American Writers.

Wrezsin, Michael. *A Rebel in Defense of Tradition: The Life and Politics of Dwight Macdonald*. Basic Books, 1994.

Yergin, Daniel. *A Shattered Peace*. Boston: Houghton Mifflin, 1977.
Zitron, Celia. *The New York City Teachers Union, 1916–1964*. Humanities Press, 1968.

VOYAGE TO COLUMBUS

Lewisohn, Ludwig. *Up Stream: An American Chronicle*. Boni and Liveright, 1922.
Thurber, James. *The Thurber Album*. Simon and Schuster, 1952.

Index

About the Author

Nora Sayre, a former film critic for *The New York Times*, is the author of *Sixties Going on Seventies*, which was nominated for a National Book Award (Contemporary Affairs) and *Running Time: Films of the Cold War*. From 1965 to 1970 she was the New York correspondent for the *New Statesman*. Her essays, articles, and reviews have also appeared in *The New York Times Book Review*, *The Nation*, *Esquire*, and many other publications. A graduate of Radcliffe College, she is currently teaching in the Writing Program at Columbia University.